RACE AND REDISTRICTING IN THE 1990s

This is the fifth volume in the Agathon series on Representation
Series Editor: Bernard Grofman

Previously published:

Electoral Laws and Their Political Consequences
edited by Bernard Grofman and Arend Lijphart

"The Federalist Papers" and the New Institutionalism
edited by Bernard Grofman and Donald Wittman

Political Gerrymandering and the Courts
edited by Bernard Grofman

Lawmaking by Initiative: Issues, Options and Comparisons
Philip L. Dubois and Floyd Feeney

RACE AND REDISTRICTING IN THE 1990s

Edited by
Bernard Grofman
University of California, Irvine

AGATHON PRESS, NEW YORK

© 1998 by Agathon Press
5648 Riverdale Avenue
Bronx, NY 10471
All Rights Reserved

Library of Congress Cataloging-in-Publication Data:
Race and redistricting in the 1990s / Edited by Bernard Grofman.
        p.   cm.   -- (Agathon series on representation ; v. 5)
                Includes bibliographical references and index.
                        ISBN 0-87586-123-7 (acid paper)
        1. United States. Congress. House--Election districts.
2. Election districts--United States. 3. Apportionment (Election
                activity. I. Grofman, Bernard. II. Series.
        JK1341.R33 1998
        328.73'07345--dc21   98-13457
                                                                CIP

PRINTED IN CANADA

Contents

Figures and Tables

I wish to dedicate this volume to two men of great wisdom and integrity:

Michael A. Hess (1952-1995), former Chief Counsel for the Republican National Committee. A key player in the redistricting battles of the 1980s and 1990s, Mike was always able to see beyond party interests to the pursuit of justice. I had the pleasure of working with him on a number of voting rights cases and I was proud to count him as a friend.

Donald Stokes (1927-1997), noted scholar of American voting behavior and Dean of the Woodrow Wilson School at Princeton from 1974 to 1992. Don's approach to bipartisan districting, as outlined in his posthumously published essay in this volume, provides an important model of how to achieve fair and reasonable districting outcomes.

They will be missed.

Acknowledgments

FOR ALMOST TWO DECADES I HAVE BEEN ACTIVELY INVOLVED in voting rights issues as a scholar and as a redistricting consultant to entities such as the Voting Rights Section of the U.S. Department of Justice, the New York City Districting Commission, the National Conference of State Legislatures, the NAACP Legal Defense Fund, the ACLU, MALDEF, AALDEF, and state and national committees of both political parties. I have served as an expert witness in over twenty cases. Over the years I have learned about the complexities of representation—theoretical, legal, and practical—from more people than I could possibly list, so I can only begin this volume with a blanket acknowledgment to the many many people—lawyers, expert witnesses, computer consultants—whom I've had the pleasure to work with (or against) and to learn so much from.

This volume was made possible by a grant from the Ford Foundation (#446740-47007) on "The Impact of Redistricting on the Representation of Racial and Ethnic Minorities." The Ford Foundation grant enabled me to reduce my teaching load over a three-year period so as to devote time to thinking about and writing about voting rights issues. I am specially indebted to Michael Lipsky of the Ford Foundation for his help and encouragement in this project. I would also like to acknowledge my debt to the scholars who were part of the Ford Foundation advisory committee for this project—Chandler Davidson, Luis Fraga, Lisa Handley, Paula McClain, and Guillermo Owen—for many helpful conversations over the years on issues related to race and redistricting and for their specific suggestions about this project. Of course, the views reflected in this volume are those of its authors and do not represent the views of the Ford Foundation.

Earlier and much shorter versions of four of the essays in this book (those by Gartner; Hagens; Handley, Grofman and Arden; and Stokes) appeared in a special minisymposium I organized on "Race and Redistricting" for the 1997 annual edition of the *National Political Science Review,* edited by Georgia Persons and published by the University of Michigan Press   In that annual, the plan to subsequently publish longer versions of these four essays in this volume is noted. Portions of my editorial comments on that minisymposium have also been incorporated into the introduction to this volume. I am indebted to Georgia Persons for permission to incorporate these materials.

Small portions of Grofman and Handley (1995a), in the *Mississippi Law Journal*, are incorporated (in updated form) into the two Grofman and Handley essays in this volume. I am indebted to Barbara Phillips Sullivan at the University of Mississippi Law School for encouraging the submission of that article to the *Mississippi Law Journal*, and for many earlier helpful discussions about voting rights issues, and to Will Montjoy of the *Mississippi Law Journal* for helpful editorial feedback.

The Schousen, Canon, and Sellers chapter on supply side effects appeared in an earlier version as Canon, Schousen, and Sellers in the *Journal of Politics* in August 1996. An earlier version of the chapter by these authors on North Carolina appeared as "A Formula for Uncertainty: Creating a Black Majority District in North Carolina" in Thomas A. Kazee, ed., *Who Runs for Congress? Ambition, Context, and Candidate Emergence.* Washington, DC: Congressional Quarterly, Inc., 1994, pp. 23-44, and is reprinted by permission of the publisher.

This volume was originally scheduled to appear in 1993. In 1993, and again in 1994, 1995, and 1996, I delayed its publication to allow changes to be made in the text because the new developments in voting rights case law beginning with *Shaw v. Reno* rendered portions of it obsolete. Even as I update these acknowledgments in June of 1998, important new districting cases are still about to be decided. For example, on March 28, 1998, a new lawsuit challenging South Carolina's Congressional redistricting was filed. Nonetheless, if this volume were ever to appear, it seemed to me that at some point I needed simply to say "Stop." Coming more than midway through the decade of the '90s and exactly ten years after the landmark *Thornburg v. Gingles* decision in 1986, I believe that 1996 makes a reasonable stopping point for discussion of the continuing evolution of voting rights case law and for the districting changes of the 1990s. Most of the chapters in the volume were completed by January 1997, although some updating of various chapters was done in early 1998. I am grateful to the authors of this volume and to Burt Lasky of Agathon Press for their understanding and forbearance about the long delay in publication.

As has been true now for more than a decade, I have benefited on this project from the invaluable secretarial assistance of Dorothy Green and Cheryl Larsson, without whose help this book would never have been finished. In addition, m present secretary, Clover Behrend, and her assistant Anna Datta played a key role in shepherding this process through to completion.

INTRODUCTION:
Race and Redistricting in the 1990s

Bernard Grofman

THE ESSAYS IN THIS VOLUME provide a portrait of how the 1990s round of redistricting treated the racial and linguistic minorities that had been given the special protections of the Voting Rights Act of 1965—African-Americans, Native Americans, Asian-Americans, and those of Spanish heritage, although most of the emphasis is on the first of these groups. While some chapters in this volume do review legal issues, unlike most other very recent work on race and redistricting (e.g., Grofman, Handley and Niemi, 1992; Aleinikoff and Issacharoff, 1993; Karlan, 1995; McDonald, 1995; McKaskle, 1995; Issacharoff, 1996; and the various essays in McClain and Stewart, 1995, and Peacock, 1997) the primary focus of this volume is not on the constitutional jurisprudence of voting rights. Instead, our focus is on the practical politics of redistricting and its consequences for racial representation.[1]

Almost all of the authors in this volume have been directly involved in the 1990s redistricting process either as a legislator (Robert Holmes), a member of the Voting Rights Section of the U.S. Department of Justice (Mark Posner), a Director of a Districting Commission (Tuckerman Babcock, Alan Gartner, Donald Stokes) or, most commonly, as an expert witness or lawyer in voting rights cases. They are thus able to bring to bear special insights as well as insider knowledge. Most of the chapters offer detailed discussion of the actual redistricting process in a single state,[2] including details of the legislative process, while others provide an overview of the consequences of 1990s districting for black and Hispanic representation[3] in congress and/or state

---

[1] Because the central focus of this volume is on racial aspects of districting, other important districting topics (e.g, one person, one vote issues, or issues related to partisan gerrymandering) will not be the subject of much attention. For more general discussions of districting see e.g., Grofman, 1992b, c; Cain, 1984; Butler and Cain, 1992.

[2] Or, in the case of the Gartner chapter, a single city—New York.

[3] The Alaska chapter deals with the representation of Native Americans.

legislatures, or consider how districting choices affect the decisions of potential minority candidates.

The book is divided into four parts: The first section deals with theoretical and empirical issues about the link between districting and descriptive representation of racial and linguistic minorities;[4] the second with legal and enforcement issues; the third contains state-specific chapters on seven of the states covered in whole or in part by Section 5 of the VRA (states which each have substantial minority populations); the last section discusses two different forms of non-partisan commissions and the lessons we may draw from them about how to improve districting.

Section I, on theoretical and empirical issues, contains three essays.

The first of these is by Lisa Handley, Bernard Grofman and Wayne Arden. It provides a detailed empirical summary of the changes in the descriptive representation of blacks and Hispanics in state legislatures that immediately followed the 1990s round of redistricting. It traces the growth in black representation at both the congressional and state legislative level in the states with the most substantial black population concentrations and shows the almost perfect causal link between that growth and the creation of black majority districts in 1992, and then provides a similar analysis for Hispanics. The Handley-Grofman-Arden joint essay also looks at the link between minority population and the likelihood of Democratic success.[5] For the South, its bottom line is a simple one: with at best rare exceptions, African-American legislators are not elected except from districts with substantial black populations. Moreover, in the South, although there is state-specific variation, high likelihood of Democratic success is strongly associated with a significant black population.

The second essay in Section I, by Schousen, Canon and Sellers, seeks to understand the characteristics of the new black House members as a function of the racial demography of the district and the nature of black-white competition. First, they consider the "collective action" problem facing potential black candidates, namely the potential that, if "too many" black candidates run, a white candidate may be the plurality winner. They suggest this problem can be largely obviated by the existence of a majority runoff requirement that acts to discourage white challengers in the Democratic primary in districts where the majority of voters in that primary are very likely to be black. They also note that both a sense of "fair play" and pressures from the minority community not to aggravate racial tensions also act to inhibit white challengers from running in newly created black majority districts. Then, they look at the likelihood that a black candidate with bi-racial appeal will be selected.

---

[4] By descriptive representation we mean the election to office of persons of a given race or ethnicity. We may distinguish the question of descriptive representation from the question of whether or not the actions of any given legislator or set of legislators are broadly representative of the communities that elected them.

[5] Related work on this point is Grofman, Griffin and Glazer (1992).

The third essay in this section, by Bernard Grofman and Lisa Handley, addresses the claim that has been made by political commentators of both the right and the left and by academic researchers (e.g., Lublin 1995a) that the creation of new majority-minority districts assured that the Republicans won solid control of the House in 1994. It also addresses the claim that the aggregate effect of racial redistricting has been to make the House less likely to adopt legislation favored by African-Americans. Grofman and Handley enter a strong (albeit partial) dissent to the view that the Voting Rights Act has had, on balance, negative consequences for black interests. However, they also note that, just as the full consequences of the 1990s redistricting lines on the fate of the Democratic party in the South were not yet visible in 1992, they were not fully realized in 1994 or 1996 either; and they argue that the future does not look good for the remaining Southern Democrats in House districts with less than 30% black population, or for the Democratic party in the South, in general.

The essays in Section II deal with legal and enforcement issues in voting rights. There is little or no dissent to the proposition that the substantial number of new black (and Hispanic) congressional districts created in the 1990s round of districting was tied to the Voting Rights Act of 1965.[6] Almost all new majority minority districts came into existence largely if not entirely in direct or anticipated response to Department of Justice preclearance powers under Section 5 of the Voting Rights Act, or as a result of actual or threatened litigation under Section 2 of the Act (as amended in 1982), or as a result of court action that took Voting Rights Act concerns into account.[7] In like manner, virtually all of the changes that have occurred in districting plans since the first round of 1990s redistricting have been triggered by court scrutiny of plans under the new constitutional test laid out in *Shaw v. Reno* as it has been further elucidated in cases like *Miller v. Johnson*. It is impossible to understand the redistricting choices of the 1990s

---

[6]Together with the Civil Rights Act of 1964 and the Immigration Reform Bill of 1965, the Voting Rights Act of 1965 is one of the cornerstones of contemporary race relations in the United States. The Act was intended to guarantee the full exercise of the franchise to blacks and later applied to other minorities. The provisions of the 1965 Act and of subsequent amendments have been upheld by the U.S. Supreme Court against constitutional challenge; moreover, its coverage has been interpreted by the Court as extending to virtually all aspects of election organization, from locations of voting booths to redistricting plans and choice of electoral systems. Thus, the Act has come to apply to far more than simple denial of the franchise.

[7]Research on the impact of voting rights concerns on 1970s and 1980s redistricting showed equally clear results: virtually all minority gains in representation in the South and southwest at the state legislative and congressional levels came about in majority-minority districts, and these districts were created largely if not entirely in response to concerns tied to Voting Rights Act enforcement or threat thereof or litigation directly under the fourteenth amendment (Grofman and Handley, 1989, 1992a; Handley and Grofman, 1994). Similar, but not quite as strong, results apply to local districting in the South (see various state chapters in Davidson and Grofman, 1994 and summary of findings in Grofman and Davidson, 1994). General discussions of voting rights case law as it applies to districting issues is found in Grofman, 1992a; Grofman, Handley, and Niemi, 1992; and various chapters in Grofman and Davidson, 1992. Grofman (1993a, 1997) and Grofman and Handley (1995a) discuss voting rights cases of the 1990s.'

without taking into account voting rights litigation and enforcement of the Voting Rights Act by the U.S. Department of Justice. As I have written elsewhere (Grofman, 1993a), in 1990s districting, the Voting Rights Act was "a brooding omnipresence."

The first essay in this section, by Bernard Grofman and Lisa Handley, offers a synoptic overview of the changes in voting rights case law in the 1990s. It focuses on the dramatic changes in districting case law that occurred when the Supreme Court, in *Shaw v. Reno*, found that districts that were drawn with race as the exclusive or overwhelmingly preponderant concern could be found to be unconstitutional. It also discusses another less known case, *LULAC. v. Clements* (1992), coming out of the Fifth Circuit *en banc*. Grofman and Handley argue that *LULAC* offers a definition of racially polarized voting that would make it very difficult for plaintiffs ever to prove polarization. Since racial polarization is the linchpin of any voting rights districting case, *LULAC* potentially has very important implications, and they note that the opinion is already being cited outside the Fifth Circuit. However, leaving aside *Shaw* and its progeny and *LULAC*, the Grofman and Handley chapter also emphasizes the remarkable continuities in voting rights case law from the 1980s to the 1990s. The chapter ends with a relatively optimistic assessment of the prospects for maintaining high levels of descriptive minority representation throughout this decade and into the next.

The second and final essay in this section, by Mark Posner, a member of the Voting Rights Section of the U.S. Department of Justice, provides a very detailed description of the role of the Department in Voting Rights Act enforcement of the Section 5 preclearance provisions that, in the 1990s round of districting, applied to 16 states in whole or in part. Posner's essay is, in his words, "not designed as a rebuttal to the Supreme Court's mistaken appraisal of the Department's enforcement of Section 5," i.e., of the claim accepted by a majority of the Court's members in cases such as *Miller v. Johnson* that the Justice Department had been pursuing a policy of maximizing the number of black safe seats to the exclusion of all other considerations. Nonetheless, by setting forth the principles and analytic methods that guided the Department in its 1990s districting reviews of over 3,000 redistricting plans, and that led to nearly 200 Section 5 objections being filed by the Department, Posner shows that judgements about the Department's policies based on only a handful of cases can be very misleading. His essay also reports a variety of statistics and other summary information about the role of the Department of Justice in 1990s redistricting, including a complete list of all objections through mid-1995, which should prove invaluable for anyone who wishes to understand what actually happened.

The essays in Section III each deal with individual case studies of redistricting, but each is also concerned with broader theoretical points. Each author was given the following charge by the editor: Each chapter was to discuss what happened in the 1990s districting in their state, with a focus on (1) alternative plans and their anticipated consequences; (2) the key state players and the positions they took; (3) the role of the Department of Justice; (4) the litigation history; and (5) the actual consequences for minority representation. Most of the authors have dealt with almost all, if not all, of these questions in their chapters. In addition, chapter authors were encouraged to consider certain special topics, such as the role of computers, or conflicts between blacks and other minorities, or the partisan implications of voting rights-related districting, if these were of particular relevance in their state.

We have placed the chapters alphabetically by state. Each of the seven states discussed in this section is one covered in whole or in part by the Justice Department preclearance provisions of Section 5 of the VRA. All but Alaska and California are southern states. While these are certainly not the only states whose redistricting efforts were substantially affected by voting rights concerns, they provide a representative illustration of the redistricting process in states covered by Section 5.

The first state chapter is by Tuckerman Babcock, who served as staff director of the Alaska Reapportionment Board. Since there are no major African-American, Hispanic or Asian-American populations in the state, Babcock's focus is on the impact of legislative districting on Alaska's Native American population (16.5 percent of the total population of the state). He also comments on the unique legal environment that affects Alaskan legislative districting, namely the fact that the legislature has no role in districting, but instead, there is a five member board which serves in an advisory role to the governor; and the fact that the Alaskan State Supreme Court is constitutionally mandated to review the actions of the Reapportionment Board. He observes that every Alaska reapportionment has been declared unconstitutional by the State Supreme Court, and argues strongly that that court has failed to develop consistent standards for judging redistricting over the past decades. Babcock also comments on what he refers to as the Section 5 "micromanagement" by the Department of Justice of the state's districting in the1990s, notably the insistence by DOJ that the population in a district which already had an Alaskan Native as incumbent be adjusted upward from 51 to 59 percent Native American.

The second state chapter, by the historian Morgan Kousser, is unique in that it provides an extensive comparison of districting in California over three different reapportionment decades. Kousser provides evidence suggesting that the effects of California districting plans on long-lasting partisan advantage has been exaggerated. Another of Kousser's most important observations is that "the concerns of ethnic groups cannot be separated from partisan politics." In California, as elsewhere, African-Americans and Latinos of Mexican descent are strongly associated with the Democratic party. He points out that, by the 1990s, minority officeholders elected from heavily minority districts created in earlier rounds of districting were in positions of power within the Democratic party. According to Kousser, 1990s plans proposed by Democrats were generally more attentive to minority election chances that those proposed by Republicans or by the Masters appointed by the State Supreme Court, who ended up reapportioning the state due to the failure of the Democratically controlled legislature and the Republican governor to agree on plans. Kousser also provides some intriguing insights into the role that the previous history of redistricting in the state played in shaping expectations for the 1990s (e.g., about what would happen if there were deadlock between the governor and the legislature) which critically shaped the behavior of key actors in the redistricting game.

The third chapter in this section is by Robert Holmes, a Georgia legislator who was intimately involved in redistricting in that state. Holmes shows that black legislators were greatly involved in shaping the districting plans that were adopted, especially as those plans impacted on African-American voters. Their ability to do so was aided by the fact that a three-term black legislator was Chair of the Senate Reapportionment Committee, and another black legislator was a senior member of both the committee in charge of redistricting the State House and the committee in charge of congressional districting. With respect to congressional districting, Holmes observes that while black legislators in the state were initially split as to districting strategy, by the end of the 1992 legislative session they had largely reached consensus to only support a congressional plan that contained three districts with black majorities, and they had agreed on criteria for black representation in the state chambers as well. However, the congressional plan passed by the legislature had only two black majority districts; proposals for plans with three black majority districts were voted down. Under Section 5, DOJ denied preclearance to the original plan, and a plan with three black-majority districts was passed, only to be invalidated in *Miller v. Johnson*. After *Miller v. Johnson* invalidated the congressional plan, white Democrats joined with Republicans in the state Senate[8] to pass a congressional plan with but a single black majority Congressional district, but that plan did not pass the House, leaving it up to a federal court to draw the state's congressional districts. The court-drawn plan, too, had but a single black majority district. Nonetheless, with the advantage of incumbency, all three black congressional incumbents were reelected in 1996 despite the fact that two of them had the black populations in their districts reduced considerably below a majority.[9]

---

[8]Holmes has a number of other observations about the nature of cooperation, or lack thereof, between black and Republican legislators. Initially part of coalition with black legislators to create black districts (whose creation Georgia Republicans saw as advantageous for their own partisan ends), the coalition first broke down amid accusations that the plans pushed by Democrats were partisan gerrymanders.

[9]See the epilogue to the Holmes chapter for details. The epilogue also discusses 1996 results in the state legislature, where there was actually an increase in the number of African-American legislators despite the fact that there were new districting plans in use that had been thought to be less advantages for minority representation.

The fourth chapter in this section is by Richard Engstrom and Jason Kirksey. Louisiana was the second state to have a plan struck down under the *Shaw* standard. Professor Engstrom was involved as an expert witness at various phases of the complicated Louisiana litigation, which involved a multiplicity of plans and several court cases. Indeed, for congressional elections in Louisiana, a different plan was in place in each of the three elections of the 1990s from 1992 to 1996. The first two plans had two black majority districts, one in New Orleans and one elsewhere. In 1992 both elected black House members; in 1994 both black incumbents were reelected even though the boundary lines of the second black majority district had been substantially revamped. However, because litigation had prohibited the 1994 plan being used again and deemed the plan unconstitutional under the *Shaw* test, the plan put in place in 1996 had only a single black majority House district. Only one black member of congress was elected in 1996, with the black incumbent of the other majority-black district choosing not to run after the black voting age population in the district had been lowered by roughly 30 percentage points from that in the 1992 plan. One of the important points made by Engstrom and Kirksey deals with the notion of black "influence districts." The federal court had claimed that districts with around 25% or so black population provided black influence; the evidence provided by Engstrom and Kirksey shows otherwise.[10]

The fifth chapter in Section III is by Patrick Sellers, David Canon and Matthew Schousen. While the authors emphasize the legal as well as political conte xt in which North Carolina districting took place, they also point out how the personal ambitions of some legislators shaped the line-drawing process. They observe that, early in the decade, "Republicans and some black leaders argued that the state should have two and perhaps even three black-majority districts," since 22 percent of the state's population is black (".22 times 12 equals 2.64 districts"). Nonetheless, the legislature opted in favor of a plan with only a single black congressional district. Interestingly, the black legislators most likely to run were a second black district to be created did not publicly protest the plan. However, a preclearance denial by the Department of Justice soon followed. Responding both to DOJ and to incumbency protection concerns, the legislature drew the subsequently infamous "I-85" district as a second majority black district. It ran for nearly 200 miles and was only the width of the interstate in some parts of the state.[11] North Carolina's congressional plan, with its peculiarly shaped districts and racially motivated irregularities in lines, served as the triggering force behind the Supreme Court's reshaping of the constitutional standards for voting rights in

[10]Engstrom and Kirksey (this volume) also note that "the influence district notion was applied in a racially selective manner....The majority African-American districts, District 2 and 4, are both over 40 percent white in voting age population,...yet neither of these districts was identified as a white influence district."

[11]In *Pope v. Blue* (1992) I testified against North Carolina's congressional plan, labelling it a patchwork crazy-quilt that violated standards of contiguity.

the 1993 landmark case of *Shaw v. Reno*.[12] Sellers, Canon and Schousen observe that "the current state of law and its interpretation by the Supreme Court leaves state legislatures in the uncomfortable position of being sued by black voters if they do not take race into account when redrawing district lines, and being sued by white voters if they are too aggressive in creating majority-minority districts."[13]

The sixth chapter in this section, on legislative and congressional districting South Carolina, is by Orville Vernon Burton, an historian who has served as an expert witness in a number of South Carolina cases. The South Carolina case makes an interesting contrast to what had gone on in neighboring states. Because of divided partisan control in the state, deadlock resulted in 1992 and a federal court drew the plans used in the 1992 elections.[14] Burton emphasizes the calculated role of Republican strategy in the state to avoid political compromise and expect to do better in the courts. According to Burton, this was consistent with a "national Republican strategy of using the federal courts for redistricting...." For 1994 the ball was back in the legislature's court, after a complicated sequence of events leading to the district court's giving deference to the legislature in seeking to devise plans that complied with the Voting Rights Act and with *Shaw*. An alliance of black Democrats and Republicans in the state House pushed a plan with a substantial increase in the number of majority-black districts. This plans was put into place in 1994 and led to further gains in black representation: in the state House, six white Democrats were replaced by black Democrats in 1994, bringing black representation up to 19% of that body. However, control of the state House also shifted to the Republicans. In Burton's view this change cannot be blamed on districting: Republicans had been making gains in the state and the shift occurred because eight elected Democrats switched parties (joining two Democrats who had already switched between 1992 and 1994).[15] Nonetheless, the "lesson" taken from the loss of the House to Republicans led Democratic state senators (both white and black) to opt for only marginal gains in black descriptive representation in the state Senate when plans for that body were redrawn in 1995.

---

[12]Neither the link between some of the most bizarre features of the plan and partisan concerns (e.g., the "u-turn" at the interstate necessary to protect the incumbent in the 6th district by keeping that district from being bisected by the 12th district), nor state claims that they were seeking to remedy past discrimination and comply with the Voting Rights Act, prevented the plan from being rejected by the Supreme Court as unconstitutional under the *Shaw* test when the case came back before it (after a remand to the district court) as *Shaw v. Hunt*.

[13]The Sellers, Canon and Schousen chapter was completed prior to a March 1998 district court decision invalidating the redrawn North Carolina congressional plan.

[14]As Burton notes, "as late as May 1994, the South Carolina legislature still had not passed a plan." Burton observes that, after *Shaw*, when other states were being challenged for having congressional districts that were "'unfair' to white voters," South Carolina was "still attempting to prove its proposed plans were not unfair to African-Americans."

[15]See, however, the discussion of the *indirect* effects of redistricting discussed in the first of the two Grofman and Handley chapters in this volume (what they refer to under the rubric of the "triple whammy").

However, the last chapter of the 1990s South Carolina redistricting story has yet to be written.[16]

The seventh and last of the state analysis chapters in Section III is on legislative redistricting in Virginia. Its author, Winnett Hagens, has been a key participant in the Norfolk State University Voting Rights Project that has provided mapping and other technical assistance to numerous minority organizations seeking to influence local and state redistricting decisions. The Hagens essay emphasizes the insider role of black legislators and the importance of minority access to computer resources and the capability to easily generate alternative plans and to evaluate plans that were proposed by others, as well as the complex interplay between racial and partisan considerations on the part of legislators and litigators. It also discusses the most recent chapter in Virginia's redistricting history, the rejection by a federal court of the boundaries for the state's lone majority-black congressional district as being in violation of the *Shaw* standard.[17]

The two essays in Section IV are also case studies of redistricting, but we have placed them in a separate section because each exemplifies a different alternative to legislative-based redistricting.

Alan Gartner served as Executive Director of the New York City Districting Commission that drew the 1990 lines for the enlarged 51 member City Council provided for in the new City Charter.[18] Gartner's essay lays out the basic elements of the redistricting process for the New York City Council.[19] He notes that the selection process for the New York City Districting Commission essentially guaranteed that spokespersons for various minority communities would have representation on the Commission. He argues, i.a., that the complex representational process that guided the City Districting Commission's activities, which had a substantial public access component, provides a good model for redistricting decision-making in multi-ethnic polities.[20] He also argues that it gave rise to lines that fairly reflected the diverse communities within New York City, despite the fact that not all minority organizations were happy with the results of the Commission's plan and DOJ required very minor changes in the lines before the plan could be precleared.

Donald Stokes served as the court-appointed non-partisan Chair of the New Jersey Apportionment Commission that drew the state's legislative and congressional districts, a post he also held in the 1980s round of district-

[16]The Burton chapter was completed in September 1996, prior to a federal court ruling on the constitutionality of South Carolina's State House and State Senate plans, and prior to the 1996 elections. Some information about subsequent events was added in early 1998.

[17] *Moon v. Meadows* (1992).

[18]I served as a voting rights consultant to the New York City Districting Commission. (However, I was not involved in the final set of changes to the plan.)

[19]Subsequently he became a court-appointed expert in the drawing of congressional lines for the State of New York.

[20]In a larger monograph from which portions of his essay for this volume is drawn, Gartner (1992) also discusses at length the influence minority organizations had on the city council districting process in New York and on the interplay between partisan and racial considerations.

ing.[21] His essay reviews that experience and its lessons for plans that seek to preserve communities of interest. In it he argues strongly in favor of the desirability of a districting commission model similar to that in New Jersey, that would remove redistricting from the control of the legislature and provide a linchpin role for an advocate of the overall public interest. To a greater extent than Gartner he is concerned with balancing the need for descriptive representation of minorities with concern for the non-fragmentation of geographically defined communities.

In the vast majority of states, redistricting is in the hands of the legislature. Good government types in the midwest and west have sought to inspire a grass-roots revolt against permitting legislatures to draw the districts from which their own members would run. Their attack on legislative control of redistricting is based on the Lockean theory that no person should be a judge in his own case, and on the practical grounds that legislatures (and governors) were botching the job and engaging in partisan and incumbent gerrymandering. Also, in California and elsewhere, in the early 1990s, Republicans put forward initiatives to take redistricting out of the hands of state legislatures, on the general theory that most state legislatures were then under Democratic control and Republicans couldn't do any worse. While the term limits movement has changed the landscape of American legislative politics, change in redistricting practices has failed to spark public interest. The number of jurisdictions that have ended (or even severely restricted) legislative control of the redistricting process has changed only minusculely since 1980.[22]

Nonetheless, alternative models of how redistricting might be done, such as the New Jersey model of a bipartisan commission with a non-partisan chair who can effectively force the parties to offer plans intended to satisfy specified criteria (Stokes, 1993; this volume)[23] or the New York City model of a racially and ethnically diverse districting commission with a first-rate technical staff and administration oriented to promoting compromise among competing interests and responding to a City Charter that lays out criteria for districting (Gartner, 1992; this volume), may well serve as inspiration for reformers as we look toward how redistricting should be done in the 21st century.[24]

---

[21] The commission was then not yet responsible for congressional redistricting.

[22] However, just as in the 1990s round of redistricting, to a greater extent than ever before, failure of governors and legislatures to agree to districting plans thrust redistricting decision-making into the hands of federal or state courts, so I would expect to see this pattern repeated in the next reapportionment round.

[23] Stokes (1993, this volume) argued that the New Jersey experience demonstrates that a mixed process of redistricting, with balanced party membership of the Apportionment Commission and a public member committed to explicit standards of public interest, can produce boundaries that are fair between the parties, responsive to the shifting tides of electoral support, and provide appropriate tradeoffs among values such as preserving geographic communities, satisfying equal population requirements, and serving the need for effective minority representation.

[24] My own view, however, is that the constraints set by Voting Rights Act Section 5 enforcement and Section 2 standards have a far greater impact on how redistricting will affect minorities than the question of who does redistricting. I hope to empirically investigate this issue in future work.

PART I
Theoretical and Empirical Issues

ELECTING MINORITY-PREFERRED CANDIDATES TO LEGISLATIVE OFFICE:
The Relationship Between Minority Percentages in Districts and the Election of Minority-Preferred Candidates[1]

Lisa Handley, Bernard Grofman, and Wayne Arden

THE ELECTIONS FOLLOWING THE 1990S ROUND of redistricting led to dramatic changes in the composition of state legislatures and the U.S. Congress. More minorities assumed legislative office following these elections than at any other time in our nation's history. Despite continuing debate over the benefits of creating majority minority districts, it is clear that the majority minority districts created in the 1990s redistricting were responsible for the significant increase in the number of African-Americans and Hispanics elected to legislative office.

Minority concentrations short of a majority also affect the election of legislators. There is a very distinct relationship between the percentage minority in a district and the party affiliation of the legislator elected: the higher the percentage minority, the greater the probability of electing a Democrat to office. If the district is a majority minority district, there is a high probability that a African-American or Hispanic Democrat will be elected. If the district is less than majority minority, but has a significant concentration of minorities, it is likely that a white Democrat will be elected to legislative office. This suggests that white Democrats are the minority-preferred candidates in districts in which minorities have influence, but are unable to elect a minority candidate.

---

[1]An earlier version of this paper was prepared for presentation at the Hendricks Symposium on Legislative Districting in the 1990's, University of Nebraska, Lincoln, Nebraska, April 8-9, 1994

13

This chapter reviews how the 1990s round of redistricting impacted the election of minority-preferred candidates, both minority and white Democrats, in Congress and state legislatures. The chapter is divided into two sections: the first section focuses specifically on majority minority districts and the election of minority candidates to office, the second section examines the relationship between minority concentrations in districts and the election of Democrats to legislative office.

MINORITY DISTRICTS AND THE ELECTION OF MINORITY CANDIDATES

To determine the impact of the 1990s round of redistricting on the creation of majority minority districts and the election of minority candidates, we have prepared two sets of tables. Both sets of tables summarize minority representation prior to the 1990s round of redistricting and following the next set of elections (1991 or 1992, depending on the legislative office and the state). One set of tables examines African-American representation in states with a black population in excess of 10 percent. The second set of tables examines Hispanic representation in states with a Hispanic population greater than 10 percent.

African-American Representation and the Creation of Majority African-American Districts

As expected, the 1990s redistricting process led to significant gains in the number of African-American legislators and majority black districts. Table 1 indicates that African-Americans were underrepresented relative to population proportions following the 1990 elections. This underrepresentation continued to be more pronounced in the South than in other parts of the country (see Grofman and Handley, 1991, for a summary of African-American representation in southern state legislatures prior to 1990). For example, in 1990 African-Americans comprised only 14 percent of the Louisiana state house despite a black population state-wide of almost 31 percent, and less than 4 percent of the Mississippi senate despite a state-wide black population of slightly less than 36 percent. The majority of southern states had no African-American representation in Congress.

Table 2 provides the results of the first post-1990 redistricting elections. The elections led to major gains in African-American representation in the South: the number of African-Americans serving in Congress rose from 5 to 17, and the number of African-American state legislators increased in every southern state - with the largest gains in Louisiana and Mississippi. In fact, the increase in African-American representation in the South far surpassed the increase elsewhere in the country. For the first time since Reconstruction, African-Americans are better represented (i.e., closer to proportional representation) in southern state legislatures than in state legislatures elsewhere in the country. Two non-southern states examined, Illinois and Michigan, actually experienced a decrease in the number of African-American state legislators.

TABLE 1. Percent African-American Elected Legislators in the South and Non-South in 1990[1]

	Percent Black Population	State House	(N)	State Senate	(N)	U.S. Congress	(N)
South							
Alabama	25.3	18.1	(105)	14.3	(35)	0.0	(7)
Arkansas	15.9	9.0	(100)	8.6	(35)	0.0	(4)
Florida	13.6	10.0	(120)	5.0	(40)	0.0	(19)
Georgia	27.0	14.4	(180)	14.3	(56)	10.0	(10)
Louisiana	30.8	14.3	(105)	10.3	(39)	12.5	(8)
Mississippi	35.6	16.4	(122)	3.8	(52)	20.0	(5)
N. Carolina	22.0	11.7	(120)	10.0	(50)	0.0	(11)
S. Carolina	29.8	12.1	(124)	13.0	(46)	0.0	(6)
Tennessee	16.0	10.1	(99)	9.1	(33)	11.1	(9)
Texas	11.9	8.7	(150)	6.5	(31)	3.7	(27)
Virginia	18.8	7.0	(100)	7.5	(40)	0.0	(10)
Total	19.2	12.1	(1325)	9.4	(457)	4.3	(116)
Non-South							
Delaware	16.9	4.9	(41)	4.8	(21)	0.0	(1)
Illinois	14.8	11.9	(118)	11.9	(59)	13.6	(22)
Maryland	24.9	17.0	(141)	14.9	(47)	12.5	(8)
Michigan	13.9	10.9	(110)	7.9	(38)	11.1	(18)
Missouri	10.7	8.0	(163)	8.8	(34)	22.2	(9)
New Jersey	13.4	7.5	(80)	5.0	(40)	7.1	(14)
New York	15.9	11.3	(150)	8.2	(61)	11.8	(34)
Ohio	10.6	11.1	(99)	6.1	(33)	4.8	(21)
Total	14.6	11.0	(902)	9.0	(333)	11.0	(127)

[1]The states listed above are states with black populations of 10 percent or greater (according to the 1990 U.S. Census). The percent African-American elected legislators reflects officeholders following the 1989/1990 elections (as reported in *Black Elected Officials: A National Roster 1991,* Joint Center for Political and Economic Studies Press, 1992).

TABLE 2. Percent African-American Elected Legislators in the South and Non-South in 1992[1]

	Percent Black Population	*State House*	*(N)*	*State Senate*	*(N)*	*U.S. Congress*	*(N)*
South							
Arkansas	15.9	10.0	(100)	8.6	(35)	0.0	(4)
Florida	13.6	11.7	(120)	10.0	(40)	13.0	(23)
Georgia	27.0	17.2	(180)	16.1	(56)	27.3	(11)
Louisiana	30.8	22.9	(105)	20.5	(39)	28.6	(7)
Mississippi	35.6	26.2	(122)	19.2	(52)	20.0	(5)
N. Carolina	22.0	15.0	(120)	12.0	(50)	16.7	(12)
S. Carolina	29.8	14.5	(124)	15.2	(46)	16.7	(6)
Tennessee	16.0	12.1	(99)	9.1	(33)	11.1	(9)
Texas	11.9	9.3	(150)	6.5	(31)	6.7	(30)
Virginia	18.8	7.0	(100)	12.5	(40)	9.1	(11)
Total	18.8	14.8	(1220)	13.5	(422)	13.6	(125)
Non-South							
Delaware	16.9	4.9	(41)	4.8	(21)	0.0	(1)
Illinois	14.8	10.2	(118)	13.6	(59)	15.0	(20)
Michigan	13.9	10.0	(110)			12.5	(16)
Missouri	10.7	8.0	(163)	8.8	(34)	22.2	(9)
New Jersey	13.4	12.5	(80)	5.0	(40)	7.7	(13)
New York	15.9	13.3	(150)	8.2	(61)	12.9	(31)
Ohio	10.6	12.1	(99)	9.1	(33)	5.3	(19)
Total	13.8	10.5	(761)	8.9	(248)	12.8	(117)

[1]The states listed above are states with black populations of 10 percent or greater, excluding Alabama and Maryland (which do not have any 1992 state legislative elections), and the Michigan state senate (which did not have any 1992 elections). The percent African-American elected legislators reflects officeholders following the 1991/1992 elections.

The primary reason for the surge in African-American representation was the increase in the number of majority black districts drawn. A comparison of Tables 3 and 4 indicates an increase in the number of majority black districts in almost every state, although the growth was greater overall in the South. In only two states—neither of which are southern—did the number of majority black districts actually decrease: Michigan drew three fewer majority black state house districts and Ohio drew one less majority black state senate district. Of the two states, however, only Michigan suffered a corresponding decrease in the number of African-American state legislators.

TABLE 3. Percent Majority African-American Districts in 1990[1]

	Percent Black Population	State House	(N)	State Senate	(N)	U.S. Congress	(N)
South							
Alabama	25.3	19.0	(105)	17.1	(35)	0.0	(7)
Florida	13.6	7.5	(120)	2.5	(40)	0.0	(19)
Georgia	27.0	18.9	(180)	19.6	(56)	10.0	(10)
Louisiana	30.8	18.1	(105)	15.4	(39)	12.5	(8)
Mississippi	35.6	26.2	(122)	26.9	(52)	20.0	(5)
N. Carolina	22.0	7.5	(120)	6.0	(50)	0.0	(11)
S. Carolina	29.8	21.0	(124)	21.7	(46)	0.0	(6)
Tennessee	16.0	11.1	(99)	9.1	(33)	11.1	(9)
Texas	11.9	6.0	(150)	3.2	(31)	0.0	(27)
Virginia	18.8	9.0	(100)	5.0	(40)	0.0	(10)
Total	19.3	14.5	(1225)	13.5	(422)	3.4	(116)
Non-South							
Delaware	16.9	4.9	(41)	4.8	(21)	0.0	(1)
Illinois	14.8	11.9	(118)	10.2	(59)	13.6	(22)
Maryland	24.9	17.0	(141)	17.0	(47)	12.5	(8)
Michigan	13.9	14.5	(110)	10.5	(38)	11.1	(18)
Missouri	10.7	8.6	(163)	11.8	(34)	11.1	(9)
New York	15.9	8.6	(150)	6.6	(61)	5.9	(34)
Ohio	10.6	4.0	(99)	6.1	(33)	4.8	(21)
Total	14.7	10.5	(822)	10.2	(239)	8.7	(127)

[1]The states listed are states with black populations of 10 percent or greater. No state legislative data was available for Arkansas or New Jersey therefore these two states have been excluded. The percentages reported in this table reflect the districting plans in place for the 1989/1990 elections. Single member districts are counted once; multimember districts (both those that are majority black and those that are not) have a value equal to the number of delegates elected.

TABLE 4. Percent Majority African-American Districts in 1992[1]

	Percent Black Population	State House	(N)	State Senate	(N)	U.S. Congress	(N)
South							
Arkansas	15.9	13.0	(100)	8.6	(35)	0.0	(4)
Florida	13.6	10.8	(120)	7.5	(40)	13.0	(23)
Georgia	27.0	23.3	(180)	23.2	(56)	27.3	(11)
Louisiana	30.8	24.8	(105)	23.1	(39)	28.6	(7)
Mississippi	35.6	31.1	(122)	23.1	(52)	20.0	(5)
N. Carolina	22.0	13.3	(120)	8.0	(50)	16.7	(12)
S. Carolina	29.8	22.6	(124)	23.9	(46)	16.7	(6)
Tennessee	16.0	11.1	(99)	9.1	(33)	11.1	(9)
Texas	11.9	7.3	(150)	3.2	(31)	6.6	(30)
Virginia	18.8	12.0	(100)	12.5	(40)	9.1	(11)
Total	18.8	17.2	(1220)	15.2	(422)	13.6	(125)
Non-South							
Delaware	16.9	4.9	(41)	4.8	(21)	0.0	(1)
Illinois	14.8	15.3	(118)	13.6	(59)	15.0	(20)
Maryland	24.9	19.9	(141)	19.1	(47)	25.0	(8)
Michigan	13.9	11.8	(110)	13.2	(38)	12.5	(16)
Missouri	10.7	8.6	(163)	11.8	(34)	11.1	(9)
New Jersey	13.4	7.5	(80)	7.5	(40)	7.7	(13)
New York	15.9	10.0	(150)	11.5	(61)	9.7	(31)
Ohio	10.6	6.1	(99)	3.0	(33)	5.3	(19)
Total	14.6	11.3	(902)	11.4	(333)	11.1	(117)

[1]The states listed are states with black populations of 10 percent or greater. Alabama has not yet redistricted its state legislature and therefore has been excluded. The percentages reported in this table reflect the districting plan in place for the 1991/1992 elections. Single member districts are counted once; multimember districts (both those that are majority black and those that are not) have a value equal to the number of delegates elected.

Not only did states draw more majority black districts, but jurisdictions were apparently also more successful in the 1990s than in the 1980s in drawing "effective" minority districts (i.e., districts in which minority voters have a realistic opportunity to elect candidates of their choice).[2] The percentage of majority black districts that elected African-Americans to office increased, as evidenced by comparing Table 5 (A) and (B) to Table 6 (A) and (B).[3] The proportion of

[2]The one notable exception is the Illinois state house. Although the number of majority black districts in the Illinois state house increased, a number of these districts failed to elect African-American candidates to office, which led to a retrogression in African-American representation.

majority black districts that elected African-Americans to office in 1992 was slightly greater than .8 (.81 in the state house and .82 in the state senate).[4] This proportion may well increase over the course of the decade as majority black districts that failed to elect African-Americans in 1992 proceed to do so in subsequent elections.

TABLE 5(A). Percentage of Majority African-American and Non-Majority African-American Districts that Elected African-American State House Members in the South and Non-South in 1990

	Percent Majority Black Districts Electing African-American Legislators	(N)	Percent Non-Majority Black Districts Electing African-American Legislators	(N)
South				
Alabama	95.0	(20)	0.0	(85)
Florida	100.0	(9)	2.7	(111)
Georgia	73.5	(34)	.7	(146)
Louisiana	78.9	(19)	0.0	(86)
Mississippi	59.4	(32)	0.0	(90)
N. Carolina	100.0	(9)	4.5	(111)
S. Carolina	61.5	(26)	0.0	(98)
Tennessee	81.8	(11)	1.1	(88)
Texas	100.0	(9)	2.8	(141)
Virginia	77.8	(9)	0.0	(91)
Total	77.0	(178)	1.3	(1047)
Non-South				
Delaware	100.0	(2)	0.0	(39)
Illinois	92.9	(14)	1.0	(104)
Maryland	87.5	(24)	3.4	(117)
Michigan	68.8	(16)	1.1	(94)
Missouri	78.6	(14)	1.3	(149)
New York	92.3	(13)	3.6	(137)
Ohio	100.0	(4)	7.4	(95)
Total	85.1	(87)	2.7	(735)

---

[3]Tables 7 (C) and 8 (C) indicate that every majority black congressional district created elected an African-American to office—and this was true in 1990 as well as 1992.

[4]The proportion of majority black districts that elect African-Americans to office depends in part on the percentage black of the district. For example, in 1992 when all districts over 50 percent black are considered, 80 percent of the districts elected African-Americans, but when only districts that are over 60 percent black are considered, 84 percent elected African-Americans. Similarly, when only districts over 65 percent black are included in the analysis, the proportion of districts that elected African-Americans increases to 86 percent. Black success may also depend on the percent of Hispanics in rhe district—a factor that needs to be controlled for (see Grofman and Handley, 1989b).

TABLE 5(B). Percentage of Majority African-American and Non-Majority African-American Districts that Elected African-American State Senate Members in the South and Non-South in 1990

	Percent Majority Black Districts Electing African-American Legislators	(N)	Percent Non-Majority Black Districts Electing African-American Legislators	(N)
South				
Alabama	83.3	(6)	0.0	(29)
Florida	100.0	(1)	2.6	(39)
Georgia	72.7	(11)	0.0	(45)
Louisiana	66.7	(6)	0.0	(33)
Mississippi	14.3	(14)	0.0	(38)
N. Carolina	100.0	(3)	4.3	(47)
S. Carolina	50.0	(10)	0.0	(36)
Tennessee	100.0	(3)	0.0	(33)
Texas	100.0	(1)	3.3	(30)
Virginia	100.0	(2)	2.6	(38)
Total	59.6	(57)	1.4	(368)
Non-South				
Delaware	100.0	(1)	0.0	(20)
Illinois	100.0	(6)	0.0	(53)
Maryland	87.5	(8)	0.0	(39)
Michigan	75.0	(4)	0.0	(34)
Missouri	75.0	(4)	0.0	(30)
New York	50.0	(4)	5.3	(57)
Ohio	0.0	(2)	6.9	(29)
Total	75.9	(29)	2.3	(262)

TABLE 5(C) . Percentage of Majority African-American and Non-Majority African-American Districts that Elected African-American Congressional Representatives in the South and Non-South in 1990

	Percent Majority Black Districts Electing African-American Legislators	(N)	Percent Non-Majority Black Districts Electing African-American Legislators	(N)
South				
Alabama	–	(0)	0.0	(7)
Arkansas	–	(0)	0.0	(4)
Florida	–	(0)	0.0	(19)
Georgia	100.0	(1)	0.0	(9)
Louisiana	100.0	(1)	0.0	(7)
Mississippi	100.0	(1)	0.0	(4)
N. Carolina	–	(0)	0.0	(11)
S. Carolina	–	(0)	0.0	(6)
Tennessee	100.0	(1)	0.0	(8)
Texas	–	(0)	3.7	(27)
Virginia	–	(0)	0.0	(10)
Total	100.0	(4)	.9	(112)

TABLE 5(C) *(continued)*. **Percentage of Majority African-American and Non-Majority African-American Districts that Elected African-American Congressional Representatives in the South and Non-South in 1990**

Non-South

Delaware	–	(0)	0.0	(1)
Illinois	100.0	(3)	0.0	(19)
Maryland	100.0	(1)	0.0	(7)
Michigan	100.0	(2)	0.0	(16)
Missouri	100.0	(1)	12.5	(8)
New Jersey	100.0	(1)	0.0	(13)
New York	100.0	(2)	6.3	(32)
Ohio	100.0	(1)	0.0	(20)
Total	100.0	(11)	2.6	(116)

TABLE 6(A). Percentage of Majority African-American and Non-Majority African-American Districts that Elected African-American State House Members in the South and Non-South in 1992

	Percent Majority Black Districts Electing African-American Legislators	(N)	*Percent Non-Majority Black Districts Electing African-American Legislators*	*(N)*
South				
Arkansas	76.9	(13)	0.0	(87)
Florida	92.3	(13)	1.9	(107)
Georgia	71.4	(42)	.7	(138)
Louisiana	92.3	(26)	0.0	(79)
Mississippi	84.2	(38)	0.0	(84)
N. Carolina	93.8	(16)	2.9	(104)
S. Carolina	64.3	(28)	0.0	(96)
Tennessee	100.0	(11)	1.1	(88)
Texas	100.0	(11)	2.2	(139)
Virginia	58.3	(12)	0.0	(88)
Total	81.0	(210)	1.0	(1010)
Non-South				
Delaware	100.0	(2)	0.0	(39)
Illinois	66.7	(18)	0.0	(100)
Michigan	76.9	(13)	1.0	(97)
Missouri	78.6	(14)	1.3	(149)
New Jersey	66.7	(6)	8.1	(74)
New York	93.3	(15)	4.4	(135)
Ohio	100.0	(6)	6.5	(93)
Total	79.7	(74)	3.1	(687)

TABLE 6(B). Percentage of Majority African-American and Non-Majority African-American Districts that Elected African-American State Senate Members in the South and Non-South in 1992

	Percent Majority Black Districts Electing African-American Legislators	(N)	Percent Non-Majority Black Districts Electing African-American Legislators	(N)
South				
Arkansas	100.0	(3)	0.0	(32)
Florida	100.0	(3)	2.7	(37)
Georgia	69.2	(13)	0.0	(43)
Louisiana	88.9	(9)	0.0	(30)
Mississippi	83.3	(12)	0.0	(40)
N. Carolina	100.0	(4)	4.3	(46)
S. Carolina	63.6	(11)	0.0	(35)
Tennessee	100.0	(3)	0.0	(30)
Texas	100.0	(1)	3.3	(30)
Virginia	100.0	(5)	0.0	(35)
Total	82.3	(64)	1.1	(358)
Non-South				
Delaware	100.0	(1)	0.0	(20)
Illinois	87.5	(8)	2.0	(51)
Missouri	75.0	(4)	0.0	(30)
New Jersey	66.7	(3)	0.0	(37)
New York	71.4	(7)	0.0	(54)
Ohio	100.0	(1)	6.3	(32)
Total	79.2	(24)	1.3	(224)

TABLE 6(C) . Percentage of Majority African-American and Non-Majority African-American Districts that Elected African-American Congressional Representatives in the South and Non-South in 1992

	Percent Majority Black Districts Electing African-American Legislators	(N)	Percent Non-Majority Black Districts Electing African-American Legislators	(N)
South				
Alabama	100.0	(1)	0.0	(6)
Arkansas	–	(0)	0.0	(4)
Florida	100.0	(3)	0.0	(20)
Georgia	100.0	(3)	0.0	(8)
Louisiana	100.0	(2)	0.0	(5)
Mississippi	100.0	(1)	0.0	(4)
N. Carolina	100.0	(2)	0.0	(10)
S. Carolina	100.0	(1)	0.0	(5)
Tennessee	100.0	(1)	0.0	(8)
Texas	100.0	(2)	0.0	(28)
Virginia	100.0	(1)	0.0	(10)
Total	100.0	(17)	0.0	(109)

TABLE 6(C) *(continued)*. **Percentage of Majority African-American and Non-Majority African-American Districts that Elected African-American Congressional Representatives in the South and Non-South in 1992**

Non-South

Delaware	-	(0)	0.0	(1)
Illinois	100.0	(3)	0.0	(17)
Maryland	100.0	(2)	0.0	(6)
Michigan	100.0	(2)	0.0	(14)
Missouri	100.0	(1)	12.5	(8)
New Jersey	100.0	(1)	0.0	(12)
New York	100.0	(3)	3.6	(28)
Ohio	100.0	(1)	0.0	(18)
Total	100.0	(13)	1.9	(104)

Tables 5 and 6 serve to illustrate another point: the vast majority of African-American legislators are elected from majority black districts. In 1990, 86 percent of the African-Americans serving in state legislatures represented majority African-American districts. In 1992, the percentage increased slightly to 89 percent. The percentage increase for Congress was more dramatic in the states studied: in 1990, 79 percent of the African-Americans in office were elected from majority black districts; in 1992, 94 percent of the African-American congressional representatives served majority black districts. Thus the gain in African-American representation cannot be attributed to an increase in the number of African-Americans being elected from non-majority black districts, at least in states with significant black populations. African-American representation increased only because the number and effectiveness of majority black districts increased.

Hispanic Representation and the Creation of Majority Hispanic Districts

The 1990s redistricting process also led to significant gains in the number of Hispanic legislators, although the increases were not as dramatic as for African-Americans. (African-American gains, especially in the South, surpassed Hispanic gains in Congress and state senates and were comparable in state houses.) African-Americans are currently better represented, proportionally, than Hispanics - although Hispanics were better represented than African-Americans in the South prior to 1992.

Table 7 indicates that Hispanics were dramatically underrepresented relative to population proportions in 1990. For example, Hispanics comprised over 25 percent of the population in California, but held only 5 percent of the state house seats and less than 8 percent of the state senate seats. In 1992, the percentage of California state house seats occupied by Hispanics increased to 10 percent but the percentage of state senate seats held by Hispanics remained the same (see Table 8). Hispanic representation actually decreased at the state legislative level in two states: Arizona and Colorado. Two states also decreased the number of majority

Hispanic districts, Colorado and Florida—although Florida maintained 3 Hispanic state senators from 1990 to 1992, despite its decrease in the number of majority Hispanic state senate seats.

TABLE 7. Percent Hispanic Elected Legislators in 1990[1]

	Percent Hispanic Population	State House	(N)	State Senate	(N)	U.S. Congress	(N)
Arizona	18.8	10.0	(60)	16.7	(30)	0.0	(5)
California	25.8	5.0	(80)	7.5	(40)	6.7	(45)
Colorado	12.9	10.8	(65)	8.6	(35)	0.0	(6)
Florida	12.2	6.7	(120)	7.5	(40)	5.3	(19)
Nevada	10.4	0.0	(42)	4.8	(21)	0.0	(2)
New Mexico	38.2	35.7	(70)	35.7	(42)	33.3	(3)
New York	12.3	2.7	(150)	3.3	(61)	2.9	(34)
Texas	25.5	13.3	(150)	16.1	(31)	14.8	(27)
Total	20.2	10.0	(737)	12.3	(300)	7.1	(141)

[1]The states listed above are states with Hispanic populations of 10 percent or greater (according to the 1990 U.S. Census). The percent Hispanic elected legislators reflects officeholders following the 1990 elections (as reported in *1991 National Roster of Hispanic Elected Officials,* National Association of Latino Elected and Appointed Officials, 1992).

TABLE 8. Percent Hispanic Elected Legislators in 1992[1]

	Percent Hispanic Population	State House	(N)	State Senate	(N)	U.S. Congress	(N)
Arizona	18.8	10.0	(60)	10.0	(30)	16.7	(6)
California	25.8	10.0	(80)	7.5	(40)	7.7	(52)
Colorado	12.9	9.2	(65)	5.7	(35)	0.0	(6)
Florida	12.2	8.3	(120)	7.5	(40)	8.7	(23)
Nevada	10.4	0.0	(42)	4.8	(21)	0.0	(2)
New Mexico	38.2	37.1	(70)	35.7	(42)	33.3	(3)
New York	12.3	4.7	(150)	6.6	(61)	6.5	(31)
Texas	25.5	18.0	(150)	19.4	(31)	16.7	(30)
Total	20.2	12.2	(737)	12.3	(300)	9.8	(153)

[1]The states listed above are states with Hispanic populations of 10 percent or greater according to the 1990 U.S. Census. The percent Hispanic elected legislators reflects officeholders following the 1992 elections.

The largest percentage increase between 1990 and 1992 in both African-American and Hispanic representation occurred at the congressional level rather than the state legislative level. This is somewhat surprising because it is easier to create minority districts at smaller levels of geography than larger levels such as congressional districts (Grofman and Handley, 1989b). One reason for the more dramatic gains at the congressional level may be the national attention focused on electing more minorities to federal office.

TABLE 9. Percent Majority Hispanic Districts in 1990[1]

	Percent Hispanic Population	State House	(N)	State Senate	(N)	U.S. Congress	(N)
California	25.8	12.5	(80)	7.5	(40)	8.9	(45)
Colorado	12.9	3.1	(65)	0.0	(35)	0.0	(6)
Florida	12.2	5.8	(120)	10.0	(40)	5.3	(19)
Nevada	10.4	0.0	(42)	0.0	(16)	0.0	(2)
New York	12.3	6.7	(150)	4.9	(61)	2.9	(34)
Texas	25.5	17.3	(150)	19.4	(31)	18.5	(27)
Total	19.9	9.1	(607)	7.2	(223)	8.3	(133)

[1]The states listed are states with Hispanic populations of 10 percent or greater. No data was available for Arizona or New Mexico therefore these two states have been excluded. The percentages reported in this table reflect the districting plan in place for the 1990 elections. Single member districts are counted once, multimember districts (both those that are majority Hispanic and those that are not) have a value equal to the number of delegates elected.

TABLE 10. Percent Majority Hispanic Districts in 1992[1]

	Percent Hispanic Population	State House	(N)	State Senate	(N)	U.S. Congress	(N)
Arizona	18.8	13.3	(30)	13.3	(30)	16.7	(6)
California	25.8	12.5	(80)	10.0	(40)	13.5	(52)
Colorado	12.9	0.0	(65)	0.0	(35)	0.0	(6)
Florida	12.2	7.5	(120)	7.5	(40)	8.7	(23)
Nevada	10.4	0.0	(42)	0.0	(16)	0.0	(2)
New Mexico	38.2	32.9	(70)	35.7	(42)	0.0	(3)
New York	12.3	7.3	(150)	6.6	(61)	6.5	(31)
Texas	25.5	20.0	(150)	22.6	(31)	23.3	(30)
Total	20.2	12.3	(707)	12.5	(295)	12.4	(153)

[1]The states listed are states with Hispanic populations of 10 percent or greater. The percentages reported in this table reflect the districting plan in place for the 1992 elections. Single member districts are counted once; multimember districts (both those that are majority Hispanic and those that are not) have a value equal to the number of delegates elected.

Why were Hispanic gains less substantial between 1990 and 1992 than African-American gains? Although Hispanic legislators appear no less likely to be elected to office from majority white seats than African-American legislators (compare Table 6 with Table 12), it appears that (1) a smaller percentage of Hispanic seats were created than African-American seats, relative to population proportions (compare Table 4 with Table 10) and (2) African-American seats were more likely to elect candidates of choice to office than Hispanic districts (compare Table 6 with Table 12). Undoubtedly, one of the primary reasons that fewer Hispanic districts were created is that it is easier to draw majority African-American seats than majority Hispanic seats: African-Americans tend to be more residentially segregated than Hispanics. Hispanic districts are less successful at electing Hispanics to office in large part because there is a greater proportion of non-voters among the Hispanic population. This is largely a product of the lower citizenship rates among the Hispanic population.

TABLE 11(A). Percentage of Majority Hispanic and Non-Majority Hispanic Districts That Elected Hispanic State House Members in 1990

	Percent Majority Hispanic Districts Electing Hispanic Legislators	(N)	Percent Non-Majority Hispanic Districts Electing Hispanic Legislators	(N)
California	30.0	(10)	1.4	(70)
Colorado	100.0	(2)	7.9	(63)
Florida	100.0	(7)	.9	(113)
Nevada	-	(0)	0.0	(42)
New York	30.0	(10)	.7	(140)
Texas	73.1	(26)	.8	(124)
Total	61.8	(55)	1.6	(552)

TABLE 11(B). Percentage of Majority Hispanic and Non-Majority Hispanic Districts That Elected Hispanic Senate Members in 1990

	Percent Majority Hispanic Districts Electing Hispanic Legislators	(N)	Percent Non-Majority Hispanic Districts Electing Hispanic Legislators	(N)
California	66.7	(3)	2.7	(37)
Colorado	–	(0)	8.6	(35)
Florida	75.0	(4)	0.0	(36)
Nevada	–	(0)	4.8	(21)
New York	66.7	(3)	0.0	(58)
Texas	66.7	(6)	4.0	(25)
Total	68.8	(16)	2.8	(212)

TABLE 11(C). Percentage of Majority Hispanic and Non-Majority Hispanic Districts That Elected Hispanic Congressional Representatives in 1990

	Percent Majority Hispanic Districts Electing Hispanic Legislators	(N)	Percent Non-Majority Hispanic Districts Electing Hispanic Legislators	(N)
Arizona	–	(0)	0.0	(5)
California	75.0	(4)	0.0	(41)
Colorado	–	(0)	0.0	(6)
Florida	100.0	(1)	0.0	(18)
Nevada	–	(0)	0.0	(2)
New Mexico	–	(0)	33.3	(3)
New York	100.0	(1)	0.0	(33)
Texas	80.0	(5)	0.0	(22)
Total	81.8	(11)	.8	(130)

TABLE 12(A). Percentage of Majority Hispanic and Non-Majority Hispanic Districts That Elected Hispanic State House Members in 1992

	Percent Majority Hispanic Districts Electing Hispanic Legislators		Percent Non-Majority Hispanic Districts Electing Hispanic Legislators	
		(N)		(N)
Arizona	62.5	(8)	1.9	(52)
California	60.0	(10)	2.9	(70)
Colorado	–	(0)	9.2	(65)
Florida	100.0	(9)	.8	(131)
Nevada	–	(0)	0.0	(42)
New Mexico	78.3	(23)	17.0	(47)
New York	63.6	(11)	0.0	(139)
Texas	86.7	(30)	.9	(120)
Total	78.0	(91)	2.9	(666)

TABLE 12(B). Percentage of Majority Hispanic and Non-Majority Hispanic Districts That Elected Hispanic State Senate Members in 1992

	Percent Majority Hispanic Districts Electing Hispanic Legislators		Percent Non-Majority Hispanic Districts Electing Hispanic Legislators	
		(N)		(N)
Arizona	50.0	(4)	3.8	(26)
California	25.0	(4)	5.6	(36)
Colorado	–	(0)	5.7	(35)
Florida	100.0	(3)	0.0	(37)
Nevada	–	(0)	4.8	(21)
New Mexico	86.7	(15)	7.4	(27)
New York	100.0	(4)	0.0	(57)
Texas	71.4	(7)	4.5	(24)
Total	75.7	(37)	3.4	(263)

TABLE 12(C). Percentage of Majority Hispanic and Non-Majority Hispanic Districts That Elected Hispanic Congressional Representatives in 1992

	Percent Majority Hispanic Districts Electing Hispanic Legislators		Percent Non-Majority Hispanic Districts Electing Hispanic Legislators	
		(N)		(N)
Arizona	100.0	(1)	0.0	(5)
California	57.1	(7)	0.0	(45)
Colorado	–	(0)	0.0	(6)
Florida	100.0	(2)	0.0	(21)
Nevada	–	(0)	0.0	(2)
New Mexico	–	(0)	33.3	(3)
New York	100.0	(2)	0.0	(29)
Texas	71.4	(7)	0.0	(23)
Total	73.7	(19)	.7	(134)

MINORITY PERCENTAGES IN LEGISLATIVE DISTRICTS AND THE ELECTION OF DEMOCRATS

In addition to measuring the impact of redistricting on African-American and Hispanic representation, we attempted to determine whether there is a relationship between the minority population percentages in a district more generally and the election of a minority-preferred candidate. We assumed that, given the large percentage of African-Americans and non-Cuban Hispanics that are Democrats, Democrats would be the candidate of choice—and this assumption appears to be correct given the strong relationship between minority concentrations across districts and the election of Democrats to legislative office.

TABLE 13. Percent Democrats in State Houses by Percent African-American in District 1990[1]

			Percent African-American in District								
South	*0-9.9*	*(N)*	*10-19.9*	*(N)*	*20-29.9*	*(N)*	*30-39.9*	*(N)*	*40-49.9*	*(N)*	*50+*	*(N)*
Alabama	59.4	(32)	75.0	(28)	91.7	(12)	85.7	(7)	100.0	(6)	100.0	(20)
Florida	41.0	(61)	71.0	(31)	90.9	(11)	100.0	(7)	100.0	(1)	100.0	(9)
Georgia	52.2	(46)	70.6	(34)	89.7	(29)	100.0	(24)	100.0	(13)	100.0	(34)
Louisiana	43.8	(16)	81.0	(21)	81.0	(21)	100.0	(19)	83.3	(6)	100.0	(19)
Mississippi	46.2	(13)	80.0	(20)	81.8	(22)	86.4	(22)	90.9	(11)	97.1	(34)
N. Carolina	37.9	(29)	52.9	(34)	83.3	(24)	95.0	(20)	100.0	(4)	100.0	(9)
S. Carolina	30.8	(13)	32.4	(34)	71.4	(21)	90.0	(20)	90.0	(10)	95.8	(24)
Tennessee	42.1	(57)	76.5	(17)	60.0	(5)	66.7	(6)	66.7	(3)	100.0	(11)
Texas	55.6	(81)	56.1	(41)	81.8	(11)	100.0	(4)	100.0	(2)	100.0	(9)
Virginia	38.9	(36)	51.7	(29)	69.2	(13)	88.9	(9)	100.0	(4)	100.0	(9)
Total	46.4	(384)	62.3	(289)	81.7	(169)	92.8	(138)	93.3	(60)	98.9	(178)
Non - South												
Illinois	43.6	(78)	93.8	(16)	83.3	(6)	100.0	(2)	100.0	(6)	100.0	(14)
Maryland	65.2	(46)	79.4	(34)	89.5	(19)	100.0	(9)	100.0	(9)	100.0	(24)
Michigan	40.8	(76)	80.0	(10)	66.7	(6)	100.0	(2)	—		100.0	(16)
Missouri	50.4	(121)	73.3	(15)	85.7	(7)	100.0	(1)	100.0	(4)	100.0	(14)
New York	46.5	(101)	95.2	(21)	100.0	(4)	100.0	(6)	100.0	(5)	100.0	(13)
Ohio	50.7	(71)	75.0	(12)	100.0	(3)	100.0	(5)	100.0	(4)	100.0	(4)
Total	48.5	(493)	83.3	(108)	86.7	(45)	100.0	(25)	100.0	(28)	100.0	(85)

[1] Information for Arkansas, Delaware and New Jersey unavailable

African-American Population Concentrations and the Election of Democrats to Office

As is evident from Tables 13-18, a very clear pattern exists between the percentage African-American in a district and the election of a Democrat. Regardless of region or type of district examined, **the higher the percentage African-American in the district, the greater the percentage of Democrats elected to office**. This pattern holds true in both 1990 and 1992, for both the South and the non-South, and for all three types of legislative districts examined—state house, state senate and congressional districts.

TABLE 14. Percent Democrats in State Senates by Percent African-American in District 1990[1]

Percent African-American in District

South	0-9.9	(N)	10-19.9	(N)	20-29.9	(N)	30-39.9	(N)	40-49.9	(N)	50+	(N)
Alabama	42.9	(7)	80.0	(10)	87.5	(8)	100.0	(2)	100.0	(2)	100.0	(6)
Florida	31.3	(16)	66.7	(18)	100.0	(4)	—		100.0	(1)	100.0	(1)
Georgia	54.5	(11)	66.7	(12)	80.0	(10)	100.0	(9)	100.0	(3)	100.0	(11)
Louisiana	0.0	(2)	77.8	(9)	100.0	(10)	100.0	(10)	50.0	(2)	83.3	(6)
Mississippi	100.0	(3)	55.6	(9)	77.8	(9)	92.3	(13)	100.0	(5)	92.3	(13)
N. Carolina	45.5	(11)	41.7	(12)	93.3	(15)	100.0	(8)	100.0	(1)	100.0	(3)
S. Carolina	60.0	(5)	50.0	(8)	76.9	(13)	75.0	(8)	100.0	(1)	100.0	(10)
Tennessee	47.4	(19)	57.1	(7)	100.0	(2)	—		100.0	(2)	100.0	(3)
Texas	64.3	(14)	70.0	(10)	100.0	(4)	—		100.0	(1)	100.0	(1)
Virginia	75.0	(12)	71.4	(14)	60.0	(5)	75.0	(4)	100.0	(3)	100.0	(2)
Total	52.0	(100)	64.2	(109)	86.3	(80)	92.6	(54)	95.2	(21)	96.4	(56)
Non - South												
Illinois	27.8	(36)	81.8	(11)	100.0	(2)	100.0	(4)	—		100.0	(6)
Maryland	56.3	(16)	90.9	(11)	83.3	(6)	100.0	(3)	100.0	(3)	100.0	(8)
Michigan	36.0	(25)	42.9	(7)	—		100.0	(1)	100.0	(1)	100.0	(4)
Missouri	57.7	(26)	100.0	(3)	100.0	(1)	—		—		100.0	(4)
New York	18.9	(37)	58.3	(12)	100.0	(3)	100.0	(3)	100.0	(2)	100.0	(4)
Ohio	22.7	(22)	33.3	(6)	100.0	(2)	100.0	(1)	100.0	(2)	100.0	(1)
Total	34.0	(162)	68.0	(50)	92.9	(14)	100.0	(12)	100.0	(8)	100.0	(27)

[1]Information for Arkansas, Delaware and New Jersey unavailable

TABLE 15. Percent Democrats in Congress by Percent African-American in District 1990

Percent African-American In District

South	0-9.9	(N)	10-19.9	(N)	20-29.9	(N)	30-39.9	(N)	40-49.9	(N)	50+	(N)
Alabama	100.0	(1)	100.0	(1)	50.0	(2)	66.7	(3)	—		—	
Arkansas	0.0	(1)	100.0	(2)	100.0	(1)	—		—		—	
Florida	42.9	(7)	37.5	(8)	66.7	(3)	100.0	(1)	—		—	
Georgia	100.0	(2)	0.0	(1)	100.0	(2)	100.0	(4)	—		100.0	(1)
Louisiana	—		0.0	(1)	66.7	(3)	33.3	(3)	—		100.0	(1)
Mississippi	—		100.0	(1)	100.0	(1)	100.0	(1)	100.0	(1)	100.0	(1)
N. Carolina	0.0	(1)	75.0	(4)	50.0	(4)	100.0	(1)	100.0	(1)	—	
S. Carolina	—		100.0	(1)	100.0	(1)	50.0	(4)	—		—	
Tennessee	50.0	(4)	50.0	(2)	100.0	(2)	—		—		100.0	(1)
Texas	57.1	(14)	85.7	(7)	80.0	(5)	100.0	(1)	—		—	
Virginia	50.0	(2)	66.7	(3)	66.7	(3)	50.0	(2)	—		—	
Total	53.1	(32)	64.5	(31)	74.1	(27)	70.0	(20)	100.0	(2)	100.0	(4)

Non - South												
Delaware	—		100.0	(1)	—		—		—		—	
Illinois	53.3	(15)	100.0	(4)	—		—		—		100.0	(3)
Maryland	50.0	(2)	0.0	(2)	100.0	(2)	—		100.0	(1)	100.0	(1)
Michigan	41.7	(12)	100.0	(3)	100.0	(1)	—		—		100.0	(2)
Missouri	57.1	(7)	—		100.0	(1)	—		—		100.0	(1)
New Jersey	33.3	(6)	71.4	(7)	—		—		—		100.0	(1)
New York	45.5	(22)	83.3	(6)	100.0	(1)	100.0	(2)	100.0	(1)	100.0	(2)
Ohio	41.7	(12)	62.5	(8)	—		—		—		100.0	(1)
Total	46.1	(76)	74.2	(31)	100.0	(5)	100.0	(2)	100.0	(2)	100.0	(11)

Overall, the probability of electing a Democrat to the state legislature and Congress decreased between 1990 and 1992.[5] Although the decline was not great (no more than 5 percent for any set of districts), it is found at all three levels; 64% to 60% in Congress; 66% to 61% in state senates; and 67% to 63% for state houses. This decline occurred in both the South and the non-South considered separately as well. In absolute terms, among states with comparable data, Democrats lost 31 house and 26 senate seats in the South and 10 house and 9 senate seats in the non-South. In Congress, Democrats lost 10 seats in the non-South and no seats in the South in 1992.[6]

---

[5]No state legislative elections were held in Alabama, Maryland and the Michigan state senate in 1991 or 1992, therefore only 16 states have been compared at the state legislative level. All 19 states have been compared at the congressional and state house level.

TABLE 16. Percent Democrats in State Houses by Percent African-American in District 1992[1]

Percent African-American In District

South	0-9.9	(N)	10-19.9	(N)	20-29.9	(N)	30-39.9	(N)	40-49.9	(N)	50+	(N)
Arkansas	83.6	(55)	100.0	(18)	100.0	(10)	75.0	(4)	—		92.3	(13)
Florida	40.0	(75)	84.6	(26)	100.0	(3)	100.0	(3)	—		100.0	(13)
Georgia	35.7	(56)	68.9	(45)	92.6	(27)	100.0	(9)	100.0	(1)	100.0	(42)
Louisiana	55.6	(18)	77.8	(27)	90.5	(21)	100.0	(12)	0.0	(1)	100.0	(26)
Mississippi	41.7	(12)	60.0	(35)	72.7	(22)	83.3	(12)	100.0	(3)	100.0	(38)
N. Carolina	38.5	(39)	46.7	(30)	95.5	(22)	87.5	(8)	100.0	(5)	100.0	(16)
S. Carolina	4.3	(23)	25.9	(27)	78.3	(23)	87.5	(16)	71.4	(7)	100.0	(28)
Tennessee	48.3	(60)	84.6	(13)	71.4	(7)	83.3	(6)	100.0	(2)	100.0	(11)
Texas	50.0	(96)	71.9	(32)	100.0	(4)	100.0	(3)	100.0	(1)	100.0	(11)
Virginia	40.5	(42)	55.6	(27)	76.9	(13)	66.7	(6)	—		100.0	(12)
Total	48.3	(476)	65.4	(280)	86.2	(152)	88.6	(79)	85.0	(20)	99.5	(210)
Non - South												
Delaware	43.8	(16)	37.5	(14)	33.3	(6)	0.0	(1)	100.0	(2)	100.0	(2)
Illinois	43.5	(85)	77.8	(9)	83.3	(6)	—		—		100.0	(18)
Michigan	34.2	(79)	87.5	(8)	71.4	(7)	100.0	(2)	100.0	(1)	100.0	(13)
Missouri	52.7	(129)	92.9	(14)	75.0	(4)	100.0	(1)	100.0	(1)	100.0	(14)
New Jersey	8.0	(50)	20.0	(10)	66.7	(12)	100.0	(2)	—		100.0	(6)
New York	51.5	(101)	100.0	(17)	100.0	(9)	100.0	(4)	100.0	(4)	100.0	(15)
Ohio	44.2	(77)	71.4	(7)	0.0	(1)	100.0	(2)	100.0	(4)	100.0	(6)
Total	42.6	(537)	70.9	(79)	73.3	(45)	91.7	(12)	100.0	(12)	100.0	(74)

[1]Alabama and Maryland did not have state house elections in 1991 or 1992.

Much of the decrease in the number of Democrats elected to office is attributable to the increase in the number of districts with less than 10 percent black populations and the lower probability of Democrats being elected from these districts. This is the only category in which the percentage of Democrats elected clearly decreased between 1990 and 1992; furthermore, this category experienced the largest increase in the number of districts—there were far more dis-

---

[6]It should be noted that as a result of reapportionment the South gained 9 congressional seats and the non-South lost 10 congressional seats.

tricts with less than 10 percent black in 1992 than there were in 1990. For example, in the non-South the number of districts with black populations below 10 increased by 24 in state houses, 14 in state senates and 2 in Congress; in the South the increase in the number of districts with less than 10 black was 69 in state houses, 37 in state senates and 19 in Congress. Moreover, following the 1992 elections, the only category in which Democrats controlled a minority of the seats were those districts below 10 percent. This is true regardless of region or level of office. In every other black percentage range, Democrats held a majority of the seats. The percentages of Democrats elected in each percentage category (0 to 10, 10 to 20, 20 to 30, 30 to 40, 40 to 50 and over 50 black), as well as the number of districts falling into each category can be found in Tables 13 and 16 for state houses, Tables 14 and 17 for state senates and Tables 15 and 18 for Congress.

TABLE 17. Percent Democrats in State Senates by Percent African-American in District 1992[1]

South	0-9.9	(N)	10-19.9	(N)	20-29.9	(N)	30-39.9	(N)	40-49.9	(N)	50+	(N)
					Percent African - American In District							
Arkansas	78.9	(19)	85.7	(7)	100.0	(4)	100.0	(2)	—		100.0	(3)
Florida	26.9	(26)	85.7	(7)	100.0	(1)	100.0	(2)	100.0	(1)	100.0	(3)
Georgia	35.7	(14)	68.8	(16)	85.7	(7)	100.0	(5)	100.0	(1)	100.0	(13)
Louisiana	25.0	(4)	72.7	(11)	100.0	(8)	100.0	(6)	100.0	(1)	100.0	(9)
Mississippi	100.0	(2)	35.7	(14)	81.8	(11)	90.0	(10)	66.7	(3)	100.0	(12)
N. Carolina	40.0	(15)	83.3	(6)	94.7	(19)	100.0	(4)	100.0	(2)	100.0	(4)
S. Carolina	33.3	(6)	41.7	(12)	37.5	(8)	100.0	(8)	100.0	(1)	100.0	(11)
Tennessee	52.4	(21)	0.0	(4)	100.0	(2)	100.0	(3)	—		100.0	(3)
Texas	55.6	(18)	50.0	(10)	100.0	(1)	—		100.0	(1)	100.0	(1)
Virginia	25.0	(24)	50.0	(14)	50.0	(6)	100.0	(1)	—		100.0	(5)
Total	43.6	(149)	57.4	(101)	82.1	(67)	97.6	(41)	90.0	(10)	100.0	(64)

Non - South	0-9.9	(N)	10-19.9	(N)	20-29.9	(N)	30-39.9	(N)	40-49.9	(N)	50+	(N)
Delaware	50.0	(8)	87.5	(8)	66.7	(3)	—		100.0	(1)	100.0	(1)
Illinois	32.6	(43)	25.0	(4)	100.0	(2)	100.0	(2)	—		100.0	(8)
Missouri	44.0	(25)	100.0	(3)	—		—		—		100.0	(4)
New Jersey	12.0	(25)	40.0	(5)	66.7	(6)	100.0	(1)	—		100.0	(3)
New York	26.2	(42)	33.3	(6)	100.0	(4)	100.0	(2)	—		100.0	(7)
Ohio	20.0	(25)	100.0	(3)	100.0	(1)	100.0	(2)	100.0	(1)	100.0	(1)
Total	28.6	(168)	62.1	(29)	81.2	(16)	100.0	(7)	100.0	(2)	100.0	(24)

[1] Alabama, Maryland and Michigan did not have state senate elections in 1991 or 1992

On the other hand, most districts over 30 percent black continue to elect Democrats to office. In fact, in the non-South, every state house, state senate and congressional district over 30 percent black elects a Democrat to office (this is true for both 1990 and 1992) except for one.[7] The pattern is not quite as stark in the South. (Actually, in the South, not even every district over 50 percent black elects a Democrat to office, at least at the state legislative level).

TABLE 18. Percent Democrats in Congress by Percent African-American in District 1992

South	0-9.9	(N)	10-19.9	(N)	20-29.9	(N)	30-39.9	(N)	40-49.9	(N)	50+	(N)
Alabama	50.0	(2)	100.0	(1)	33.3	(3)	—		—		100.0	(1)
Arkansas	0.0	(1)	100.0	(2)	0.0	(1)	—		—		—	
Florida	25.0	(16)	66.7	(3)	100.0	(1)	—		—		100.0	(3)
Georgia	50.0	(2)	50.0	(4)	50.0	(2)	—		—		100.0	(3)
Louisiana	—		33.3	(3)	50.0	(2)	—		—		100.0	(2)
Mississippi	—		100.0	(1)	100.0	(1)	100.0	(1)	100.0	(1)	100.0	(1)
N. Carolina	0.0	(4)	100.0	(2)	100.0	(4)	—		—		100.0	(2)
S. Carolina	—		0.0	(1)	33.3	(3)	100.0	(1)	—		100.0	(1)
Tennessee	50.0	(4)	66.7	(3)	100.0	(1)	—		—		100.0	(1)
Texas	52.6	(19)	100.0	(7)	100.0	(2)	—		—		100.0	(2)
Virginia	66.7	(3)	40.0	(5)	100.0	(1)	100.0	(1)	—		100.0	(1)
Total	39.2	(51)	68.8	(32)	66.7	(21)	100.0	(3)	100.0	(1)	100.0	(17)

Non-South	0-9.9	(N)	10-19.9	(N)	20-29.9	(N)	30-39.9	(N)	40-49.9	(N)	50+	(N)
Delaware	—		0.0	(1)	—		—		—		—	
Illinois	46.7	(15)	100.0	(2)	—		—		—		100.0	(3)
Maryland	0.0	(3)	66.7	(3)	—		—		—		100.0	(2)
Michigan	50.0	(12)	100.0	(2)	—		—		—		100.0	(2)
Missouri	57.1	(7)	—		100.0	(1)	—		—		100.0	(1)
New Jersey	16.7	(6)	83.3	(6)	—		—		—		100.0	(1)
New York	50.0	(22)	33.3	(3)	—		100.0	(3)	—		100.0	(3)
Ohio	38.5	(13)	100.0	(3)	0.0	(1)	100.0	(1)	—		100.0	(1)
Total	43.6	(78)	75.0	(20)	50.0	(2)	100.0	(4)	—		100.0	(13)

Percent African - American In District

Not surprisingly, the categories of districts that experienced the largest decrease in number were those districts with black populations between 30 and 50 percent. For example, in the South there were 18 fewer congressional districts, 90 fewer state house districts and 22 fewer senate seats with black populations between 30 and 50 percent. In the non-South, the decrease in districts with black populations between 30 and 50 percent was 16 in state houses, 5 in state senates and no change in congressional districts. This decrease in districts between 30

---

[7]The exception is a 31% black state house district in Delaware that elects a Republican to office.

and 50 percent black is not unexpected given the increase in the number of districts over 50 percent black—the logical place to begin drawing additional majority black districts is in areas of the state with substantial black populations and no currently existing majority black district. Since Democrats control an overwhelming percentage of districts between 30 and 50 percent black, some of the Democratic losses in 1992 must be attributed to the elimination of these strong minority influence districts.

A review of the relationship between black population concentrations and the election of Democrats to office in the individual states across the region reveals some differences across states. South Carolina and New Jersey are the least likely to elect Democrats at low black percentages, Arkansas appears to be the most likely. In 1992, all congressional and legislative districts in Florida, Texas and New York with black populations greater than 20 percent elected Democrats to office. On the other hand, black percentages of 50 percent or more were required before every district in Louisiana, Mississippi and South Carolina elected a Democrat.[8] Overall, the patterns in the South and non-South, especially with regard to Congress, are becoming increasingly similar. This is due in large part to the decreasing likelihood of Democrats being elected from the South, particularly from districts less than 10 percent black.

Hispanic Population Concentrations and the Election of Democrats to Office

Although the pattern is not as marked, the same relationship noted for African-American population concentrations and the election of Democrats exists for Hispanics: the higher the percentage of Hispanics in districts, the greater the percentage of Democrats elected to office.[9] This is true of all three levels of legislative districts but, as will be discussed below, there are some significant differences in the three levels of offices studied.

In states with Hispanic populations greater than 10 percent, the probability of electing a Democrat to the state house and Congress actually increased between 1990 and 1992, while the probability of electing Democrats to the state senate decreased slightly. The percentage of seats held by Democrats increased from 58 in 1990 to 61 in 1992 in the seven state houses considered (Table 19); but the percentage of the seats held by Democrats in the state senates decreased from 54 to 50 (Table 20). In actual numbers, Democrats gained 24 house and 4 congressional seats (these states gained 8 seats as a result of reapportionment) and lost 9 state senate seats.

The Hispanic population percentage which elects a majority of Democrats to

---

[8]In 1990, no category of districts we analyzed in these three states elected only Democrats.

[9]We analyzed seven of the eight states with Hispanic populations greater than 10 percent. The states reviewed were Arizona, California, Colorado, Nevada, New Mexico, New York and Texas. Florida, although it has an Hispanic population greater than 10 percent, was excluded because of the large number of Cuban voters who exhibit little similarity with non-Cuban Hispanics (and tend to vote for Republicans rather than Democrats).

office is dependent on the level of office. For example, in 1992 Democrats held 62 of the state house districts with Hispanic populations between 10 and 20 percent (see Table 19), however, Democrats did not control a majority of state senate seats until the Hispanic population concentration reached 30 to 40 percent—at which point Democrats were elected to 78 percent of the seats (see Table 20). Furthermore, there is no category of state house districts or congressional districts that elect only Democrats; but all state senate districts over 40 Hispanic elect Democrats to office (see Table 21).

Since the populations of New York and Texas are both over 10 percent black and 10 percent Hispanic, a more detailed review of these two states provides a good indication of the role played by these two groups in electing Democrats to office. In New York, there appears to be little measurable difference between the two minority groups; in the New York Assembly, Democrats control all of districts over 10 percent black and all of the districts over 10 percent Hispanic (see Tables 16 and 19). The likelihood of electing a Democrat to the state senate or to Congress in New York is also comparable regardless of whether a district contains a significant African-American or Hispanic population.

TABLE 19: Percent Democrats in State Houses by Percent Hispanic in District
1992

1992	0-9.9	(N)	10-19.9	(N)	20-29.9	(N)	30-39.9	(N)	40-49.9	(N)	50+	(N)
				Percent Hispanic in District								
Arizona	9.1	(22)	36.4	(22)	100.0	(2)	83.3	(6)	—		100.0	(8)
California	33.3	(9)	61.8	(34)	35.7	(14)	60.0	(5)	87.5	(8)	100.0	(10)
Colorado	35.0	(40)	71.4	(14)	60.0	(5)	0.0	(1)	80.0	(5)	—	
Nevada	60.0	(25)	81.3	(16)	—		100.0	(1)	—		—	
New Mexico	100.0	(2)	38.5	(13)	52.8	(17)	85.7	(7)	100.0	(8)	100.0	(23)
New York	50.5	(99)	100.0	(23)	100.0	(13)	100.0	(3)	100.0	(1)	100.0	(11)
Texas	45.8	(48)	51.1	(45)	66.7	(15)	71.4	(7)	100.0	(5)	93.3	(30)
Total	44.1	(245)	61.7	(167)	63.6	(66)	76.7	(30)	92.6	(27)	97.6	(82)

1990[1]

1990	0-9.9	(N)	10-19.9	(N)	20-29.9	(N)	30-39.9	(N)	40-49.9	(N)	50+	(N)
				Percent Hispanic in District								
California	36.4	(11)	51.9	(27)	35.3	(17)	91.7	(12)	100.0	(2)	100.0	(10)
Colorado	30.8	(39)	50.0	(10)	55.6	(9)	100.0	(1)	50.0	(4)	100.0	(2)
Nevada	36.0	(25)	71.4	(14)	100.0	(2)	100.0	(1)	—		—	
New York	45.5	(99)	95.7	(23)	100.0	(14)	100.0	(1)	100.0	(3)	100.0	(10)
Texas	73.5	(34)	42.5	(40)	66.7	(21)	72.7	(11)	83.3	(6)	88.4	(26)
Total	45.7	(208)	59.6	(114)	65.1	(63)	84.6	(26)	80.0	(15)	93.8	(48)

[1]Information for Arizona and New Mexico not available

TABLE 20: Percent Democrats in State Senates by Percent Hispanic in District
1992

Percent Hispanic in District

1992	*0-9.9*	*(N)*	*10-19.9*	*(N)*	*20-29.9*	*(N)*	*30-39.9*	*(N)*	*40-49.9*	*(N)*	*50+*	*(N)*
Arizona	18.2	(11)	27.3	(11)	100.0	(1)	66.7	(3)	----		100.0	(4)
California	50.0	(2)	46.7	(15)	50.0	(12)	100.0	(2)	100.0	(3)	100.0	(3)
Colorado	23.8	(21)	75.0	(8)	50.0	(2)	100.0	(2)	100.0	(2)	----	
Nevada	33.3	(12)	66.7	(9)	----		----		----		----	
New Mexico	100.0	(1)	28.6	(7)	22.2	(9)	57.1	(7)	100.0	(3)	100.0	(15)
New York	21.6	(37)	64.3	(14)	66.7	(3)	100.0	(2)	100.0	(1)	100.0	(4)
Texas	33.3	(9)	30.0	(10)	100.0	(3)	100.0	(2)	----		100.0	(7)
Total	25.8	(93)	48.6	(74)	50.0	(30)	77.8	(18)	100.0	(9)	100.0	(33)

1990[1]

Percent Hispanic In District

1990	*0-9.9*	*(N)*	*10-19.9*	*(N)*	*20-29.9*	*(N)*	*30-39.9*	*(N)*	*40-49.9*	*(N)*	*50+*	*(N)*
California	100.0	(2)	53.3	(15)	62.5	(8)	85.7	(7)	66.7	(3)	100.0	(3)
Colorado	10.5	(19)	28.6	(7)	83.3	(6)	----		100.0	(3)	----	
Nevada	40.0	(15)	83.3	(6)	----		----		----		----	
New York	23.7	(38)	54.5	(11)	85.7	(7)	----		100.0	(2)	100.0	(3)
Texas	71.4	(7)	50.0	(8)	85.7	(7)	100.0	(1)	100.0	(1)	83.3	(6)
Total	29.6	(81)	53.2	(47)	78.6	(28)	87.5	(8)	89.9	(9)	91.7	(12)

[1]Information for Arizona and New Mexico is unavailable

In Texas, on the other hand, there appears to be a difference in the ability of the two minority groups to affect the election of a Democrat. As discussed previously, every district in Texas with a black population over 20 percent elects a Democrat to office (see Tables 16, 17 and 18). This is not the case in districts with Hispanic populations greater than 20 percent; in fact, no category elects only Democrats except for state senate districts over 20 percent Hispanic. The differences between Hispanic and African-American population concentrations appear to be narrowing, at least at the state legislative level, when the 1990 and 1992 tables are compared.

Some possible explanations for the differences between the African-American and the Hispanic population percentages necessary to elect Democrats to office include: (1) the large number of non-citizens in the Hispanic community who are ineligible to vote; and, (2) the lower proportion of Hispanic voters compared with African-American voters who are Democrats. For example, in New York—where a large proportion of the Hispanics are Puerto Rican and thus eligible to vote—the difference between African-Americans and Hispanics in their ability to elect Democrats to office is minimal.

Table 21. Percent Democrats in Congress by Percent Hispanic in District

1992
Percent Hispanic In District

1992	0-9.9	(N)	10-19.9	(N)	20-29.9	(N)	30-39.9	(N)	40-49.9	(N)	50+	(N)
Arizona	0.0	(1)	50.0	(4)	----		----		----		100.0	(1)
California	33.3	(3)	70.0	(20)	16.7	(12)	71.4	(7)	75.0	(4)	100.0	(6)
Colorado	33.3	(3)	0.0	(2)	100.0	(1)	----		----		----	
Nevada	0.0	(1)	100.0	(1)	----		----		----		----	
New Mexico	----		----		----		50.0	(2)	0.0	(1)	----	
New York	35.0	(20)	100.0	(6)	100.0	(2)	----		100.0	(1)	100.0	(2)
Texas	50.0	(8)	66.7	(12)	100.0	(3)	----		----		85.7	(7)
Total	36.1	(36)	68.9	(45)	44.4	(18)	66.7	(9)	66.7	(6)	93.8	(16)

1990
Percent Hispanic In District

1990	0-9.9	(N)	10-19.9	(N)	20-29.9	(N)	30-39.9	(N)	40-49.9	(N)	50+	(N)
Arizona	0.0	(1)	0.0	(3)	----		----		100.0	(1)	----	
California	33.3	(6)	58.8	(17)	33.3	(6)	77.8	(9)	66.7	(3)	100.0	(4)
Colorado	0.0	(2)	66.7	(3)	100.0	(1)	----		----		----	
Nevada	0.0	(1)	100.0	(1)	----		----		----		----	
New Mexico	----		----		----		33.3	(3)	----		----	
New York	36.8	(19)	87.5	(8)	100.0	(4)	----		100.0	(2)	100.0	(1)
Texas	57.1	(7)	80.0	(5)	62.5	(8)	0.0	(1)	100.0	(1)	100.0	(5)
Total	36.1	(36)	64.9	(37)	63.2	(19)	61.5	(13)	85.7	(7)	100.0	(10)

CONCLUSION

The 1990s redistricting process led to significant growth in the number of African-American and Hispanic elected officials. These gains were due to the increase in the number of majority minority districts created; they were not the result of additional minority representatives being elected from majority white districts. In fact, in 1992 fewer African-Americans represented majority white districts than in 1990. Thus, we have found no evidence to indicate that majority minority districts are no longer necessary to ensure African-Americans and Hispanics fair representation in our legislative bodies.

Our research also indicates a strong relationship between the minority composition of a district and the likelihood of electing a Democrat to office. The majority of districts over 10 percent black or Hispanic elect Democrats. For example, in 1992 Democrats controlled an overwhelming majority of districts containing black populations in excess of 10 percent, but a minority of districts with black populations less than 10 percent. Democratic losses in the first post-redistricting elections appear to be the result of an increase in the number of overwhelmingly white districts and the lower probability of Democrats being elected from these districts.

REPRESENTATION AND AMBITION IN THE NEW AFRICAN-AMERICAN CONGRESSIONAL DISTRICTS: The Supply-Side Effects

Matthew M. Schousen, David T. Canon, and Patrick J. Sellers

THE GOAL OF EMPOWERING MINORITIES through redistricting has been attacked from all sides (Guinier, 1991a: 1134-53; Thernstrom, 1987: 237-38). Though our study will not resolve this normative debate, it offers a new perspective from which to assess the viability of this approach to black empowerment: the supply-side of redistricting.[1] The traditional demand-side perspective on minority redistricting includes studies of vote dilution (Davidson, 1984; Schockley, 1991), racial bloc voting (Chapter 4 of this volume; Grofman, 1991; Loewen, 1990; McCrary, 1990; Schockley, 1991), run-off elections (Bullock and Smith, 1990; Ballard, 1991), political geography and demographics (Grofman and Handley, 1989a, 1989b; Niemi, Grofman, Carlucci, and Hofeller, 1990; Niemi and Brace, 1993), racial transitions and incumbency advantage (Vanderleeuw, 1991), and the partisan implications of black-majority districts (Brace, Grofman, and Handley, 1987).

In contrast, our supply-side perspective examines how individual politicians respond to the changing electoral context imposed by new district lines and how, in turn, their decisions shape the electoral choices and outcomes in a given district. Rather than simply assuming that goals for minority representation are translated into a specific configuration of district lines with predictable conse-

---

[1] The "supply-side" perspective of politics has provided new explanations for divided government (Jacobson, 1990; Ehrenhalt, 1991), partisan realignments (Hurley, 1991; Canon and Sousa, 1992), and the impact of economic variables on election outcomes (Jacobson and Kernell, 1983). But, there is no systematic analysis of the relationship between redistricting and candidate behavior. The only study of the supply-side of redistricting and minority representation is an analysis of black mayoral elections that concludes black incumbents deter future black challengers (Watson, 1984).

quences, the supply-side perspective cautions that all outcomes are dependent on the calculations of potential candidates. We argue that individual politicians acting in their own self-interest create a collective action problem for a majority in the black community that may tip the balance of power to a minority of black voters and white moderates in the district, or in extreme cases undermine the central goal of electing black representatives. Ironically, the collective action problem is most likely in newly created black-majority districts because of the absence of institutions that could channel the ambition of competing black candidates.

We examine this collective action problem with a unique data set that includes the race of every candidate in House districts that were at least 30% black in 1972, 1982, and 1992.[2] The first section of the chapter assesses the goals of racial redistricting and explores the impact of the collective action problem on prospects for attaining those goals. Next we examine the pervasiveness of the collective action problem and describe how it has helped produce a shift from "traditional" black leadership—leaders who had their roots in the civil rights movement and in the African-American community they would represent—to more centrist, "new style" leaders who work more closely with whites in mainstream politics.

THE COLLECTIVE GOAL AND THE COLLECTIVE ACTION PROBLEM

A central political goal of the civil rights movement in the last twenty years has been to elect more black politicians. Most individuals in the black community have agreed on this collective goal for symbolic and policy reasons: black leaders serve as role models for the community, stimulate political participation, provide the political system with greater legitimacy, and enhance the likelihood of substantive representation (Clay, 1993; Guinier, 1991a: 1091). The election of African-Americans is a collective good in the classic sense: it is non-exclusive (once it is provided to a given district or state no voter can be prevented from "consuming" the symbolic good) and indivisible (one person's enjoying the representation does not detract from another's consuming the good).

The collective nature of this goal was emphasized by former Rep. Mervyn Dymally (D-CA), "(T)he black power movement is based on a concept of community. Black self-interest focuses not on the ambition of a particular individual, but on the entire black community" (1971, 50). Ironically, personal

---

[2]We only examine black districts, though many of the same problems are evident in the new Hispanic-majority districts. The central theoretical reason for excluding the new Hispanic districts is that bloc voting is not as pervasive in the Hispanic community as in the black community, and thus one of the assumptions of our theory is not met. The 30% cutoff was chosen because below that level, blacks have very little chance of being elected. The only exception in the current House is Gary Franks (R-CT). Franks shows that black conservatives may have increasing opportunities in the Republican Party, but in most districts the Democratic Party is the only realistic outlet for black candidates. We therefore limit our study to Democratic primaries.

ambition may undermine the provision of the public good (i.e., prevent the black community in a congressional district from electing a black to Congress). When new black-majority districts were created in 1992, dozens of black politicians had a realistic chance of being elected for the first time in history. This pent-up supply of black politicians, the absence of political institutions capable of channeling ambition, and racial bloc voting create a potential collective action problem for the black community analogous to Hardin's "tragedy of the commons" (Hardin, 1968; Olson, 1965). For example, if one white candidate and four black candidates run in a district that is 51% black, the white candidate will probably win. In such cases, the collective good for the African-American community can only be provided if the individual ambitions of various politicians can be controlled. Many politicians voluntarily sacrificed their political interests for the collective good, but altruistic behavior cannot be relied upon to solve this collective action problem. Institutional arrangements are generally required, but the most obvious solutions—selective recruitment and endorsements by groups or parties—are rarely successful in an era of candidate-centered campaigns.

The collective action problem is most likely in districts where blacks have a slim majority. In urban districts such as in Detroit (15th district), Baltimore (7th), and New York City (11th), the coordination problem is not evident because the districts are more than 70% black. A white candidate probably would not win under any circumstances (for example, if a white won a divided primary, the black community could unite behind a single independent candidate in the general election and probably prevail). But as the percentage of black voters falls closer to 50%, the likelihood of a white candidate winning the primary increases. [3]

Personal ambition is not the only cause of a collective action problem; policy considerations may also encourage more than one black candidate to run. For example, if a moderate black is running against a moderate white in a new black-majority district, a liberal black may be unwilling to sacrifice his or her policy views, simply to gain more symbolic representation in Congress. These concerns may lead the liberal black to enter the race, despite the possibility that his or her candidacy might split the black vote and help elect the white candidate. In this way, concerns about the nature of the public good to be provided (the type of black elected to Congress and the substantive representation he or she provides) may undermine the provision of that good (the election of a black to Congress).[4]

Policy differences among black candidates typically do not lead to the election of a white. Instead, the collective action problem is likely to affect substan-

---

[3] Obviously there is a coordination problem for white candidates as well, but their ability to affect the outcome of the election is limited. If the black community solves the coordination problem in a black-majority district, a white candidate will probably not win, even if he or she is the only white running. White Democrats have won elections in black-majority districts (Peter Rodino, D-NJ, and Lindy Boggs, D-LA, were the two most recent), but currently there are no white representatives in black-majority districts.

tive representation: in primaries with several black candidates, a black moderate may win the election with the plurality support of a small number of blacks and most of the white Democrats in the district. Many whites are not comfortable with an activist civil rights, redistributive agenda, and are especially threatened by black separatist rhetoric (Edsall and Edsall, 1991, especially chap. 3). These swing voters support moderate blacks over liberal blacks, which creates an opportunity for strategic behavior by black moderates who may pursue the centrist voters. Later in this chapter we explore in greater detail these differences in the substantive representation provided by these "new style" black politicians who actively cultivate biracial coalitions, and "traditional" black politicians who rely on the votes of their black constituents.

These substantive disagreements within the African-American community raise fundamental questions about defining "representatives of their choice." The political science and legal literature on the topic, the Supreme Court, and Congress assume that if given the opportunity (through black-majority districts) blacks will elect leaders who represent their interests.[5] But even disregarding the small but growing black political right (Walter Williams, Thomas Sowell, Clarence Thomas, Shelby Steele, The Lincoln Institute, etc.), *black interests are not monolithic*. If there are several black candidates, each representing a different part of the ideological spectrum and pursuing different political coalitions, it may not be possible to define a single representative of choice.

The remainder of this chapter investigates the implications of these issues. How often does the collective action problem affect the African-American community's efforts to elect a black to Congress, either by allowing a white to defeat a divided black field or by permitting swing white voters to determine the type of substantive representation that the black community receives?

---

[4] This fits our theoretical formulation of the collective good as the election of a black to Congress. With many collective action problems, individuals derive identical levels of benefits from the provision of the public good. For example, all ships passing a lighthouse at night receive a similar benefit from the light. This assumption does not necessarily hold in black-influence or black-majority districts, because different voters may value the contrasting policy platforms of competing candidates differently. Liberal voters may derive substantial benefits from the policy positions of a leftist candidate, while moderate voters may receive less utility from those positions. Conversely, centrist voters will receive greater benefits from the policy stands of a moderate candidate than will liberal voters. Thus, while all members of the black community may prefer that a collective good be provided (e.g., a black elected to Congress), the community may find it difficult to agree on the type of black candidate to be elected.

[5] Justice White's concurring opinion in *Thornburg v. Gingles* (1986) considers a scenario with black Democratic and Republican nominees. But, we have not encountered a discussion of the vote dilution standard in the context of a Democratic primary with black candidates who represent different factions within the black constituency. Until recently, the courts have assumed monolithic black interests. A recent series of Supreme Court decisions (*Shaw v. Reno* 1993, *Miller v. Johnson* 1995, and *Shaw v. Hunt* 1996) signal that the Court is questioning the validity of the assumption of monolithic black interests. Sandra Day O'Connor, writing for the majority in *Shaw v. Reno*, said that the North Carolina redistricting plan "reinforces the perception that members of the same racial group regardless of their age, education, economic status, or the community in which they live think alike, share the same political interests, and will prefer the same candidates at the polls. We have rejected such perceptions elsewhere as impermissible racial stereotypes" (125 L Ed 2d 511, 113 S Ct, 529).

TESTING THE SUPPLY-SIDE MODEL

To address these questions, we collected data on the race of the candidates and other variables in all House districts with at least 30% black population in 1972, 1982, and 1992. Collecting the data on race was much more difficult than we had anticipated. But after 239 phone interviews, we ascertained the race of the candidates in all 144 districts (see Appendix A for a discussion of our data collection techniques and interviews).

Descriptive data on the level of candidate activity in black districts will reveal if there is any basis for a collective action problem. If new districts release a pent-up supply of black candidates, there should be a significant increase in the number of black candidates in 1992 when compared with 1972 and 1982. As is shown in Table 1, black candidate activity increased substantially in 1992 in districts that were at least 30% black, while there were fewer white challengers in these districts. More than twice as many black candidates ran in black districts in 1992 (80) than in 1972 and 1982 combined (37). Fifty-four of the black candidates in 1992 ran in the 14 new black-influence or black-majority districts. At the same time, the number of whites running fell from 111 in 1972 and 1982 to 45 in 1992. The pattern of increased activity in new districts holds in 1972 and 1982 as well, but there were only 5 new districts in 1972 and 3 new districts in 1982 that were created to enhance black representation, compared with 15 in 1992. Therefore, the mean levels of the number and quality of candidates are much lower for 1972 and 1982 than in 1992. The averages per district are shown in Table 1.

TABLE 1. Candidate Activity in Democratic Primaries in Districts That Are at Least 30% Black

	All candidates			Candidates receiving at least 5% of the primary vote		
	1972	*1982*	*1992*	*1972*	*1982*	*1992*
Black challengers						
Mean number	.40	.36	1.7***	.36	.34	1.43***
Mean quality of pool	.96	.81	4.55***	.92	.79	4.17***
White challengers						
Mean number	1.30	1.13	.96	1.10	1.00	.55**
Mean quality of pool	2.56	2.49	1.74	2.36	2.36	1.30*
Number of districts	50	47	47	50	47	47

*Differences between 1972 and 1992 are significant at the .05 level
**Differences between 1972 and 1992 are significant at the .025 level
***Differences between 1972 and 1992 are significant at the .01 level

Note: This table includes only challengers, not incumbents. The differences would be greater for blacks if incumbents were included. The quality of the pool is derived from a four-level measure of quality that is summed across all candidates. Candidates who have held significant elective office receive a four, minor elective and other public office is a three, ambitious amateurs are a two, and regular amateurs are a one. See Canon (1990, 87-92, 165-67) for a more extended discussion of this variable.

An important consequence of this trend is that black voters now have a greater opportunity to elect a "representative of their choice" (even though it may be a second choice, as we discuss more fully below). Supply-side considerations (the absence of black candidates) denied black voters the opportunity to vote for a serious candidate (defined as one who receives at least 30% of the vote) in 64% of the black districts in 1972 and 55% in 1982. This percentage decreased dramatically in 1992 to 25.5%.

This trend marks an especially significant departure from previous patterns in southern politics. Malcolm Jewell notes that candidate activity in southern state legislative primaries in the 1960s was the lowest in the "black belt" (counties with at least 40% black population). He says that these counties were "run by a small clique of politicians hostile to innovation who have maintained a closed political circle, partly to minimize competition and open controversy that might possibly encourage Negro registration and voting" (1967, 34). In 1992, these same areas stimulated a much higher rate of candidate activity than is typical in comparable congressional races. In all incumbent primaries between 1972 and 1988 (n=3,915), 63.9% of incumbents were unopposed. The average quality of the candidate pool (as defined in Table 1) was only .64; in open-seat races it was 6.75 (n=722). In black districts in 1992, the candidate pool quality averaged 1.93 for incumbent primaries (n=30, only 40% were unopposed) and 14.59 in open-seat races (n=17).[6] Clearly black districts in 1992 were a hotbed for activity, rather than a weak spot in participatory democracy.

IMPACT ON SYMBOLIC REPRESENTATION

Nearly four black candidates, on average, ran in every new black district in 1992. Given these levels of candidate activity, blacks should have faced a collective action problem in these districts. Counter to our expectations, however, opportunistic whites did not take advantage of the split black vote in most of these districts. Like much of American society, congressional campaigns remain largely segregated. Of the 144 races in black districts in 1972, 1982, and 1992, only 40 (27.8%) had at least one black candidate and one white candidate. In most of these races, one of the candidates did not run a serious campaign. Only 11 districts (7.6%) had a candidate of each race who received at least 30% of the vote in the Democratic primary.

As a result, there was only one district where a black candidate lost because of a collective action problem (the Ohio 1st in 1992). In four others, the black nominee would have lost had it not been for the runoff election (Florida 23rd, Georgia 2nd, North Carolina 1st, and the special election to fill Mike Espy's seat in the Mississippi 2nd).[7] Four of the five were new black-

---

[6] Data collected from *Congressional Quarterly Weekly Report* by two of the authors for a study of congressional primary elections from 1972-1988.

influence or black-majority districts (the exception was the Mississippi 2nd, which was created in 1982).

The rather surprising absence of a collective action problem requires an explanation. A central reason is a sense of fairness among potential white candidates and the perception that it is "the blacks' turn." Two white Democratic state legislators whom we interviewed cited the creation of the black-majority district as their main reason for not running in the North Carolina 1st. One said, "The first district was created to elect a minority candidate and I think that is a good thing. I would not want to stand in the way of that. I would never consider running in the 1st, not now or in the future." The other also cited "not wanting to step on toes" in the new district, but also was realistic in recognizing she would not be able to win because she is white (personal interviews, 5/28/92). The aggregate data presented in Table 1 also support this conclusion (recall that the mean number of non-frivolous white challengers in black districts fell by almost 50% between 1982 and 1992).

Sometimes the decision of whites not to run in black districts was not entirely voluntary. Pressure from the black community contributed to incumbent Robin Tallon's decision not to run for reelection in the newly created black-majority 6th district in South Carolina. Despite having to face a constituency with 60% new voters, Tallon originally announced his plans to run for reelection, saying that his campaign would "promote racial harmony" (Duncan, 1992: 2536). Tallon had always received strong support from the 40% of the black voters in the old 6th District in each of his elections since 1982. However, Phil Duncan reported that his "decision to run met with considerable criticism from the black community; some of the black aspirants for the 6th faulted him for trying to block minority political empowerment." Tallon had a change of heart just minutes before the filing period closed on June 25th. He decided not to run, saying that his campaign would "further divide the races (and) cause racial disharmony and unrest" (Duncan, 1992: 2536). Districts with runoff elections also may deter whites from running in black majority districts, just as blacks were deterred by runoffs when the districts were black majority. For example, according to a state party official, Claude Harris, the incumbent in the Alabama 7th, would have run in the new black majority district had it not been for the runoff; instead he retired (personal interview, April 5, 1993).

---

[7] However, one cannot make firm conclusions about the impact of the runoff provision on the behavior of candidates and voters. If several black candidates split the black vote and one white candidate wins the initial round of a two-stage primary, one cannot assume that the same white would have emerged the winner in a plurality-vote system. The same black candidates might have solved their collective action problem and united behind a single candidate if the runoff primary had not helped ensure the eventual election of an African-American. Similarly, black voters may be more strategic in their behavior in a plurality election, supporting a candidate who might be their second choice (but black) to avoid electing a white candidate. A parallel argument for the motivations of white candidates and voters in white majority districts is made by Gregory G. Ballard (1991, 1153). See also, V.O. Key (1956, 410, 420-23).

IMPACT ON SUBSTANTIVE REPRESENTATION

Although our data indicate that the segregation of campaigns and runoff provisions generally further the goal of electing more blacks, the collective action problem may greatly alter the substantive representation received by the black community in congressional districts, tipping the balance of power in the district, in some cases, to white voters. Ideological and policy disagreements within the black community help produce this outcome by encouraging different types of black candidates to run for Congress. As we note above, moderate white voters, especially in the south, will be more likely to support "new style" black candidates who cultivate biracial coalitions than "traditional" blacks who appeal primarily to their African-American constituents.

"Traditional" black candidates, with backgrounds in the civil rights movement and black churches, typically come from the liberal wing of the Democratic party. These candidates tend to think of themselves and the black community as political outsiders who must form political organizations separate from the larger white community in order to battle for a greater share of the political pie. Many of these black politicians have little or no prior experience in party and elective politics, and more importantly, value their outsider status (Dymally, 1971; Holden, 1973). This outlook was especially prominent in the early stages of the "black electoral success" period. According to one black politician who was elected mayor of a Southern city in 1969, "Black elected officials in the South can not become hung up on party politics and be thus bound up by party loyalty....In the South the black man can be rendered useless if he allows himself to be put in the pocket of the party boss or if he allows himself to come up through the party structure" (Howard Lee, quoted in Dymally, 1971: 76). Adam Clayton Powell more explicitly described the value of remaining independent from the white establishment: "Black organizations must be black-led. The extent to which black organizations are led by whites, to that precise extent are they diluted of their black potential for ultimate control and direction....Black people must support and push black candidates for political office first..." (quoted in Dymally, 1971: 65-166). More recently, Bennie Thompson, who was elected to replace Mike Espy in Mississippi, emphasized this separatist position. Espy was noted for his moderation on racial issues and his appeals to white voters. Thompson criticized this moderation, saying that blacks voters "don't like how the district has gone back to the plantation owners." Thompson vowed to return more power to blacks and consistently rejected biracial politics during the campaign, saying, "You've got to be one or the other. Ain't no fence. The fence is torn down now" (*Congressional Quarterly* 3/6/93, 537).

Not all black politicians or members of the black community support "traditional" black positions. In the late 1980s and early 1990s more and more black politicians began advocating a moderate approach that emphasizes compromise and accommodation with the white community rather than confrontation and separation (Perry, 1990). These "new style" black politicians tend to follow more mainstream lines of career development and are more closely tied to the party establishment. Sanford Bishop, for example, served in the Georgia state legislature for 16 years before defeating white incumbent Charles Hatcher (D-GA) in a 1992 primary. The black challenger campaigned on his political experience, arguing that he "represents a new generation of leadership" (Duncan, 1992: 2536). In Louisiana's 4th district, state senator Cleo Fields campaigned hard for the support of white voters. According to *Congressional Quarterly*, "Fields has always played down racial issues and done as much as possible to raise the comfort level of his white constituents. At one point in the campaign, he distanced himself from Jones (his runoff opponent, a black state senator), who attacked a white newspaper editor as 'some racist cracker'" (*Congressional Quarterly*, 1993: 90).

Aggregate-level evidence suggests that the electoral climate facing black candidates has gradually changed to favor "new style" blacks over "traditional" ones. In the 38 congressional districts that elected blacks in 1992, the percentage of black voters fell five points from the level of the previous decade (61.8% in 1982 to 56.5% in 1992; the percentage of white voters climbed from 31.7% to 36.3% in these same districts). As Strickland and Whicker argue, blacks who are political insiders and project a conservative image are more likely to appeal to white voters. They say, "Only by demonstrating expertise can black candidates in black-white contests overcome individual racism where individuals assume that blacks are inferior and less able to govern" (1992, 208-209). Table 2 suggests that the "new style" black politicians are increasingly taking advantage of the changed electoral environments by appealing to white voters. From 1972 to 1980, 38.5% of the blacks elected to the U.S. House had no previous elective experience, and only 15.4% had more than ten years of previous experience. The pattern changes significantly in 1992. Of the 16 new black members elected, only one (6.2%) had no prior experience. Eleven (68.8%) had more than ten years of political experience, which makes them far more experienced than the average new white member of Congress.

TABLE 2. Prior Political Experience of Black Members of the U.S. House, 1972-1992

Prior experience in public office	Year elected to Congress		
	1972-1980	*1982-1990*	*1992*
No experience	38.5%	23.5%	6.2%
More than zero years, but less than ten years of experience	46.1%	47.1%	25%
Ten or more years of experience	15.4%	29.4%	68.8%
Number of members	13	17	16

The dramatic success of "new style" black congressional candidates can be attributed in part to the dynamics of the collective action problem and substantive representation described above. Democratic primaries in newly created black-influence and black-majority districts often pit one or more liberal "traditional" black candidates against one or more moderate "new style" black candidates. If the black community splits its support between traditional and new style candidates, whites can play a pivotal role in deciding which candidate will represent the district. In districts with both a new style black and traditional black candidate, the presence of a white candidate can influence the outcome of the Democratic primary in one of two ways. In states without runoff elections, a divided black vote can translate into a victory for the white candidate. In states with runoffs, the new style black candidate has to compete with the white candidate for moderate voters, thus creating a greater likelihood that the traditional black candidate will win. If no white candidate enters the race, we argue that moderate white voters will support the new style black candidate and greatly increase his or her chances of winning the election. However, if the blacks solve their collective action problem and unite behind a single candidate, a traditional black will win.

Because data on the coalitional and ideological politics of black candidates in Democratic primaries is both scarce and difficult to collect, we test our hypotheses only for the 1992 election. We examined the 17 congressional districts in which a newly elected black candidate emerged from the Democratic primaries and the new black influence district (the Ohio 1st) in which a black did not win.[8] Sixteen of the 18 cases support our theory. In seven districts a white candidate competed with at least one liberal black and one moderate black candidate. Either a liberal black won as the moderate vote was split (CA37, FL3, FL23, GA11, NC1, MS2), or a white won because of the divided black vote (OH1). In seven other districts no white candidate emerged, and one of the black moderate candidates defeated one or more black liberal (AL7, IL1, IL2, LA4, MD4, NC12 and SC6). In two districts (FL17 and TX30), a dominant black candidate ran with no white opposition. In these cases, there is no collective action problem and a liberal black who is strongly supported by the African-American community wins. Two cases were not were not consistent with our theory. In the Georgia 2nd, Sanford Bishop defeated a white incumbent Charles Hatcher, and in the Virginia 3rd, Robert Scott won a low turnout (15%), issueless primary over two black moderates. In the Georgia case our theory predicted that a traditional black should have won, but Bishop clearly ran as a new style black, touting his legislative experience and attacking Hatcher for his 819 overdrafts. In Virginia, ideology and racial politics simply did not emerge in this contest between three similar black candidates. The most conservative of the three candidates, Jacqueline G. Epps, should have won, according to the expectations of our theory (with white support in a divided black field). But, Scott used his superior name-recognition and fund-raising ability to win this low-key race.

---

[8] We included the special election to fill Mike Espy's seat in this analysis. To ascertain the ideological positions of the various candidates we conducted 30 personal interviews and consulted newspaper articles, *Congressional Quarterly Weekly Report*, and various editions of the *Almanac of American Politics*.

This limited test of our supply-side theory suggests that the presence or absence of a white candidate can strongly influence the type of candidate who wins the Democratic primary in black-influence or black-majority districts.[9] Ironically, in newly created districts of this type, the black community is often unable to agree on the type of candidate that best represents its interests, and thus white voters play the decisive role in determining how the district is represented. While this may be good or bad, depending on one's normative perspective, the debate thus far has ignored this issue. We expect that these supply-side effects will have a significant impact on the type of representation that the new black districts receive. Candidates elected from biracial coalitions are likely to exhibit more moderate behavior and pursue different policy agendas than "traditional" African-Americans elected from a unified black electorate. These substantive effects are an important topic for future research.[10]

Appendix A—Data Collection and Interviews.

The first set of interviews conducted for this study was part of an in-depth case study of the candidate emergence process in the North Carolina 1st in 1992 (Canon, Schousen, and Sellers, 1994). We conducted 37 interviews with 34 people, including newspaper reporters, Democratic Party chairs of the most populous counties in the district, members of the General Assembly, a member of the U.S. Congress, and all of the identified potential candidates. The interviews ranged in length from twenty minutes to more than two hours, with an average length of about one hour. All but five of the interviews were face-to-face (citing time constraints, three candidates and two informants would only agree to phone interviews).

In the second stage of the project, we collected data on the race of all candidates in 1972, 1982, and 1992 in districts that were at least 30% black. This proved much more difficult that we thought it would be. We were a bit surprised to discover that no institution systematically records the race of House candidates. We called the Joint Center for Political Studies, the Black Congressional Caucus, the Urban League, the NAACP, Vote America, the Democratic National Committee, and the Democratic Congressional Campaign Committee. The Joint Center was the most helpful; one of the researchers working on the *Roster of Black Elected Officials* told us that they considered expanding their research to include candidates who lose, but they did not have sufficient funding. After pursuing those dead-ends, we naively assumed that we would be able to identify the race of House candidates from the public record. Many futile hours at the micro-

---

[9]The same pattern of coalitional politics should be evident even in the post-*Shaw v. Hunt* era in which creating black-majority districts will become increasingly difficult, as long as the bloc of African-American voters is sufficiency large.

[10] One of the authors (David Canon) is currently working on a book, *Race, Representation, and Redistricting, in the United States Congress*, that will examine the impact of supply-side effects on behavior in Congress. The book will also address the normative issues that are not tackled here.

film machines and pouring through *Congressional Quarterly Weekly Report* disabused of us that notion. There were two problems with the public record: first, minor candidates (those receiving less than 10% of the vote) often were mentioned only in passing, and second, the race of leading candidates was not noted in some cases. Next, we called party officials (starting with the state party headquarters in each relevant state), newspaper reporters, campaign workers, offices of incumbents who were still in office (this approach was especially useful for 1992), and the candidates themselves to fill in the substantial gaps. After 239 phone interviews, ranging in length from a minute or two ("Nope, don't know anything about that campaign. Try Mr. X. He would know"), to more than a half an hour, we were able to identify the race of all the candidates.

ESTIMATING THE IMPACT OF VOTING-RIGHTS-RELATED DISTRICTING ON DEMOCRATIC STRENGTH IN THE U.S. HOUSE OF REPRESENTATIVES

Bernard Grofman and Lisa Handley

WHILE THIS ASSERTION HAS BEEN DENIED BY CIVIL RIGHTS GROUPS such as the NAACP Legal Defense and Educational Fund (NAACP LDF, 1994), there appears to be a widespread agreement across party and ideological lines that the creation of a large number of new majority black districts in the South (and, perhaps to a lesser extent, the creation of new majority black and majority Hispanic districts elsewhere in the country) contributed in no small part to the change in party control of the House that occurred between 1990 and 1994. For example, according to George Will (1995), "(r)acial gerrymandering is one reason that Newt Gingrich is speaker." More recently, the Voting Rights Act has been blamed for the continuing Republican control of the House in 1996 despite the reelection of a Democratic president. Thus, the argument is made that gains in descriptive minority representation have come only at the cost of probable defeat of minority-supported initiatives in the House.[1]

In addition, the claim has been made (e.g., by Lublin, 1997) that there is, in general, a trade-off between descriptive representation of minorities and the ability of minorities to gain policy outcomes to their liking which holds even if Democrats were to have remained (or to become again) the majority party in the House (or in any given Southern state legislature).

Here we focus on African-African representation in the House in 1992 and

---

[1]Lublin (1995b) observes that "the aggregate effect of racial redistricting has been to make the House less likely to adopt legislation favored by African Americans."

1994. By comparing the results of the congressional elections in 1992 and 1994 under the 1990s lines with earlier outcomes, we provide new empirical evidence on the extent to which 1990s redistricting leading to the creation of new black majority congressional seats (1) negatively impacted Democratic seat share, and/or (2) negatively impacted mean and median congressional liberalism. While our results suggest that the *direct* impact of racial redistricting on Democratic congressional losses in the South has been somewhat exaggerated, we offer a theory of what we call the "triple whammy" that leads us to an extremely negative view of the long run prospects for the Democratic party in the South. In our view of what has been happening in the South, race and realignment go hand in hand.

DATA ANALYSIS

Impact of Districting/Distribution of Black Population on Democratic Seat Share

We believe it important to distinguish between three easy-to-confuse questions. The first is "Did the Democrats suffer greater losses between 1990 and 1994 in the areas of the country where (new) black seats were drawn than elsewhere?" The second is "If the districting lines in 1990 had been used (in the South) in 1994 , would Democrats have done better; and, the flip side, if the districting lines in 1994 had been used (in the South) in 1990, would the Democrats have done worse?" The third is "Would the optimal arrangement of black voting strength across congressional districts have permitted the Democrats (in the South) to hold on to some of the seats they lost?" The answers to these different questions need not point in the same direction vis-a-vis the partisan consequences of districting. Which question you answer largely determines whether you conclude that the Voting Rights Act proved very costly to House Democrats in the 1990s.

For the 1994 versus 1990 comparison, our answer to the first question is no;[2] our answer to the second question is yes, but not to any great extent; and our answer to the third question is yes for sure, but not nearly as many seats as you might think, although more than one would conclude in looking only at the answers to the previous two questions.

Let us look first at the question, "Did the Democrats suffer greater losses between 1990 and 1994 in the areas of the country where (new) black seats were drawn than elsewhere?" Taking this question as the relevant question to be answered, the civil rights attorney Laughlin McDonald (1995) asserts that the impact of the VRA on the Democratic party has been much exaggerated. He points out that in the nine states that drew new predominantly minority districts after the 1990 census, Democrats lost 19% of their 1992 seats in the 1994 election; in the 41 other states, they lost 21%.[3] Moreover, even if the Democrats had

---

[2] However, we would have to answer yes to the first question for a 1996 versus 1994 comparison.

[3] Moreover, in House elections, a swing ratio near 2 has characterized the past several decades (Brady and Grofman, 1991). Given the striking decline in Democratic mean congressional vote share from 1992 to 1994, a seat loss of 52 seats is not that out of line.

retained every one of their 1992 House seats in the nine states that drew new black majority seats—completely bucking the national trend—the Republicans would *still* have gained control of the House in 1994.

Of course, looking at only a single year can be misleading. In *1992* most of the limited number of Democratic losses did occur in the nine states with new majority minority seats; thus looking only at 1994 results understates the impact of 1990s districting on Republican gains. But even taking these Democratic 1992 losses into account does not change the basic result that Republican congressional gains between 1990 and 1994 occurred virtually everywhere. Between 1994 and 1996, however, the Republicans gained a handful of Southern seats in the House (some by virtue of incumbents changing their party affiliation) at the same time as they were losing seats elsewhere in the nation. But, on average, at least for elections to the House, Republicans also gained more votes compared with 1994 in the South than elsewhere.

The answer to the second question posed above, "If the districting lines in 1990 had been used in 1994 (and in 1992), would Democrats have done better; and, the flip side, if the districting lines in 1994 had been used in 1990, would the Democrats have done worse?" is a subject of some dispute in the literature. For example, Lublin (1995a, b), who looks at seats decided by relatively small margins which lost substantial black population between 1990 and 1992 and which shifted to the Republicans by 1994, notes that many of these seats could have been kept in Democratic hands if the black population in the district had been kept at its previous levels.   Lublin (1995a, emphasis ours) concludes that "the creation of new majority-minority districts assured that the Republicans won *solid* control of the House in 1994." However, we should not read too much into this claim.   Even using Lublin's method of calculation, it seems to us unlikely that drawing new black majority seats during the 1990s round of districting cost the Democrats more than 10 of the 62 seats they dropped between 1990 and 1994.

More importantly, if we look at the question of the link between Republican gains and districting using a methodology that is sensitive to the overall consequences of changes in the distribution of black strength for the probability of Democratic success rather than just singling out just those districts where the loss of black population might have affected close contests, we get an estimate of the impact of racial districting that is considerably lower than that obtained by Lublin. In net terms, taking into account countervailing factors such as the certainty of Democratic success in the new heavily black seats, we find that as few as 2-5 of the 24 Southern congressional seats lost by the Democrats between 1990 and 1994 might be seen as the direct result of the racial aspects of 1990s redistricting. The rest of the Democratic losses are attributable to a quite simple fact—Republican congressional candidates across the board got a lot more votes in the South in 1994 than they did in 1992 and fewer votes in 1992 than in 1990 as well. Indeed, Republicans showed greater vote gains in 1994 in the deep South than in the rest of the country.[4]

Before we can explain the basis for our empirical results about this second question, we need to lay some methodological groundwork.

Let us imagine a population (e.g., an electorate) decomposed into a set of mutually exclusive and exhaustive categories, C_1 through C_n. These may be based on characteristics such as attitudes or demographic attributes. Let Y be the variable whose change in value we seek to account for, i.e., let Y be the dependent variable (e.g., turnout). Let p_{it} be the proportion of the total population that group i comprises at time t. Let y_{it} be the (perhaps estimated) value of the dependent variable in the ith group at time t. We wish to explain the change in Y over time, i.e., to account for

$$\Delta Y = Y_0 - Y_t$$

as a function of changes in composition (i.e., differences between p_{it} and p_{i0}, in each of the categories), and changes in behavior (i.e., differences between y_{it} and y_{i0}, in each of the categories).[5]

Now let

(1) $\Delta Y_i = y_{i0} - y_{it}$

(2) $\Delta P_i = p_{i0} - p_{it}$

Abramson and Aldrich (1982) use the formula in Eq. (3) below as a measure of the impact on behavior (in their case turnout) of changes in the variables (e.g., partisanship) they study.[6]

(3) $$\dfrac{\displaystyle\sum_{i=1} y_{it}\Delta p_i}{\Delta Y}$$

The numerator of Eq. (3) is the difference between the value of the independent variable that would have been found had the proportion of the population in each category remained unchanged from time 0 to time t while the behavior of each of the population groups was that found at time t, and the value of the independent variable that actually obtained at time t,[7] i.e., it can be thought of as a measure of the compositional change.[8]

---

[4] It is also important to note that, thanks to reapportionment and sun-belt population gains relative to the rest of the country, there were more 9 seats in 1994 (or 1992) in the South than in 1990. Thus, 1990s Republican gains in vote share had a greater impact on Republican seat gain in the South relative to 1990 than in areas of the country with constant or declining congressional delegation size.

[5] For example, using the notation of Cassel and Luskin (1981: 1327-28), $p_{it} = s_{ijkt}$ where, in their notation, i indicates the proportion of the electorate in the ith category of partisanship, j the jth category of efficacy, and k the kth category of some third variable, while t is, as here, a subscript for time. This example demonstrates how the C_1 categories can be based on one or more polychotomous variables.

[6] Their notation is somewhat different from ours.

[7] The expression shown in Eq. (3) is what Cassel and Luskin (1988) denote as A_1.

Cassel and Luskin (1988) strongly critique Eq. (3) as a measure of the contribution of compositional change (to total turnout decline) by noting that the value of the expression in Eq. (3) can readily exceed one.[9] We can also readily provide examples in which its value is negative. Cassel and Luskin take such findings to mean that the expression cannot possibly measure the proportion of the change in behavior (turnout) that can be accounted for by any given factor. In like manner it can be shown that the equation analogous to Eq. (3) for attributing the magnitude of *behavioral* change, shown as Eq. (4) below, is also flawed in that it can take on values below zero or above one.

$$(4)\quad \frac{\sum\limits_{i=1} p_{it}\Delta Y_i}{\Delta Y}$$

To understand what is going on we make use of the following algebraic identity:

$$(5)\quad Y_0 - Y_t = \sum_{i=1}^{n} y_{it}\Delta P_i \qquad \text{(a) composition effect}$$

$$+ \sum_{i=1}^{n} p_{it}\Delta Y_i \qquad \text{(b) behavioral effect}$$

$$+ \sum_{i=1}^{n} \Delta P_i \Delta Y_i \qquad \text{(c) interaction effect}$$

Like Abramson and Aldrich we treat Expression (5a), which has a ΔP_i term in it, as a measure of compositional change for a fixed value of the y_i, namely y_{it}. In like manner we treat Expression (5b), which has a ΔY_i term in it, as a measure of behavioral change for a fixed value of the p_i, namely p_{it}.[10] However, *we have added an interaction term to complete the algebraic identity.*

---

[8]A similar formula is used by Boyd (1981) and Cavanagh (1982), each of whom looks at the effects on turnout of growth in the proportion of the eligible electorate falling into the oldest and the youngest age cohorts, and at the turnout consequences of permitting eighteen-year-olds to vote. Both authors estimate effects by computing a hypothetical turnout in 1976 on the assumption that age-specific turnout rates had stayed constant over the period and that the only thing that changed was the proportion of eligibles who fell into each age grouping. Each then takes the difference between hypothetical turnout and actual turnout (normalized by the total decline in turnout) to be the measure of age-related compositional changes, i.e., they calculate an expression identical to that of Expression (3) except that except that y_{i0} is used instead of y_{it} In our terminology here the C_i are age segments of the population and Y again is turnout.

[9]Categories based on efficacy, partisanship, etc. See earlier footnote .

[10]We may readily develop an analogue to Expression (5) where we look at the value of our fixed parameters at time zero rather than at time t. See below.

This decomposition model has been used in published work by only a few political scientists (Grofman and Handley, 1991; Krehbiel and Wright, 1993). John Jackson, at the University of Michigan, like one of the present authors, independently derived the above methodology, but then discovered it to be already known in the sociology literature (John Jackson, personal communication, October 1989). Eq. (5) provides a useful methodology to estimate the relative magnitude of changes in districting lines (composition) and changes in voting (behavior) on Democratic congressional success from 1990 to 1994 (and/or from 1990 to 1992).

For the states with above 10% black population, we show in Table 1 the percent Democratic in the House in 1994 by percent African-American in the district. The format for this table parallels that in Tables 15 and 18 (page 30 and page 33) in the Handley, Grofman and Arden chapter in this volume. Those earlier tables show data for 1990 and 1992, respectively.

We shall make use of the data in these tables and the formulas of Eq. (5) to calculate the impact of redistricting related changes in the distribution of black population across districts on Democratic seat share in the House for the South. It is in the South where we expect large effects to be present. If they are not found there, they will be found elsewhere in the nation. When we calculate the three formulas shown in Eq. (5) for the data in Table 1 in this chapter and Table 15 in the Handley, Grofman, and Arden chapter for the eleven Southern states for which data is provided, what we are doing is as if we were rerunning the 1994 House elections in the South with 1990s district lines and rerunning the 1990 House elections in the South with 1994 levels of Republican success in the various racial categories.[11] Similarly, when we calculate the three formulas shown in Eq. (5) for the data in Tables 18 and 15 in the Handley, Grofman, and Arden chapter, what we are doing is as if we were rerunning the 1992 election with 1990s district lines and rerunning the 1990 election with 1992 levels of Republican success in the various racial categories

Performing these calculations for the 1990 to 1994 comparison, we find that a 17% decline from 1990 to 1994 in the percentage of House seats held by Democrats in the (eleven state) South is apportioned into 17 points of behavioral change (i.e., increased Republican vote share) and only 4 points of compositional (i.e., redistricting-related) change, with -4 points of interaction effect. If we allocate the interaction equally to the compositional and behavioral components, then only 2 percentage points, equaling a little over 2 seats (2/17 x .17 x 125) would be attributed to the impact of race-related districting in the South. If, more plausibly, we allocate the interaction effect in proportion to the magnitude of the behavioral and compositional effects, we would still only attribute 4 Southern seats (4/21 x .17 x 125) to the race-related effects of 1990s districting. Even if we allocate the interaction effect entirely to the compositional component, we would still only attribute 5 seats (4/17 x .17 x 125) to the race-related effects of 1990s

---

[11]Because we do our calculation in percentage terms, there is an additional factor that needs to be taken into account, namely the additional nine seats added to Southern congressional delegations after the 1990 census.

**TABLE 1. Percent Democrats in Congress by Percent African-American in District
1994**

Percent African-American In District

South	0-9.9	(N)	10-19.9	(N)	20-29.9	(N)	30-39.9	(N)	40-49.9	(N)	50+	(N)
Alabama	50.0	(2)	100.0	(1)	33.3	(3)	—		—		100.0	(1)
Arkansas	0.0	(1)	100.0	(2)	0.0	(1)	—		—		—	—
Florida	18.8	(16)	33.3	(3)	100.0	(1)	—		—		100.0	(3)
Georgia	50.0	(2)	0.0	(4)	0.0	(2)	—		—		100.0	(3)
Louisiana	—		33.3	(3)	50.0	(2)	—		—		100.0	(2)
Mississippi	—		100.0	(1)	0.0	(1)	100.0	(1)	100.0	(1)	100.0	(1)
N. Carolina	0.0	(4)	50.0	(2)	25.0	(4)	—		—		100.0	(2)
S. Carolina	—		0.0	(1)	0.0	(3)	100.0	(1)	—		100.0	(1)
Tennessee	25.0	(4)	33.3	(3)	100.0	(1)	—		—		100.0	(1)
Texas	52.6	(19)	100.0	(7)	50.0	(2)	—		—		100.0	(2)
Virginia	33.3	(3)	40.0	(5)	100.0	(1)	100.0	(1)	—		100.0	(1)
Total	33.3	(51)	53.1	(32)	33.3	(19)	100.0	(3)	100.0	(1)	100.0	(17)
Non - South												
Delaware	—		0.0	(1)	—		—		—		—	
Illinois	33.3	(15)	100.0	(2)	—		—		—		100.0	(3)
Maryland	0.0	(3)	66.7	(3)	—		—		—		100.0	(2)
Michigan	41.7	(12)	100.0	(2)	—		—		—		100.0	(2)
Missouri	57.1	(7)	—		100.0	(1)	—		—		100.0	(1)
New Jersey	16.7	(6)	50.0	(6)	—		—		—		100.0	(1)
New York	45.5	(22)	33.3	(3)	—		100.0	(3)	—		100.0	(3)
Ohio	15.4	(13)	100.0	(3)	0.0	(1)	0.0	(1)	—		100.0	(1)
Pennsylvania	44.4	(18)	100.0	(1)	—		—		—		100.0	(2)
Total	36.5	(96)	66.7	(21)	50.0	(2)	75.0	(4)	—		100.0	(15)

districting. Thus, the *direct* effect on Democratic seats of changes in the distribution of black population across Southern districts[12] is at least a two-seat loss in the House for the Democrats and at most a five-seat loss for the Democrats.[13]

---

[12]Of course there are also some non-South states with substantial black populations, but the partisan effects of black population shifts across House districts in these states is of a much smaller magnitude than for the South.

[13]Using a variety of statistical methods, Petrocik and Desposato (1995) reach nuanced and relatively conservative conclusions about the impact of race-related districting on Democratic success that are not that different from those of the present authors. They note (p. 16, emphasis in original) that "had the political mood been less hostile (especially in 1994) it's doubtful that Democratic losses would been so large. They also emphasize that Democrats in the South did a rather good job of redrawing lines given the two severe constraints they faced: (1) the need to draw additional black majority seats lest plans be denied preclearance; (2) a reduction in both the number of and the loyalty of Democratic party identifiers in the South (see esp Figure 2). In particular, they argue that many of the black voters used to form the new black majority seats were pulled from districts that were already Republican, thus minimizing the costs to Democrats; and that the burden of running in a district with radically redrawn district lines was placed on Republican incumbents to the greatest extent possible. Nonetheless, since there were more Democratic seats to begin with, more 1990 Democratic incumbents were impacted by changes in their old district lines than were Republican incumbents. They also point that, especially in 1994, there was both a decline in black turnout relative to white turnout in the South and a major decline in the willingness of white voters to support Democratic congressional candidates. Their bottom line is that "New voters, the loss of loyal black voters, and the anti-Democratic mood were all necessary for the losses."

However, this estimate of redistricting effects is almost certainly an understatement because it skips over what happened in 1992. One reason the Republicans got more votes in 1994 than in 1990 is that 1990s line drawing impacted white Democratic incumbents. There were somewhat fewer white (Southern) Democratic incumbents in 1994 than there otherwise might have been as a result of the 1992 elections, [14] and some Democratic incumbents were induced to withdraw from politics prior to the 1992 election.[15] Thus, some of the impact of the 1990s line drawing on Democratic seat loss will be missed if we simply do a 1994 versus 1990 comparison.[16] Taking these earlier effects into account would increase the importance of the VRA as a factor in Southern Democratic congressional decline, and would give estimates of the magnitude of the racial districting effect that come somewhat closer to the magnitude of the effect estimated by Lublin. But, even taking into account both direct effects in 1994 and the continuing effects of the 1992 election and pre-election choices made by Democratic officeholders, we would still conclude that the consequences of drawing new black majority seats cannot be blamed for the shift in control of the House in 1994.

Now let us turn to the third of our questions about redistricting impact: "Would the optimal arrangement of black voting strength across congressional districts have permitted the Democrats to hold on to some of the seats they lost?"

In 1994, in the South, districts with between 20 and 30 percent black population show evidence of a possible backlash effect in that these districts are actually less likely to elect Democrats than districts with only 10-20 percent black populations. Thus, based on 1994 election results, in the South, it would appear that Democrats would have been well-advised to avoid creating districts with between 20 and 30 percent black population. By turning two districts with 20-30 percent black population into one district with 30-40 percent black population and one district with 0-10 percent black population, they would have raised the expected number of Democratic successes in 1994 in the two seats from .67 to 1.33.

---

[14] Using an eight state definition of the South, and using a methodology that draws on ideas in Gleaming and King (1994), Hill (1995) estimates that redistricting cost the Democrats four seats in the South in 1992.

[15] Performing analogous calculations to those above for the 1990 to 1992 comparison, we find that a 5% decline in the percentage of seats in the (eleven state) South from 1990 to 1992 held by Democrats is apportioned into 5 points of behavioral change (i.e., increased Republican vote share) and 6 points of compositional (i.e., redistricting-related) change, with -6 points of interaction effect. If we allocate the interaction equally to the compositional and behavioral components, then only 3 percentage points, equaling a little under 4 seats (3/5 x .05 x 125) would be attributed to the impact of race-related districting. This result does not really change much if we allocate the interaction effect in proportion to the magnitude of the behavioral and compositional effects. Even if we allocate the interaction effect to the compositional component to the greatest extent possible, we would still only attribute 6 seats (5/5 x .05 x 125) to the race-related effects of 1990s districting in 1992.

[16] Also, some half-dozen white Democratic House members shifted their allegiance to the Republican party in the 1990s. As we discuss later, we see some of these changes as responsive to a new climate in the South in which the Democratic party is increasingly seen as the party of blacks, both in terms of voters and, increasingly, in terms of office-holders as well.

Based on calculations like these, we can show that, in theory, *ceteris paribus*, had the Democrats made near optimal use of black voters to shore up Democratic seats in the South against the Republican tide, as many as 10-11 seats might have been saved. However, this maximum estimate of 10-11 seats is unrealistic, because, given the geography, it would have been impossible without excessively tortuous lines to convert a large proportion of the 20 to 30 percent black population districts into the districts with between 30 and 40 percent black population that were optimal for Democratic election chances in the South. Moreover, even if compactness could have been achieved given the constraints of geography, gerrymandering that would have been optimal from the perspective of maximizing Democratic congressional seat share in the South (i.e., districts with 30 to 40 percent black population) would seem to be incompatible with the creation of districts from which African-Americans would have had a realistic chance of being elected to Congress from that region, since the latter (except where there are already black incumbents in place) appear to require black populations closer to 50 percent (see e.g., Grofman and Handley, 1995a; Handley, Grofman, and Arden, this volume, and references cited therein; cf. Cavanagh, 1995; Cameron, Epstein, and O'Halloran, 1995).

In the non-South, in 1994, in contrast, districts with 10-20 percent black population seemed desirable to maximize Democratic chances. These findings parallel those in Grofman, Griffin and Glazer (1992). Higher black populations are needed to maximize Democratic success in the South than in the non-South, and spreading black population so as to avoid creating majority black districts is desirable in both South and non-South from the standpoint of maximizing the aggregate election chances of (white) Democrats. However, there is one very important difference between the conclusions reached from examining the data in Table 1 and that reached in the earlier analyses of Grofman, Griffin and Glazer (1992). In the 1990s, in the South, as Democratic support has continued to fall among white Southerners, an even higher black population share is now optimal from the standpoint of maximizing Democratic chances in the House than was true in previous decades. In the 1980s, in the South, what had been optimal for Democratic chances was to maximize the number of districts with between 20 and 30 percent black population. Now, such districts are no longer safe.

Of course, we must be cautious in trying to use the Grofman, Griffin, Glazer (1992) methodology to second-guess (Democratic) districting strategies; the methodology only provides an estimate of the partisanly optimal allocation rule, and it neglects complications such as geographic constraints and incumbency advantages.[17] Moreover, our belief about what is the best districting strategy with respect to black population placement from a partisan point of view may change with new election results, as is evident from our earlier point about the difference between the Grofman, Griffin and Glazer (1992) findings for the South in the

---

[17] Very similar notes of caution are sounded in Hill (1995: 400).

1980s and our own findings for that region in 1994. [18] Another important point to note is that, as can be seen by reviewing the data in Table 1, it is harder for Democrats to make districting mistakes in the non-South than in the South with respect to how best to locate black population for purposes of partisan advantage.

Impact of Districting/Black Population Distribution on Mean and Median Congressional Liberalism

Lublin (1995a, b) argues that Republican gains made possible by the creation of (additional) black seats, especially those in the South, has the net effect of reducing congressional liberalism, and thus reducing the likelihood that bills supported by black legislators will pass. Also, he notes that the creation of such districts made it more likely that Republicans would win/keep control of Congress. We have already commented on the extent to which Republican gains that can be linked to the VRA can be said to have caused a change in partisan control of the House. Here we wish to evaluate the claim that the net effect of creating black seats is a loss for congressional liberalism. We believe this claim is wrong. Only insofar as the spillover effects of the new seats vis-a-vis Democratic loss operate to shift partisan control of the House will creating new black seats reduce the liberalism of House policy outcomes.

Even if we posit that every new black congressional seat in the South led to a net loss of one white Democrat, [19] calculations using the methodology in Grofman, Griffin, and Glazer (1992), updated by using 1994 ADA scores, shows that creating black seats is pretty much a wash as far as mean liberalism. the average black southern congress member has an ADA score of 85; the average white southern Democrat has an ADA score of only 46 or so, with only minimal variation as a function of how black the seat is in population (except for a couple of seats in the 40-50% black population range where there is evidence of backlash insofar as these district representatives are actually less liberal than those from

---

[18] Indeed, in our view, the definitive word on how best to understand what population percentage is now needed to give black House candidates in the South a realistic opportunity to be elected has yet been written. In the 1960s and early 1970s, the lack of black registration was the principal barrier to black electoral success. In the late 1970s and through the mid-1980s the principal reason that blacks could not be elected from non-majority black seats was that blacks could not win the Democratic primary given polarized voting patterns and the advantages possessed by white incumbents. Now, the principal barrier to black electoral success in a district that is, say, 35-40% black, is no longer the Democratic primary; rather it is the general election. Because so many whites in the South have become Republicans, for any given (substantial) black population proportion, black success in the Democratic primaries is easier to achieve than it ever has been. On the other hand, being the nominee of the Democratic party is no longer anything like the royal road to inevitable success that it once was, especially if you are black. Growing Republican strength in the South has reversed the relative importance of primaries and generals as barriers to black representation. Republican gains have made it easier for blacks to get elected (in primaries) while Republican gains have also made it harder for blacks to get elected (in general elections). The exact nature of the trade-off between these two countervailing effects is subtle. Modeling the effects of this two-stage electoral game on both partisan and minority representation is a task on which the present authors are currently engaged.

[19] It is highly implausible that we can expect a net loss of more than one Democratic seat for each new black majority seat created—at least in terms of the direct effects of districting.

districts with fewer blacks). In 1994, the average southern Republican has an ADA score around 6, independent of how black in population the district is, with mean decile scores ranging between 4 and 8. thus if we replace two white southern Democrats with a Republican and a black Democrat, we go from a combined ADA of 92 to a combined ADA of 93. Yes, white Republicans are a lot more conservative than white Democrats, but black southern Democrats are equally more liberal than white Democrats elected from non-majority black seats!

Lublin (1995b) argues that the correct way to look at roll-call voting impact is in terms of medians rather than means. In the scenario above the median member of Congress remains the same if we replace two moderates with one extreme conservative and one extreme liberal.[20] However, even though the impact on race-related districting on the overall House median is a wash, since we would argue that the location of the median party voter in the majority party is also important for policy outcomes in the House, if Democrats control congress, policy liberalism is almost certainly aided by the election of black Democrats who shift the Democratic median to the left; on the other hand, if Republicans control congress, policy liberalism is harmed by the election of very conservative Southern Republicans who shift the Republican median even farther to the right. Thus, given the 1994 and 1996 election results, gains in descriptive minority representation have required a price to be paid in terms of negative consequences for policy liberalism in House votes.[21]

DISCUSSION

We have shown that

(1) Through 1994, Democrats did not suffer greater levels of decline in those states where black majority districts had been drawn than in those states where they had not been.

(2) Given the substantial increase in support for Republican congressional candidates from 1990 to 1994, the Republican seat gains in Congress were generally consistent with previous patterns of seats-votes relationships over the past two decades.

(3) Almost all of the Democratic congressional loss in the South from 1990 to 1994 can be attributed to one simple fact: namely, Republican candidates made substantial vote gains in virtually all districts.

(4) Given the national scope of the Republican 1994 tidal wave, even had no

---

[20]Lublin's counterexamples rest on an attempt to determine median voters by simulating outcomes of certain important (and close) roll calls under alternative districting schemes, with hypothetical votes recreated using Poole-Rosenthal "Nominate" scores (Poole and Rosenthal, 1987). The problem with this method is that it relies on a string of complicated projections. Because the predictive equations are far from perfect, results based on a precise location for the median voter are highly suspect.

[21] Of course, even this analysis is still perhaps too simplistic. The rise to power of the extreme conservative wing of the Republican party in the House may have led Newt Gingrich to overreach, provoking a voter backlash to conservative initiatives.

new black majority seats been drawn in the 1990s districting round, the Republicans would still have gained control of the House.

(5) Had there been no need to create additional black seats and had African-American voters in the South been treated as "sandbags" and optimally deployed to protect Democratic beachheads from the Republican tide, even skillful partisan gerrymandering could not have reduced the level of Democratic congressional loss between 1990 and 1994 by more than at most 10-11 seats in the South.

(6) For all practical purposes, unless there is a black incumbent already in place, Southern districts that are not majority black do not elect African-Americans (at least ones who are candidates of choice of the African-American community) to the House. Thus, gerrymandering that appears to have been optimal from the perspective of maximizing Democratic congressional seat share in the South (i.e, districts with a 30-40% black population) appears incompatible with the creation of districts from which African-Americans have in the past had a realistic chance of being elected to Congress from the South.

(7) The consequences for Democratic success of a failure to "optimally" allocate black population across districts are (considerably) greater in the South than in the non-South.

(8) The implications of Democratic districting for congressional liberalism appears a wash, were Democrats to have kept control of the House. Even if every new black majority seat in the South led, on balance, to the replacement of a white Democrat with a Republican, the mean liberalism of the combination of one new Republican and one new black Democrat would be virtually indistinguishable from the mean liberalism of the two white Southern Democrats who had been replaced.

MORE SPECULATIVE CONCLUSIONS

We propose the following general conceptual framework for thinking about the impact of race-conscious districting in the South—what we call the theory of the "triple whammy." This theory has three components: (1) *ceteris paribus*, reducing black population proportion in a district reduces the likelihood that the district will be won by a Democrat, and, on balance, creating black majority seats is not an "optimal" allocation of black votes from the standpoint of maximizing the number of Democrats to be elected, especially in the South. (2) The "blackening" of the Democratic party in the South has a kind of chain reaction effect, making it ever less likely that Democrats will regain white support as the center of gravity within the Democratic party in the South shifts toward black interests (cf. Edsall and Edsall, 1991). (3) We can expect a kind of top-down realignment based on "progressive ambition," as the incumbency advantage shifts to the Republicans, in which the potential for Republican success at the congressional level makes it more likely that strong Republican candidates will seek state legislative office as a springboard to the higher and more desirable office,[22] and the increased Republican state legislative strength in the South will provide an increased pool of strong Republican congressional candidates which will make it more likely that Republicans will be able to hold on to their recent gains in congressional seats in the South. Eventually Republican gains will even percolate down to lower levels of office in most Southern states.[23]

When Lyndon Johnson pushed for the passage of the Voting Rights Act of 1965, he did so with the belief that it might doom the Democratic party's future chances in the South, although he also recognized that without it, the Democratic party in the South was probably doomed anyway (Grofman and Davidson, 1994). Over the past 30 years, the greatest loss of Democratic strength at the presidential level has taken place in the South, with the decline greatest in the areas of the South with the greatest black population, despite the fact that these voters (some not enfranchised until the late 1960s) vote solidly Democratic (Grofman and Handley, 1995).

If we look at the relationship between Democratic vote shares and black percentage in congressional districts in the South, we find that, while it used to be true that Democrats had a better than 50% chance of winning even the districts where there was minimal black voting strength (Grofman, Griffin and Glazer, 1992), by 1994, it was only in districts with more than 30% black population that Southern Democrats could be sure of winning more than half the seats (see Table 1 [page 57]; Tables 15 and 18 in Handley, Grofman and Arden [page 30 and page 33, this volume]).

As black population becomes ever more key to Democratic success in the South, and as Republicans win more and more of the heavily white seats, the character of the Democratic constituency and of Democratic elected officials begins to change accordingly.   Increasingly, in the South, the Republicans will become even more the white party and the Democrats the party of blacks. Consider two groups, B and W, and their support levels for the Democratic party, P_{BD} and P_{WD}. The strength of each group within the Democratic party is given by

---

[22] Similarly, we would argue that one reason for recent Republican House gains in the South is the fact that Republicans have been doing better in recruiting House candidates due in part to the fact that Republicans now have a realistic chance to be elected to the U.S. Senate in most Southern states, and being a Republican member of the House is a good place from which to seek a Senate seat.

[23] This model of "top-down" realignment (Brunell and Grofman, 1998, forthcoming) begins at the presidential level. It is in voting for president that the cracks in the "Solid South" first appeared, next in U.S. Senate elections, then in gubernatorial elections, then in House elections, and only very recently in elections for lower office. However, this realignment has been what Brunell and Grofman (1998, forthcoming) call a "glacial realignment," whose pace has been hindered by the rise of "candidate-centered politics" (Wattenberg, 1991) and, in the South, by the long shadow cast by the Civil War. But, like an avalanche, this realignment picked up speed in 1994 and began sweeping congressional Democrats out of its path. In 1996 despite a Democratic presidential victory and net losses overall, the Republicans made gains in the House in the South. The solid South was an historical anomaly; once the Democratic party began to change its stance on civil rights after WWII, and especially after Lyndon Johnson's "great betrayal" in supporting passage of the Civil Rights Act of 1964 and the Voting Rights Act of 1965, no one would ever be able to put Humpty-Dumpty together again (cf. Huckfeldt and Kohfeld, 1989; Carmines and Stimson, 1989).

$BP_{BD}/(BP_{BD} + WP_{WD})$. As P_{WD} goes down, then this ratio goes up. Thus, the greater the decline in white support for the Democrats, the greater the proportion of that party's support that comes from black voters and the more visible blacks will be in the Democratic coalition.[24]

The same kind of argument applies at the office-holder level. A majority of Democratic party leaders in some Southern states are now black. In Georgia, thanks to the 1994 election debacle and one party switch by a Democratic incumbent, there were *no* white Democratic members of the 1994 Georgia congressional delegation.

Prior to the 1996 election one of the present authors made a bet with a congressional specialist that few of the House seats in the South that changed partisan affiliation in 1992 and 1994 would return to Democratic control and that the Republicans would make a net gain of House seats in the South regardless of what happened to them elsewhere in the country or for president. That prediction was an accurate one. Moreover, the full consequences of the 1990s districting have yet to be felt. In particular, we can anticipate further limited net congressional Democratic losses in the South over the remainder of the decade, as those few seats in which George Bush got more votes than Clinton in 1992 that are still in the hands of Democrats shift into Republican hands.[25] Indeed, in Congress, in the deep South, only in districts with at least a 30% black population are Democrats likely to be safe.

In our (admittedly pessimistic) view, the Democratic party in the deep South (with the probable notable exceptions of Mississippi and Louisiana) will eventually become a minority party at all levels of government. As it does so, it will necessarily become more and more a party of blacks, with an increasing proportion of African-Americans among its diminishing number of elected officials. The Republican party will be the party supported by most whites—as has long been true in the deep South in terms of presidential voting, and has already become true at the congressional level.

Shaw v. Reno will not rescue the Democratic party in the South by permitting them to return to earlier ways of using black voters as "sandbags." First of all, contrary to some interpretations of its significance, Shaw does not overthrow the *Thornburg v. Gingles* guidelines (see discussion in Grofman, 1997; Grofman and Handley, 1995a; Grofman and Handley, chap. 5 this volume). Second, and probably even more importantly, even though a number of Southern states already have been forced to redraw congressional lines in the light of *Shaw v. Reno*-type challenges and others will be forced to do so, as we can see from the results of the

---

[24] Analogously, recent Democratic presidential nominees have received well over 20% of their total votes from African-Americans, making blacks a highly visible component of the national Democratic coalition—as reflected in the racial composition of delegates to recent Democratic National Conventions in which blacks have made up between 20% and 25% of the delegates.

[25] The growing Republican strength in the South also means that the regional peculiarities that fostered split-ticket voting for congress and president will be decreasing (Grofman, McDonald, Koetzle, and Brunell, 1996).

1996 House elections, Democrats still failed to make net gains in the South despite doing so elsewhere in the country. Because white support for the Democratic party in the South is already so weakened and the top-down realignment in the South has already progressed quite far, it will take more than a handful of changes in congressional (or legislative) district lines to return the Democratic party to dominance in Dixie[26]

---

[26]Of course, the South will never be as solidly Republican as it had been solidly Democratic for the obvious reason the blacks will anchor the Democratic party in the South and some whites will join them—especially when economic hard times (or fear thereof) remind Bubba that, while the "new" Republicans love their country they also love their country clubs, and that, even if Republicans are right that "welfare" is just another code word for "giving money to blacks," it can be even more important to decode "free men and free markets" as "low-wage jobs without health care, pension rights, or concern for worker safety."

PART TWO
Legal and Enforcement Issues

VOTING RIGHTS IN THE 1990S:
An Overview[1]

Bernard Grofman and Lisa Handley

IN THIS ESSAY WE WILL PROVIDE A BRIEF OVERVIEW OF CHANGES in voting rights case law in the 1990s. Because we have written extensively about voting rights in the past, our approach here will be a synoptic one, and we refer the reader to our earlier work for further details.[2] Our principal focus will be on issues related to race and redistricting. Thus, we will not cover, except in passing, legal issues related to one person, one vote or to partisan gerrymandering.

We may divide the modern voting rights era into five periods:

(1) In the period from 1962-1965, after *Baker v. Carr* but prior to the passage of the Voting Rights Act of 1965, one person, one vote issues are central (see Grofman, 1992b, c).

(2) From 1965-1970, the focus is on removing barriers to black registration and voting in the South (Alt, 1994).

(3) Beginning in the 1970s, and especially for legislative and congressional districting, the Section 5 powers of the U.S. Department of Justice are at the heart of voting rights jurisprudence (Grofman, Handley, and Niemi, 1992). Because the Department of Justice is concerned that multimember districts may operate to submerge black voting, by the mid-1980s, because of Justice Department pre-clearance denials (or threat of denial) the number of multimember districts used for legislative elections in the South is drastically reduced (Niemi, Hill, and Grofman, 1985).

---

[1] We are indebted to Dorothy Green and Chau Tran for library assistance. This research was partly supported by a grant from the Ford Foundation, #446740-47007, "The Impact of Redistricting on the Representation of Racial and Ethnic Minorities," to the first-named author. The views expressed in this paper are solely those of the authors and do not reflect those of the Ford Foundation.

[2] See especially Grofman, 1985, 1992a; and Grofman, Handley, and Niemi, 1992 for voting rights case law prior to the 1990s; and Grofman and Handley, 1995a; and Grofman, 1997 for more recent developments. Portions of this essay were taken from Grofman and Handley, 1995a.

(4) In 1982, Section 2 of the Voting Rights Act is amended to assure that a finding of discriminatory purpose will not be needed before a districting plan can be held to violate the Voting Rights Act. Although this change was intended to restore a legal status quo ante (See Grofman, Handley, and Niemi, 1992), the new language of Section 2, especially as interpreted by the Supreme Court in 1986 in the landmark case of *Thornburg v. Gingles*, leads to a wave of successful challenges to local use of at-large elections throughout the South (see Davidson and Grofman, 1994). The Section 2 standard is also held to be applicable to single member district plans (Grofman and Handley, 1992).

For congressional and legislative districtings in the 1990s, a combination of Section 5 actions by the Department of Justice, and (to a much lesser extent) the threat of litigation under Section 2 of the Act, yielded major gains in minority representation. In states covered by Section 5, as a result of strong enforcement pressures from the Department and greater technical sophistication about map-drawing possibilities, the initial 1990s districtings gave rise to a huge increase in the number of black majority seats in Congress—far higher than in any previous decade. Also there were large, if not quite as startling, gains in the number of majority-minority seats in state legislatures in the South and Southwest (Handley, Grofman and Arden, this volume), especially in heavily black states like Georgia and Mississippi.[3] A very high proportion of the majority black districts that have been created have elected minority candidates of choice (Handley, Grofman, and Arden, this volume). There were gains in Hispanic representation as well, also coming largely from the newly drawn majority-minority seats (Handley, Grofman, and Arden, this volume).

(5) With its 1993 decision in *Shaw v. Reno,* the voting rights tide turns (somewhat unexpectedly) in a much more conservative direction. In districting, the Supreme Court majority in *Shaw* and subsequent cases finds an overemphasis on the racial characteristics of districts to the exclusion of other representational concerns to violate constitutionally protected rights. Unfortunately, however, the exact nature of the rights that are being violated is, to put it mildly, less than clear (see discussion in e.g., Karlan, 1993; McDonald, 1995; cf. Pildes and Niemi, 1993). The Court arguably leaves at least equally obscure the crucial operational question of how to determine when race is such a "preponderant" factor that a given plan must be struck down as unconstitutional, although peculiarities in district lines based on purely racial considerations are taken to be prima facie evidence for possible unconstitutionality (see Grofman, 1993a, Grofman and Handley, 1995a; Grofman, 1997).[4]

---

[3] Deep south states have a long history of contesting any attempt to provide black representational gains through redistricting (see e.g., Parker, 1990).

[4] For other perspectives on *Shaw v. Reno,* see e.g., Pildes and Niemi, 1993; Aleinikoff and Issacharoff, 1993; Karlan, 1995; Kousser, 1995b; McDonald, 1995; McKaskle, 1995; Issacharoff, 1996; and the various essays in McClain and Stewart, 1995; and Peacock, 1997.

1990S REDISTRICTING PRIOR TO *SHAW V. RENO*

Critical to the dramatic gains in minority representation that took place in the early 1990s have been a number of key factors, most of which are directly related to the Voting Rights Act,[5] including: (a) an insider rather than outsider position for minorities with respect to legislative and congressional districting in the 1990s in many states that reflects previous gains in minority representation (see e.g., Holmes, this volume; Hagens, this volume); (b) the computer revolution that made it possible for minority legislators and minority advocacy groups to generate a plethora of plans to be produced at the click of a mouse, and allowed for fine-tuning of variants;[6] (c) vigorous enforcement of Section 5 of the Act by the Voting Rights Section of the Department of Justice;[7] (d) until quite recently, remarkable continuity in voting rights case law, with the three-pronged test in *Thornburg v. Gingles* (1986) defining the parameters of minority vote dilution for jurisdictions not covered by Section 5;[8] and (e) a Republican strategy that resisted bipartisan agreements on districting plans and sought to use litigation under the provisions of the Act to force major changes in district lines, with the expectation that such changes would inevitably benefit the Republican minority by concentrating Democrats in heavily minority districts and, in the process, displacing a number of white Democratic incumbents.[9]

THE 1990S LEGAL BACKLASH TO VOTING RIGHTS ACT ENFORCEMENT

Shaw v. Reno and Its Progeny

The Voting Rights Act has long been seen as one of the most successful pieces of legislation of the post-WW II period, whose consequences include a dramatic growth in black registration and black voter turnout, especially in the period immediately after its passage (Alt, 1994), and even more dramatic long-run gains in the number of black (and to a lesser extent, Hispanic) elected officials.[10] Recently, however, it has come under increasing attack as having outlived its usefulness and having been perverted to purposes not intended by its framers.[11] The strange shape of some majority-minority districts helped trigger a scholarly and public backlash against the Voting Rights Act in the 1990s[12] and, arguably, is the direct antecedent to the Supreme Court's opinion in *Shaw v. Reno*.[13]

---

[5] Grofman (1993a) notes that the Voting Rights Act is often most influential where its impact is least visible. By anticipating how courts and DOJ will interpret the Act, legislators frequently make changes they would not otherwise have made to reduce the likelihood of a plan being overturned. Consequently, even if a plan is overturned in court or denied preclearance, the difference between what was rejected and what eventually becomes law may not seem that large. Yet, without the influence of the Voting Rights Act, the proposed redistricting plan almost certainly would have looked quite different. Grofman (1993a: 1263) characterized the Act as a "brooding omnipresence" in redistricting decision making in the 90's.

[6] For example, Hagens (this volume) shows how the ready computer access of minority legislators and groups seeking to foster minority interests affected the redistricting bargaining process in Virginia.

While we can understand popular disgust at some of the lines drawn ostensibly in the name of fostering minority voting rights: (a) many of the more bizarre features of the legislative and congressional plans of the 1990s reflect partisan or incumbent protection calculations (just as in previous decades) and thus should not be blamed entirely on the Voting Rights Act; and (b) compactness is a criterion of limited importance.[14] Nonetheless, the shape of districts such as North Carolina's 12th CD suggested to the media, the public, and most importantly, to many members of the Supreme Court, that, in the 1990s, race had (except for population equality)[15] become the only real criterion governing redistricting, and that "maximizing" had replaced "equal opportunity" as the standard.[16]

In *Shaw v. Reno*, the Court created a new constitutional cause of challenge to a districting plan, namely that a plan had an impermissible racial motive—to segregate the races—allowing a plan to be struck down even if did not have impermissible consequences in terms of diluting the voting strength of any group. In *Shaw*, a five member majority on the Supreme Court viewed a North Carolina congressional district (the 12th North Carolina CD) that had been consciously drawn with a black majority as potentially violative of the Equal Protection Clause of the 14th Amendment because the nature of the startlingly irregularities in its shape suggested to them that the district could have no legitimate purpose other than to assure racial representation. A second Supreme Court decision, *Shaw v. Hunt,* struck down the plan, reversing the three-judge panel that had upheld its constitutionality (see Sellers, Canon, and Schousen, page 269 this volume). Because of the delay caused by the several rounds of litigation, a new congressional plan for North Carolina will not be put into place until the 1998 election.[17]

After *Shaw*, with the *Miller v. Johnson* decision, which overturned a Georgia

---

[7] One of the puzzles of voting rights enforcement is why the Department of Justice under Republican presidents such as Bush pursued a generally tough enforcement policy in the area of voting rights while regressing or retrenching in all other civil rights domains. One standard answer is that it is all a Republican plot. In this view, in the 1990s round of districting Republican officials under Bush ordered DOJ try to create as many highly concentrated minority districts as they could in order to pack Democrats. But, this is far too simplistic: there are a number of instances where DOJ actions under the Bush Administration (as in the Los Angeles County Board of Supervisors case) directly harmed Republican interests. As one of us has argued elsewhere (Grofman, 1993a), the civil service professionals at the Voting Rights section of DOJ seek to enforce the Act in a completely non-partisan fashion and they are highly competent (albeit overworked). While there is some interference from political appointees at DOJ, all in all, this interference is minimal.

Nonetheless, Republican belief that strict voting rights enforcement would in the long-run benefit Republican interests has acted to shield the Voting Rights Section from the conservative backlash that has crippled civil rights enforcement in other areas--permitting DOJ staff in the Voting Rights Section to, by and large, just do their job and enforce the Act as they see it, especially with respect to Section 5. When Clinton came into office, after his retreat on the Lani Guinier appointment there was an initial period when there was no Assistant Attorney General (AAG) for Civil Rights—conducive to a maintenance of previous enforcement policies—and when Deval Patrick was appointed AAG, he, too, was committed to vigorous enforcement of the Act. All in all, there has been remarkable continuity in DOJ voting rights policies from Bush to Clinton, with the present AAG vigorously defending the preclearance denials made by his Republican predecessor. See further discussion of these points in Grofman (1993a).

congressional district that was nowhere near as ill-compact as the North Carolina 12th, but whose creation could be laid almost entirely to insistence by the Department of Justice that Georgia go from one majority black congressional district in the 1980s redistricting round to three such districts in the 1990s (see Holmes, this volume), it is clear that the Supreme Court majority is anxious to put curbs on DOJ's use of its preclearance authority,[18] and it is also clear that ill-compactness is not a necessary condition for a district to be struck down as violative of *Shaw*.[19]

The *Shaw v. Reno* decision can be attacked on a variety of grounds. In particular, it creates a new constitutional standard that is hard to interpret and it places a burden of presumptive constitutional illegitimacy on tortuously shaped black majority districts that it does not place on similarly ugly white majority districts.[20] On the face of it, *Shaw*, *Miller*, and related subsequent decisions[21] might appear incompatible with the requirements of the Voting Rights Act for race-conscious districting to remedy vote dilution, and thus they appear to threaten the dramatic black (and Hispanic) gains in representation that have been brought about over the past several decades through the creation of majority-minority districts. Moreover, *Shaw* and subsequent decisions have already led to the voting rights bar being put on the defensive, defending *Shaw*-type claims, with few new voting rights challenges being brought; and to a greater unwillingness of those defendant jurisdictions faced with Section 2 lawsuits to agree to draw majority-minority districts as part of an out-of-court settlement, since they can take refuge in the claim that the remedial district(s) violates *Shaw*.[22] Nonetheless, we are not as concerned about the dangers of *Shaw* and its progeny as are some other voting rights specialists.

---

[8]Prior to *Shaw*, despite several opportunities to revisit the *Thornburg v. Gingles* decision and make it harder to prove a violation of Section 2 of the Act, the Court had reiterated that *Thornburg* defines the Section 2 test for minority vote dilution. Indeed, cases decided early in the 1990s applied the *Thornburg* test to judicial elections for the first time (albeit this was an interpretation that federal courts would subsequently backtrack from: see Karlan, 1997 forthcoming). While the decision in *Presley v. Etowah County* (1992) suggested that the Supreme court was not really prepared to advance voting rights case law to go beyond the issues covered in *Thornburg*, it did not really represent a retrenchment (see discussion of this case in Grofman and Handley, 1995). Similarly, the failure of federal courts to require a statistical adjustment for census minority undercount could also not be taken to be a retrenchment of previous voting rights standards. In general, the standards for operationalizing one person, one vote remained unchanged in the 1990s. Also, (with the partial exception of *Republican Party of North Carolina v. Hunt*) the potential for a districting plan to be held unconstitutional as a partisan gerrymander (Grofman, 1990) went unrealized in the 1990s (see discussion in Grofman and Handley, 1995a). Arguably, the closest thing to a genuine change in voting rights case law prior to *Shaw* was that the Supreme Court signaled to federal courts that they should defer more to state court jurisdiction in the initial phases of redistricting litigation than some federal courts had shown themselves wont to (Karlan, 1993). This was a minor course correction, with no direct implications for substantive doctrine.

[9] See further elaboration of this argument in Grofman (1993a).

[10]There has been a long history of bipartisan support for strong voting rights enforcement. Also, voting rights law was seen as fundamentally distinct in many ways from other areas of 14th Amendment jurisprudence, permitting even conservative justices to assent to color-conscious choices so as to safeguard fundamental rights (see further discussion of these points in Grofman, 1993a: 1243-1247; Grofman and Handley, 1995a).

While the 5-4 lineups in *Shaw* and *Miller v. Johnson*, and the intemperate tone of some of the opinions in these (and other) cases, suggest that the Court is strongly polarized around voting rights issues and that there are Justices on the Court who wish an almost total reversal of the current interpretation and implementation of the VRA, [23] there is every reason to expect that extreme anti-VRA views will remain in a minority on the Supreme Court, at least for the near future. Justice O'Connor, whose orientation is relatively case-specific and fact-specific, holds the pivotal vote (Grofman, 1997).

Moreover, if we look at the Supreme Court's 1995 *per curiam* affirmance of the California districting plans created under the auspices of the California Supreme Court in *DeWitt v. Wilson*, we see that majority-minority districts can be sustained, as long as it can also be shown that factors other than racial balance were important in the districting decision-making as to the number of and configuration of these majority-minority districts. Also, as yet (February 1998), *Thornburg* is far from dead, especially since there are ways to make *Thornburg* and *Shaw* compatible (Grofman, 1997).

Finally, as one of us has written elsewhere (Grofman, 1997), the most important implications of *Shaw* hold only at the level of congressional districting: "(G)iven the degree of residential segregation in the U.S., drawing relatively compact and clearly contiguous black districts at the local level (or even for most

---

[11]In the 1980s we had already seen the beginnings of a backlash to the Act, especially among Republicans. In 1982 Republicans like Senator Orrin Hatch opposed the Act's extension, and initially so did Ronald Reagan. Opponents of the Act claimed that Section 5 had become an unreasonable intrusion of the federal government into state affairs and that the new language of Section 2 of the Act was tantamount to a quota system. Similarly, Abigail Thernstrom (1985, 1987), in work which received considerable scholarly attention, and others (e.g., Schuck, 1987), argued that the Act had been distorted beyond the intent of its framers and was being enforced by the Department of Justice in an inappropriately rigid and aggressive manner. Nonetheless, this point of view had little or no impact on Voting Rights Act enforcement in the 1990s round of districting.

[12]In addition, (white) Democrats have been concerned with the supposed partisan implications of drawing heavily minority districts that tend to soak up Democrats (see the previous chapter by Grofman and Handley, this volume).

[13]The current negative reaction to the VRA also cannot be understood without taking into account constitutional and normative arguments about ideas about equality and competing individualistic and group-oriented conceptions of rights. For critics of the Act, such as George Will or Abigail Thernstrom, the VRA has come to embody an idea of tribalistic representation that is incompatible with a commitment to a color-blind society, and thus incompatible with the "proper" interpretation of the fourteenth amendment's "equal protection" clause. As Will (1995) puts it: "The creation of 'majority-minority' districts expresses the ideology of 'identity politics': you are whatever your racial or ethnic group is. But that ideology, promulgated by political entrepreneurs with a stake in the racial and ethnic spoils system, is false regarding the facts of human differences, and bad as an aspiration and an exhortation." For discussion of the normative debate about voting rights in this essay see, e.g., Davidson and Grofman, 1994 (esp. Grofman and Davidson, 1992b); Grofman, 1993a.

[14]See further discussion of the compactness issue in Grofman (1993a). Also see Niemi, Grofman, Carlucci and Hofeller (1990) and Pildes and Niemi (1993).

[15]We might also note in passing that, in our view, an overemphasis on strict population equality has often been carried to the point of absurdity and led to disregard for preserving political subunit boundaries or creating districts that mapped onto (re)cognizable communities of interest. See e.g., Stokes (1993: 22), Grofman (1992c: 786-788).

state legislatures) is not that difficult." Moreover, even at the congressional level, the results of elections in 1996 suggest that, with the strong advantage given by incumbency,[24] black candidates can continue to win in reconfigured districts (such as those in Georgia and Texas) when those districts remain very heavily black in population, even if not majority black (see e.g. the discussion of the 1996 congressional results in Georgia in the concluding epilogue in Holmes, this volume).

LULAC v. Clements and the Definition of Racially Polarized Voting

Important as *Shaw* is as a brake on further gains in descriptive minority representation, and certain as *Shaw*-related litigation is to lead to the defeat of some minority officeholders when districts become reconfigured,[25] in our view, the greatest potential for a major setback in minority representation lies not in *Shaw* and its progeny, but in the potential consequences of another much less visible case, *LULAC v. Clements*.[26] In *LULAC*, a majority of the 5th circuit, in an *en banc* ruling, reinterpreted the definition of racial bloc voting in a fashion that we see as incompatible with the descriptive approach to the presence or absence of racial bloc voting taken in Thornburg. The *LULAC* court moved away from the straightforward question of whether or not minority candidates of choice regularly lose because of white bloc voting into a consideration of whether or not other factors, such as straight party-line voting, could explain the racial differences in voting patterns. The *LULAC* line

---

[16]Elsewhere, one of us has argued that this is a mischaracterization of 1990s case law and DOJ enforcement practices (Grofman, l993a). See esp. Posner (this volume) and the discussion in *Moon v. Harris* (1997) of the DOJ stance in Virginia. The three judge court in *Moon* observes (1997 WL 57432, 8) that "the record reflects no indication that the Department of Justice advocated a 'maximization' policy for Congressional districts in Virginia. Indeed, the acting head of the Voting Rights Section of the Department of Justice spoke in Richmond prior to the redistricting process and stated that the Department did not read the VRA to require that, if a majority black district could be created, it must be."

[17] At the time of writing (February 1998), it is not clear whether this plan will be a legislative one or one drawn by the courts.

[18] For example, the three judge court in *Diaz v. Silver* (1997), the New York congressional voting case, asserts that "The Supreme Court had found that DOJ had unlawfully interpreted the VRA to require the maximization of majority-minority districts." (slip op. at p. 61; cf. the totally different, and we believe far more accurate, interpretation of the DOJ position with respect to maximization set forth in 1997 by the three judge court in *Moon v. Harris* quoted in an earlier footnote).

[19] For example, the three judge court in *Diaz v. Silver* (1997) asserts that "the fact that a district is compact does not immunize it from scrutiny. Compactness or its absence would not itself excuse racially motivated districting" (slip op. at p. 78).

[20] *Shaw* is jurisprudentially excessive because it creates a new constitutional violation when it could have addressed the perceived problem in a more efficient and focused manner merely by correcting legislative misinterpretations of Section 2 (and Section 5). The Supreme Court failed to appreciate the political/legal dynamic that led to the creation of majority-minority districts. Thus, it crafted an overbroad remedy, when it could, in our view, have achieved the same end with far less travail by choosing a different case to send a message to legislatures (and to lower courts and the Department of Justice) about how better to interpret the geographical compactness element of *Thornburg's* three-pronged test for Section 2 vote dilution and/or the Section 5 preclearance denial standard.

[21] See, e.g., Engstrom and Kirksey, this volume, for discussion of the various *Hays* decisions, the *Shaw*-related litigation in Louisiana.

of argument has now been taken up by other circuits,[27] and is likely to be a major source of contention in future voting rights cases, despite the fact that, arguably, it flies in the face of Justice Brennan's position in *Thornburg* that only the fact of racial polarization, not evidence as to the reasons for the existence of that polarization, is needed to demonstrate a dilutive impact. [28]

According to Judge Higginbotham, who wrote the *LULAC* majority opinion, in partisan elections, racially polarized voting occurs only "where Democrats lose because they are black, not where blacks lose because they are Democrats." Thus, *LULAC* stands for the proposition that, even if minority voters support the minority candidate in overwhelming numbers and non-minority voters oppose the minority candidate in overwhelming numbers, if it can be demonstrated that minority voters supported the minority candidate not only because s/he was black/Hispanic but because he was a Democrat, while non-minority voters opposed that candidate not only because s/he was minority but because that candidate was a Democrat (and thus not a Republican), then voting is not racially polarized.

If we accept this definition of polarized voting, in general elections where candidates run on party labels, polarized voting will be roughly as scarce as hen's teeth, since blacks (and Mexican-Americans) vote overwhelmingly Democratic, while a majority of whites in most areas of the South now support Republican.[29] Thus *LULAC* represents the possibility of a total turnaround in voting rights case law, since proving polarization in voting patterns is the linchpin of minority voting rights claims with respect to districting.

However, even if we grant Judge Higginbotham's premise that the simple descriptive fact of polarized voting is not enough to show that voting is polarized in a legally relevant way (which conflicts with Justice Brennan's views in

---

[22] Moreover, in the redistricting taking place next century, it seems likely that jurisdictions covered under Section 5 of the Act will be much more likely to challenge the Department of Justice's Section 5 preclearance denials in D.C. court by arguing that no constitutional remedy is possible because any remedy plan would require ill-shaped districts.

[23] For example, *Hall v. Holder* (l994), is important not for its decision, a relatively narrow holding that legislative size was not litigable under the VRA because there were no clear standards as to how large a legislature should be, but because the concurring opinion by Justice Thomas (joined by Justice Scalia) is a complete repudiation of the past several decades of voting rights jurisprudence. Their opinion claims that earlier court decisions were wrong in accepting the fact that the VRA applied to issues of vote dilution, and it also makes a strong normative argument against the creation of what they call racial "safe boroughs."

[24] Various students of congressional elections have found the advantages of incumbency (e.g., name recognition, better access to campaign funding) to be worth from 6 to 10 percentage points of vote share in a general election over what a candidate of the same party running when the seat is open could be expected to achieve.

[25] See, for example, Engstrom and Kirksey (this volume) for a discussion of what happened when Louisiana congressional lines were redrawn after a successful *Shaw*-type challenge.

[26] *LULAC v. Clements*, 999 F. 2d 831(5th Cir. 1993), cert denied 114 S. Ct. 878 (1994). *LULAC* also breaks new ground in upholding the applicability of Section 2 of the Voting Rights Act to judges. We will not discuss that aspect of the case here, since subsequent cases have led to a backsliding from the practical import of that aspect of the opinion (see Karlan, 1997 forthcoming).

[27] See esp. *Lewis v. Alamance County*, 99 F 3rd 600 (4th Cir. November 4, 1996).

Thornburg), for the Higginbotham argument to make sense we must be able to treat party and race as independent factors and to statistically separate out their effects. The latter is very difficult to do, and if we try to do so using cross-sectional data, we would be mistaking the true causal link between race, partisanship and voting behavior. It can readily be shown that the affiliations of white voters in the South and black voters in the South have fluctuated directly with the nature of the racial policies espoused by the Democratic and Republican parties.[30] Moreover, the political affiliations of white voters in the South can be directly related to the racial context in which they find themselves, with whites in the most heavily black areas having deserted the Democratic party almost entirely (Grofman and Handley, 1995b; Huckfeldt and Kohfeld, 1989; cf. Carmines and Stimson, 1989).[31]

DISCUSSION

While decisions such as *Shaw* would probably have turned out the same even if the Justices in the majority had been persuaded to change their minds about certain important and mistaken factual claims about the supposed present-day irrelevance of race in American politics and American society,[32] it seems plausible to believe that normative/constitutional judgments are shaped at least in part by views about consequences, and thus by views about social facts.[33] In this light, we would like

---

[28] The definition of polarized voting used by the Supreme Court in *Beer v. U.S.* and elaborated in *Thornburg*, is simply that whites and blacks vote for different candidates, and, in particular, that whites regularly oppose black candidates who have the support of the black community. If the standard definition of racially polarized voting is used, then, at least in the South, the evidence for racially polarized voting is considerable, although there are not many examples of blacks losing in white majority seats because black candidates are discouraged from ever seeking election in such constituencies. *LULAC* sneaks an intent requirement back into Section 2 jurisprudence because it moves from the test for racially polarized voting based simply on the presence or absence of differences in the support levels of black and white (or Hispanic and non-Hispanic) voters vis a vis the minority candidate(s) of choice that is specified in *Thornburg* to a test that requires consideration of the factors that determine how voters voted, and thus to a test of whether or not the intent lying behind the decision of white/Anglo voters to not support the minority candidate could be regarded as racial in motivation. We regard the 5th circuit reinterpretation of the definition of racially polarized voting as incompatible with the test for bloc voting used in *Thornburg*.

[29] In our view, however, it is also critical to understand what happens in party primaries, where polarized voting patterns may also be found. If voting is polarized in the primaries of one or both parties, whether or not it is also polarized in the general may be irrelevant to a determination that minority voting strength has been diluted through the presence of polarized voting.

[30] The first cracks in the Democratic solid South, white desertions by the droves, came in 1948 in response to Truman's desegregation stance, and the pattern was repeated in 1964, in response to Lyndon Johnson's civil rights policies. Blacks finally deserted the party of Lincoln, to vote for Lyndon Johnson and succeeding Democratic presidential nominees in proportions above 90 percent, only after passage of the Civil Rights Act of 1964. Today, the two major parties stand for very different positions with respect to civil rights, and, as we tend to forget, which party is on which side has flip-flopped over the past 30 years.

[31] A considerably more detailed discussion of the problems with the *LULAC* decision, one from which much of the material above has been drawn, is found in Grofman and Handley (1995a). Also, see Grofman (1985; 1991a; 1991b; 1993b; 1993c; 1995) for a general discussion of how to measure racially polarized voting and other related issues.

to believe that the Supreme Court majority in cases such as *Shaw* would not have been quite so fervent in their denunciation of the evils of black majority seats and in their likening of such seats to racial apartheid if they had been better grounded in empirical reality about the continuing existence of barriers to minority electoral success from non majority-minority districts,[34] or the fact that (because of racial discrimination) blacks do perceive important political interests in common with one another simply because they are black,[35] or recognized the limited truth to the claim that a focus on descriptive representation, on balance, harms minority interests by helping conservative Republicans to get elected.[36]

Justice O'Connor's opinion in Shaw seeks a moral high ground by attacking districts for whites and districts for blacks (or other minorities) as tantamount to *Shaw* apartheid. However, if (at least in the absence of minority incumbents) voting is heavily polarized along racial lines (in primaries and/or general elections), and minority candidates usually lose, then drawing districts with no attention to their demography may mean that only (non-Hispanic) whites can be expected to win election. We must be careful that a zeal to end overreliance on racial considerations in the districting process not retard the integration of the halls of our legislatures. While most of us would prefer to live in a color-blind society, we live in a "'second-best' world where color conscious problems require color-conscious remedies" (Grofman and Davidson, 1992b), even if that merely means being attentive to the continuing massive residential segregation of minority groups (Massey and Denton, 1993).[37]

---

[32]In his dissenting opinion in Miller, Justice Stevens (joined by Justice Ginsburg) approvingly quotes various social scientists about the continuing significance of racial and ethnic divisions in American life. Unfortunately, most of the works quoted by Justices Stevens and Ginsburg are twenty or more years old. However, more current works making the same point are easily found (see below).

[33]Like a number of other social scientists (see esp. Kousser, 1995b: 18-19), we are bothered by the remarkably casual way in which Supreme Court Justices throw out empirical assertions that lack factual grounding as if they were simply so obvious as to not need supporting justification. For example, Shaw is misguided in its views that the majority-minority districts that have been created can be directly analogized to "racial apartheid." Usually these districts are the most racially balanced districts in a state.

[34]See Handley, Grofman, and Arden (this volume).

[35]If we look at the similarities between white and black attitudes on a large variety of issues, from foreign policy to abortion, it is possible to argue that blacks and whites are really not that different in attitudes, but such an analysis is quite misleading about things that matter most. When it comes to attitudes and beliefs linked to race, the empirical evidence is overwhelming that the gap between whites and blacks remains huge. As Kousser (1995b) summarizes the evidence: "(W)hites and blacks see entirely different worlds. In the white view, there is little remaining prejudice or public or private discrimination, and there is consequently little need for government programs to do something about it. In the black view, prejudice and discrimination are pervasive, and government at all levels should act to remedy this serious plight" (Kousser, 1995b: 35). Related arguments and evidence is found in other recent sources such as Welch, 1991; Tate, 1993; and Dawson, 1994. Dawson (1994), for example argues that, for blacks, race is more important than class (or other factors) in defining self-identity (or having it defined for one by others).

[36] For evaluation of this claim see the previous chapter by Grofman and Handley (this volume) and references therein.

[37] The Voting Rights Act may be far from perfect, but the need for it remains. As Maurice Chevalier responded when asked how he liked being old: "Consider the alternative."

Despite *Shaw v. Reno* and its progeny, we prefer to end this essay on a reasonably hopeful note. As we argued above, we see *Shaw* as limited in its probable impact.[38] We would prefer to emphasize how far we have come since the passage of the Voting Rights Act.[39] In large part because of the Voting Rights Act, the 1990s round of redistricting, like that in previous decades, led to substantial growth in the number of minority officials in Congress and in state legislatures.[40] Even though more majority-minority districts will fall to *Shaw*-type challenges,[41] not all (or even most) districts will be (successfully) challenged, and the incumbents in many redrawn districts will continue to be reelected even though minority population in the district will be reduced somewhat below a majority.

---

[38]Also, even though we are both highly skeptical about taking compactness too seriously, especially as compared to other factors such as preserving communities of interest, we do believe that contiguity of district boundaries is, in general, desirable, and one of the present authors testified against the North Carolina 12th congressional district on the grounds that the plan in which was embedded was a patchwork crazy quilt lacking rational state purpose (Grofman, 1992a). In his testimony, however, Grofman indicated that the North Carolina plan was very nearly *sui generis* in its bizarreness (also see Grofman, 1993a: 1260-1263.

[39]Indeed, even in the worst case scenario, to the extent that we do go backwards in minority electoral success, it will be toward the status quo circa 1980, not that circa 1890.

[40]Also, some additional districts in which minorities have a realistic opportunity to elect candidates of choice will be created by new Section 2 challenges to at-large systems at the local level.

[41]For example, congressional districts in Virginia and New York were struck down by three-judge federal courts as unconstitutional under *Shaw*, and even the substantially redrawn North Carolina congressional districts were struck down in March 1998.

POST-1990 REDISTRICTINGS AND THE PRECLEARANCE REQUIREMENT OF SECTION 5 OF THE VOTING RIGHTS ACT

MARK A. POSNER

THIS ESSAY CHRONICLES, ANALYZES, AND EXPLAINS an important and controversial period in the application of Section 5 of the Voting Rights Act to state and local redistricting plans—the period from April 1991, shortly after the 1990 Census was released, until mid-1995, when the Supreme Court issued its watershed decision in *Miller v. Johnson*, rewriting the law of redistricting, sharply criticizing the manner in which the Department of Justice conducted its review of post-1990 redistricting plans and, at least to some degree, restarting a post-1990 redistricting cycle that otherwise had generally reached its conclusion.

In 1965, Congress took up an historic challenge, to end the "blight of racial discrimination in voting...[which had] infected the electoral process in parts of our county for nearly a century,"[1] by enacting the Voting Rights Act of 1965.[2] Central to the Act's remedial scheme is Section 5,[3] which places a federal "preclearance" barrier against the adoption of any new voting practice or procedure (by covered states and localities) whose purpose or effect is to discriminate against minority voters. For 30 years thereafter, Congress, the federal courts, and the Department of Justice worked hand-in-hand to make the promise of Section 5 a very potent reality.

The drawing of districts from which officials are elected, whether through a redistricting or the adoption of a districting plan to implement a new district method of election, is one of the most important voting changes that a jurisdiction may adopt, and the review of redistrictings and districtings has been an integral part of Section 5 enforcement efforts from the beginning. For those jurisdictions subject to Section 5, the knowledge that their redistricting or districting plan would be closely scrutinized by a federal preclearance official (the Attorney General or the District Court for the District of Columbia) has exerted a strong influence on their districting choices. Where those choices have been tainted by a discriminatory purpose or effect, Section 5 preclearance has been

---

[1]*South Carolina v. Katzenbach*, 383 U.S. 301, 308 (1966).
[2]Pub. L. No. 89-110, 79 Stat. 437 (1965).
[3]42 U.S.C. § 1973c (1988).

denied, requiring the adoption of new, nondiscriminatory plans. From Congress to state legislatures to local governing bodies, the application of Section 5 to redistricting and districting plans has played a major role in minority voters making dramatic strides toward achieving an equal opportunity to elect candidates of their choice to office.

The role of Section 5 in redistrictings has expanded, from the 1970s to the 1980s to the 1990s, as court decisions and legislation have (directly or indirectly) subjected an increasing number of redistricting and districting plans to Section 5 review. Initially, it was the Supreme Court's Fourteenth Amendment "one-person, one-vote" decisions which gathered force with the passage of time leading more jurisdictions to determine that redistricting was a constitutional necessity.[4] In 1975, Congress amended the Section 5 coverage test resulting in the State of Texas becoming covered,[5] which nearly doubled the number of voting changes submitted for Section 5 review.[6] Also in the 1970s, the federal courts developed a constitutional "vote dilution" claim for challenging at-large election systems.[7] In 1982, Congress incorporated that law into Section 2 of the Voting Rights Act[8] which was followed by court decisions that generally adopted a liberal interpretation of the revised statute.[9] The 1982 amendment resulted in hundreds of counties, cities, and school districts covered by Section 5 changing to district election systems, either voluntarily, under threat of a lawsuit, or in the context of federal court litigation.

On June 29, 1995, the Supreme Court decided *Miller v. Johnson,*[10] its second

---

[4]The Supreme Court initially held that "one-person, one-vote" applies to congressional districting plans. *Wesberry v. Sanders*, 376 U.S. 1 (1964). This was followed by decisions applying the requirement to state legislative plans, *Reynolds v. Sims*, 377 U.S. 533 (1964), and to local government apportionment. *Hadley v. Junior College District of Metropolitan Kansas City*, 397 U.S. 50 (1970); *Avery v. Midland County*, 390 U.S. 474 (1968).

[5]Pub. L. No. 94-73, 89 Stat. 400 (1975).

[6]Since Texas has become covered under Section 5, the state and its subjurisdictions have accounted for approximately 40 percent of the changes submitted for administrative Section 5 review, and about 30 percent of all submitted redistricting and districting plans.

All statistics cited in this essay are taken from statistics and data compilations maintained by the Voting Section of the United States Department of Justice's Civil Rights Division.

[7]The leading decisions were *White v. Regester*, 412 U.S. 755 (1973), and *Zimmer v. McKeithen*, 485 F.2d 1297 (5th Cir. 1973) (en banc), *aff'd on other grounds sub nom.*, *East Carroll Parish School Board v. Marshall*, 424 U.S. 636 (1976).

[8]Pub. L. No. 97-205, 96 Stat. 131 (1982). The 1982 amendment effectively reversed the Supreme Court's decision in *Mobile v. Bolden*, 446 U.S. 55 (1980), where the Court held that plaintiffs would need to satisfy a stiff test of discriminatory purpose in order to prevail in a challenge to an at-large method of election. The 1982 amendment instead adopted a "results" test, patterned on the pre-*Mobile* constitutional vote dilution standard.

[9]See, *e.g.*, *Thornburg v. Gingles*, 478 U.S. 30 (1986); *Garza and United States v. County of Los Angeles*, 918 F.2d 763 (9th Cir. 1990), *cert. denied*, 498 U.S. 1028 (1991); *Collins v. City of Norfolk*, 883 F.2d 1232 (4th Cir. 1989), *cert. denied*, 498 U.S. 938 (1990); *Gomez v. City of Watsonville*, 863 F.2d 1407 (9th Cir. 1988), *cert. denied*, 489 U.S. 1080 (1989); *United States v. Dallas County Commission*, 850 F.2d 1430 (11th Cir. 1988), *cert. denied*, 490 U.S. 1030 (1989) (county commission); *United States v. Dallas County Commission*, 850 F.2d 1433 (11th Cir. 1988), *cert. denied*, 490 U.S. 1030 (1989) (county school board); *Campos v. City of Baytown*, 840 F.2d 1240 (5th Cir. 1988); *Citizens for a Better Gretna v. City of Gretna*, 834 F.2d 496 (5th Cir. 1987), *cert. denied*, 492 U.S. 905 (1989); *McMillan v. Escambia County*, 748 F.2d 1037 (5th Cir. 1984); *Ketchum v. Byrne*, 740 F.2d 1398, (7th Cir. 1984), *cert. denied*, 471 U.S. 1135 (1985); *Jones v. City of Lubbock*, 727 F.2d 364 (5th Cir. 1984); *Jeffers v. Clinton*, 730 F. Supp. 196 (E.D. Ark. 1989) and 756 F. Supp. 1195 (E.D. Ark. 1990) (three-judge court), *aff'd mem.*, 498 U.S. 1019 (1991).

ruling on the new constitutional claim of racial gerrymandering. The Court (by a five to four vote) held that Georgia's congressional redistricting plan, which had been adopted in response to the Attorney General's objections to two earlier plans, was impermissibly based on race, and sharply criticized the manner in which the Department of Justice exercised its Section 5 preclearance authority in reviewing redistricting plans. Specifically, the Court concluded that, at least in the review of the Georgia plans and perhaps in other reviews as well, the Department had implemented a policy of maximizing the number of majority-minority districts by denying preclearance to plans that could have included additional majority-minority districts but did not. The Court admonished that this policy raised "serious constitutional concerns."[11] The Court noted, but did not accept, the Department's denial that any such policy existed. More recently, in *Shaw v. Hunt*[12] the Court (again split five to four) held that the Department had applied the same maximization policy in denying preclearance to North Carolina's post-1990 congressional plan.

While this essay is not designed as a rebuttal to the Supreme Court's mistaken appraisal of the Department's enforcement of Section 5, by setting forth the principles and analytic methods that guided the Department in its 1990s redistricting reviews it demonstrates that no "maximization" policy existed. The Court's belief reflects a review of only three Section 5 objections. Moreover, the *Miller* determination (on which *Shaw* then largely piggybacked) was based on a narrowly circumscribed district court record. The United States, as defendant-intervenor in the case, did not seek to defend its Section 5 review process or demonstrate that the objections were properly grounded on the Section 5 legal standard because, in its view, it was sufficient that the objections were proper on their face and there was no collusion between the Department and the State of Georgia regarding the state's decision to remedy the objections by adopting a new plan.[13] This essay, on the other hand, relies on the entire width and breath of the Department's experience in reviewing post-1990 redistrictings, which involved the receipt of nearly 3,000 redistricting plans and nearly 200 objections.

The essay is divided into three sections. First, it sets the stage for the post-1990 Section 5 reviews by summarizing the basic requirements of Section 5 as applied to redistricting and districting plans, also noting the important developments in districting technology and census data that were inaugurated with the

---

[10]515 U.S. 900 (1995).

[11]*Id.* at 926. The Court made this finding in ruling that the Section 5 objections did not provide a compelling state interest justifying the adoption of what it concluded was a racially gerrymandered plan. Thus, the plan failed the constitutional test of strict scrutiny.

[12]517 U.S. 899 (1996).

[13]As noted *infra*, only the District Court for the District of Columbia (and not local district courts such as the court in *Miller*) may, under the Voting Rights Act, consider (in a *de novo* review) the propriety of the Attorney General's Section 5 objections. Sections 5 and 14(b) of the Voting Rights Act, 42 U.S.C. §§ 1973c, 1973*l*(b). In the Supreme Court in *Miller*, the Department argued that "[g]iven the Attorney General's important role in the Section 5 statutory scheme, a State should be able to act on the assumption that the Attorney General has correctly objected to its plan, unless the objection is clearly insupportable." Br. for the United States at 30.

1990 Census. The second section reports a variety of statistics and other summary information to provide an overview of the Section 5 determinations made by the Attorney General, as well as by the District Court for the District of Columbia, regarding the post-1990 redistricting and districting plans. The third section describes the analytic framework employed by the Department of Justice in making these determinations and examines the manner in which the Department addressed a number of specific districting issues.[14]

I. LEGAL AND TECHNOLOGICAL BACKDROP FOR POST-1990 SECTION 5 REVIEWS

A. Overview of Section 5 Requirements

Section 5 of the Voting Rights Act, 42 U.S.C. § 1973c (1988), requires that covered jurisdictions obtain federal approval (preclearance) whenever they "enact or seek to administer" a change in a voting practice or procedure,[15] including redistricting plans.[16] Preclearance is to be obtained before the voting change is implemented,[17] and may be obtained through one of two alternative methods—either by making an administrative request to the Attorney General or by seeking a declaratory judgment against the United States before a three-judge panel of the United States District Court for the District of Columbia. A judicial preclearance action is considered *de novo*, and may be filed without first making an administrative submission or after preclearance is denied by the Attorney General.[18] The administrative preclearance process was designed by Congress to provide an expeditious means by which jurisdictions may obtain preclearance,[19] and almost all jurisdictions utilize the administrative preclearance procedure with relatively few filing declaratory judgment actions in the history of Section 5.[20]

To obtain preclearance (whether from the Attorney General or the district court), the jurisdiction has the burden of demonstrating that its voting change "does not have the purpose and will not have the effect of denying or abridging the right to vote on account of race or color, or [membership in a language minor-

---

[14]In the remainder of this essay, the term "redistricting" generally will be used to refer to both redistricting and districting plans.

[15]Section 5 applies whenever a covered jurisdiction "shall enact or seek to administer any voting qualification or prerequisite to voting, or standard, practice, or procedure with respect to voting different from that in force or effect" on the jurisdiction's coverage date, which (depending on the jurisdiction) is November 1 of 1964, 1968, or 1972.

[16]*Georgia v. United States*, 411 U.S. 526 (1973); Procedures for the Administration of Section 5 (hereafter "Section 5 Procedures"), 28 C.F.R. § 51.13(e).

[17]*E.g., Clark v. Roemer*, 500 U.S. 646 (1991); *United States v. Board of Supervisors of Warren County*, 429 U.S. 642 (1977); *Connor v. Waller*, 421 U.S. 656 (1975) (per curiam. § Section 5 Procedures, 28 C.F.R. § 51.10.

[18]Preclearance determinations by the Attorney General are not subject to judicial review. *Morris v. Gressette*, 432 U.S. 491 (1977); *Harris v. Bell*, 562 F.2d 772 (D.C. Cir. 1977); Section 5 Procedures, 28 C.F.R. § 51.49.

[19]*Morris v. Gressette, supra. See also McCain v. Lybrand*, 465 U.S. 236 (1984).

[20]From the enactment of Section 5 in 1965 through July 1, 1995, the Attorney General received approximately 270,000 changes for Section 5 review. Only 55 declaratory judgment actions were filed in this period (which sought preclearance for somewhat more than 55 voting changes).

ity group]."[21] The Act defines "membership in a language minority group" to include "persons who are American Indian, Asian American, Alaskan Natives or of Spanish heritage."[22] During the time period in question, the Attorney General's Procedures for the Administration of Section 5 also specified that a change could not be precleared if it presented a "clear violation" of the "results" test of Section 2 of the Voting Rights Act, 42 U.S.C. § 1973 (1988),[23] which prohibits the use of voting practices or procedures that deny minority voters an equal opportunity to elect candidates of their choice. In 1997, the Supreme Court held that preclearance may not be denied based on a Section 2 violation.[24] While this ruling is significant, Section 2 played only a very minor role in the Attorney General's Section 5 redistricting determinations following the 1990 Census; only one redistricting objection relied exclusively on Section 2.[25] Accordingly, the Supreme Court's ruling has minimal relevance here.

Section 5 applies to nine states in their entirety—the States of Alabama, Alaska, Arizona, Georgia, Louisiana, Mississippi, South Carolina, Texas, and Virginia—and to substantial portions of two other states—New York (the Bronx, Brooklyn, and Manhattan) and North Carolina (40 of the state's 100 counties).[26] In addition, relatively small portions of California, Florida, Michigan, New Hampshire, and South Dakota are covered.[27] Where 80 entire state is covered, all statewide redistricting plans and all local plans are subject to preclearance. In the case of a partially covered state, statewide plans must be precleared to the extent they impact on the political subdivisions that are covered, and all local plans in the covered subdivisions must be precleared.

A requirement of federal preclearance also may arise as a result of voting rights litigation. Under Section 3(c) of the Voting Rights Act, 42 U.S.C. § 1973a(c) (1988), a federal district court may remedy a Fourteenth or Fifteenth Amendment violation in part by ordering that the defendant jurisdiction be subject to the same preclearance requirements as in Section 5, for a specified period of time and for specified types of voting changes. Preclearance is obtained from the Attorney General or from that local district court.[28] Several significant post-1990 redistrictings were subject to preclearance pursuant to Section 3(c), including the New Mexico house and senate plans and the redistricting for the Los Angeles County board of supervisors.[29]

Preclearance is required irrespective of the method by which a covered jurisdiction adopts a redistricting plan. Thus, a plan must be precleared whether it is adopted

---

[21]42 U.S.C. § 1973c (1988). Section 5 places the burden of proof on covered jurisdictions in judicial preclearance actions, *South Carolina v. Katzenbach, supra,* and the Attorney General's Section 5 Procedures similarly require that jurisdictions bear the burden of proof in administrative preclearance proceedings. 28 C.F.R. § 51.52. In *Georgia v. United States, supra,* the Supreme Court rejected a challenge to the Attorney General's interpretation of the Act in this regard.

[22]Section 14(c)(3), 42 U.S.C. § 1973*l*(c)(3).

[23]Section 5 Procedures, 28 C.F.R. § 51.55(b)(2).

[24]*Reno v. Bossier Parish School Board,* 117 S. Ct. 1491 (1997).

[25]This objection was to the redistricting plan for the Texas Senate (interposed on March 9, 1992). For a description of the circumstances relevant to that objection, see note 52 *infra.*

by a legislative body, a state court, or a redistricting commission.[30] In addition, if a jurisdiction proposes or agrees to a plan to resolve a federal voting rights lawsuit (such that the plan reflects the policy choices of the jurisdiction), preclearance is required even though the plan also must be approved by the district court.[31] On the other hand, a plan prepared by the federal court itself is not subject to preclearance.[32]

---

[26]The coverage formula, set forth in Section 4(b) of the Voting Rights Act, 42 U.S.C. § 1973b(b) (1988), specifies a two-part test for Section 5 coverage: 1) on November 1 of 1964, 1968, or 1972, the state or political subdivision "maintained...any test or device" related to voting (as determined by the Attorney General); and 2) less than 50 percent of the jurisdiction's voting age residents were registered to vote on November 1 of 1964, 1968, or 1972, or less than 50 percent of the voting age residents voted in the presidential election of 1964, 1968, or 1972 (as determined by the Director of the Census). For purposes of determining coverage using the 1964 and 1968 dates, Section 4 defines "test or device" to include certain requirements imposed as a prerequisite to voting or registering to vote, such as literacy tests and moral fitness tests. With respect to the 1972 coverage date, Section 4(f)(3) provides that "test or device" also includes the use of English-only elections in jurisdictions where more than five percent of the voting age citizens "are members of a single language minority" (defined in Section 14(c)(3), 42 U.S.C. § 1973*l*(c)(3), as including "persons who are American Indian, Asian American, Alaskan Native or of Spanish heritage").

For each coverage date, coverage first was determined on a state-by-state basis and then, for those states not covered in their entirety, the coverage formula was applied to each "political subdivision" in those states ("political subdivision" is defined in Section 14(c)(2), 42 U.S.C. § 1973*l*(c)(2), as "any county or parish, except that where registration for voting is not conducted under the supervision of a county or parish, the term shall include any other subdivision of a State which conducts registration for voting").

Section 4(b) also specifies that coverage determinations by the Attorney General and the Director of the Census are not reviewable in court, which was upheld by the Supreme Court in *Briscoe v. Bell*, 432 U.S. 404 (1977). Section 4(a) sets forth a procedure by which a jurisdiction that meets the coverage test may "bail out" from coverage. For a discussion of the bailout procedure, see Paul F. Hancock and Lora L. Tredway, "The Bailout Standard of the Voting Rights Act: An Incentive to End Discrimination," 17 Urb. Law. 379 (1985).

The Supreme Court upheld the constitutionality of the coverage procedure in *South Carolina v. Katzenbach*, *supra*, and subsequently reaffirmed the constitutionality of Section 5 in *City of Rome v. United States*, 446 U.S. 156 (1980).

Jurisdictions subject to Section 5 also are subject to certain other special provisions of the Act dealing with federal registration examiners and election observers. Sections 6-9 of the Voting Rights Act, 42 U.S.C. §§ 1973d-g.

[27]In these states, the following areas are covered by Section 5: four counties in California (Kings, Merced, Monterey, and Yuba); five counties in Florida (Collier, Hardee, Hendry, Hillsborough (where the City of Tampa is located), and Monroe); two townships in Michigan (Clyde and Buena Vista); ten towns in New Hampshire (Rindge Town, Millsfield Township, Pinkhams Grant, Stewartstown Town, Stratford Town, Benton Town, Antrim Town, Boscawen Town, Newington Town, and Unity Town); and two counties in South Dakota (Shannon and Todd). The complete listing of all Section 5 covered jurisdictions, including their applicable coverage dates, is set forth in the appendix to the Section 5 Procedures. 28 C.F.R. Pt. 51.

[28]The Section 5 Procedures specify that Section 3(c) submissions to the Attorney General are processed in the same manner as Section 5 submissions. 28 C.F.R. § 51.8.

[29]*Sanchez v. Anaya*, No. 82-0067M (D.N.M. Dec. 17, 1984) (coverage for state legislative redistrictings in New Mexico following the 1990 Census); *Garza and United States v. County of Los Angeles*, Nos. CV 88-5143 EN (Ex) and CV 88-5435 KN (Ex) (C.D. Cal. Apr. 26, 1991) (coverage for any change affecting the method of electing the county board of supervisors through 2002).

In addition, during the time period in question, four individual counties in New Mexico were required to obtain preclearance for all voting changes including redistrictings. *United States v. McKinley County*, No. 86-0029-C (D.N.M. Jan. 13, 1986) (until January 1996); *United States v. Socorro County*, No. 93-1244 JP (D.N.M. Apr. 11, 1994) (until December 2003); *United States v. Cibola County*, No. 93-1134 LH/LFG (D.N.M. Apr. 21, 1994) (until March 2004); *United States v. Sandoval County*, No. 88-1457-SC (D.N.M. Sept. 9, 1994) (at a minimum, until ten years following entry of the order). The State of Arkansas and its political subdivisions were covered under Section 3(c) but only with respect to changes relating to the use of a majority vote requirement in general elections. *Jeffers v. Clinton*, 740 F. Supp. 585, 626-27 (E.D. Ark. 1990), *app. dis.*, 498 U.S. 1129 (1991) (coverage until further order of the court).

When a jurisdiction files an administrative preclearance request, Section 5 specifies that the Attorney General has 60 days in which to interpose an objection (i.e., deny preclearance), and that if no action is taken within the 60-day review period, the submitted change is precleared by operation of law. The administrative preclearance process is governed by the Attorney General's Procedures for the Administration of Section 5,[33] which define the specific steps a jurisdiction must take to seek administrative preclearance and the procedures followed by the Attorney General in responding; the process is relatively informal compared to federal court litigation.[34] The Section 5 Procedures include a provision allowing the Attorney General to send a written request for additional information to the submitting jurisdiction and the operative 60-day period then begins anew when the jurisdiction provides a complete response to that request.[35] The Procedures also provide that a jurisdiction may request that the Attorney General reconsider and withdraw an objection.[36]

Where preclearance is denied, the jurisdiction continues to be prohibited

---

[30]For example, following the 1990 Census all three statewide plans for California (for Congress and the two houses of the state legislature) were adopted by the state supreme court, and then precleared by the Attorney General on February 19 and 28, 1992. The plans adopted for the 1992 elections for the Alaska legislature also were ordered by the state courts, and were precleared on July 8, 1992. In New York City, the responsibility for drawing the city council redistricting plan is assigned to a redistricting commission. The Attorney General interposed an objection on July 19, 1991 to the initial plan adopted by the commission and precleared a remedial plan on July 26, 1991.

[31]*McDaniel v. Sanchez*, 452 U.S. 130 (1981); Section 5 Procedures, 28 C.F.R. § 51.18. Such plans include those embodied in a consent decree and plans offered to the court as a remedy by the defendant jurisdiction but opposed by the plaintiff.

[32]*Connor v. Johnson*, 402 U.S. 690 (1971) (per curiam); *Texas v. United States*, 785 F. Supp. 201 (D.D.C. 1992); Section 5 Procedures, 28 C.F.R. § 51.18. The United States has taken the position that a plan prepared by a litigant other than the defendant jurisdiction, which does not reflect the jurisdiction's policy choices and which is ordered into effect by a federal district court, also is not subject to Section 5. Br. for the United States as Amicus Curiae at 11-15, *Slagle v. Terrazas*, 506 U.S. 801 (1992), *aff'ing mem.*, 789 F. Supp. 828 (W.D. Tex. 1991) (No. 91-1540). *See also* 28 C.F.R. § 51.18.

If a court-ordered plan that was not subject to preclearance is subsequently adopted by the Section 5 jurisdiction, the plan may then be subject to Section 5 preclearance for use in future elections. *Statewide Reapportionment Advisory Committee v. Campbell*, No. 3:91-3310-1 (D.S.C. Aug. 22, 1994); 28 C.F.R. § 51.18.

[33]28 C.F.R. Pt. 51.

[34]The administrative preclearance process is begun by a jurisdiction sending a written request to the Attorney General that identifies the changes for which preclearance is sought. The Section 5 Procedures specify the information that should be included with the request, the manner in which the Attorney General processes requests, the permissible responses by the Attorney General, and the general substantive standards applied by the Attorney General.

Unlike federal court litigation, there are no parties in an administrative preclearance proceeding, the process is not adversarial, there is no testimony taken, and the Attorney General does not have subpoena power. The Attorney General considers any and all information provided by the submitting jurisdiction (which, for a redistricting, typically may include a letter describing and explaining the new plan, the enacting legislation or ordinance, demographic information and district maps, transcripts or minutes of meetings, newspaper articles, and election returns). The Attorney General also considers any written comments submitted by interested persons, and gathers additional information through telephone interviews. It is rare for an on-site investigation to be conducted because of the overwhelming number of submissions that must be reviewed, the Attorney General's limited staff, and the limited time allowed for conducting Section 5 reviews.

[35]Section 5 Procedures, 28 C.F.R. § 51.37. *Georgia v. United States*, 411 U.S. 526 (1973) (upholding the Attorney General's regulation regarding the right to toll the 60-day period by requesting additional information). The 60-day period also is restarted when the submitting jurisdiction provides material supplemental information to the Attorney General. 28 C.F.R. § 51.39.

[36]Section 5 Procedures, 28 C.F.R. §§ 51.45, 51.47, 51.48. The Section 5 Procedures also permit the Attorney General to initiate a reconsideration review. 28 C.F.R. § 51.46.

under Section 5 from implementing the voting change. Although Section 5 generally contemplates that the affected jurisdiction may continue to implement the existing practice or procedure, a new plan usually must be adopted following a redistricting objection since the existing plan typically does not comply with the Fourteenth Amendment's "one-person, one-vote" requirement. With respect to first-time districting plans (i.e., plans adopted in connection with a change to district elections from an at-large election method or an appointive system), the jurisdiction also may find it necessary to adopt a new plan rather than return to the old election or selection system.[37] If a jurisdiction does not voluntarily adopt a new redistricting or districting plan after preclearance is denied, that decision may be challenged through litigation (e.g., claiming a "one-person, one-vote" violation or a Section 2 violation).[38]

The Attorney General's decisionmaking authority under Section 5 has been delegated to the Assistant Attorney General for Civil Rights.[39] The Assistant Attorney General makes all decisions with respect to objections, requests for reconsideration of objections, and other significant or controversial matters (e.g., all statewide redistrictings following the 1990 Census). The Assistant Attorney General has authorized the Chief of the Division's Voting Section generally to act on the Attorney General's behalf in all other matters.[40] The staff of the Voting Section is responsible for the receipt, investigation, and analysis of all submitted voting changes.

Each Section 5 decision by the Attorney General is formalized in a letter sent to the submitting jurisdiction. Objection and reconsideration letters provide a description of the concerns that prompted the decision to object or to withdraw or not withdraw the reconsidered objection. Preclearance letters generally consist of a standard letter that does not address the basis for the preclearance decision.

B. Technological Changes

The 1990 Census sparked a technological revolution in the drawing and review of redistricting plans. For the first time, the Census Bureau placed the country's census geography (with its associated population data) on computer. This made it possible for any entity or individual possessing the computer-readable census data and "geographic information system" ("GIS") software to quickly and simply use the census data to draw redistricting plans or review plans drawn by others. The use of census data to draw or review plans was not something new in the 1990s. But the GIS software provided a new and powerful lens through

---

[37]For example, a Section 2 suit may be pending against the jurisdiction, and either the court has determined that the at-large system violates Section 2 or the jurisdiction does not wish to litigate that issue. Or state law may preclude a return to the prior system.

[38]The United States may file suit under Section 2, but lacks authority to file suit based on a constitutional violation.

[39]Section 5 Procedures, 28 C.F.R. § 51.3.

[40]Section 5 Procedures, 28 C.F.R. § 51.3. Should the Chief of the Voting Section disagree with a recommendation by Section staff to interpose an objection, the submission is forwarded to the Assistant Attorney General for decision.

which the precise location and size of minority population concentrations could be determined.

Section 5 jurisdictions, as well as private voting rights groups, widely utilized GIS in creating plans. The Voting Section of the Civil Rights Division similarly utilized GIS in reviewing submitted plans, and GIS played a profound and crucial role in allowing the Attorney General to closely scrutinize in a timely manner the very large number of plans submitted for preclearance following the 1990 Census. Previously, the Department often had asked jurisdictions submitting redistricting plans to identify the location of minority population concentrations and, in some submissions, had its own staff go through the painstaking process of transferring census data from a computer printout to a census map on which the new and existing district lines were overlaid.

In addition, the Census Bureau for the first time in the 1990 Census provided demographic information for the entire country by small geographic units, known as census blocks, rather than using census blocks and, in some rural areas, larger enumeration districts. This allowed jurisdictions greater flexibility in drafting district lines and a heightened ability to identify the location of minority population concentrations.

II. PRECLEARANCE DETERMINATIONS REGARDING POST-1990 REDISTRICTING PLANS

A. Overview

The 1990s saw a record level of Section 5 redistricting activity. From April 1991 through the first half of 1995, the Attorney General received nearly 3,000 redistricting plans for Section 5 review (2,822).[41] This was almost twice the number of plans submitted in a comparable period following the 1980 Census, and about seven times the number submitted following the 1970 Census.[42] In response, the Attorney General precleared 93 percent (2,348) of the post-1990 plans for which a merits determination was made (i.e., plans precleared or objected-to) and interposed objections to seven percent (183 plans).[43] No merits determination was made on a portion of the submitted plans (slightly over ten percent of the total plans submitted), either because a merits determination was inappropriate or because the plans still were pending review as of July 1, 1995.[44]

The rate of objection in the 1990s was almost identical to the 1980s rate, when the Attorney General interposed objections to eight percent of the plans for which a merits determination was made. While the necessary statistical informa-

---

[41]The 1990s submissions included a small number of pre-1990 plans which jurisdictions had failed to submit for preclearance at the time they were adopted.

[42]For calendar years 1981 through 1984, approximately 1,500 redistrictings plans were submitted to the Attorney General for Section 5 review, and from 1971 through 1974 approximately 400 plans were submitted.

[43]During this period, there was one instance in which the Attorney General interposed an objection to a redistricting plan and then later withdrew the objection (to a county redistricting plan in Mississippi). The Section 5 determination for this plan is included in the preclearance total and not in the figure for the number of plans to which objections were interposed.

tion is not available to compute this percentage for the 1970s, the objection rate was substantially higher in that period—the Attorney General objected to approximately 14 percent of all plans submitted then (including plans for which a merits determination was not made).[45]

In absolute terms, the 183 post-1990 redistricting objections represent a record number. They constitute about 40 percent of all redistricting objections interposed since the Voting Rights Act was adopted in 1965, about one and two-thirds times the number of objections interposed from April 1981 through June 1985, and over three times the number of objections interposed from April 1971 through June 1975.[46]

The large increase in the absolute number of objections following the 1990 Census is only in part attributable to the increase in the number of plans submitted. While a large portion of the increase in submitted plans was due to the adoption of district election systems following the 1982 amendment to Section 2, only a modest number (14 percent) of the objected-to plans were from jurisdictions that either were adopting their first redistricting plan following the post-1982 adoption of a district method of election or were adopting a districting plan for the first time (as part of a change from an at-large election system or an appointed board). Even if these first-time redistrictings and districtings are discounted, the absolute number of plans to which objections were interposed still increased substantially from the 1980s to the 1990s.[47]

Another notable aspect of the post-1990 objections was the significant increase in the number of objections involving discrimination against Hispanic Americans. Objections were interposed on this basis to statewide plans in Ari-

---

[44]No merits determination could be made for 286 plans, either because the plan was voluntarily withdrawn from Section 5 review before a determination was made, Section 5 Procedures, 28 C.F.R. § 51.25, or because the plan was not ripe for review or had become moot (*e.g.*, certain plans were adopted with a sunset provision that was triggered before a Section 5 determination could be made). 28 C.F.R. §§ 51.22, 51.35.

Another 46 plans submitted during this time period were pending review as of July 1, 1995, *i.e.*, were under active review but the 60-day review period had not yet expired (36 plans), or the Attorney General had made a written request for additional information and the jurisdiction had not yet responded (10 plans).

The number reported for the total number of submitted plans is slightly less than the sum of the plans precleared, objected to, under consideration as of July 1, 1995, or for which the Attorney made no determination. This is because there were a small number of plans already pending review as of April 1991, *i.e.*, the beginning of the reporting period used in this article.

[45]From April 1981 through June 1985, objections were interposed to approximately 108 redistricting plans (there also were five plans where objections were interposed and then later withdrawn). From April 1971 through June 1975, there were approximately 58 redistricting objections (with an additional two that were subsequently withdrawn).

[46]As of June 30, 1995, the Attorney General had interposed objections to approximately 460 redistricting plans since the adoption of Section 5.

Another way to describe the scope of the post-1990 redistricting objection activity is that if the Section 5 preclearance mechanism did not exist, the Department would have had to successfully prosecute approximately 118 lawsuits under Section 2 of the Act between April 1991 and June 1995 in order to have achieved the same result (118 represents the number of individual states and local jurisdictions where objections were interposed to statewide and local redistricting plans).

[47]Discounting the post-1990 objections to these first-time redistrictings and districtings, the post-1990 total still is about one and a half times greater than the number of redistricting objections in the comparable 1980s period.

zona, New Mexico, New York, and Texas, and to local plans for three counties and a community college district in Arizona, two counties in California, the New York City Council, and, in Texas, 11 counties, two cities (Dallas and Houston), four school districts, a water district, and plans for justices of the peace and constables in five counties. In contrast, during the same time period in the 1980s, objections based on discrimination against Hispanic voters were interposed to statewide plans in New York and Texas, and to local plans only for the New York City Council and one county in Texas.

Following the 1990 Census (through the middle of 1995), jurisdictions filed only eight declaratory judgment actions seeking preclearance from the District of Columbia Court for a post-1990 redistricting plan. The district court granted preclearance in one case over the opposition of the United States (for a Louisiana school board plan), however, that decision recently was vacated and remanded by the Supreme Court; in two other cases the district court granted preclearance with the United States' concurrence (for the Texas Senate plan and a plan for a Mississippi county governing body). The other suits were dismissed without a ruling on the merits (see Appendix I-A, page 111). In fact, since the passage of the Act, there have been only nine decisions on the merits regarding redistricting plans in declaratory judgment actions (see Appendix I-B, page 112).

B. Statewide Redistricting Plans

From April 1991 through June 1995, the Attorney General interposed Section 5 objections to 30 statewide redistricting plans for congressional delegations, state legislatures and a state board of education. Preclearance was granted to 53 statewide plans (including initial plans and plans adopted to remedy objections).[48]

The plans to which objections were interposed are as follows:

State	Plans
Alabama	Congressional
Alaska	House and Senate
Arizona	House (2 plans) and Senate (2 plans)
Florida	Senate
Georgia	Congressional (2 plans), House (3 plans), and Senate (2 plans)
Louisiana	House, Senate, and Board of Elementary and Secondary Education
Mississippi	House and Senate (2 plans)
New Mexico	Senate[49]
New York	Assembly
No. Carolina	Congressional, House, and Senate
So. Carolina	House
Texas	House and Senate
Virginia	House

---

[48]There were another 14 redistrictings precleared that made limited changes to statewide plans that previously had been precleared, and two limited redistrictings were precleared where the prior statewide plan was court-ordered.

[49]As of July 1995, the objection to the New Mexico Senate plan was the only objection interposed under Section 3(c) of the Voting Rights Act, 42 U.S.C. § 1973b(c) (1988), since the adoption of the Act.

Generally, all other statewide plans in the covered states were precleared, except as noted below.[50]

Following the statewide objections, the affected states uniformly complied with Section 5. No state sought to implement a plan to which the Attorney General objected, and after the objections were interposed the states generally adopted new plans which were precleared and then implemented. In a few instances, the objected-to plan was replaced for the 1992 elections by a plan ordered into effect by a federal district court based on exigent circumstances, i.e., there was insufficient time for the state to develop a remedial plan and hold elections as scheduled. This occurred with respect to the Alabama congressional plan, the Arizona legislative plans, and the Texas House plan. Arizona and Texas subsequently adopted and obtained preclearance for remedial plans, while Alabama is continuing to implement the court-drawn plan for congressional elections.[51]

---

[50]Following the 1980 Census, the Attorney General interposed objections to 27 statewide plans, as follows:

State	Plans
Alabama	House (2 plans) and Senate (2 plans)
Arizona	House and Senate
Georgia	Congressional, House, and Senate
Louisiana	House
Mississippi	Congressional
New York	Congressional, Assembly, and Senate
No. Carolina	Congressional, House (3 plans), and Senate (2 plans)
So. Carolina	House
Texas	Congressional, House, and Senate
Virginia	House (2 plans) and Senate

[51]In Alabama, the legislature initially failed to adopt a congressional redistricting plan and suit was filed in the local federal district court to obtain a new plan. After trial and four days before judgment was entered, the state legislature adopted a plan. The three-judge district court then entered an order on March 9, 1992 adopting its own plan for the 1992 elections, with the proviso that if the legislature's plan was precleared within 18 days of the order that plan would be used instead. *Wesch v. Hunt*, 785 F. Supp. 1491 (S.D. Ala.), *aff'd mem. sub nom.*, *Camp v. Wesch*, 504 U.S. 902 (1992). The Attorney General interposed an objection to the legislative plan on March 27, 1992. The district court declined to reopen its judgment and reconsider its plan in light of the objection, and this decision was summarily affirmed by the Supreme Court. *Figures v. Hunt*, 506 U.S. 809 (1993).

The Attorney General interposed an objection to the redistricting plans for the Arizona House and Senate on June 10, 1992. Immediately thereafter, the legislature adopted a new plan. On June 19, 1992, a local three-judge district court ordered the interim use of that plan for the 1992 elections. *Arizonans for Fair Representation v. Symington*, No. CIV 92-256-PHX-SMM (D. Ariz.). About a month later, the state submitted this plan to the Attorney General for preclearance, and on August 12, 1992 the Attorney General interposed an objection. The court then declined to reconsider its decision in light of the objection, which was summarily affirmed by the Supreme Court. *Arizona Hispanic Community Forum v. Symington*, 506 U.S. 969 (1992).

The Attorney General interposed an objection to the plan for the Texas House of Representatives on November 12, 1992. On December 24, 1992, the local district court ordered into effect a plan that altered the legislative plan with respect to those districts whose configuration was the basis for the Attorney General's objection. *Terrazas v. Slagle*, 789 F. Supp. 828 (W.D. Tex. 1991).

In addition, the following events transpired with respect to the redistricting plans for the Mississippi House and Senate. After the Attorney General interposed objections to both plans in 1991, a three-judge district court ordered that the existing, precleared 1982 plans be used on an interim basis for the regular 1991 elections. *Watkins v. Mabus*, 771 F. Supp. 789 (S.D. Miss.), *aff'd mem. in part and vacated as moot in part*, 502 U.S. 954 (1991). The state legislature adopted new plans in 1992 which the Attorney General precleared (the Attorney General interposed an objection to the initial 1992 Senate plan and then precleared the second 1992 Senate plan). The district court then ordered special House and Senate elections in 1992 pursuant to the precleared plans to elect persons to complete the remainder of the regular four-year terms. *Watkins v. Fordice*, 791 F. Supp. 646 (S.D. Miss. 1992).

In addition, there were a few instances where, as an initial matter (i.e., not following an objection), states were unable to adopt the requisite statewide plans and, as a result, federal district courts stepped in and imposed court-ordered plans for the 1992 elections. This occurred with respect to the Arizona congressional plan, all three South Carolina plans (for Congress, the state House, and the state Senate), the Texas Senate plan, as well as the Florida and Michigan congressional plans (where Section 5 coverage is limited).[52] South Carolina, Texas, and Florida subsequently adopted and obtained preclearance for new plans.

C. Local Redistricting Plans

From April 1991 through June 1995, the Attorney General interposed Section 5 objections to 153 redistricting plans (for 122 different elected bodies) for counties, cities, and school districts, as well as plans used to elect certain other local officials.[53] These included objections to the plans for the three largest cities covered in whole or in part by Section 5, New York City and Dallas and Houston, Texas. Preclearance was granted to 2,279 local plans.

The local plan objections may be summarized as follows:[54]

State	Total	Local Jurisdictions
Alabama	7	Two cities and one school district (including objections to two plans for each city and to three plans for the school district)
Arizona	5	Three county governing bodies and one college district (including objections to two plans for the college district)
California	2	Two county governing bodies

---

[52]*Arizonans for Fair Representation v. Symington*, No. 92-256-PHX-SMM (D. Ariz. May 5, 1992), *aff'd mem. sub nom.*, *Hispanic Chamber of Commerce v. Arizonans for Fair Representation*, 507 U.S. 981 (1993) (Arizona); *Burton v. Sheheen*, 793 F. Supp. 1329 (D.S.C. 1992), *vacated and remanded sub nom.*, *Statewide Reapportionment Advisory Committee v. Theodore*, 508 U.S. 968 (1993) (South Carolina) (vacated in light of position taken by the United States in its brief as amicus curiae, urging remand for the district court to determine whether its plans complied with Section 2 of the Act); *De Grandy v. Wetherell*, 794 F. Supp. 1076 (N.D. Fla. 1992) (Florida); *Good v. Austin*, 800 F. Supp. 557 (E.D. & W.D. Mich. 1992) (Michigan).

Texas' efforts to adopt a post-1990 plan for its state Senate may be chronicled as follows. The legislature enacted a plan in 1991 and submitted it to the Attorney General for Section 5 preclearance. However, before the Section 5 determination was made, the plan was withdrawn from review (as permitted by 28 C.F.R. § 51.25) and a new plan was submitted that was the product of a settlement in a state court redistricting suit. That plan was precleared but subsequently was invalidated by the Texas Supreme Court. *Terrazas v. Ramirez*, 829 S.W.2d 712 (1991).

A federal district court then ordered its plan into effect. *Terrazas v. Slagle*, 789 F. Supp. 828 (W.D. Tex. 1991), *aff'd mem. sub nom.*, *Richards v. Terrazas*, 504 U.S. 939 (1992) and *Slagle v. Terrazas*, 506 U.S. 801 (1992). At the time the district court initially acted, the Texas legislature had not adopted a substitute plan. Shortly thereafter, the legislature adopted a plan, however, the district court declined to put the legislature's plan into effect based primarily on its determination that doing so would delay the 1992 elections. An alternative basis for the district court's decision was a preliminary determination that the legislature's plan violated Section 2 of the Voting Rights Act. The Attorney General interposed an objection to the legislature's plan on March 9, 1992 based upon the federal court's ruling that the state's plan would violate Section 2; subsequently, with the Attorney General's concurrence, the District Court for the District of Columbia precleared the plan. *Texas v. United States*, 802 F. Supp. 481 (1992). After the 1992 elections were held, the district court held that the plan did not violate Section 2. 821 F. Supp. 1162 (1993). Accordingly, the legislature's plan was implemented in the 1994 elections.

[53]This does not include the one instance where an objection to a local redistricting plan later was withdrawn. For the same period in the 1980s, the Attorney General interposed objections to approximately 81 local plans, not including five plans to which objections were interposed and then later withdrawn.

Georgia	5	One county governing body, three cities, and one school district
Louisiana	50	Seventeen parish governing bodies, seven cities, fourteen school districts, and one plan for parish justices of the peace/constables (including objections to three plans for two parish governing bodies, two plans for three parish governing bodies, three plans for one school district, two plans for another school district, and two plans for one city)
Mississippi	43	Twenty-five county governing bodies, six cities, and two plans for justice court/constables (including objections to three plans for one county governing body and two plans for eight county governing bodies)
New York	1	New York City
So. Carolina	11	Four county governing bodies, four cities, and two school districts (including objections to two plans for one city)
Texas	28	Twelve county governing bodies, two cities, four school districts, one water district, and five plans for justices of the peace/constables (including objections to three plans for one county governing body, two plans for one city, and two plans for one school district)
Virginia	1	One county governing body.

Appendix II (page 114) lists the individual jurisdictions where objections were interposed.

The vast majority of local plans to which objections were interposed were for jurisdictions whose district methods of election pre-date the 1982 amendment of Section 2.[55] Thus, as noted previously, the large increase in the number of post-1990 objections may not simply be traced to the flood of new redistrictings that resulted from election method changes prompted by the 1982 amendment to Section 2. In addition, a large number of the post-1990 redistricting objections concerned elective bodies where no redistricting objection was interposed following the 1980 Census. However, there also were some "repeat offenders" (particularly in Mississippi), where post-1990 objections followed redistricting objections in the 1980s or in 1990.[56]

Nearly all local jurisdictions complied with Section 5 by not implementing plans to which objections were interposed. There were a few exceptions to this record of Section 5 compliance, notably involving jurisdictions in Arizona and Texas. In response to these violations, lawsuits were filed by the United States and private plaintiffs to enforce Section 5, and the district courts generally enjoined the violations (see Appendix I-C, page 112).

---

[54]In Louisiana and South Carolina, there were objections interposed where the same plan was to be used for the both the parish/county governing body and the local school district, and in Texas there were objections where the same plan was to be used for the county governing body and for the election of justices of the peace and constables. For statistical purposes, the Justice Department has counted each such objection as an objection to two plans since state law did not require that the entities involved use the same plan. In Mississippi, on the other hand, the governing boards of countywide school districts and county election commissioners are required to be elected using the board of supervisors redistricting plan. Accordingly, the Department has counted each objection to a supervisor plan as one objection.

[55]Of the 153 local plans to which objections were interposed, only 25 of the plans were for jurisdictions (20 jurisdictions) that adopted a district method of election following the 1982 amendment to Section 2.

Following the objections, some jurisdictions were able to adopt and obtain preclearance for a new plan prior to their next regularly scheduled election. Others delayed their elections until a precleared plan was obtained (notably, parish governing bodies in Louisiana) or held elections under their pre-1990, precleared plans (notably, county governing bodies in Mississippi). As of July 1995, about 84 percent of the jurisdictions where objections were interposed had obtained preclearance for new plans (and another five percent had new plans pending before the Attorney General or had objections interposed only recently, during the second quarter of 1995).

D. Deterrent Effect of Section 5

Statistics concerning the number of plans that were precleared or to which objections were interposed describe only one aspect of the impact of Section 5 on the plans adopted during the first half of this decade. It is clear that before any preclearance review was conducted, district boundaries often were configured to protect and enhance minority electoral opportunity in part because of the plan-drawers' knowledge that their districting choices would be scrutinized for discriminatory purpose and effect under Section 5.

There are a number of reasons why Section 5 had a strong deterrent effect. By the 1990s, state and local officials, and their demographers, had become intimately familiar with the substantive requirements of Section 5. In addition, the large body of objections interposed since the passage of the Voting Rights Act in 1965, and the near complete absence of any success in Section 5 preclearance actions in the District of Columbia Court, were tangible evidence that Section 5 posed a significant barrier to implementing a discriminatory plan. Moreover, Congress' adoption of the Section 2 "results" standard in 1982, and the subsequent explication of that standard by the Supreme Court in *Thornburg v. Gingles*[57] and by the lower courts in redistricting litigation,[58] sent a powerful message to Section 5 jurisdictions that the Voting Rights Act would not permit the adoption of dilutive plans. Finally, minority leaders and the organizations

---

[56]The jurisdictions where a post-1990 Census objection followed an objection in the 1980s or in 1990 may be summarized as follows:

State	Local Jurisdictions
Alabama	One city (two post-1990 objections)
Georgia	One city
Louisiana	Two parish governing bodies and one school district (two post-1990 objections to one of the parish governing bodies)
Mississippi	Eleven county governing bodies (including three post-1990 objections for one governing body and two post-1990 objections for five governing bodies)
New York	New York City
South Carolina	One county governing body
Texas	One school district

[57]478 U.S. 30 (1986).

[58]See, *e.g.*, *Garza and United States v. County of Los Angeles*, 918 F.2d 763 (9th Cir. 1990), *cert. denied*, 498 U.S. 1028 (1991) (Los Angeles County board of supervisors plan found to violate Section 2); *Jeffers v. Clinton*, 730 F. Supp. 196 (E.D. Ark. 1989) and 756 F. Supp. 1195 (E.D. Ark. 1990) (three-judge court), *aff'd mem.*, 498 U.S. 1019 (1991) (Arkansas legislative plan found to violate Section 2). See also cases cited in note 9 *supra*.

that assist them were well prepared following the 1990 Census to advocate the adoption of plans that would provide minority voters an opportunity to elect candidates of their choice.

There also were specific efforts made by the Department of Justice in the early 1990s to promote compliance with Section 5. The Assistant Attorney General for Civil Rights and the leadership of the Voting Section made numerous speeches at conferences attended by state and local officials, government and private attorneys, and demographers and legislative support staff in which the Department explained the principles that would be applied in enforcing Section 5. The Department emphasized that it would closely scrutinize submitted plans to ensure that they satisfied the preclearance standards. However, the Department also emphasized that it did not require that plans maximize the number of majority-minority districts or that plans provide proportional representation.[59]

Toward the end of the post-1990 redistricting cycle, in June 1993 and then in June 1995, the Supreme Court issued its twin decisions in *Shaw v. Reno*[60] and *Miller v. Johnson*[61] holding that, in certain limited circumstances, the intentional creation of a majority-minority district will trigger strict scrutiny under the Fourteenth Amendment. In *Shaw*, the Court held that strict scrutiny is invoked when a plan "is so bizarre on its face that it is 'unexplainable on grounds other than race.'"[62] Then, in *Miller*, the Court expanded this test holding that strict scrutiny applies when "race was the predominant" redistricting criterion; the Court explained that this test would be met when the decisionmaker "subordinated traditional race-neutral districting principles, including but not limited to compactness, contiguity, respect for political subdivisions or communities defined by actual shared interests, to racial considerations."[63] In *Miller*, the Court held that a new black-majority congressional district in Georgia was unconstitutionally racially gerrymandered, and in 1996 the Court issued two more decisions finding constitutional violations involving new black-majority and Hispanic-majority districts in North Carolina and Texas.[64] However, a majority of the Court rejected the view that any consideration of race in redistricting is prohibited,[65] and, on the same day it decided *Miller*, the Court summarily affirmed a district court's ruling that California's congressional and legislative redistricting plans—which include numerous majority-minority districts—were not premised on an unconstitutional use of race.[66]

---

[59]See, *e.g.*, "Remarks of [Assistant Attorney General] John R. Dunne," 14 Cardozo L. Rev. 1127 (1993).

[60]509 U.S. 630 (1993).

[61]515 U.S. 900 (1995).

[62]509 U.S. at 644.

[63]515 U.S. at 916. The Court explained that "[a] State is free to recognize communities that have a particular racial makeup [without triggering the strict scrutiny standard], provided its action is directed toward some common thread of relevant interests." *Id.* at 920. However, the Court upheld the district court's finding that the use of race in drawing the challenged Georgia district could not be sanctioned on this ground.

[64]*Bush v. Vera*, 517 U.S. 952 (1996) (Texas); *Shaw v. Hunt*, 517 U.S. 899 (1996) (N. Carolina).

[65]*Bush v. Vera*, 517 U.S. at __, 116 S. Ct. at 1951-1952.

Clearly, the Supreme Court's rulings will have a substantial influence on state and local decisionmakers in future redistrictings, particularly when the issue is whether to provide minority citizens with a greater electoral opportunity than existed under the current plan. In part, of course, this will reflect the concern for redistricting in a constitutional manner. However, the ambiguity of the constitutional standard enunciated in *Shaw* and *Miller* also may compromise the positive deterrent effect of Section 5, to the extent that jurisdictions (either in good faith or for illicit reasons) may place less value on recognizing communities defined both by race and "actual shared interests." Initially, the decisions' effect on future redistricting behavior will be evidenced most particularly in those jurisdictions where established post-1990 plans are ruled unconstitutional. The more widespread effect on Section 5 jurisdictions likely will not be felt until the redistrictings following the 2000 Census. Most Section 5 jurisdictions had completed their redistricting efforts before *Shaw* was decided in 1993.[67] Also, *Shaw* represented a more limited ruling than *Miller* since it pointed only to bizarrely shaped majority-minority districts as those which would be constitutionally suspect and, by June 1995 when *Miller* was handed down, nearly all Section 5 jurisdictions had completed redistricting.[68]

III. THE ATTORNEY GENERAL'S SUBSTANTIVE FRAMEWORK IN REVIEWING POST-1990 REDISTRICTING PLANS

In describing the analytic framework relied upon by the Attorney General in reviewing the post-1990 redistricting plans, it is useful at the outset to emphasize several general propositions.

First, the touchstone for each redistricting determination was the "purpose and effect" test of Section 5. In applying this test, the Attorney General followed the analytic framework established by the courts as well as the principles and standards of review set forth in the Attorney General's Procedures for the Administration of Section 5.[69] The Attorney General did not implement any policy of maximizing the number of majority-minority districts nor did the Attorney General seek to mandate proportional representation. Although the Supreme Court in *Miller* criticized the Department's application of the Section 5 test, the decision did not alter that test.

---

[66]*DeWitt v. Wilson*, 856 F. Supp. 1409 (E.D. Ca. 1994), *aff'd mem.*, 515 u.s. 1170 (1995). More recently the Court affirmed district court rulings approving a black-minority legislative district in Florida and a Hispanic-majority congressional district in Chicago. *Lawyer* v. *Department of Justice* 117 S. Ct. 2186 (1997)' *King* v. *State Board of Elections*, 979 F. Supp. 619 (N.D. Ill. 1997), *aff'd mem. sub. nom. King* v. *Illinois Board of Elections*, 118 S. Ct. 877 (1998).

[67]Approximately three-quarters of the redistricting plans submitted between April 1991 and July 1, 1995 were submitted before the Supreme Court's decision in *Shaw*.

[68]The redistricting and districting plans submitted for administrative Section 5 review during the year following *Miller* constitute only about five percent of all plans submitted beginning in April 1991.

[69]28 C.F.R. Pt. 51, Subpt. F.

The determination whether a plan should be precleared or was objectionable rested on a case-specific analysis of the individual facts relevant to the particular jurisdiction. As stated by the Supreme Court in *Thornburg v. Gingles* (in discussing Section 2 of the Act), Voting Rights Act determinations depend "upon a searching practical evaluation of the past and present reality,...and on a functional view of the political process."[70] Thus, under Section 5, a practice that is legal and proper in one jurisdiction may be illegal and improper in another.[71]

The great majority of the redistricting objections were based on the purpose prong of the Section 5 test. Because discriminatory purpose rarely is disclosed by explicit statements by officials, the purpose analysis involved the application of the long-established analytic framework to determine whether discriminatory purpose should be inferred, keeping in mind that under Section 5 the jurisdiction bears the burden of demonstrating the absence of discrimination. In applying this approach to the review of post-1990 redistrictings, the Department of Justice took a broad view of the purpose test. However, that did not represent any *de facto* use of a policy of maximization or proportional representation.

Underlying the "purpose and effect" test the question in each redistricting review typically was whether the submitted plan discriminated by: a) not providing for one or more additional majority-minority districts; and/or b) affording too low of a minority percentage in a proposed majority-minority district to allow minority voters a realistic electoral opportunity. As set forth in the Section 5 Procedures, in map-drawing terms the issue was whether the proposed districts divided ("fragmented") or overconcentrated ("packed") minority population concentrations. In that regard, fragmentation was viewed as including the decision to separate minority concentrations that are located reasonably close to one another such that inclusion of the concentrations in one district would not violate traditional race-neutral districting principles.[72]

Finally, the consideration of any partisan political interests has no part to play in the administration of Section 5. With a few possible exceptions since the enactment of the Voting Rights Act in 1965, political interests have not governed

---

[70]478 U.S. at 45 (internal quotation marks omitted), *quoting* S. Rep. No. 417, 97th Cong., 2d Sess. 30 & n.120 (1982), *reprinted in* 1982 U.S.C.C.A.N. 177, 208.

[71]The Attorney General's case-specific approach to applying the Voting Rights Act previously has been described in James P. Turner, "Case-Specific Implementation of the Voting Rights Act," in *Controversies in Minority Voting* (Bernard Grofman and Chandler Davidson, eds., 1992). Mr. Turner was a longtime Deputy Assistant Attorney General in the Civil Rights Division and served as Acting Assistant Attorney General on a number of occasions, including most recently from January 1993 until the confirmation of Deval Patrick as Assistant Attorney General in March 1994.

[72]Section 5 Procedures, 28 C.F.R. §§ 51.58, 51.59. As the Supreme Court pointed out in *Johnson v. De Grandy*, 512 U.S. 997 (1994), some fragmentation and packing of a minority group may be inevitable in a redistricting plan and fragmentation or packing must result in some cognizable minimization of voting strength in order to make out a Section 2 results violation. Similarly, under Section 5, fragmentation and packing are significant, but not decision determinative, factors in reaching the ultimate conclusion whether a plan passes muster.

the application of the Voting Rights Act in any national administration, and this high standard was met in the review of the post-1990 redistricting plans. As noted by other commentators, there were a number of high visibility Voting Rights Act determinations in recent years where the determination was not what was advocated by the local political leaders of the national administration's political party.[73]

A. Overview of Section 5 Preclearance Standard

1. Retrogressive Effect

As interpreted by the Supreme Court in its 1976 decision in *Beer v. United States*,[74] the effect prong of the Section 5 test requires that covered jurisdictions demonstrate that their voting changes will not "lead to a retrogression in the position of…minorities with respect to their effective exercise of the electoral franchise."[75] Retrogression is a legal determination based on a finding that minority electoral opportunity has been meaningfully reduced, and that the reduction was avoidable.

The benchmark for judging whether a change is retrogressive is the existing practice or procedure, so long as that practice or procedure is legally enforceable under Section 5 (i.e., was in place as of the date of Section 5 coverage, was precleared, or was court-ordered and thus not subject to preclearance).[76] As applied to redistrictings, the retrogression analysis generally involves a comparison of the electoral opportunity provided by the proposed plan to that provided by the existing plan. The existing plan is analyzed using the most recent census data since the retrogression standard safeguards the level of minority voting strength present at the time the submission is being reviewed.[77] While the existing plan typically

---

[73]Bernard Grofman, "Would Vince Lombardi Have Been Right If He Had Said: 'When It Comes to Redistricting, Race Isn't Everything, It's the Only Thing'?," 14 Cardozo L. Rev. 1237, 1254-1256 (1993) (discussing: the Department of Justice's successful Section 2 litigation against the redistricting plan for the Los Angeles County Board of Supervisors (*Garza and United States v. County of Los Angeles, supra*); preclearance of the Virginia House plan in July 1991; and preclearance of the North Carolina congressional plan in February 1992); Frank R. Parker, "Voting Rights Enforcement in the Bush Administration: The Four-Year Record," in *New Opportunities: Civil Rights At a Crossroads* (Citizens' Commission on Civil Rights, 1993) (noting that every redistricting objection arose out of circumstances where minority leaders opposed the plan, and also noting the July 1991 preclearance of the Virginia House plan). While the examples cited by these commentators occurred during the Bush Administration, in the Clinton Administration, for example, an objection was interposed to the South Carolina House plan (in May 1994) which was drawn by Democratic legislators and opposed by the Republican governor.

There are two essential checks on any tendency of a political appointee in the Department of Justice to permit political interests to enter into the Section 5 calculation. First, Section 5 decisions are guided by a large body of precedent, which includes not only court decisions and the Section 5 Procedures but also the large number of prior Section 5 determinations. These past Section 5 decisions are not binding precedent in a technical sense, but indicate analytic approaches that the Department seeks uniformly to follow unless there is a sound legal or policy reason for making a departure. Secondly, as described previously, the Department's internal decisionmaking process is a "bottom-up" process. All Section 5 submission reviews are conducted by the career, nonpolitical staff of the Voting Section, and all matters reviewed by the Assistant Attorney General are presented for decision with the analyses and recommendations made by the career Section staff and leadership.

[74]425 U.S. 130 (1976).

[75]*Id.* at 141.

[76]Section 5 Procedures, 28 C.F.R. § 51.54(b); *Texas v. United States*, 785 F. Supp. 201 (D.D.C. 1992).

is malapportioned and thus is no longer capable of implementation, a jurisdiction typically has available a variety of alternative plans that satisfy the "one-person, one-vote" test, follow sound districting principles, and maintain or augment minority electoral opportunity. However, a meaningful reduction in minority opportunity that is constitutionally unavoidable because of the "one-person, one-vote" requirement would not violate the retrogression standard.[78]

Although application of the retrogression test to redistrictings may engender some difficult factual questions, Section 5 jurisdictions generally understood (by the 1990s) its essential meaning and few retrogression objections were interposed to post-1990 redistrictings.[79] Often those objections also involved purpose concerns.

An example of a retrogression objection was the objection interposed on September 28, 1993 to the House and Senate plans for the State of Alaska. As stated in the February 11, 1994 letter denying the state's request to withdraw the objection, the focus of concern was "the effect upon Alaskan Native voters of the boundary lines for House District 36 and Senate District R, which includes all of House District 36…[which] result[ed] in reductions in the Alaskan Native share of the voting age population in House District 36 (from 55.7 percent to 50.6 percent) and in Senate District R (from 33.5 percent to 30.5 percent)." In its request for reconsideration, the state argued that despite the presence of polarized voting, there was sufficient white crossover voting that the reductions would not adversely affect the ability of Alaskan Native voters to elect their preferred candidates. The Attorney General maintained the objection noting that the Department's analysis of the electoral data showed that the reductions "would make it more difficult for Alaskan Native voters to elect candidates of their choice, even though the defeat of the Alaskan Natives' preferred candidates might not be ensured by the proposed reductions."[80]

---

[77]*City of Rome v. United States*, 446 U.S. 156, 186 (1980); *Texas v. United States*, 866 F. Supp. 20 (D.D.C. 1994); *Texas v. United States*, 785 F. Supp. 201 (D.D.C. 1992); *Mississippi v. United States*, 490 F. Supp. 569, 582 (D.D.C. 1979), *aff'd mem.*, 444 U.S. 1050 (1980); Section 5 Procedures, 28 C.F.R. § 51.54(b)(2).

The Voting Rights Act does not require that Section 5 analyses be based on the population data published in the decennial censuses. As a matter of practice, the Department relies on the census data as being presumptively accurate, however, where that data are unavailable (*e.g.*, where district lines split census blocks) or are out of date or incorrect, the Department will rely on population surveys or estimates prepared by the Section 5 jurisdiction (or, alternatively, by other interested persons) if prepared in a manner that indicates they are accurate and reliable.

[78]Comments to Revision of Procedures for the Administration of Section 5 of the Voting Rights Act of 1965, 52 Fed. Reg. 488 (1987). Section 5 also does not freeze in place those aspects of a redistricting plan that have been found to represent an unconstitutional racial gerrymander. *Abrams v. Johnson,* 117 S. Ct. 1925, 1939 (1997).

[79]Where the change under review is an initial districting plan (adopted in connection with a change to a district method of election), the new plan must be compared with the overall method of election or selection previously in effect (subject to the proviso that this method is lawful under Section 5). This typically involves a comparison between the submitted plan and an at-large election method or an appointive system, which typically does not suggest any retrogression.

[80]In addition, as set forth in both the initial objection letter and the reconsideration letter, there also were purpose concerns that underlay the objection.

2. *Discriminatory Purpose*

Almost all the Section 5 objections interposed by the Attorney General to redistricting plans during the first half of this decade were based on the purpose prong of the Section 5 test.

Both the Attorney General and the federal courts consistently have construed the Section 5 purpose test as being co-extensive with the constitutional prohibition on enacting redistricting plans (or other voting practices and procedures) that minimize minority electoral opportunity for a discriminatory reason, and that is the approach that was used by the Attorney General in reviewing post-1990 redistricting plans.[81] To show the absence of discriminatory purpose, a Section 5 jurisdiction must demonstrate that the choices underlying the redistricting plan were not tainted, even in part, by an invidious purpose. It is not sufficient to establish that there are some legitimate, nondiscriminatory reasons for the plan.[82] Moreover, the fact that a redistricting plan is ameliorative, or at least not retrogressive, does not (by itself) demonstrate that the plan also is free of a discriminatory purpose. A plan may improve minority electoral opportunity to some extent (or at least not worsen it) but still may minimize minority electoral opportunity for an invidious reason, and such plans may not be precleared.[83] But the Department has not considered that discriminatory intent is demonstrated by the mere fact that a plan does not include as many majority-minority districts as it might.

As the Supreme Court recently confirmed,[84] the analytic framework used in Section 5 in evaluating whether a voting change has a prohibited discriminatory purpose is the framework laid out by the Court in *Arlington Heights v. Metropolitan Housing Development Corp.*[85] for evaluating whether a challenged practice

---

[81] *City of Pleasant Grove v. United States*, 479 U.S. 462, 469- 472 (1987); *City of Port Arthur v. United States*, 459 U.S. 159, 168 (1982); *City of Richmond v. United States*, 422 U.S. 358, 378-379 (1975).

However, in *Reno v. Bossier Parish School Board*, 520 U.S. 471 (1997), the Supreme Court recently raised as a possibility (but did not hold) that the Section 5 purpose test is limited to the question whether a change was enacted with an intent to retrogress minority electoral opportunity. The Court did not decide the issue (or undertake any analysis of the question) because, regardless of what the ultimate question is under the Section 5 purpose test, the district court in *Bossier* apparently had used the wrong analytic framework in deciding that the school board's redistricting plan satisfied that test (and thus a remand was necessary). Justices Breyer and Stevens, in their separate opinions in *Bossier*, explained that both the language of Section 5 and the underlying congressional intent, as well as the Court's prior Section 5 decisions, require that the Section 5 purpose test be construed as being equivalent to the constitutional test of purpose to minimize minority electoral opportunity. On remand, however, the district court declined to decide this issue. *Bossier Parish School Board v. Reno*, No. 94-1495 (D.D.C. May 1, 1998).

[82] *Village of Arlington Heights v. Metropolitan Housing Development Corp.*, 429 U.S. 252, 265-66 (1977). *Accord, Texas v. United States*, 866 F. Supp. 20 (D.D.C. 1994); *Busbee v. Smith*, 549 F. Supp. 494, 516-17 (D.D.C. 1982), *aff'd mem.*, 459 U.S. 1166 (1983).

[83] *City of Pleasant Grove v. United States, supra*; *City of Port Arthur v. United States, supra*; *City of Richmond v. United States, supra*; *Busbee v. Smith, supra*. The Supreme Court's decisions in *Miller*, 515 U.S. at 923-924, and *Shaw v. Hunt*, 517 U.S. at __, 116 S. Ct. at 1904, are not to the contrary. Although the Court criticized the Department of Justice's enforcement of Section 5, the Court agreed that, notwithstanding the fact that the plans to which the Attorney General objected increased the number of black-majority congressional districts in Georgia and North Carolina, the Department properly required the states to demonstrate the absence of discriminatory purpose.

[84] *Reno v. Bossier Parish School Board, supra.*

has an unconstitutional discriminatory purpose. The Attorney General's Procedures for the Administration of Section 5 further define the relevant analytic factors.[86]

As stated in *Arlington Heights*, "[d]etermining whether invidious discriminatory purpose was a motivating factor demands a sensitive inquiry into such circumstantial and direct evidence of intent as may be available."[87] The Court noted that "an important starting point"[88] for the purpose inquiry is an analysis of the impact of the official action at issue. Thus, the starting (but not the ending) point in reviewing redistricting plans is an analysis of the extent to which the submitted plan fairly reflects minority voting strength in the context of prevailing voting patterns.[89] The analysis then branches out to consideration of such matters as the reasons proffered by the jurisdiction for its selection of the particular district lines, the reasons proffered for rejecting available alternative configurations, the extent to which the proposed plan adheres to or deviates from the jurisdiction's stated districting criteria, and the process leading to the adoption of the plan (including the opportunity for, and response to, minority input).[90] In actual practice, these different points of inquiry tend to merge together and reflect back on one another, as in each submission the pieces of the factual puzzle are fit together to reach an overall judgment as to whether the submitted plan was tainted by an invidious purpose.

Overall, the Section 5 objections interposed by the Attorney General to the post-1990 redistrictings reflected the view that where a plan substantially minimized minority voting strength, and that minimization was not required by adherence to traditional race-neutral districting principles, the jurisdiction bore the burden of demonstrating through specific evidence that discriminatory purpose did not play a role in the selection of the district lines. The conscious choice of district lines that have the foreseeable effect of minimizing minority voting strength is significant evidence of discriminatory purpose.[91] However, the Supreme Court's rulings in *Miller* and *Shaw v. Hunt* suggest that, where a plan is ameliorative, that fact now may go a long way toward

---

[85]429 U.S. 252 (1977).

[86]28 C.F.R. §§ 51.57-51.59.

[87]429 U.S. at 266.

[88]*Id.*

[89]In the Section 5 context, the Supreme Court has characterized a districting plan that provides a full and appropriate electoral opportunity to minority voters as one that "afford[s] them representation reasonably equivalent to their political strength in the... community" or, alternatively, one that "fairly reflects the strength of the [minority] community." *City of Richmond v. United States*, 422 U.S. at 370, 371. *See also Johnson v. De Grandy*, 512 U.S. 997, 1013-1014, 1020 (1994)(proportional representation, or lack thereof, is probative evidence as to whether a redistricting plan provides minority voters with the equal electoral opportunity required by Section 2 of the Act); 512 U.S. at 1025 (O'Connor, J., concurring; same). However, a plan may fairly reflect minority voting strength but nevertheless be the product of an invidious purpose. *City of Port Arthur v. United States*, 459 U.S. at 168. *See also Johnson v. De Grandy*, 512 U.S. at 1017-1021 (proportional representation is not an absolute defense to a Section 2 "results" claim).

[90]429 U.S. at 267-268. See also Section 5 Procedures, 28 C.F.R. §§ 51.57, 51.59(e)-(g).

demonstrating the absence of a discriminatory purpose.

B. Specific Redistricting Issues

1. Voting Patterns

An integral part of every review of a redistricting plan under Section 5 is an analysis of voting patterns, particularly with respect to elections for the electoral body for which the districts were drawn.

The threshold question in this regard is whether voting is polarized between minority and white voters, and if so, whether the polarization is at a level that is electorally significant. As noted by the Supreme Court in *Thornburg v. Gingles*, "courts and commentators agree that racial bloc voting is a key element of a vote dilution claim."[92] Simply put, it is only where voting is polarized between minority and white voters that the choice of district lines may affect the opportunity of minority voters *qua* minority voters to elect candidates of their choice.[93] The two complementary aspects of this inquiry, as described in *Gingles*, are whether minority voters are politically cohesive and whether white voters cast their votes sufficiently as a bloc to defeat the minority's preferred candidate in an election district.[94]

Accordingly, consideration was given to the polarization question in every post-1990 redistricting submission, and where serious concerns arose as to the propriety of a submitted plan, the Department closely scrutinized the electoral circumstances to determine whether and to what extent voting was polarized.[95] As with all other aspects of the Section 5 review, the analysis in each submission was case-specific and jurisdiction-specific. Nonetheless, in carrying out the reviews of the post-1990 plans, the Department commonly (although not universally) found that voting was racially or ethnically polarized in the jurisdictions at issue, although the level of polarization varied.

The Attorney General also considered, on a case-specific basis, factors other than polarization that may influence the electoral significance of a particular minority population percentage in a particular redistricting plan. This typically included such factors as the extent to which the minority voting age population percentage is less than the minority population percentage; the

---

[91] As stated in the Senate Report for the 1982 Voting Rights Act amendments regarding proof of discriminatory purpose under Section 2, "the normal inferences to be drawn from the foreseeability of defendant's actions... 'is one type of quite relevant evidence of racially discriminatory purpose.'" S. Rep. No. 417, 97th Cong., 2d Sess. 27 n.108, *quoting Dayton Board of Education v. Brinkman*, 443 U.S. 526, 536 n.9 (1979), *reprinted in* 1982 U.S.C.C.A.N. 177, 205.

[92] 478 U.S. at 55.

[93] "Not only does voting along racial lines deprive minority voters of their preferred representatives..., it also allows those elected to ignore minority interests without fear of political consequences,... leaving the minority effectively unrepresented." *Thornburg v. Gingles*, 478 U.S. at 48 n.11 (internal quotation marks omitted).

[94] As further explained by the Court in *Gingles*, "[i]f the minority group is not politically cohesive, it cannot be said that the selection of a multimember electoral structure [or the selection of particular district lines] thwarts distinctive minority group interests." *Id.* at 51. The Court also noted "that in the absence of significant white bloc voting it cannot be said that the ability of minority voters to elect their chosen representatives is inferior to that of white voters." *Id.* at 49 n.15.

extent to which eligible minority persons are registered to vote at a lower rate than eligible whites; the extent to which minority registered voters turn out at a lower rate than whites; and whether there is any population present in the jurisdiction that is legally precluded from voting or that in practice does not vote in local elections (such as a noncitizen population or the residents of a military base). Since the analysis is case-specific, the Attorney General has not subscribed to and has not in any way enforced the so-called "65 percent rule."[96]

The Attorney General's analysis of these factors yielded a variety of results. There were instances where a post-1990 plan was precleared that included one or more majority-minority districts less than 65 percent minority in total population, although there were available alternative plans in which a 65 percent minority district was drawn. For example, on August 23, 1993, the Attorney General precleared a new method of election (four districts and two at large) and districting plan for the City of Warner Robins, Georgia. The plan included one black-majority district that was 61 percent black in total population; this district in turn was 55 percent black in voting age population and 53 percent black in voter registration. The city had rejected six-district and five-district plans in which the district would have been, respectively, 67 percent and 66 percent black in population. The analysis indicated that while voting was polarized, black voters would have a realistic opportunity to elect their preferred candidate in the proposed district.

On the other hand, there were some instances where an objection was interposed although the proposed district at issue was greater than 65 percent minority in total population. For example, on June 24, 1992, the Attorney General interposed an objection to the plan for the New York state Assembly. The proposed plan, in northern Manhattan, unnecessarily split a

---

[95]To assess whether voting is racially or ethnically polarized, the Section 5 analysis focuses on evidence from a variety of sources. This may involve, most importantly, an analysis of election returns for the subject electoral body, and also may include an examination of exogenous elections where appropriate. Where possible, the Department of Justice makes use of the well-established techniques of ecological regression analysis and extreme case precinct analysis, relying on the Voting Section statistician to perform the necessary calculations. Election returns also are studied to determine the existence of any patterns as to where, when, and by what margin minority candidates are elected or defeated.

In assessing whether polarized voting is present, the analysis typically examines only those elections in which a minority candidate offered for election, unless there is evidence that a particular white candidate was sponsored by the minority community. *Collins v. City of Norfolk*, 883 F.2d 1232 (4th Cir. 1989), *cert. denied*, 498 U.S. 938 (1990); *Campos v. City of Baytown*, 840 F.2d 1240 (5th Cir. 1988), *cert. denied*, 492 U.S. 905 (1989); *Citizens for a Better Gretna v. City of Gretna*, 834 F.2d 496 (5th Cir. 1987), *cert. denied*, 492 U.S. 905 (1989). However, the Department recognizes that the Act protects the opportunity of minority voters to elect their preferred candidates irrespective of the candidates' race or ethnic origin and does not protect minority candidates *per se*.

[96]That "rule" posits that the voting age population, registration, and turnout factors each produces a five percentage point drop in the minority share of the district population such that a district must be at least 65 percent minority in total population in order for the minority group to constitute 50 percent of the voters present at the polls on election day. See, *e.g.*, *United Jewish Organizations of Williamsburgh, Inc. v. Carey*, 430 U.S. 144 (1977); *Ketchum v. Byrne*, 740 F.2d 1398 (7th Cir. 1984), *cert. denied*, 471 U.S. 1135 (1985); *Mississippi v. United States*, 490 F. Supp. 569 (D.D.C. 1979), *aff'd mem.*, 444 U.S. 1050 (1980).

geographically compact Hispanic population between two Assembly districts (in the context of polarized voting), thus minimizing Hispanic voting strength. The proposed district was 73 percent Hispanic in total population, but a substantial portion of the Hispanic population in the district were not citizens.

Another recurrent question was whether different minority groups should be combined in assessing electoral potential when a jurisdiction has a significant number of residents of different groups. The Attorney General's approach again was to employ a functional, case-specific analysis. Where the electoral analysis indicated that minority groups are politically cohesive with each other, that was factored into the Section 5 analysis. Where they are not cohesive, then the analysis proceeded to determine the impact of the submitted plan on each separate group. This approach rejects the view that the Act itself precludes combining minority groups as a matter of law.[97]

This functional approach, for example, led to different conclusions with respect to redistricting plans affecting two different areas of Texas. As set forth in a March 30, 1992 objection letter regarding a redistricting plan for the Lubbock Independent School District, the Attorney General relied in part on a finding that blacks and Hispanics in the school district formed electoral coalitions. On the other hand, in connection with the November 18, 1991 preclearance of the Texas congressional plan, the Attorney General rejected an allegation of discriminatory line-drawing in connection the state's decision not to draw a district in the Dallas-Fort Worth area that was majority-minority only if the black and Hispanic populations were combined. Even if the two minority populations were to coalesce, the alternative only would have been an influence district and significant questions were raised as to whether the minority communities combined in this district (blacks and Hispanics in both Dallas and Tarrant Counties) would form an electoral coalition in congressional elections.[98]

2. Treatment of Minority Population Concentrations by the Submitted Plan and Available Alternative Plans
Another key element of every post-1990 redistricting review was a close analysis of the interplay between the demography of the jurisdiction and the proposed district lines, and the extent to which alternative plans were available that complied with traditional districting principles but combined or separated minority population concentrations in a manner which, given the prevailing voting patterns, would have yielded districts with significantly different minority percentages.

---

[97]The courts of appeals that have addressed this issue under Section 2 of the Voting Rights Act are split. *Concerned Citizens v. Hardee County*, 906 F.2d 524 (11th Cir. 1990) (minority coalition claims are permissible under Section 2); *Campos v. City of Baytown*, 840 F.2d at 1244 (same). *Contra, Nixon v. Kent County*, 76 F.3d 1381 (6th Cir. 1996) (en banc).

[98]In *Terrazas v. Slagle*, 821 F. Supp. 1162 (W.D. Tex. 1993), the district court rejected a Section 2 challenge to the state Senate redistricting plan which was predicated on the failure to draw a Dallas-Fort Worth black/Hispanic influence district in that plan. The court found for the state in part because plaintiffs failed to provide any evidence that blacks and Hispanics would form an electoral coalition.

As set forth in the Section 5 Procedures, the map analysis involves a review of whether the plan minimizes minority voting strength by fragmenting or packing minority population concentrations.[99] To the extent that a proposed plan does one or both of these things, the flip side of this inquiry is an examination of what alternative plans would yield if the potentially problematic features of the submitted plan were reduced or eliminated.

In analyzing what districting options were objectively available to the jurisdiction, the Attorney General factored in certain districting principles that either are constitutionally mandated or generally reflect the accepted manner in which districts should be drawn.

At the constitutional level, plans of course must adhere to the Fourteenth Amendment's "one-person, one-vote" principle.[100] In practice, however, this requirement often imposes only a very flexible limit on the districting options, especially with the advent of the GIS technology. In addition, *Shaw v. Reno*[101] and *Miller v. Johnson*[102] now impose a constitutional limit on the extent to which race may predominate in redistricting decisionmaking.

The Section 5 Procedures note other, non-constitutional considerations, including the legitimate governmental interests of the jurisdiction, and compactness and contiguity.[103] In that regard, the Attorney General did not consider as "available" any alternative plan that included districts so noncompact as to be extreme or bizarre.[104] Typically, post-1990 plans included contiguous districts that were roughly compact, and the post-1990 objections were premised on the existence of fragmentation or packing which, if cured, would yield a plan that would include contiguous districts of similar compactness.

However, the mere existence of an alternative plan that is constitutionally acceptable, with compact and contiguous districts, and with more majority-minority districts than the submitted plan, did not result in the Attorney General interposing a "purpose" Section 5 objection. For example, in 1994, the Attorney General precleared a redistricting plan for the boards of commissioners and education in Dougherty County, Georgia, although the plan was opposed by some minority leaders who favored an alternative plan that included an additional majority-minority district.

3. Rationale for the Adopted Plan

---

[99]28 C.F.R. § 51.59(c) & (d).

[100] *See generally New York City Board of Estimate v. Morris*, 489 U.S. 688 (1989), and cases cited therein. However, the equal apportionment requirement does not apply to districts used to elect judicial officers. *Wells v. Edwards*, 347 F. Supp. 453 (M.D. La. 1972), *aff'd mem.*, 409 U.S. 1095 (1973) (one-person, one-vote inapplicable to judicial elections); *Holshouser v. Scott*, 335 F. Supp. 928 (M.D.N.C.), *aff'd mem.*, 409 U.S. 807 (1972) (same); *Chisom v. Roemer*, 501 U.S. 380 (1991) (approving holding in *Wells*).

[101]509 U.S. 630 (1993).

[102]515 U.S. 900 (1995).

[103]28 C.F.R. § 51.59(e) & (f).

[104]This is the longstanding approach of the Department of Justice to the compactness issue. Drew S. Days, III and Lani Guinier, "Enforcement of Section 5 of the Voting Rights Act," in *Minority Vote Dilution* 171 (Chandler Davidson ed., 1984).

a. Neutral Justifications. The primary explanation that typically was advanced by a jurisdiction for its submitted redistricting plan was the need to adhere to the "one-person, one-vote" requirement. But since that requirement usually leaves open a variety of districting options, it was rare for that to explain the particular district lines selected or to justify the adoption of a dilutive plan.

After *Shaw* and *Miller*, jurisdictions also may justify the plan selected by contending that alternatives would have threatened an unconstitutional racial gerrymander. As with any other justification offered by a jurisdiction, the Attorney General would evaluate that claim to determine whether the concern was valid or was a pretext for intentionally minimizing minority voting strength. After *Shaw*, and during the period covered by this essay, there were only a few instances in which jurisdictions raised this issue.

There were a variety of other criteria, neutral on their face, that jurisdictions cited in their submissions of post-1990 plans. These included such things as respect for other political boundaries (e.g., municipal or township boundaries, precinct boundaries, and the boundaries of districts used to elect other bodies), "least change" (i.e., minimizing changes in the existing plan), and equalization of duties (typically, equalizing the road mileage that each county commissioner or supervisor is responsible for). The Section 5 Procedures require the Attorney General to scrutinize such justifications to determine whether they are "reasonable and legitimate."[105] For example, the justifications were reviewed to determine whether they were applied consistently (both between districts, and historically between plans), the extent to which the district lines selected in fact reflected the criteria, and the extent to which the criteria in fact were discussed or employed during the redistricting process.

b. Incumbency Protection. A major concern that underlay most (if not almost all) post-1990 plans was incumbency protection. Incumbency protection in and of itself is not precluded by the Voting Rights Act. However, where incumbency protection is tied to racial discrimination, the plan may be objectionable.

Incumbency protection may become intertwined with a purpose to minimize minority voting strength where voting is racially or ethnically polarized and white voters historically have been overrepresented in electing a jurisdiction's officials. In these circumstances, it may be necessary to minimize a district's minority population percentage in order to protect the re-election chances of an incumbent official who is the choice of white voters but not minority voters. Thus, in reviewing post-1990 plans, the Attorney General interposed objections where the interests of incumbents favored by white voters were protected at the expense of minority electoral opportunity. Such incumbency protection efforts typically were related to the unnecessary fragmentation of minority communities or the needless packing of minority residents into a minimal number of districts.[106]

An example of an objection where incumbency protection was an issue was the May 2, 1994 objection to the redistricting plan for the South Carolina House

---

[105]28 C.F.R. § 51.57(a).

of Representatives. The plan was adopted after the Supreme Court vacated a court-ordered plan used in the 1992 House elections on the ground that the district court had failed to adequately apply Section 2.[107] The objection letter summarized the basis for the objection as follows:

> [O]ur analysis reveals that the redistricting process was designed to ensure incumbency protection, not compliance with the Voting Rights Act. Without analyzing the Voting Rights Act concerns that the Supreme Court directed should be considered before the 1992 redistricting plan could be used again, the House opted for a least-change approach that limited revisions only to those that each district's incumbent would accept. The state has not advanced state policy considerations served by the proposed plan other than incumbency protection and the ease of administering a plan essentially the same as the 1992 plan.
>
> The state, fully aware of alternative redistricting configurations that created additional black-majority districts, rejected them without considering them seriously. The proposed plan...fragments and packs black population concentrations to avoid drawing additional black-majority districts or enhancing the existing black majorities....Overall, the state has failed to justify its redistricting plan on legitimate, nonracial grounds.[108]

c. Jurisdiction's Knowledge of Alternative Plans. To conclude that a plan was tainted by discriminatory purpose, the Attorney General must determine that the jurisdiction was aware that an alternative configuration was available that would have provided for greater minority electoral opportunity. In considering this issue in the review of post-1990 redistrictings, the Attorney General again followed a functional, case-specific approach.

In some redistrictings, alternative plans that more fairly reflected minority voting strength were developed during the redistricting process by the minority community or by the jurisdiction itself. However, the Attorney General did not consider it necessary that this occur in order to conclude that a plan was the product of a discriminatory purpose. It sometimes was probative that minority citizens suggested a particular districting approach which the jurisdiction then decided not to incorporate in its plan. Or, in some circumstances, the well-known demographic characteristics of the jurisdiction (particularly the location and size of

---

[106]See, *e.g.*, *Garza and United States v. County of Los Angeles*, 918 F.2d 763, 771 (9th Cir. 1990), *cert. denied*, 498 U.S. 1028 (1992); *Ketchum v. Byrne*, 740 F.2d 1398, 1408-09 (7th Cir. 1984), *cert. denied*, 471 U.S. 1135 (1985). The Attorney General's position in this regard was articulated in numerous Section 5 objection letters, including, for example, the letters in which objections were interposed to post-1990 statewide plans.

Section 5 concerns also may arise where a plan manipulates the districts to which incumbents or potential minority challengers are assigned, *e.g.*, by drawing a noncompact district in order to maintain a white incumbent in his or her district or by purposefully excluding potential strong minority challengers. On the other hand, the Attorney General did not interpose any post-1990 objections requiring that district lines be manipulated to exclude white incumbents from their districts in order to promote minority electoral opportunity.

[107]*Burton v. Sheheen*, 793 F. Supp. 1329 (D.S.C. 1992), *vacated and remanded sub nom.*, *Statewide Reapportionment Advisory Committee v. Theodore*, 508 U.S. 968 (1993).

[108]The plan adopted by the state following the objection was precleared but then was struck down as being an unconstitutional racial gerrymander. *Able v. Wilkins*, 946 F. Supp. 1174 (D.S.C. 1996). A new remedial plan was precleared, and was upheld by the same court when the racial gerrymander claim was renewed. *Able v. Wilkins*, No. 3:96-0003 (Apr. 25, 1997).

minority concentrations) indicated readily available alternatives to the plan adopted by the jurisdiction. It also was relevant whether the jurisdiction provided an adequate opportunity for minority input during the districting process. In considering the jurisdiction's awareness of alternative plans, the Attorney General recognized that minority citizens may have lacked the expertise and resources to prepare a formal alternative plan.

4. Increase in Minority Population Percentages from 1980 to 1990
In a number of Section 5 jurisdictions, there was a substantial increase in the minority population percentage from 1980 to 1990, particularly in the West and Southwest involving Hispanic population. The Attorney General carefully monitored redistricting plans adopted by these jurisdictions to determine whether the new plans recognized the enhanced minority population share or sought to fragment or pack minority concentrations to counter growing minority electoral strength.

For example, on October 4, 1991, the Attorney General interposed an objection to the redistricting plan for the City of Houston, Texas. The city is governed by a 14-member council and a mayor, who also is a member of the council, with nine councilmembers elected from single-member districts and five councilmembers and the mayor elected at large. As discussed in the objection letter, from 1980 to 1990 the city's Hispanic population grew by 60 percent, increasing from 18 to 28 percent of the total city population, while the black population percentage remained essentially unchanged and the white percentage decreased from 52 to 41 percent. Although the city claimed that it sought to recognize the growing Hispanic population in drawing its new districts, the submitted plan—like the existing plan—provided only one district in which Hispanic voters would have the opportunity to elect a candidate of their choice and fragmented the remainder of the community into a number of adjoining districts. Alternative plans developed during the redistricting process demonstrated that, by avoiding such fragmentation, the plan would contain two districts in which Hispanics would constitute a majority of the voting age population. The objection letter concluded that the goal of recognizing the Hispanic growth appeared to have been subordinated by the city to a concern for drawing districts that would protect the re-election chances of white incumbent councilmembers.

5. Who Controls the Elective Body
Particularly difficult post-1990 determinations were presented where jurisdictions were majority-minority in population and the redistricting dispute was over whether the plan would favor white or minority voters with regard to the opportunity to elect a majority of the governing board. In these circumstances, alternative plans developed by various parties during the redistricting process often were drawn with full awareness as to which group would be benefited by the plan. These submissions required a particularly sensitive examination of the facts and difficult judgments to distinguish between a motivation to adopt a racially fair plan and an invidious purpose to minimize minority voting strength. On a number of occasions objections were interposed, not based on any abstract judgment as to

which group should have the opportunity to control the elected body, but based on a factual determination that the jurisdiction had failed to demonstrate the absence of discriminatory purpose.

6. Influence Districts

A small number of objections involved discrimination regarding the drawing of so-called "influence" districts, i.e., districts that would not be majority-minority under any available districting scenario. Thus, these objections did not raise either of the basic districting questions that characterized the review of almost all post-1990 redistrictings—whether additional majority-minority districts may have been drawn or whether the minority percentage in a proposed majority-minority district may have been higher.

In general, the Section 5 "purpose and effect" test applies equally to a claim that minority voting strength was unnecessarily minimized by failing to draw a stronger "influence" district.[109] However, from a functional perspective, it typically is less likely that such a claim will arise or that it will lead to an objection. In the context of polarized voting, it often is of relatively little electoral significance for minority voters whether a somewhat stronger or somewhat weaker influence district is drawn since, in either case, minority voters generally will not enjoy a realistic opportunity to elect their preferred candidate. In addition, minority voting strength in an influence district may be reduced in order to accommodate requests from the minority community to draw an additional majority-minority district or augment the minority percentage in an existing majority-minority district. The absence of a significant electoral impact would make it less likely that any discriminatory purpose was present. With respect to retrogression, a nonmeaningful reduction in minority voting strength would not render a plan retrogressive.

An example of an "influence district" objection was the February 22, 1993 objection to the redistricting plan for the three-member board of supervisors of Graham County, Arizona. According to the 1990 Census, the county is 25 percent Hispanic, 15 percent Native American, and 2 percent black. By fragmenting the Hispanic population, the plan reduced the Hispanic proportion of one district from 39 to 33 percent, whereas in a plan free of such fragmentation that Hispanic proportion likely would have modestly increased. As set forth in the objection letter, the analysis indicated that in the context of local voting patterns, the fragmentation significantly minimized Hispanic voting strength and the county failed to provide any nonracial explanation for its districting choices.

7. Minority Participation

---

[109]The Supreme Court has not yet decided whether a failure to draw a stronger influence district may violate the Section 2 results standard. See, *e.g.*, *Johnson v. De Grandy*, 512 U.S. 997 (1994). A number of courts of appeals, however, have held that the results test does not apply to influence district claims and that a plaintiff must demonstrate that additional districts may be drawn in which minority residents would constitute a majority of the voting age population. *E.g.*, *Brewer v. Ham*, 876 F.2d 448 (5th Cir. 1989); *McNeil v. Springfield Park District*, 851 F.2d 937 (7th Cir. 1988), *cert. denied*, 490 U.S. 1031 (1989). In addition, one court of appeals has further specified that minorities must constitute a majority of the alternative district's citizen voting age population. *Romero v. City of Pomona*, 883 F.2d 1418 (9th Cir. 1989).

The minority residents of Section 5 jurisdictions play a crucial role in ensuring that nondiscriminatory plans are adopted and in the Attorney General's enforcement of Section 5.

The Section 5 Procedures specifically recognize that an important factor in Section 5 determinations is "[t]he extent to which the jurisdiction afforded members of racial and language minority groups an opportunity to participate in the decision to make the change."[110] If minority citizens are included in the decision-making process, it is more likely that a redistricting plan that fairly reflects their political and community interests will be adopted. On the other hand, if minorities are excluded from the decisionmaking process, that may be highly probative of an effort to minimize minority electoral opportunity.

In the 1990s, minority leaders and groups were much better prepared to offer specific alternative redistricting plans and suggestions to state and local officials, and often made use of the new GIS technology. Where this occurred and a plan was adopted that was opposed by the minority community, minority citizens then were in a much stronger position to argue discriminatory purpose to the Attorney General than if they had not raised specific concerns during the redistricting process. The Attorney General also relies on minority contacts in the Section 5 jurisdictions to provide their analysis of the local electoral dynamics and their perspective on the process that led to the adoption of the submitted plan.

Often where there was minority opposition to a post-1990 plan, minority leaders and groups were in general agreement about the plan's purpose and effect. In some instances, there was a diversity of viewpoints. That sometimes involved, for example, a situation where minority incumbent officials voted for the submitted plan while other minority leaders opposed it. This split could indicate the absence of a discriminatory purpose; however, the support offered by minority incumbents did not automatically validate a plan as the Attorney General on occasion found that their support was based only on their interest in protecting their own re-election chances or their belief that they were not in a position to express opposition to the plan.

In practice, there were few instances where an objection was interposed to a post-1990 plan in the absence of minority opposition, since absent any local controversy it is unlikely that the Attorney General would conclude that federal action barring the change is necessary or appropriate. On the other hand, plans were precleared despite minority opposition. In the end, the Attorney General in each submission considered all the information provided by the jurisdiction and interested citizens and made an independent judgment as to whether the plan should be precleared.

IV. CONCLUSION

The adoption of redistricting plans following the decennial census has become an important and integral part of the American political process. For minority voters,

---

[110] 28 C.F.R. § 51.57(c).

redistricting may offer a unique opportunity to remedy past discrimination through the adoption of new plans that fairly reflect minority voting strength. However, in part because redistricting decisions may be controlled by officials who do not owe their election to minority voters, the process also poses the danger that discrimination may taint the new plan.

The Voting Rights Act, and Section 5 in particular, have provided minority voters with a powerful institutional means by which to ensure that redistricting is accomplished in a nondiscriminatory manner, and the Attorney General vigorously enforced Section 5 following the 1990 Census to effectuate the congressional mandate. In order to carefully scrutinize each of the enormous number of redistrictings submitted following the 1990 Census, the Department of Justice committed personnel and resources to undertake a "state of the art" review process. The result has been that political opportunity in the 1990s is apportioned in a fair, nondiscriminatory manner to a degree not before seen in American political history. The extent to which, following the Supreme Court's lead, we now recede from this high water mark remains an open question.

APPENDIX I: SECTION 5 REDISTRICTING CASES AND DECISIONS

A. The eight cases in which jurisdictions sought judicial preclearance for a post-1990 redistricting plan are as follows, in chronological order of filing:

1. *Bolivar County, Mississippi v. United States*, No. 91-2186, filed August 26, 1991, seeking preclearance of a redistricting plan for the county board of supervisors to which the Attorney General had interposed an objection; on December 20, 1994, the court granted preclearance to a revised plan, with the concurrence of the United States.

2. *Texas v. United States*, No. 91-2383, filed September 20, 1991, seeking preclearance of congressional, state House and Senate, and state board of education redistricting plans; the Senate plan was precleared by the district court with the concurrence of the United States (802 F. Supp. 481 (D.D.C. 1992)); the congressional and board of education plans were precleared by the Attorney General pursuant to submissions made by the state prior to filing the declaratory judgment action; and the claim regarding the state House plan was not pursued after the Attorney General interposed an objection to the plan.

3. *Walker v. United States*, No. 92-0480, filed February 24, 1992, seeking preclearance of a redistricting plan for the commissioners court, justices of the peace, and constables in Gregg County, Texas; at the time suit was filed, the county had pending before the Attorney General a request for administrative preclearance of the same plan, and after suit was filed the Attorney General interposed an objection to the plan; the suit was voluntarily dismissed after the Attorney General precleared a subsequently adopted remedial plan.

4. *Ellis County, Texas v. United States*, No. 92-1110, filed May 11, 1992, seeking preclearance of a redistricting plan for the county commissioners court to which the Attorney General had interposed an objection; the complaint was dismissed as moot by the district court in an unreported opinion dated October 6, 1992; the county subsequently obtained administrative preclearance from the Attorney General for a remedial plan.

5. *Calhoun County, Texas v. United States*, No. 92-1890, filed August 18, 1992, seeking preclearance of redistricting plans for the county commissioners court, and for justices of the peace and constables, to which the Attorney General had interposed objections; the suit was voluntarily dismissed after the Attorney General granted administrative preclearance to remedial plans adopted by the county.

6. *Lee County, Mississippi v. United States*, No. 93-0708, filed April 6, 1993, seeking preclearance of a redistricting plan for the county board of supervisors to which the Attorney General had interposed an objection; the suit was voluntarily dismissed and a remedial plan subsequently was adopted and precleared.

7. *Castro County, Texas v. United States*, No. 93-1792, filed August 25, 1993, seeking preclearance of a redistricting plan for the county commissioners court to which the Attorney General had interposed an objection; the suit was dismissed and the county obtained administrative preclearance from the Attorney General for a remedial plan.

8. *Bossier Parish School Board v. Reno*, 907 F. Supp. 434 (D.D.C. 1995), *vacated and remanded*, 520 U.S. 471 (1997), *on remand*, No. 94-1495 (May 1, 1998), filed July 14, 1994, seeking preclearance of a redistricting plan to which the Attorney General had interposed an objection; on November 2, 1995, the court granted preclearance, on May 12, 1997 the Supreme Court vacated and remanded and on May 1, 1998, the district court again granted preclearance.

B. In addition to the decisions regarding the Bossier Parish, Louisiana School Board, the Bolivar County, Mississippi Board of Supervisors, and the Texas state Senate (set forth in part A of this Appendix), the other judicial section 5 preclearance decisions are (in chronological order of decision):

1. *Beer v. United States*, 374 F. Supp. 363 (D.D.C. 1974) (declaratory judgment denied for redistricting plan for New Orleans City Council), *vacated and remanded*, 425 U.S. 130 (1976), *on remand*, No. 1495-73 (July 29, 1976) (declaratory judgment granted).

2. *Donnell v. United States*, No. 78-0392 (D.D.C. July 31, 1979), *aff'd mem.*, 444 U.S. 1059 (1980) (declaratory judgment denied for redistricting plan for the Warren County, Mississippi Board of Supervisors).

3. *Mississippi v. United States*, 490 F. Supp. 569 (D.D.C. 1979), *aff'd mem.*, 444 U.S. 1050 (1980) (declaratory judgment granted for redistricting plans for the state House and Senate).

4. *City of Port Arthur v. United States*, 517 F. Supp. 987 (D.D.C. 1981) (declaratory judgment denied for districting plan for Port Arthur, Texas City Council), *aff'd on other grounds*, 459 U.S. 159 (1982).

5. *Senate of California v. United States*, No. 81-2767 (D.D.C. Apr. 26, 1982) (declaratory judgment granted without opposition to redistricting plan for the California state Senate).

6. *Busbee v. Smith*, 549 F. Supp. 494 (D.D.C. 1982), *aff'd mem.*, 459 U.S. 1116 (1983) (declaratory judgment denied for congressional redistricting plan for the State of Georgia).

C. The cases in which relief was granted in local district courts to prevent implementation of unprecleared post-1990 redistricting plans are:

1. *Casares v. Cochran County, Texas*, No. 5-92-CV-184-C (N.D. Tex. Oct. 9, 1992) (injunction against further implementation of commissioners court plan which was implemented in the March 10, 1992 primary and to which the Attorney General

objected on April 6, 1992; settlement thereafter provided for special election implementing a subsequently adopted, precleared plan).

2. *Dallas County Board of Education v. Jones*, No. 92-0583-B-M (S.D. Ala. Sep. 28, 1992) (injunction against further implementation of redistricting plan for Alabama school district which had not been submitted for preclearance either to the Attorney General or the District of Columbia Court but which had been implemented in a June 2, 1992 primary; a court-ordered plan was then imposed).

3. *Daniel v. Bailey County, Texas*, No. 5-92-CV-0171-C (N.D. Tex. Oct. 28, 1992) (agreed order permitting conduct of 1992 election pursuant to a commissioners court plan to which the Attorney General objected on April 6, 1992, and approving settlement plan (subsequently precleared) for use in future elections; election district at issue in objection was not up for election until 1994).

4. *Gamez v. Deaf Smith County, Texas*, No. 2-92-CV-0115-J (N.D. Tex. July 16, 1992) (1992 special primary election ordered to implement precleared commissioners court plan after March 10, 1992 primary held pursuant to a plan to which the Attorney General objected on April 10, 1992).

5. *Gant v. Ellis County Commissioners' Court*, No. 3-92-CV-0395-D (N.D. Tex. Mar. 4, 1992) (injunction against implementation of commissioners court plan to which the Attorney General subsequently objected on March 30, 1992; a remedial plan subsequently was precleared).

6. *Hoskins v. Hannah*, No. G-92-12 (S.D. Tex. Jan. 24, 1992) (injunction against implementation of plan for justices of the peace and constables in Galveston County, Texas to which the Attorney General subsequently objected on March 17, 1992; settlement provided for a special 1992 primary election for constable pursuant to a plan also embodied in the settlement and subsequently precleared).

7. *LULAC v. Monahans-Wickett-Pyote Independent School District*, No. P-92-CA-007 (W.D. Tex. Apr. 16, 1992) (injunction against implementation of plan for Texas school district to which the Attorney General objected on March 30, 1992; a remedial plan subsequently was precleared).

8. *Mexican American Political Action Committee v. Calhoun County, Texas*, No. V-92-013 (S.D. Tex. Nov. 5, 1992) (order based on parties' stipulations shortening terms of office of county commissioner and constable elected in 1992 using plans to which the Attorney General objected on March 17, 1992, and providing a special election for these offices pursuant to subsequently adopted, precleared plans).

9. *Puerto Rican Legal Defense & Education Fund v. City of New York*, 769 F. Supp. 74 (E.D.N.Y. 1991) (temporary restraining order granted by single judge barring commencement of candidate petitioning process for qualification for the party primaries pursuant to city council redistricting plan then pending review with the Attorney General), *vacated and injunction denied*, No. CV 91 2026 (E.D.N.Y. June 18, 1991) (three-judge court), *further relief granted*, (E.D.N.Y. July 30, 1991) (three-judge court) (modifying candidate qualification procedures for party primaries pursuant to city council plan precleared July 26, 1991 following Attorney General's objection to initial plan on July 19, 1991).

10. *Reyna v. Castro County, Texas*, C.A. No. 2-92-CV-168-J (N.D. Tex. Oct. 14, 1992) (injunction against further implementation of commissioners court plan implemented in the March 10, 1992 primary and to which the Attorney General objected on March 30, 1992); *Castro County, Texas v. United States*, No. 93-1792 (D.D.C. Dec. 17, 1993) (injunction barring county from taking any action to seek to implement the commis-

sioners court plan to which the Attorney General objected on March 10, 1993 and with respect to which the county was seeking judicial preclearance in this case).

11. *United States v. Graham County*, No. CIV-93-598 (D. Ariz. Apr. 18, 1994) (settlement enjoining the county from implementing the redistricting plan to which the Attorney General objected on February 22, 1993, and requiring the county to engage in outreach efforts in the minority community with respect to the plan that subsequently was precleared by the Attorney General).

12. *United States v. Yuma County*, No. 92-2024 (D. Ariz. Oct. 30, 1992 & Mar. 12, 1993) (consent orders enjoining implementation of plans for the Yuma County, Arizona board of supervisors and the Arizona Western College District (Yuma County portion) to which the Attorney General interposed objections on September 28, 1992, and requiring that the county hold special elections under precleared plans).

The cases in which relief was denied or otherwise not granted are:

1. *Almager v. Gaines County, Texas*, No. 5-92-CV-66-W (N.D. Tex. June 1, 1993) (case dismissed pursuant to joint motion; Attorney General objected to initial post-1990 commissioners court plan on July 14, 1992 and subsequently precleared a remedial plan adopted by county with plaintiff's concurrence; election district at issue in objection was not up for election until 1994).

2. *Campos v. City of Houston*, 776 F. Supp. 304 (S.D. Tex. 1991) (City of Houston, Texas ordered to conduct its November 1991 election pursuant to a plan to which the Attorney General had objected on October 4, 1991, despite availability of redistricting plan precleared by the Attorney General on October 12, 1991), *stay pending appeal denied*, 502 U.S. 1301 (1991) (Scalia, Circuit Justice), *vacated and remanded*, 968 F.2d 446 (5th Cir. 1992), *cert. denied*, 508 U.S. 941 (1993); *United States v. City of Houston*, 800 F. Supp. 504 (S.D. Tex. 1992) (court declined to order special election to implement the plan precleared on October 12, 1991).

3. *Craig v. Gregg County, Texas*, No. 6-92-CV-128 (E.D. Tex. June 1, 1992) (court denied joint motion for special primary election for commissioners court and constables after March 10, 1992 primary held pursuant to redistricting plan to which the Attorney General objected on March 17, 1992; court previously had not granted plaintiff's request for an injunction against holding the primary using the unprecleared plan).

4. *Lopez v. Hale County, Texas*, 797 F. Supp. 547 (N.D. Tex. 1992), *aff'd mem.* 506 U.S. 1042 (1993) (court declined to enjoin implementation of commissioners court plan to which the Attorney General objected on April 10, 1992, based in part on the fact that the election district that was the subject of the objection was not up for election until 1994; a remedial plan subsequently was precleared).

APPENDIX II: POST-1990 OBJECTIONS TO LOCAL REDISTRICTING PLANS

Alabama
Dallas County Board of Education: 5/1/92; 7/21/92; 12/24/92
Greensboro (Hale County): 12/4/92; 1/3/94
Selma (Dallas County): 11/12/92; 3/15/93

Arizona

Arizona Western College District (Yuma County portion): 9/28/92 (2 plans)
Graham County (board of supervisors): 2/22/93
La Paz County (board of supervisors): 7/17/92
Yuma County (board of supervisors): 9/28/92

California
Merced County (board of supervisors): 4/3/92
Monterey County (board of supervisors): 2/26/93

Georgia
Griffin (Spalding County): 11/30/92
Macon (Bibb and Jones Counties): 12/20/94
Monroe (Walton County): 10/22/93
Randolph County (board of commissioners and school board): 6/28/93

Louisiana
Bienville Parish (police jury): 9/27/91
Bossier Parish (school board): 8/30/93
Catahoula Parish (police jury): 10/25/91
Concordia Parish (police jury): 12/23/91; 8/28/92
DeSoto Parish (police jury): 10/15/91
Desoto Parish (school board): 4/25/94
East Carroll Parish: 12/20/91 (police jury and school board); 8/21/92 (police jury only); 1/4/93 (police jury and school board); 8/19/94 (school board only)
Evangeline Parish (school board): 5/24/93
Franklin Parish (police jury): 11/25/91 (2 plans)
Iberville Parish (school board): 6/21/93; 11/24/93
Jackson Parish (police jury): 10/8/91
Jennings (Jefferson Davis): 3/8/93
Lafayette Parish (parish council): 10/18/93
Lafayette Parish (school board): 9/21/92
Madison Parish (police jury and school board): 4/10/92
Minden (Webster Parish): 10/17/94
Morehouse Parish: 9/27/91 (police jury); 5/26/92 (police jury); 9/14/92 (police jury); 3/26/93 (justice court)
Pointe Coupee Parish (police jury): 2/7/92; 9/10/92
Richland Parish (police jury): 1/2/92
St. Francisville (West Feliciana Parish): 5/18/93
St. Landry Parish (police jury and school board): 12/16/91
St. Martin Parish (police jury and school board): 10/25/91
St. Martinville (St. Martin Parish): 11/9/92
St. Mary Parish (school board): 8/30/93
Tallulah (Madison Parish): 8/30/93
Terrebonne Parish (council): 1/3/92
Vermillion Parish (school board): 12/30/92
Ville Platte (Evangeline Parish): 12/13/93; 4/3/95
Washington Parish (school board): 6/21/93
Webster Parish (police jury and school board): 12/24/91
West Carroll Parish (school board): 3/30/93
West Feliciana Parish (police jury): 10/25/91

Winnsboro (Franklin Parish): 11/22/94

Mississippi
Adams County (board of supervisors): 1/30/95
Amite County (board of supervisors): 8/23/91; 11/30/92
Attala County (board of supervisors): 1/13/92
Benton County (board of supervisors): 9/9/91
Bolivar County (board of supervisors): 7/15/91; 8/23/91
Canton (Madison County): 12/21/93
Carroll County (board of supervisors): 4/18/94
Charleston (Tallahatchie County): 6/4/93
Chickasaw County (board of supervisors): 3/26/93; 4/11/95
Clarke County (board of supervisors and justice court): 9/24/91
Forrest County (board of supervisors): 10/7/91
Gloster (Amite County): 3/30/93
Greenville (Washington County): 2/22/93
Harrison County (board of supervisors): 9/9/91
Hinds County (board of supervisors): 7/19/91
Jefferson Davis County (board of supervisors): 9/13/91
Lauderdale County (board of supervisors): 10/7/91
Lee County (board of supervisors): 8/23/91; 3/22/93
Leflore County (board of supervisors): 10/21/91
Marshall County (board of supervisors): 9/30/91; 10/13/92
Monroe County (board of supervisors): 4/26/91; 9/17/93; 3/20/95
Montgomery County (justice court): 9/16/91
Okolona (Chickasaw County): 10/29/93
Oktibbeha County (board of supervisors): 9/30/91
Pearl River County (board of supervisors): 11/25/91
Perry County (board of supervisors): 11/19/91
Quitman (Clarke County): 12/19/94
Sunflower County (board of supervisors): 10/25/91; 5/21/92
Tallahatchie County (board of supervisors): 4/27/92
Tate County (board of supervisors): 7/2/91; 10/11/91
Union County (board of supervisors): 8/2/91; 6/20/95
Walthall County (board of supervisors): 9/30/91

New York
New York City: 7/19/91

South Carolina
Bennettsville (Marlboro County): 2/6/95
Dorchester County (council): 8/28/92
Johnston (Edgefield County): 6/5/92; 7/6/93
Lee County (council and school district): 2/8/93
Marion County (council and school district): 1/5/93
Norway (Orangeburg County): 11/9/92
Orangeburg County (council): 7/21/92
Rock Hill (York County): 1/17/92

Texas

Bailey County (commissioners court and justices of the peace/constables): 4/6/92
Calhoun County (commissioners court and justices of the peace/constables): 3/17/92
Castro County (commissioners court): 3/30/92; 10/6/92; 5/10/93
Cochran County (commissioners court): 4/6/92
Dallas (Dallas County et al.): 5/6/91 (2 plans)
Deaf Smith County (commissioners court): 4/10/92
Del Valle Independent School District (Travis County): 12/24/91; 7/31/92
Ellis County (commissioners court): 3/30/92
Gaines County (commissioners court): 7/14/92
Galveston County (justices of the peace/constables): 3/17/92
Gonzales Underground Water Conservation District (Gonzales County): 10/31/94
Gregg County (commissioners court and justices of the peace/ constables): 3/17/92
Hale County (commissioners court): 4/10/92
Houston (Harris County et al.): 10/4/91
Lubbock Independent School District (Lubbock County): 3/30/92
Monahans-Wickett-Pyote Independent School District (Ward County): 3/30/92
McCulloch County (commissioners court): 6/4/93
Refugio Independent School District (Refugio County): 4/22/91
Terrell County (commissioners court): 4/6/92
Wharton County (commissioners court and justices of the peace/ constables): 8/30/93

Virginia
Powhatan County (board of supervisors): 11/12/91

PART III

Case Studies

PREDICTABLY UNPREDICTABLE:
The Alaskan State Supreme Court and Reapportionment

Tuckerman Babcock

ALASKANS MAY NOT LIKE TO ADMIT IT, but we are not unique in every respect. Like every other state at least once every ten years the Alaskan state legislature must be reapportioned.

On the other hand, the Alaskan State Supreme Court, if not unique among all state courts, comes close. This court has crafted a legacy that is as predictable as it is unpredictable. Since the first reapportionment case decided by the State Supreme Court in 1965, there have been three decades of reapportionment.[1] Predictably, each decennial reapportionment is challenged, predictably the State Supreme Court finds the Governor's first plan unconstitutional, and predictably the State Supreme Court allows the second plan to go forward.

Each Opinion is written to explain the constitutional violation or violations compelling the Court to conclude that all, or part, of the first plan of each decade be dismissed as unconstitutional. What is unpredictable for those responsible for redistricting in Alaska[2] is embodied in the fact that the Court never applies the same rules twice. Each initial plan has been found unconstitutional, but each for different reasons. A constitutional issue that catches the Court's attention in one case is ignored in the next. An innovative solution in one cycle becomes a fundamental flaw in the next. With that tradition, the would-be Alaskan redistricter might as well ignore (1) whatever reasoning has been advanced by the State Supreme Court; (2) any district designed in the past that has been allowed to

---

[1] *Wade v. Nolan*, 414 P.2d (Alaska 1966), *Egan v. Hammond*, 502 P.2d (Alaska 1972), Masters Plan 1972, *Groh v. Egan*, 526 P.2d (Alaska 1974), *Carpenter v. Hammond*, 667 P.2d (Alaska 1983), *Kenai Peninsula Borough v. State* 743 P.2d (Alaska 1987) and *Southeast Conference v. Hickel*, CN 1JU-91-1608 Civil, SCN S-5165, December 29, 1995 opinion.

[2] State of Alaska, Constitution, Article VI

stand or have even proposed by the court; and, therefore, (3) strike for as much political advantage as possible without fear of unnecessarily endangering the plan. The implication for those inclined to egregious partisan gerrymandering is clear: follow the federal rules to secure approval by Justice, and go for all you can get stateside because the only rule the State Courts follow is that the first plan will be thrown out. In Alaska, a wise redistricter must accept that the first plan will fall. Then, if history is any guide, the second plan, however amended, will stand. Beside the predictable unpredictability of the State Court, what else confounds redistricting in Alaska?

Alaska is the Last Frontier. The last state where, at close to one person per square mile, Frederick Jackson Turner's thesis may still be put to the test. A minuscule one percent of the land is inhabited and just 3 percent is privately owned. Geographically, Alaska sprawls across an area more than twice the size of Texas; boasts more coastline than the contiguous 48 states combined; displays glaciers as large as some other states; and offers the highest mountain in North America, Mount McKinley. Alaska houses the smallest population (after the 1990 census one can quibble with Wyoming on this point); is crisscrossed by the fewest roads and has the most airports. Finally, an item of vital interest to reapportionment, although not an item of interest, I am sure, to the more than 1,000,000 tourists who visit each year, is that Alaska's geography and population of 550,000 require the most expansive and least populated legislative districts in the nation.

For 1991 those facts were complicated by a decade of skyrocketing population. At just over 33 percent, Alaska enjoyed the greatest percentage increase in the United States. Growth was wildly uneven around the state, causing an explosion in overall deviation of House districts from 14.9 percent in 1984 to 82.5 percent in 1990. House district deviations exceeded 75 percent within every geographic area of the state.

There is no concentration of Asian, Hispanic, or African-American population sufficient to form even 25 percent of any legislative district. However, Native Americans in Alaska make up 15.6 percent of the statewide population (a decline from 16.0 percent in 1980) and can provide a majority or substantial minority in several districts. Certain minorities in Alaska, just as in every other state in the Union, are protected from discriminatory districting by Section 2 of the Voting Rights Act. In addition, Alaska suffers the burden of mandatory preclearance under Section 5.[3] This requirement is particularly onerous because, perhaps

---

[3]This requirement for preclearance is not related to any historical example of actual discrimination or harm. Indeed, Alaska was allowed to opt out of the Voting Rights Act preclearance requirements during the 1970s. Alaska was covered again solely because a certain percentage of the population has a first language other than English. Despite the fact that no discrimination has ever been demonstrated, the U.S. Justice Department took from November 1991 to April 1992 to approve the first plan and actually entered an objection to the second plan in 1994. In a ludicrous example of micromanagement, U.S. Justice Department attorney Steve Rosenbaum, Chief of the Voting Rights Act Section, insisted that approximately 2,000 people be moved around involving six communities. The effect was to increase the voting age population in a single house district from 51 percent Alaska Native to 59 percent Alaska Native. The district already had an Alaska Native incumbent Representative.

unique among states, there is virtually no evidence of racially polarized voting.[4]

The State Constitution mandates a House of 40 and a Senate of 20. Article VI of the State Constitution provides for a five member advisory board appointed by the Governor (members are appointed without regard to political affiliation and cannot also serve on any other government panel, board, commission or be federal, state or local government employees). The five serve at the pleasure of the Governor and need not be confirmed by the Legislature. In fact, the State Constitution provides no participation in reapportionment for the legislature other than appropriation of funds to carry out the task. The State Constitution limits the Court to a review for constitutionality and gives them the authority to compel the Governor to reapportion. This specific limitation on the discretion of the judiciary to adopt plans of their own was ignored in 1972 (at the request of the Governor), was followed in 1983 when an unconstitutional plan was sent back to the Governor for amendment, and then was ignored in 1992 over the earnest objection of the Governor when the Court appointed three Masters and drew up their own plan in a couple of weeks.[5]

The U.S. Bureau of the Census PL94-171 data showed statewide population in April 1990 at 550,043. The Constitution states that after receiving the population figures from the census, this five member board is allowed just 90 days to recommend a final plan to the Governor. After receiving the Board's recommendation, the Governor is allowed 90 days to review the plan and make any change he chooses so long as he describes his change in writing.

Alaska elected a new Governor in November of 1990, Walter J. Hickel, an Alaska Independence Party member who also had been elected Governor in 1966 as a Republican. Governor Hickel took office on December 3, 1990 and in January 1991 replaced the five-member board that had been appointed by former Governor Steve Cowper, a Democrat.[6] The Board retained staff, hired consultants, and for legal advice relied on Virginia Ragle, an assistant attorney general. The Board also relied on the Voting Rights Act expertise of Charles J. Cooper of Potts, Pittman, Shaw and Trowbridge in Washington, D.C.

All of Alaska is covered under Section 5 of the 1965 Voting Rights Act, as amended in 1982, which requires all election law changes to secure preclearance from the U.S. Department of Justice. The Act applies to Alaska not because of any

---

[4]*Racially Polarized Voting in Alaska*, a study done for the Reapportionment Board, 1991, by Bernard Grofman.

[5]The first Alaskan redistricting in 1961 escaped unchallenged in state court. The redistricting dealt only with a few House districts because the Alaska Senate was based on geography, not population.

[6]Unlike the process in the huge majority of states, the Attorney General in Alaska is appointed by the Governor, is confirmed by the Legislature, and serves at the pleasure of the Governor. Governor Cowper's term expired on noon on December 3, 1990. Draft reapportionment plans were adopted by his reapportionment board on the morning of December 3, 1990. These draft plans were adopted in the absence of population figures from the U.S. Bureau of the Census and these preliminary plans were jettisoned by Governor Hickel's reapportionment board. All public testimony collected by the Cowper board regarding preferred alignments was adopted.

evidence of past racial animus but because turnout was below an arbitrary threshold in areas where English was not the primary language. The 1982 amendments had never been applied to an Alaskan redistricting. In fact, until presented with a revised plan in 1993, no objection had ever been lodged by the U.S. Department of Justice against any redistricting in Alaska.[7] Indeed, no federal court has ever ruled specifically on the constitutionality of any Alaskan redistricting.

Yet, every Alaskan reapportionment had been declared unconstitutional by the State Supreme Court. There were five previous cases going into this round. Despite rigorous analysis of prior court decisions, and great hopes on the part of the Governor and the Reapportionment Board, the 1991 reapportionment met the same fate as every preceding plan: at least some part of the plan was declared unconstitutional by the State Supreme Court (May 1992).

The 1991 Board took some two months to develop priorities for redistricting. Guidelines directed staff on the development of redistricting scenarios. Both the Board's attorney and contract attorneys advised that every effort must be made to protect individuals covered by the Voting Rights Act from avoidable retrogression in their ability to elect candidates of their choice.[8] The Board was urged not to pair incumbents who belonged to a protected race or language group with incumbents who did not belong to such a group. The Board was advised to devise so-called "influence" districts where people protected by the Voting Rights Act constituted at least 25 percent of the population. Despite honest misgivings about the prevalence or even existence of significant racially polarized voting patterns in Alaska, the Board followed that advice with gusto to help ensure approval by Justice and to preserve as many rural districts as possible. The Board, and their legal advisors, simply held out little hope of convincing the Justice Department that Alaska was not subject to the pernicious polarization and discrimination that gave rise to the Voting Rights Act in the first place.[9] The State had successfully bailed out before the 1975 amendments but did not try to bail out in time following the 1982 amendments.

The Board decided to shoot for keeping overall statewide population ine-

---

[7]In 1994 the U.S. Department of Justice objected to House District 36 because it dropped from 55.6 percent Alaska Native voting age population (VAP) to 50.2 percent. The Governor directed the Attorney General to amend the plan to please Justice attorneys. The Attorney General also negotiated a settlement with the lone challenger to the 1994 plan, the Matanuska-Susitna Borough. The settlement eliminated the 23 percent influence the Borough had in a fourth House district and concentrated Borough population in three overpopulated and underrepresented House districts. The Borough insisted on reducing their influence in the legislature in order to place residents only in districts dominated by Borough voters.

[8]How can there be retrogression in the ability of a protected group to elect candidates of their choice in the absence of racially polarized voting by the unprotected majority that might usually ensure the defeat of candidates supported by the protected group? Despite Professor Grofman's analysis, the conclusions of the State Supreme Court and the powerful legislative positions held by Alaska Natives (the only significant protected group in Alaska), Section 5 applies to Alaska and the Department of Justice must be appeased. This can lead to ridiculous micromanagement. At least one subset (Athabascan Indians) of the protected group (Alaska Natives) succeeded in persuading Justice to threaten an objection if a single town of 500 people was not moved from one district to another.

quality among districts to under 2 percent (they later relaxed that standard to 10 percent) while at the same time designing districts avoiding retrogression and respecting individual ethnic and linguistic groups.

The Board held 12 public hearings and incorporated 32 public hearings held by the previous Board. They considered six scenarios for Southeast Alaska; twelve for Rural Alaska; eight for Fairbanks; ten for Anchorage and four for Southcentral Alaska. The Board reviewed in detail three final plans and adopted portions of two.

The final plan included a statewide deviation under 10 percent and an average deviation under 2 percent; the lowest overall and average deviations in state history.[10]

The plan provided for uniform single member districts where each district would elect a single representative and a single senator; the first time in state history that a uniform electoral apportionment was adopted.[11]

The plan maintained the number of Native American majority districts while increasing the percentages of Native Americans in every influence district. This was accomplished despite the drop from 16 percent to 15.6 percent in statewide Native American population. This was the first plan in state history where rural Alaska (where Alaskan Natives are generally in the majority) did not lose at least one seat in the Legislature.[12]

In order to accomplish those ends many Representatives and Senators, both Republican and Democrat, were paired in single-member districts and some towns and boroughs were divided between House or Senate districts. These divisions generated strong opposition from some citizens, towns, boroughs, the State Democratic Party, and five powerful Native American corporations.[13]

---

[9]In the last 20 years not a single unprotected group candidate defeated a protected group candidate as a result of racially polarized for the state legislature. The only instance of racially polarized voting discovered by Professor Grofman's analysis took place in a district with just 18 percent protected group VAP. In 1996, among other examples, an Alaska Native woman was reelected in a House District four percent Alaska Native VAP with 70 percent of the vote. She defeated a white male challenger in the primary. An Alaska Native man defeated two white men and a black man for his party's nomination and went on to defeat an incumbent white woman for the State Senate. The District had 5 percent Alaska Native VAP. An Alaska Native Representative challenged an incumbent Alaska Native State Senator in a District with 25 percent Alaska Native VAP and went on to defeat a white challenger by a wide margin for the open Senate seat.

[10]The Courts gave short shrift to population equality. In *Southeast Conference v. Hickel*, both the Superior Court and Supreme Court used the 16.45 percent deviation allowed in *Mahan v. Howell*, 410 U.S. 315 (1973) as though it was perfectly acceptable in order to satisfy other objectives. Judge Weeks wrote: "The courts have approved deviations of up to 10 percent as a matter of course and up to 16.4 percent with justifications like many that the board ignored." When the Court was through revising the plan, population deviation was 16.33 percent.

[11]Under the preceding reapportionment, the 40 House members had been elected from 14 single and 13 double-member districts while the 20 Senators were elected using five different types of district configurations.

[12] That plan revised under direction from the State Courts eliminated one of two Native majority Senate districts and reduced two influence districts, one to 36 percent from 41 percent and the other from 48 percent to 25 percent.

[13]The cases were consolidated under *Southeast Conference v. Hickel*.

Following the Governor's reapportionment proclamation, the Constitution, Article VI, Section 8, allows just 30 days for filing challenges in superior court. Suits were filed against portions of the plan by the Southeast Conference representing cities in Southeast Alaska protesting division of their communities, the Matanuska-Susitna Borough against unwelcome division of their political subdivision and by the Arctic Slope Regional Corporation and the Tanana Chiefs Conference opposed to pairing Inupiat Eskimo with Athabascan Indians instead of the traditional pairing of Yupik Eskimo with Athabascan Indians. The Yupik Eskimo community, represented by the Fish and Game Fund, filed suit to defend the Governor's plan. The Democratic Party filed suit on procedural grounds that eventually demonstrated mistakes in advertising but whose broad hints of gerrymandering were apparently ignored by the Supreme Court in their decision and were not officially part of either the Superior Court or Supreme Court decisions. Indeed, no party brought charges of partisan gerrymandering before the court although many did not hesitate to imply the worst to the press. In court, Arctic Slope and Tanana Chiefs claimed that local incumbents representing their regions were targeted because of their opposition to the Governor in the Legislature. Pending preclearance, the plan could not be put into effect and little progress was made in state court.

The Board finished their work on June 11, 1991. The Governor proclaimed a plan on September 5, 1991. The plan was submitted to the U.S. Justice Department for preclearance on November 8, 1991 and was reviewed by Justice for some five months before it was precleared on April 10, 1992. It was the first statewide plan in the United States to receive preclearance without objection from Justice following the 1990 census.

The same interests filing suit in state court carried their opposition to the Justice Department. However, the Governor had active allies for his reapportionment before Justice. Native American groups in Alaska were divided. Support for the Governor's plan came from five of the nine Alaska Native legislators and five of the twelve Native Regional Corporations established under the Alaska Native Land Claims Settlement Act of 1971. Opposition to the plan came from the remaining four Alaska Native legislators and from five of the twelve Native Regional Corporations. Two Native Corporations and the Alaska Federation of Natives took no public position.

Representatives of the Governor flew twice to Washington, D.C. to meet with Justice Department officials. More information was requested by Justice on December 31, 1991, and a response from the State was sent back to Washington on February 11, 1992. If the pointed questions of the December 31 Justice letter are any guide, they gave considerable weight to objections raised by the opponents of the Governor's plan.

Nevertheless, after additional information and lobbying by Alaska Natives in support of the Governor's plan, the Justice Department eventually entered no objection to the reapportionment. A Justice Department attorney, Robert Kengle, seemed to be focused on Athabascan Indians and the effect the plan had on their status in a single legislative district. The State countered that (a) the Voting Rights Act did not apply separately to each group of Native Americans in Alaska, and, in any case, (b) the position of Athabascan Indians did not avoidably retrogress under the Governor's plan. They actually increased their statistical advantage. The Athabascan were simply paired with Inupiat Eskimo instead of Yupik Eskimo. While the State did not agree with Mr. Kengle that individual Native American groups had to be considered for purposes of the Voting Rights Act, the Board took individual groups into consideration for socio-economic reasons.

Oddly enough, it was the condition of the Yupik Eskimo and efforts by the Board and Governor to unify the Yupik that led to fierce opposition by Inupiat Eskimo and Athabascan Indian organizations. Traditionally, reapportionment relied on dividing Yupik Eskimo communities along the Western Alaskan coast to round out population for districts otherwise dominated by Inupiat Eskimo to the north and using Yupik Eskimo communities along the Yukon and Kuskokwim Rivers to shore up the underpopulated Interior Alaska where Athabascan Indians predominated.

The 1991 Board united the Yupik into two districts and combined the Inupiat and Athabascan into two. Yupik Eskimo dominated two districts, one district was dominated by Inupiat Eskimo, and one district combined the remaining Inupiat Eskimo population with rural Athabascans. The Athabascans and non-Natives living in the Athabascan region of the new district made up more than 55 percent of that new district population.

Once Justice approved the Governor's plan on April 10, 1992, State litigation resumed in earnest. The original complaints filed in September 1991 did not come to trial until April 16, 1992. After a 16-day trial, a Superior Court Judge from Southeast Alaska issued a harsh 106-page Opinion on May 11, 1992 that rejected nine House districts and invalidated the plan. The Judge, who had no experience with reapportionment, was nonetheless unequivocal in his denunciation of the attitude of members of the Board. He criticized the process the Board followed as inadequate and stated in his Opinion that the chair of the Board was evasive in testifying, sometimes "misleading to the point that only persistence in counsel's questioning brought out the truth."[14]

Alaska includes a military population of approximately 55,000 service personnel and their dependents. This represented 10 percent of the total population recorded by the Census for Alaska. The Superior Court also ruled that the Board failed to take a "hard look" at whether non-resident military could be identified and deducted from the population base for reapportionment.[15] According to earlier rulings by the State Supreme Court, the State Constitution permits the deduc-

---

[14]Superior Court Judge Larry Weeks wrote that the Board Chairman was contradicted by his deposition testimony at least ten times. Interestingly, the Chair of the Reapportionment Board was elected in 1992 to the State House and reelected in 1994 and 1996.

[15]*Southeast Conference v. Hickel.*

tion of non-resident military from the reapportionment base if nonresidents can be identified.

The Governor appealed. The State Supreme Court took ten days to uphold the Superior Court that certain districts violated the State Constitution and reversed Judge Weeks with respect to the population base, ruling instead that the Governor's inclusion of all military and dependents was reasonable.

The Supreme Court stated that the Board and Governor had needlessly sacrificed socio-economic integration and compactness in order to bolster Native American districts and to achieve "excessive" population equality.[16] The Court even managed to find a lack of contiguity. The 1992 Court held that the Board had an affirmative responsibility to apply the "as nearly as practicable" standards for contiguity, compactness, and relative socio-economic integration outlined in Article VI, Section 6 of the State Constitution and further decreed that political subdivisions inherently represented integrated socio-economic areas.[17] The Court insisted that these state constitutional mandates could be sacrificed only when mandated by the Voting Rights Act.

The State Supreme Court reached its conclusion in June, 1992. The Court's decision and remedy so late in the year required—for the first time in state history—canceling some local school board elections and postponement of the statewide primary for three weeks. In a 3-2 decision it also ordered the Superior Court to adopt an interim plan. Rather than remand reapportionment to the Governor, the Court ignored the plain language of the State Constitution which reads:

> Governor Hickel and Attorney General Charles E. Cole were outraged at the usurpation of constitutional authority granted to the Governor and publicly denounced the court, but with elections pending, they participated in the Court's adoption of an interim plan. Ultimately, the 1992 interim plan left some 75 percent of Alaskans in the districts the Governor originally placed them; the Court adopted a revised map prepared and submitted by the Governor.

Was the Court's plan any better? Most people in Southeast Alaska think so. Statewide, the Alaska Native community remained divided. No changes were made to urban Alaska. The Matanuska-Susitna Borough was still divided, although in seven instead of nine districts. The plan adopted by the Court meandered back and forth across highways in rural Alaska for several hundred miles and divided the tiny Lake and Peninsula Borough (population 1,668) in half, separating the people of that Borough into two house and two

---

[16]After the Court was through revising the Governor's plan overall population deviation leaped from 9.2 percent to 16.33 percent, as high as any in the United States.

[17]This innovative ruling left organized boroughs (counties) with preferential status while leaving those communities in rural areas of Alaska not organized into boroughs (some 60 percent of the area of Alaska), apparently requiring a greater burden of proof before their interest in being districted together equaled boroughs. The Constitution simply states that political subdivision boundaries may be considered.

senate districts. This latter result was not required by the Voting Rights Act nor did it adhere to the latest Opinion by the Supreme Court regarding the recently discovered preeminence of Boroughs as perfect representations of socio-economic integration.[18]

Was there any way to avoid this fate for the Governor's plan? Can the Governor and Board in 2001 look for clues in the rulings of the Alaska Supreme Court?

I think not. The 1991 Board attempted to avoid the fate of the 1971 and 1981 boards by following the court's own rules to no avail.[19] The 1992 court reversed or ignored their previous reasoning and conclusions.[20]

Three examples should serve to illustrate this point.

ADAK 1972 and 1992

In 1972 the State Supreme Court's own interim plan decided where to place the naval military base of Adak, which sits some 900 miles out at the western edge of the Aleutian chain. This Court-drawn House district skirted around the rest of the Aleutians (an island chain) for more than 1,100 miles until Adak was finally combined with the City of Kodiak, but not the rest of the Kodiak Borough. Zero evidence of socio-economic integration existed and none was referred to by the Court's Masters who devised the scheme. It is impossible to conceive a district less compact. It resembled a 1,100-mile hose with bulbs of population at both ends. It was contiguous only over more than 1,000 miles of water. It was adopted by the Court.

The 1991 reapportionment board took the isolated military base and aligned it over water (about 1,000 miles) with Southwest Alaska. The obvious Court precedent may have deterred the six plaintiffs who filed suit against portions of the Governor's plan from objecting to this, but it did not deter our imaginative State Supreme Court. Acting on its own motion, *sua sponte*, without so much as a reference to the model of its own 1972 plan,[21] the 1992 Court

---

[18]It was a result of revisions made by Judge Weeks to the plan adopted by his own Masters. He moved a town in the east where people had complained (Cordova) and exchanged them for a town in the north east (Tok) and dividing the Lake and Peninsula Borough. Once Tok was moved and the little Borough divided, people promptly complained. Judge Weeks ignored them. His tinkering serves as excellent evidence of the perplexity in reapportionment and the trials of attempting to accommodate public opinion. People complain largely when something they dislike happens to them. Until it happens they don't have anything to complain about. Where do you draw the line, both literally and figuratively, with public testimony?

[19]During the 1991-92 reapportionment process, the Board carefully reviewed the Court's own prior plans to attempt to discern what it was the Court might find acceptable. The Board applied all previous tests discovered by the Court in the past by which proposed new districts might by measured. Every district proposed by the Reapportionment Board and Governor Hickel had its counterpart in districts previously endorsed or designed by the Court.

[20]The final decision in *Southeast Conference v. Hickel* included yet another new proclamation from the eminent jurists of the State Supreme Court. Perhaps they were a little embarrassed by the similarities between districts designed or approved by them in the past and the new districts adopted by Governor Hickel but declared unconstitutional by the Court. How did they deal with this ticklish problem? The 1992 Court declared that all Court plans were interim in nature and need not necessarily be constitutional.

rejected the pairing of Adak Naval Base over water with the Lower Yukon River area some 800 miles distant, proclaiming such a district "plainly erroneous." This conclusion was reached despite the substantial improvement in the percentage of Native Americans in House and Senate districts and the endorsement of the plan by all three Alaska Native Regional Corporations whose population was affected.

One Iceworm Is Fine, Two Are a Crowd

The 1983 Supreme Court held that a new House district, stretching for some 800 miles, winding its way through islands and up inland waterways from Annette Island in the South, to Yakutat in the north, was socio-economically integrated except for the City of Cordova.[22] This district was described as the "Iceworm" district by the Court. In order to permit such a novel construction— previous districts had centered on communities moving from north to south. To justify the elongated and weaving Iceworm district the 1983 Court stated in their Opinion that they believed all of Southeast Alaska was socio-economically integrated.

The 1991 plan divided the region and some towns in Southeast to create two districts (instead of one) stretching the length of the region in order to unite almost all Native Americans living in Southeast Alaska in two house districts and one senate district. Such districts would ensure political integration of Southeast House districts and enhance Alaska Native voting influence.

However, the 1992 Court ruled that those districts were not socio-economically integrated as nearly as practicable and ruled them unconstitutional. What is incredible is that the 1983 court admitted that dividing the Southeastern region of Alaska into districts North and South would lead to greater socio-economic integration but elected to defer to the Governor and his Board who desired to maximize Alaska Native influence. This 1981 effort to maximize was not a result of a Justice Department objection, nor was it to avoid retrogression, and the Court admitted it was not required by the Voting Rights Act. Yet the 1983 court concluded a single Iceworm was fine as long as it was confined to Southeast Alaska. They ruled that a district not as socio-economically integrated as practicable was within the proper discretion of the Governor. The 1992 Court proclaimed the opposite. Now the constitution was reinterpreted to require adherence to borough boundaries and to maximize socio-economic integration! Yet, except for one member, the membership of the Court was identical.[23]

---

[21] In the written decision that followed six months later the Court decreed that since Court plans were interim in nature, they did not have to be constitutional. *Southeast Conference v. Hickel.*

[22] *Carpenter v. Hammond*

[23] The new member had been the Superior Court judge who ruled the whole 1981 plan constitutional and had been overruled by the State Supreme Court.

Borough Busters, That Was Then, This Is Now

In 1982, the Kenai Peninsula Borough population justified 1.5 Senate and 3 House districts. However, the 1984 revised plan divided the Kenai Peninsula Borough into four House districts and three Senate districts. The local government challenged the 1984 plan arguing that their right to equal representation was violated. The 1987 Court dismissed their claim utterly.

In 1992, the Matanuska-Susitna Borough population justified just under 1.5 Senate and three House districts. It was, and is, the fastest growing area in Alaska. The 1992 plan divided the Matanuska-Susitna Borough[24] (Mat-Su) into five House districts and four Senate districts. In the Governor's plan, Mat-Su residents were the majority in two House seats, held 44 and 48 percent of the population in two more, and made up 20 percent in a fifth. In the Senate, the people of the Mat-Su made up a solid 72 percent in one district, 40 percent in a second, 24 percent in a third and 10 percent in a fourth.

The 1987 Court, ruling on the revised 1984 plan, concluded that they should not draw a fine line with respect to whether areas are socio-economically integrated as nearly as practicable. The Court found that the Nikiski portion of the Kenai Peninsula Borough was socio-economically integrated with Anchorage despite the fact that the interaction of North Kenai with South Anchorage is compromised by being 100 miles apart by road, sharing no common services, looking to different daily newspapers and communities where only a very few residents commute.[25]

That was then, this is now. The 1992 Court concluded that Wasilla is not socio-economically integrated as nearly as practicable with Eagle River. This comic conclusion is made notwithstanding the fact that these communities are both members of the same telephone and electric cooperatives, are less than 25 miles apart, share only one daily paper; moreover, up to 40 percent of each community's workforce commutes together into Anchorage on a daily basis.

Every member of the Court who participated in the 1987 ruling participated in 1992. During the intervening five years the Court apparently discovered that Boroughs were actually ideal socio-economic integrated units and that to divide a borough any more than absolutely necessary was an obvious violation of the constitution.[26] The 1992 Court ruled that these 1992 Matanuska-Susitna districts violated the state constitutional provisions mandating socio-economically integrated districts.[27]

The 1992 Court trotted out the description the delegates to the state constitutional convention gave to their concept of socio-economic integration: [W]here

---

[24]The fastest growing Borough in Alaska during the 1980s and 1990s according to the U.S. Census and the Alaska Department of Labor.

[25]*Kenai Peninsula Borough v. State*

[26]How this Opinion squared with the needless division of the Lake and Peninsula Borough (population 1,668) designed by Judge Weeks and adopted by the Supreme Court remains a mystery. The Governor's final plan (March 1994) reunited the tiny Borough.

[27]Interestingly, the Court's own Masters and the final plan adopted by the Governor maintained a Wasilla-Eagle River House District.

people live together and work together and earn their living together, where people do that, they should be logically grouped that way. A socio-economic unit is described as: "an economic unit inhabited by people. In other words, the stress is placed on the canton idea, a group of people living within a geographic unit, following if possible, similar economic pursuits.[28]

The 1992 Court announced that all boroughs (counties, municipalities) inherently represented integrated socio-economic units, the antiquity or size of the borough notwithstanding. However, the Matansuka-Susitna Borough was compelled by the Legislature in 1965 to organize as a local government. The Borough is the size of West Virginia and was simply modeled after an existing state legislative district. As for being a perfect socio-economic ideal, in the last thirty years, the Borough has contracted once and sought expansion at least twice.[29]

Some Neighbors Are More Socio-economically Integrated Than Others

The 1992 Court went on to declare a new constitutional principle: that it was unconstitutional for any political subdivision of the state to be divided so that excess population went in more adjoining districts than necessary.

Obviously, this could not have been the understanding of the 1991 Board, because no plan had ever been designed with that in mind. Indeed, the Constitution merely states that the Reapportionment Board may consider political subdivisions while drawing districts but gives them no greater weight. On the contrary, the Board determined that equal population, enhancement of the numbers of people protected by the Voting Rights Act, and uniform legislative representation were the primary goals superior to adhering to political subdivision boundaries. Naively, the Board believed the plain constitutional language, prior rulings by the Court, and the Court's own examples when they took a direct hand in drawing districts were safe guides.

For example, the 1992 Court writes:

> It is axiomatic that a district composed wholly of land belonging to a single borough is adequately integrated....We recognize that it may be necessary to divide a borough so that its excess population is allocated to a district situated elsewhere. However, where possible, all of a municipality's excess population should go to one other district in order to maximize effective representation of the excess group. This result is compelled not only by the article VI, section 6 requirements, but also by the state equal protection clause which guarantees the right to proportional geographic representation.[30]

While this constitutional principle may be "axiomatic," the 1987 Court approved a plan dividing the Kenai Peninsula Borough in five House seats and three Senate seats.

---

[28] Minutes of the Alaska Constitutional Convention, 3 PACC 1873 (January 12, 1956).

[29] In 1996, the Alaska Local Boundary Commission recommended to the Legislature the approval of an application by northeastern residents seeking to break away from the Matanuska-Susitna Borough.

[30] Kenai 1352, 1369 and 1372-73 and Southeast Conference, p.29.

Once again, the 1992 Court ignored several of its own previous rulings and discovered heretofore unobserved state constitutional standards. Every decade, without prejudice toward whether the Governor was Democrat, Republican or Alaskan Independence, the Court has found the Governor's plan unconstitutional. In each case the Court has applied heretofore undiscovered rules to justify judicial interloping.

Reviewing Alaska history, we find that the State Supreme Court has substituted its own judgment for Governors Egan and Hickel, compelled Governor's Egan and Hammond to amend their plans, and reprimanded Governor Sheffield by declaring his plan unconstitutional.[31]

The Governor proclaimed a new reapportionment on March 25, 1994. No suits were filed protesting the plan during the 30-day period allowed by the state constitution. It is preposterous to suggest that no suit was filed because Governor Hickel managed to please everyone. Indeed, in 1995 a Yupik Eskimo group had dropped a case pending in federal court and citizens from Nenana to Glennallen were outraged that there were no suits in state court. Even in the election for Governor in 1994, no party or individual filed suit even on the hope that a new Governor might have an opportunity to craft a plan more to their liking. It is reasonable to surmise that the absence of a state challenge was less because the Democratic Party was delighted with the Governor's plan than because everyone recognized the futility of a second round victory in state court. What else can this be due to other than the predictability of our State Supreme Court?

My conclusion is that the State Supreme Court believes every Governor will use reapportionment to create districts that benefit their political agenda, whether party oriented or incumbent oriented. Consequently, the Court believes only by declaring a plan unconstitutional can they exercise restraint on the unbridled political maneuvering of the Governor.

The Governor has absolute authority to reapportion through a reapportionment board that serves at his pleasure. However, the first plan of any governor will be declared unconstitutional by the State Supreme Court. What empirical evidence exists is irrefutable. No effort to read past decisions will spare even the most apolitical Governor or Board from the censure of the Court. The perverse effect of this judicial strategy eliminates whatever meager incentive exists for a governor to practice restraint, work to compromise, or to any real degree rein in political manipulation during reapportionment, round one. Such is the legacy of Alaska's predictably unpredictable reapportionment process.

---

[31]The 1987 Court found a senate district unconstitutional, concluding that the design of one of the multi-member Senate districts intentionally discriminated against the people of Anchorage and violated their right to equal protection under the Alaska Constitution. In what stands out as a singularly bizarre action the 1987 Court proclaimed that their declaration that the district was unconstitutional was remedy enough. Kenai 1373.

REAPPORTIONMENT WARS:
Party, Race, and Redistricting In California, 1971-1992[1]

Morgan Kousser

I. INTRODUCTION: THE TEN YEARS' WAR

THE 1980S WAS THE DECADE OF REAPPORTIONMENT IN CALIFORNIA POLITICS. Ever since 1910, when Los Angeles passed San Francisco in population and the first urban-rural and sectional conflict over redistricting bitterly divided the state's legislature, the issue has disrupted politics every ten years. (Wilkening, 1977.) But never before has it lasted for the entire decade, coloring political events nationally as well as locally and spilling over into the next reapportionment cycle. From 1981 to 1991, Republicans contended that if only they could obtain a "fair" reapportionment through a court or commission, they would control the congressional delegation and that of the lower house of the state legislature. Attempting to overturn what they considered partisan gerrymanders, the GOP sponsored seven largely unsuccessful referenda on the subject from 1982 to 1990 and flirted with leaders of minority groups, offering them safely "packed" seats at the expense of Anglo Democrats.

In 1991-92, the Republicans, led by newly elected Gov. Pete Wilson, finally got their wish, adamantly refusing to compromise or even negotiate seriously with the Democratic majority in the legislature and thereby insuring that their partisan allies on the state's courts would superintend the drawing of the new districts. Although Democrats and, to a lesser extent, Latino groups were displeased with the resulting boundaries, Republicans were jubilant. Nonetheless, Democrats carried the 1992 elections for the state Assembly and Senate and for Congress by almost exactly the same margins as with the old "gerrymandered" lines of the 1980s. These results called into question the dogma held so unquestion-

---

[1] Micah Altman, Tim Hodson, Daniel Hays Lowenstein, and Jonathan Steinberg made this a better paper with their helpful comments on earlier drafts. Most writers on California reapportionment have been participants in the process. E.g., Baker, 1962; Cain, 1984; Hinderaker and Waters, 1952; Lowell and Craigie, 1985; Quinn, 1981 and 1984; Wilkening, 1977. Although I have never helped to draw a district, I did serve as an expert witness for most of the members of the Democratic congressional delegation in an unsuccessful federal court challenge to the 1991 Special Masters' Plan.

ingly during the 1980s by political elites of both parties in the state that the exact placement of district lines was the key to political control of the state.[2] Although the fortunes of individual politicians can often be dramatically affected by redistricting, it may be much more difficult, at least in a state as large and complex as California, to transform the statewide results by line-drawing.

This chapter reviews the extraordinarily complicated and conflicted course of redistricting in California from the 1970s through the 1990s and applies new and revealing measures of the partisan effects of redistricting to determine the significance of redistricting in changing the balance of political power in the state.[3] Using evidence not only from plans that were adopted, but from those that were rejected, it simulates the outcomes in actual elections under a range of alternative plans. It gives explicit, easily replicable answers to the question of how election outcomes would have differed if other redistricting schemes had been chosen. In particular, it assesses the effect of the so-called "Burton gerrymander" of congressional seats in the 1980s, which has been credited with "derailing the Reagan Revolution" in national politics. (Quinn, 1984, introduction, 1.)

A second purpose of the chapter is to assess the importance for political parties and ethnic minority groups of the constraints on redistricting imposed by national, legal, and constitutional standards. Is it safe now to withdraw Congress and the federal courts from the "political thicket" of redistricting, except perhaps to protect the rights of allegedly beleaguered Anglo majorities, as some people claim?[4] A quick glance at reapportionment politics in the period from 1920 through 1965 in California suggests how important judicial intervention has been in the past. The state's 1879 constitution mandated reapportionment once a decade and required that districts contain equal numbers of people. Nevertheless, the urban-rural conflict in the increasingly urbanized state of the 1920s prevented agreement over redistricting in the 1921, 1923, and 1925 legislatures, and in 1926, the Farm Bureau Federation led a referendum campaign to malapportion the state senate by constitutional amendment. No county could have more than one state senator, and not more than three counties could compose a state senate district. By 1960, the ratio of the population of the largest to the smallest senate district was 422:1. (Baker, 1962, 51.) Lobbyists, personified by the notorious Artie Samish (Samish and Thomas, 1971), dictated many of the state's policies, while the Republican party and the reactionary urban press, led by the *Los Ange-*

---

[2]For similar questioning about the 1950s and 60s in California, see Way, 1962, 261, and Quinn 1984, ch.1,40; and for other states, Basehart and Comer, 1991.

[3]As Tim Hodson pointed out in a personal communication, the stories might have been somewhat different if I had included more information on the considerably less partisan state senate, with its longer terms and, at least recently, higher proportion of experienced members. The problem is that because numbers of senate districts often get rearranged during redistricting and four-year terms may overlap the redistricting year, some members' terms may be extended, in effect, to six years, making it very difficult to measure the effect of redistricting systematically.

[4] This is the implication of the views of U.S. Supreme Court Justices Clarence Thomas and Antonin Scalia, putting together their concurrence in *Holder* v. *Hall*, 114 S.Ct. 2581 (1994) and their assent to *Miller* v. *Johnson*, 115 S.Ct. 2475 (1995).

les Times, denounced any attempt to overturn the grossly unequal apportionment rules for the senate as a plot by "un-American," communist-dominated unions to impose "boss rule" on the state and to tax worthy farmers to provide social welfare schemes for poor city-dwellers. (Barclay, 1951; Hinderaker and Waters, 1952). Initiative measures to decrease the malapportionment failed in 1928, 1948, 1960, and 1962. (Baker, 1962; Quinn, 1981.) Naturally, because the vast majority of politically active Latinos and African-Americans lived in the cities, there were no minority state senators, although Los Angeles and Oakland did elect a string of black representatives to the Assembly. It was only after the equal state apportionment case of *Reynolds* v. *Sims* (377 U.S. 533) in 1964 that urban areas received their fair numbers of representatives and that it became possible to elect members of minority groups to the state senate.

Such Supreme Court decisions not only guarded democracy in general, they also constrained the ability of those who drew district lines to distort the results by party or other group. If there were no limit to the size of districts, it would be simple enough to pack opposing partisans into a few districts and create the maximum number of seats for one's own party, faction, or race. A population equality requirement, however, imposed a severe constraint on the ability of redistricters to manipulate outcomes. (Quinn, 1984, Ch. 1, 20-32 gives examples of the pre-*Reynolds* situation.) Moreover, the 1965 Voting Rights Act and its subsequent expansion by Congress and the courts forced state officials to pay special attention to the impact of line-drawing on the ability of members of minority groups to elect candidates of their choice, and by the 1990s, some attempted to extend interpretations of the Act to safeguard the ability to *influence* the election of candidates.

A third goal of the chapter is to trace the evolution of racial and partisan representation in the state and the connection between them. Which party (if either of them) has been more sympathetic to the claims of ethnic minorities and how has the level and expression of sympathy changed over time? How have "nonpartisan" or at least non-legislative redistricting institutions treated minorities? Would ethnic minorities be better off in the future if reapportionment were removed from legislative control?

Fourth, how have court-ordered and partisan plans differed? This question assumes particular importance because of the strong likelihood of deadlock and litigation in redistricting in California and throughout the country in the post-millennial redistrictings. Are ethnic minorities better off trusting the courts than the legislature? Have court-ordered plans in the past been neutral in their effects on political parties?

The nation's most heavily populated and culturally diverse state, California, has been the focal point of conflict over social and economic policy since the 1960s—from higher education policy to tax limitation to welfare "reform" to prison building to immigration restriction to affirmative action. But in many ways, the centerpiece of its political battles has been redistricting, an amazingly expensive, seemingly almost continuous conflict that fostered or blighted political careers and, some have said, strongly affected public policy for the nation. What can we learn from the Golden State's reapportionment wars?

II. THE 1970S: MINORITIES, MAJORITIES, AND MASTERS

A. A "Balanced and Representative Plan"

The reapportionment struggle of the 1970s so closely paralleled and so directly affected that of the 1990s that the earlier battle deserves detailed attention here. Despite a pro-Democratic redistricting in 1965, when the state faced up to the strict equal population standards that federal courts had imposed after *Baker* v. *Carr*, Republicans gained a slight majority in the lower house, the Assembly, in the 1968 election. Assuming that his party would retain control in 1970, and would therefore be able to design a partisan reapportionment, Rep. Jerry Lewis of the Elections and Constitutional Amendments Committee drafted a memo outlining Republican plans. "In my judgment," he proclaimed, "our number one criteria [sic] should be a program designed to establish districts in California that will elect the highest possible number of Republicans to the State Legislature and the House of Representatives. A second item for consideration is to include in the plan Democrat [sic] districts with sizable majority [sic] for those who are measured to be the 'least effective members' of the minority party....I believe we have an unusually good opportunity to develop a 'balanced and representative plan' which in reality is totally designed for partisan purposes." [5] Unfortunately for the GOP, the party lost its Assembly majority in the 1970 elections, and Democrats retained a slim majority in the State Senate. To add mortification to defeat, Lewis's revealing memo was left in the Committee files when the Democrats took over. When Lewis gave an especially sanctimonious speech on the floor denouncing the Democrats for engaging in what he termed partisan gerrymandering, Democratic Speaker Bob Moretti whipped out the memo, quoting the pertinent passages, no doubt to Democratic guffaws and Republican chagrin.[6] In fact, both parties viewed reapportionment as primarily a partisan battle—the Democrats were just a bit more open about it.

With Ronald Reagan in the governor's chair and thin Democratic majorities in both houses of the legislature and in the congressional delegation, the 1971 redistricting should have been a compromise, an incumbent gerrymander that did not overly advantage or disadvantage either party. It nearly happened that way. In late 1971, Governor Reagan, the Democratic state legislative majority, and the 38 incumbent members of Congress from both parties[7] had agreed on boundaries for the congressional and State Senate seats and had just settled on a redistricting of

---

[5]Reproduced in Lowenstein, 1972, vol. II, Exhibit E, and quoted in Brown and Lowenstein, 1990, 67-68.

[6]Jerry Gillam, "Assembly Approves Redistricting Plan; Court Test Expected," *Los Angeles Times*, Nov. 24, 1971, 3.

the State Assembly when a millionaire Anglo Republican upset a Latino Democrat in a special election. Attracting state and national attention in his effort to become the third Latino in the Assembly, Richard Alatorre was a solid favorite to carry a heavily Democratic, ethnically and culturally diverse district in Los Angeles. Alatorre was derailed, Democrats charged, by a series of "dirty tricks" in a West Coast Watergate campaign managed by the future Los Angeles county chairman of the "Committee to Reelect the President"—i.e., Richard Nixon. (Kousser, 1991, 655-56).

Having won the district, Republicans demanded that it be redrawn to favor the Republican victor. (Waxman, 1972.) Outraged Democrats refused, and the deal collapsed when Gov. Reagan refused to pledge to endorse agreements negotiated by Republicans in the legislature. After a stormy confrontation between Reagan and the Republican legislative caucus, Democrats passed their own redistricting bill for the Assembly and the bipartisan bills for the other two bodies on Dec. 20, 1971, Reagan immediately vetoed all of them, and power passed to the State Supreme Court.[8] Thus, the 20-year partisan battle over reapportionment in California was set off when an attempt by Democrats to increase ethnic minority representation was blocked by Republicans. Partisan and ethnic factors in California reapportionment are inseparably intertwined.

Attorneys representing Latinos and African-Americans filed briefs asking the California Supreme Court to reject the legislative plans as ethnically discriminatory, claiming that they protected Anglo incumbents, rather than creating more districts where members of minority groups would have a chance to elect candidates of their choice. Democrats pointed to increased minority opportunities in their original plans, criticized the proposed Republican plans for endangering four of the seven currently minority-held seats in the Assembly, and underlined the extreme partisan nature of the compact-looking Republican plan, which paired or put in marginal seats nearly every Democratic leader in both houses of the legislature. Although Republicans claimed to be creating three new "minority districts," two of them considerably overlapped areas then represented by major Democratic incumbents, pointedly forcing Democrats to choose between Anglo leaders and minority challengers. (Lowenstein, 1972; D'Agostino, 1972; Quinn, 1984, ch. 4, 9-10.) In a separate brief, Republican State Controller Houston Flournoy asked the court to adopt the Republican plans, which the legislature had voted down, on the grounds that they provided for more competitive districts.[9] Brushing aside all of these arguments without so much as a comment, the high court quickly and unanimously issued a ruling that merely carried the redistricting battle over until

---

[7]A court-ordered, but not court-designed plan in 1967 had produced a bipartisan incumbent gerrymander for congressional seats. (Mayhew, 1971, 282.)

[8]William Endicott, "Reapportionment Plan Favoring GOP Studied," *Los Angeles Times*, Jan. 5, 1972, I-24 ; "Assembly Democrats Reject Remapping Bid," *ibid.*, Jan. 6, 1972, I-2; Richard Bergholz, "32 Congressmen Petition Court to Overrule Redistricting Veto," *ibid.*, Jan. 7, 1972, I-3; Quinn, 1984, ch. 4, 17-20.

after the 1972 elections. (*Legislature* v. *Reinecke*, 10 Cal. 3d 396 (1973).)

Chief Justice Donald Wright, a Reagan appointee, began by jettisoning the only redistricting commission that California has ever had. One portion of the 1926 Farm Bureau Federation Amendment had provided for a Reapportionment Commission composed of certain statewide elected officials, which was to act if the legislature and the governor could not agree on a reapportionment plan. Although the rest of the 1926 Amendment had previously been declared contrary to the U.S. Constitution's Equal Protection Clause (*Silver* v. *Brown*, 63 Cal.2d 270 (1965)), it was not absolutely clear whether the Commission was so inter- twined with the Senate apportionment scheme that it had to die, as well. Reason- ing that the 1926 plan was adopted in a referendum as part of a coherent whole, the court ruled that the Commission had to follow the malapportioned Senate into oblivion. It is significant to note that while the case was pending in the Supreme Court, the Republican-dominated Commission was focusing on a plan drafted by Alan Heslop and Thomas Hofeller, the Republicans' chief political consultants on reapportionment, that, the *Los Angeles Times* opined, "would wipe out the Democratic majority in both the Senate and Assembly."[10]

Because the state's population gains entitled it to five more members of Con- gress than it had had in the 1960s, the court had to decide whether to adopt the legislature's proposed congressional lines temporarily, to use the lines drawn in 1967 and elect the extra five members of Congress at-large (as some Republicans proposed), or to draw districts itself. Operating under a February 23 deadline for candidates qualifying for the June 1972 primaries, the court ruled on Jan. 18, one day after the final briefs were due in the case and less than a month after Reagan's veto, that it had no time to draw districts itself and provide for public comment on them. It rejected statewide at-large elections because they would burden candi- dates with massive expenses and confuse voters by offering them choices for too many offices. Since all 38 incumbent congresspersons had endorsed the legisla- ture's bipartisan plan, the court did, too.[11]

Despite uneven population growth that seriously unbalanced the populations across districts, the court ruled that the 1972 State Assembly and Senate elections

---

[9]"Minority Groups Ask for Rejection of Bills," *Los Angeles Times*, Jan. 18, 1972, I-18 ; "High Court Asked to Void Democrats' Redistricting Bills," *ibid.*, I-3. Nothing in state or federal law explic- itly favors competitive districts. Regression estimates by methods detailed in Kousser, 1995a, show that had the Republican plan been in effect in 1972, Democrats would probably have won 46 (out of 80) seats in the Assembly, rather than the 51 that they actually carried under the old 1965 lines. Under the Masters' Plan, Democrats would have won only 42 races in 1972. After the extraordinary registra- tion and behavioral shifts in a Democratic direction in 1973-74, all of the plans would have provided for huge Democratic majorities, the Republican plan protecting the most Republican seats, 28.

[10]William Endicott, "Reapportionment Plan Favoring GOP Studied," *Los Angeles Times*, Jan. 5, 1972, I-24; Quinn, 1984, ch. 4, 8. Hofeller had drawn the basic plans that the Republicans had pre- sented in the legislature. Controller Flournoy, who advocated the Republican plans before the Supreme Court, was a member of the Reapportionment Commission.

[11]Glazer et al., 1987, 694-97, find that California was one of only two states in the country in which there was a significant partisan congressional gerrymander in 1970-72. Democrats, they believe, gained about one seat by it.

would be held under the same arrangement as in 1970. Democrats, whose districts had generally lost population or gained less than the more suburbanized Republicans during the 1960s, were satisfied with this ruling, and the Republicans could at least solace themselves with the fact that the court had rejected the Democratic legislature's proposals. Finally, the court gave the legislature further time to cut a deal that would go into effect for the 1974 elections. Otherwise, it would appoint three Appeals Court judges as "special masters" and come up with a program of its own.

Republican Lt. Gov. Ed Reinecke, a rather taciturn member of the now moribund Reapportionment Commission and a man with no previous or subsequent reputation for special solicitude toward minority groups, comically overreacted to the court's opinion. It was the "most shocking instance of poor logic and bad judgment on the part of the Supreme Court I've ever seen in my existence...a total copout." The legislature, he declared, had "fragmented" minority communities "for the purpose of perpetuating the liberal Caucasians in office....this is an example of why the people of this country as well as this state took to the streets. They saw there was no relief by working within the system. In fact I must say that today I would join them."[12] While avoiding Reinecke's graphically ludicrous hyperbole, Governor Ronald Reagan no doubt evoked similar hilarity in Sacramento watering holes with his comment that "There is only one way to do reapportionment—feed into the computer all of the factors except political registration. That should not be a part of it." Democrats claimed that the Republican plans would have overturned their majority in the Assembly and guaranteed Republican dominance for a decade.[13]

The legislature then somewhat desultorily resumed its effort at a compromise, the serious action taking place in the closely divided Senate, in which Democrats enjoyed a bare two-seat majority. (See Table 1.) In the 1971 plan, Elections and Reapportionment Committee chairman Mervyn Dymally, the only African-American in the Senate, had solidified his own district, bolstered the black population of a district then represented by an Anglo Democrat, offering blacks the possibility of doubling their numbers in the Senate during the coming years, and created a district centered in East Los Angeles that was designed to elect the first Latino to the Senate since 1911.[14] After the Supreme Court decision, the Republicans and nearly half of the Democrats, led by conservative Democrat George Zenovich of Fresno and Republican John Harmer of Glendale, proposed a new alignment that moved Dymally's district east, into the heavily Latino area of East Los Angeles, and reduced the black per-

---

[12]Tom Goff, "Reagan, Reinecke Denounce Court; Legislative Leaders Praise Action," *Los Angeles Times*, Jan. 19, 1972, I-14.

[13]Tom Goff, "Governor Urges Redistricting Plan Without Partisan Politics," *Los Angeles Times*, Jan. 21, 1972, I-3.

[14]Dymally called increased Latino representation "the most pressing political business in California." Quoted in Wilkening, 1977, 249.

centage of the second district that Dymally had drawn from 52% to 27%. The scheme effectively capped combined black and Latino representation in the Senate at one and potentially pitted Dymally against ambitious Latinos in the remaining district. Three Republican Senators stalked out of an Elections and Reapportionment Committee meeting when Herman Sillas, the Chairman of the California Advisory Committee to the U.S. Commission on Civil Rights, charged that the plan was "fathered by racism and nurtured by hate and fear." Before he left, John Harmer denounced the Mexican-American Sillas as "a discredit to his people."[15] Eventually, Zenovich and Harmer strung together a district stretching east from East Los Angeles through Orange and Riverside counties, finally terminating in San Bernardino. Uncharacteristically disregarding political reality, Harmer termed this a "Mexican-American district" despite the fact that it was only 47% Spanish-surnamed in population and no doubt much less in registered voters.[16]

TABLE 1. The Partisan Balance among Legislators in California, 1970-94 Elections

Election	Assembly		Senate		Congress	
Year	D	R	D	R	D	R
1970	43	37	21	19	20	18
72	51	29	22	18	23	20
74	55	25	25	15	28	15
76	57	23	26	14	29	14
78	50	30	26	14	26	17
80	47	33	21	19	22	21
82	48	32	23	17	28	17
84	47	33	25	15	27	18
86	44	36	24	15*	27	18
88	47	33	24	15*	27	18
90	48	32	24	13**	30	19
92	48	32	22	13**	30	22
94	39	41	21	17***	27	25

*One independent
**Two Independents and three vacancies
***Three Independents
Source: *California Journal*, selected issues, 1970-94

[15]Jerry Gillam, "Reapportionment Plan Favoring Democrats Gains in Assembly," *Los Angeles Times*, Feb. 16, 1973, I-3; "3 GOP State Senators Walk Out of Redistricting Hearing," *ibid.*, Feb. 9. 1973, I-3; Herman Sillas, "Dear State Senators, Whatever Happened to East Los Angeles? (It's Missing)," *ibid.*, Feb. 21, 1973, II-7. The quoted phrase is as reported by Sillas.

[16]"Senators Deadlock on Latin Districting Plan," Los Angeles Times, Mar. 23, 1972, I-2; "Senate Panel 'Packed' in Surprise Maneuver," ibid., Mar. 29, 1972, I-21; Tom Goff, "'Bipartisan' Redistricting Plan OK'd by State Senate 25 to 13," ibid., May 24, 1973, I-3; Lowenstein 1972, I, 14-15.

B. The Masters' Plan: "Flagrant Democratic Gerrymandering"?

The Assembly deadlocked until the State Supreme Court appointment of three Special Masters in May 1973 pressured the lower house into passing a bipartisan plan which, despite overwhelming support from incumbents of both parties, was vetoed (again) by Gov. Reagan.[17] The three Masters were all retired Anglo judges, two Democrats, Harold F. Collins of Los Angeles and Alvin E. Weinberger of San Francisco, and one Republican, Martin J. Coughlin of Los Angeles. All had been appointed to their highest judicial positions by Democratic Governor Pat Brown, though two had originally been selected for judgeships by Republican Governor Earl Warren. (California Journal, 1973.) No one seems to have noted publicly the absence of any minorities or women on the panel. Because of past discrimination, of course, there were few or no retired black, Latino, or female judges at the time. In hearings before the Masters, however, representatives of black, Latino, and women's groups denounced the revised legislative plans as incumbent gerrymanders and urged more attention to minority groups and less to incumbents, especially in the Senate.[18]

Unveiled in September 1973, the plans, which were actually drawn by the Masters' staffers, law professor Paul McKaskle and political scientist Gordon Baker, appeared likely to decimate incumbents, especially in the Senate, placing the homes of 29 members of the Assembly (18 Democrats and 11 Republicans) and 18 Senators (10 Democrats and 8 Republicans) in districts that contained at least one other incumbent. (Wilkening, 1977, 401-02.) They also substantially increased the possibilities for minorities in the Senate, returning, in effect, to Dymally's proposed configuration in Los Angeles and securing recently won Assembly seats for blacks and Latinos.[19] (See Table 2.) Popular accounts seemed to indicate that the Masters' plans also improved the opportunities for ethnic minorities in the other two bodies. "Mexican Americans and blacks are the winners and long-entrenched incumbent legislators are the losers in a state Supreme Court-sponsored reapportionment that could make major changes in California politics," began the lead story in the *Los Angeles Times*. Herman Sillas exuberantly announced "It's a great day," while Stephen Reinhardt, vice chairman of the

---

[17]"The Job of Reapportionment," *Los Angeles Times*, Nov. 13, 1972, II-8; "Jerry Gillam, "Assembly Remapping Plan Shelved by Democrats; GOP Lies Charged," *ibid.*, Mar. 9, 1973, I-3; "Pact Near on Redistricting of Assembly," *ibid.*, May 11, 1973, I-28; Tom Goff, "Assembly Redistricting Bill OK Seen by Moretti," *ibid.*, May 19, 1973, I-3; Jerry Gillam, "Assembly Approves Reapportionment Proposal 63 to 12," *ibid.*, May 18, 1973, I-1; "Reagan Urged to Veto Bill on Redistricting," *ibid.*, May 26, 1973, I-22; Jerry Gillam, "Assembly Reapportion Plan Hit by Veto Threat," *ibid.*, June 13, 1973, II-1; Gillam, "Last-Chance Reapportionment Plan Given to Reagan; Veto Expected," *ibid.*, June 15, 1973, I-3; Tom Goff, "State Reapportionment Plan Vetoed by Reagan," *ibid.*, June 28, 1973, II-1; "Senate Democrats Fail to Override Reagan's Veto of Redistricting Bill," *ibid.*, June 29, 1973, I-3; *California Journal 1972.*

[18]Richard Bergholz, "State Supreme Court Preparing Its Own Reapportionment Plan," *Los Angeles Times*, June 19, 1973, II-1.

[19]Daryl Lembke, "Panel Submits Remapping Plan to California Supreme Court," *Los Angeles Times*, Sept. 1, 1973, I-1.

California state advisory committee to the U.S. Commission on Civil Rights, called the plan "outstanding, particularly because it attempts to provide more representation for racial minorities." Editorially, the *Times* announced that "The recommendations would end the practice of gerrymandering Mexican-Americans, blacks and other minorities into ethnic voting pockets in order to dilute their political effectiveness....The masters' plan is particularly attractive because it redresses the wrong done for so long to Mexican-Americans and other minorities."[20] In fact, African-Americans had increased their representation in the Assembly in 1972 from five to six, and Latinos, from two to five, and that election produced a second black Member of Congress, as well. (*California Journal*, 1972a.) In the Senate and in the Congress, the McKaskle boundaries were more favorable to minorities than the bipartisan lines drawn by the 1973 legislature had been, although in the Assembly, the number of members of minority groups elected actually decreased after the 1974 election, as Ray Gonzales of Bakersfield went down to defeat.[21]

TABLE 2. Ethnic Minority Legislators in California, 1970-1994

ELECTION	ASSEMBLY			SENATE			CONGRESS		
YEAR	B	L	A	B	L	A	B	L	A
1970	5	2	1	1	0	1	1	1	0
72	6	5	1	1	0	1	2	1	0
74	6	4	1	2	2	1	3	1	1
76	6	4	1	2	2	1	3	1	1
78	6	3	1	2	3	1	3	1	1
80	5	4	0	2	3	0	4	1	2
82	6	4	0	2	3	0	4	3	2
84	6	4	0	2	3	0	4	1	2
86	6	4	0	2	3	0	4	3	2
88	7	4	0	2	3	0	4	3	2
90	7	4	0	2	3	0	4	3	2
92	7	7	1	2	3	0	4	4	3
94	7	9	1	2	4	00	4	4	3

Source: *California Journal*, selected issues, 1970-94, and Professor Fernando Guerrera, personal communication, June 22, 1993.

The partisan consequences of the McKaskle-Baker plan were even less clear. Apparently a glance at 1970 registration totals and the numbers of the new districts

---

[20]Bill Boyarsky, "Redistricting Plan: New Faces in '74," *Los Angeles Times*, Sept. 3, 1973, I-1; Daryl Lembke, "High Court Hears Complaints on Computerized Remap Plan," *ibid.*, Oct. 31, 1973, I-3; "Finally: Sensible Reapportionment," *ibid.*, Oct. 30, 1973, II-6.

[21]A systematic comparison of the "Spanish heritage" population in the congressional districts drawn by the Democrats and the Masters indicates no substantial differences. The Masters packed Latinos into Edward Roybal's district, the only one that elected a Latino before 1982, leaving slightly smaller populations to influence surrounding districts than the Democrats provided. Thus, the Democrats drew three districts in which the population was 35% Latino or more, and two more in which the proportion was 25%, while McKaskle drew only two over 35% and one more that was 26%. In practical political terms, there was little difference between the two plans. I have not located ethnic percentages for voters in Senate or Assembly districts.

that would have been carried by the 1970 candidates for Governor and U.S. Senator[22] convinced the Masters and their staff that their plan was "neither politically unfair nor unfair to incumbents, but may result in fewer 'safe seats' and more 'competitive seats'." Yet seven years later, former Democratic Assembly Speaker Jesse Unruh remarked that "There was a hell of a lot more flagrant Democratic gerrymandering (in the court plan) than I ever would have had the guts to do in my most arrogant moment."[23] Blessed with less hindsight, the Speaker in 1973, Bob Moretti, predicted that Democrats would win 45 to 49 of the 80 Assembly seats under the proposal, while GOP Assembly Floor Leader Bob Beverly thought it gave Republicans a good chance to take control of the body. Democratic Congressman Phil Burton pronounced the Masters' congressional districts "fair, just and equitable. This plan unites more communities than ours did and eliminates the dilution of the minority group vote." But similarly cheery was Gordon Luce, the chairman of the Republican State Central Committee, who declared the plan "an enormous improvement over the gerrymander advanced by the Democratic leadership in the Legislature." An editorial writer for the *Los Angeles Times* went so far as to suggest that the Masters' Plan might represent "the death of gerrymandering."[24] The knowledgeable editor of the *California Journal*, Ed Salzman, predicted only one or two seat changes in the party balance in each legislative body and calculated that only about 10 of the 163 incumbents in the Assembly, Senate, and Congress would lose their seats as a result of the redistricting.[25]

Because they did not have to obtain majorities of the legislator, the support of the Governor, and at least the acquiescence of members of Congress, the McKaskle-Baker districts were certain to look more regular than the legislators' districts on a map that contained neither geological nor sociological features—which was how they were usually presented to the public. The bitter clashes of self-interest, partisan interest, and ideological interest that deeply divide California politicians can only be compromised in reapportionment by drawing oddly-shaped districts.[26] Moreover, the 20th century American media's habitual scorn for politicians and the "scientific" mystique that surrounded computers in the early 1970s also helped to insure an enthusiastic public response for the court-

---

[22]Tables of these figures, but no further analyses, are in the Masters' files at the Institute for Governmental Studies, University of California, Berkeley.

[23]Daryl Lembke, "Panel Submits Remapping Plan to California Supreme Court," *Los Angeles Times*, Sept. 1, 1973, I-1; Richard Bergholz, "A Challenge: Fair Plan for Redistricting," *ibid.*, Dec. 7, 1980, I-3.

[24]Tom Goff, "Can Find No Reason to Oppose Panel Remapping Plan—Moretti," *Los Angeles Times*, Sept. 6, 1973, I-3; Paul Houston, "State Redistricting Plan Perils 4 Congressmen," *ibid.*, Sept. 9, 1973, I-3; Bill Boyarsky, "Redistricting Plan: New Faces in '74," *ibid.*, Sept. 3, 1973, I-1; "The Death of Gerrymandering?" *ibid.*, Sept. 5, 1973, II-6.

[25]Salzman, 1973. Similarly, Richard Bergholz of the *Los Angeles Times* predicted that Democrats would win 20-23 seats in Congress, 18-22 in the Senate, and 44-51 in the Assembly. Bergholz, "Both Parties Optimistic Over Redistricting Plan: Democrats Expect to Retain 23-20 Margin in Congress; GOP Sees Chance to Narrow Gap," *Los Angeles Times*, Nov. 29, 1973, I-1.

[26]Tom Goff, "State Remapping Appears Headed Back to Courts," *Los Angeles Times*, Mar. 21, 1972, I-3.

ordered scheme. Thus, the *Times* reported that at a hearing on the proposal, politician-complainants were "fighting for their political skins," against McKaskle-Baker, which was "Devised by feeding population data into a computer..."[27] These images of squarish districts mechanically drawn by supposedly disinterested technicians who were insulated from the pressures of politics or publicity were to recur repeatedly over the next two decades—pristine technocracy, as opposed to the messy, imperfect compromises that characterized the legislative process. It is one of the ironies of the late twentieth century that citizens of the world's foremost democratic country put so little trust in the officials they elect, have so little understanding of the process by which laws are made, and accept so readily the intervention of unknown and unaccountable "experts" in making fundamental policy.

When the districts were drawn in the summer of 1973, no one could have foreseen that by the time of the 1974 elections, the oil price shock would rumble through the economy, producing a sharp recession, and that President Nixon would resign and be pardoned in the aftermath of a scandal that would severely damage the reputation of the Republican party. The result was a dramatic victory for the Democrats in the nation generally and in California, in particular. In the Assembly, Democrats made a net gain of seven, giving them their largest majority since 1877. In the Senate, they won 17 of 20 of the four-year seats up for election in 1974, raising their total by a net of three. In the Congress, Democrats picked up five seats in what state Democratic party chair John Burton called a repudiation of "the party of Watergate." Suggesting in November 1973 that the Masters' Plan had reduced partisan margins in seats across the state, Michael Berman, a Democratic political consultant and staffer of the Assembly Elections and Reapportionment Committee, had predicted a 30-seat turnover in the Assembly. Although the Democratic surge probably reduced the carnage, there were 23 new members of the Assembly elected in 1974.[28] To what degree was the Democratic triumph the result of redistricting, and to what degree, of other factors? How well would each party have done under the 1972, rather than the 1974 boundaries?

One way to answer this question is provided by *Congressional Quarterly* retabulations of the results of the 1968, 1970, and 1972 congressional elections using the McKaskle-Baker boundaries. (*Congressional Quarterly*, 1974.) In 1968, Democrats actually won 21 of the 38 districts. If those votes had been cast in the 43 districts drawn by the Masters, Democrats would have won only 19, while Republicans would have carried 24. In 1970, Democrats won 20 of 38 seats (52.6%), and would have been victorious in 23 of 43 (53.5%) under the

---

[27]Daryl Lembke, "High Court Hears Complaints on Computerized Remap Plan," *Los Angeles Times*, Oct. 31, 1973, I-3.

[28]Daryl Lembke, "Court Orders State Remapping, Ignores Factor of Incumbency," *Los Angeles Times*, Nov. 29, 1973, I-1; Kathy Burke, "Rep. Burton Predicts Democratic Landslide," *ibid.*, Aug. 29, 1974, II-2; Robert Shogan, "GOP Founders in Riptides, Watergate, Pardon, Economy," *ibid.*, Nov. 5, 1974, I-1; George Skelton, "Democrats Take 72 of 100 Races," *ibid.*, Nov. 7, 1974, I-1; William Endicott, "State's Democrats Add Four Seats in Congress," *ibid.*, Nov. 7, 1974, I-3.

Masters' plan.[29] In 1972, Democrats won 23 of the 43 under the bipartisan proposal put into place temporarily by the state Supreme Court; they would have won 25 under the Masters' plan. In the actual election of 1974, Democrats won 28 congressional seats. By this measure, then, the Masters' districts probably gave the Democrats at most one or two congressional seats, compared with the districts drawn by Democratic-majority legislatures in 1965 for the Assembly and Senate and in 1971 for Congress, while the Watergate scandal and the recession accounted for two or more of the five-seat gain.

A second approach to the question is to place the 1972 and 1974 elections in the context of general trends over the whole period from 1970 to 1994. Figures 1 and 2 illustrate several aspects of these trends for congressional and Assembly races, tracking differences in party registration and estimates of the margin between Democratic and Republican candidates in hypothetical districts where the party registration was that in an average district, a district where 55% of the total registrants were Democrats and 40% were Republicans, and one where the proportions were 55% and 38%.[30] (The figures will be discussed again at later points in this chapter.)

1974 was certainly a landslide year for the Democrats. In a district where the registration was 57.5% Democratic and 35.5% Republican, the average Democratic vote margin was 22% in Congressional and 18% in Assembly races—an increase from 9% and 12%, respectively, in 1972. Similarly, Democratic margins more than doubled from 1972 to 1974 in hypothetical 55/40 and 55/38 districts. These results suggest that the effects of the Watergate, recession, and pardon issues spilled over into Assembly contests and that they outweighed line-drawing in their importance for the 1974 results.

---

[29]*Congressional Quarterly* (1973) also retabulated the 1970 results by the 1972 districts. If the 1970 election had been held within the 1972 boundaries, Democrats, by this measure, would have won 22 of the 43, one less than under the 1974 boundaries.

[30]The Senate is omitted because the small number of elections (its terms are for four years) makes it less predictable. Total registration, rather than two-party registration is used because the percentages of third-party or no-party registrants differ considerably in size and behavior from district to district. The 55% Democratic and/or 38-40% Republican rule of thumb for competitive seats is repeatedly mentioned. See, e.g., Way, 1962, 253; Salzman, 1974; D'Agostino, 1972, 3. In the 1972 congressional contests, Democrats lost only 3 districts that were 55% or more Democratic, and Republicans lost only one that was 38% or more Republican; in the Assembly, the analogous figures were eight and ten. In 1981, a report in the *Los Angeles Times* highlighted Senate districts that were 55% and above Democratic and remarked that "Republicans can win in districts where their registration is as low as 40%." Claudia Luther and Jerry Gillam, "Democrat in State Senate Unveil Redistricting Plan," *Los Angeles Times*, Sept. 3, 1981, I-1. By 1991, an insider newsletter called a district "safe" for the Democrats if it was 54% or more Democratic, and safe for the Republicans if it was 40% or more Republican. Dick Rosengarten, *Calpeek: California Political Week*, 13, #45 (Dec. 9, 1991), 3. The 38% rule is referred to in Daniel M. Weintraub, "Incumbents Come First in Redistricting, Speaker Says," *Los Angeles Times*, Aug. 30, 1991, A-3; Weintraub, "Remap Plans Would Add 4 House Seats in Southland," *ibid.*, Sept. 12, 1991, A1. Edmond Costantini and Charles Dannehl, "Party Registration and Party Vote: Democratic Fall-Off in Legislative Elections," *Legislative Studies Quarterly*, 18 (1993), 33 indicates that a district in which the Democratic percentage of the two-party registration in California legislative races from 1972 through 1990 was 56% would be rated a "virtual toss-up."

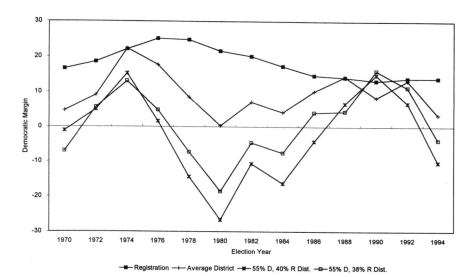

Figure 1. Democratic Margins in Congressional Contests, 1970-1994

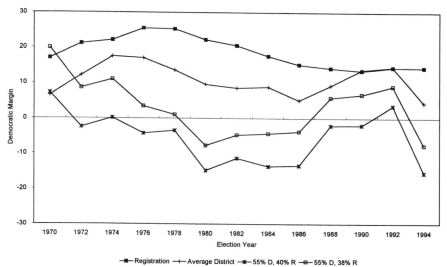

Figure 2. Democratic Margins in State Assembly Contests, 1970-1994

A third approach, explained in detail in Kousser, 1995, implies that Democrats might have done even better if the 1972 lines had been in effect in 1974 and for the rest of the decade. Using methods somewhat more sophisticated than, but essentially similar to those that produced the results for hypothetical districts in Figures 1 and 2, I estimate how well the candidates of each party would have fared in 1972 if the relationships between registration by party and the vote had been the same as they were in 1974. Conversely, I estimate how many seats each party would have won in 1974 if the relationships between registration and voting had been the same as those in 1972. If voters had behaved as they did in 1974, but the 1972 lines (and patterns and levels of party registration) had been in effect, my estimate is that the Democrats would have won 30 congressional seats, instead of 23. Had they behaved as in 1972, but within the 1974 boundaries, they would have won 29, instead of 28.[31] The Assembly results are similar. In actuality, Democrats won 51 and 55 seats in the November, 1972 and November, 1974 elections. Had the lines been those of 1972 and the behavior that of 1974, Democrats would have won 57 seats; in the opposite case, 58.[32]

TABLE 3. What If Voters Had Behaved as in 1972,
But in the 1974 Districts, and Vice Versa?

Boundaries in Effect	Behavioral Pattern*	
	1972	1974
Panel A: Congress		
1972	23**	29
1974	30	28
Panel B: Assembly		
1972	51	58
1974	57	55

*Patterns are the regression relationships estimated from the rows for 1972 and 1974, respectively in Table 1, Kousser, 1995.
**Number or estimated number of Democratic victories

A fourth approach is to compare the degree of "packing" of Democrats and Republicans into overwhelmingly partisan districts in 1972 with that at the time that the Masters' districts were announced in 1973.[33] Although any definition of "packing" is time-bound and somewhat arbitrary, let us define one empirically. In

---

[31]These estimates, of course, do not allow for the idiosyncrasies of individual campaigns. If one uses the regressions for 1974 and computes the number of districts that the Democrats "should" have carried on the basis of party registration alone, the result is 33. In other words, the estimate in the text of 29 seats in 1974 if the behavior pattern had been that of 1972 is actually 4 seats less than the estimate if the 1974 behavior pattern and the 1974 districts are used.

[32]Again, the estimates from same-year regressions show higher numbers than the actual numbers of Democratic victories—54 and 62, respectively. It should also be noted that the "1972" lines for the Assembly were actually those adopted in 1965, which were kept in effect for 1972 by the State Supreme Court.

1972, Democrats won every congressional district that was 36% Republican or less (to the nearest percentage point) and lost every one that was 39% Republican or more. In the Assembly in 1972, Democrats won 39 of the 41 districts that were 36% Republican or less, and lost 24 of the 33 districts that were 39% Republican or more.[34] Suppose we allow for some uncertainty by defining relatively "safe" districts at the time as 34% Republican or below, and 41% Republican or above. Then the number of safe Democratic districts in the Masters' plan was 36 in the Assembly, while the number in 1972 was 33; and the numbers of safe Republican districts were 23 and 27, respectively. In the Congress, the numbers of safe Democratic districts were 17 and 18, while the numbers of safe Republican districts were 14 and 17. By these definitions, the Masters' plan had about the same number of "competitive" districts in the Assembly as the previous plan had, but McKaskle-Baker was somewhat more favorable to Democrats than the scheme that it replaced. For Congress, McKaskle drew four more competitive districts and three fewer safe Republican ones.

Overall, then, three retired judges who had been appointed by a Democratic governor, superintending a redistricting by a former poverty lawyer (McKaskle), produced lines that were very similar in their prospective effects to districts that had been drawn by legislatures containing Democratic majorities.[35] It is not surprising, then, that after 1974, Assembly Democratic leaders believed that the courts would not deal with them unfairly, especially if advised by McKaskle.[36]

III. THE 1980S: THE "BURTON GERRYMANDER" AND ITS CONSEQUENCES

A. Burton, Berman, and the Two Roses

As the next round of redistricting approached, the political situation in California had changed considerably. Six percent fewer voters registered with one of the two

---

[33]The Masters' papers at the Institute for Governmental Studies, University of California, Berkeley, indicate that they aggregated only the 1970 registration figures into their districts. A comparison of these with partisan registration margins in the actual 1970 Assembly districts, using the same technique as in figures 3-7, below, shows almost no difference in competitiveness between the Masters' Plan and the 1965 legislature's plan. A similar comparison, using 1973 data, between the Masters' Plan and Senate Bill 195, the compromise that was vetoed by Gov. Reagan in 1973, similarly demonstrates no visible differences within the competitive range of districts.

[34]As Kousser, 1995a, Table 1 shows, election outcomes are considerably more dependent on the level of Republican than of Democratic registration.

[35]More informal analyses come to the same conclusion. Butler and Cain, 1992, 37; Quinn, 1984, ch. 4, 73-74.

[36]It would be going too far, however, to agree with *California Journal* editor Ed Salzman, who announced in June 1974 that "With hindsight, it is easy to see that the Republican Party would have been better off with any of the various compromise reapportionment plans developed by the Legislature." (Salzman, 1974.) Similarly (and contradictorily) Quinn Chapter 4, 58, 65, states that Republicans would have won "far more seats" under the 1973 compromise districts than under the McKaskle Plan, but also that McKaskle's lines "did not favor one party or another." Since the compromise congressional proposal was almost exactly the same as that used for the 1972 elections, it seems nearly certain that Democrats would have been at least as well off with the 1972 as with the McKaskle lines. Gov. Reagan and his advisers correctly recognized their partisan interest in not compromising with the legislature in 1971-73, swapping a certain disadvantage for an unknown one.

major parties in 1980 than in 1972, and the volatility of voters and their tendency to split tickets rose with the amount of political independence. Although Democrat Jerry Brown had replaced Republican Ronald Reagan as governor and the Democrats still held the edge in both houses of the legislature and the state's congressional delegation, their majorities had been much reduced by the reverberations of the Proposition 13 (property tax reduction) campaign in 1978 and the electoral thunder of Ronald Reagan's presidential campaign in 1980. After the 1976 election, the numbers of Democratic seats in the Assembly, Senate, and Congress, respectively were 57, 26, and 29; after the 1980 election, 49, 21, and 22. While Republicans wished to lock in their recent gains with favorable district lines, Democrats wanted to reclaim several close districts that they had previously controlled. The Democratic majority on the State Supreme Court was more solid, 6 to 1, but Republicans had already backed an almost-successful campaign against the state's first female Chief Justice, Rose Bird, three of the Jerry Brown-appointed Justices were subject to voter rejection on the 1982 ballot, and Republicans hoped that threatened judges would veto any partisan Democratic reapportionment. If all else failed, Republicans believed that they might be able to cut a deal with the Democrats. It was this last belief that so inflamed the fight for the Assembly Speakership.

Since Jess Unruh modernized the California legislature during the 1960s, the Speaker has been the state's second most powerful official, centrally coordinating fundraising and campaign planning, controlling the agenda and appointing all committee chairs in the Assembly, doling out or denying perquisites, and using these powers to foster or blight legislation and careers.[37] (Crouch et al., 1967, 137-38.) Because the Speaker is elected by the members of the Assembly and can theoretically be replaced at any time, she must particularly concerned with redistricting. In 1980, Republicans were frantic over the prospect that Howard Berman might become Speaker and his brother Michael might be in charge of reapportionment.[38]

In 1974, Assemblyman Leo McCarthy of San Francisco, with the help of the Bermans, had challenged Bob Moretti as Speaker and beaten Willie Brown of San Francisco for the post after Moretti dropped out of the contest. Howard Berman had become Majority Leader, with the promise of ascending to the Speakership eventually. By 1979, Berman, chafing at being second in command, challenged McCarthy directly, winning 27 of 50 votes in the Democratic caucus.

---

[37] Crouch et al., 1967, 137-38.

[38] A political organizer from the age of 16, Michael Berman managed his first successful Assembly campaign, an upset of a 26-year Assembly incumbent, before he was 21 years old. With his brother and the victor in the upset, Henry Waxman, Michael became the core of what eventually became known as the "Berman-Waxman Machine," which was in fact a loose grouping of Jewish, African-American, and Latino liberal Democratic politicians in Los Angeles. Waxman chaired the Assembly Elections and Reapportionment Committee in 1971, and Michael was a consultant to that committee. W.B. Rood, "Michael Rows the Boat for Berman," *Los Angeles Times*, Jan. 28, 1980, I-3. On Republican fears, see Claudia Luther, "Democrats Get Slow Start on Redistricting," *ibid.*, March 8, 1981, I-3.

At this point, bitter McCarthy supporters refused to solidify behind Berman on the Assembly floor, Assembly Republicans refused to vote for either side, McCarthy retained his position, and the battle was put off until after the 1980 elections. In those elections, McCarthy and Berman actively supported different Democratic candidates, Berman's allies won more seats, and McCarthy dropped out of the race, but threw his support to his former enemy Willie Brown. When five Democrats defected from Berman and the Democratic caucus deadlocked, the Assembly Republican leadership decided to vote for Brown in return for veto power over Republican committee assignments and a rather vague promise of partisan fairness in redistricting.[39]

Republicans deployed four more weapons during the 1981 reapportionment. Although attempts during the 1970s to set up a reapportionment commission had failed, Republicans and nonpartisan "good government" supporters had successfully backed a toothless initiative in June 1980. Proposition 6 required all public bodies to pay attention to contiguity and city, county, and regional boundaries during reapportionment, but never defined these terms, provided no method of enforcement or advice on how to resolve contradictory objectives, and contained no protections for ethnic minorities.[40] Republican businessmen also financed a computerized reapportionment center at the Rose Institute of Claremont McKenna College in Southern California. Led by Alan Heslop and Tom Hofeller, two veterans of the Republican redistricting efforts of 1971, Rose invited Latinos to use their facilities without charge in hopes that their push for more Latino representation would at the least embarrass Democrats, and at the most, reduce the overall number of Democratic seats. Although Hofeller denied that Rose was "a Republican appendage," Assembly Republican Minority Leader Carol Hallett announced long before any proposed reapportionment was produced that "The Rose Institute plan (whenever it emerges) is a Republican plan."[41] Among the

---

[39]Al Martinez, "Speakership Fight: a Study in Power," *Los Angeles Times*, Feb. 19, 1980, I-3; Claudia Luther and Robert Fairbanks, "Willie Brown Vies for Speaker's Post," *ibid.*, Nov. 21, 1980, I-3; "Chicanos Take Plea to Capital," *ibid.*, Dec. 1, 1980, II-4; Claudia Luther and Tracy Wood, "Willie Brown New Assembly Speaker," *ibid.*, Dec. 2, 1980, I-1; Kenneth Reich, "Reapportionment: L.A.'s Time to Pay the Piper," *ibid.*, Jan. 4, 1981, II-1; Claudia Luther and Jerry Gillam, "2 Redistricting Plans Advance in Legislature," *ibid.*, Sept. 12, 1981, I-1; Luther, "Speaker's Crown Firmly Affixed," *ibid.*, Sept. 28, 1981, I-3. After Brown proved less nonpartisan in redistricting than they had hoped, Republicans tried—unsuccessfully—to play Howard Berman off against the Speaker. Quinn, ch. 5, 48-50.

[40]Art. XXI, Sec. 1, State Constitution; *California Journal*, 1972a; Walter A. Zelman, "It's Time to Defeat Rep. Gerry Mander," *Los Angeles Times*, April 20, 1979, II-7; "Fairer Apportionment: Yes on 6," *ibid.*, May 16, 1980, II-6; Richard Bergholz, "New Lines: Both Parties Are Worried," *ibid.*, Jan. 4, 1981, I-1.

[41]Richard Bergholz, "New Lines: Both Parties Are Worried," *Los Angeles Times*, Jan. 4, 1981, I-1; Henry Mendoza, "Latinos Backed on Political Concern," *ibid.*, Feb. 1, 1981, II-4; Claudia Luther, "Latinos Warn on Reapportionment," *ibid.*, Feb. 21, 1981, II-1; Richard Santillan, "For Chicanos, a Louder Voice," *ibid.*, March 5, 1981, II-7; Claudia Luther, "Latinos May Get Little in Redistricting," *ibid.*, April 30, 1981, I-3; Jerry Gillam, "Latinos Seek New Assembly District," *ibid.*, May 5, 1981, I-23; Kenneth Reich, "Latino Coalition Submits Plan to Increase State Representation," *ibid.*, II-4; Kenneth Reich, "Top Democrats Cool to Reapportionment Plan," *ibid.*, June 17, 1981, I-3.

Democrats whose districts the Rose plan ultimately splintered was Speaker Willie Brown—not a move aimed at conciliation.[42] The third weapon, the threat of legal suits, finally proved no more efficacious than the previous two, while the fourth, a statewide referendum on accepting or rejecting the Democrats' plans, ultimately proved to be a pyrrhic victory for the GOP, as we shall see below.

Minority legislators had more power in shaping a reapportionment plan that was ultimately put into effect in 1981 than at any other time in California's history. In 1971, Mervyn Dymally had been head of the Senate Elections and Reapportionment Committee, but Gov. Reagan had vetoed his plan, a conservative coalition had taken control of the committee, Reagan had vetoed even their effort, and the Masters' plan had superseded everything anyway. Ten years later, Assemblyman Richard Alatorre, who had been pledged to Howard Berman in the Speakership contest, went over to Willie Brown and was named chairman of the Assembly Elections and Reapportionment Committee.[43] Together with the Speaker, an African-American, Alatorre made sure that minority concerns were taken into account in the redistricting of all three legislative bodies. Latino activists also pressured Brown and Alatorre, openly threatening to join Republicans in court if reapportionment plans disappointed them, storming out of committee hearings, and even sitting in at the Speaker's office.[44]

The actual districts that were drawn for the Congress and the Assembly satisfied blacks, delighted Latinos, and reassured Democratic politicians. Comprising a relatively stable proportion of the population and heavily concentrated geographically, African-Americans from California were already represented proportionately in all three bodies, and the new lines threatened no black incumbent or major aspirant.[45] Latinos, angered because the State Senate plan did not create another Latino district in Los Angeles, were, however, "pleasantly surprised...shocked favorably" by Alatorre's concentration of Latino areas into potential "influence districts" for the State Assembly and pleased that the number of Latinos from California in Congress seemed likely to triple under the new boundaries.[46] The plans also conciliated Howard Berman and his allies Assemblymen Mel Levine and Rick Lehman by tailor-making congressional seats for them, thus simultaneously promoting them and removing them from Sacramento.[47]

Republicans, however, exploded, especially over the congressional plan drawn by liberal Democratic Congressman Phil Burton of San Francisco. Report-

---

[42]Claudia Luther, "Legislators to Determine Own Survival," *Los Angeles Times*, June 28, 1981, I-3.

[43]"Chicanos Take Plea to Capital," *Los Angeles Times*, Dec. 1, 1980, II-4; Kenneth Reich, "Reapportionment: L.A.'s Time to Pay the Piper," *ibid.*, Jan. 4, 1981, II-1; Claudia Luther, "Latinos Warn on Reapportionment," *ibid.*, Feb. 21, 1981, II-1.

[44]Claudia Luther, "Latino Walkout Climaxes Session on Redistricting," *Los Angeles Times*, Aug. 5, 1981, I-21; Luther and Jerry Gillam, "GOP Bloc Threatens to Delay Bills in Rift Over Redistricting," *ibid.*, Aug. 25, 1981, I-3.

[45]Tracy Wood, "Remap Fight Pits Pair of Democrats," *Los Angeles Times*, Dec. 23, 1982, I-3; Wood, "Democrats Seek to Add to Margin in Congress," *ibid.*, Dec. 28, 1982, I-3.

edly relying only on a mechanical adding machine, his encyclopedic knowledge of the political proclivities of Northern California, and the expertise on the L.A. area of Michael Berman and Cal State–Long Beach Prof. Leroy Hardy, Burton drew irregular districts that punished his particular enemies and protected his friends.[48] In high dudgeon, one Republican denounced the Burton plan as an "outrageous, blatant, partisan carving up of the people," another likened it to the Jewish Holocaust, while a third, adding one more insensitive religious metaphor, compared Speaker Brown to the contemporary Iranian theocrat, the Ayatollah Khomeini.[49] Claiming that the Burton redistricting would cost them between six and ten seats in Congress,[50] the Republicans put a referendum on the June 1982 ballot that allowed voters to reject the plans for each of the legislative bodies. At the same time, they asked the State Supreme Court and a federal district court to suspend the new district lines and either establish different temporary lines or run the 1982 elections within the districts that had been used in 1980. The GOP also joined with the good government group Common Cause in sponsoring a referendum on a reapportionment commission which, if approved on the November 1982 ballot, would draw wholly new districts for subsequent elections.[51]

As in 1971, the State Supreme Court unanimously decided to put the new congressional districts into effect immediately, because otherwise, the two additional members of Congress would have to be selected at-large, which was illegal under a 1967 federal law. But unlike the case decided a decade earlier, the Court also ruled that the 1982 elections for the Assembly and the Senate should be held in the new districts. For a four-three majority, Chief Justice Rose Bird wrote that to use the old, by now severely malapportioned districts would violate the equal population requirement that courts had ruled to be

---

[46]Claudia Luther and Jerry Gillam, "Democrats in State Senate unveil Redistricting Plan," *Los Angeles Times*, Sept. 3, 1981, I-1; Maria L. La Ganga, "Latino Group Urges Veto of Remapping," *ibid.*, Sept. 5, 1981, I-24; Claudia Luther and Jerry Gillam, "Assembly Remapping Plan Unveiled; GOP Vows Fight," *ibid.*, Sept. 9, 1981, I-1; Frank del Olmo, "Latinos Get a Break in Assembly Remapping," *ibid.*, Nov. 5, 1981, II-11. Prof. Bruce Cain became Alatorre's chief redistricting consultant, battling the Rose computers at Claremont McKenna College with the Caltech mainframe, twenty miles down the road. From the beginning, the focus of this bitter rivalry was on Latinos, whom both sides sought to woo and use.

[47]Claudia Luther, "Speakers' Crown Firmly Affixed," *Los Angeles Times*, Sept. 28, 1981, I-3.

[48]Butler and Cain, *1992*, 42; Ellen Hume, "Plan to Ensure Congress Seat for Latino May Be Backfiring," *Los Angeles Times*, April 18, 1982, II-1; Quinn, 1984, ch. 5, 14-25.

[49]Claudia Luther and Jerry Gillam, "2 Redistricting Plans Advance in Legislature," *Los Angeles Times*, Sept. 12, 1981, I-1; Luther and Gillam, "3 Plans for State Redistricting OK'd," *ibid.*, Sept. 16, 1981, I-1.

[50]These guesses imply that what the Republicans considered a "fair" redistricting would have produced Republican majorities in the congressional delegation ranging from 27-18 to 31-14, a rather audacious claim in a state where Democratic registrants outnumbered Republican by 55%-33% in 1980.

[51]George Skelton, "GOP Opens Drive for Remapping Measure," *Los Angeles Times*, Sept. 23, 1981, I-3; Claudia Luther, "GOP to Aid Remapping Reform Bid," *ibid.*, Dec. 6, 1981, I-3; Charles Maher, "GOP Congressmen Ask Judges to Remap State," *ibid.*, Dec. 15, 1981, I-3; Claudia Luther, "Court Views Choices in Districting Battle," *ibid.*, Jan. 12, 1982, I-3; Luther and Richard Bergholz, "Campaign Launched for Remap Initiative," *ibid.*, Feb. 3, 1982, I-3.

implicit in the federal and state constitutions. She rejected Republican arguments that even though both houses of the legislature had passed the measures and Gov. Jerry Brown had signed them, they should not be considered enacted until the electorate had had a chance to veto them—as Governor Reagan had vetoed the 1971 lines—in the first initiative on a particular redistricting plan in the state's history. Republicans responded by threatening to join an ongoing recall effort against the four Jerry Brown-appointed members of the Court, and the party did oppose three of them in the November election.[52] In the federal court, Republican moves for a temporary injunction against the plans on the grounds that they favored the Democratic party, that they had not yet been pre-cleared by the U.S. Department of Justice, and that shifts in Senate lines would prevent some voters from selecting senators for six years were unceremoniously rejected.[53] The GOP was more successful in the June referendum, as voters objected to each of the Democratic plans by margins of 62-65%, setting the stage for a vote on a redistricting commission.[54]

Written by Republican activist and attorney Vigo Nielsen, Jr. and backed by Common Cause—and $400,000 from the state Republican party—the complicated 10-person commission plan appeared, on the surface at least, so carefully balanced between the two major political parties that it was likely to result in a bipartisan gerrymander.[55] (Proponents of the plan, numbered Proposition 14 on the November ballot, did not stress this implication of their handiwork.) Six members were to be representatives of the two major parties selected by partisan caucuses in the Assembly and Senate and by the state party chairpersons. Four "independent" members who were, in the words of the initiative, to "bring ethnic, social and geographic diversity to the commission," were to be chosen by a two-thirds vote of the seven most senior justices on the State Court of Appeals.[56] Since it took seven votes to adopt a plan in the commission, at least one partisan from each side would have to approve

[52]Philip Hager, "Court Backs Remapping Plan and Ballot Challenge," *Los Angeles Times*, Jan. 29, 1982, I-1; Richard Bergholz, "GOP Will Take Aim at Ruling on Redistricting," *ibid.*, Feb. 1, 1982, I-3; Philip Hager, "GOP-Backed Group Begins Drive to Unseat Justices Named by Brown," *ibid.*, Sept. 30, 1982, I-3; election returns, *ibid.*, I-16; Salzman, 1982a. The insider view of the Republicans' chief redistricting consultant for the Assembly in 1981 makes it clear that it was this decision, not those concerning capital punishment, that really motivated the Republican leadership of Bird's eventually successful recall. (Quinn, 1984, ch.5, 78.)

[53]Claudia Luther, "GOP Renews Challenge on Redistricting," *Los Angeles Times*, Feb. 9, 1982, I-3; Charles Maher, "Judge Refuses to Stop Remapping," *ibid.*, Feb. 11, 1982, I-16; "Court Denies Districting Plea," *ibid.*, March 23, 1982, I-17.

[54]Claudia Luther, "Remapping Challenge May Be Just Warm-Up," *Los Angeles Times*, May 10, 1982, I-3; "Election Districts: No, Yes, Yes," *ibid.*, May 21, 1982, II-6; Claudia Luther, "Initiative to Create Redistricting Commission Qualifies for Ballot," *ibid.*, June 22, 1982, I-3.

[55] Richard Bergholz, "GOP Will Take Aim at Ruling on Redistricting," *Los Angeles Times*, Feb. 1, 1982, I-3. Details on the commission plan are taken from Salzman, 1982b.

[56]Michael Asimow and Walter Zelman, "Prop. 14: Is It Real 'Reform'?" *Los Angeles Times*, Oct. 10, 1982, IV-3. To guard in another way against partisanship, no more than four of the seven Appeals Court justices who nominated independent commission members could have been members of the same political party at the time that they had been named to the Appeals Court.

any redistricting. If the commission deadlocked, the State Supreme Court had 60 days to draw up a proposal, probably using the commission and its staff as special masters.[57]

While the commission was directed to encourage electoral competition, there was no mention of protection of the rights of ethnic minorities as a goal of its plans—an omission that Democrats and representatives of minority groups harshly attacked.[58] The reapportionment commission, said Assembly Democratic caucus leader Don Bosco, "would relegate the most important decision the Legislature makes to a bunch of old, white, upper-middle class men." Just as members of ethnic minorities had finally gained power in the legislature, *Los Angeles Times* editorialist Frank del Olmo and Speaker Willie Brown charged separately, it was proposed to take it away and give it to a body that was not likely to have "the kind of ethnic, racial and sexual balance found in the Legislature." Echoing similar comments by the California Teachers' Association and the State Advisory Committee to the U.S. Commission on Civil Rights, Senate Majority Leader David Roberti noted that "There's less for minorities in the Common Cause plan than there was in the process the Legislature underwent."[59] While surely self-serving, the Democrats' comments were not untrue. By 1981, ethnic minorities were such an important part of the Democratic coalition, not only in the electorate, but also in the legislative and congressional delegations, that white Democrats had no alternative but to satisfy most of their redistricting demands. No bipartisan or nonpartisan commission offered so certain a prospect of influence.

Attracting only 79% of the number of votes that were cast for Republican George Deukmejian for governor the same day, the commission proposition went down to a stunning 55%-45% defeat. Faced with a tough nationwide campaign in the midst of the highest unemployment since the Great Depression, the Republican National Committee reneged on a promise to provide $300,000 for the Proposition 14 campaign. In California itself, Republicans strained every bit of financial muscle they had to defeat Tom Bradley, the first serious black candidate for governor in the state's history, a feat that they accomplished, after a subtly racist campaign, by a margin of only 50,000 votes out of 7.5 million cast. (Pettigrew and Alston, 1988.) Extreme conservatives focused on defeating a handgun control initiative on the same ballot. Without a serious campaign in

---

[57]This provision would pressure the party that did not have a majority on the Supreme Court to compromise, for fear that if it did not, the Supreme Court would put the commission's plan into effect, anyway. It is noteworthy that the elaborate nonpartisan rules did not apply to the State Supreme Court, which was not prohibited from dividing along party lines or given any nonpartisan guidelines. For other evaluations, see Bill Billiter, "Prop. 14: Election Reform or a Trojan Horse?" *Los Angeles Times*, Oct. 14, 1982, I-C-1.

[58]The national Common Cause "Model State Constitution" and statutory provisions also included no protections for ethnic minorities. (Adams, 1977.)

[59]Claudia Luther and Richard Bergholz, "Campaign Launched for Remap Initiative," *Los Angeles Times*, Feb. 3, 1982, I-3; "Civil Rights Panel Opposes Redistricting Commission," *ibid.*, Oct. 15, 1982, I-11; Frank Del Olmo, "Prop. 14 Endangers Latinos' Gains," *ibid.*, Oct. 28, 1982, II-11.

its behalf, the complex reapportionment proposition was lost in the cacophony of other contests. Two weeks before election day, 48% of Californians polled had not decided how they would vote on Proposition 14, and they apparently decided that, when in doubt, they would abstain or vote no.[60] After the election, but before Deukmejian took office, Democrats passed and Gov. Jerry Brown signed plans that offered additional protection to enough Republican legislators to obtain a two-thirds majority and consequent "urgency" status, thus precluding another referendum. In most cases, however, the new boundaries, drawn with the assistance of Michael Berman, were only slightly different from those that the voters had rejected in June. Republicans put up only lackadaisical resistance, Senate Minority Leader Bill Campbell remarking, "I'm sick and tired of reapportionment."[61]

Other Republicans, however, persisted. When in February, 1983, national GOP operatives turned down a proposal by California state leaders that the Republican National Committee commit $1 million to a new campaign to redraw California districts, right-wing Assemblyman Don Sebastiani, young heir to his family's wine fortune, funded an initiative initially without asking for money from the official Republican party.[62] Republican campaign consultants who were angry at the Burton Plan because its safe districts robbed them of the business that might come their way if more competitive districts encouraged more active campaigns eagerly signed on with Sebastiani. (Quinn ch. 5, 99.)[63] Phrased as a statute, rather than an amendment to the State Constitution, the initiative largely consisted of Assembly, Senate, and congressional district maps drawn at the Rose Institute by Republican political consultant Joseph Shumate. Responding to right-wing pressure, the Republican State Committee pledged $300,000 for the Sebastiani Initiative, and Gov. Deukmejian set a special election for Dec. 13, 1983, a date whose proximity to religious holidays was a patent attempt to guarantee a low turnout.[64] Charging that it would

---

[60]Election returns, *Los Angeles Times*, Nov. 4, 1982, I-16; Richard Bergholz, "State GOP Wants Party Help for Remap Fight," *ibid.*, Feb. 2, 1983, I-3; Brazil 1982.

[61]Tracy Wood, "Senate Quiets Fears, Passes Its Reapportionment Plan," *Los Angeles Times*, Dec. 24, 1982, I-3; Lowell and Craigie, 1985, 249.

[62]Herbert A. Sample and Richard Bergholz, "Remap Referendum Called Impractical," *Los Angeles Times*, Jan. 7, 1983, I-3; Bergholz, "New GOP Strategy on Redistricting Develops," *ibid.*, Feb. 4, 1983, I-3; Bergholz, "New Effort to Overturn Reapportionment Begins," *ibid.*, Feb. 24, 1983, I-21; Bergholz, "GOP Assemblyman Announces Petition Drive to Get Redistricting Plan on Ballot," *ibid.*, 1983, I-22. For a sympathetic version of the events surrounding the initiative by Sebastiani's lawyers, see Lowell and Craigie, 1985. In legal papers, they charged, astoundingly, that the legislature's plan diluted minority votes, presumably meaning that it did so more than the Sebastiani plan.

[63]While it may be doubted that more competitive districts will improve the quality of policymaking or invigorate democratic participation, there is no question that it would increase the demand for political consultants—a consequence not often mentioned in debates over the issue.

[64]Richard Bergholz, "GOP Weighs Effort to Redraw Voting Districts," *Los Angeles Times*, May 25, 1983, I-23; John Balzar and Douglas Shuit, "Redistricting Election Ordered," *ibid.*, July 19, 1983, I-3; Balzar, "Democrats Facing Uphill fight on Remapping Plan," *ibid.*, Aug. 19, 1983, I-1; William Schneider, "Voter Turnout Is Key To Sebastiani's Hopes," *ibid.*, Aug. 21, 1983, IV-1.

reduce the power of minorities and women, and that the state constitutional provision mandating a reapportionment every decade should be interpreted to mean exactly one, and no more, Democrats successfully sued in the State Supreme Court to keep voters from considering the Sebastiani Initiative. As an example, the lawyers pointed out that the plan reduced the Latino population percentage in Edward Roybal's Los Angeles congressional district from 63% to 16%, and placed his home in the most Republican district in the state. It also moved a conservative Anglo area into a second Latino-majority Los Angeles congressional district, endangered at least one Los Angeles congressional seat then held by a black incumbent, removed the homes of State Senator Art Torres, Assemblyman Richard Alatorre, and Speaker Willie Brown from their current districts, packed blacks into a Bay Area congressional seat in which blacks had been able to elect their candidate of choice since 1968, and completely redrew Democratic districts throughout the state. Democrats quipped that Sebastiani has jammed so many African-Americans into one Los Angeles Assembly district that it had more blacks in it "than any district this side of Lagos, Nigeria." (Quinn, 1984, ch. 5, 110.) The justices' vote went strictly along party lines.[65] The main emphasis in the opinion was on the once-a-decade provision of the State Constitution. (*Legislature* v. *Deukmejian*, 34 Cal. 3d 658 (1983).)

After Sebastiani's judicial rejection, Common Cause Executive Director Walter Zelman sought a compromise—a reapportionment commission that would control the 1991 redistricting, but not continue the effort to overthrow the current lines. Adamant Republicans refused. When Sebastiani announced plans for an initiative that would write new lines into the State Constitution, thereby circumventing the State Supreme Court decision, Gov. Deukmejian muscled him aside, putting his chief political operative, Sal Russo, in charge of a campaign to establish a redistricting commission by state constitutional amendment. Instead of the balanced bipartisanship of the 1982 Common Cause/Republican Commission proposal, Deukmejian's commission, which would draw new boundaries for all state elections from 1986 on, was to be comprised of current Appeals Court justices. After the State Judicial Council objected that the task was too political for sitting judges to be involved in, Deukmejian substituted retired Appeals Court

---

[65]Sebastiani's plan, which made no effort to protect minority or female incumbents, was not helped by his right-wing radicalism—he was the only member of the Assembly to vote against making Martin Luther King, Jr.'s birthday a state holiday—and his penchant for insensitive comments, such his statement on the Assembly floor that he approved of female astronauts "as long as they have a one-way ticket." Keith Love, "Sebastiani Redistricting Plan a Political Time Bomb," *Los Angeles Times*, July 10, 1983, I-1; John Balzar and Douglas Shuit, "Redistricting Election Ordered," *ibid.*, July 19, 1983, I-3; Philip Hager, "Democrats Ask State Supreme Court to Stop Redistricting Vote," *ibid.*, July 20, 1983, I-3; Philip Hager, "Court to Hear Challenge to Remap Election," *ibid.*, Aug. 3, 1983, I-1; Hager, "State High Court Asked to Halt Remapping Vote," *ibid.*, Aug. 6, 1983, II-1; Douglas Shuit, "Blacks to Fight Remap Plan as 'Resegregation'," *ibid.*, Aug. 27, 1983, I-25; Philip Hager, "Remapping Issue Moves Into Court," *ibid.*, Sept. 1, 1983, I-3; Hager, "High Court Cancels Redistricting Vote," *ibid.*, Sept. 16, 1983, I-1.

justices.[66] Refusing all offers of compromise from the Democrats, Republican leaders declared that the 1981 district lines made Democratic incumbents so safe that they would target only a handful of them in 1984 (a self-fulfilling prophesy), instead spending $4 million on qualifying and seeking to pass the initiative, which became known as Proposition 39.[67]

Matching the Republicans dollar for dollar, billboard for billboard, and simplistic TV commercial for commercial, the Democrats capitalized on the weariness of the public and the media with the reapportionment issue and the widespread skepticism that partisan politics could ever be entirely removed from reapportionment.[68] Deukmejian's billboards read "Fairness, not politics," while one Democratic TV commercial featured an actor dressed like a judge raising his hand and pronouncing "In keeping with Proposition 39, I swear to protect my political party," and another ended with the slogan "Say no to the politicians."[69] More substantively, Democrats charged that 34 of the 38 current retired Appellate Court judges were white males whose average age was 73, whose current law practices might pose conflicts of interests with their reapportionment duties, and whose actions would not be accountable to the voters. The only female among the 38, former U.S. Secretary of Education Shirley Hufstedler, denounced Prop. 39 because it would "shut out of the reapportionment process such traditionally underrepresented groups as women and Hispanics," and Latino activist Cesar Chavez denounced the proposal before Latino community groups in Los Angeles and Orange counties.[70] Even President Reagan's landslide reelection victory could not save Prop. 39, which lost by the same

---

[66]Walter A. Zelman, "Time's Up on Sacramento's Game-Playing," *Los Angeles Times*, Sept. 19, 1983, II-5; John Balzar, "Deukmejian Seeks to Form Nonpartisan Remap Panel," *ibid.*, Oct. 2, 1983, I-1; Balzar, "Sebastiani to Work for New Remap Effort," *ibid.*, Oct. 3, 1983, I-1; Balzar, "Governor's Aide Will Lead GOP Remap Effort," *ibid.*, Oct. 12, 1983, I-3; Douglas Shuit, "Deukmejian remap Plan Hits Legal Snag," *ibid.*, Nov. 10, 1983, I-3; Shuit and Balzar, "Deukmejian Sets Remap Proposal Before Judges," *ibid.*, Nov. 18, 1983, I-3; Jerry Gillam, "Remap Panel Plan Amended by Governor," *ibid.*, Dec. 2, 1983, I-3; William Endicott, "Governor Sets Redistricting Board in Motion," *ibid.*, Jan. 21, 1984, II-1; William Kahrl, "Deukmejian Comes Out Ahead—Except in Party," *ibid.*, Nov. 14, 1984, II-5.

[67]Bill Lockyer, "Let's End the War of Reapportionment With Fair Principles," *Los Angeles Times*, Oct. 5, 1983, II-7; Keith Love, "State GOP to Lower Its Sights in '84," *ibid.*, Nov. 5, 1983, I-25; Jerry Gillam, "Democrats Draw Up Remap Plan," *ibid.*, Dec. 1, 1983, I-3; Gillam and John Balzar, "Democrat Proposal for Remap Panel Advances," *ibid.*, March 8, 1984, I-3; Carl Ingram, "remap Panel Chief Clashes With Colleagues, Resigns," *ibid.*, March 9, 1984, I-3; Balzar, "GOP Remap Plan Trounced in Assembly," *ibid.*, May 2, 1984, I-3; Balzar, "Prop. 39—the Battle that Could Determine the Game," *ibid.*, Sept. 10, 1984, I-3; Ingram and Gillam, "Racing Industry's $2.6 million Fights Lottery," *ibid.*, Oct. 30, 1984, I-13.

[68]Editorial, "Enough is Enough," *Los Angeles Times*, Oct. 5, 1983, II-61; John Balzar, "Deukmejian, Unfazed by Prop. 39 Loss, Vows to 'Reform' State Remapping Laws," *ibid.*, Nov. 8, 1984, I-3.

[69]John Balzar, "Prop. 39—the Battle that Could Determine the Game," *Los Angeles Times*, Sept. 10, 1984, I-3; Balzar, "Remapping Plan Causes Turmoil on Wide Front," *ibid.*, Oct. 16, 1984, I-3.

[70]John Balzar, "Prop. 39—the Battle that Could Determine the Game," *Los Angeles Times*, Sept. 10, 1984, I-3; Gerald F. Uelmen, "Don't Plunge Judges Into Political Thicket," *ibid.*, Sept. 19, 1984, II-5; "Chavez Recruits Opposition to 4 Ballot Initiatives," *ibid.*, Oct. 6, 1984, I-30; Balzer, "Remapping Plan Causes Turmoil on Wide Front," *ibid.*, Oct. 16, 1984, I-3; editorial, "Reapportionment: No on 39," *ibid.*, Oct. 31, 1984, II-4.

55%-45% margin that Prop. 14 had two years earlier.[71]

Still, they did not stop. In February 1985, Sebastiani proposed a two-part initiative—first, his maps, and second, a constitutional amendment preventing the State Supreme Court from overturning them. Although Sebastiani had become "a folk hero" among conservative Republicans through his reapportionment efforts, Deukmejian and other Republican leaders shunted Sebastiani aside again, but continued *Badham* v. *Eu,* a legal challenge to the congressional reapportionment, in federal court.[72] When a Republican attorney charged that the Burton plan was "the most egregious partisan gerrymander, not only of this decade but any other decade as well," Democratic attorneys answered that, in contrast to cases of racial gerrymandering, Republicans in California could hardly argue that they had been "shut out" of the political process, and that political parties did not deserve more protection from the courts in this regard than ethnic minorities enjoyed. A three-judge panel agreed with the Democrats in a party-line vote, and in 1989 the U.S. Supreme Court, after some apparent behind-the-scenes maneuvering, summarily affirmed the district court's dismissal of the Republicans' case. Only three Justices wished to hear the case, the first to come before them since they had ruled political gerrymandering a justiciable issue in 1986.[73] (*Badham* v. *Eu,* 694 F.Supp. 664 (N.D.Cal., 1988), aff'd mem. 109 S.Ct. 829 (1989).)

B. Did Phil Burton Singlehandedly Reverse the "Reagan Revolution"?

How partisan were the plans drawn in 1981, especially the "Burton Plan" for Congress? How true were Republican claims that the reapportionment cost them six or more seats in Congress and that it "preordain[ed] election results for a decade"? (Quinn, 1984, ch. 5, 56; Atwater, 1990, 670-71.) How did the habits and identifications of the voters change over the 1980s, and what implications did these changes have for the redistricting of the 1990s? How did minorities fare under the Democratic plans? Were sporadic Republican charges that Democrats split minority communities in order to insure the election of Anglo Democrats true?

The *Congressional Quarterly* retabulations imply that the Burton/Berman lines adopted in 1982 helped the Democrats somewhat in years in which voting trends were generally favorable to the party, but might have hurt them slightly in "bad years."[74] Democrats won the most congressional seats that they had ever

---

[71]John Balzar, "Deukmejian, Unfazed by Prop. 39 Loss, Vows to 'Reform' State Remapping Laws," *Los Angeles Times,* Nov. 8, 1984, I-3.

[72]John Balzar, "Sebastiani Revives Reapportionment," *Los Angeles Times,* Feb. 13, 1985, I-3; Philip Hager, "GOP Presses Challenge to '82 California Remapping," *ibid.,* Dec. 4, 1986, I-3.

[73]Philip Hager, "Judges Question GOP's Bid to Dump California Remap Plan," *Los Angeles Times,* Dec. 6, 1986, II-1; Philip Hager, "Court Upholds Democrats' '82 State Reapportionment," *ibid.,* April 23, 1988, I-1; David G. Savage, "Court Rejects GOP Bid to Overturn District Lines," *ibid.,* Oct. 4, 1988, I-3; Savage, "High Court Revives Political Remapping Case," *ibid.,* Nov. 15, 1988, I-3; Savage, "Justices Deny GOP Appeal of California Redistricting," *ibid.,* Jan. 18, 1989, I-1.

[74]Curiously, the *CQ* data do not appear to have been mentioned during the public debate in California over the "Burton Plan." It has been employed as an index of the intent of the redistricters by Born, 1985.

won in the state, 29 of 43, or 67.4%, in 1976. If the 1976 congressional votes are tabulated in the 1982 lines, the Democrats would have won 31 of 45, or 68.9%. In 1978, Democrats actually won 26 of 43, or 60.5%; the aggregated totals under the Burton plan would have been 26 of 45, or 57.8%. In the 1980 election, which Republicans touted throughout the decade as the proper election to use to determine the effect of the "Burton gerrymander,"[75] Democrats won 22 of 43 seats, or 51.2%, but if the Burton plan had been in effect, they would have carried only 21 of 45, or 46.7%.

Trends depicted in Figures 1 and 2 (page 147) also lend little support to the Republicans' charges. Although the Democratic advantage in voter registration dropped for a decade from its high point in 1976, it roughly flattened out after that, and the decline was offset by an apparent increase in party loyalty by those who did register as Democrats and a decrease among Republicans. As Senate Majority Leader David Roberti remarked at the time, "what is happening is that very, very conservative Democrats are now registering Republican. They are registering the way they vote."[76] In hypothetical congressional and Assembly districts in which 55% of the total registrants were Democrats and either 38% or 40% were Republicans, 1980 marked the low point for the Democrats. Democrats could expect to have carried a "55/40" congressional district by 15% in 1974, to have lost it by 27% in 1980, but to have won it by a 15% margin in 1990. In the Assembly, the figures are less dramatic, but there was still an estimated 15% swing over the period. The wide variation in such numbers suggests that redistricting did not produce a static political system, as the bare statistics on the number of seats switching from one party to another might seem to imply, and that it was unrealistic for Republicans to expect to do as well the rest of the decade, particularly in congressional races, as they did in the extraordinary year of 1980.[77]

Table 4 applies the behavioral patterns of the 1982 and 1984 elections to the registration patterns and boundary lines of 1980, and vice versa. It parallels Table 3 (page 148) and was estimated in the same manner. If the ordinary least-squares regression relationships between voting and registration in congressional districts had been those of 1982, but the Democratic and Republican registration percentages been the same as the 1980 boundaries, Democrats would have won 27 of 43 seats (62.2%), instead of the 22 of 43 (51.1%) that they actually won in 1980. This suggests that the 1980 party balance in congressional seats is a very misleading baseline with which to compare the results under the Burton plan. In the Assembly, the comparable figures are 49 and 47. The trends in 1982, a year of

[75]Computed from data in: *Congressional Quarterly,* 1983, 33-85. Curiously, the anonymous author of the narrative section on California redistricting in the same volume (p. 29) does not appear to have bothered to make these calculations.

[76]Jerry Gillam and Douglas Shuit, "GOP Faces Hard Road in Senate Campaign," *Los Angeles Times,* Nov. 14, 1985, I-3.

[77]Daniel M. Weintraub and Jerry Gillam, "Remap Process No Longer a Narrow Political Concern," *Los Angeles Times,* March 11, 1990, A1.

Republican recession, were simply more favorable to the Democrats than those of 1980, a year of Democratic inflation.

TABLE 4. What If Voters Had Behaved as in 1982 and 1984, but in the 1980 Districts, and Vice Versa?

Boundaries in Effect	Behavioral Pattern		
	1980	1982	1984
Panel A: Congress			
1980	22	27	28
1982	26	28	–
1984	22	–	27
Panel B: Assembly			
1980	47	49	57
1982	50	48	–
1984	41	–	47

Entries are numbers of seats won or estimated to b e won by Democrats.

To estimate the effect of changing boundaries, one should read down the columns of Table 4 and similar tables, thus keeping the behavior constant, but varying the boundaries. In a bad Democratic year such as 1980, the 1982 Burton boundaries seem to have gained the Democrats at most three seats,[78] while those of 1984[79] actually lost them 2.2% of the seats (22 of 45 in 1984 vs. 22 of 43 in 1980). The pattern is very similar in the Assembly. In 1982, the boundaries seem to have made little difference in the outcomes, as Democrats are predicted to have won a half of a percentage point more seats under the Masters' Plan than under Burton, and one more Assembly seat. In 1984, when President Reagan's coattails disappeared, the Democrats might well have won an additional congressional seat and as many as ten Assembly seats if they had still been operating under the Masters' Plan. These results suggest that Burton and Berman were quite risk averse, padding the margins of incumbents, instead of gambling that a series of

---

[78] 26 of 45 is 57.8%. Applying this percentage to the 43 districts the State had in the 1970s gives 24.8 seats, or 25 rounded off. Democrats actually won 22 of 43 in 1980, and 25-22=3.

[79] 1984 was actually a good year for Democrats below the Presidential level in California, as Republicans targeted only two marginal Democratic congressmen in 1984, both parties concentrated on Proposition 39, and every political observer knew very early that turnout in the presidential contest between Walter Mondale and Ronald Reagan would make little difference in Reagan Country. Therefore, neither party's vote for Congress or the Assembly was very high, and there were few close contests, especially for Congress.

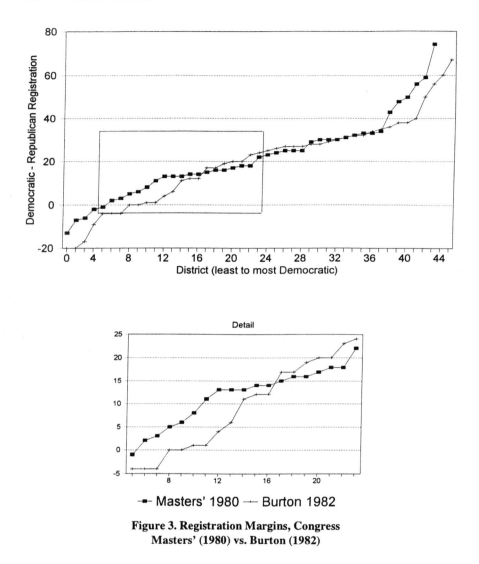

**Figure 3. Registration Margins, Congress
Masters' (1980) vs. Burton (1982)**

close districts might fall their party's way. While such a strategy reduces turn-over, it does not maximize partisan gains. By this measure, the Burton partisan gerrymander was largely a fiction.

A final way to gauge the difference between the Burton Plan and the 1970s Masters' Plan is to subtract the Republican from the Democratic registration in each district in 1980 and again in 1982, order each series (separately) from the most Republican to the most Democratic district, and graph one plan against

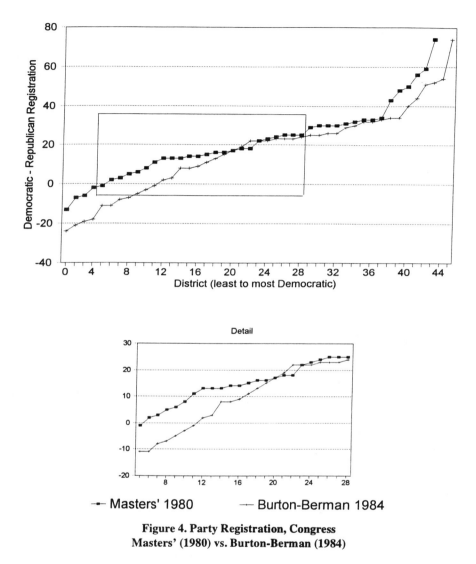

Figure 4. Party Registration, Congress
Masters' (1980) vs. Burton-Berman (1984)

another. Figure 3 compares registration figures from the last year of the Masters' Plan, 1980, against those of the first Burton Plan as it stood at the time of the 1982 election. Figure 4 compares 1980 with the amended Burton Plan, using November 1984 statistics.

Figure 3 shows that while Burton packed somewhat larger percentages of Republicans into safely Republican districts, McKaskle had packed more Democrats into overwhelmingly Democratic districts. Figure 4 demonstrates that the revised congressional plan, which enough Republican members of Congress and the legislature preferred to allow to pass easily, created even safer Republican districts. In the range of competitive districts, however, the more detailed inset graphs above Figures 3 and 4 make clear how little the registration patterns of the three plans differed. Democrats won only two congressional districts in 1982 in which they enjoyed a registration margin over the Republicans of less than 20%. In the roughly competitive terrain of 10% to 30% Democratic registration margins, there was little to distinguish the court-ordered plan of the 1970s from the "partisan gerrymander" of the 1980s. The Burton Plan created slightly more districts with about a 20% Democratic registration margin, while McKaskle's plan, by 1980, had more at approximately the 15% level. Shifts in the party balance over the decade, the influence of economic events or scandals, or the presence of especially attractive or unattractive candidates could easily outweigh such tiny registration differences. Analogous graphs for the Assembly, not presented here, yield similar conclusions.

In a 1991 press conference on redistricting, Speaker Willie Brown asserted that Republicans failed to capture control of the Assembly during the 1980s not because of partisan gerrymandering, but "because they have fielded inferior candidates and run poor campaigns."[80] Before he died in 1983, Congressman Phil Burton described his strategy in redistricting: "The most important thing you do, before anything else, is you get yourself in a position (to) draw the lines for (your own) district. Then, you draw them for all your friends before you draw anyone else's."[81] These two statements illuminate the preceding statistical comparisons of the plans of the 1970s and 80s. By concentrating their money and energy on repealing the Democrats' boundary lines, Republicans may not only have failed to target their funds wisely. They may also have created such low expectations of victory as to discourage better potential candidates from running and potential supporters from contributing time and funds to them. Railing against reapportionment, in other words, may have been self-defeating for the GOP. Burton's typically crusty boast reflects widely known facts: He buttressed the congressional district of his brother John Burton (who, however, declined to run for reelection in 1982), collapsed that of his bitter opponent Congressman John Rousselot, and drew three districts for Howard Berman and his allies and two more designed to elect Latinos. After accomplishing this—all six of these Democratic districts had at least a 27% registration advantage in 1982—even Phil Burton and Michael Berman could not do much more than protect enough incumbents to get a plan through the legisla-

---

[80]Daniel M. Weintraub, "Incumbents Come First in Redistricting, Speaker Says," *Los Angeles Times*, Aug. 30, 1991, A3. Tim Hodson noted instructive examples: Assembly campaigns in Santa Barbara in 1982 and 1984 and in Riverside in 1984, and Senate elections in Los Angeles in 1985, and Santa Barbara, Riverside, and coastal northern California throughout the decade.

[81]Quoted in Baker, 1989, 13.

ture. Although it was in their interest to claim as much credit as they could, they simply did not have extra Democratic voters left over to change the face of California politics for a decade.[82]

IV. THE 1990S: BACK INTO THE JUDICIAL THICKET

A. "The Maximum Number of Republican Seats"

Less than a year after losing their judicial challenge to the California reapportionment of the 1980s, Republicans began their campaign to control the redistricting of 1991. In fact, they might be said to have begun it in 1986, when they fervently supported a campaign to replace the Democratic majority on the State Supreme Court with a Republican one. Republicans, *Los Angeles Times* reporter John Balzar noted, "lead the opposition to the chief justice," Rose Bird, charging that she "has sided with Democrats, or at least liberals, on some key cases over the years—in particular, protecting a Democrat-drawn reapportionment plan for the Legislature and Congress from a GOP initiative challenge, a ruling that partisans on both sides take personally to this day." According to Bird's defenders, the opposition's $9 million campaign against her, led by Republican Gov. George Deukmejian, amounted to "the slease parade of 1986,...an unheard-of intrusion by the executive branch into the...independence of the judiciary."[83] After spearheading the defeat of the state's first female Chief Justice, its first Latino liberal Associate Justice, and another liberal Anglo, Deukmejian appointed his former law partner Malcolm Lucas, like him an Anglo male conservative, as Chief Justice.

Reapportionment was the Republican National Committee's "No. 1 national goal" in the 1990 election cycle, according to National Chairman Lee Atwater, and "the governorship of California has more than any other single thing to do with the national reapportionment than anything I can think of." Closer to home, Assembly Minority Leader Bill Jones asserted that "Reapportionment is the whole ballgame....The political landscape in California will be shaped in no small part by that for the next 10 to 20 years."[84] Coupled with the push to elect nationally ambitious Pete Wilson governor, Republicans sponsored two initiatives on the subject for the June 1990 ballot. Written by "top Republican activists," proposition 118 aimed at forcing a bipartisan plan by requiring that it be passed by two-thirds of both houses of the legislature, signed by the governor,

---

[82]For a similar general conclusion about reapportionment in the 1970s and 80s throughout the country, see Niemi and Jackman, 1991, 199.

[83]John Balzar, "GOP Relishes, and Democrats Fear, Impact of Bird Campaign," *Los Angeles Times*, Feb. 10, 1986, I-3; untitled story, *ibid.*, April 18, 1986, I-2; Frank Clifford, "Supreme Court: An Ominous Question," *ibid.*, I-1. The leading ostensible issue in the campaign against Bird and the other Democrats on the Court was the death penalty. In the nine years since the Republicans took over the Court, the State has executed two persons.

[84]Robert Shogan, "'90 California Governor Race Seen as Key to Redistricting," *Los Angeles Times*, Oct. 26, 1989, A3; Daniel M. Weintraub, "Lawmakers' Fall Session Is Sure to Be Divisive," *ibid.*, Aug. 18, 1991, A3.

and ratified by the voters. If the legislature did not act by July 15 in the year after the census, the State Supreme Court (by 1990, safely Republican) would take over. A competing proposition, backed by other Republicans, would take effect if it got a larger majority than Proposition 118 did. Proposition 119 proposed to establish a judge-appointed commission of five Democrats, five Republicans, and two independents, chosen with concern for racial, ethnic, gender, and geographic diversity, to consider plans submitted to it by interested groups.

Although both propositions established guidelines about following geographic and city-county boundaries and requiring "competitive" districts, neither mentioned protection of ethnic voters, leaving the propositions open to charges by Democrats that "both measures are designed to aid Republicans by concentrating ethnic minorities into a few districts," and that by scrambling current boundaries, they would "unseat minority and women legislators, who only recently have begun to make gains after decades of being shut out of office." Others claimed that it would decrease congressional support for the environment, since it would reduce the number of Northern California members whose districts touched the coast, where voters of both parties tended to be more environmentalist. Common Cause, the National Organization for Women, the Sierra Club, the League of Conservation Voters, and the Mexican-American Legal Defense and Education Fund (MALDEF) opposed both propositions, while major corporations such as Chevron, Hewlett Packard, and TransAmerica Insurance Company supplemented the Republican National Committee's $675,000 contribution in favor of them. With Democratic candidates pooling funds to oppose the measures and organized labor and other Democratically-oriented interest groups joining them, the grand total of spending in the campaigns for and against the initiatives topped $6 million.[85]

Once again, the Democrats surprisingly turned back redistricting initiatives. In early May of 1990, fewer than one in four voters felt they knew enough to express opinions on Propositions 118 and 119, but when read descriptions of them, solid pluralities backed both. Yet a month later, after another skillful TV and direct mail campaign directed for the Democrats by Michael Berman, the electors vetoed both propositions by 2-1 margins, nearly half of self-identified Republicans joining 80% of the Democrats in defeating them.[86] November, however, brought more cheerful news for the GOP, as voters not only moved U.S.

---

[85]Daniel M. Weintraub and Jerry Gillam, "Remap Process No Longer a Narrow Political Concern," *Los Angeles Times,* March 11, 1990, A1; Joe Scott, "Old Allies Go to War Over Remap," *ibid.,* April 1, 1990, M5; Weintraub, "Common Cause Opposes Plan for Redistricting Commission," *ibid.,* May 2, 1990, A3; Weintraub, "Brown Calls Redistricting Propositions GOP 'Fraud,'" *ibid.,* May 9, 1990, A3; Weintraub, "Fraud Charges Traded on Redistricting Propositions," *ibid.,* May 17, 1990, A3; Weintraub, "Voters Could Radically Alter Redistricting," *ibid.,* May 27, 1990, A3; Weintraub, "Redistricting Measures Costliest on the Ballot," *ibid.,* June 2, 1990, A29.

[86]George Skelton, "Feinstein Widens Support, Increases Lead," *Los Angeles Times,* May 6, 1990, A1; Daniel Weintraub, "Voters Could Radically Alter Redistricting," *ibid.,* May 27, 1990, A3; Daniel Hays Lowenstein, "The Message That Voters Sent in Rejecting Propositions 118 and 119," *ibid.,* June 17, 1990, M5.

Senator Pete Wilson into the Governor's mansion, but also limited members of the Assembly to three two-year terms and Senators to two four-year terms and sliced legislative staffs by a third. Using Wilson's veto power, Republicans would be able to block any reapportionment that they did not like, and even if they did not get just the districts they desired, they would at least be able to retire experienced Democrats, especially their nemesis Speaker Willie Brown, later in the decade.[87] And according to the Democrats' national reapportionment leader, Congressman Vic Fazio of Sacramento, some Republicans hoped to wield enough power in reapportionment to reduce the Democratic congressional delegation from 26 of 45 in 1990 to 20 of 52 in 1992.[88]

The Democratic strategy on reapportionment in 1991 was simple: conciliate minority groups and make a deal with either conservative or moderate Republicans. Thus, they made Peter Chacon, a San Diego Latino, chairman of the Assembly Elections and Reapportionment Committee, named Sen. Art Torres to the Senate Elections and Reapportionment Committee, appointed Latinos as counsels to each committee, and instructed redistricting technicians to group together nearby areas of ethnic minority concentration. When MALDEF had trouble with the technical details of some of its plans, Democrats offered assistance without distorting MALDEF's intentions. The Assembly Democrats' preferred sets of plans (referred to as "Plan A" for each house) were primarily negotiating documents, Democratic daydreams floated in order to be bargained away or pressed in court, should the negotiations with the Republicans deadlock. To conservative Republicans, the Democrats offered a set of plans, termed "Plan B," that concentrated Republican seats in areas thought to be strongly anti-abortion and anti-gun control, and they managed to obtain the endorsement of Georgia Congressman Newt Gingrich for the congressional version of this scheme. Another set of plans, designated "Plan C," created seats in areas where Republicans were considered more likely to be pro-choice and pro-environment, which was believed to be attractive to the supposedly "moderate" Pete Wilson. The three plans constituted a public announcement that the Democrats were willing to bargain with anyone.[89]

The less partisan Senate managed a bipartisan compromise, which passed, 37-0. The same Senate plan was attached to all three of the Assembly Democrats'

---

[87]Republican Assembly candidates often seemed to run against Brown as much as against their actual opponents, and their pamphlets sometimes featured photos of Brown and made transparent appeals to racial bigotry in their references to him. Dan Morain, "Speaker's Rearranging of Assembly Is Lesson in Power," *Los Angeles Times*, Jan. 1, 1993, A25.

[88]William J. Eaton, "Fazio Sees Battle Over 100 New House Seats in Remap," *Los Angeles Times*, Nov. 9, 1990, A4.

[89]Daniel M. Weintraub, "Remap Plans Would Add 4 House Seats in Southland," *Los Angeles Times*, Sept. 12, 1991, A1; Weintraub and Mark Gladstone, "Lawmakers Miss Deadline for Redrawing Districts," *ibid.*, Sept. 14, 1991, A22; Gladstone, "Redistricting Expertise Brings Berman Back to Sacramento," *ibid.*, B1; Weintraub, "Bipartisan Redistricting Deal Taking Shape," *ibid.*, Sept. 15, 1991, A3; Weintraub, "Wilson Demands Remap Changes That Favor GOP," *ibid.*, Sept. 19, 1991, A3; Weintraub, "Democrats Pass Redistricting Plans," *ibid.*, Sept. 20, 1991, A3.

proposals. Although Senators favored presenting their plan to Gov. Wilson separately, partly in hopes that he might honor the Senate compromise, and partly because a unanimously-passed bipartisan plan might appeal to the State Supreme Court if it were not attached to a partisan plan, Speaker Brown refused to allow the separation, probably to increase the pressure on the Governor not to veto everything.[90]

Gov. Wilson's strategy was even simpler: Refuse to negotiate or to let any other Republican seriously negotiate with the Democratic majorities in the Assembly, Senate, or Congress, appoint a "commission" without consulting any Democratic or minority group leader, veto all legislative plans, turn the issue over to the State Supreme Court—which Wilson aides privately referred to during this period as "Pete's law firm"—and suggest that the Court's special masters use the Commission's proposal as a starting point.[91] From time to time, the Governor and other Republicans, as well as the Democratic leaders, issued various "good government" statements, such as that Wilson wanted "an honest reapportionment, one that favors people over politicians," and from time to time, Republicans murmured nice things about ethnic minorities. "We think we have a lot in common with some of those minority groups," the Governor's aide Marty Wilson declared awkwardly. But when they came to define "fair" districts, Republican leaders acknowledged that they were fundamentally interested in partisan advantage. A "fair district," Assembly Minority Leader Bill Jones announced, was one in which Republican registration was at least 38% and which George Bush had carried in 1988. "Our position," said Congressman John Doolittle, the spokesman for California's Republican delegation in reapportionment matters in 1991, "has always been to push for the maximum number of Republican seats."[92]

At first, some blacks and Latinos thought that Republicans might deal with them. Black Republican Steve Hamilton, vice chair of the nationalist Congress of Racial Equality, charged that "The current districts take advantage of blacks.

---

[90]Tim Hodson, a principal staff member in the Senate reapportionment, helped me to understand the significance of the Senate's actions.

[91]Wilson spent approximately $1.5 million of his campaign funds on Republican efforts during the 1991 redistricting. Daniel M. Weintraub, "Brown Leads Campaign Race for Cash," *Los Angeles Times*, Feb. 1, 1994, C1.

[92]Richard C. Paddock, "Big Population Gains Will drive State Redistricting," *Los Angeles Times*, March 25, 1991, A1; Daniel M. Weintraub and Alan C. Miller, "Governor Stops Plan to Negotiate Remap Deal," *ibid.*, May 23, 1991, A3; Weintraub, "Wilson Outlines redistricting Strategy," *ibid.*, July 19, 1991, A3; Jerry Gillam, "Wilson Picks Redistricting Panel," *ibid.*, July 27, 1991, A21; Sherry Bebitch Jeffe, "This Year's Reapportionment Script is Still Full of Question Marks," *ibid.*, Aug. 18, 1991, M6; Weintraub, "Wilson Asks Court Takeover of Redistricting," *ibid.*, Sept. 7, 1991, A1; Weintraub and Mark Gladstone, "Lawmakers Miss Deadline for Redrawing Districts," *ibid.*, Sept. 14, 1991, A22; Weintraub, "Bipartisan Redistricting Deal Taking Shape," *ibid.*, Sept. 15, 1991, A3; Weintraub and Carl Ingram, "Chance Fading for Bipartisan Deal on Reapportionment," *ibid.*, Sept. 17, 1991, A3; Sherry Bebitch Jeffe, "Wilson Under Fire," *ibid.*, Sept. 22, 1991, M1; Weintraub, "Remap Bills Are Vetoed by Wilson," *ibid.*, Sept. 24, 1991, A1; Philip Hager and Weintraub, "Redistricting Task Goes to State Justices," *ibid.*, Sept. 26, 1991, A3.

You're nothing more than a pawn." Not only was his charge patently false,[93] but his solution, to pack more blacks into districts that already elected black representatives, thereby reducing black influence in surrounding districts and overall, aimed more at assisting Anglo Republicans than the people he claimed to speak for. Bay Area Republicans circulated maps that lumped all minorities together and shifted lines allegedly to create several minority influence districts and assuredly to increase the number of districts potentially winnable by the GOP. Seeking to avoid being captured by either side, MALDEF, the Asian Pacific Legal Center, and California Rural Legal Assistance worked independently of either party, proposing partial plans for minority areas that did not take into account the spillover effects on predominantly Anglo districts—demonstrating a naivete that Democratic politicians of all ethnic groups decried and Republicans applauded. Pointing out that without Democratic control of the legislature, African-American and Latino officials would lose powerful committee chairs and control of committee majorities, Speaker Willie Brown argued that MALDEF's plan "would be worse for minorities" in the long run than Democratically-produced proposals for the Assembly.[94] In the end, all the maneuvering was irrelevant, because Gov. Wilson refused to negotiate with anyone and even used White House pressure to shepherd any straying Republicans back into the compliant fold.[95]

A month and a half before the legislature's scheduled adjournment, Wilson appointed an ethnically, sexually, and nominally politically balanced six-person reapportionment panel: two retired Republican judges, one of whom was Asian-American; a female black Republican expert on Russian politics who had served on the staff of the National Security Council under President Bush; and three Democrats, including one Latino, ranging in age from 70 to 83.[96] None of them appears to have held elective office or had any previous experience in reapportionment. No doubt their races, genders, and political affiliations were sufficient qualification, since they scotched predictable charges of partisanship and insensitivity to minority group and female concerns.[97] Their two chief consultants were Prof. Gordon Baker, the junior member of the 1973 McKaskle-Baker team and a political scientist at the University of California at Santa Barbara whose standards for redistricting in a 1989 article ignored the effect on minority ethnic

---

[93]The proportion of African-Americans in the Assembly, Senate, and Congress from the state, 7.9%, was slightly higher than their proportion in the general population, 7.4%.

[94]Daniel M. Weintraub, "Minorities Get GOP Support in Remap Battle," *Los Angeles Times*, Aug. 26, 1991, A3; Irene Chang, "Asians, Latinos Join in Proposal for Remapping," *ibid*, Aug. 31, 1991, B2; Bill Boyarsky, "New Agenda for Asians and Latinos," *ibid*., Sept. 4, 1991, B2; Weintraub, "Proposed Senate Districts Protect Most Incumbents," *ibid*., Sept. 5, 1991, A3; Weintraub, "Latinos Offer Own Plan for Redistricting," *ibid*., Sept. 6, 1991, A3; Weintraub and Carl Ingram, "Chance Fading for Bipartisan Deal on Reapportionment," *ibid*., Sept. 17, 1991, A3.

[95]Daniel N. Weintraub, "Bipartisan Redistricting Deal Taking Shape," *Los Angeles Times*, Sept. 15, 1991, A3.

[96]Jerry Gillam, "Wilson Picks Redistricting Panel," *Los Angeles Times*, July 27, 1991, A21.

[97]Daniel M. Weintraub, "Wilson Outlines Redistricting Strategy," *Los Angeles Times*, July 19, 1991, A3.

groups, and Prof. Richard Morrill, a Geographer at the University of Washington, who had drawn plans for the Rose Institute in 1981.[98] Unfortunately for Wilson's strategy, his Commission took much longer to draw districts than expected, robbing him of a debating point against the Legislature.[99] When the Commission's plans were revealed, moreover, they decimated districts then represented by members of minority groups, reducing the number of congressional seats winnable by blacks in Los Angeles from three to one and the number of probable Latino seats in all three bodies from 10 to 5. In the Assembly, the professors had overconcentrated blacks in one Los Angeles Assembly district and set up a probable confrontation between African-Americans and Latinos in another. As a consequence, the Governor had to bring in his redistricting consultant, Joe Shumate, the author of the 1983 Sebastiani Plan, to fix up the minority districts to fight an almost certain Voting Rights Act challenge.[100] (See Table 5, page 175, for further details.) No further demonstration of the effect of "balanced" commissions or "nonpartisan" consultants on minority representation is necessary.

Stymied by Wilson, Democrats in mid-September mechanically passed three plans for each legislative body, perhaps hoping that Wilson would finally choose one, but more probably out of frustration. "I'm at the breaking point," said Speaker Brown, the veteran of more drawn-out legislative struggles than any other legislative leader in the state's history. "I do better letting the courts rip me off....Not from Day 1 did I believe that the governor and [Assembly Republican leader Bill] Jones wanted to do anything except have me deliver the Democratic Party to them. I, of course, was not going to do that."[101] Immediately vetoing all three, Wilson turned over the task to the State Supreme Court, which appointed as Special Masters three retired Anglo[102]

---

[98]Baker, 1989. On Morrill's 1981 plan, see Cain, 1984, 13-14.

[99]Daniel M. Weintraub, "Wilson Asks Court Takeover of Redistricting," *Los Angeles Times*, Sept. 7, 1991, A1.

[100]Daniel M. Weintraub, "Wilson Panel Remap Plan Would Help Republicans," *Los Angeles Times*, Oct. 12, 1991, A31. Under the Governor's Commission's plan, the black population percentages in the three most heavily African-American congressional districts in Los Angeles County were 57.3, 20.7, and 14.7. One district was heavily packed, and black incumbents would have lost one and probably two of the three seats. By contrast, the Democrats' plans spread the black population around in the three seats, making their percentages 40.5, 38.3, and 30.1 and keeping the boundaries relatively stable, and the final Masters' Plan set the same percentages at 40.3, 42.7, and 33.6. Under each of these plans, given contemporary voting patterns in the area, black incumbents would quite probably retain their seats.

In the Assembly, the black population percentages in the relevant districts in Los Angeles under the Commission plan were 53.9, 40, 32, 25.5, and 21; under the Democratic plans, they were 38.6, 35.8, 33.8, 29, and 24.8. While the Latino population percentages were generally high in all of these districts, Democrats made sure they were always substantially below the black percentages, avoiding interethnic confrontations. By contrast, the Commission's 21% black district was 75.1% Latino in population and 26.2% Latino in registration.

[101]Daniel M. Weintraub, "Democrats Pass Redistricting Plans," *Los Angeles Times*, Sept. 20, 1991, A3 (first part of quotation); Weintraub and Carl Ingram, "Chance Fading for Bipartisan Deal on Reapportionment," *ibid.*, Sept. 17, 1991, A3 (quotation after elision). Republicans and some Democrats thought at first that this was just another of the Speaker's negotiating ploys.

judges, two Republicans and one nominal Democrat, all of whom had been appointed to the bench by Republican governors. The Masters, in turn, relied chiefly on University of San Francisco law professor Paul McKaskle, who had drawn the 1973 Court-sponsored plans.[103]

Speaking as though electoral boundaries had nothing to do with electing people, the Special Masters claimed to have acted utterly apolitically. "We had no agenda, no political purpose, and we did not consider any political consequences," announced George A. Brown, a Reagan appointee to the bench from the conservative Central Valley county of Kern.[104] Nonetheless, the immediate reaction to the plans from *Los Angeles Times* pundit Sherry Bebitch Jeffe was that it portended "a Democratic disaster of major proportions: their majority in the Assembly is at risk; their margin in the state Senate is likely to decline, and their lopsided domination of the state's congressional delegation is at an end." Rose Institute Republican Alan Heslop declared that Pete Wilson and Willie Brown "rolled the dice. It seems to me the governor won and won pretty big. Willie Brown lost and may have lost in a decisive fashion and a rather permanent fashion." Republican leaders in Sacramento were said to be "overjoyed," predicting that Republicans would win majorities in the Assembly and congressional delegations and 19 of the 40 seats in the Senate, while Assembly Democrat Steve Peace denounced the Masters' plan as a "partisan gerrymander of gigantic proportions," and an unidentified associate of the Berman-Waxman group asserted that "It looks like a partisan Republican plan drawn by a partisan Republican court." The seats of Democratic reapportionment leaders seemed especially targeted: Congressman Vic Fazio's Sacramento-area district was extensively reshaped and made much more conservative, while the Berman-Waxman allies' West Los Angeles seats in Congress were reduced from four to two, and the residences of three of their Assembly allies were placed in the same district.[105] The

---

[102]One judge, Rafael Galceran, had a Spanish surname, though he was born in Jackson, Mississippi in 1921 (Livermore, 1985/86, 295) and was completely unknown to the Latino legal community in Los Angeles county, where he lived, in 1991. "When I testified before the Masters," said MALDEF reapportionment leader Arturo Vargas (personal communication, Aug. 2, 1995), "all I remember is looking up at three old white men."

[103]Daniel M. Weintraub, "Remap Bills Are Vetoed by Wilson," *Los Angeles Times*, Sept. 24, 1991, A1; Philip Hager and Weintraub, "Redistricting Task Goes to State Justices," *ibid.*, Sept. 26, 1991, A3; Hager, "Wilson Asks Federal Court to Stay Out of Redistricting Fight," *ibid.*, Oct. 9, 1991, A3; Hager, "How Panel Redrew the Political Map," *ibid.*, Dec. 8, 1992, A3.

[104]Philip Hager, "How Panel Redrew the Political Map," *Los Angeles Times*, Dec. 8, 1992, A3. Intentionally or unintentionally, the State Supreme Court distorted what had transpired when they claimed that "the parties and amici curiae uniformly confirmed at oral argument that the process employed by the Masters was entirely free of political bias or intent." *Wilson v. Eu*, 1 Cal.4th 707, 719 (1992). In fact, what the Democratic attorneys said in oral argument was that they were not prepared to make an affirmative case that the plan had a partisan intent—a "Scotch verdict," rather than a "not guilty" verdict, and they argued strenuously that the plan had a pro-Republican effect or bias.

[105]Jeffe, "Why Republicans May Rue Their Heartfelt Support for Term Limits," *Los Angeles Times*, Dec. 8, 1991, M6; Daniel M. Weintraub, "Wilson Got His Wish in Remap Plan," *ibid.*, Dec. 5, 1991, A3; Weintraub, "Remap Could Bring Major Gains for GOP," *ibid.*, Dec. 4, 1991, A1; Bill Stall and Alan C. Miller, "Plan Would Carve Up Democratic Stronghold," *ibid.*, Dec. 4, 1991, A25.

district of the longtime Democratic Senate leader David Roberti, who had negotiated the compromise Senate proposal, was completely collapsed, leaving him a district to run in only because of the forced resignation on corruption charges of another Senator, and shortly thereafter making Roberti the nation's first victim of term limits.

Minority reaction to the Masters' Plan was unfavorable, if less harsh. One much more secure black Assembly district could have been drawn in Los Angeles county, and African-American Congressman Julian Dixon's seat gained affluent Jewish Democrats and lost Anglo Republicans, setting up a potential intraparty, interethnic battle in case the popular Dixon retired.[106] The rapidly growing Latino population gained another congressional seat in Los Angeles in this and every other proposed plan, but the Masters' configuration substituted Anglo for black and Latino Democrats in the adjoining Latino seat held by Edward Roybal since 1962. Only the unwillingness of the Berman-Waxman alliance to back a non-Latino candidate kept the seat in Latino hands when Roybal retired in 1992. In Los Angeles county, MALDEF's proposed plan created six Assembly and three State Senate districts in which Latinos comprised at least 40% of the estimated registered voters. Comparable numbers in the Masters' Plan were four and two.[107]

McKaskle also believed that legally he had more responsibility to adhere to the vague state judicially created criteria of compactness and minimizing the crossing of political boundaries than he did to join centers of minority population—unless they could obviously control the politics of a district. And while in considering "majority-minority" or "control" districts, the Masters did consider the ethnicity of the other people in the districts, they claimed not to have considered the political composition of the others in "influence districts"—that is, those in which minorities could not by themselves elect a candidate of choice, but where they could strongly affect the choice of the district. (*Wilson* v. *Eu*, 1 Cal. 4th 707, 714-15, 722, 751-53, 767-69, 775-78, 790-91 (1992).)

Yet to blind oneself to partisanship (if that is what the Masters really did) is to endanger minority positions and restrict minority influence. As the Dixon and Roybal examples above spotlight, to control an overwhelmingly Democratic district, minorities need to compose a larger proportion of the population than in a district with a somewhat larger proportion of Republicans, because the crucial contest in the Democratic district will be the primary. Moreover, to place African-Americans or Democratic Latinos in a district that Republicans can easily carry will deprive the minorities of nearly all influence over the winning office-

---

[106]When two longtime Anglo Democratic incumbents were thrown into the same district, Carson City Councilwoman Juanita M. McDonald, an African-American, won a startling upset victory in the primary and faced no Republican opposition in the general election.

[107]Daniel M. Weintraub, "Latino Group Seeks to Alter Remap Plans," *Los Angeles Times*, Dec. 17, 1991, A3.

holder. Their votes will be almost entirely wasted.[108] Even before mainstream California Republicans embraced the anti-immigrant Proposition 187 in 1994 and the effort to end affirmative action for underrepresented minorities in 1995-96, members of the party had based campaigns on the immigrant "invasion" from the south, circulated scurrilous anti-Latino doggerel in the legislature, and run anti-welfare TV ads that featured black and brown "welfare mothers."[109] Since all such ethnically divisive efforts help to insure that African-Americans and Latinos will remain loyal Democrats, partisan and minority group concerns will necessarily continue to overlap in redistricting.

Table 5 summarizes the ethnic percentages in each of the 45 congressional districts in the Burton-Berman reapportionment (as of 1990), and in the 52 districts in the 1991 Masters' Plan and the seven alternative plans. Except for the egregious design of the Governor's Commission, which clearly overconcentrated the black population and the Latino registration, the contrast between the plans lies more in districts in which minorities could influence the result than in those which they could effectively dominate by their numbers. Pro-Democratic plans (1990, A, B, C, and MALDEF) concentrated minorities, while pro-Republican plans (the Masters' plan, the Commission's, Shumate, and Jones) scattered them. Thus, the favorite plans of the Democrats, A and C, created two more districts than any of the Republican plans in which the black population made up 10% or more, and Plan A drew two or three more districts in which the Latino registration was above 20% than any of the Republican plans did.

Equally important, the Republican plans tended, much more than the Democratic plans, to dilute ethnic minority influence by adding minority voters to Republican districts. For instance, congressional Plan A created 11 districts in which the Latino population percentage was between 30% and 60%—which, in contemporary California, will usually produce too low a percentage of Latino registrants and potential crossover voters to elect a candidate of choice of the Latino community—and where the Democratic registration margin over the Republicans

---

[108]Examples are the heavily black and brown Los Angeles county community of Pomona, tacked onto the predominantly Republican Orange county 41st Congressional District, and rural, 65% Latino Imperial county, tacked onto the heavily Republican San Diego suburbs in the 52nd Congressional District. The victorious Republicans in these two districts averaged 97 (where 100 is the most conservative) on the *Congressional Quarterly* "conservative coalition" index in 1993 and 1994. The average score for Latino members of Congress from Southern California in the same years was 26.

[109]"Bill (Tax Reduction) Hoge for Assembly," "Invasion: U.S.A." (pamphlet, 1992, in author's possession); English Language Political Action Committee, "Protect English: Vote Against Feinstein For U.S. Senator November 3, 1992," (pamphlet, 1992, in author's possession); Eric Bailey and Dan Morain, "Anti-Immigration Bills Flood Legislature," *Los Angeles Times*, May 3, 1993, A3; Morain and Mark Gladstone, "Racist Verse Stirs Up Anger in Assembly," *ibid.*, May 19, 1993, A3; Gladstone, "Assemblyman Takes Heat for Anti-Immigrant Poem," *ibid.*, May 20, 1993, A3. TV ads for Gov. Wilson's proposal to cut Aid to Families with Dependent Children by 25% spotlighted minorities. The November 1992 ballot proposition was rejected by the voters of the state. In the summer of 1993, Gov. Wilson sought to raise his 15% approval rating by calling for the repeal of the citizenship section of the 14th Amendment, and he rode his endorsement of Prop. 187 to reelection and the launching of his 1996 presidential bid.

was 15% or more.[110] By contrast, the Masters' plan contained only 9 such districts, that of the Governor's Commission, 8, and the Jones or Republican plan, 7. Since Latinos and, even more so, African-Americans are reliable Democratic voters, it is in the interests of Democrats to concentrate them in influence districts, just as it is in the interests of Republicans to disperse or waste those minorities who cannot be packed into a minimal number of districts.[111] At least as interpreted by most political professionals in the state in 1991, the Voting Rights Act kept Republicans from overpacking minorities and kept Democrats from spreading them into a maximum number of influence districts, rather than first creating minority control districts, and then joining the remaining clusters to increase minority (and Democratic) power. Even apart from the necessity of complying with the Voting Rights Act and the ideological affinity between Anglo and minority Democrats, Democrats are likely to be more responsive than Republicans are to minority concerns in reapportionment because minorities are now firmly entrenched in the Democratic leadership and because minority voters form appreciable proportions of the coalitions required to elect Anglo Democrats.

Challenges to the Masters' plans by Democrats and representatives of MALDEF and the NAACP in the State Supreme Court and before a three-judge federal panel were brushed aside after brief hearings on straight party-line votes, each of the ten judges voting for the party of the person who had appointed her or him.[112]

B. Was The Masters' Plan Nonpartisan?

The initial election under the new lines was a Republican disaster, as Bill Clinton became the first Democratic presidential candidate to carry the state since 1964 and the first to carry San Diego county since 1944, and Democrats won two U.S. Senate seats. Under the Masters' plan, Democratic dominance of the congressional delegation declined by only one-tenth of one percent of the seats, and the party exactly maintained its 1990 margins in the Assembly and Senate. Three weeks before the election, Republican State Chairman Jim

---

[110]As Figures 1 and 2 (page 147) show, a 15% Democratic registration margin was approximately the minimum needed for the district to be fairly reliably Democratic in 1990 or 1992. In 1994, the necessary margin was about 20%. Because of the geographic and economic segregation of Anglos from ethnic minorities in contemporary California, minorities will usually automatically fall into overwhelmingly Democratic electoral districts. Thus, the fact that the Republican plans create both fewer Latino influence districts and fewer still that are contained in districts generally winnable by Democrats constitutes *prima facie* evidence of intentional discrimination.

[111]For a much extended argument about influence districts, see Kousser, 1993.

[112]Philip Hager, "Court Rejects Appeal of Redistricting Plan," *Los Angeles Times*, Jan. 29, 1992, A3. Federal Judge Thomas Tang, a Democrat, concurred with his two Republican colleagues on the narrow ground that, without a full hearing, the Voting Rights Act challenge to the Masters' Plan had not been conclusively proven—a position with which the plaintiffs did not disagree. The cases were *Wilson v. Eu, 1 Cal. 4th 707 (1992)* and *Members of the California Democratic Congressional Delegation v. Eu* (Case No. C 91 3383 FMS, N.D. CA). Speaker Willie Brown had reportedly had so much faith in the partisan fairness of Paul McKaskle that he allowed legislative Democrats to drop any prospective federal court challenge until it was too late to file. The NAACP apparently did not object to the congressional plan before the State Supreme Court, but did before the federal court.

TABLE 5. Ethnic Percentages for 1990 & 1991 Congressional Plans

Decile	Proposed Plans								
	1990 Plan	Masters	A	B	C	Gov. Com.	Shumate	Jones	MALDEF
Panel A: Black Population									
0-9.9	29	43	41	43	41	43	44		42
10-19.9	11	5	7	5	7	5	4		6
20-29.9	1	0	0	0	1	2	0		1
30-39.9	1	2	3	2	1	1	3		2
40.49.9	2	2	1	2	2	0	1		1
50-59.9	1	0	0	0	0	1	0		0
Panel B: Latino Population									
0-9.9	6	4	7	6	3	6	6	5	4
10-19.9	17	20	23	21	26	20	19	21	25
20-29.9	6	12	4	10	7	11	13	12	8
30-39.9	9	6	8	6	7	5	5	6	4
40-49.9	3	4	4	3	3	4	3	0	4
50.-59.9	1	3	2	2	2	4	4	5	5
60-69.9	3	2	3	3	3	1	1	2	1
70-79.9	0	0	0	0	0	1	0	1	0
80-89.9	0	1	1	1	1	0	1	0	1
Panel C: Latino Registration (estimate)									
0-9.9	22	27	29	29	29	27	28	27	31
10-19.9	19	18	14	15	15	18	20	18	13
20-29.9	1	2	5	4	4	5	1	2	3
30-39.9	2	2	2	2	2	1	2	3	3
40-49.9	1	3	2	2	2	0	3	2	2
50-59.9	0	0	0	0	0	1	0	0	0

*Entries are numbers of districts with stated percentages of population.
Masters' = 1991 Special Masters Plans (Feb. 1, 1992 registration data).
Plans A, B, C = Plans passed by Democratic legislature.
Gov. Com. = Plans drawn by Gov. Wilson's "nonpartisan" commission.
Shumate = Modification of Governor's Commission plans by Gov. Wilson's redistricting consultant.
Jones = Plans offered by Republicans in legislature.
MALDEF = Plans offered by Mexican-American Legal Defense & Education Fund.
Source: Computed from data supplied by Pactech Data Research

Dignan was predicting that the GOP would carry 26-29 congressional contests, but the party ended up with only 22, two of those extremely close GOP victories.[113] Why was the Republicans' faith in reapportionment frustrated, temporarily, at least, and what might have happened under other redistricting plans?

Certainly the recession, the deepest and longest in California since the Second World War, was the dominant force in the election results.[114] Particularly affecting Republican strongholds in Southern California, the economic downturn made George Bush so unpopular that he did not appear west of the Sierra Nevada mountains after October 1. Second was the fact that Democrats nominated more experienced and moderate candidates who often raised considerable sums. Thus, Vic Fazio spent $1.6 million, the fourth largest amount for a congressional candidate in the country, to defend his considerably altered Sacramento district against far-right gun lobbyist H.L. Richardson, Jane Harmon amplified her appeal with her husband's family's fortune in an open seat contest against conservative anti-abortionist Joan Milke Flores, and liberal Democrat Tony Beilenson survived the addition of Ventura county suburbs to his West Los Angeles district by conducting a well-tailored and well-financed campaign against Tom McClintock, the leader of the self-described "cavemen" faction of Assembly Republicans. Frank Riggs, a clear-cut Republican loser, was the only congressional incumbent of either party to fall, though several were endangered and eight retired. Nearly a quarter of the Republican primaries for the Assembly featured bitter conservative-moderate contests, and while conservatives won eleven of them, they lost five of those seats in November. Especially in Southern California, some of these were candidates of what might be termed the "bizarre right," including one who was caught on audio tape declaring his belief that the U.S. Air Force and four states had "official witches"[115] and another "Christian" candidate who equated his Jewish opponent's pro-choice stance with support for the Nazi Holocaust. Democrats picked up a few seats where, according to the registration percentages, they should never have had a chance. Third, Democrats energized by their party's presidential and U.S. Senate nominations registered more than twice as many new voters as the Republicans between May and October, increasing their statewide registration margin over the Republicans from nine percent to twelve percent, and outregistering the Republicans for the first time in the last four presidential election years.

---

[113]Patt Morrison, "Congress Races Being Run on Road Full of Potholes," *Los Angeles Times*, Oct. 13, 1992, A1.

[114]In this paragraph, I draw on the excellent detailed analysis in *California Journal*, 1992, as well as Daniel M. Weintraub and Mark Gladstone, "GOP Loses 2 Assembly Seats Despite Remap," *Los Angeles Times*, Nov. 5, 1992, A1; George Skelton, "Wilson Hints at Softer Style After Election Drubbing," *ibid.*, Nov. 5, 1992, A1; Glenn F. Bunting and Dan Morain, "Democrats Win 10-Seat Edge in Congressional Delegation," *ibid.*, Nov. 5, 1992, A3.

[115]In a 1994 rematch, this candidate won, allowing him to hunt whomever he wants to in Sacramento.

The registration drive often nudged districts that had seemed likely to go Republican in December 1991, when the Masters' Plan was announced, over into the competitive category, just as it bolstered marginally Democratic districts.[116]

Like the simulations from the elections and districting schemes of the 1970s and 1980s, simulations comparing the 1990, 1992, and 1994 contests undercut the notion that the Democratic redistricting of the 1980s drastically changed partisan outcomes. The first row of Table 6 (Plan A), which is computed in the same way that Tables 3 and 4 were, estimates what might have happened if the boundaries in effect had been those of the 1980s, but the relationships between voting and partisan registration had been those of 1992 or

TABLE 6: What If Voters Had Behaved as in 1990, 1992, or 1994, But Under Different Redistricting Arrangements?

	Behavioral Pattern					
	Congress			Assembly		
	Year					
	1990	1992	1994	1990	1992	1994
Plans						
Actual Lines						
1990	26**	28**	25**	48	48	40
Masters' (Nov. 1992, 1994)	–	30	27	–	48	39
Proposed Plans (Feb. 1, 1992)						
Plan A	32	33	28	50	48	41
Plan B	27	28	26	49	47	40
Plan C	30	31	27	49	46	39
MALDEF	30	30	24	47	43	38
Governor's Commission	29	28	19	45	41	33
Shumate	26	28	22	45	40	35
Jones	25	24	24	44	43	36
Masters' (Feb. 1992)	26	28	22	45	41	37

*Entries are numbers of seats won or estimated to be won by Democrats.
**of 45 seats—all other congressional results are of 52 seats.
Behavioral Pattern = Based on regression of relationships between election outcomes and registration in the stated year.
1990 = 1984 redistricting plans, with registration data as of 1990.
Masters' Actual = 1991 Special Masters' Plans (Nov. 1992 and 1994 registration data).
Plans A, B, C = Plans offered by Democratic legislature.
Maldef = Plans offered by Mexican-American Legal Defense & Education Fund.
Gov. Com = Plans drawn by Gov. Wilson's "nonpartisan" committee.
Shumate = Modification of Governor's Commission plans by Gov. Wilson's redistricting consultant.
Jones = Plans offered by Republicans in legislature.
Masters' Proposed = Special Masters' Plan with registration data as of Feb. 1, 1992.
Source: Computed from data supplied by Pactech Data Research.

---

[116]The Republican registration as a percentage of all voters declined in 17 of the 18 most competitive Assembly districts from January to September 1992. Daniel M. Weintraub, "GOP Bid for Assembly Control Becomes Long Shot," *Los Angeles Times*, Oct. 5, 1992, A1; Patt Morrison, "Congress Races Being Run on Road Full of Potholes," *ibid.*, Oct. 13, 1992, A1.

1994, instead of 1990. The differences between what actually happened in 1990 (Democrats won 26 and 48 seats, respectively, in Congress and the Assembly) and what could have been expected to happen if the voters had behaved as in 1992 are small. In a landslide Democratic year like 1992, under the "Burton gerrymander," the Democrats would have won 28 of 45 (62.2%) of the congressional seats, instead of the 30 of 52 (57.7%) that they did win in 1992 under the Masters' Plan. (Compare the first and second rows of the table.) The Assembly would likely have contained 48 Democrats, instead of the 47 actually elected in 1992. In a good year for the Democrats, then, the Burton plan would have given the Democrats approximately two more congressional seats than the Masters' Plan with the registration patterns of November 1992. These patterns were, as has been noted above, significantly more favorable for the Democrats than the patterns had been in 1990 or during the fall of 1991, when the Masters' Plan was drafted. (Compare row 2 with row 8.)

Nonetheless, reapportionment plans that were not adopted would probably have changed the outcomes dramatically. Rows 3-8 of Table 6 show how many seats Democrats could have expected to win under each of the plans if the relationships between party registration and voting had been those observed in the 1990, 1992, or 1994 elections.[117] If the relationships between party registration and voting had been the same as in 1990, Democrats could have expected to win 32 seats in Congress under the most pro-Democratic plan, Plan A, while under the plan proposed by the Republicans, termed the "Jones Plan" in the table, Democrats were likely to win only 25. For the Assembly, the expected difference in the two plans was six seats in 1990. Under the conditions of 1990, results under the Masters' plans tracked those under the more openly pro-Republican Jones and Shumate plans much more closely than under the plans proposed by the Democrats. Since it reflects the consequences that keen political observers might reasonably have anticipated on the basis of the most relevant recent data, columns 1 and 4 of these rows of Table 6 give the best indications of the partisan intent of each plan.[118]

As the extent of the 1992 Republican debacle in California became clear, some Democratic insiders claimed privately that the party was better off with the Masters' lines than they would have been with the plans they had fought for so hard, reasoning that some of the supposedly large number of marginally pro-Republican districts in the Masters' plan would wash ashore in the Democratic tide. However plausible the reasoning, Table 6 suggests that it is wrong. If the behavioral relationships in 1992 had been just as they were under the Masters'

---

[117]The Masters' Plan is listed in row 8 with its registration as of February 1992, to make its registration patterns comparable with the proposed plans that were not adopted. In row 2, its registration is as of November 1992 and November 1994, respectively.

[118]Even if the contentions of the Governor's Commission and the Special Masters that they ignored partisan considerations are credited, no one else ignored the partisan consequences of their plans, and those consequences played a large role in the reception each group gave to the "nonpartisan" plans.

Plan, but Plan A had been in effect, Democrats would have won 35, instead of 30 seats in Congress, and the same number, 48, in the Assembly. Under Plans B and C and the MALDEF Plan for Congress, which Democrats ended up backing during the federal court challenge to the Masters' Plan, Democrats would have carried from one to three more seats than under the Masters' Plan. For the Assembly, they would likely have done much better under Plans A, B, and C, and somewhat better under the MALDEF plan than under the Masters' plan. The most striking differences in Table 6, however, are between the Jones or Republican plan for Congress and the Masters', Commission, and Shumate plans for the Assembly, on the one hand, and all the other plans, on the other. The Masters' plan with the registration percentages at the time it was approved, as well as the Governor's Commission plan and its modification by Shumate would have been likely to give Democrats the barest of Assembly majorities. The Jones Plan so artfully packed Democrats into as few districts as possible that even in a year of Republican disaster—Democrats won 57.1% of the two-party vote for Congress in the average district—Republicans would be expected to win 28 of the 52 congressional seats (53.8%).[119] The difference between Plan A and the Jones Plan was nearly as large as the national swing in congressional seats in 1992!

Although the party registration percentages in California barely budged between November 1992 and November 1994, the national surge in the tendency to vote Republican (Ladd, 1995) cost California Democrats 9 Assembly and 3 congressional seats in 1994, several on each side being decided by extremely close margins. Had the Burton plan been in effect, Democrats would probably have held two more seats in Congress, and Plan A would have given them one more. (See Table 6.) Likewise, the Democratic plans of the 1980s or 90s might well have retained slight Democratic majorities in the Assembly. The contrast with the Republican and Masters' plans is again stark. Although Democrats won 51.7 % in the average California congressional district and 52.3% in the average Assembly district, the esthetically correct Governor's Commission plan would have awarded them only 36.5% of the congressional and 41.3% of the Assembly seats. The Republicans would likely have won fewer congressional seats in their banner year of 1994 under the Jones plan than under the Masters' plan.

Why different plans would be likely to lead to different results is made strikingly clear in Figure 5, which compares Democratic registration margins in the 52-seat Jones congressional plan with those in the 45-seat Burton-Berman plan of the 1980s. The upper right-hand corner shows that the Jones plan contained many more heavily Democratic districts than the 1982 plan, which enabled it to shave Democratic totals elsewhere. In the crucial central portion

---

[119]The Democrats' margins in an average district in 1992 would have been approximately the same under almost all of the proposed plans. See Kousser, 1995a, Appendix B.

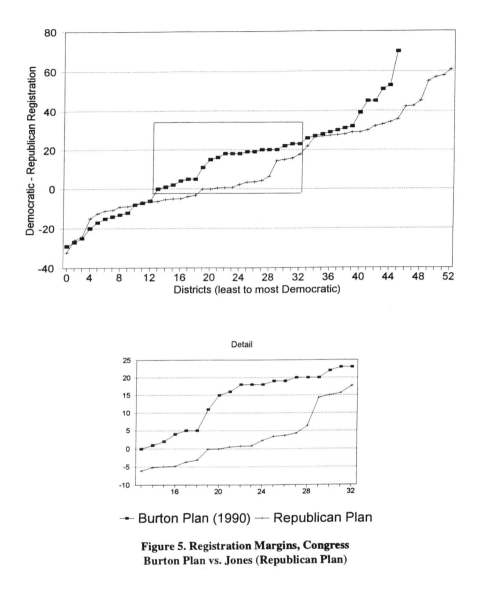

Figure 5. Registration Margins, Congress
Burton Plan vs. Jones (Republican Plan)

of the graph, Republicans created as many districts as possible in which the Democratic margin was below five percent, and then jumped to fairly safely Democratic districts in which Democratic margins were fifteen percent or more. The apparent Democratic strategy was the mirror image of that of the

Republicans—pack Republicans and create as few districts with less than a five percent margin and as many with fifteen or more percent as possible. Three points follow: First, both parties had incentives to establish as few highly competitive districts as possible, and they acted in accord with those incentives. Second, the technicians of both parties were sufficiently competent that they could simultaneously maximize their potential number of victories in "good" years and minimize their losses in somewhat worse years.[120] Third, although comparisons between plans are instructive and clearly demonstrate their intentions, it is impossible to determine which is less partisan without choosing some "fair point" or making an inescapably arbitrary definition of a competitive range of districts.[121] For instance, the Jones plan contained only four districts in which the registration gap in Figure 5 was more than 6% and less than 20%, while the Burton plan, as of 1990, contained 11. On the other hand, 10 of the Jones plan's districts had registration margins of between 0 and 6%, while this was true in only 6 of the Burton plan's districts. What is the legally or social scientifically correct fair point, and how would one practically apply a standard based on the widely discussed principle of symmetry? (Gottlieb, 1988)

Figures 6 and 7 show that the 1991 Masters' plan for Congress resembled the Jones plan much more closely than it did Plan A.[122] The Masters' plan packed Democrats more and Republicans less than Plan A did, and the registration gap between Democrats and Republicans was consistently less in the middle range of the Masters' plan than it was in Plan A. Both created about the same number of highly competitive districts. Figure 7 demonstrates that there were only subtle differences between the Masters' plan (using February 1992 registration data) and the Jones plan. Essentially, the Jones plan had somewhat larger jumps in the center portion of the graph, while the pattern of registration differences in the Masters' plan climbed a bit more smoothly. Although such tiny distinctions could lead to as much as a four-seat shift in such a very good Democratic year as 1992, they would become unimportant in a more normal election year.

---

[120]If the relation between votes and registration were that of 1980 (which is unlikely, since Republican voters grew increasingly less loyal and Democrats more loyal during the 1980s), then all the congressional plans of 1991 would imply a Republican congressional landslide of 32-33 of the 52 seats.

[121]Even the most statistically complex attempts to estimate partisan bias in redistricting plans make such arbitrary assumptions, as, for instance, Gelman and King's decision to calculate Bayesian posterior distributions of hypothetical seats-votes curves between the voting percentages of 45% and 55%, or Campagna's decision, using a simpler but parallel model, to set the range at 40% to 60%. See Gelman and King, 1990, 278; Campagna, 1991.

[122]The patterns of other Democratic plans and the MALDEF plan, and their contrast with the other pro-Republican plans are very similar, as are the contrasts for the Assembly plans.

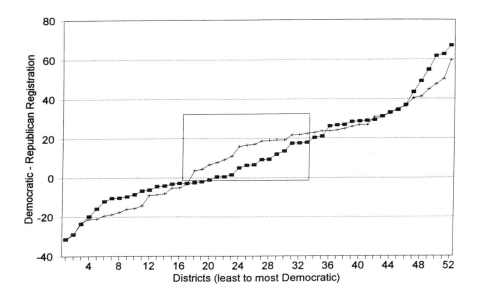

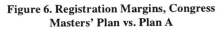

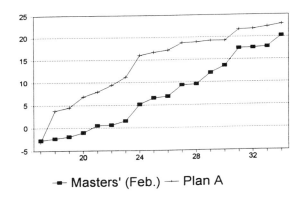

Figure 6. Registration Margins, Congress
Masters' Plan vs. Plan A

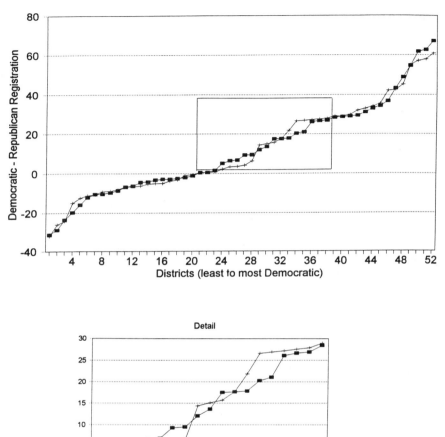

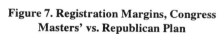

**Figure 7. Registration Margins, Congress
Masters' vs. Republican Plan**

C. Judicial Challenges to the Masters' Plan

The opinion in *Wilson* v. *Eu* by the Republican Chief Justice[123] scornfully dismissed charges by the Assembly Democrats that the Masters' Plan was biased in favor of his party, characterizing their comparison of the districts with the 1990 gubernatorial election returns as "dubious" and a second test based on registration statistics as "of similarly doubtful utility." "Yet predictions of future election contests are quite obviously speculative and imprecise, involving the weighing of countless variables," Chief Justice Lucas declared. Purported attempts by the Masters to comply with the Voting Rights Act and the various amorphous state criteria for redistricting, he asserted without evidence or further argument, would automatically produce plans that were as fair to all concerned as any devised by the legislature—and that is all that was required.[124]

Lucas's argument was disingenuous, false, and illogical. It was disingenuous for the head of a court that had been taken over through an eight-year-long, highly partisan series of expensive election campaigns to dismiss summarily, without offering any reasoning or evidence himself, the plausible attempts by his Democratic foes to gauge the partisan effect of the Masters' plan. When everyone else freely discussed what they agreed were the likely pro-Republican consequences of the Masters' districts, Lucas's pose of innocent ignorance was unconvincing. It is false because, as I show elsewhere (Kousser, 1995a), winners in the Assembly and Congress can usually be predicted about 90% of the time by one who knows only major party registration statistics in each district. If the Justices wished to test the predictive power of party registration on voting, they had only to look in the mirror, because every Republican Justice voted for the Masters' plan and the one Democratic Justice voted against it. Lucas's stance was illogical because the assertion that—allegedly—pursuing goals of ethnic fairness, compactness, etc. would guarantee the attainment of the wholly different goal of partisan fairness is a *non sequitur.*[125] Whatever the criterion of partisan fairness, it must be related only to the partisanship of outcomes. And the much closer resemblance of the registration patterns of the Masters' plans to

---

[123]Chief Justice Lucas continues to be an active and open partisan. Three years before the 1998 gubernatorial election, Lucas, in an infraction of the State Judicial Code of Conduct, publicly endorsed State Attorney General Dan Lungren, who argued *Wilson* v. *Eu*, and who has often argued major cases before the California Supreme Court, for Governor. Maura Dolan, "Justice Says He's Sorry About Endorsement," *Los Angeles Times*, Aug. 10, 1995, A3.

[124] *Wilson* v. *Eu*, 1 Cal.4th 707, 727 (1992). For similar comments, see *Davis* v. *Bandemer*, 106 S.Ct. 2797, 2825 (1986), (O'Connor, J., concurring.) In contrast to 1973, when McKaskle assessed the partisan consequences of his plan and found it fair, this time he listed a long series of possible complications with such a measurement. In fact, as Kousser, 1995, Tables 1 and 2 show, outcomes were less, not more predictable in the 1970s than in the 1980s. The Report's discussion seems, therefore, less a cautious recognition of complexity than a rationalization of a recognized partisan outcome. *Ibid.*, 795.

[125]In fact, application of many of the popular redistricting criteria are likely to lead to pro-Republican outcomes. See Lowenstein and Steinberg, 1985.

those of the Republicans than to those of the Democrats suggests that the predictable partisan effects of the Masters' schemes tilted toward the party of the majority of the Supreme Court and of the Masters' panel.[126] While it may not be possible to determine the degree of partisanship of any particular plan in an absolute sense, it is demonstrably simple to compare one plan with another. If courts want to be considered more than just another venue for cutthroat reapportionment politics, they should take the effort to assess partisan consequences more seriously than the Deukmejian Court did.[127]

After the U.S. Supreme Court's 1993 decision in *Shaw* v. *Reno* (113 S.Ct. 2816) that "racial gerrymandering" was justiciable, two Richmond, California attorneys, seemingly unconnected to any party or interest group, filed a federal court challenge to the Masters' Plan and to other aspects of the state election code, including, quirkily, the provision that prevents a person from running for more than one congressional seat in the state at the same time. Pointing out that the Masters' Report openly admitted—indeed, emphasized—that the Masters had taken account of the racial characteristics of the population in order to draw districts that would "withstand section 2 [Voting Rights Act] challenges under any foreseeable combination of factual circumstances and legal rulings," and that in Los Angeles County, they started "by tracing a line around census tracts with majority or near majority Latino population," (*Wilson* v. *Eu*, 1 Cal.4th 707, 745, 776 (1992)), the Anglo plaintiffs charged that they and other white people had been discriminated against.[128] Taking race into account at all in districting, they claimed, "segregated" voters in violation of *Brown* v. *Board of Education* (347 U.S. 483 (1954)) and set up racial "quotas," which fell afoul of *University of California Regents* v. *Bakke* (438 U.S. 265 (1978)). (Smith and DeWitt, 1995.)

A three-judge panel consisting of one Democrat and two ethnic minority Republicans, in a six-page opinion written by Ninth Circuit Judge Procter Ralph Hug, Jr., a Carter appointee, concluded that the Masters' districts did not

---

[126]A telltale indication of the partisan bias of the Masters' panel is the treatment of the proposed Republican and Democratic plans in the panel's report. The report dismissed the Democrats' plans for having "calculated partisan political consequences (the details of which are unknown)," while the presentations in favor of the Republican plans were said to be "clear and persuasive." The Masters refused to adopt the Republican plans, they claimed, only because they were flawed in (unspecified) detail and presented late in the process. *Wilson* v. *Eu*, 1 Cal. 4th 707, 765, 768 (1992).

[127]U.S. Supreme Court Justice Byron White noted in *Gaffney* v. *Cummings,* 93 S.Ct. 2321, 2332 (1992) that a "politically mindless approach may produce, whether intended or not, the most grossly gerrymandered results; and, in any event, it is most unlikely that the political impact of such a plan would remain undiscovered by the time it was proposed or adopted, in which event the results would be both known and, if not changed, intended." As governor, Deukmejian led the campaigns to reject Bird and the other Democrats, and he appointed a majority of the membership of the court that sat in *Wilson* v. *Eu*.

[128]They also contended that allocating seats on the basis of population, rather than proportionally to registration or to votes actually cast systematically discriminated against Anglos, because minorities registered and voted in smaller proportions. The three-judge panel scornfully dismissed this argument that the effects of past discrimination should justify more, not less, present and future discrimination, and the Supreme Court affirmed this finding without comment. (Smith and DeWitt 1995; *DeWitt* v. *Wilson*, 115 S.Ct. 2637(1995)).

violate "the narrow holding of *Shaw*," because race was not the "sole" criterion used for drawing districts and because the resulting districts did not have "extremely irregular district boundaries." According to Hug, the Masters' Report indicated that they had engaged in "a judicious and proper balancing of the many factors appropriate to redistricting....[W]here race is considered only in applying traditional redistricting principles along with the requirements of the Voting Rights Act,...strict scrutiny is not required. However, if it were required, we conclude that this California redistricting plan has been narrowly tailored to meet a compelling state interest." (*DeWitt* v. *Wilson*, 856 F.Supp. 1409, 1413, 1415 (1994).) The compelling interest was apparently compliance with the Voting Rights Act, and an informal "eyeball" evaluation of compactness was all that the Court felt necessary to satisfy narrow tailoring. On the same day that the U.S. Supreme Court decided *Miller* v. *Johnson*, which held that a districting plan would be subject to strict scrutiny only if race were the "predominant factor motivating the legislature's opinion," disregarding "traditional race-neutral districting principles," it summarily affirmed Hug's decision in *DeWitt*. (115 S.Ct. 2637(1995)). The implication seemed to be that even if race were admittedly the predominant motive for drawing minority opportunity districts, those districts could be sustained if they did not appear too irregular to a judge's glance and if their boundaries did not cross more jurisdictional lines than necessary. This, at least, was the interpretation of the pivotal Supreme Court Justice, Sandra Day O'Connor, on the issue. (*Bush* v. *Vera*, 116 S.Ct. 1941, 1951 (1996))

V. CONCLUSION: POLITICS, COURTS, AND MINORITY VOTING RIGHTS

What lessons should we draw from the reapportionment experiences of the nation's most populous state for three decades? First, constraints matter. Had there been no *Reynolds v. Sims*, and had the passions of reapportionment been as high as they were, it is difficult to imagine that one party or another would have refrained from creating massively overpopulated and underpopulated districts. Given the chance, Republicans might have made Los Angeles county one Senate district, as it had been before 1965, while Democrats might have crammed Orange and San Diego counties and as many affluent suburbs of Los Angeles county into as few districts as they pleased. Depending on which party controlled reapportionment, the lack of an equal population standard might have more gravely disadvantaged Latinos and especially African-Americans, concentrated as they are in major urban areas, than the lack of the Voting Rights Act would have. Nonetheless, without the Voting Rights Act, the ability of Republicans to pack ethnic minorities (as in the 1991 congressional and Assembly plans of the Governor's Commission) and of Democrats to place them in areas that maximized Democratic, but not necessarily minority political power would have been much greater.

Second, history matters. The experience of deadlock and a court-ordered reapportionment drawn by Paul McKaskle in the 1970s, and of the reapportionment decisions of the Bird Court in the 1980s created expectations on both sides of the partisan divide in the 1990s. Speaker Willie Brown believed that McKaskle would be unlikely to create plans that would be as bad for Democrats as those that the Republicans were offering, which reduced his incentive to compromise. Republicans believed that the State Supreme Court had acted in a pro-Democratic fashion in both the 1970s and 1980s, and they were sure that their Court would reverse the sign of partisanship, but retain the intensity in the 1990s, so Gov. Wilson and the state and national Republican leadership never seriously considered compromises with the Democrats. The Republican furor over the "Burton gerrymander" fueled referendum campaign after campaign in the 1980s, fired their special effort to keep the governorship in 1990, and consumed them with a desire for revenge. Republican bitterness over failing to gain control of reapportionment during the 1980s stimulated their successful effort to limit legislative and congressional terms.

Third, the concerns of ethnic groups cannot be separated from partisan politics. The redistricting deal of 1971 unraveled because the Democratic party's effort to elect a third Latino to the Assembly (from a district in which only about 20% of the registered voters were Latino) failed in one of the roughest campaigns that Republicans have ever run in the state. The only reapportionment in three decades in California controlled by the legislature, that of the 1980s, tripled the number of Latino members of Congress and drew numerous districts that increased the influence of minority ethnic groups. All of the pro-Republican plans of 1991, including the Masters' plan, scattered blacks and Latinos, diluting their influence far more than the MALDEF or Democratic plans did. The Republican strategy of bashing minorities for 9 out of every 10 years and then courting some of them during the redistricting year lost its viability as Democrats gradually and somewhat grudgingly agreed to draw districts where African-Americans or Latinos enjoyed good chances to elect candidates of their choice. As the minorities elected became key Democratic leaders, the Republicans abandoned all pretenses of conciliating minorities and consequently, the interests between Democrats and minority constituents became even more strongly positive.

Fourth, having to take account of incumbency in order to pass a plan in a legislature dampens partisanship in redistricting, while being able to write on a much cleaner slate allows partisanship (or any other motive) much freer rein. Like other self-interested individuals, legislative incumbents generally prefer individual safety and certainty to the good of some larger group, such as their political party. Indeed, incumbent self-interest is undoubtedly a much more effective constraint in redistricting run by a legislature than such nebulous concepts as "compactness" or "communities of interest," which can easily be manipulated to rationalize any plan.[129] Two important implications of this reflection follow: First, reapportionment by commission may allow a more partisan plan to be put into force. While every redistricting commission proposal made during the 1980s recognized this obvious danger by institutionalizing some scheme of partisan balance, the Governor's Commission, appointed by Gov. Wilson alone, and the Special Masters, appointed solely by the State Supreme Court in 1973 and 1991, made only small gestures toward bipartisan control, and, as Tables 3 (page 148) and 6 page 177 and Figure 7 (page 183) demonstrate, all three produced plans that reflected the partisan interests of those who appointed them. Second, when six- and eight-year term limits in the state legislature remove incumbency as a softening factor in reapportionment in the year 2001, partisan advantage is likely to become an even more important motive, and conflict is likely to be even more virulent—difficult as that may be to believe. If one party controls all four of the most relevant political bodies (the Assembly, the Senate, the governorship, and the State Supreme Court) during the redistricting, the "Burton gerrymander" may seem tame by comparison with the plan that will emerge. If control is split, or perhaps even if it is not, the State Supreme Court will be trumps, as in 1991. If a political monopoly by one party seems likely in 1998 or 2000, the other party will presumably seek to pass a commission initiative, and the intellectually unedifying spectacles of the 1980s, which did so much to bring the state government into disrepute, will be revisited.

Fifth, despite extreme claims by some journalists and scholars, redistricters who have to get plans ratified by legislatures have not, in the past, at least, been able to perform partisan miracles. In a 1992 article, Professors James Fay and Kay Lawson assert, without presenting any evidence whatsoever, that in California reapportionment, "Whichever party rules the game can give itself about a three-to-two advantage in the House delegation."[130] Yet as a close analysis of the "Burton gerrymander" has shown, and as other careful scholars have argued more generally, the overall effects of redistricting on the partisan balance have

---

[129]A good example of rationalization on the basis of a supposed "community of interest" may be found in "Declaration of Joseph Shumate in Support of Defendant Pete Wilson's Opposition to Plaintiffs' Motion for Preliminary Injunction," filed in connection with *Members of the California Democratic Congressional Delegation* v. *Eu* (Case No. 91-3383 FMS Civil, U.S. District Court, Northern District of California), 8-9. Defending the Masters' congressional plan, Wilson's redistricting consultant defends the decrease in the Latino population percentage in District 30 on the grounds that it was necessary to avoid splitting the "Koreatown" section of the city of Los Angeles. There are only three difficulties with this position. First, the Masters' did in fact split the generally recognized bounds of that unincorporated area almost exactly in half. Second, only 13% of the Koreans in Los Angeles county in 1984 were registered to vote. Third, of that 13%, about a fifth did not register with a major party, and many others, perhaps a majority of those remaining, were Republicans. (Nakanishi, 1991.) Since the district was overwhelmingly Democratic, Koreans would be extremely unlikely to compose more than five percent of the decisive Democratic primary electorate—a proportion much lower than the Masters or Shumate attempted to corral in black or Latino influence districts.

[130]Fay and Lawson, 1992, 27. It is not clear what they mean by a "three-to-two" advantage—a higher seats/votes ratio? 60% of the delegation?

been small to nonexistent.[131] Why, then, have such exaggerated tales persisted? One reason, it seems likely, is the inattention and cynicism of the public, which is ready to believe almost anything bad about legislators. Another is the self-interest of all the insiders. Phil Burton and other reapportionment experts basked in their reputations as wizards who put a curse on the evil opposition. Republican losers consoled themselves with the thought that the outcomes were beyond their control, that they and their ideas were not really rejected in a fair contest. Others, by exaggerating the effect of current or past districting schemes, tried to promote "reforms" that they believed would help their party by mandating "compact" and/or "competitive" districts, districts in which (they hope) their superior financial resources will prove decisive, and which will in any event limit the number of seats that the more geographically concentrated Democrats can win. (Atwater, 1990.) Journalists tried to convince themselves and their readers that their stories on arcane subjects really mattered. In sum, the effect of redistricting may be blown out of proportion because participants may want to puff their reputations or justify what they have done or had done to them, while citizens may seek to rationalize their alienation and apathy.

Sixth, term limits have swept experienced ethnic minority politicians, especially Speaker Willie Brown, out of the legislature, No minority politician—and few Anglo politicians—with experience in redistricting is likely to be in the California legislature in 2001, even assuming that the legislature has any real power over that reapportionment. As a result of the term-limit "reform," real power, in this and other legislative activities, will pass to lobbyists and unelected and unknown technicians, with little effective oversight from the transient, unprofessional politicians that term limits guarantee.

Finally, if *Shaw* v. *Reno* and *Bush* v. *Vera* encourage redistricters to exalt esthetics over the social and political reality of continued racial polarization and discrimination, and if *Miller* prevents those interested in redistricting from explicitly talking about its ethnic consequences and encourages challenges from Anglo voters to every minority opportunity district, then the state could easily end up with plans like those of the Governor's Commission, under which the chances for minorities to elect or even to influence the election of candidates of their choice would be drastically reduced. Across the nation in 1991, minority organizations participated in redistricting more than they ever had before, and they had on their side the pressure of the Voting Rights Act, interpreted by the U.S. Department of Justice to require states and localities to offer special justifications for rejecting proposed or possible minority opportunity districts. In California, everyone except the Governor's Commission appeared to accept as a first principle the Ninth Circuit Court's statement in *Garza* v. *Los Angeles County Board of Supervisors* that "The deliberate construction of minority controlled voting districts is exactly what the Voting Rights Act

---

[131]Glazer *et al.*, 1987; Butler and Cain, 1992, 8-10.

authorizes." (918 F.2d 763, 776 (1990), quoted in *Wilson* v. *Eu*, 1 Cal.4th 707, 717 (1992).) Without the leverage that that interpretation of the law gave them, members of minority groups would have had much less power to force politicians, judges, and bureaucrats to listen to them, and the discussions of minority representation in the news media and in the corridors of power would have been much less open and informative. If courts and Republican politicians insist on a "color blind" reapportionment in 2001, only the public is likely to be kept in the dark, and the resultant plans are likely to insure that the legislators become, in their ethnic characteristics, more like those of the 1950s and '60s than like the multi-hued group elected during the 1990s.

REAPPORTIONMENT STRATEGIES IN THE 1990s: The Case of Georgia

Robert A. Holmes

ONE YEAR AFTER EACH DECENNIAL CENSUS the Georgia General Assembly undertakes the task of redrawing the state legislative and Congressional districts. For most state legislators this may be the most important activity they are involved in during their tenure. This high stakes legislative battle involves decisions which will directly affect their political survival.

The struggle of the Georgia Legislative Black Caucus (GLBC) to carve out three Black Majority Congressional districts and 41 State House and 13 Senate districts in Georgia during the Special Session from August 19 to September 4, 1991, the regular session of the Georgia General Assembly from January 13 to March 31, 1992, and the 1995 special session held after the Supreme Court declared unconstitutional the 11th Congressional District, were among the most intense, combative, and divisive political battles in the history of Georgia state politics. The intensity of the battles caused many white legislators in metro-Atlanta and North Georgia as well as GLBC members to challenge the nation's longest tenured (23 years) House Speaker, Tom Murphy, on two critical actions: 1) the maps which he supported; and 2) the composition of the conference committee, which included three white males from rural South Georgia. Several meetings of the House and Senate conference committees on reapportionment lasted until well past midnight, and charges of "sell-out," "racism," and "political favoritism," and attacks on the personal integrity of legislators involved in the map drawing were pervasive. During the 1991 special session, the GLBC was split into two factions of almost equal size over the feasibility of creating two majority-Black Congressional and one "influence" (approximately 40 percent Black) district versus three majority-Black districts. A similar division was evident over how many "electable" state House and Senate seats it was feasible to create. Both factions went to Washington, D.C. to meet with officials of the U.S.

Department of Justice. During the last days of the 1992 legislative session the Justice Department had not approved the Georgia House and Senate plans, and the Georgia General Assembly leadership accused it of holding them hostage until the legislature enacted an acceptable three-majority-Black Congressional district plan.

At a meeting attended by 32 of the 35 GLBC members, they voted unanimously to support a three Black majority Congressional district plan. The contrasting positions within the GLBC are reflected in the following statements. First, Representative Michael Thurmond, Chair of the GLRC of Athens, who embraced the two-majority-Black House leadership plan commented: "Two birds in the hand is (sic) better than one possible influence district in the bush." Black Senate Reapportionment Committee Chairman Eugene Walker, said it was impossible to draw three "legitimate" Black Congressional districts. And Representative Calvin Smyre, the first Black to serve as a Governor's Floor Leader (1987-91) and a member of the Georgia State and National Democratic Committees, indicated that at best only a marginal 51 percent district could be created, which would not allow the election of a Black Congressperson, and asked rhetorically: "Are we trying to create districts on paper? Or do we want to get Blacks elected to the districts we draw."

Led by Mary Young-Cummings, Representatives Tyrone Brooks, Cynthia McKinney, and John White, several GLBC members disagreed with the Thurmond/Smyre/Walker position and labeled it a sellout. Representative John White told a group of capitol reporters:

> There are a few of us who don't see eye-to-eye with him (Thurmond) on this question. We believe that we ought to maximize in every way we can. Those Black legislators who are acquiescing will be faced with an angry Black public when that public understands that they're been sold short. We may not win it (the 3rd Black district) in this coming election, but if we don't draw it, we won't ever win it.

A similar debate ensued in 1995 over whether three Congressional Black majority districts could be retained and if state legislative districts should be redrawn to avoid another court suit even though it might result in several existing Black majority districts becoming majority white.

THE GLBC REDISTRICTING/REAPPORTIONMENT STRATEGY

Reapportionment in Georgia in 1991-92 and 1995 was in many ways a repeat of what occurred a decade earlier. (Holmes, 1984). Many of the same strategies and techniques were employed by the Georgia Legislative Black Caucus (GLBC) in it's efforts to maximize the number of majority-Black Congressional and state legislative districts. Black lawmakers attempted to utilize the following techniques:

1. Negotiate with the White legislative leadership in the Georgia General Assembly to increase Black majority districts.
2. Formulate alternative reapportionment plans to be submitted to the House Legislative and Congressional Reapportionment and Senate Reapportionment Committees.
3. Utilize the threats of appealing to the U.S. Department of Justice under Sec-

tion 5 of the Voting Rights Act (VRA) or filing a suit in the Federal District Court to pressure the legislature to "do the right thing."

4. Form tacit coalitions with Republican legislators to achieve mutually beneficial goals.

5. Develop a multifaceted strategy using three different groups of Black legislators: 1) "Insiders," Black members of the House and Senate Reapportionment Committees; 2) "Outsiders," Black legislators who would develop maximum ("Max Black") majority-Black district plans to be used as leverage to increase the Black districts in the Committee plans; and 3) a GLBC Task Force on Reapportionment which would develop alternative compromise plans.

Four of these major techniques were utilized in 1981, but the fifth was a new development resulting from a conscious effort on the part of the Georgia Legislative Black Caucus to achieve its goals without the lengthy and time consuming effort of having to go through the Justice Department, the federal district court and the U.S. Supreme Court as occurred in 1981.

Shortly after the adjournment of the legislative session in March 1991, the Chairmen of the House and Senate Reapportionment Committees sent out guidelines to the members and announced a schedule of 13 joint public hearings in the 10 Congressional Districts to receive public comments. Upon the advice of Speaker Murphy, the House Chair divided the state into 18 arbitrary multicounty geographical districts which were designated as "work areas" whose legislators were to meet and draw the number of districts specified based on the ideal size of 35,900 population.

The GLBC Executive Committee met to discuss reapportionment issues. A consensus was reached that the Chair of the GLBC should appoint a task force on reapportionment to devise strategies and plans prior to the convening of the anticipated August 1991 special legislative session on reapportionment. It was believed that this development would enhance considerably the ability of Black Georgians to be more effective in the 1991 redistricting political process. A conscious effort was made to appoint legislators who were not members of the General Assembly Reapportionment Committees to the Task Force.

There were two important developments that were different from 1981. Senator Eugene Walker, a three-term Black legislator, was the Chair of the Senate Reapportionment Committee, and Representative Georganna Sinkfield was one of the senior members of the House Legislative and Congressional Reapportionment Committee. These two Black legislators, in their capacities as "insiders," were to lead the push for more Black districts within their committees. Representatives Tyrone Brooks and Cynthia McKinney were the lead "outsiders" who worked with American Civil Liberties Union lawyer, Kathy Wilde, to develop "Max Black Plans" for the Congressional, State Senate and State House districts. They attempted to use census data to develop the highest number of Black majority legislative and Congressional districts that was statistically possible. They designed a Congressional plan that had three majority-Black districts, a House of Representatives plan that had 51 Black majority legislative seats, and a Senate plan that had 15

Black majority senatorial districts. The GLBC Task Force worked to develop alternative plans that would serve as a middle ground between the proposals pushed by the White House and Senate leadership and those plans developed by Brooks/McKinney. GLBC Task Force members from the seven urban areas in the state attempted to work with their white colleagues in the "work areas" to draw their own districts and to create a maximum number of new Black majority districts within their metro area as well as adjacent rural counties.

The GLBC Task Force comprised a cross section of Black legislators throughout Georgia. All 35 incumbent Black legislators were from the major metropolitan areas (Atlanta, Albany, Augusta, Columbus, Macon, and Savannah) in the state, and they were asked to develop a consensus concerning House and Senate plans for their particular areas. Also, the three Black members who served on the House Reapportionment Committee, including Representative McKinney, and one other Black Senator, Sanford Bishop, who served on the Senate Reappointment Committee, from different areas in the state were also asked to develop majority-Black legislative and Congressional districts for the rural areas in close geographic proximity to them. A statewide map was to be drawn which would include the maximum number of majority-Black districts that the GLBC could agree upon. This composite plan would be presented as a statewide alternative plan to the House and Senate committees' recommendations. This three-tiered strategy adopted by the GLBC was one which it was thought would provide the most effective means by which Blacks could ensure that they could have an opportunity to significantly increase the number of majority-Black legislative districts in the 1992 election.

The Caucus Task Force members began meeting in mid-May 1991, and the legislators from the seven metro areas were asked to submit their plans to the chair of the Task Force by July 1, 1991. This was to provide time for the integration of the individual area plans prior to the holding of a general GLBC meeting at a late July 1991 retreat to discuss the Congressional, House, and Senate proposals.

Governor Zell Miller announced in mid-July that he would convene a special session of the Georgia General Assembly on August 19, 1991 to deal with reapportionment, budget reductions, and local legislation.

On July 27-28, 1991, 30 of the 35 members of the GLBC attended a retreat at Lake Lanier Islands, Georgia to focus on and discuss the various redistricting and reapportionment plans proposed by its members. Unfortunately, not all of the metro plans were completed by the deadline and a consensus could not be reached on several of the area plans. Concerning the Congressional proposal, some GLBC members pushed for three majority-Black districts while others supported two majority-Black and a third influence district (about 40 percent Black) because creating a third would involve splitting at least three of the metro core cities (Columbus, Macon, and Savannah) into two separate Congressional districts each. At the end of the retreat, it was agreed that another attempt would be made to meet the next week to finalize the three GLBC plans. At a dinner meeting held on August 4th at Black-owned Pashcal's Hotel in Atlanta, a consensus was reached on several rural districts, but there remained some disagreement in the Augusta area. Still another meeting was called by the Chair of the GLBC, for the evening of August 19, 1991 at Pashcal's' Hotel, the first day of the special session, to discuss the GLBC's House and Senate plans. Concerning these proposals, the GLBC Chair, Representative Michael Thurmond, wrote in a confidential memo to the Black legislators:

> I am proud that these plans, which reflect the collective effort of the Caucus, maximize the voting strength of African-American citizens in the State. The Caucus' plans include the delegation plans from those delegations with Caucus members. Incumbent Caucus members are protected, while maximizing the number of other majority-Black districts, particularly in rural Georgia. We have considered Black populations, voting age population, registered voters, voting patterns, and pools of local elected officials (such as city councilpersons, school board members, and county commissioners).
>
> Many of you worked long and difficult hours to develop these plans. I want to thank those of you who served on the house and senate reapportionment committees...; we owe a special debt of gratitude to the Caucus' reapportionment committee; Representatives Cynthia McKinney and Tyrone Brooks played a major role in the development of the Caucus' plans, often adopting unpopular positions in the best interest of the State's Black citizens.

Thirty-two of the 35 Black legislators attended this session, and after more than two hours of discussion, a consensus was reached that the GLBC would support a 42-majority-Black State House district plan (compared with 29 in the 1981 reapportionment plan); a 13-majority-Black Senate plan (compared with 9 in 1981); and a 3-majority-Black district Congressional plan (compared with 1 in 1981). GLBC Chair Thurmond agreed to contact the Legislative Legal Counsel's office to have the final State House plan drafted so it could be introduced in the General Assembly during the first week of the special session.

Given the varied approaches to drawing the district lines, there were considerable differences in the three plans to be proposed in the Special Session.

TABLE 1. 1992 Special Session.
Comparison of Plans for Redistricting/Reapportionment of Majority-Black Districts

	House	Senate	Congress
House/Senate Committees/ Plans	35	10	2
GLBC Task Force Plans	42	13	3
Brooks/McKinney "Max Plans"	51	15	3

THE 1991 SPECIAL SESSION

On August 19, 1991 the Special Session of the Georgia General Assembly convened in an attempt to complete the redistricting/reapportionment process begun after the regular session by the House and Senate Reapportionment Committees.

Georgia comes under the provisions of the 1965 Voting Rights Act as amended in 1982 which requires that the legislature avoid diluting Black voting strength and pre-clear all voting changes with the U.S. Department of Justice. Indications were that Georgia would be held to a strict standard of creating as many majority-Black districts as possible in order to elect the maximum number of Black legislators.

This goal was supported by Republicans, who believed that the more majority-Black districts that are created, the better the chances of electing more Republicans. They believed that the concentration of Black voters into districts drawn to maximize their political strength will have the effect of packing white suburban voters into areas that may be fertile soil for Republican candidates.

Republican optimism was promoted by the population shifts in Georgia between 1980 and 1990. South Georgia, a solidly Democratic area, lost legislative seats while many of the new state House and Senate seats to be created were in metro Atlanta's rapidly growing suburbs which were strongly Republican.

State Legislative Reapportionment

Each house in the General Assembly was responsible for its own redistricting. Both had the responsibility of drawing Congressional districts. The Georgia Legislative Black Caucus (GLBC) proposed a 42-Black-majority district plan for the House and a 13-majority-Black Senate district plan. The compromise plan adopted by the Senate, SB 1 EX, provided for ten districts in which African-Americans make up a majority of the population. This compared with eight such districts that existed. The House approved a plan (HB 8 EX, Hanner 131 and others) which created 35-majority-Black districts. In 1991, 28 members of the House were Black. If Blacks were elected in each majority-Black legislative district, Black representation in the state Senate could be raised to 21 percent and in the state House to 17 percent under the GLBC plans. The Black population in Georgia is 27 percent.

While the GLBC Chairman Thurmond indicated the Caucus would not challenge the results of the House plan, individual Black legislators promised to bring suit in federal district court.

Congress

After the U.S. Census Bureau count of the 1990 population, Georgia gained a seat in Congress, thus increasing its representation from 10 to 11. At the Special Session the Assembly's job was to draw the lines of the new Eleventh District and to redraw all other Congressional district lines to create districts of relatively equal populations (a variance of 1 percent is permitted).

Congressional redistricting was the most controversial aspect of the special session. With regard to Congress, the General Assembly, after days of lobbying by incumbent Congressmen, long and acrimonious conference committee meetings (one ended at 3 a.m.), and intense negotiations, adopted a new Congressional map. The Senate approved the plan SB 2 EX, by a vote of 36-17. The house vote was 107-66. The final vote on September 5 resulted in a splitting of the votes of Black legislators and Republicans. This came several days after an earlier plan on August 31 had been defeated in the House (75 yeas and 86 nays) with much of the opposition coming from Black legislators, Republicans, and lawmakers from Atlanta's suburbs.

The new Congressional map created a second majority-Black district (the Eleventh) in addition to the Fifth District. The new district stretched from South Dekalb County east to Augusta and south to Macon. GLBC member Bob Holmes submitted a map with a third majority-Black Congressional district (57.6%) in South Georgia, but there was no House or Senate leadership support for the proposal.

Speaker Murphy led the move to break up Congressman Newt Gingrich's Sixth district and divided it among four Congressional districts. For example, the Fifth District, currently represented by Representative John Lewis, was given half the Atlanta airport (with the other half in the Third District) along with the home of Republican Minority Whip Gingrich. This raised the possibility of a contest between Representative Gingrich and the incumbent Representative Richard Ray. The home of Fourth District Congressman Ben Jones was put into the new Tenth District. Because members of Congress do not have to live in a district to run in it, Mr. Jones could have run again in a redrawn Fourth District. A significant portion of Representative Newt Gingrich's old district was moved into the Third District. In addition, the new Sixth District, then located in Atlanta's northern suburbs, became strongly Republican. Redistricting in Georgia was to be reviewed by the Justice Department and if it survived this agency's scrutiny, it was certain to be challenged in the courts. Republicans claimed that they had been the victims of partisan gerrymandering in the state to keep Republican gains to a minimum. All three plans appeared to be subject to challenge on the basis of not providing African-Americans with the maximum opportunity to increase Black representation. Several individuals and organizations threatened to bring suit against the reapportionment plans on the grounds that they failed to meet this standard.

During the special session held from August 19 to September 4, 1991, a House redistricting plan was passed which provided for 35 majority-Black districts (three did not have Black majority voting age populations); a Senate plan included 10 such districts; and the adopted Congressional plan had two majority-Black districts. As was noted, several members of the GLBC and leaders of civic/community organizations across the state said they would ask the Justice Department to reject all three plans.

Several Georgia delegations of opponents and proponents of the plans went to Washington, D.C. to meet with Justice Department officials to state their respective positions. On the morning that several Black legislators and more than 30 civil rights leaders from Georgia were to board a bus for their trip to Washington, Representative Tyrone Brooks proved to be clairvoyant when he remarked, "I am more confident today than ever before that Georgia's reapportionment plan is in serious trouble. When we convene in January, we will have to deal with reapportionment again."[1]

THE 1992 SESSION OF THE GENERAL ASSEMBLY
Although the Voting Rights Act of 1965 gives the Justice Department a 60-day review period, this period can be prolonged if additional information is

---

[1]Charles Walston, "Brooks: Redistricting will be redone" *Atlanta Journal/Constitution,* 2 November 1991.

requested from the state—which is what occurred. The state did not submit the plans and accompanying documents until October 1, almost one month after they were adopted. Rumors abounded as to when Justice would render its decision, but no reply had been received by the day the General Assembly convened for its regular session on January 13, 1992. Legislators became even more anxious because Washington still had not notified the state as the legislature began its traditional recess (one week after convening) to hold budget hearings. As the legislators left the Capitol for their break, Representative Bob Hanner, chairman of the House Reapportionment Committee, remained until he received word that a response would not be forthcoming that week. Expressing his frustrations, Hanner feared the Justice Department would notify the state so late in the session that it would be difficult to redraw the maps before the General Assembly adjourned.

Finally, on Tuesday, January 21, a letter was received by Mark Cohen, Senior Assistant Attorney General for Georgia, from John Dunne, U.S. Assistant Attorney General for Civil Rights. Dunne said the dilution of minority voting strength seemed to be a deliberate policy of the legislature in its drawing of all three plans. He noted that numerous opportunities were available to draw more minority districts and that several alternative proposals submitted by Black legislators had been rejected. It was pointed out also that the state plans were designed "to benefit incumbents and minimize Black voting strength." (Dunne, 1992a) Powerful House and Senate members' districts were drawn first, and this resulted in fragmentation of several concentrations of Black communities throughout Georgia.

Concerning the Congressional Plan, as noted, Speaker Tom Murphy attempted to destroy Republican Congressman Newt Gingrich's district, which then had a ripple effect on the 10 other districts. Also, several parts of the district represented by Georgia's only Black Congressman (John Lewis) were extended into suburban counties such as Clayton, Coweta, and Fayette, which had large white population concentrations. Justice also questioned why minority communities in central Georgia were divided among two districts rather than united in a new majority-Black 11th district. Finally, the GLBC had supported the creation of a majority-Black 2nd Congressional district, but the state plan had created a 39.4 percent "influence district." The Dunne letter said the plan "did not recognize...the Black voting potential of the large concentrations of minorities in Southwest Georgia." Concerning the reapportionment process itself, the Washington officials asserted that it "discouraged alternative plans from being presented and debated," and it "rushed the process in order to manipulate the adoption of plans that minimized minority voting strength overall."

Senator Gene Walker and Representative Bob Hanner, chairs of the legislature's reapportionment committees, expressed disappointment regarding the federal agency's actions and its statement about the racial motivation of the state. Walker lamented, "I'm certain that we operated in good faith. I'm disappointed in the kind of tone they used. I'm Black, and I'm not a racist." And Hanner stated simply, "It's very disturbing." But Representative Brooks said the legislature was to blame because it ignored the warnings of the GLBC that the plan would not be approved because it failed to protect Black voters' interest. The Reapportionment Committee chairs urged their colleagues to start immediately on the state plans so that they could remedy the deficiencies and avoid a delay in primary elections. Senator Culver Kidd remarked, "It would behoove each and every one of us to try to have something ready to drop in when the legislature reconvenes." Senator Walker concurred, saying, "That's my hope, that we can achieve something like that. But right now, I just want to let the process unfold a little bit and give us an opportunity to reflect on it."[2]

By the middle of the two-week recess, three of Georgia's incumbent Congressmen, Lindsey Thomas, Ed Jenkins, and Doug Barnard, had announced they would not seek reelection. The question arose concerning whether several state legislators who either had announced or were expected to announce their candidacies for Congress should participate in the redistricting process. Reactions were mixed as Senator Don Johnson asked to be removed from the Senate Reapportionment Committee "to avoid any appearance of impropriety." Representative Mike Thurmond said he had not announced his candidacy so he could remain neutral. He remarked, "My responsibility is to help develop a fair plan statewide....I think it creates serious ethical quandaries when you mix personal ambition with public responsibility." On the other hand, Representative Cynthia McKinney said there was no conflict in helping to draw a district from which she might run, commenting, "If I draw a plan that provides for the needs of all Georgians to be fairly represented, and others draw plans that do not, then the people benefit because I was around to draw a plan."[3]

The Senate and House decided to hold public hearings during the recess to get more citizen input. Much of the focus was on Southwest Georgia and the goal was to have a draft plan ready when the legislature reconvened on February 3. However, Representative Brooks warned that if moving with such haste resulted in the adoption of plans that did not protect minority voting interests, then Blacks would again appeal to the Justice Department to object. Black Representative J.E. "Billy" McKinney testified before the Senate Reapportionment Committee that since five of its members were running for Congress, he doubted their ability to be fair or objective. And he told the House committee, "We've spent a whole lot of our money to get your plan rejected. The fight will not end. The fight will go on. This whole fight is about power."[4]

---

[2]Rhonda Cook and Gary Hendricks, "Black vote was minimized, so redistricting starts again today," Ibid. 22 January 1992 and Mickey Higginbotham, "Lawmakers again face redistricting," *The Times* (Gainesville). 22 January 1992.

[3]"Who should draw state's districts?" *The Valdosta Daily Times*, 24 January 1992.

[4]Rhonda Cook, "Blacks Renew Push for More South Districts," *Atlanta Journal/Constitution*, 29 January 1992.

HOUSE AND SENATE REAPPORTIONMENT

The GLBC made a concerted effort to ensure Black representation in the General Assembly from rural areas of the state. All 35 Black legislators who served during the 1991-92 session were from the six urban centers (Albany, Atlanta, Augusta, Columbus, Macon and Savannah). The last Black legislator from a rural Black Belt county literally was run out of office in 1907! A major road block had been that many committee chairmen and top leaders in the General Assembly were from rural regions. Expressing the urgency of the need to remedy this situation, GLBC chair Thurmond observed, "One of our primary objectives was to seek political empowerment for rural Georgia. I believe we have reached an historic point in this state. It is a victory that we have committed ourselves to doing what is necessary." The proposed House plan seemed to focus on tampering with majorities in the earlier plans rather than creating more Black districts. Representative Brooks expressed the sentiments of the majority of Black members when he said, "The Legislature has simply not gone far enough when it comes to Blacks and poor people, those voices just aren't there." The ten rural counties with the highest percentage of Black populations (Randolph-57.9 percent; Macon-58.7 percent; Calhoun-58.7 percent; Terrell-59.9 percent; Warren-60.2 percent; Clay-60.8 percent; Taliaferro-60.0 percent; Talbot-62.3 percent; Stewart-63.3 percent; and Hancock-79.4 percent) all had white legislators. Black Burke County Commissioner Herman Lodge said, "What people need is to have somebody in government who is going to look out for their interests. I feel we just don't have representation." [5]

The attempt to put the revised state House and Senate plans on a fast track met with a few delays as members sought to fine-tune some of the districts to which the Justice Department had objected. For example, there were efforts to create three additional majority-Black House districts—one combining Burke with Augusta/Richmond County, a second involving Columbus/Muscogee and Chattahoochee Counties, and a third—Dooly, Crisp, Macon, Peach, and Houston counties—the "Heart of Georgia" district. Representative Brooks again warned the House leadership that if they did not address these districts Justice would again reject their plan. The Senate plan only added one more majority-Black district for a total of 11.[6] A decision was made to address the Congressional plan later in the session.

On January 30, the Senate Reapportionment Committee passed a plan creating 12 majority-Black districts. However, two of them had only slim majorities, such as a 50.7 percent district in Southwest Georgia which contained two incumbents. The plan also increased Black majorities in four Black incumbents' districts. Senator Walker said that the General Assembly had effectively addressed the concerns of the Justice Department and that he expected it would approve the maps.

---

[5]"Rural Georgia had no black vote," *Atlanta Journal/Constitution*, 12 February 1992.

[6]Kenneth Edelstein, "New redistricting lines don't end old grievances," *Columbus Ledger-Enquirer*, February 1992.

However, after Senator Garner and two Black Senators, David Scott and San-ford Bishop, met with a Justice Department attorney for four hours on March 9th, Garner predicted, "The Senate plan's coming back, the House plan's coming back." Representative Brooks asserted that, "Its amazing that these legislators can sit so many days...and still not do the right thing. Obviously, this doesn't meet the letter of the law." And Representative Billy McKinney argued that a 50 percent Black district was simply an "influence district and not one where a Black person could be elected."[7]

The House Committee's revised plan contained 38 majority-Black districts, including three with no incumbents, and it increased the Black percentage in eight districts. The House passed this plan 128-37. The two plans were then submitted to the Justice Department.

Several Black legislators voted against both plans, but the GLBC Chair, Repre-sentative Thurmond, held a press conference at which he asserted that the Caucus had endorsed the plan! He said:

> This plan addresses the eight areas of concern when you consider the totality of cir-cumstances. This is not a perfect plan. Some judgment calls were made.   We are here convinced that we can do the right thing. We stand ready to defend and advocate on behalf of this plan.[8]

Thurmond and three other Black legislators met on March 11 with Justice offi-cials and attempted to convince them that creating three additional marginal Black districts would not result in more Blacks being elected in middle Georgia, east cen-tral Georgia and Columbus. Senator Majority Leader Wayne Garner was more blunt in his view of federal officials, "We deal in practicality. They deal in theory. It's hard to bring those two together." His point was that drawing more Black dis-tricts based on population alone does not help to elect more Blacks because other factors such as low voter registration, low turnout, and lack of political awareness need to be considered. However, Representative Brooks said he would ask the Jus-tice Department to object to the plans. Two Cobb County Republican activists filed a suit in federal district court in Atlanta in which they asked the court to redistrict the state if the legislature did not get all three plans approved by March 13.[9]

CONGRESSIONAL REDISTRICTING

Redrawing the Congressional lines proved to be an even more difficult task. The most divisive issue was over the creation of a third majority-Black district in South-west Georgia, the 2nd Congressional District of Congressman Charles Hatcher. The legislative leadership had agreed to a configuration of a second majority-Black 11th district which stretched from South Dekalb east to (Augusta) Richmond

---

[7]Rhonda Cook, "Blacks attack Senate panel's redistricting plan," *Atlanta Journal/Constitution,* 31 January 1992.

[8]Cited in M. Elizabeth Neal, "Lawmakers approve revised map with more black districts," *Mari-etta Daily Journal,* 1 February 1992.

[9]Rhonda Cook, "Feds urged to set redistricting deadline," *Atlanta Journal/Constitution,* 13 Febru-ary 1992.

County and south to (Macon) Bibb County. The only way to create a third majority-Black district was to include parts of Columbus and Macon along with Albany and the Black Belt rural counties. The House and Senate passed different plans, and hoped that a conference committee could reconcile them. The House plan passed 116-49 and simply increased the 2nd district by only two percentage points. The Senate made more substantive charges in its plan, which passed 35-17. Its plan pushed the 11th district into Savannah and created a majority-Black 2nd district by including parts of Albany, Columbus, Macon and Valdosta.

Speaker Murphy angered some GLBC members as well as North Georgia legislators by appointing three rural South Georgia legislators to the conference committee, including a second-term legislator (Representative Sonny Dixon) instead of a five-term Black Atlanta legislator, Representative Georganna Sinkfield. After almost two weeks of negotiations, the Senate conferees backed away from their insistence on a third majority-Black district and supported a 49 percent 2nd district. The conference committee report was adopted on February 26 by the House 102-54 and in the Senate 37-13. Under this plan Savannah would remain in the 2nd district. Lt. Governor Pierre Howard said,

> The Senate was never anxious to go to Chatham with the 11th District to begin with. We were just trying to do what the Justice Department was requiring. What we seem to be getting from the Justice Department is that the 11th District going all the way to Savannah can disadvantage a minority candidate.[10]

Howard was alluding to the assertion that the cost of running in three major metro media markets (Atlanta, Augusta, and Savannah) would make it very difficult for a Black candidate to win. Representative Thurmond again embraced the adopted plan, commenting, "Two birds in the hand is (sic) better than one possible influence district in the bush." Other Black legislators said that at best only a 51 percent Black district could be created, which would not allow the election of a Black Congressman. This argument was similar to the position taken by Senator. Walker during the special session when he said, "We looked seriously at the possibility of drawing three legitimate Black districts. [But] we couldn't do it and legitimately draw the other eight, too." This was a rather strange argument in view of the fact that three different GLBC members had drafted and submitted plans with a third district having 58.2 percent (Brooks and McKinney), 57.6 percent (Holmes) and 53.4 percent (Bishop) majority-Black populations. Therefore, other Black legislators disagreed with the Thurmond/Walker position. Representative McKinney said the districts needed to have as high a Black percentage as possible to get Black representation. And Representative Brooks called the three media market issue raised by Lt. Governor Howard, "nonsense," "poppycock," and "irrelevant" to reapportionment.[11]

The Senate conferees expressed optimism that the plan would be approved by

---

[10]Sonja Ross, "Idea of 3rd black seat loses steam in capitol*," Gwinnett Daily News*, 27 February 1992.

[11]Rhonda Cook, "Waiting starts for Feds' view of new districts," *Atlanta Journal/Constitution*, 28 February 1992.

Justice. Senator Wayne Garner, the majority leader and one of the Senate conferees, said, "I don't think Justice is going to take the full 60 days...and I think they'll approve it." Representative Sonny Dixon, one of the House conference committee members, said, "From all indications, we have met the Justice Department objections. I believe we have exhausted every opportunity to maximize minority voting strength." Senator Bishop seemed resigned to acceptance of the revised plan by Justice officials, saying, "It is a plan the state of Georgia can defend. It does not unduly dilute minority voting strength." However, Representative Brooks said, "This plan is worse than the plan that went to Washington last September." He surmised that "the plan will be right back here in our laps in a few days." Warning against taking the issue to the courts as was done in 1981, Brooks asserted, "the taxes of this state will be used to defend a hopeless case." Concern was expressed regarding whether a decision would be made prior to the April 27 qualifying date for the Democratic primary election. Senator Walker noted that Justice was aware of the election dates and suggested it would act in good faith by rendering a decision in a timely manner.[12]

As happened in 1991, different groups of Black legislators met with Justice officials to support the plan. And other groups, such as the Concerned Black Clergy, urged Justice to again reject all three plans. Senator Garner returned to Atlanta after a four-hour meeting in Washington and surmised that the plan would be rejected; "I believe we'll have it back by the end of the week." Representative Calvin Smyre and three other Black legislators asked Justice not to require the changes in Muscogee County which could create three rather than two majority-Black State House seats! Justice officials also suggested that two additional Black majority districts could have been drawn in Southwest and middle Georgia and others could have been strengthened by having a higher Black percentage. Representative Smyre said the two incumbent Black state legislators would be put at risk by the attempt to create a third seat in Columbus, and asked, "Are we trying to create districts on paper? Or do we want to get blacks elected to the districts we draw?" On the other hand Representative White asserted, "Those Black legislators who are acquiescing will be faced with an angry Black public when that public understands that they've been sold short." He added, "We may not win it in this coming election, but if we don't draw it, we won't ever win it."[13]

Members of the Concerned Black Clergy (CBC) criticized the three plans passed by the legislature and sent a delegation to Washington to express their opposition to them. Dr. Joseph Lowery, President of the Southern Christian Leadership Conference, along with Reverend Bernie Mitchell of Savannah and Lonnie Miley, a City Councilman from Macon, met with Assistant Attorney General John Dunne. They focused on the Congressional Plan. In a March 17 letter to Dunne, Lowery

---

[12]Charles W. Walston, "Senate remapping plan faces pessimism," *Atlanta Journal/Constitution*, March 12 1992.

[13]Ken Edelstein, "Assembly's mood pessimistic on redistricting plans." *Columbus Ledger-Enquirer*, 12 March 1992.

noted that the legislature had rejected four plans with 3 majority-Black districts. He charged that the adopted plan "does not fairly and equitable represent the 30 percent Black population of Georgia." Representative Cynthia McKinney said, "The community leaders know who's supporting them and who's supporting the (State) leadership." Representative Thurmond then indicated he had supported the three Congressional Districts plan in discussions with federal officials.[14]

The week after returning to Georgia, Thurmond held a joint press conference at the Capitol with the Concerned Black Clergy, whose president said, "The organization is perplexed by the fact that some members of the Black Caucus would go to the Justice Department to plead on behalf of the state's plan." To which Representative Thurmond responded that the Caucus supports three Congressional districts, but "there is some disagreement how they should be configured."[15]

On March 20, 1992, Dunne informed the state of his decision. In the letter, he said that while the state had remedied several of the objections noted in the January 21 letter, the "Heart of Georgia" district continued to "fragment and submerge significant Black population concentrations" by splitting Black voters in Houston County into three majority white districts. Dunne also objected to fragmentation in Southwest Georgia "to insure the reelection of white incumbents," the failure to create a third Black majority district in Muscogee/Chattahoochee, and the inclusion of part of Columbia County in Augusta/Richmond to maintain a majority white (4-3) delegation. Similar objections to giving priority to protecting incumbents over Black interests were raised about the configuration of several Senate districts in the Atlanta metro area which Dunne alleged "minimized Black voting potential." Also, it was pointed out that three districts with majority-Black voting age populations could have been created in the central and southwest parts of the state. Finally, he noted that the legislative leaders apparently had decided to create only two voting age Black Congressional districts. He said the Senate had attempted to draw a third district by including parts of Chatham in the 11th. Dunne said the state had split counties and cities in other areas of the state, but refused to do so in the 2nd Congressional district, thereby diminishing the effectiveness of the minority electorate.(Dunne, 1992b)

Of course, reactions of Georgia lawmakers were mixed. A House conferee, Representative Sonny Dixon, lamented, "I couldn't be more disappointed. I feel like I've been punched in the stomach. The question is, can we pass a plan that goes as far as we are being pushed?" Representative Hanner complained, "I'm very disappointed with what came back. I'm very surprised." On the other hand, Representative Cynthia McKinney was "ecstatic" and called the Justice Department action "a landmark decision." Lt. Governor Howard said Dunne made clear what needed to be done and urged the General Assembly "to act with dispatch" to remedy the

---

[14]Sharyn Wizda, "SCLC President meets with Justice official," *Gwinnett Daily News*, 19 March 1992 and "Feds reviewing redistricting plans, *"Rome News-Tribune*, 13 March 1992.

[15]Charles Walston, "Black caucus leader joins call to revise district plan," *Atlanta Journal/Constitution*, 10 March 1992.

problems so the courts will not step in and draw the districts."[16] The need to move quickly was obvious because there were only five working days left in the forty day 1992 legislative session.

As legislators headed home for what they had hoped would be the last week-end of the session, the legislative staff and two committees went back to the draw-ing board. A March 21, 1992 *Atlanta Constitution* editorial criticized the legislature's approach as doing as "little as possible to see how much they could get away with." It urged the General Assembly to address the Justice Department's objections as quickly as possible.

During the weekend, the House and Senate Committee hammered out plans for the Senate, House and Congress. Both chambers worked late into the night. Close to midnight on the 37th day of the session, the Senate voted to create three additional majority-Black Senate districts. The new 11th district was over 200 miles long and C-shaped, with a 54 percent Black population. Senators from the area called it "an abomination." They added part of Dekalb County with Clayton to increase the Black VAP to 63 percent in one district and enhanced the 55th district to 60 percent by reducing the Black percentage in the 43rd District, whose incum-bent was Senator Walker. This adopted plan had 13 majority-Black districts. The House also added three new Black majority VAP districts, one of which was that of the Majority Leader, Representative Larry Walker. The legislative leader remarked, "I'm going to have a 59 percent [Black] district. But I am displeased with the pro-cess, with the fact that, apparently an American Civil Liberties Union lawyer can sit here in Atlanta and tell us if this plan is going to be approved."[17] The two plans were submitted to the Justice Department, but several weeks went by without any response from the federal agency.

There were rumors that Justice was holding the revised House and Senate plans hostage until the legislature enacted an acceptable three majority-Black district Congressional plan. The official word out of Washington was that a com-puter malfunction was the reason that a reply had not been given on the two plans. To which Senate Majority Leader Garner said, "I suspect that if one of these Congressional maps is agreed to, it would start the computer up." Repre-sentative Hanner feared that it would be very difficult to pass a plan because of the opposition from white legislators in Columbus, Macon, Savannah, some northern counties as well as several southern counties. On March 26 the com-mittee presented the new map, and its members criticized the Justice Depart-ment for coercing them into drawing "bizarrely shaped districts." Representative Dixon remarked, "To exploit the Voting Rights Act, to mandate gerrymandering, rendering asunder these regions for negligible differences in the numbers, is an absolutely baffling mystery to me."[18] On Sunday, March 30 the Justice Depart-

---

[16]James Salzer, "Redistricting Map Booted Back to State," *Athens Daily News/Athens Banner,* 21 March 1992.

[17]Charles Walston and Steve Harvey, "Districting plan no. 3 approved," *The Atlanta Journal/Con-stitution,* 25 March 1992.

ment again rejected the House district plan, and now there were only two working days left in the session. Representative Thurmond said, "I think the Justice Department needs to butt out of our legislative business. I don't think Congress intended for the (Voting Rights) Act to be administered in such a petty, vindictive and partisan way." Once again, the Justice Department called for another Black majority district in the Columbus area. It said the House plan "packed" the two majority-Black districts to protect a white incumbent. This change was made and sent back to Washington along with a major increase in the Black percentage in Senator Eugene Walker's district.[19]

On the last day of the session, the House passed a Congressional plan by a single vote with Speaker Murphy having to cast a vote to make the required 91 needed for a constitutional majority. The Senate also approved the plan. The plan contained three majority-Black Congressional districts with percentages of 56.52 (2nd), 62.27 (5th), and 64.07 (11th). Before the vote, several speakers asked members to reject the plan. One notable speech was given by House Majority Whip Denmark Groover, who said: "The time has come when you and I…must show some steel in our backbone. I'm not prepared to vote for a plan which jerks the heart out of the county in which I live. I am not prepared to vote for a plan in which, for the third time, we have made concessions that has (sic) emasculated areas of community interest." Representative Brooks also spoke against the plan, saying a larger Black percentage could have been drawn in the new 2nd district and noted there was still some fragmentation which dilutes the Black vote. He promised to ask Justice to object to the plan so the legislature could draw a better one in a second special session. However, ACLU attorney Kathy Wilde said she felt the plan would be approved by Justice, saying, "I don't think its the best plan, but I think it's a decent plan."[20]

Finally, on April 2, 1992, the Justice Department approved the House, Senate and Congressional Plans. Brooks said, "We got 98 percent of what we were fighting for." The final maps contained 41 House, 13 Senate and 3 Congressional Black majority districts. The two committee chairs breathed sighs of relief, but expressed regrets at the outcome. Hanner said, "I'm not happy at all with what we had to do to the state to get it approved." Commenting on the elongated rural districts in south Georgia, such as the 130-mile-long, 58.8 percent Black 158th district, he said, "I believe it actually hurts the Blacks in those areas when you just reach in and get a finger to maximize Black voting strength." And Senator Walker said, "It caused some serious political pain for me and a host of my colleagues."[21] The only good thing that most legislators could say about the reapportionment/redistricting process is: Thank God it only happens once a decade!

---

[18]James Salzer, "Congressional districts take bizarre turns in new plan" *Athens Daily News/Athens Banner,* 27 March 1992.

[19]Steve Harvey, "House districts rejected again," *Atlanta Journal/Constitution,* 30 March 1992.

[20]Steve Harvey, "House districts rejected again," *Atlanta Journal/Constitution,* 30 March 1992.

[21]David Savage, "The redistricting triangle," *State Legislature* (September 1995): 20-24.

REFLECTIONS ON THE 1991-92 SESSION

The decennial struggle over redrawing state lines is perhaps the most difficult activity in which any legislator becomes involved during their tenure. It is a struggle for political survival which necessarily makes political enemies out of neighbors since everyone seeks to maximize his or her own position. The Black legislators had a powerful ally in the U.S. Department of Justice, which enabled them to leverage their position and achieve most of their goals. As a result of reapportionment, the makeup of the 1993-94 legislature seemed destined to change from the 1991-92 body. It would most likely become more suburban, more urban, more Black, more female and more Republican. Also, with four of the ten incumbent Congressmen not running for reelection and the open 11th Congressional district, 18 members of the House and Senate offered their candidacies. Thus the Georgia Congressional delegation will likely have many new faces.

The GLBC's three-tiered strategy had worked to perfection up until the last 10 days of the 1991 special legislative session, at which time it appears that the personal agenda's of some caucus members took priority over the interests of Black Georgians. Three incidents illustrate this point. First, the Chair of the GLBC "forgot" to get the Legislative Counsel to draw up an actual bill incorporating the Caucus's 42 House district Black-majority plan. Consequently, a floor substitute bill had to be offered. Since the main bill was adopted, there was never a vote taken on the substitute because it was now out of order. Second, after Justice objected to the legislature's 35 Black district plan, and the General Assembly subsequently sent up a 38 Black-majority district plan, the Chair and five other Caucus members flew up to Washington, D.C. to meet with Justice Department officials to express their support of the legislative leadership's plan. Third, there were reports that the Caucus Chair and a few other Black legislators actively lobbied against the creation of a three Black Congressional district plan in conference committee and with the Lt. Governor. And Senator Walker strongly backed the 11-majority-Black district Senate plan.

The General Assembly leadership continued to adamantly oppose the creation of a third viable Black Congressional district up until March 31, the very last day of the regular 1992 legislative session. In his objection letter of March 20, 1992, Assistant Attorney General John Dunne once again objected to all three redistricting plans because in each case he said there were no logical reasons why the state had not adopted any of the alternative plans that had been presented which would have eliminated the fragmentation of certain Black areas in the adopted Senate and House plans. One week before adjournment, the legislature adopted a 41-Black-majority district House plan and a 13-Black-majority district Senate plan. Dunne noted that the Georgia legislative leadership had attempted to limit Black voting potential to two Congressional districts, and had refused to seriously consider various alternative plans which would not have diminished Black potential voting strength in a Southwest district, including parts of Albany, Columbus and Macon with their heavy concentrations of Blacks. Approximately one hour before adjournment on the last night of the session, the General Assembly adopted a Congressional plan with a 56.7 percent Black majority Southwest Georgia district, but only after the House Speaker cast his vote to provide the one vote margin of victory! The Justice Department approved all three plans the following week.

It seems clear that the 1991-92 strategy of the Georgia Legislative Black Caucus yielded more effective results than the 1981 round of reapportionment. The three tiered strategy proved to be a most productive innovation, but there were some problems because as the Caucus did not maintain its unity until the end. In fact, the majority of its members actually voted to support the two-majority-Black District Congressional Plan to which Justice objected. While the Chairman had expressed support for three majority-Black Districts during the Special Session, he, in fact, went to Washington. D.C. to speak in favor of the House committee's two-majority-Black district plan that passed the General Assembly, as did Representative Georganna Sinkfield, the senior Black member of the House Reapportionment Committee. A majority of the GLBC did not oppose the final version of the penultimate plan adopted by the General Assembly. In fact, only one Black Senator voted against the conference committee report on February 27, 1992 which included a 49.15 percent Black 2nd Congressional district while five (5) had voted for it and 3 did not vote! On the same conference report, 10 Black House members opposed it, 8 voted for it and 8 did not vote! However, 14 GLBC members and a host of Black organizations, such as the NAACP, and the SCLC, the Concerned Black Clergy, wrote letters, called and traveled to Washington, D.C. to voice their objections. They prevailed and Justice forced the white state leaders to approve a viable third Black majority Congressional district on the final day of the legislative session.

It seems clear that the members of the GLBC gained valuable experience from the reapportionment political process in 1981 and did, in fact, learn some important lessons and attempted to apply those lessons to the 1991-92 process. The final outcome of their legislative efforts to draw the maximum number of majority-Black seats was greatly facilitated by the new strategy. While there were new opportunities created to elect more minorities to legislative seats, it also seemed clear that the results of the GLBC strategy would not be immediately realized in the 1992 elections. This was likely to be the case for two reasons. First, many of the newly created Black majority legislative districts had powerful white incumbents, such as House Majority Leader Larry Walker, chairman of the House Agriculture Committee Henry Reeves, a 26-year veteran, Bob Hanna, Chair of the House Reapportionment Committee, Jimmy Lord, Chair of the Insurance Committee, and other close allies of Speaker Tom Murphy. Second, the lines were drawn extremely late, less than four months prior to primary election day which left inadequate time for candidates to organize, register and mobilize the Black electorate in rural areas. Concerning this situation, GLBC Chair Representative Michael Thurmond made a very sage remark which warrants repeating here: "This is not the final evaluation of reapportionment. It takes at least two elections until you see results."

THE AFTERMATH OF THE 1992 REDISTRICTING PROCESS

In the 1992 General Assembly elections, Blacks increased their representation from 28 to 31 in the House and from 6 to 9 in the Senate while the GOP more than doubled its membership in the House from 25 to 52. Blacks increased their numbers in the Congressional delegation from one to three and Republicans went from one to four Congressmen. Blacks gained one additional seat each in the 1994 election to raise their numbers to 32 in the House and grew to 10 in the Senate. The GOP gained 15 additional House seats for a total of 67, increased their numbers to 21 in the Senate and to 8 in the U.S. House of Representatives.

In the 1992 Congressional elections, State Representative Cynthia McKinney won a hard fought Democratic primary election for the newly created Eleventh Congressional seat. Among the opponents she defeated were State Senator Eugene Walker, Chair of the Senate Reapportionment Committee, and Representative Michael Thurmond, Chair of the GLBC. In the primary runoff, her challenger was white Democrat Charles DeLoach. McKinney won the election and became the first Black woman to be elected to Congress from Georgia. Also, Black Senator Sanford Bishop defeated incumbent Congressman Charles Hatcher in the 2nd Congressional District, and 5th District Congressman John Lewis easily won reelection. Blacks won three of the 11 contested Congressional seats, Republicans were victorious in seven districts, as was one white Democrat (he changed to the Republican party after the 1994 election).

Miller v. Johnson

Five persons from the 11th District, including defeated candidate George DeLoach, filed a suit in the United States District Court for the Southern District of Georgia stating that racial gerrymandering was used to create the district in violation of the Equal Protection Clause (14th Amendment), which prohibits race biased decision-making. The contention of the plaintiffs was that the configuration of the district was based exclusively on racial considerations. A 1982 amendment to the VRA sought to help minorities "to elect representatives of their choice" and the Supreme Court in *Thornburg v. Gingles* (1986) prohibited state legislatures from diluting minority voting strength. After the 1990 census, the U.S. Justice Department decided to prod Southern states to draw the maximum number of majority minority legislative districts. Critics of this thrust called it "racial gerrymandering."

In 1993, the Supreme Court addressed this issue in *Shaw v. Reno*, but did not issue a clear ruling. However, two years later on June 26, 1995 in *Miller v. Johnson*, the court clarified its position concerning whether the bizarre shape or racial rationale was a key factor in determining the constitutionality of a redistricting plan. Asserting that race neutral principles, such as compactness, communities of shared interest, and respect for political subdivisions were factors to be considered, the Court declared in a 5-4 decision that if race were the predominant factor, then this was impermissible and the plan was unconstitutional. (*Miller v. Johnson* 115 S Ct 2475 (1995))

More specifically, the Southern District Court of Georgia declared unconstitutional the 11th Congressional District because the Georgia General Assembly had used race as the predominant factor in drawing the districts. The state agreed, arguing that the Justice department refused to preclear two earlier plans with two majority-Black districts. Speaker Thomas Murphy and Lt. Governor Pierre Howard made no effort to defend the plan adopted by the Georgia legislature and they were critical of it in their court testimony. The District Court said the VRA did not require race based districting nor the maximization of Black representation. It said race cannot be used as the leading factor in policy making and that the Justice Department had exceeded its authority in forcing states to create as many majority-Black Districts as possible. (Savage, 1995)

Justice Kennedy, writing for the five-member majority of the U.S. Supreme Court, said there was no rational explanation except separating voters on the basis of race that explained the bizarre geographic configuration of the Eleventh Congressional district. He noted that the redistricting was not based on either a compelling state interest to eradicate the effects of past discrimination or traditional principles, such as communities of interest. The majority opinion noted the involvement of the Justice Department in demanding race based revisions of plans submitted by the General Assembly and the findings of the U.S. District Court for the Southern District of Georgia which ruled 2-1 that the Eleventh District was racially gerrymandered and violated the Equal Protection Clause. The defendants stipulated that race was the overriding factor and the evidence was overwhelming that this was the Georgia General Assembly's intent. Kennedy said the District Court had applied the correct analysis in concluding that Georgia was responding to Justice Department's pressure to create three majority-Black districts. Attorney General Mike Bowers' written objections to these demands were cited in which he claimed that the state's efforts to meet the Justice Department's demand would "violate all reasonable standards of compactness and contiguity."

Finally, Speaker Tom Murphy and Lt. Governor Pierre Howard testified that the legislature did not create the Eleventh District to remedy past discrimination, but only to satisfy Justice's preclearance demands of a "Black maximization policy." The federal agency has interpreted Section 2 of the Voting Rights Act (VRA) to mean that whenever possible, the state must draw a majority-Black district. Finally, Associate Justice Kennedy said the VRA purpose was to stop official efforts to abridge or dilute minority voting rights and eradicate discrimination in the electoral process. He said the Justice Department's "shortsighted and unauthorized" application of the VRA would continue racial stereotyping prohibited by the 14th amendment. Thus, the Supreme Court affirmed the District court's decision and remanded the case for further proceedings.

The four dissenting Justices led by Justice Stevens asserted that the court had misapplied the term gerrymander because the white plaintiffs were not legally injured and, therefore, had no cause of action or standing under the Shaw decision. Stevens wrote that the issue was the exact opposite of the earlier cases which had frustrated African-Americans from participating in the political process because the Georgia districting plan sought to improve diversity by increasing the likelihood of

Black representation. Traditional gerrymandering had sought to maintain the dominant white group's power and not share it with an underrepresented group and thus violated the Equal Protection Clause. He said a plan which favors the politically weak does not violate the equal protection provision and a state is permitted to adopt such policies to promote fair representation for different groups.

Justice Ginsburg said legislative districting was a political business which should be left to the state legislatures except where intervention was necessary to prevent dilution of minority voting strength. She accused the court of adopting a new unwarranted standard. Because of past practices of exclusion of Blacks from the political process, state legislatures must sometime consider race as a factor relevant to drawing of district lines and concentrate members of the group in one district for legitimate purposes. She also reiterated that reapportionment is primarily the duty and responsibility of the state legislatures, not the federal courts. The courts should intervene only in exceptional situations to secure equal voting rights denied by states such as Georgia. It was also noted that significant consideration was given to traditional districting factors and the political process of compromises and trades. The dissenters asserted that the geographical configurations were not any more irregular than the 1980s reapportionment districts and that the adopted plan had respected boundaries of the majority of political subdivisions. In fact, the percentage of intact counties was greater in the 11th district than the average of seven other Congressional districts. Traditional districting principles, such as compactness, contiguity, and respect for political subdivisions were said to be objective factors that may serve to defeat a claim that a district has been gerrymandered on racial lines, but the majority's decision ended this situation. She observed that a plethora of litigation will be required under the Miller standard and will involve the federal judiciary's involvement to an unwarranted extent. She argued that the court should have supported the plan that resulted from Georgia's political process.

The Aftermath of the *Miller v. Johnson* Decision

The Supreme Court's decision on June 26, 1995 to sustain the federal district court's ruling sent political shock waves through Georgia and Southern politics. ACLU attorney Laughlin McDonald said "I really fear this court is sending us back to the dark days of the 19th century." Black Georgia leaders said the decision was an attack on Black political gains and would lead to suits challenging Black majority districts at all levels of government. Many pundits said Republicans would be losers and the winners would be mostly white Democrats.[22] The court ruling placed hundreds of Black legislators, county commissioners, city councilmen, and school board members at risk. Black elected officials and community leaders as well as Georgia's eight-member Republican Congressional delegation expressed concern that the Georgia General Assembly would wipe out two of the majority-Black Congressional districts as well as reverse GOP gains of 1994 and increase the number of white Democratic Congresspersons.

---

[22]"Will Democrats get back on map?" *Atlanta Journal/Constitution,* 30 June 1995.

After meeting with Speaker Thomas B. Murphy and Lt. Governor Pierre Howard and some members of the House and Senate Democratic leadership (only one of the 10 legislators present was Black), Governor Miller issued a call for a special legislative session to convene on August 14, 1995. He listed four items that could be considered: 1) Congressional redistricting; 2) House and Senate reapportionment; 3) Driving Under the Influence (DUI) legislation; and 4) bills affecting local political jurisdictions. (Miller 1995) The consideration of General Assembly seats came as a surprise since there was no court ruling/mandate nor had a suit been filed in federal district court concerning the issue. However, A. Lee Parks, the attorney for the plaintiffs in *Miller v. Johnson* had threatened to file a suit against 17 House and 5 Senate districts alleging that the legislature had drawn racially gerrymandered districts relying on the predominance of race in drawing legislative district boundaries.

A confidential memorandum written by Parks' law partner, Larry Chesin, noted that there are "several instances of racial gerrymandering...that are fairly blatant," but ironically white Democrats won several of these seats. He cautioned that state legislative districts have a different meaning, that the many irregularly configured districts makes disregard of "traditional districting principles more difficult to establish." Chesin further noted that since smaller areas are involved in state legislative districts, it would be easier to establish communities of interest.[23]

Speculation was rampant concerning the possible growing fissure between white and Black Democratic legislators, prospects for a Black-GOP coalition to maintain three African-American majority-Black and the eight Republican Congressional Districts, (the 66 GOP and 32 Black members in the House and 21 Republicans and 10 Black Senators constituted majorities in both chambers of the legislature). There was considerable debate on the subject of why General Assembly districts were included in the Governor's call, scenarios regarding the types of maps that would be drawn, implications regarding the impact of the General Assembly's actions on other challenges to majority-Black District cases in Florida, Louisiana, North Carolina, and Texas, and finally, whether redistricting would be done by the federal court itself or the state legislature. There was uncertainty regarding whether the Georgia legislature would redraw only the 11th Congressional district and readjust the adjacent 1st, 4th and 10th districts or redraw the entire state's Congressional and state legislative districts.

There was considerable conjecture regarding several white Democratic lawmakers. Some were contemplating a switch to the GOP and would have to make a critical decision whether to vote with or against the Republican position on Congressional redistricting, and other white Democrats not contemplating jumping to the other party would be challenged to work closely with their Black Democratic colleagues. He noted that the likely challenge to state legislative districts based on the principle set forth in *Miller v. Johnson* would be a significant factor in General

---

[23]Memorandum from Larry Chesin to Lee Parks regarding Georgia House and Senate districts. July 21, 1995.

Assembly members' actions on Congressional redistricting as "any double crosses, deals or allies established" might alienate Black Democrats. Congressperson Cynthia McKinney said she would fight to keep her district intact while GOP member John Linder surmised that he might have to move to get reelected.[24]

The GLBC had scheduled a strategic planning retreat at Lake Lanier Island in mid-July 1995, and its leadership decided to add the reapportionment issue to the agenda. Prior to the session, the GLBC Chairperson, Senator Diane Harvey Johnson, had appointed a task force on redistricting to devise a Congressional plan, to negotiate with the General Assembly leadership, to monitor the work of the Senate and House Reapportionment committees, and to regularly report to and dialog with the full caucus on such matters. Civil Rights organizations led by the SCLC and NAACP along with a Black ministers group (Concerned Black Clergy) said the Democratic party should stop making Blacks the culprits for their losses of Congressional seats and warned them about reducing the number of Black majority districts and representation.[25] They and Black lawmakers were concerned that the General Assembly leadership would destroy the Black majority districts by dispersing Black loyal Democratic voters among several districts, thus enhancing the electoral prospects of white Democrats.

The GLBC emerged from its retreat exposing the slogan "3 Seats, No Retreat" and its chair presented to the House and Senate legislative reapportionment committees the plan delineated in Table 2, which embodied this concept. The plan made changes in the three majority-Black districts and reduced the Black percentages from 56.62 to 54.45 (2nd), 62.27 to 56.70 (5th) and 64.04 to 56.56 (11th).

TABLE 2. Georgia Congressional Districts:
Plan Presented by the Georgia Legislative Black Caucus
1995 Special Session

District	White	%White	Black	%Black	Total VAP	White VAP	%White VAP	Black VAP	%Black VAP
1	398607	67.74	179805	30.56	426375	301018	70.60	118451	27.78
2	259587	44.11	320418	54.45	414393	200257	48.33	208194	50.24
3	455817	77.39	124222	21.09	431175	341617	79.23	83421	19.35
4	509790	86.38	51161	8.67	450110	392142	87.12	37193	8.26
5	240478	40.84	333895	56.70	447848	203393	45.42	233875	52.22
6	526103	89.34	45908	7.80	440796	396858	90.03	32183	7.30
7	506077	85.96	76946	13.07	427992	372984	87.15	51123	11.94
8	435636	73.98	146096	24.81	423174	325735	76.97	92566	21.87
9	568015	96.38	14588	2.48	437597	422418	96.53	10530	2.41
10	454892	77.25	120640	20.49	437714	346904	79.25	81129	18.53
11	245146	41.65	332886	56.56	413739	187088	45.22	219477	53.05

In a surprise move, the Southern District of Georgia Federal Court issued an order on August 2nd, less than two weeks before the special session of the legislature was to convene, setting a hearing date of August 22 and inviting the parties to

---

[24]"Who Will Draw the Lines?" *Georgia Legislative News,* 7 August 1995.

[25]Joan Kirchner, "Clergy joins fight to keep 3 black seats," *The Atlanta Voice,* 29 July - 4 August, 1995.

the suit to submit plans and ideas "narrowly conceived" to "cause minimal disruption to the political processes of the State of Georgia" by August 15 (one day after the special legislative session was to begin). The judges also asked the parties to explain why the court should not draw a redistricting plan![26] Once again speculation was rampant concerning the court's action and its timing, which seemed to pre-empt the legislature's authority to draft a Congressional plan, an action apparently contemplated in 1995 before the Supreme Court agreed to hear the case. Also, it was surmised that the order was an effort to caution the legislature about making major changes in the map.

In a meeting held a few days after the court order was issued, there was a meeting involving the GLBC Reapportionment Task Force, Speaker Murphy, the House leadership, and Georgia Attorney General Bowers. A Black House member suggested that the defendants (the Speaker, Governor, Lt. Governor and Secretary of State) write to the court and ask for a delay, but the suggestion was rejected on the grounds that it might "anger" the court. Attorney General Bowers suggested that a progress report on the General Assembly's actions during the special session would be sufficient. However, House Speaker Murphy attempted to use the August 2nd court order to get the GLBC to agree to a Congressional plan prior to the convening of the legislature.

While the district court's intentions were unknown and the court action was said to be "highly unusual," there was a consensus that the General Assembly should try to draw a map. Joint meetings of the Senate and House Reapportionment Committees began on July 31. Senator Peg Blitch, the Senate Chair, expressed frustration at the lack of guidance from the federal district court and the conflicting legal advise concerning what the proper remedy should be from several lawyers who presented testimony before the Committees. Pamela Susan Karlan, a professor of law at the University of Virginia, who was an adviser to the GLBC, told the panel, "you are walking a tightrope right now. Whichever way you draw the districts, someone is going to sue." Congresswoman Cynthia McKinney, along with the GOP, joined the GLBC in urging the legislature to make the minimum changes required and not completely redraw the state map.[27]

While much of the public focus was on redrawing the Congressional boundaries prior to the convening of the special session, once it opened on August 14 the legislature focused on state House and Senate reapportionment. For the entire first week, the Reapportionment staff huddled with groups of state legislator's from different parts of the state in an effort to reshape their districts. It seemed clear that the "real agenda" of the House leadership was to protect white Democratic committee chairs, the Majority Leader, and a few other close allies of Speaker Murphy.

---

[26]U.S. District Court for the Southern District of Georgia, Augusta Division, No. CV 194-008. Filed 2 August 1995 (5:03 p.m.).

[27]Mark Sherman, "Redrawn districts expected to face challenge," *Atlanta Journal/Constitution,* 3 August 1995 and Herbert Denmark, Jr. "Black caucus launches effort to maintain seats," *The Atlanta Voice,* 5-11 August 1995.

Observing this development, the *Atlanta Journal* editorialized that the General Assembly had apparently forgotten why it had been called into session—to fix the 11th Congressional District. With only two working days before the scheduled court hearing date on August 22, neither chamber had considered a Congressional plan. Noting the legislature's leadership said it was trying to take a proactive stance to protect the state districts from suffering the same fate that befell the 11th Congressional district, the newspaper said there had been no suit filed against the state districts. It accused the General Assembly of playing politics in trying to help some powerful members to get reelected in 1996 rather than redrawing the lines during the regular cycle after each 10-year census. A second criticism was that the leadership was attempting to divert attention from the hard task of responding to the Supreme Court's ruling. It was conjectured that the Democratic leaders recognized they couldn't get the votes of Black lawmakers to pass the type of plan desired by them, one majority-Black district, and their strategy seemed to be to wait for the court to draw such a Congressional redistricting plan. The paper urged the legislature to return to its original task and to only redraw state legislative districts for "compelling legal reasons."[28]

Despite this criticism, the legislature moved ahead. While several Black legislators also expressed concern about the new strategy by the legislative leadership, others, whose districts were mentioned as targets by the plaintiffs' attorneys, began to negotiate individually with their legislative colleagues in their region to redraw their districts.

In the Senate, two majority-Black districts represented by white Democrats were reduced from 62 percent to 43 percent and from 59 percent to 42 percent Black by the Senate Committee with only one of the four Black members of the Committee voting no. Senate David Scott, who served as Chair of the GLBC Task Force on Reapportionment, voted against this dilution of majority-Black Senate districts. An attempt by the Governor's floor leader, Senator Mark Taylor of Albany, to reduce his district below 50 percent Black was unsuccessful, but it did decrease from 56 to 52 percent. Scott said the Senate was illegally trying to change the 1992 plan. The Senate plan also helped the reelection prospects of other Democratic Senate leaders, such as Senator Terrell Starr (Chair of Finance) and Senator Jake Pollard (Chair of Insurance) who had the number of Black voters increased in their districts by approximately 13 percent each to help withstand prospective GOP challengers.

The House Committee made even more extensive changes in the state House map by making reductions in 10 formerly majority-Black districts. Among the key legislators affected were the Majority Leader Larry Walker (59.04 to 26.03 percent), House Agriculture Chair Henry Reeves (63.10 to 27.20 percent) and Representative Bob Hanna, Chair of the Natural Resources and Environment Committee (62.22 to 43.11 percent). However, Black Representative Eugene Tillman saw his district slashed from a 57.29 percent Black voting age population to 38 percent, and

---

[28]"Fix the 11th district, change state lines later," *The Atlanta Journal,* 17 August 1995.

GLBC Vice Chair Carl Von Epps' district was reduced from 60.07 to 55.68 percent Black. Overall, the Committee made changes in 69 House districts despite claims by the leadership that its only purpose was to take preemptive steps to avoid a threatened law suit against 17 districts.

The GLBC held several meetings to discuss the strategy that should be followed when the House reapportionment bill reached the floor. After one marathon meeting lasting over four hours, there was unanimous agreement among the 32 Black House members to vote against it. They were perturbed over the fact that there had been no formal consultation with the Caucus before the House leaders made the drastic reductions in the Black population in several house districts. House GOP Minority Leader Bob Irvin attacked the Democratic leadership's actions as "a deliberate assault on both Black and Republican districts using the Supreme Court as a poor excuse. It's a deliberate calculated attempt to undo the elections that resulted in more blacks and Republicans being down here."[29] In response, the House leadership increased Representative Tillman's district up to 48 percent and Von Epps to 55 percent. However, several GLBC members argued that its members should still vote against the plan in order to use it as leverage to force passage of an acceptable Congressional redistricting plan. It was suggested that the two plans be "paired" and that no action be taken unless there was agreement on both. When the leadership decided to push the plan on the House floor, a tacit GLBC-GOP coalition managed to narrowly block the passage of the measure by a vote of 89 to 87, two votes short of a constitutional majority. While 10 Republicans voted with the White Democrats, all 32 Black legislators opposed it. Majority Leader Walker served notice that he would ask for reconsideration of the vote the next day.

In the Senate, the members of the Caucus split down the middle (5-5) on the vote to pass that chamber's plan. Senator Scott led the opposition calling the plan a "terrible mistake" and excoriated his Democratic colleagues who supported the plan for diluting the Black vote by "dismantling Black majority districts" and then expecting Blacks to support the Democratic party. Senate GLBC members who voted for the plan justified their position on the grounds that they "got the best deal" possible to preserve incumbents seats. And Senator Charles Walker, Senate Democratic Majority Caucus Chair and one of the three Senate conferees on the Budget, said "I can hardly lose something I never had"—a reference to the fact that the diluted districts were currently represented by white Democrats. This seemed to contradict the 1991 position of the Caucus members John White and Mike Thurmond who asserted that the seats created in 1991 may not be won in the 1992 or 1994 elections, but if they were not drawn then Blacks would never have the opportunity to win them.

With the August 22 Federal court public hearing less than 12 hours away, the Georgia House committee passed a Congressional plan that was similar to one outlined by Speaker Murphy and the plaintiffs attorney Lee Parks! Its primary feature

---

[29]Alexander, Kathy and Mark Sherman, "2 Houses Try to Reduce Majority-Black Districts," *Atlanta Journal/Constitution,* 22 August 1995.

was one Black-majority district (Congressman John Lewis), and two 40 percent districts which confined Congressperson McKinney's district to two counties in metro Atlanta (Dekalb and Clayton) and pushed Congressman Bishop's residence out of his own district into one currently represented by GOP Congressman Mac Collins.

In a New York Times Op-Ed article (August 23, 1995) titled "Georgia's Unholy Alliance," attorney A. Lee Parks lamented the fact that no white Democrats were in the Georgia Congressional delegation because Blacks were concentrated in a few districts. He criticized the effort of Black and GOP legislators to block the special session from adopting a plan that would recoup power for the Democratic Party, and urged Blacks to work with white Democrats against the Republican party. Parks said they should seek to elect candidates based on biracial coalitions. He warned that the federal court would draw the plan if the legislature did not seize the opportunity.

At the August 22 hearing, the federal judges again criticized the Justice Department and blamed it for the current predicament. Judge Bowen said the state had been "bludgeoned into passing a monstrosity Congressional redistricting plan." They then set a deadline of October 15th for the General Assembly to draw a new plan and secure approval from either the Justice Department or the Washington, D.C. federal district court.

It was believed that failure to pass the reapportionment plan on the House districts would enhance Black and Republican leverage in the Congressional redistricting battle. As long as both plans were on the table, Blacks would be able to bargain for a better deal in protecting incumbent Black lawmakers in the state House, Senate and Congressional delegations. However, this opportunity was lost as several GLBC members voted in favor of reconsideration of the failed plan despite pleas from many Caucus members who argued that to do so would be a step backward and reduce their ability to secure passage of a plan to protect the three incumbent Black Congresspersons. Several publicly proclaimed their allegiance to the Democratic party and called their previous unanimous vote on the plan along with a solid 85 percent Republican support merely a coincidence rather than an alliance or coalition. After a lengthy GLBC meeting marked by an acrimonious debate over the indefensibility of voluntarily dismantling several majority-Black districts currently represented by white Democrats and reducing the Black VAP below 50 percent in four others, 26 of the 32 GLBC members in the House reversed their previous position and voted for the Democratic leadership's plan. Table 3 shows changes in 11 majority-Black House districts.

After the adoption of the State Senate and House reapportionment plans, Walter Butler, President of the Georgia Conference of the NAACP, and other civil right leaders criticized the action of the General Assembly. In a letter sent to Caucus members, Butler called the vote "an attempt to turn back the clock on the voting rights of African-Americans in the state," which constituted "retrogression and vote dilution" in violation of Sections 2 and 5 of the Voting Rights Act. He called the reapportionment of state legislative districts unwarranted because there was no legal challenge or court ruling requiring such action, and he noted that the Supreme

Court decision dealt only with the 11th Congressional District. Criticizing the GLBC members who voted for the plans, Butler wrote:

> The most disturbing aspect of the plans adopted is that for the first time since the passage of the 1965 Voting Rights Act, significant numbers of African-American state legislators have voted to dilute the voting strength of African-American voters. The decision by several members of this caucus to support plans to reduce the number of majority-Black districts sets a dangerous precedent. The actions of some of the Black legislators will make it harder to convince the Department of Justice to interpose an objection to these discriminatory plans. Even worse, by siding with the white majority against the voting rights of African-Americans, Black legislators have made future litigation against these plans more difficult, time consuming and costly. (Butler, August 25, 1995)

Table 3. Major Changes in Majority-Black House Districts*
1995 Special Session
(percentages)

	1992 %	1992 %	1995 %	1995 %	
	Black Pop.	Voting Age Pop. (VAP)	Black Pop.	Voting Age Pop.	Decrease
Jimmy Lord (121), Chair, Insurance Committee	62.60	58.84	53.60	49.83	- 9
Larry Walker (141), Majority Leader	59.06	54.04	26.03	23.90	-33.03
Tom Bordeaux (151) Governor's Assistant Floor Leader	61.14	56.25	51.65	46.88	- 9.94
Bob Hanner (159), Chair, Natural Resources & Environment Committee	62.22	57.43	43.11	40.39	-19.11
Henry Reaves, (178) Chair, Agriculture Committee	63.10	58.01	27.20	24.64	-35.9
Gerald Greene, (158) Secretary, Appropriations Committee	63.62	58.79	55.70	50.89	- 7.92
Kermit Bates (179)	63.28	59.13	37.32	33.51	-25.96
Frank Bailey (70)	57.24	54.18	52.90	50.05	- 4.34
Mickey Channell (111)	54.45	50.11	36.57	32.64	-17.88
E.C. Tillman (173) (Black Legislator)	60.58	57.29	48.12	47.48	-12.46
Carl Von Epps (31) (Black Legislator	60.07	51.07	55.68	47.27	- 4.39

*Source: Compiled by author.

THE CONGRESSIONAL REDISTRICTING BATTLE

The original House Reapportionment Committee's Congressional plan that was voted on the floor was so bad that it received only 19 votes in the House and 2 in the Senate. The GLBC Task Force members worked long into the night and on weekends in an effort to craft a plan that could gain the support of the white Democratic leadership. Finally, on August 24, a plan that seemed to offer the possibility of reelecting the 3 Black incumbent Congresspersons and 3 or 4 white Democrats was agreed to and introduced by Speaker Murphy as a floor substitute. The plan passed the House 103 to 66 with all GLBC members voting in favor. It contained two majority-Black districts (the 5th at 56.31 percent and the 11th at 53.37 percent) while the 2nd had a 49.5 percent Black population. This plan passed after a vote to defeat (62 to 108) a plan backed by the Georgia GOP that had been submitted to the federal district court by Congressman John Lewis and Speaker Newt Gingrich. Under this plan, the 5th district was 57.1 percent Black, the 11th had a 54.85 Black majority and District 2 was 49.36 percent Black. The House plan that passed was then submitted to the three-judge federal court panel as a status report representing action by the General Assembly to meet the court's mandate.[30]

Charges of betrayal were made in the Senate after a reapportionment plan with only one majority-Black Congressional district was passed 34-21 in a racially polarized vote. Senator Mark Taylor, the Governor's Floor Leader, who was believed to be interested in running for the 2nd Congressional District seat, introduced the plan as a floor substitute. In an obvious appeal to the "angry white male" Senators, Taylor urged them to support his plan "if you're tired of paying for the sins of your fathers and grandfathers." However, Black Senator Ed Harbison said, "to put it plainly, it (the plan) stinks and represents a deliberate attack" against Black Congressmen. And his colleague, Senator Charles Walker, accused Taylor of trying to further his own Congressional ambitions. All 10 Black Senators voted against the plan drawn by Senator Mark Taylor, but a coalition of GOP and white Democratic lawmakers voted overwhelmingly in support of it. Unlike the House version, the Senate plan did not put Speaker Gingrich and Congressman Bob Barr in the same district, but it "kicked" Congressman Bishop out of his 2nd Congressional District and put him in the 3rd District. However, Speaker Murphy objected to their placing Cobb county in his 7th District.[31] It was clear that the two bodies were too far apart for a quick resolution of their plans and that a conference committee would have to try to work out their major differences. It was known that Black Senator Charles Walker was to be a Senate conferee, and Speaker Murphy indicated he would place veteran Black legislator David Lucas on the House con-

---

[30]Civil Action File No. CV 194-008 by Defendants, Zell Miller, Pierre Howard, Thomas Murphy and Max Cleland, 30 August 1995.

[31]Dick Pettys, "Black Democrats are betrayed," *Augusta Focus* 31 August - 6 September 1995 Mark Sherman and Kathy Alexander "Senate would reduce majority black districts to 1," *Atlanta Journal/Constitution,* 31 August 1995.

ference committee and require unanimity among the three House negotiators on any agreed upon conference committee plan.

A coalition of Black civil rights organizations condemned the Senate action as "racist and absurd." Their statement accused the White Democrats and Republicans of "abandoning and emasculating" the Voting Rights Act and compared Senator Mark Taylor to California Governor Pete Wilson, who launched his bid for the GOP Presidential nomination by initiating anti-affirmative action and anti-immigrant policies. The leaders urged the General Assembly to adopt a plan similar to the House passed two Black majority and one heavy influence district. Finally, they threatened to file a lawsuit under Section 2 and they urged the Department of Justice to reject the plan under Section 5 because the plan diluted Black voting strength. Concerning the state legislative district plans, they said the Senate and House bills represented vote dilution and retrogression. The group planned a series of town hall meetings in the state to educate/inform the public regarding these efforts to dilute Black voting strength. The concluding sentence stated, "We have come too far, marched too long, prayed too hard, wept too bitterly, bled to profusely, and died too young to let anybody turn back the clock on our journey to justice."(Joint Statement For the Preservation of African-American Voting Rights)

A Black-owned newspaper, *Augusta Focus* (August 31, 1995), editorialized that white Democrats were apparently seeking affirmative action in terms of Congressional representation. It said that Black ad hoc coalitions with Republicans could be useful, but that there was no significant commonality of interest or philosophy between the two groups. Instead, Blacks were urged to adopt an independent posture because the traditional alliance with white Democrats would not work when political survival was at stake.

When the Senate and House each insisted on their positions on the respective maps, a conference committee was appointed. The Black legislators were still reeling from the white Democrat-Republican Senate action and tried to stake out their position and effect an acceptable compromise. The GLBC gave up its battle to secure three majority-Black districts and some expressed concern that House Republicans and Democrats might somehow coalesce and pass a plan close to the Senate version. The House negotiators focused on Speaker Murphy's priority of getting Cobb county completely out of the 7th District, thus placing two Republican Congressmen, Barr and Gingrich, in the same district. This was obviously unacceptable to House and Senate Republicans. There was also the recognition that even if the six conferees agreed on a map, there was no certainty of passage in either the House or Senate. Many political games were being played with multiple agendas, including efforts of several Senators to position themselves for a Congressional race. For examples, Senator Taylor, whose plan would push Congressman Bishop into the 3rd district and cut the Black VAP to 39 percent, has already been mentioned. Senate Majority leader Sonny Perdue was said to be interested in the 8th Congressional District seat and favored a plan which added the northern majority-Black portion of the city of Macon (Bibb county) into the district and shifted incumbent GOP Congressman Saxby Chamblee's home county of Colquitt out of the district. Lt. Governor Pierre Howard's former Executive Assistant, Lewis Massey, reportedly had his sights on the 9th district and sought to move Clarke county (home of his Alma Mater, the University of Georgia) from the 10th to the 9th district.

Eleven days after the conference committee had been appointed, the frustration level of the Senate led to the passage of a resolution to adjourn the special session by a vote of 30 to 21 with seven of the 10 GLBC members voting in favor of the resolution. However, by a 73 to 88 vote, with all GLBC members opposing the *sine die* resolution, the House refused to end the special session. Speaker Murphy had reportedly sent a state plane to fly in some legislators who had left the Capitol to return home to their places of business in an attempt to muster enough votes to pass the adjournment resolution. The House also convened on Saturday, September 9 with the expectation that its members would have an opportunity to vote on a conference committee plan. There was a vote to reconsider the failed vote to adjourn *sine die,* and it passed 82 to 70. However, this was still nine votes shy of the 91 votes needed to adjourn.

The session then turned into a surrealistic, Rod Serling "Twilight Zone" event. Some days had lasted from 10 a.m. until 1 a.m. with members being asked to "stand at ease pending the call of the Chair" for 2 or 3 hours at a time, only to reconvene for 2-3 minutes and then recess again for an undetermined amount of time. Factionalism existed among the GOP as well as white and Black Democrats. Speaker Newt Gingrich urged his Republican colleagues to end the session to minimize the possible damage that could happen if the Democrats united. Most of the GOP House members publicly rejected his request, some from the House floor, while an overwhelming majority of the Republican Senators heeded his call! Meanwhile, many House GLBC members became suspicious of a possible move by dissident House Democrats and Republicans to pass a one-majority-Black Congressional plan. This fear came to outweigh the concern that the federal district court might draw the plan. Tempers flared almost continuously among the Senate and House conferees as each blamed the deadlock on the other side. Black Representative David Lucas, accused the Democratic Senate negotiators of "cutting a deal with the devil" in voting for a one-majority-Black district plan which helped Republicans rather than the Black Democratic Congressmen. Senator Jack Hill retorted that the House was being unreasonable in its insistence on dealing with the 7th district first per Speaker Murphy's request. Citing their "fixation" on this part of the map, he said, "Let's be real clear that one fix the blame where the blame ought to be—your unwillingness to negotiate on the rest of the map until the 7th is completed." After the conferees adjourned Sunday night at 10 p.m., the Speaker said the legislature should go home.[32] After another day of acrimonious negotiations, a clear majority of the House members had had enough. When they returned from a lunch

---

[32]Mark Sherman, "Sniping the order of the day in redistricting negotiations," *Atlanta Journal/ Constitution,* 11 September 1995.

break, the members voted 102 to 50 to adjourn *sine die* and the Senate voted 40 to 13 to go home.

The media were very critical of the General Assembly for staying in session for more than five weeks at a cost of $500,000 ($25,000 per day) and leaving without accomplishing their task. The legislature was accused of abdicating its responsibility to the federal judges. The General Assembly had spent most of its time on state legislative districts for the first two weeks of the special session which was a clear indication of the legislators' priorities—"to protect their own political interests." The media blamed all three factions of the General Assembly (Republicans, African-Americans and white Democrats) for putting "their narrow political agendas ahead of the larger interests of the voters, thus resulting in a deadlock."[33]

Columnist Tom Baxter called the session "a watershed event" which marked the end of the old monolithic politics of the past. Neither presiding officer could hold his body together. Several observers commented that the era of Speaker Murphy's 22-year control of the Georgia House of Representatives had come to an end. Others surmised that a Black-Republican-dissident Democrat Coalition similar to what happened in North Carolina in the 1980s, which enabled Blacks to elect Black House Speaker Daniel T. Blue, could happen in Georgia in 1997. Another scenario was that a Republican-White Democrat alliance which passed the Senate Congressional plan, might become the controlling force in future sessions. Speaker Newt Gingrich said he was glad the session had ended because the legislature was "on the verge of becoming destructive." Congressperson Cynthia McKinney called it a shame that the legislature decided "to throw in the towel." Reverend Joseph Lowery blamed white Democratic Senators for their refusal to agree to a modified version of the House-passed Congressional plan. Congressman Bishop said the legislature did its best, but there were too many "serious disagreements." GOP Congressman John Linder said he was happy that the court would decide the matter rather than the "spiteful Speaker (Murphy)." And Lt. Governor Howard said that any map passed by the legislature would have been suspect because of the focus on race in drawing any plan.[34] Representative Denny Dobbs perhaps best characterized the reason why the special session ended without drawing new Congressional lines when he said, "We just split up into too many factions..." Black and white Democrats were split over how many majority-Black districts to draw. And Republican efforts to retain their eight Congressional seats caused them to refuse to compromise. Even the specter of court intervention proved insufficient to force action by the General Assembly. The GOP decided to take their chances with the court rather than accept a House map placing Congressmen Gingrich and Barr in the same district. Black legislators, who observed the momentum in the House shifting to the Senate version, decided they too would take their chances with the federal judges. And White Democrats became confident that the judges would reconfigure

---

[33]"Maps lead to nowhere," *Macon Telegraph*, 14 September 1995.

[34]Tom Baxter, "Failed map-makers lost their sense of direction," *Atlanta Journal/Constitution*, 13 September 1995.

the 11th district and disperse Black voters into other adjacent districts, thus increasing the prospects of electing more white Democratic Congressmen. According to the House Reapportionment Committee Chair, Representative Tommy Smith, "There's a large segment of the General Assembly that has felt from the beginning that the courts would draw it (Congressional plan) more to their liking."[35]

CONCLUSION

The GLBC retained its unity on Congressional redistricting, but this was not enough to gain the support of their White House or Senate Democratic colleagues. The fragile coalition of Democrats was fractionalized, perhaps beyond repair. It remains to be seen whether this division will carry over into future sessions of the General Assembly. It has long been said that legislative reapportionment is politics in its rawest form and many General Assembly members found out just how ugly the process can be. As Senator Mark Taylor said, "if the people could have seen this process, they would have been outraged."

Finally, on December 13, 1995, federal district judges Dudley H. Bowen, Jr. and B. Avant Edenfield put an end to the speculation concerning what the Georgia Congressional map would look like as they released the new Congressional map they had drawn. After the special session ended, Attorney Parks filed a suit against the 2nd Congressional district and the court also declared it unconstitutional. The judges' map made drastic changes, shifting more than 60 percent of Georgia's residents into new Congressional districts, and reduced the number with Black majorities from three to one.

The plan drawn by the court was the one under which the 1996 elections would take place. The options of African-American Georgians were somewhat limited: 1) the plan could be appealed, 2) an attempt could be made to get a Supreme Court justice to block the implementation of the plan; and 3) the legislature could make another attempt to redraw the map during a regular or a special session in 1996. However, Governor Miller said enough money had already been spent on reapportionment legal matters, and Lt. Governor Howard said he did not want to deal with reapportionment in 1996. President Clinton asked the Solicitor General to prepare a petition asking the Supreme Court to rehear the Georgia Case, but the Court refused. Still a third law suit was filed by Attorney A. Lee Parks against the state legislative district plans. The district court again ruled in favor of the plaintiffs. It drew a plan which was a modified version of the one passed by the General Assembly in the 1995 Special session and ordered that the 1996 elections be held under these plans. There is a possibility that another, permanent plan will have to be either drawn by the General Assembly or the federal court under which future elections will occur up to 2000.

The court plan made far reaching changes in seven of the 11 Congressional dis-

---

[35]Mark Sherman and Mike Christensen, "Democratic leaders take the heat," and Kathey Alexander, "Retreat on redistricting," *Atlanta Journal/Constitution,* 13 September 1995.

tricts, including putting two Black Democratic Congressmen in the same districts with two white GOP incumbents-in the 4th (Cynthia McKinney and John Linder) and the 3rd (Sanford Bishop and Saxby Chambliss). Two districts, the 8th and 11th, were left without an incumbent. Table 5 compares the new plan with the 1992 plan in terms of the Black population by each Congressional district. While Congressman John Lewis' district was untouched, Congressman Bishop's second district had its Black percentage reduced from 50.52 to 39.21 percent while Congresswoman McKinney's 11th district was reduced from 64.07 to 11.79 percent Black.

TABLE 4. Georgia Congressional Map Drawn by Federal District Court (1996)

District Number	Total Pop % Deviation	Black Pop % of Total	VAP % of Total	Black VAP % of VAP
1	589546	133616	429079	87200
	0.10	22.66	72.78	20.32
2	591681	334433	416052	217320
	0.47	56.52	70.32	52.23
3	591712	105893	429385	70042
	0.47	17.90	72.57	16.31
4	588293	67968	448179	48225
	-0.11	11.55	76.18	10.76
5	586485	365206	440910	253413
	-0.41	62.27	75.18	57.47
6	587118	35366	438847	25567
	-0.31	6.02	74.75	5.83
7	588071	75813	431939	50533
	-0.15	12.89	73.45	11.70
8	591249	124253	427130	78517
	0.39	21.02	72.24	18.38
9	586222	21516	436725	15161
	-0.46	3.67	74.50	3.47
10	591644	106916	439254	72631
	0.46	18.07	74.24	16.54
11	586195	375585	413413	249533
	-0.46	64.07	70.52	60.36

Perhaps the most significant changes were in the creation of four districts with Black populations between 30.55 and 39.21 percent. Such districts are considered ideal for white Democratic candidates because they have a strong Democratic base of Black voters and a core of "Yellow Dog (white Democrats)," and this coalition is likely to constitute more than 50 percent of the electorate. Thus, the prospects are good for three or four new Democrats to be elected in the 1996 general election, and for the number of Black Congresspersons to decline to one or two.

Supporters of the VRA were devastated and said the decision voided the application of this historic legislation. They surmised that in other states where minority districts have been challenged that Georgia would be used as a model, thus leading to a decrease in minority Congressional seats in 1996 as well as further reductions in the next round of redistricting after the year 2000 census. Essentially, the plan adhered closely to the one submitted by the plaintiffs' attorney, A. Lee Parks. Several incumbent GOP Congressmen accused the two judges, both of whom were Democrats, of playing politics. Congressman John Linder said Speaker Murphy managed to get the court to do what he was unable to push through the legislature—namely to draw a map favoring white Democrats.

TABLE 5. Comparison of Old and New Congressional Maps

District	Black % Change	1995 Black Population	1995 Black Percentage	1992 Black Population	1992 Black Percentage
1	+7.89	179,809	30.55	133,616	22.66
2	-17.31	230,419	39.21	334,433	56.52
3	+6.76	145,377	24.66	105,893	17.90
4	-25.05	215,700	36.60	67,968	11.55
5	-0.28	365,330	61.99	365,206	62.27
6	-0.36	37,597	6.38	35,366	6.02
7	-0.32	7,787	13.21	75,513	12.89
8	+10.05	182,636	31.07	124,253	21.02
9	-0.02	21,520	3.65	21,516	3.67
10	+19.48	220,803	37.55	106,916	18.07
11	-52.28	69,503	11.79	375,585	64.07

Source: U.S. District Court of the Southern District of Georgia.

As this text goes to press, the general primary and runoff elections have been held in Georgia. Regarding the Congressional primary on July 9, 1996, both Congresspersons Bishop and McKinney moved their residences into their new districts and won with more than 60 percent of the vote in the general primary election against multiple white challengers. It should be noted that Black voters in both of their districts comprise close to a majority of the electorate in the Democratic party primaries and also that they both managed to gain more than 20 percent of the white vote in their respective districts. However, McKinney faces strong Republican opposition in the 4th Congressional District, while Bishop is rated a heavy favorite to prevail in the November 6th general election.

In the General Assembly, all Black incumbents won their Democratic primary elections in cases where they had challengers. However, seven of them face GOP opposition. In the general election, in three of these cases, there is uncertainty as to the outcome. (See Epilogue, page 227.)

LESSONS LEARNED

As noted above, in the 1991-92 round of reapportionment/redistricting politics, Black legislators used a multifaceted strategy involving five techniques. However, during the 1995 special session, The GLBC did not use either the threat to appeal to the DOJ, form an alliance with the GOP, or use the three separate groups approach (Insider, Outsider, and Task Force). Its efforts focused primarily on negotiating with the Democratic leadership and forming a task force to develop alternative plans and lead the negotiation effort.

As noted above, 26 of the 32 House GLBC members and 5 of the 10 Black Senators discarded the opportunity of aspiring Black office seekers in nine House districts and two Senate districts to gain more General Assembly seats without securing anything in return, except a small decrease in the Black population percentage in the districts of two incumbent GLBC members. This happened despite the unity displayed in the first vote on the House plan and without any new development occurring prior to the second vote. The State NAACP President, Walter Butler, noted this precedent of Black legislators voting to dilute African-American voting strength. Interestingly, there was a reluctance to vote a second time with the GOP to maintain the opportunity for more Blacks to win state legislative seats currently held by white Democrats.

In fact, the incumbent Black representatives were also forgoing the opportunity to assume additional chairmanships in the House which would have been possible with the likely defeat of four white Democratic chairmen. For example, the Chair of the Insurance Committee had already announced his plans to retire from his seat, then a 62 percent Black-majority district, but announced for reelection stands after his district was reduced to a 49.83 Black voting age population. Likewise, the Chair of the Agriculture Committee had won his election in 1994 by only 7 votes in a 63.1 percent Black-majority district. His district was not only reduced to 27.2 Black percent, but his African-American female opponent in the 1994 election had her residence moved from his district into another.

Unlike the Congressional situation where there was the allegation that the GOP had benefited the 1992 district configuration, the maintenance of the 1992 state legislative map would only benefit Democratic political aspirants. It may have been possible for Blacks to win six to eight new seats in the House, but this prospect may have been eliminated.

Party loyalty apparently was given the highest priority by 26 GLBC members who sought to be good team players and Democratic party loyalists on the state plan. They also asserted that they had protected two Black incumbents and got the best deal possible.

The GLBC stood firm in its demand for three majority-Black Congressional districts, but Senate Democratic favored a plan that would create a map designed to boost the electoral prospects for white Democratic Congressional aspirants. Ultimately, the federal district court did impose a map which reflected this position. However, initially they failed to achieve this goals, as both Bishop and McKinney prevailed in their Democratic primary contests without a runoff. It remains to be seen whether the GOP will capitalize on the split between white and Black Democrats by winning one or both of these seats in the general election on November 6, 1996.

EPILOGUE

As noted, there was great uncertainty concerning the ability of 2nd District Congressman Sanford Bishop and Fourth District Congresswoman Cynthia McKinney to retain their seats in their drastically reconfigured districts, which were now only approximately 35 percent African-American. It was feared that their greatest threats would come in the July 9 Democratic Party primary election because districts containing a Black population between 30 and 40 percent were deemed ideal for a white Democratic candidate. With a solid base of Black Democratic votes, a victory could be secured by gaining only 25-30 percent of the white electorate.

Both Bishop and McKinney faced multiple challenges in the Democratic primary, with McKinney facing the more formidable task. Among her three primary opponents were Attorney Comer Yates, who had been a candidate in the 4th District general election in 1994 against incumbent Republican John Linder, and State Senator Ronald Slotin. Yates had the backing of some of the most powerful officials in the state Democratic Party after he announced his candidacy even before the three-judge panel finalized the Congressional district boundaries. Rather surprisingly, both McKinney and Bishop won their primary elections without runoffs, with each receiving approximately 60 percent of the votes.

While not proving that majority-Black districts were no longer necessary to elect Blacks, it did show the power of incumbency. Both had outstanding records of accomplishments that showed they could do the job, both had great name recognition, and both were able to raise considerably more money that their opponents.

In the general election, McKinney faced Republican John Mitnick, who sought to link her with Minister Louis Farrakhan and to subtly inject race into the election. McKinney's father, State Representative Billy McKinney, responded by calling her opponent a "racist Jew." Much of the election contest focused on personalities rather than issues. McKinney prevailed in the November 5 general election, winning 57.8 percent to 42.2 percent for Mitnick. Bishop's race was a low key affair, and he too defeated his opponent, Darrell Ealum, by 54 to 46 percent. McKinney commented that her victory should not be interpreted to mean that majority-Black districts are unnecessary. She noted that she was able to win only because she had had the opportunity to serve in Congress from the 11th District from 1993 to 1996 and to prove herself.

The District Court had approved an interim plan for the state House and Senate elections that combined features of the 1992 plan and the one adopted for the 1995 special session. There was concern that as many as four incumbent Black legislators were vulnerable because of a decrease in Black voters in their districts. However, there was actually a net gain of two members for the GLBC, as a Clark Atlanta University history professor, Vincent Forte, won the Atlanta Senate seat vacated by Ron Slotin, who had resigned to run for Congress, and a Black attorney, Arnold Ragas, upset a 16-year Republican House member in suburban DeKalb county. This increased the total of Georgia Black legislators to 44, thus giving Georgia the largest number of Black legislators in the nation.

The election outcome bodes well for Black legislators and demonstrates the power of incumbency. There are indications that although they managed to retain their numbers, consideration may need to be given to considering alternatives to single member majority districts to make further gains. Congresswoman Cynthia McKinney and State Representative Bob Holmes are sponsoring legislation calling for use of alternative non-racial voting systems such as cumulative voting, limited voting, and the single transferable vote. These new electoral arrangements may be critical new factors in the next reapportionment battle in the 21st century.

RACE AND REPRESENTATIONAL DISTRICTING IN LOUISIANA

Richard L. Engstrom and Jason F. Kirksey

FOLLOWING THE 1990 CENSUS A NUMBER OF STATES adopted congressional districts that made the original "gerrymander" of 1812, in Essex County, Massachusetts (Figure 1), look like a model of compactness. Louisiana was among that group. Louisiana's entry in the contest for the least compact district in America was the new Fourth Congressional District (Figure 2). It was said to resemble the mark of Zorro, "a giant and somewhat shaky 'Z'".[1] Its perimeter was 2,558 miles long, exceeding that of any other congressional district in the country except Alaska's at-large district (Huckabee 1994, 20, 38-45). It was ranked as the fourth least compact district in the nation according to one quantitative measure, eleventh according to another (Huckabee 1994, 38-45; Pildes and Niemi 1993, 565).

District Four was called a "gerrymander" by people preoccupied with the shapes of individual districts. It was not a gerrymander, however, if by gerrymander one means a districting plan that dilutes the voting strength of a cohesive group of voters within a particular political jurisdiction.[2] There were no allegations that the plan the district was a part of, adopted in 1992, was a political or partisan gerrymander. And while there was an allegation that the plan was unfair to African-Americans (discussed below), this was not an allegation made by the state's African-American community. Indeed, the district was designed to empower African-American voters, not discriminate against them.

The shape of District Four was directly related to its purpose. It was designed to be a majority African-American district, one that would provide African-American voters with a viable opportunity to elect a candidate of their choice to the United

---

[1] *Hays v. State of Louisiana*, 839 F.Supp. 1188, 1199 (W.D. La. 1993).
[2] See, e.g., the entries for "gerrymandering" in Plano and Greenberg (1993: 140) and Renstrom and Rogers (1989: 108).

FIGURE 1. The "Original" 1812 Gerrymander
Source: E. Griffith: The Rise and Development of the Gerrymander 18 (1907).

States Congress. This was accomplished by linking dispersed concentrations of African-Americans across the state into a district. This search and include policy dictated the shape of the district. The result was a district boundary allegedly longer than the boundary around the state itself.[3] African-Americans, according to the 1990 Census, constituted 66.4 percent of all of the people residing in the district, and 62.6 percent of those of voting age. The state's voter registration data revealed that, as of June 1992, African-Americans constituted 63.2 percent of the people registered to vote in the district. Percentages such as these could only be attained by creating a district that was severely contorted.

RACIAL FAIRNESS VERSUS COMPACTNESS

The Fourth District was one of two majority African-American districts in the new plan. The other was the Second District, based in New Orleans. This was essentially a modification of the Second District in the previous plan, a majority

---

[3]This comparison, which was never documented, was asserted in the post-trial brief of the plaintiffs challenging this district in *Hays*. Memorandum in Support of the Plaintiffs' Claims that Act 42 of the 1992 Louisiana Violates the Voting Rights Act, p. 5 (hereinafter Plaintiffs' Memorandum).

Figure 2. Louisiana's Fourth Congressional District, 1992
Source: *Washington Post,* November 3, 1992

African-American district that had, in 1990, elected William Jefferson to be its representative. Jefferson was the first African-American to serve in Congress from Louisiana since Reconstruction. The new Second District was 61.0 percent African-American in total population, and 56.2 percent in voting age population. Voter registration in June 1992 was 60.0 percent African-American.

By providing two viable African-American districts, the new congressional districting plan offered the state's African-American minority an opportunity to be proportionally represented, in a descriptive sense (see Pitkin, 1967, 60-91), in Louisiana's delegation to the U.S. House of Representatives. According to the 1990 census, African-Americans constituted 30.8 percent of the state's population, and 27.7 percent of its residents of voting age. The state's voter registration figures for June, 1992, revealed that African-Americans constituted 27.9 percent of the state's registered voters. Two districts would be 28.6 percent of the state's new total of seven (down from eight) congressional districts.

Given the distribution of the minority population across the state, it was not possible to create a second majority African-American district with boundaries that remotely resembled a rectangle. While District Four, as adopted, was one of several possible designs for a viable African-American district outside the New Orleans metropolitan area, all of the alternatives were far from compact. The presence of a second African-American district in the 1992 plan, therefore, reflected an important policy decision by the state—drawing districts that would be racially fair had a higher priority than drawing districts that would be pleasingly shaped.[4]

DEPARTURE FROM PAST PRACTICE

The adoption of District Four constituted a significant departure from past state-wide districting experiences in Louisiana. Never before had the state engaged in such an affirmative effort to empower, electorally, its African-American minority. The usual practice, in contrast, had been to adopt districting plans that diluted the voting strength of African-Americans. These plans would then be invalidated under the Voting Rights Act, by either the United States Attorney General or a federal court, for being racially unfair. Revised plans providing the minority with more electoral opportunities would then be adopted by the state in response to these adverse decisions by federal authorities (see Engstrom et. al., 1994, 111-112, 117-120).

The congressional districts that the new plan would replace had themselves been drawn in response to a federal court decision that invalidated, on racial grounds, the first plan the state had adopted following the 1980 census. Although a majority African-American district could have been created within the City of New Orleans, the state plan, adopted in 1981, failed to contain such a district. The state chose instead to divide the city, and its African-American voters, into two districts, each of which extended into white suburban areas and had white majorities in population and voter registration. This was accomplished by drawing a contorted and racially selective district boundary through the city that left one of the districts with a shape resembling that of a duck, resulting in the scheme being referred to derisively as the "gerryduck" (Engstrom, 1986). That plan was invalidated by a federal district court in 1983, however. The dispersion of the African-American vote was found to be a violation of section 2 of the Voting Rights Act, which prohibits the use of electoral arrangements that have dilutive consequences.[5] The state then adopted another plan that year, one containing a New Orleans-based majority African-American district, the Second District, the first majority African-American congressional district in Louisiana this century.

The state's preference for districting plans that dilute the minority's voting strength was evident again in 1991, in its first efforts to redraw representational

---

[4]On the issue of conflicting districting criteria generally, see Butler and Cain (1992, 65-90).

[5]*Major* v. *Treen*, 574 F. Supp. 325 (E.D. La. 1983).

district boundaries following the 1990 census. The state adopted three statewide districting plans that year, and all were disapproved by the Attorney General. These plans were for the two chambers of the state legislature and for the state Board of Elementary and Secondary Education (BESE). Each of these plans was rejected by the Attorney General for being unfair to the African-American minority.

In sharp contrast to the state's usual practice, the new congressional District Four was adopted in 1992 in an effort to avoid another invalidation, rather than as a direct response to one.

PRECLEARANCE AND THE 1991 REJECTIONS

While District Four was not a direct response to an invalidation of another congressional plan, it was clearly a reaction to the state's legal responsibility under the Voting Rights Act to be fair to its African-American minority. Due to its history of race-based disfranchisement (see Engstrom et. al., 1994, 104-108), Louisiana is subject to the *preclearance* provision contained in section 5 of the Voting Rights Act. Under this provision, any change that the state makes in its election laws and procedures, including any changes it makes in election districts, may not be implemented until either the federal Attorney General or the United States District Court in Washington, D.C. has concluded that the change does not have a racially discriminatory purpose or effect.[6] The state's resistance to creating electoral opportunities for African-Americans had resulted in the failure to obtain preclearance for many of its past redistricting efforts.

The state's failure to gain preclearance for its initial post-1990 census state legislative districting plans kept intact a record of consistent rejection. Never has the state gained preclearance for its initial redistricting plans for both chambers of the legislature. The first legislative plans subject to this requirement were those adopted in response to the 1970 census. Both the state house and Senate plans adopted following that census were objected to by the Attorney General. Both were replaced by plans imposed by the federal judiciary (Halpin and Engstrom, 1973, 52-57, 63-65). Following the 1980 census, the state gained preclearance for its new Senate districts, but not those for the lower house. Preclearance was not obtained until the House districts were redrawn a second time (Weber, 1993, 112-113, and Engstrom et. al., 1994, 111-112). The Attorney General's rejections of the initial plans for both chambers following the 1990 census extended the post-census rejection record to three-for-three.

By 1990 African-Americans had constituted a majority of the registered voters in 15 of the 105 state House districts and five of the 39 state Senate districts. At the time of redistricting, each of these districts (and only these districts) was represented by an African-American legislator. New plans for both the House and the

---

[6]79 Stat. 439, as amended, 42 U.S.C. sec. 1973c.

Senate, bringing the districts into compliance with the basic "one person, one vote" rule following the 1990 census, could be created that would increase significantly the number of districts with African-American registration majorities.[7]

Redistricting the State House, 1991

During a special session of the legislature in 1991, a new plan for the House was adopted that satisfied the "one person, one vote" standard and also increased the number of districts in which African-American voters would have a viable opportunity to elect candidates of their choice. No district in the plan deviated from the ideal, or average, district population by as much as five percentage points. The most populous district was 4.98 percentage points above the ideal, while the least populous was 4.86 percentage points below. The plan contained 20 districts with African-American population majorities, 19 of which also had African-American voter registration majorities.

Although the House plan expanded the number of African-American districts, it was opposed by the African-American members of both legislative chambers. This opposition was based on the fact that many more electoral opportunities for African-Americans could have been created. Amendments that would have increased the number of African-American districts were offered, but defeated. All 14 African-American members of the House at that time voted against passage of the plan, while the other House members voted 71 to 15 in favor of it. In the Senate, four of the five African-American members opposed the plan (one African-American member was absent), while 25 of the 26 white members voting on the plan voted for it.[8]

This initial House plan, like its predecessors in 1971 and 1981, failed to survive section 5 scrutiny. Preclearance was again denied when the Attorney General concluded that the plan had both a discriminatory purpose and a discriminatory effect. The Attorney General identified seven areas in the state where African-American voters had been either unnecessarily packed (overconcentrated) into one or a few districts or unnecessarily cracked (dispersed) across two or more districts. Districting decisions were found to be driven by a desire to retain white voting majorities. The Attorney General concluded that alternative sets of districts, "drawn as logically as in the proposed plan," could have been adopted that would have provided African-Americans with more electoral opportunities.[9]

---

[7]The Louisiana Constitution specifies that the districts for each chamber of the state legislature must be single-member districts. The only state constitutional constraint on the drawing of these districts is that they be apportioned on a population basis "as equally as is practicable". La. Const, Art. III, sec. 1(A) and 6(A).

[8] In the House, all 17 Republicans voted in favor of the plan, as did 54 of the 68 white Democrats casting votes on it. One Independent voted in opposition. In the Senate, all four Republicans voting on the plan were in favor (two were absent), while white Democrats split 21 to five in favor.

[9]Letter from John R. Dunne, Assistant Attorney General of the United States, to Hon. Jimmy N. Dimos, Speaker, Louisiana House of Representatives (July 15, 1991).

Following the failure to gain preclearance, another House plan was adopted. Fifty-one of the districts in the initial plan were altered in this revision. The population deviations in the revised plan remained under five percentage points (the largest being +4.99 and -4.98), while the number of districts with African-American population majorities now increased to 26, with 25 also having African-American voter registration majorities.

African-American registered voters were much more efficiently distributed across districts in the revised plan. The overall increase of six more districts with voter registration majorities in the second plan was due primarily to more districts being created in which African-Americans constituted between 55 and 60 percent of the registered voters. Whereas 42.7 percent of the African-Americans registered to vote was included in the 19 districts with African-American registration majorities in the initial plan, 53.0 percent were included in the 25 districts with registration majorities in the revised plan.

The revised plan was supported by the African-American legislators. In the House, 14 of the 15 African-American members voted for the plan (with one absent), while the other members divided 48 to 27 in favor. In the Senate, all five African-American members voted for the revised plan, compared with 24 of the 29 other members voting on it.[10] The Attorney General granted preclearance to this plan, and elections were held under it in October of 1991, with runoffs in November.[11] African-American candidates were elected in 23 of the 25 House districts with African-American voter registration majorities. An African-American was also elected in the other district with an African-American population majority, a New Orleans district that at the time of the election had a slight African-American plurality (49.8 percent) in registered voters.

Redistricting the State Senate, 1991

A new plan for the state Senate was also adopted during the special session. Deviations from perfect population equality among the districts were again kept below five percentage points, as the largest district deviated from the ideal by 4.98 percentage points and the smallest by 4.86. The plan contained eight districts with African-American population majorities, seven of which also had African-American voter registration majorities.

This plan also was opposed by the African-American legislators, again because more minority electoral opportunities could have been created. As with

---

[10]Ten of the 14 Republicans voting on the plan in the House voted for it (three were absent), compared to 38 of 58 white Democrats. In the Senate, two Republicans supported it and three opposed it (with one absent), while white Democrats voting on it split 22 to two in favor.

[11]Under Louisiana's election law, all of the candidates for a state legislative or congressional seat, regardless of their party affiliations, compete in a single primary election in which all registered voters may participate. The party affiliations of the candidates are identified on the primary ballot. If no candidate receives a majority of the votes cast in the primary election, a runoff election is held between the top two vote recipients, again regardless of the candidates' party affiliations. On the adoption and use of this election system in Louisiana, see Hadley (1986).

the House plan, amendments to the Senate plan that would have created additional opportunities were offered, but rejected. All five of the African-American senators voted against the plan, while 23 of the 33 white senators voting on it opposed it. On the House side, 13 of the 14 African-American members voted against it (one was absent), compared with only 5 of the 76 white members voting on it.[12]

The Senate plan also failed to survive section 5 scrutiny. The Attorney General objected to it for the same reason the African-American legislators opposed it; additional districts with African-American majorities could easily have been created. The Attorney General specifically identified two areas of the state where the African-American voting strength had been cracked, and concluded that in both areas this was due to an effort to protect white incumbents. In the Monroe area in northeast Louisiana the reelection concerns of white senators were found to be "the primary, if not exclusive, reason" for the division of African-American voters across districts. In the Lafayette area in southwest Louisiana African-American voters were split between districts in order to keep their presence in one of the districts at a level "considered acceptable to [the] white incumbent". Although the protection of incumbents does not by itself violate any federal law, the Attorney General pointed out that it cannot be done "at the expense of black voters".[13]

The Senate plan was revised in response to the Attorney General's objection. While 20 districts were affected in some way by the changes, the major change was the creation of two additional districts with African-American voter registration majorities in the areas identified by the Attorney General. This brought the number of districts with African-American majorities, in both population and voter registration, to nine. A district was created in the Monroe area that was 60.5 percent African-American in registration. Another was created in the Lafayette area that was 57.2 percent in registration. Whereas 37.3 percent of the state's African-American registered voters were in seven districts with African-American registration majorities in the initial plan, 48.1 percent were in nine districts with registration majorities in the revised arrangement.

The revised plan was supported by all five of the African-American state senators and all 14 of the African-American House members voting on the plan (one was absent). Their white colleagues in the Senate split 24 to 5 in favor of the plan, while the white members of the House supported it by a vote of 47 to 29.[14]

---

[12]In the Senate, five Republicans voted for it and one against it, while the white Democrats split 18 to 9 in favor of the plan. In the House, only one Republican and four white Democrats opposed the plan.

[13] Letter from John R. Dunne, Assistant Attorney General of the United States, to Hon. Samuel B. Nunez, President, Louisiana Senate, and Hon. Dennis Bagneris, Chairman, Louisiana Senate Committee on Senate and Governmental Affairs (June 28, 1991).

[14]Republicans in the Senate split three to two in opposition to the plan (with one absent), while the white Democrats voting on the plan divided 22 to 2 in favor. In the House, 11 of the Republicans voting on the plan favored it, and four opposed it. The white Democrats in the House supported it 36 to 25.

The Attorney General granted preclearance to this plan, which was then used in the 1991 Senate elections. Eight African-Americans won Senate seats in those elections, each from a district with an African-American registration majority.

Redistricting BESE, 1991

The Attorney General's rejection of the initial state House and Senate plans no doubt influenced the decision to create two majority African-American districts in the congressional plan the following year. But probably of more importance was the Attorney General's objection, a few months later, to the state's plan for its Board of Elementary and Secondary Education (BESE). BESE is an 11-member body of which eight members are elected, each from a single-member district. The BESE plan, therefore, would contain just one more district than the new congressional plan. There was already, as in the malapportioned congressional plan, one BESE district in which African-Americans were a majority of the registered voters. Like its congressional counterpart, this was a New Orleans-based district in which an African-American had already been elected. A second district with an African-American majority could have been created in the new BESE plan, but was not. The Attorney General's rejection of this eight district plan with a single African-American district was a much more immediate precedent for the forthcoming congressional redistricting than the earlier objections to the state legislative plans.

The initial BESE plan was adopted during the regular legislative session of 1991. The most populous district in the plan deviated from the ideal district population by 1.85 percentage points, while the least populous deviated by 1.69. The plan retained a majority African-American district in the New Orleans area. This new district's population was 63.6 percent African-American, while its voter registration was 58.5 percent African-American. The highest African-American registration percentage in any of the remaining seven districts was 35.8.

Two African-American majority districts in voter registration could have been created, and African-American legislators therefore opposed this plan. In the House, all 10 African-American members voting on the plan opposed it (five were absent), while in the Senate, all five African-Americans voted against it. The rest of the House members voted 76 to 5 in favor of passage, while in the Senate the white members voted 23 to 8 in favor of the plan.[15]

The Attorney General objected to this plan because of the failure to create a second majority African-American district. In denying preclearance, the Attorney General noted that a number of other configurations could have provided two such districts. The focus of the objection was three adjacent districts in which African-Americans constituted 38.4, 31.7, and 28.0 percent of the

[15]All 17 Republicans in the House supported the plan, as did all 58 white Democrats and the one Independent voting on it. Five of the six Republicans in the Senate supported it, along with 23 of the 25 white Democrats voting on it.

residents respectively, and 35.8, 28.2, and 22.2 percent of the registered voters. An alternative configuration could have included many of these African-Americans in a single district. In a comment that would be directly applicable to the congressional context as well, it was specifically noted in the objection that:

> ...it appears that the significant concentrations of black voters in northeastern Louisiana and in the parishes bordering the State of Mississippi, both along the river and the state's southern border, can be combined in a way that recognizes the black voting potential in these areas.[16]

The state adopted a second plan during the 1992 regular session of the legislature. The most populous district in the revised plan had only 467 more people residing in it than the least populous. The maximum deviations from precise population equality were only +0.06 percentage points and -0.03. The 1992 plan contained two majority African-American districts. The New Orleans based district was now 63.8 percent African-American in population, 61.9 percent in voter registration. A second district, containing the concentrations specifically identified by the Attorney General, was 65.5 percent African-American in population and 61.9 percent in registration. All 21 African-American legislators in the House who voted on it favored the plan (the remaining three were absent); in the Senate, all seven voted in favor (with one absent). White members of the House split 42 to 30 in favor, and the white senators 20 to seven.[17] This plan was precleared by the Attorney General and used in the 1992 election, in which African-Americans were elected in both of the majority African-American districts.

The Attorney General's objection to the initial BESE plan because it did not contain a second majority African-American district was directly applicable to the forthcoming congressional redistricting task. African-Americans in northeastern Louisiana could be combined with those along the Mississippi River and in the parishes under the State of Mississippi within a congressional district as well. While a congressional district would have to be more populous than a BESE district, given that there would be seven rather than eight districts, that did not preclude the creation of a second majority minority district. Two contiguous, viable African-American congressional districts could be created. In light of the BESE objection, it was reasonable to assume that two such districts would be necessary if preclearance was to be obtained, at least from the Attorney General, for any congressional plan.[18]

---

[16] Letter from John R. Dunne, Assistant Attorney General of the United States, to Angie Rogers LaPlace, Assistant Attorney General, State of Louisiana (October 1, 1991).

[17] In the House, the Republicans split nine to five in opposition to the plan, while the white Democrats voted 37 to 20 in favor. In the Senate, the Republicans split three in favor and two against (with two absent), while the white Democrats favored the plan 17 to five.

[18] Preclearance may also be granted by the United States District Court for the District of Columbia.

CONGRESSIONAL REDISTRICTING

Due to insufficient population growth, Louisiana lost a seat in the United States House of Representatives following the 1990 census. The old eight-district plan therefore had to be replaced with a new seven-district scheme. A new set of districts received legislative approval in May of 1992, during the first regular session of the newly elected legislature, and was agreed to by the new governor, Edwin Edwards, on June 1. This plan, as noted above, contained two viable African-American districts, one more than the plan it would replace.

The adoption of two majority African-American districts was stimulated by a perception that two such districts would be necessary if a plan was to be precleared by the Attorney General. Contributing to this perception, along with the objection to the BESE plan, were decisions by the Attorney General denying preclearance to the congressional redistricting plans of three other southern states. These decisions, announced after the objection to the BESE plan, served to reinforce the inference that if Louisiana were to gain preclearance for a congressional plan, that plan would have to include two viable African-American districts.

The North Carolina, Georgia, and Alabama Rejections

North Carolina's new congressional districts were the subject of the first objection. North Carolina had gained a congressional seat as a consequence of the census, bringing its total to 12. Although none of that state's existing districts had an African-American majority within it, two such districts could be created in a 12-district plan. The plan the state adopted in 1991, however, contained only one. While it would have been the state's first majority African-American congressional district this century, being the first was not a justification for being the only, and in December, 1991, the Attorney General declined to preclear the plan.[19]

The state subsequently adopted, in 1992, another plan containing a second African-American district. This second minority district was about 160 miles long and so narrow at points that it relied upon a highway, Interstate 85, for contiguity. North Carolina's revised plan was granted preclearance by the Attorney General and, while the Louisiana legislature was in session, withstood two challenges in federal court. One challenge was a partisan gerrymandering claim brought by Republicans, the other a racial gerrymandering claim brought by white voters. The state prevailed, at least in 1992, with summary judgment motions on both claims.[20]

About a month after the North Carolina objection, the Attorney General

---

[19] Letter from John R. Dunne, Assistant Attorney General of the United States, to Tiare B. Smiley, Special Deputy Attorney General, State of North Carolina (December 18, 1991).

[20] *Pope v. Blue*, 809 F. Supp. 392 (W.D. N.C. 1992) and *Shaw v. Barr*, 808 F. Supp. 461 (E.D. N.C. 1992). The rejection of the partisan gerrymandering claim was summarily affirmed by the Supreme Court, *Pope v. Blue*, 506 U.S. 801 (1992), but the rejection of the racial gerrymandering claim was subsequently reversed, and the case remanded for further consideration, in *Shaw v. Reno*, 509 U.S. 630 (1993).

objected to Georgia's new congressional districting plan. Georgia had also gained a congressional seat, bringing its House delegation to 11. Its new 11-district plan contained two majority African-American districts, one more than in the 10-district plan it was to replace. Despite this increase, the Attorney General found that the plan still fragmented the African-American electorate. A third district with an African-American majority in voting age population could have been created in the southwestern portion of the state. In addition, the electoral opportunities provided by each of the districts that had African-American majorities could have been enhanced easily. African-Americans constituted 62.2 and 60.6 percent of the general population and 57.8 and 56.6 percent of the voting age population in these two districts. These figures, the Attorney General noted, could have been increased by simply replacing white residents within these districts with African-Americans residing in areas adjacent to the districts.[21]

The Georgia legislature adopted a second set of congressional districts the day after Louisiana's legislature convened in 1992. This second plan added a third majority African-American district. This district, which was 56.6 percent African-American in total population and 52.0 percent in voting age population, kept the concentrations of African-Americans in the southwestern portion of the state intact. The African-American percentages of the total and voting age populations in one of the other majority minority districts were increased from 60.6 to 64.1 and from 56.6 to 60.4, respectively. The other majority minority district was altered only slightly, with the total population percentage increasing from 62.1 to 62.3 and the voting age percentage declining from 57.8 to 57.5.

The third objection by the Attorney General concerned a congressional redistricting plan for Alabama. The state had adopted a new seven-district plan that contained one district in which African-Americans constituted a majority of the registered voters. As in North Carolina, this would have been the first majority minority district this century in Alabama. Three days before the start of Louisiana's legislative session, however, the Attorney General objected to Alabama's plan because two districts with African-American voting age majorities could have been created.[22]

As a result of this objection, Alabama's new congressional districts, at least for the 1992 elections, were determined by a federal court. A three-judge district court in Alabama had adopted an interim plan that was to go into effect if pre-clearance was not obtained for the state's plan. The plan imposed by the court also contained one district in which African-Americans constituted a majority of the registered voters. Although the African-American intervenors in the litigation[23] had included a plan containing two majority African-American districts in

---

[21] Letter from John R. Dunne, Assistant Attorney General of the United States, to Mark H. Cohen, Senior Assistant Attorney General, State of Georgia (January 21, 1992).

[22] Letter from John R. Dunne, Assistant Attorney General of the United States, to Hon. Jimmy Evans, Attorney General, State of Alabama (March 27, 1992).

[23] The suit was brought initially by Paul Charles Wesch, a Republican Party official in Mobile County.

voting age population among the plans they presented to the court, in neither of those districts did African-Americans constitute a majority of the registered voters. In rejecting this plan, the court noted that it failed to comply with the "one person, one vote" requirement and that the intervenors themselves had questioned whether either of the two African-American districts had a sufficient minority presence to provide the minority with a viable opportunity to elect a candidate of the its choice.[24]

In Louisiana two congressional districts could be created in which African-Americans constituted not only a majority of the voting age population, but a majority of the registered voters as well. Given that fact, and the Attorney General's objections to the congressional plans of these other states, it was reasonable to infer that the Attorney General would not grant preclearance to a new Louisiana plan unless that plan contained two viable minority districts. Indeed, these objections, along with that to the BESE plan, resulted in two majority-minority districts being widely viewed as a basic legal requirement, just as was creating districts with only minimal deviations from the average district population. Being widely recognized as a "requirement," however, was not the same as being well received. Many of the state's white legislators no doubt shared the attitude expressed by state Representative Jerry LeBlanc, who was quoted as saying, "I don't like it...but these are the cards that are dealt to us by the federal government and we have to play with them."[25]

This perception of "the cards" applied as well to the other redistricting tasks still before the legislature in 1992. As already noted, a second BESE plan with two African-American districts was adopted that year. In addition, the state created the first majority African-American district (62.1 percent African-American in population, 60.3 percent in voter registration) for its five-member Public Service Commission, the state's main regulatory body for public utilities. An African-American was elected to serve on that body for the first time, from that district, later that year. In stark contrast to the state's failure to gain preclearance for any of its initial redistricting efforts in 1991, all three statewide redistricting plans adopted in 1992 were granted preclearance by the Attorney General.[26]

The 1992 Context

The virtual certainty of having redistricting plans denied preclearance had not been sufficient to deter the state from adopting dilutive schemes in the past. The

---

[24] *Wesch* v. *Hunt*, 785 F. Supp 1491 (S.D. Ala. 1992).

[25] Quoted in Mike Hasten, "Surprised House Passes Remap Plan," *Advertiser* (Lafayette), May 6, 1992.

[26] In addition, the state also settled two voting rights lawsuits concerning the election of judges, settlements that created many new opportunities for African-American voters to elect judicial candidates of their choice (see Engstrom, Halpin, Hill, and Caridas-Butterworth, 1994: 121-124). These opportunities, not surprisingly (see Engstrom, 1989), resulted in the election of numerous African-Americans to judicial positions throughout the state, including that of Justice of the Louisiana Supreme Court.

legislature's behavior in 1992, however, was less defiant. Much of this change was no doubt attributable to turnover in both the legislature and the governor's office resulting from the 1991 elections. As already noted, the 1991 state legislative elections were held under the plans precleared by the Attorney General. The result was a substantial increase in the number of African-American legislators. African-Americans now held over 20 percent of the seats in each chamber, and they could be expected to be particularly cohesive on an issue like congressional redistricting (as well as on the other statewide redistricting tasks). Their numbers and cohesion would make them a more significant voting bloc in redistricting politics than they had been previously.

Probably of more importance, however, was the change in the gubernatorial office resulting from the 1991 election. Edwin Edwards, a former three-term governor, had replaced Charles "Buddy" Roemer, the previous governor who had given his assent to the dilutive plans adopted in 1991. Edwards had been heavily dependent on the state's African-American voters in his victory over ex-Ku Klux Klan leader David Duke in 1991. Indeed, a statewide exit poll of the gubernatorial runoff between Duke and Edwards revealed that Duke had been the choice of the state's white voters by a margin of 10 percentage points (55 percent to 45 percent). The African-American voters, however, cast 96 percent of their votes for Edwards, providing him with a comfortable victory overall (61 percent of the total vote).[27] Edwards made it clear before the start of the legislative session that he supported creating two African-American congressional districts, which he maintained would be necessary for preclearance. A gubernatorial veto was therefore likely for any plan that fell short of that standard.[28]

When the legislature met in 1992, therefore, both federal law and gubernatorial approval appeared to require that two of the state's seven congressional districts contain viable African-American electoral majorities. The fact that this could not be accomplished through districts with compact shapes did not appear to be a serious impediment. Compact districts were not required by either federal or state law, and compactness certainly had not been a districting criterion that the state had taken seriously in the past.[29] The real issue going into the 1992 session of the legislature therefore was not whether to create a second majority-minority district, but rather, as a Baton Rouge newspaper editorialized, "where and how such a district will be configured".[30]

The Adoption of District Four

The debate over "where and how" to create a second African-American district revolved around two basic variants. Both combined African-Americans in the

---

[27]The exit poll was conducted by Voter Research and Surveys, a polling organization created by the four major television networks, ABC, CBS, CNN, and NBC.

[28]See, e.g., Marsha Shuler, "EWE Favors 2nd Majority Black House District," *Advocate* (Baton Rouge), March 11, 1992, or Marsha Shuler, "McMains Submits Another Plan for Reapportionment," *Advocate* (Baton Rouge), April 9, 1992.

Monroe area, in northeastern Louisiana, with African-Americans in Baton Rouge, in central Louisiana. This linkage was accomplished by including in the district a long and relatively narrow strip of lightly populated but heavily African-American areas along the west bank of the Mississippi River, where the river forms the state boundary between Louisiana and Mississippi. Both variants also extended west into Alexandria, in the center of the state, and into Lafayette, in the southern part, as well as east into the parishes under the southern boundary of Mississippi. The major difference was whether another approximately 38,000 African-American registered voters, which would constitute close to 20 percent of the total African-American registration within the district, would be from the northern or southern sections of the state.

The decision concerning the new minority district had more than racial implications, of course. One of the state's incumbent congressmen, Democrat Billy Tauzin, was quoted as saying that "How you shape it shapes all the others."[31] While there was, in fact, considerable discretion in the design of the other six districts, regardless of where the second minority district was located, there was also no doubt that the structure of the new minority district could have an impact on the reelection prospects of particular members of the congressional delegation. Which of these incumbents were treated more favorably would, in turn, have partisan consequences.

None of the incumbent members of Congress had announced any plans to terminate their congressional service in 1992. With the loss of a seat overall, and the creation of a second African-American district, it was clear that two of the seven white incumbents would probably have their congressional tenure terminated (or at least interrupted) involuntarily. Different districting designs would have different implications for these white incumbents. The loss of a seat had meant that every district in the old eight-district plan was now underpopulated. The least underpopulated was 7.4 percent below the new seven-district ideal; the most, 22.7 percent below. Every incumbent's district therefore was vulnerable to drastic revision. The fact that four of the white incumbents were Republicans and

---

[29]The 1969 congressional redistricting plan, for example, contained a district that extended from the Sabine River at the Texas-Louisiana border all the way to Lake Pontchartrain in the southeastern part of the state (see Engstrom, 1980). It was, like the Massachusetts gerrymander of 1812, the subject of a political cartoon, with eyes, a mouth, and hands added to highlight the noncompact shape of the district [*Times-Picayune* (New Orleans), June 4, 1969]. The next time the legislature revised the congressional districts, in 1972, "partisan politics had dictated that geographical compactness should be ignored" (Weber, 1993, 111). The 1972 plan, for example, also contained a "narrow, elongated" district, the motivation for which was "to ensure the election of a Democratic congressman" (Weber, 1993, 111). The state's next set of congressional districts, adopted in 1981, contained the infamous "gerryduck" district, and was found to be a racial gerrymander that violated the Voting Rights Act [see *Major* v. *Treen*, 574 F.Supp. 325 (1983), and Engstrom 1986].

[30]"Reflections on Redistricting for Congress," *Sunday Advocate* (Baton Rouge), March 15, 1992. See also the testimony in *Hays* of state Representative Robert Adley, Transcript (August 26, 1992), at 45, 69, 74-75.

[31] The Honorable Billy Tauzin, quoted in Joan McKinney, "Remap Plan Unraveling on Way to Senate," *Advocate* (Baton Rouge) April 12, 1992.

three were Democrats added a serious partisan dimension to the incumbent concerns as well. Although Louisiana politics are rarely acutely partisan (see Parent, 1988), this was a context in which partisan concerns could be expected to be, and were, elevated. Indeed, the dean of the state's delegation in the U.S. House, Democrat Jerry Huckaby, noted prior to the legislative session: "The Louisiana delegation has traditionally been a delegation—not four Democrats and four Republicans—but this has made us into Democrats and Republicans."[32]

The state Senate initially passed a bill containing a southern variation for the new minority district. In this version, the district was extended into southeastern and south-central Louisiana. The district, which was 61.6 percent African-American in population and 59.2 percent in voter registration, was widely reported to have been designed to favor state senator Cleo Fields, an African-American from Baton Rouge who was expected to be a candidate in the new majority minority district. Fields had unsuccessfully challenged the Republican incumbent in the old Eighth District, Clyde Holloway, in 1990. Although he received only 29.6 percent of the vote in that election, he is estimated to have received 84.7 percent of the votes that had been cast by African-Americans.[33] Over 30,000 of the additional African-American registered voters included in this southern extension were from the old Eighth District, and Fields' previous exposure among these voters was expected to benefit his candidacy. All of the African-American senators voted in favor of the bill except Charles D. Jones, of Monroe, who was expected to be an opponent of Fields in the new minority district.

The five white majority districts in this plan had pronounced partisan consequences. The three white Democratic incumbents, Huckaby, Tauzin, and Jimmy Hayes, were each placed in a district in which no other incumbent resided. So also was Republican incumbent Bob Livingston. The other three Republican incumbents, however, Holloway, Richard Baker, and Jim McCrery, were all placed in the same district. This arrangement was widely regarded to have been designed to protect primarily Huckaby, the most senior member of the state's delegation, who had been implicated in the recent House banking scandal.[34] The plan kept Huckaby separated from the other congressman from North Louisiana, McCrery, whom he reportedly did not want to run against.[35] It also placed over

---

[32]Quoted in Bruce Alpert and Jack Wardlaw, "La. Delegation Awaits its Fate in Redistricting," *Times-Picayune* (New Orleans), March 15, 1992.

[33]These estimates, and others presented below, are derived from bivariate ecological regression analyses in which the votes cast in precincts are regressed onto the racial composition of the precincts (the African-American percentage of the registered voters for elections prior to 1988, the African-American percentage of the people signing-in to vote for elections in or after 1988). For an illustration of this methodology applied to Louisiana elections, see Engstrom , 1989.

[34]Huckaby had 88 overdrafts listed with the House "bank," ranking him 36th among the 303 members and former members of the House with overdrafts identified in the *Washington Post*, on April 17, 1992.

[35]Indeed, one of his Democratic colleagues was quoted as saying that being placed in the same district with McCrery was an "anathema to Huckaby. He does not want to face McCrery." The Hon. Billy Tauzin, quoted in Joan McKinney, "Remap Plan Unraveling on Way to Senate," *Advocate* (Baton Rouge), April 12, 1992.

87,000 African-American registered voters in Huckaby's district, an increase of about 6,000 over his previous district. This African-American presence, constituting 27.0 percent of all of the registered voters in the district, was expected to help Huckaby with any challenge from a Republican candidate, even though Huckaby himself had a very conservative voting record in Congress.[36] The plan was described by one Republican state senator as "a Jerry Huckaby-gerrymandered plan,"[37] and by McCrery as "gerrymandering at its highest level."[38] All five of the Republican senators voting on the plan opposed it (one was absent), while the white Democrats split 13 to 11 in favor (with one absent). Combined with the votes of the seven African-American senators (all Democrats), the plan received the minimum number of votes necessary for passage, 20. Republicans made it clear that they would challenge the arrangement in court if it was ultimately adopted by the state.[39]

This version of the plan would not be adopted, however. It was pronounced "dead on arrival" when it reached the state house, where a coalition including African-American and Republican legislators backed what was referred to as a "consensus" plan.[40] The second minority district in this plan extended northwest, rather than south. Sherman Copelin, the African-American representative who sponsored the plan, complained that the new minority district in the plan passed by the Senate did not contain enough African-American voters to ensure that African-Americans would elect a candidate of their choice.[41] The northern version extended the district west, under the Louisiana-Arkansas border, all the way to the Shreveport area in the northwestern corner of the state, where over 30,000 African-American registered voters were brought into the district. The percentage of African-Americans among the registered voters in this district was 63.2, almost 4 percentage points higher than the second minority district in the other version.

---

[36]Huckaby's support for the "conservative coalition" in the House, as identified by Congressional Quarterly, averaged 96 percent for the years 1987 through 1991. He voted against the Civil Rights Act in both 1990 and 1991.

[37]State senator Max Jordan, quoted in "Senate OKs Remap Plan," *News-Star* (Monroe), May 1, 1992.

[38]Quoted in Jack Wardlaw, "Lawmakers OK Rival Plans in Redistricting," *Times-Picayune* (New Orleans), May 1, 1992.

[39]See "Senate OKs Remap Plan," *News-Star* (Monroe), May 1, 1992. The Republican incumbents did file a suit in federal court on May 25, asserting that the state was unlikely to adopt a plan in sufficient time for it to be precleared and implemented prior to the candidate qualifying period, and requesting that the court therefore adopt a plan. They also informed the court that they were prepared to submit a plan for the court's consideration. Complaint for Declaratory Judgment, Injunctive and Other Relief, *Baker* v. *McKeithen*, CV92-0973 (W.D. La. 1992). The Republican incumbents had earlier established the Committee for Fair Representation for the purpose of supporting their interests in the redistricting process through lobbying and, if necessary, litigation. See Joan McKinney, "Reapportionment Round 1," *Sunday Advocate*, (Baton Rouge), March 8, 1992.

[40]Marsha Shuler and Bill McMahon, "Congressional Remap Plans Advance in Legislature," *The Advocate* (Baton Rouge), May 1, 1992, and Marsha Shuler, "Lawmakers See House Remap Plan Thriving, Senate Bill Dying," *The Advocate*, May 4, 1992.

[41]Jack Wardlaw, "Lawmakers OK Rival Plans in Redistricting," *Times-Picayune* (New Orleans), May 1, 1992.

This plan also treated the white incumbents more equitably, at least in partisan terms. While Republicans Baker and Holloway would continue to reside in the same district, McCrery and Huckaby were placed together in a north Louisiana district. The more northern version of the minority district reduced the number of African-American registered voters available to be placed in Huckaby's district, which in this plan would be 18.6 percent, (compared with 27.0 percent in the plan passed by the Senate). If McCrery, who had been quoted as saying "If I have to run against Huckaby, so be it,"[42] were reelected from that district, then the loss of two white incumbents would be shared equally between the two parties (assuming, of course, that both Baker and Holloway were not defeated in their new district, an unlikely occurrence).

This plan, in which the largest and smallest districts were only 0.01 and 0.006 percentage points respectively above and below the ideal district population, passed the House by a vote of 61 to 41. All 24 African-American representatives (all Democrats) voted for it, as did 12 of the 14 Republicans. White Democrats, as a group, did not support it. Only 25 voted for it, while 39 voted against it (with three absent). The House adopted the plan a second time, in the form of a House amendment to the Senate-passed bill. Group support remained the same, except white Democrats split 26 to 40 this time (with only one absent). The Senate acceded to the Copelin plan by accepting the House amendment. The vote in the Senate was 22 to 13. Five of the African-American senators (including Jones) voted for it, with two against (and one, Fields, absent). All six Republican senators supported it, while the white Democrats split evenly, 11 to 11 (with three absent). The largest and smallest districts in the plan were only 0.01 and 0.006 percentage points above and below the ideal district population, respectively. It became the state's plan when Governor Edwards signed the bill on June 1, and became law when the Attorney General granted preclearance on July 6.[43]

HAYS V. LOUISIANA

Following preclearance of the plan, a lawsuit was filed seeking to prevent it from being used in the 1992 congressional elections. The plaintiffs in this case, *Hays* v. *Louisiana*, were two white, one Asian-American, and one African-American resident of Huckaby's old district in north Louisiana.[44] They argued, essentially, that the plan was unfair to minority voters because it overconcentrated African-Americans in the Second and the Fourth Districts. Some of the African-Americans should be removed from these districts, they maintained, and placed in adjoining districts so that they would have more "influence" on the elections in these other districts. This argument, needless to say, fueled

---

[42]Debbie Edney, "McCrery Says Reapportionment Unfair," *News-Star* (Monroe), April 24, 1992.

[43]Letter from John R. Dunne, Assistant Attorney General of the United States, to Angie Rogers LaPlace, Assistant Attorney General, State of Louisiana (July 6, 1992).

[44]See note 1, *supra*. The case was originally filed in a state court, but was removed to and tried before a three-judge federal district court upon petition by the State.

speculation that the suit was little more than an effort to get the judiciary to do what the legislature had not done, which was enhance Huckaby's reelection prospects by increasing the African-American vote in his new district.[45]

The plaintiffs described the state's plan as "a sophisticated voter dilution scheme" that violated both the Constitution and the Voting Rights Act.[46] They claimed that the Second and the Fourth Districts were both safe, "super-majority" African-American districts into which minority voters had been unnecessarily "packed,"[47] while all of the other districts were safe white districts. The plan therefore would assure that two African-Americans and five whites would be elected, resulting, according to them, in "the functional disenfranchisement" of the African-American voters in the white districts and the white voters in the African-American districts.[48]

This disfranchisement, the plaintiffs further maintained, was intentional. The scheme, they argued, was "the 'illegitimate' child" of an "illicit political love affair" between African-American leaders and the Republican Party.[49] Although the plaintiffs had explicitly stated that they were not alleging that there had been any partisan bias behind the formulation of the plan,[50] they did maintain that "partisanship was indirectly impacted through manipulation of racial composition of the districts."[51] Their explanation for the joint support of African-Americans and Republicans for the plan was:

> The super-majority or "safe" district is treasured by black elected officials, while the reduction in black influence in the remaining majority white [districts] is supported by the Republican Party as an effort to eliminate the effectiveness of the black minority in the remaining districts.[52]

The plaintiffs proposed that Districts Two and Four be reduced to racially "competitive" districts. This would allow African-American voters to be dispersed among districts in such a way that they could constitute at least 20 percent of the registered voters in three other districts, rather than just one, and therefore have "an opportunity to influence" the elections in those three districts.[53] Such a scheme would not only be more fair to African-Americans,

---

[45]While not made explicit, this motivation was no doubt implied in the post-trial brief for the Louisiana Legislative Black Caucus, which maintained that "this lawsuit is simply a vehicle for a few disgruntled white people who lost a political battle and are trying to get this Court to interfere with the political process and reverse the result." Memorandum of Amicus Curiae Louisiana Legislative Black Caucus, at 7 (hereinafter Black Caucus's Memorandum).

[46]Plaintiffs' Memorandum, at 27.

[47]Plaintiffs' Memorandum, at 5, 13, 16, and Weber testimony, (August 26, 1992) at 118-119, 126-127, and 177, and (August 27, 1992) at 317.

[48]Plaintiffs' Memorandum, at 11.

[49]*Id.*, at 14.

[50]Complaint Seeking Permanent Injunction and Declaratory Judgment and Motion for Preliminary Injunction, at 2 (hereinafter Plaintiffs' Complaint).

[51]Plaintiffs' Memorandum, at 15.

[52]*Id.*, at 15.

[53]Weber testimony, (August 26, 1992) at 224-245.

they argued, it would also allow the districts to better reflect "the traditional criteria of contiguity, compactness, minimal violation of existing political subdivision boundaries and substantial commonalities of interest."[54]

The plaintiffs introduced a plan purporting to accomplish these goals. The African-American voting age percentage in District Four was reduced to 53.7 in this plan, and the voter registration percentage to 53.5. In District Two, the African-American voting age population (VAP) was reduced to 55.9 percent, and the registration to a reported 60.2 percent. (A variation of the plan affecting only two districts in the New Orleans area brought the VAP percentage in District Two down further, to 52.8; registration figures were not provided for this variant.) The African-American VAP percentages for the three so-called "influence" districts in the plaintiffs' plan were 25.2, 21.2, and 19.9, while the voter registration percentages were 23.5, 20.6, and 20.5.

The extent to which the greater dispersion of the African-American vote within the plaintiffs' plan would significantly enhance minority "influence" in the majority white districts was seriously questioned by all three judges on the court.[55] The state's plan had three districts that were 19.5, 19.5, and 17.7 percent African-American in VAP, and 21.3, 18.8, and 17.8 percent in voter registration. The differences in the plans in this respect, as one judge noted, were in fact *de minimus*.[56] And while the plaintiffs' plan did divide fewer parishes into more than a one district than did the state's plan (16 compared with 28), the extent to which it satisfied any notion of compactness or commonality of interest was also seriously questioned by the judges.[57] One district in the plaintiffs' plan ran the length of the state, from the Arkansas border to the Gulf of Mexico.[58] Indeed, so noncompact were some of the plaintiffs' districts that one judge queried, "If I've got to take a craziness, why should I take yours over the legislature's?"[59]

The plaintiffs responded to the judges' concerns by suggesting that the African-American voters could be even more dispersed. Relying on the testimony of a political scientist, they argued that districts in which African-Americans constituted only 40 to 45 percent of the voting age population would still be racially "competitive."[60] Districts Two and Four therefore could be further "unpacked," and the other districts drawn more consistently with the other criteria.[61]

---

[54]Plaintiffs' Memorandum, at 33.

[55]See the questions and comments from the bench of the Honorable Jacques L. Wiener, Jr., the Honorable John M. Shaw, and the Honorable Donald E. Walter, Transcript (August 26, 1992), at 219-222, 226-227.

[56]*Id.*, at 221-222.

[57]*Id.*, at 191, 199, and 205-206, and Transcript (August 27,1992), at 313-316.

[58]Transcript (August 27, 1992) at 313-314.

[59]*Id.*, at 313-314.

[60]Plaintiffs' Memorandum, at 14, 16, 31-33; Weber testimony, (August 26, 1992) at 198, 218-219, and (August 27, 1992), at 330, 391.

[61]Plaintiffs' Memorandum, at 33; Weber testimony, (August 26, 1992), at 198-199, 202-203, 209-210, 218-219.

The state acknowledged that "The primary motive for drawing these districts was to enhance black voters' ability to elect the candidates of their choice,"[62] but argued that neither of the two majority African-American districts was a "packed" district. Evidence was presented showing that voting in the state's congressional elections had been racially polarized. In the elections held under the previous districting arrangement, voters had been presented with the choice between or among African-American and white candidates on seven occasions, and on each occasion they had responded in a racially divided manner. The African-American voters preferred an African-American candidate and the white voters a white candidate.[63] Given the racial divisions in Louisiana politics, the state argued, "viable" minority districts would need to be majority minority districts.[64]

Districts Two and Four, in which African-Americans would constitute 60.0 and 63.2 percent of the registered voters, were described by state's expert witness as providing African-Americans with "two really good shots" at electing the candidates of their choice, but not a guarantee of such.[65] In the previous year's state legislative elections, it was pointed out, white candidates who had not been the choice of African-American voters had won in three districts in which African-Americans were a majority of the registered voters. The African-American voters in each of these districts overwhelmingly preferred African-American candidates.[66] One of these districts was a state senate district in which African-Americans constituted 60.9 percent of the VAP and, at the time of the election, 56.3 percent of the voter registration.[67] Higher rates of voter participation and cohesion among the whites allowed the white candidate to win, despite that candidate's support among the African-American voters being estimated at only 15.7 percent.[68] Given this experience, it was argued that neither Districts Two and Four could be considered so disproportionately African-American that minority votes would be "wasted" in them.[69] Indeed, an African-American state legislator testified

---

[62]Post Trial Brief of Defendants, p. 10 (hereinafter Defendants' Memorandum).

[63]These elections were the 1984 and 1990 primary elections in the old District Two, and the 1986 primary and runoff, 1988 primary and runoff, and 1990 primary in the old District Eight. Testimony of Richard L. Engstrom, Transcript (August 27, 1992), at 337-342 (hereinafter Engstrom testimony); Defendants' Exhibits 2, 3, 7, and 8.

Racially polarized voting is certainly not unique to congressional elections in Louisiana. For judicial findings of racially polarized voting in other types of elections across the state, see e.g., *Clark* v. *Edwards*, 725 F. Supp. 285, (M.D. La. 1988), *East Jefferson Coalition for Leadership and Development* v. *Parish of Jefferson*, 691 F. Supp. 991 (E.D. La. 1988), *Citizens for a Better Gretna* v. *City of Gretna*, 636 F. Supp. 1113 (E.D. La. 1986), and *Major* v. *Treen*, 574 F. Supp. 325 (E.D. La. 1983).

[64]Engstrom testimony, at 342, 386. See also the testimony of state representative Willie Hunter, Jr., concerning racial differences in political participation, Transcript (August 26, 1992), at 249, 259-260 (hereinafter Hunter testimony).

[65]Engstrom testimony, at 343; see also Hunter testimony, at 251, 258.

[66]Engstrom testimony, at 344-346; Defendants' Exhibit 6.

[67]See Plaintiffs' Exhibit 8.

[68]Defendants' Exhibit 6.

that the new Fourth congressional district could likewise be won by a white candidate who was not the preference of African-American voters.[70]

The state also argued that there was no evidence to support the plaintiffs' theory about "influence" districts. The notion that a 20 percent minority presence was somehow a threshold at which minority voters could be expected to influence election outcomes was flatly rejected.[71] The state's own experience, it was maintained, contradicted that suggestion.[72] Among the seven majority white districts in the previous plan, the district with the most African-Americans was the Eighth, which had a VAP that was 36 percent African-American in both 1980 and 1990.[73] Voter registration in the district was 36.3 percent by 1992. The white incumbent in this district, Holloway, had never received as much as 10 percent of the votes cast by the district's African-American voters. African-American candidates who had been overwhelmingly favored by the African-American voters had attempted to unseat him in 1988 and 1990, but were unsuccessful due to the strong support for Holloway among white voters.[74] Not only had African-American voters had little influence on these election outcomes, they also had little influence, the state argued, on Holloway himself. When asked whether African-American voters within the old Eighth District had any influence over Holloway, an African-American state legislator responded, "No, certainly not,"[75] a conclusion supported by testimony concerning Holloway's voting record in Congress.[76] Indeed, the state's own expert witness acknowledged that Holloway's votes in Congress had been "unresponsive" to the concerns of African-Americans.[77]

The minimal increases in the number of African-Americans in the majority white districts in the plaintiffs' plan compared to the state's plan, it was argued, could not be said to significantly benefit minority voters.[78] This was especially the case if the consequent reduction in the African-American voting strength in Districts Two or Four would place the group's opportunity to elect candidates of their choice in those districts at risk, as was the case in the plaintiffs' plan.[79] The plaintiffs' proposal, the state maintained, amounted to leaving the five white districts safe but making the two African-American districts at best "marginal," or "competitive," an arrangement that could hardly be considered more racially fair than the state's plan.[80]

---

[69]Engstrom testimony, at 345-346, 352.

[70]Hunter testimony, at 262-265.

[71]Engstrom testimony, at 346-8, 352.

[72]Defendants' Memorandum, at 6; United States' Memorandum, at 7.

[73]Plaintiffs' Exhibit 6.

[74]Engstrom testimony, at 347-348, 357-358. Defendants' Exhibits 4, 5, 7, and 8.

[75]Hunter testimony, at 268.

[76]Engstrom testimony, at 358-359; Weber testimony (August 27, 1992), at 280-281.

[77]Weber testimony, at 280-281.

[78]Defendants' Memorandum, at 5-6, 8-9; see also United States' Memorandum, at 16 n.12.

[79]Engstrom testimony, at 343-344, 347, 349-351; Hunter testimony, at 259-260. See also Black Caucus's Memorandum, at 7.

[80]Engstrom testimony, at 351, 359, 376-377.

The state defended its districts by arguing that they were "functional and perform the very purpose for which they were enacted."[81] The state intended to provide African-American voters with viable opportunities to elect two candidates of their choice to Congress. In doing so, it recognized that "commonalities of interest" are not limited to people who happen to reside in close geographical proximity to one another. Witnesses testified that African-Americans across the state share social and economic problems that, due to their race, are particularly intense. Consequently, African-Americans residing in Baton Rouge, for example, may feel that they have more in common with African-Americans in Shreveport than with whites in Baton Rouge.[82] The state acknowledged that the districts "may not be pleasing to the eye," but that in itself did not make them legally infirm.[83]

The court denied the plaintiffs' request that the forthcoming congressional elections be enjoined. It also, in a brief memorandum ruling, rejected the plaintiffs' claim that the state's plan was unconstitutional. No decision was reached, however, on whether the plan was a violation of the Voting Rights Act. Supplemental briefs were specifically requested on whether the voting strength of either whites or blacks was being diluted by the plan, or by any particular district within it.[84]

THE 1992 ELECTIONS

The primary elections for congressional seats under the state's plan were held in October 1992, with runoffs, where necessary, on the same day as the presidential election that year. As a result of these elections, the number of African-Americans serving in Congress from Louisiana increased to two. None of the white candidates that ran in the majority African-American districts could be classified as strong candidates (see, e.g., Jacobson, 1992: 168, 177). The African-American incumbent in the new Second District, William Jefferson, was reelected easily in the primary. Jefferson had only two opponents, a white independent who had been an unsuccessful candidate for Congress on four previous occasions, and an African-American councilwoman from suburban Kenner, in the Jefferson Parish portion of the district. Voter registration in the Second District was 60.2 percent African-American at the time of the primary, and 58.3 percent of those signing-in to vote that day were African-Americans. Jefferson won 73.5 percent of the votes cast. He was the overwhelming choice of the African-American voters, receiving an estimated 90.3 percent of the votes cast by them. And while he was the plurality choice of the other voters, he did not receive a majority of the votes cast by them. Jefferson is esti-

---

[81]Defendants' Memorandum, at 11.

[82]Hunter testimony, at 248, 254-255; Engstrom testimony, at 385-386.

[83]Defendants' memorandum, at 11; see also Black Caucus's Memorandum, at 6, and United States' Memorandum, at 12.

[84]Memorandum Ruling and Order, Hays v. State of Louisiana, Civ. No. 92-1522 (W.D. La. August 27, 1992).

mated to have received a vote from only 48.5 percent of the whites voting in this election. The white independent candidate, Roger Johnson, finished second among white voters, receiving an estimated 26.2 percent of their votes.

An African-American was also elected in the new Fourth District. The contest in this majority African-American district, in which there was no incumbent, drew a field of eight candidates. Six of these candidates were African-Americans. Both of the white candidates were Republicans who had never held elective office. As expected, state senators Fields and Jones were among the candidates, and they had to faced each other in a runoff. The district's voter registration was 63.3 percent African-American at the time of the primary, and 65.8 percent of those signing in to vote in that election were African-American. Fields had a commanding lead over Jones in the primary, receiving 47.8 percent of the votes compared with Jones's 14.0. Fields received an estimated 60.8 percent of the votes cast by African-Americans in the primary, while Jones was the second preference of this group, at 18.6 percent. White voters cast a plurality of their votes for one of the white candidates, Steve Myers, a Baton Rouge attorney who had unsuccessfully sought a state legislative seat in 1991. Myers received an estimated 23.1 percent of the votes cast by whites, while Fields was the second choice of white voters, with 22.5 percent.

The African-American voter registration percentage in the Fourth District at the time of the runoff election was 63.1 percent. Among those signing in to vote that day, 60.4 percent were African-American. Fields won the election, receiving 73.9 percent of the votes cast. He is estimated to have received a vote from 79.2 percent of the African-Americans voting in the runoff, and 64.7 percent of the whites.

The three white incumbents who had been placed in districts of their own in the new plan were, like Jefferson, reelected by large margins in the primaries. This included Livingston, the Republican in the new First District, and Democrats Tauzin and Hayes, in the Third and the Seventh, respectively. Despite having five opponents, Livingston received 72.7 percent of the votes cast in his primary. Tauzin won 81.7 percent of the primary vote against a single opponent in his district, and Hayes won 73.0 percent against two opponents (one of whom was his brother).

The other two districts each contained two incumbents. Republicans Holloway and Baker, along with a Democratic state senator, Ned Randolph, were candidates in the new Sixth District, while Democrat Huckaby, Republican McCrery, and three other candidates competed in the new Fifth District. In both districts, the incumbents had to face each other again in runoff elections. In the Sixth District, Republicans Holloway and Baker received 36.7 and 33.1 percent of the vote, respectively, in the primary, while Randolph received 30.2 percent. Baker then edged Holloway in the runoff, receiving 50.6 percent of the vote. In the Fifth District, McCrery led the primary by a substantial margin, receiving 44.1 percent of the votes, while Huckaby received 29.4. In the runoff, McCrery won with 63.0

percent of the votes. One incumbent from each party therefore lost their seat following the redistricting, leaving the state's new seven-member House delegation at four Democrats and three Republicans.

The 1992 elections, it turned out, were the only elections held under this districting configuration. The following summer the United States Supreme Court, in the case involving congressional districts in North Carolina, *Shaw* v. *Reno*, established a new standard for evaluating racial gerrymandering claims under the Fourteenth Amendment.[85] The federal court in Louisiana therefore revisited the *Hays* plaintiffs' gerrymandering allegation in light of this new precedent, and further elections under the arrangement were precluded as a result of that evaluation.

Hays v. *Louisiana*, Round II

The federal court in Louisiana never did rule on the Voting Rights Act issue on which it had requested post-trial briefs in 1992. The court instead returned, in 1993, to one of the plaintiffs' claims that it had expressly denied the previous year, that the Fourth District was a "racial gerrymander" that violated the equal protection clause of the Fourteenth Amendment. This issue was resuscitated when the Supreme Court held in *Shaw* that race-based districting, even when designed to benefit rather than harm an African-American minority, must be "strictly scrutinized" under the Fourteenth Amendment. In *Shaw* the Court took a district-specific approach to the concept of gerrymandering, divorcing it from any requirement that the voting strength of a cognizable group be systematically diluted by a set of districts.[86] If a district is drawn solely for the purpose of separating voters along racial lines, and "traditional districting principles" are disregarded in the process, strict scrutiny must be applied. To survive such scrutiny, a state must have a "compelling interest" in basing the district on race, and the district itself must be "narrowly tailored" to satisfy that interest.[87]

As noted above, the state had argued in 1992 that "The primary motive for drawing these districts was to enhance the ability of black voters to elect the candidates of their choice."[88] In 1993, in the post-*Shaw* context, the state argued that despite this motive, the actual *shape* of District Four was the result of partisan and incumbent politics, rather than race, and therefore strict scrutiny was not necessary. Testimony about the districting process was elicited from Fields, Congressman Hayes, and an African-American state senator, Marc Morial. This testimony revealed that a majority of the legislators believed that the Justice Department would not preclear a plan that did not include a second majority African-American district, and therefore the issue before the legislature was, as Fields expressed it, "Where do we create it?"[89] The shape of the Fourth District,

---

[85] 509 U.S. 630 (1993).

[86] Compare this with the treatment of the partisan gerrymandering issue in *Gaffney* v. *Cummings*, 412 U.S. 735 (1973), and *Davis* v. *Bandemer*, 478 U.S. 109 (1986).

[87] *Shaw* v. *Reno*, 509 U.S. 630 (1993).

[88] Post Trial Brief of Defendants, p. 10 (hereinafter Defendants' Memorandum).

especially the extension along the northern border of the state, was said to be driven by partisan and incumbent considerations rather than race. According to Fields, "Politics led the district to look the way it looked."[90] In addition, the state presented statistical evidence concerning the demographic and socioeconomic characteristics of the districts that it argued demonstrated that District Four was a "coherent" district within which there were "commonalities" other than race.[91] The court dismissed these arguments as "no more than disingenuous, *post hoc* rationalizations."[92] It found the districting principles of compactness, contiguity, and respect for political subdivisions and "commonality of interests" to have been "cavalierly" disregarded in the creation of the Fourth District. "No one could claim," the court stated, "that District 4 is compact, at least not with a straight face." And while the district was unquestionably contiguous, it was quite narrow in places, prompting the court to say that it satisfied this principle "only hypertechnically and thus cynically." Twenty-eight of the state's 64 parishes (counties) were divided in the plan, compared with only seven in the previous eight-district arrangement. District Four itself included only four whole parishes and parts of 24 others. Most of the major municipalities had also been divided in the plan. District Four was ultimately characterized as an "un-district" that included "bits of every religious, ethnic, economic, social, and topographical type found in Louisiana."[93] While politics might have affected "the general location of the gerrymander," the court concluded, it was "the core decision" to create a second majority African-American district that caused these deviations from traditional districting principles.[94]

The state argued that there were "compelling" reasons for the Fourth District. If African-American voters were not provided with two viable opportunities to elect congressmen of their choice, it maintained, the plan would not be in compliance with the Voting Rights Act. As noted above, it was widely believed that a plan without two majority African-American districts would be denied section 5 preclearance. Such a plan could also be vulnerable, the state argued, to invalidation under section 2 of that Act, which prohibits election arrangements that result in minority vote dilution. (The state's first effort at congressional districting following the 1980 census was precleared but then found to conflict with that provision.)[95] The state also maintained that the districting plan was justified as a remedial measure that would help politically empower the state's African-Americans. While African-Americans constituted close to 30 percent of the state's pop-

---

[89]Testimony of Cleo Fields, Transcript (August 20, 1993), at 7, 18 (hereinafter, Fields testimony).

[90]*Id.*, at 18. See also the testimony of Marc Morial, Transcript (August 19, 1993, morning session), at 11-24 (hereinafter Morial testimony), and the testimony of James A. Hayes, Transcript (August 19, 1993, afternoon session), at 37-38.

[91]See the expert witness testimony of Allan J. Lichtman, Transcript (August 20, 1993), at 41-94.

[92]*Hays* v. *State of Louisiana*, 839 F.Supp. 1188, 1201 (W.D. La. 1993).

[93]*Id.*, at 1200-1201.

[94]*Hays* (1993), at 1201.

[95]See *Major* v. *Treen*, 574 F.Supp. 325 (E.D. La. 1983).

ulation, the state's congressional delegation had been exclusively white until 1991 and largely unresponsive to African-American interests. State senator Morial testified that this "history of legislative indifference to the black population of this state is something that the creation of a second majority black district seeks to address."[96] The history of discrimination had also resulted in severe disparities in the socioeconomic characteristics of the state's white and African-American residents, disparities that usually result in levels of political participation among African-Americans that are lower than those for whites. District Four was therefore constructed to have a voter registration over 60 percent African-American so that minority voters would have a viable opportunity to elect a candidate of their choice.[97]

The court found it unnecessary to rule on the state's compelling interest arguments because, in its opinion, even *if* the reasons for a second majority African-American district were compelling, District Four had not been "narrowly tailored" to achieved them.[98] According to the court, District 4 contained more African-Americans than necessary to provide the group with a reasonable opportunity to elect an African-American. In the court's view:

> ...a district with a black voting age population of not more than 55%—and probably less—would have been adequate to ensure that blacks could elect a candidate of their choice, assuming they chose to exercise their franchise and assuming the candidate of their choice had more than a modicum of appeal for non-black voters.[99]

Such a district could have been created, the court added, with "substantially less violence to traditional redistricting principles."[100] The state's plan was found therefore to fail the strict scrutiny test, and further elections under it were prohibited.

CONGRESSIONAL DISTRICTING, 1994

The legislature, not surprisingly, interpreted the *Hays* decision to mean that a second majority-minority district would be permitted, provided it was not over 55 percent in voting age population and did not deviate from traditional districting criteria as dramatically as District Four in the 1992 plan. Just such a district was adopted during a special legislative session in 1994.[101]

---

[96]Morial testimony, at 14.

[97]See Morial testimony, at 15-16; Fields testimony, at 15-17; and the testimony of State Senator Tom Greene, Transcript (August 20, 1993), at 121-122.

[98]The court did provide an extensive footnote, however, expressing its opinion that neither section 2 nor section 5 of the Voting Rights Act required the state to create a second majority African-American district, and castigating the Justice Department for in effect requiring the state to adopt one. *Hays* (1993), at 1196-1197, n.21. In addition, one member of the three-judge panel did explicitly reject the state's "compelling interests" arguments, finding them "so slim that they reek of the pretextual and the contrived." *Id.*, at 1218, (Walters, J., concurring).

[99]*Id.*, at 1208.

[100] *Id.*, at 1208.

A new version of a majority African-American Fourth District was developed by the staff of the state senate. For many years the congressional district with the highest percentage of African-Americans, outside of the New Orleans area, had been the Eighth. In a plan adopted in 1969, following Supreme Court decisions tightening the one person, one vote requirement for congressional districts (see Engstrom, 1980), the Eighth stretched from the middle of the state's western border with Texas all the way to Lake Pontchartrain in the southeastern part of the state. The district was elongated, with its eastern portion considerably more narrow than the western part. It shared borders with all of the other congressional districts except the two containing parts of New Orleans. It was, by any standard, not compact. Indeed, it was the subject of the traditional political cartoon at districting time, highlighted by an artist's addition of eyes, mouth, and hands.[102] Subsequent versions of the Eighth were more wedge-shaped districts running from Rapides Parish in the center of the state down to Lake Pontchartrain. The "Old Eighth" became the conceptual basis for a new Fourth District, modified to bring it close to 55 percent African-American in voting age population.

The new Fourth District was also wedged-shaped (Figure 3). It ran from Caddo Parish in the northwestern corner of the state to Ascension Parish in the southeast, a distance of about 250 miles. It included three entire parishes and parts of 12 others. African-Americans constituted 58.4 percent of the population and 54.4 percent of the voting age population of the district, according to 1990 census figures. They also constituted, as of 1994, 55.3 percent of the registered voters. A plan including this district was agreed to by the state's congressional delegation. District Two, the other majority African-American district, was changed very little by the plan, retaining a 61.0 percent African-American population and 60.7 percent African-American voter registration in 1994. The African-American percentage of registered voters in the other five districts ranged from 9.6 to 23.7. Congressman McCrery was quoted as saying, concerning the congressional delegation, "I wouldn't say we're all in favor of it, but nobody expressed any grave reservations in terms of their own particular districts. We said if the plan was passed by the Legislature we could live with it."[103] The plan, in which both the largest and smallest districts deviated from the ideal population

---

[101]Despite the *Hays* court's belief that neither section 2 nor section 5 required the state to adopt two districts with African-American majorities (see note 98, *infra.*), it was still widely believed that a plan without two would not be granted preclearance by the Justice Department. If there had been any ambiguity about this, it was dispelled when the Justice Department took the position, in an *amicus curiae* brief in support of the state's appeal of the *Hays* decision, that the *Hays* court was in error. Brief for the United States as Amicus Curiae, *State of Louisiana et al., v. Hays et al.*, No. 93-1539, at 12-13, n.3. In addition, just prior to final passage of the new districting plan, the Assistant Attorney General for Civil Rights provided attorneys representing the Louisiana Legislative Black Caucus a letter indicating that two majority African-American districts would be required for preclearance, a letter that was circulated among legislators. See Letter from Deval L. Patrick, Assistant Attorney General, to Brenda Wright and Robert McDuff, April 20, 1994 (via facsimile transmission).

[102]*Times-Picayune* (New Orleans), June 4, 1969.

[103]*Times* (Shreveport), March 27, 1994, at 1A.

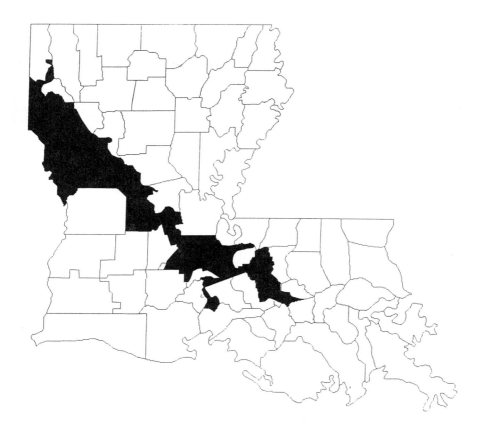

FIGURE 3. Louisiana's Fourth District. 1994

by only 0.01 of a percentage point, was passed by a vote of 61 to 43 in the House and then 21 to 15 in the Senate. All 24 African-American members of the House voted in favor of the plan, as did seven of the eight African-American senators (one being absent). White members of the House and Senate voted in opposition to the plan, however. In the House, 37 voted in favor and 43 against (with one absent), and in the Senate, 14 voted in favor and 15 against (with two absent).[104] The new districts were precleared by the Department of Justice, but before elections could be held in them, another hearing was held in the *Hays* case.

---

[104]White Democrats in the House were divided, with 32 voting in favor of the plan and 31 against it. House Republicans split five in favor and 11 against. In the Senate, 13 of the white Democrats voted in favor of the plan and nine against it, while only one Republican voted for it and six Republicans voted against it.

Hays v. *Louisiana*, **Round III**

The plaintiffs in the *Hays* case were not satisfied with the state's second effort at revising congressional districts. They therefore continued their *Shaw* challenge, describing the new plan as only "a slightly less egregious racial gerrymander" than its predecessor.[105] Traditional districting criteria continued to be sacrificed, they argued, in a quest for racially determined districts. The mark of Zorro, in their opinion, had simply been replaced by "a racial dagger."[106] They also maintained that the state had no compelling interest in the creation of a second majority African-American district, and that even if it had, District Four was still not narrowly tailored. This version of District Four, they argued, was also "packed" with more African-Americans than necessary to provide that group with a "realistic chance" to elect a candidate of its choice.[107] Indeed, according to the plaintiffs, "districts within thirty-five (35%) to forty-five (45%) percent black citizens" would be sufficient to provide African-Americans in Louisiana with such a chance.[108]

The court agreed that the new Fourth District was a racial gerrymander, stating that "we called for major surgery. [This] is at best a cosmetic makeover."[109] The state's argument that the new Fourth was based on the old Eighth and therefore consistent with past districting practices was rebuffed as "mere pretext." In the court's opinion, "The State did not imitate the 'old Eighth' for tradition's sake. ...New District Four was drafted with the specific intent of ensuring a second majority-minority Congressional district."[110] References to the old Eighth, a majority white district, were even dismissed as irrelevant, because the constitutionality of that district had never been challenged in court.[111] The court likewise rejected the state's other argument, that District Four followed the Red River valley and consequently reflected a "commonality of interest," as "clearly a *post hoc* rationalization."[112]

The court flatly rejected the plaintiffs' assertion that African-Americans in

---

[105]Memoranda in Support of Motion for Preliminary Injunction and Adoption of an Interim Congressional Districting Plan for the 1994 Congressional Elections in the State of Louisiana, at 12.

[106]*Id.*, at 27.

[107]*Id.*, at 15.

[108]*Id.*, at 17.

[109]*Hays v. State of Louisiana*, 862 F.Supp. 119, 122, n.1 (W.D. La 1994).

[110]*Id.*

[111]*Id.*, at 122, and at 127 (Shaw, J., concurring). The court, however, did not identify any grounds for such a challenge. The only features of the Eighth referenced by the court were its shape and its purpose—it was a "bizarre" district designed to ensure "the reelection of Congressman Gillis Long" *Id.*, at 122. (In fact, the incumbent at the time the district initially assumed its bizarre shape was Speedy Long, not Gillis Long. The district had been extended into the southeastern part of the state initially in 1967, and further in that direction in 1969. Gillis replaced Speedy in 1973.) Neither of these features, without more, violates the Constitution. Compactness is not a requirement of congressional districts in either federal, see *Shaw* v. *Reno*, 509 U.S. 630, 647 (1993), or state law, and there is no constitutional prohibition against protecting incumbents, see *White* v. *Weiser*, 412 U.S. 783, 791 (1973). The basis for such a challenge is therefore unclear.

[112]*Hays* (1994), at 122.

Louisiana have a realistic chance to elect candidates of their choice in districts that range from 35 to 45 percent African-American, and also their characterization of District Four as a "packed" district.[113] But the court also said that the legislature had misinterpreted its 1993 decision "as approving a racially gerrymandered district if it contained no more than 55% minority registered voters."[114] The state, the court said, had no compelling interest in basing districts on race. A second majority African-American district was not required, in the court's opinion, by either section 2 or section 5 of the Voting Rights Act.[115] And the state's claim that a second district was needed to remedy past and present discrimination was also rejected. The court stated:

> Without concrete evidence of the lingering effects of past discrimination or continuing legal prejudice in voting laws and procedures, coupled with specific remedies, we cannot agree that the re-segregation of Louisiana by racially configured voting districts is warranted.[116]

The court replaced the state's plan with one of its own that contained only a single majority African-American district. The Second District in the New Orleans area was 60.7 percent African-American in population, 56.1 percent in voting age population, and as of 1994, 60.3 percent in voter registration. Five of the other districts had African-American registration percentages ranging from 22.7 to 27.7, while one was only 9.7 percent. The court said it had "ignore[d] all political considerations" in developing the plan, which split only six parishes and one town of about 3,000 residents.[117] The largest and smallest districts deviated by only 0.01 of a percentage point from the ideal district population. All of the districts except the Second resembled rectangles (Figure 4). Both Congressman Fields and Congressman Baker resided in the Sixth District in this arrangement, a district that was 27.5 percent African-American in voter registration.

The 1994 election did not proceed under the court drawn plan, however. The Supreme Court stayed the lower court's ruling, allowing the election to be held under the state's second plan. All of the incumbents won reelection in the October primary. Fields did not draw a major white opponent in the new Fourth District, which was 55.3 percent African-American in voter registration at the time of the election. Turnout among registered voters in that district was essentially the same for whites and African-Americans, 45.0 percent and 45.4 percent, respectively. Fields is estimated to have received over 99 percent of the votes cast by African-Americans and about 32 percent of those cast by whites, leaving him with just under 70 percent overall. All of the other incumbents won

---

[113]See Transcript (July 21, 1994, afternoon session), at 18-19.

[114]*Hays* (1994), at 122.

[115]*Id.*, at 123-124.

[116]*Id.*, at 124.

[117]*Id.*, at 125.

with over 70 percent of the vote except Hayes, who was challenged by former congressman Holloway for the Seventh District seat. Hayes received 53 percent of the votes to win in the primary. The state's second plan, however, like its first, was used for only one election. The *Hays* litigation continued, and ultimately resulted in the court's plan being used for the 1996 election.

Hays v. *Louisiana*, Round IV

The Supreme Court heard the state's appeal of the *Hays* ruling in 1995 and, without dissent, vacated the lower court's decision.[118] The gerrymandering and strict scrutiny findings were not addressed in the Court's controlling opinion however. The decision was vacated because the plaintiffs, the Court concluded, did not have standing to sue over the district lines. Continuing to view the concept of gerrymandering as a district-specific phenomenon, the Court held that the plaintiffs lacked standing to sue because none of them lived in the allegedly gerrymandered district. The plaintiffs were not residents of the Fourth District in the 1994 plan, but rather the adjacent Fifth. While the racial composition of the Fifth was of course affected by the design of the Fourth, the Court found nothing in the record to indicate that "the legislature intended District 5 to have any particular racial composition." The spillover effect of the Fourth on the Fifth, by itself, did not constitute a "cognizable injury" under the Fourteenth Amendment.[119]

The same day the Supreme Court handed down its ruling in *Hays* it also decided *Miller* v. *Johnson*, in which a majority African-American congressional district in Georgia was struck down.[120] The Georgia district was in several respects similar to the 1994 version of the Fourth in Louisiana. It traversed much of the state, with most of its African-American population located at the ends of the district and in extensions reaching out to urban concentrations. It also had been adopted in order to satisfy the preclearance requirements of the Department of Justice.

The Supreme Court ruling in *Hays* presented nothing more than a procedural hurdle requiring additional plaintiffs to be added to the lawsuit. Once this was done, another hearing was held by the district court in 1995. This two-day hearing produced, the court concluded, "nothing but essentially redundant, cumulative evidence" because the facts had not changed.[121] The defendant's race-neutral explanations for District Four were dismissed as "frivolous."[122] The court found that "the State considered only race in determining which pockets of voters to pull in and which pockets of voters to push out," and had done so to satisfy the Justice Department's demand for two majority-minority districts.[123] In this respect, the Supreme Court's *Miller* decision provided the district court with what it called "a 'Goose' case", which in Louisiana refers to a "commanding precedent, factually on

---

[118] *United States* v. *Hays*, 515 U.S. 737 (1995).

[119] *Id.*, sl. op. at 9.

[120] 515 U.S. 900 (1995).

[121] *Hays* v. *State of Louisiana*, 839 F.Supp. 1188 (WD La 1993), (sl. op. at 13).

all fours."[124] The state's compelling interest arguments were again rejected, for the same reasons as before, and "the heavy-handed confection" of District Four was found to fall short of the "narrow tailoring" standard.[125]

The court readopted the districting plan it had created the previous year, and even claimed that its plan, despite dismantling one of the two majority-African-American districts, "empowers more black voters" than the state's plan.[126] This assertion was premised on the rather simplistic notion that any district that is at least 25 percent African-American in voting age population is a minority "influence district."[127] The court noted that none of the majority white districts in the state's plan met this criterion (although one was only 0.6 percentage points below that figure), while three of the districts in the court's plan did. Districts Four, Five, and Six in the court's plan had voting age populations that were, respectively, 29.3, 27.8, and 29.4 percent African-American. African-Americans in these districts would presumably "influence" election outcomes and the subsequent behavior of the people elected to represent these districts. The "influence" that African-Americans would have in these three districts, according to the court, would empower the state's African-Americans more than actually having a second representative in Congress chosen by and accountable to the voters in a majority African-American district.

The notion that African-Americans will influence the outcomes of elections in any districts in which they constitute at least 25 percent of the voting age popu-

---

[122]*Id.*, at 15. The court repeated its observation that the constitutionality of the "Old Eighth" District had never been challenged (see *supra.*, note 111), and this time offered a reason why this was somehow relevant. The court stated:

> We suspect that if challenged today, that district would meet the same fate as District 4, as it was formed unabashedly with the intention of gathering minority voters into one district to ensure the re-election of longtime Louisiana Congressman Gillis Long.

Id., at 19, n.48.

The state had cited versions of the old Eighth, however, going back to the late 1960s (specifically 1967 and 1969), when the incumbent was Speedy O. Long, not Gillis Long. This was when the departure from compactness began, in the form of the long, relatively narrow extension of the district into the southeastern part of the state. The 1967 version of the district was 32.4 percent nonwhite, while the 1969 version, which went further into the southeast, was 30.7 percent white (according to the 1970 census). The 1972 revision, less elongated that its predecessors, brought the district to 36.2 percent African-American, while the 1982 version brought that percentage up to 38.3. By no stretch of the imagination could any of these versions of the district be said to have been "an effort to segregate voters into separate voting districts because of their race" [*Shaw* v. *Reno*, 504 U.S. 630, 658 (1993).

The *Hays* court's suspicion that the old Eighth would be found unconstitutional today also appears to be in conflict with the rejection of most of the racial gerrymandering allegations in the Texas congressional redistricting case, *Vera* v. *Bush*, 861 F.Supp. 1304 (S.D. Tex. 1994). These allegations concerned the deliberate manipulation of the boundaries of majority white districts in order to increase the number of African-Americans in them and thereby enhance the reelection prospects of the white Democratic incumbents. *Id.*, at 1304, 1326-1328, 1344-1345.

[123]*Hays* (1996), at 16-17.
[124]*Id.*, at 14, n.13.
[125]*Id.*, at 24.
[126]*Id.*, at 7, n.17.
[127]*Id.*

lation is certainly dubious, especially in light of the court's simultaneous acknowledgment that "racial bloc voting is a fact of contemporary Louisiana politics."[128] There was no suggestion that African-Americans will be able to elect the candidates of their choice in these districts if those candidates are African-Americans. Indeed, the court had unequivocally rejected, during the 1994 hearing, the plaintiffs' assertion that African-Americans can elect candidates of their choice in districts that are 35 percent African-American.[129] Nor did the court cite any evidence demonstrating that African-American voters could be expected to determine which of the various white candidates in these districts would be elected. There was no evidence indicating that white voters in these districts are so systematically and predictably divided that the African-Americans would constitute a swing vote, effectively choosing between or among the candidates most preferred by the white voters. Indeed, within one of the court's so-called "minority influence" districts, District Five, a former Grand Wizard of the Ku Klux Klan, David Duke, won a majority of the votes in both the 1990 election for a U.S. Senate seat and the 1991 runoff election for Governor.[130]

Nor was there any evidence indicating that the people chosen to represent districts in which African-Americans constitute 25 percent or more of the voting age population will behave, after elections, in a manner responsive to that portion of their constituency. As noted above, Clyde Holloway had not been responsive to minority interests while serving as the congressman for the Eighth District. That district was 36 percent African-American in voting age, the highest among the seven majority white districts in the state. Expert witnesses for both the plaintiffs and the defendants had testified in 1992 that as a congressman, Holloway had not been responsive to the interests of the African-Americans in the district.[131] Further evidence introduced at the 1994 hearing revealed that, from 1987 through 1990, Holloway had voted in favor of civil rights measures endorsed by the Leadership Conference on Civil Rights only 6 percent of the time. He had opposed, for example, both the House and the conference committee versions of the Civil Rights Act in 1990, and was even one of the few Republicans to oppose the bipartisan compromise that resulted in the Civil Rights Act of 1991.[132] It is not surprising, therefore, that all of the African-Americans witnesses in the *Hays* litigation, including the only African-American among the plaintiffs, expressed a preference for the creation of two majority African-American districts.[133]

The influence district notion was applied in a racially selective manner by the court as well. The majority African-American districts, Districts Two and Four, are both over 40 percent *white* in voting age population (40.7 and 44.7,

---

[128]*Id.*

[129]Transcript, (July 21, 1994, afternoon session), at 18-19.

[130]See Ronald E. Weber, Report on Liability Issues Related to Louisiana Act 1 Congressional Districts for Hearing in *Hays* vs. *State of Louisiana*, Plaintiffs' Exhibit 8.

[131]See text at *supra.*, note 77.

[132]Declaration of Richard L. Engstrom, State Exh. 13.

[133]Testimony of Edward L. Adams, Transcript (August 26, 1992), at 235.

respectively), yet neither of these districts was identified as a white influence district. Indeed, the court specifically found the whites in District Four to be in a situation comparable to the African-Americans in the three districts the court described as "bleached," rather than the African-Americans in the so-called minority influence districts. The three "bleached" districts, One, Three, and Seven, have voting age populations that are only 10.1, 18.4, and 16.5 percent African-American. According to the court, "...office holders and office seekers no longer need to heed the voices of the minority residents of their districts— here, the whites of District 4, the blacks of the other, 'bleached' districts."[134] The basis for this racial distinction in influence districts, especially curious given the court's rather adamant agreement in 1994 that District Four was not a "packed" district, was never articulated by the court.[135]

THE 1996 ELECTIONS

Prior to the 1996 congressional elections, the plan imposed by the court in *Hays* was adopted by the state itself. The 1995 state elections had brought a new governor and legislature to Baton Rouge. The new governor was Mike Foster, a former Democratic state senator who switched to the Republican Party just prior to the gubernatorial primary. Foster won the governor's office by defeating Congressman Fields in a runoff election in which the vote was severely divided along racial lines. (Fields received well over 90 percent of the votes cast by African-Americans in that election, while Foster received close to 90 percent of those cast by whites.) Foster called a special session of the legislature in 1996, one purpose of which was to adopt the *Hays* court's districting plan "in its entirety and without change".[136]

The new House had 22 African-American members, two fewer than it had after the 1991 elections. Two white candidates who had won special elections in majority African-American districts in New Orleans in 1994 and 1995 were reelected in the regular 1995 election.[137] The new Senate had nine African-American members, one more than after the 1991 elections. The new African-American senator won the only majority African-American Senate district that had not been carried by an African-American candidate in 1991. (The white incumbent in this district did not seek reelection after being indicted in a scandal involving the state's video poker industry.) Both legislative chambers were more Republican than previously. The number of Republicans in

---

[134]Ironically, the African-American incumbent in District Four, Fields, has been identified as an example of a "new style" African-American candidate who reaches out to white voters in an effort to create a moderate biracial coalition. See Canon, Schousen, and Sellers, 1996.

[135]On the issues of whether 55 percent constituted "packing" and whether 35 percent provided African-Americans with a "realistic chance" to elect the candidate of their choice, Judge Shaw stated, from the bench in 1994, "We will not seriously entertain any cross-examination to the contrary on those two points. We are convinced already." Transcript (July 21, 1994, afternoon session), at 19.

[136]Call for Special Session, Item No. 123.

the House increased from 16 following the 1991 elections to 27 after the 1995 elections (including two members who switched their party affiliations). On the Senate side, the number doubled, from seven following the 1991 elections to 14 after the 1995 elections (again including one member who switched to the Republican Party). This new legislature adopted the court's plan by a vote of 61 to 40 in the House and 20 to 19 in the Senate. All 21 of the African-American House members voting on the plan opposed it (the remaining member was absent), as did all nine African-Americans in the Senate. White members of the House voted in favor of the plan, 61 to 19, while white senators favored it by a vote of 20 to 10.[138] Following this change in the status of the plan, the Supreme Court dismissed the state's appeal of the *Hays* decision as moot.[139]

The court's plan, in its new incarnation as the state's plan, had to be submitted to the Justice Department for preclearance under section 5 of the Voting Rights Act. In August, prior to the 1996 elections, preclearance was denied. The department maintained that the state could have adopted a plan with two "reasonably compact" districts that would each provide black voters with a "reasonable opportunity" to elect candidates of their choice. The state's latest plan, in the department's opinion, would therefore "clearly violate" Section 2 of the Voting Rights Act, necessitating that preclearance be withheld. According to the Justice Department:

> ...we have a situation where both the State and the federal court have acknowledged that electoral politics in Louisiana remain polarized by race; where black candidates

---

[137] A special election was held in state House district 102 in 1994. African-Americans had constituted a plurality of the voter registration in this district in 1991, when it was won by an African-American candidate (see Llorens, Parsons, and Perry, 1996) who was later elected to the New Orleans city council. The 1994 special election to fill this seat drew a field of seven candidates. The district had an African-American majority in voter registration at the time of the special election, 51.2 percent, but African-Americans constituted a minority of those signing in to vote in both the special primary (43.9 percent) and the runoff (44.1 percent). The runoff was a biracial contest in which about 90 percent of the white voters voted for the white candidate and about 90 percent of the African-Americans voters voted for the African-American candidate. This resulted in the white candidate winning 55.5 percent of the votes.

House district 95 was also the subject of a special election after the African-American incumbent won a state Senate seat in a majority African-American district. This House district was 74.6 percent African-American in voter registration at the time of the 1995 special election. The African-American vote in the primary was dispersed across a nine-candidate field, while about two-thirds of the votes cast by the white voters went to a white Democrat. This white candidate lead the primary with 39.5 percent of the votes. His runoff opponent was an African-American Republican who had received only 15.5 percent of the votes, edging an African-American Democrat for the other runoff position by three votes. The white Democrat was subsequently favored over the African-American Republican by both the white and the African-American voters in the runoff. He received about 70 percent of the votes cast by whites and 57 percent of those cast by African-Americans.

[138] White Democrats in the House voted in favor of the plan by a vote of 35 to 18 (with three absent), while House Republicans were almost unanimously in favor, 26 to one. In the Senate, white Democrats split eight to eight over the plan, while Republicans supported it by a vote of 12 to two.

[139] *Louisiana v. Hays*, 114 S. Ct 2731, 512 U.S. 1230 (1994); 115 S Ct. 2431, 515 U.S. 737 (1995).

continue in the main to be the choice of black voters and white candidates of white voters with limited crossover; where a second district can be created in a way that respects Louisiana's districting traditions and provides black citizens a reasonable opportunity to elect candidates of choice; and a redistricting plan...which fails to respond to any of these realities.[140]

The 1996 elections were conducted using the court-ordered plan. The result left Louisiana with only one African-American congressman. Mr. Jefferson was reelected without opposition in the Second District. No African-Americans candidates contested any of the six white districts. Mr. Fields, who had been placed in the new Sixth District along with Republican Richard Baker, declined to run for reelection. Conservative Republican incumbents were easily reelected in two of the so-called "influence districts"; Jim McCrery winning 71.4 percent of the vote in the new Fourth District and Baker 69.3 percent in the Sixth. There was no incumbent in the remaining "influence district," the Fifth, which was won by another conservative Republican, John Cooksey. Cooksey won 58.3 percent of the vote in a runoff against Democrat Francis Thompson, who in the primary had edged former Republican congressman Holloway out of the runoff by 1.0 percentage point (27.7 percent to 26.7). White Republican incumbents were unopposed in the First and Third Districts, while a Democrat, Chris Johns, won an open seat in the Seventh District in a runoff with another Democrat. (A Republican candidate failed to make the runoff in the Seventh by only 12 votes.)[141]

CONCLUSION

Redistricting following the 1990 census resulted in significant increases in African-American representation in Louisiana. The number of state House districts in which African-Americans constituted a plurality of the registered voters increased from 15 to 26; the number of such districts for the state senate increased from five to nine. African-Americans have been elected in all but two of these districts, and in no others. On two other statewide governing bodies, the Board of Elementary and Secondary Education and the Public Service Commission, the number of majority African-American districts increased

---

[140]Letter from Deval L. Patrick, Assistant Attorney General, Civil Rights Division, U.S. Department of Justice, to E. Kay Kirkpatrick, Director, Civil Division, Department of Justice, State of Louisiana, August 12, 1996. The Louisiana Legislative Black Caucus had asked the Supreme Court for a rehearing on the issue of mootness because the state's plan had not been precleared under section 5 at the time the Supreme Court dismissed the appeal in *Hays*. See Petition for Rehearing, Louisiana Legislative Black Caucus, et al., vs. Hays, et al., No. 95-1682 (July 19,1996). Following the Justice Department's denial of preclearance, the Supreme Court invited the plaintiffs in *Hays* to respond to this petition (___ U.S. ___, October 7, 1996).

[141]Billy Tauzin, the incumbent in the Third District, switched his party affiliation to the Republican Party, as did Jimmie Hayes, the incumbent in the Seventh. Hayes did not contest the House seat, however, but ran instead for the U.S. Senate seat vacated by Democrat J. Bennett Johnson. Hayes failed to make the runoff in the Senate election.

from one to two and from zero to one, respectively. African-American candidates were also elected in each of these districts, and only these districts.

The number of majority African-American districts for the U.S. House increased only temporarily, however. There were two such districts, rather than one, in the elections of 1992 and 1994, but the number reverted back to one for the election of 1996. As a consequence of the different district configurations, there were two African-Americans serving in the Louisiana congressional delegation from 1993 through 1996, but only one when the 105th Congress opened in 1997. This tight correspondence between the racial composition of electoral districts in Louisiana and the race of the representatives of those districts reflects the fact that race is the major demographic division in the state's politics. No other demographic variable divides Louisiana voters like race. These increases in African-American representation would not have occurred if Louisiana had not been subject to the preclearance requirement of the Voting Rights Act. The gains in the state legislature and on BESE resulted directly from the Justice Department's refusal to preclear dilutive redistricting plans for these bodies, and the gains on the Public Service Commission and in the U.S. House resulted from the perception that the creation of new majority African-American districts would be necessary to obtain preclearance. These gains, none of which resulted in the underrepresentation of the state's white majority, are now at risk, however, as a result of the Supreme Court's objections to the benign application of racial considerations in the districting process.

The Supreme Court's recent decisions in redistricting cases have elevated the importance of districting criteria such as compactness, respect for preexisting political boundaries, and the recognition of nonracial "communities of interest" above that of racial fairness. This has occurred despite the fact that these criteria have not been well defined, clearly measured, nor rigorously applied in the past. The representational benefits that result from the application of these criteria, moreover, are at best ambiguous (see Engstrom, 1995). Yet these criteria may now be employed as justifications for limiting the ability of African-Americans to elect candidates of their choice.

Louisiana's experience with congressional redistricting highlights this consequence of the recent Supreme Court decisions. One of the most obvious "communities of interest" in the state, its African-American minority, has had its representation reduced in order to accommodate districting criteria that relate far more to a concern for "appearances"[142] than to the "fair and effective representation" of the residents of the state.[143] If this revision in the hierarchy of districting goals is to be permanent (five of the justices currently on

---

[142]See *Shaw* v. *Reno*, 509 U.S. 630, 647 (1993).

[143]In *Reynolds* v. *Sims*, the Supreme Court declared that "achieving fair and effective representation for all citizens" is the basic aim of apportionment or districting. 377 U.S. 533, 565-566 (1964). See also *Gaffney* v. *Cummings*, 412 U.S, 735 (1973).

the Court support it while the other four are vigorously opposed), then Louisiana should reevaluate its continued reliance on the single member district election system.

Louisiana is a state in which African-Americans suffer from the effects of both past and present discrimination. It is a state in which a majority of the white voters, as recently as 1990 and 1991, have voted for a former Grand Wizard of the Ku Klux Klan and self-identified "racialist", David Duke.[144] It is a state, in short, in which racial fairness needs to be a preeminent representational goal. Without state authorities feeling that the Voting Rights Act requires the benign consideration of race in their redistricting decisions, that goal is not likely to be attained through the medium of single member districts. Racial fairness, to put it bluntly, has never been a "traditional districting principle" in Louisiana.

A federal court in Georgia, while invalidating a majority African-American congressional district in that state, noted that "The time has come to contemplate more innovative means of ensuring minority representation in democratic institutions," and admonished the Georgia legislature to find "new solutions" to the problem of minority underrepresentation.[145] Louisiana's legislature would be well advised to do the same. Other types of election systems, equally if not more democratic than single member districts, could be adopted to elect Louisiana's delegation to the U.S. House, as well as other representative bodies with governing authority in the state. These other systems would be more likely to result in "fair and effective representation" than single member districts drawn under the new constraints imposed by the Supreme Court.

Modified multi-seat election systems, such as limited, cumulative, or preference voting, could be employed to provide opportunities for not just geographically concentrated groups to elect candidates of their choice, but geographically dispersed groups as well.[146] Minority electoral opportunities within these systems are not dependent on, or are at least much less dependent on, where district lines are placed. Race therefore does not have to be "the predominate factor" in the design of districts within these arrangements (see, e.g., Engstrom, 1992). The larger districts associated with these electoral arrangements allow districting criteria-like compactness and respect for political subdivision boundaries to be accommodated without necessarily having an adverse impact on minority electoral opportunities. Indeed, these systems are more likely to provide opportuni-

---

[144]This occurred in the U.S. Senate election of 1990 and the gubernatorial election of 1991 (see Rose, 1992, and Rose with Esolen, 1992).

[145]*Johnson* v. *Miller*, 864 F.Supp. 1354, 1393 (S.D. Ga. 1994).

[146]A federal statute currently requires the use of single member districts in elections for the U.S. House of Representatives. 2 U.S.C. sec. 2c (1988). Legislation has been introduced, however, to permit the use of multi-member districts, provided they are combined with limited, cumulative, or preference voting systems. See the Voters' Choice Act (H.R. 2545) introduced in the 104th Congress by Rep. Cynthia McKinney of Georgia.

ties for actual "communities of interest," whether geographically concentrated or not, to be directly represented within legislative bodies (Morrill, 1996). The goal of "fair and effective representation" in Louisiana is much more likely to be realized through these types of arrangements than through single member districts drawn under the districting constraints now imposed by the United States Supreme Court.

CONGRESSIONAL REDISTRICTING IN NORTH CAROLINA

Patrick J. Sellers, David T. Canon, and Matthew M. Schousen

CONGRESSIONAL REDISTRICTING IN NORTH CAROLINA was thrown into the center of the national debate over minority redistricting in the summer of 1993 when the Supreme Court severely criticized the state's plan as a racial gerrymander that "bears and uncomfortable resemblance to political apartheid" [*Shaw v. Reno* 1993]. The confluence of forces that produced this controversial plan make it one of the most interesting and instructive case studies of the politics of empowering minority voters through racial redistricting. Ambitious African-American office-holders, self-interested Republican party officials and Democratic House incumbents, Section 5 pre-clearance procedures, computer technology, and white backlash against the new black districts all played important roles in the unfolding drama.

Though it is impossible at this early juncture to assess the long-term effects of redistricting in North Carolina, the most obvious short-run consequence was to redistribute power toward black voters, black community leaders, and black politicians. In a state that had not elected a black to Congress since 1899, two new black-majority districts attracted a very strong field of African-American politicians who gave a new voice to black voters. Some of the black candidates campaigned with the explicit message that "it's our turn." Even the black candidates who attempted to create biracial coalitions, such as Mel Watt in the 12th District and Willie Riddick in the 1st, gave more attention to the concerns of black voters than had been true in previous elections.

The other short-run effect of the redistricting process was confusion and uncertainty. The state legislature debated ten redistricting plans, including one that was passed (plan #6) only to be rejected by the U.S. Justice Department. A second plan (plan #10) was written into law only weeks before the beginning of the filing period for congressional primaries. A lawsuit filed by the North Carolina Republican Party extend the filing period by one week, but a federal judge dismissed the suit ruling that the new plan met federal requirements. The uncertainty affected potential candidates who were deciding whether to run, incumbents who were trying to map out reelection campaigns, and voters who did not know which district they were in. After a series of court cases, including two decisions by the Supreme Court, the district lines remain unsettled as lawmakers return to the drawing board to create new districts for the 1998 elections.

Ultimately two African-Americans were elected in 1992 and reelected in 1994 from two newly created black-majority districts. Voters chose Mel Watt in the new 12th District and Eva Clayton from the redesigned 1st District. Both candidates won hotly contested primaries in 1992 (Clayton was forced into a runoff with a white candidate, Walter Jones, Jr., the son of the late incumbent who had represented the district for 26 years), but easily defeated the token Republican opposition in the fall. Both representatives have been prominent in congressional politics, especially Clayton who was elected president of the huge freshman class in the 103rd Congress.

This essay explores the forces that shaped congressional redistricting in North Carolina. We begin by examining the strategic and legal context of redistricting. We then turn to the interplay between the competing groups, individuals, and courts as the various redistricting plans unfolded. We conclude by pointing out the significance of the redistricting process in North Carolina's congressional elections.

SETTING THE STAGE

The Players

The conflicting preferences of individuals and groups involved in redistricting created a protracted process that was heated, confusing, and controversial. Civil rights advocates viewed the addition of one House seat in North Carolina (from 11 to 12) as an opportunity to create one or more minority-controlled districts. Progressively ambitious African-American state lawmakers looked forward to carving out districts that would provide outlets for their ambition. U.S. House incumbents and other state legislators with more static ambition hoped to protect their existing turf, or even make it more secure.

The two major political parties also had a stake in the redistricting process, hoping to strengthen their respective positions in the state. The Democrats held a seven to four advantage in congressional seats in 1990. The party hoped to keep that edge, strengthen their incumbents' seats, or even increase their advantage. Republicans, on the other hand, wanted to use the creation of minority districts to concentrate Democratic voters in a few districts, thereby weakening Democratic incumbents in neighboring districts and increasing Republicans' chances to pick up a few seats.

Other groups such as the National Association for the Advancement of Colored People (NAACP) and the American Civil Liberties Union (ACLU) urged the creation of a second black district. But as we will discuss below, there was a split within the black community over the wisdom of this strategy. Technical support for redistricting largely came from the state legislature, but some Democratic House incumbents also got involved with the help of a New York-based political action committee. The National Committee for Effective Congress (NCEC), known for supporting Democrats, provided a computer and data base that enabled House members to draw up potential district maps. When asked about the Democrats' reliance on the NCEC, Rep. Tim Valentine (D) responded that North Carolina congressmen were not paying for the services; the national Democratic Party had engaged the NCEC to help "handle redistricting issues." Rep. David Price (D) added that "it helped to have our own resource so if we wanted to suggest something we weren't totally out to lunch" [*News and Observer*, August 25, 1991]. A prominent North Carolina group, the Black Leadership Caucus (BLC), did not get involved in the redistricting process. But, the group played an active role in the recruitment process by trying to ensure that blacks would be elected in the new black-majority districts.

Legal Requirements for Redistricting

The North Carolina General Assembly was keenly aware of the political and legal pressures to create at least one black-majority district. Twenty-two percent of the state's 6.6 million people are black. Consequently, Republicans and some black leaders argued that the state should have two and perhaps even three black-majority districts (.22 times 12 equals 2.64 districts). This view received support from the 1982 Voting Rights Act Amendment, and its subsequent interpretations by the Supreme Court and the Justice Department. The 1986 Supreme Court decision *Thornburg v. Gingles* made it possible for a minority group to claim discrimination if "(i) it is sufficiently large and geographically compact to constitute a majority in a single-member district, (ii) it is politically cohesive, and (iii) its preferred candidates are usually defeated as a result of bloc voting by a white majority" [Research Division, North Carolina General Assembly 1991, 10; also see Chapters 2, 3, and 5 of this volume].

The first condition established in *Gingles*, size and compactness, created some problems for the redistricting committee. Unlike some northern states, such as Illinois or Michigan, or even southern states such as Georgia, North Carolina does not have an African-American population that is concentrated in large urban areas. Instead, the minority population is scattered in smaller urban areas such as Charlotte, Durham, Raleigh, Wilmington, Winston-Salem, and Greensboro and in the rural northeastern part of the state. Only three counties are at least 50 percent black, and when added together they are not nearly large enough to comprise a single congressional district (Figure 1). Therefore, North Carolina lacked the luxury enjoyed by many states of debating the minimum percentage of black voters needed to guarantee the election of an African-American (see Chapter 1 of this volume). Instead, the North Carolina legislature had to use creative cartography to scrape together enough black voters to make a single black-majority district.

The Research Division of the state legislature advised the redistricting committees that they could ignore the compactness standard: "Neither the State nor

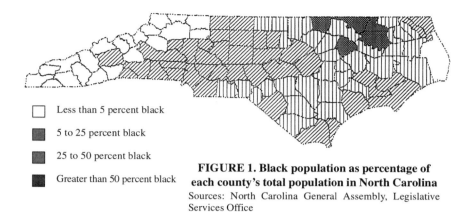

Less than 5 percent black

5 to 25 percent black

25 to 50 percent black

Greater than 50 percent black

FIGURE 1. Black population as percentage of each county's total population in North Carolina
Sources: North Carolina General Assembly, Legislative Services Office

federal constitution requires districts to be compact. Critics often refer to the lack of compactness of a particular district or group of districts as gerrymandering, but no court has ever struck down a plan merely on the basis that it did not appear to be compact" [Research Division, North Carolina General Assembly 1991, 12]. The legislature certainly followed this advice with impunity![1]

While North Carolina's new districts are not geographically compact, they meet the other two conditions laid out in the *Gingles* decision. The black vote in North Carolina is cohesive; between 90 and 95 percent of black voters cast ballots for Democratic candidates in statewide elections. As noted above, it has also been more than 90 years since a black North Carolinian has served in Congress (George H. White, from 1897-1901). This legacy made it clear to the redistricting committees that any redistricting plan had to include at least one black-majority district.

One final legal question had to be considered by the redistricting committees: the legal status of partisan gerrymanders. The redistricting committees wanted to protect Democratic incumbents, but they were concerned that contorted districts lines would not be viewed favorably by the courts. Historically the Court has been reluctant to enter this "political thicket," acknowledging that redistricting is an inherently partisan process. In *Davis v. Bandemer* [1986], however, the Court recognized the justiciability of partisan gerrymander claims, but they failed to overrule the Indiana redistricting plan. The Court argued that an electoral system is discriminatory only when "it consistently degrades a voter's or group of voters' influence on the political process." Fur-

---

[1]For an excellent discussion of different measures of compactness and how different values are traded off in the redistricting process see Butler and Cain [1992, 60-90], Niemi, Grofman, Carlucci, and Hofeller [1990]; and Young [1988]. Neimi et al., argue that compactness will become a more important standard in redistricting cases in the 1990s. This prediction may be coming true as Justice O'Connor noted in *Shaw v. Reno* [1993] that "appearances matter" in the creation of districts. However, in the 1995 decision, *Miller v. Johnson*, the Court did not emphasize the importance of "appearances."

thermore, the aggrieved party must prove intent to discriminate and actual discriminatory effects over a period of at least two elections [Research Division, North Carolina General Assembly 1991, 11]. The consequences of this vaguely worded decision are unclear. Some argue that the partisan gerrymanders could be struck down if a stronger case is presented than the one used in Indiana. Others say that the discrimination suffered by parties must be comparable to that experienced by minorities in the South [Butler and Cain, 1992, 33-36]. The Court seems to be leaning toward the latter interpretation. In *Badham v. Eu* [1988], the Court refused to strike down the 1981 California redistricting plan, claiming that the standard of unconstitutional discriminatory effect had not been met. Two rulings by the Supreme Court concerning the North Carolina plan affirm this position but raised new doubts concerned racial gerrymanders. We are getting ahead of our story.

ACT I—THE DRAMA UNFOLDS: PLAN #6

Early in 1991, the North Carolina General Assembly appointed redistricting committees to take up the task of creating the new state legislative and congressional districts. In addition to the legal constraint to create a new black-majority district, the committees were confronted with a political task—to protect as many Democratic incumbents as possible. As the redistricting drama unfolded, one other factor grew increasingly important: unlike many states that have a bipartisan process, North Carolina's redistricting process was completely dominated by the Democrats who firmly controlled the state legislature and thus the redistricting committees (Senate: 19 Democrats to 7 Republicans, House: 19 Democrats to 9 Republicans). Furthermore, the Republican governor, Jim Martin, was the only state executive in the nation without veto power.

Members on the redistricting committees were not motivated solely by broad partisan goals. Some professed altruistic aims of creating fair districts, but others were blunt about their desire to make sure that the redrawing of congressional district lines did not adversely affect their own districts. Still others had their sights on higher office, either in moving from the state House to the state Senate or moving from the state level to the national level. [personal interviews, August, 1991-March, 1992].[2] One important feature of both the House and Senate committees was the prominent role of black lawmakers. Six of the ten black House members and three of the five black senators (all Democrats) sat on the redistricting committees. Thus, 60 percent of the black House and Senate members were on the redistricting committees, compared with only 20

---

[2]We conducted 37 interviews with 34 people, including newspaper reporters, Democratic Party county chairs, members of the General Assembly, a member of the U.S. Congress, and most of the candidates running in the black-majority districts. The interviews ranged in length from twenty minutes to more than two hours, with an average length of about one hour. All but five of the interviews were face to face. Most of the interviews were conducted from August 1991 to May 1992. These interviews were initially conducted as part of an in-depth case study of the candidate emergence process in North Carolina's 1st congressional district in 1992. [See Canon, Schousen, and Sellers, 1994].

percent of the whites in the House (22 of 110) and 49 percent of the whites in the Senate (23 of 47). Of the nine black lawmakers on the two committees, two actually ran for a U.S. House seat in 1992 (Mickey Michaux and Thomas Hardaway) and three others were often mentioned in the newspapers as strong potential candidates (Toby Fitch, Howard Hunter, and Frank Ballance). We discuss the influence of these black lawmakers on the creation of black congressional districts later in the chapter.

Two initial questions confronted the redistricting committees as they considered how to create at least one minority district: 1) which minority groups should be considered in creating the new district? and 2) where would the district or districts be located? Answering the first question was relatively easy. Unlike states such as California or Texas, North Carolina does not have a large Hispanic population. Since the state is only one percent Hispanic and one percent Native American, it was clear that the focus of minority representation would be on African-Americans. Although Republicans and the NAACP made a brief appeal for three minority districts (two black majority and one black and American Indian majority), their argument fell on deaf ears because most members of the black community rejected the notion that Native American and African-Americans jointly represent a cohesive minority community.[3]

Answering the second question was also relatively straightforward as long as only one black district was created. According to state Rep. Thomas Hardaway (D), a black member of the House redistricting committee, the obvious place to put the district was in northeastern North Carolina because that is the "black belt" of the state (see Figure 1). In July and August of 1991, the state House and Senate worked out the details of redistricting plan #6, which included a single black-majority congressional district in the northeastern part of the state (see Figure 2).

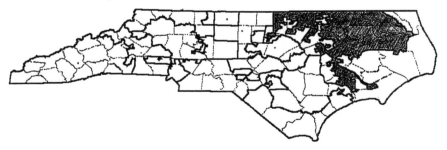

FIGURE 2. Redistricting Plan #6
Proposed by Democrats, June 1991. Approved by General Assembly, September 1991. Rejected by Justice Department, December 1991.

---

[3]While the North Carolina legislature did have one Native American member (State Rep. Adolph Dial), the Indian community did not have much interest in congressional redistricting. They were active in trying to create more native American Indian majority districts at the state level [personal interview, October 14, 1993].

The contorted shapes of the resulting congressional districts, however, provoked immediate controversy. Political commentators poked fun at the shape of the new minority-majority district, calling it "modern art," "political pornography," "a bug splattered on a windshield," and the work of an "eight month old baby" or a "chimpanzee playing with a felt-tip pen." Underlying the humor were serious concerns about the new district. In what would be an uneasy alliance, the Republican Party, the NAACP, and the ACLU criticized the new plan for serving the interests of congressional incumbents more than the interests of minorities.

Republican legislators argued that the Democrats did not create a second black majority congressional seat because they wanted to preserve as many safe Democratic seats as possible. Under plan #6, the seven districts that were currently controlled by Democrats were likely to remain so. The Republican would also keep their four districts, and the new 12th district would have a majority of Republican voters. Thus, the balance of power would still favor the Democrats, but now the margin would be seven to five instead of seven to four.

As an alternative to the Democratic plan, the Republicans suggested creating a second black-majority district in the southern part of the state running from Charlotte to Wilmington. The obvious motivation behind this concern for minority representation is the partisan advantage gained by concentrating the traditionally strong Democratic black vote in two districts. Under this Republican alternative, called "the Balmer Plan" for its author, state Rep. David Balmer, the GOP would create two strongly Democratic black-majority districts and protect all four Republican incumbents (see Figure 3). In addition, three other districts would be dominated by conservative white voters who have a history of voting for Republicans such as Senator Jesse Helms and Governor James Martin. Consequently, Republicans could have held a seven-to-five majority in the North Carolina congressional delegation under this plan.

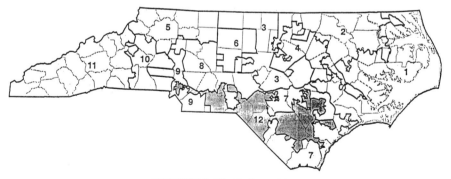

FIGURE 3. The Balmer Plan
Proposed by Republicans, June 1991. Rejected by General Assembly, September 1991.

While they could not support the Balmer plan, members of the black community were torn between Democratic party loyalty and the desire to create more than one black-majority district. Moderate black state legislators, such as Daniel T. Blue, the first black Speaker of the North Carolina House, argued that a single black-majority district would be the best way to increase power for minorities. He worried that a second black congressional seat could isolate blacks on "political reservations"[4] and "provide major gains for Republicans" [*News and Observer*, December 20, 1991]. Even progressively ambitious black lawmakers such as Mickey Michaux and Toby Fitch, who would probably have benefited from a second minority district, favored the Democratic plan for a single black-majority district. But in an interview with the *Durham Herald-Sun*, Michaux admitted that the single minority district was not popular in the black community, and so most black lawmakers kept a "low profile" in the debate [*Durham Herald-Sun*, January 8, 1992]. Leaders in the black community who were not so closely tied to the Democratic Party, such as Mary L. Peeler, executive director for the North Carolina branch of the NAACP, argued that "...we wanted to see a maximization of the black voting strength in North Carolina" [*News and Observer*, August 18, 1991]. The ACLU joined the NAACP in rejecting the single black majority congressional district plan. For these groups, the question was one of fairness. In a state that was 22 percent black, one of twelve House seats was simply not enough. Despite this resistance, the General Assembly finally approved plan #6 and its single black district in September.

Because the Republican governor of North Carolina lacked veto power, plan #6 became law. Progressively ambitious candidates begin gearing up for the 1992 congressional primaries. Consistent with the expectations of ambition theory and previous work on the candidate-centered nature of congressional campaigns [Jacobson and Kernell, 1983; Canon, 1990], quality challengers emerged in the two new districts that did not appear to have incumbents running. In the newly created 12th congressional district, the absence of an incumbent and the fact that the district had more registered Republicans than Democrats quickly attracted two quality white Republican candidates. N.C. Rep. Coy Privette (R) announced that he would be running in the 12th. His motivation for entering the race stemmed from the fact that the new district included his current state House district (Cabarrus County) and the county in which he was raised (Iredell County). Joining Privette in the Republican primary was Alan Pugh, an aide to Governor Martin. Pugh quit his job, rented a headquarters in the 12th district, hired a campaign manager and a political consultant, and raised over $10,000 over the next several months [*Charlotte Observer*, May 14, 1992].

Activity in the new 1st district was also heavy, but it was mostly on the Dem-

---

[4]This debate also rages in the black community nationally. Carol Swain echoes Blue's sentiment, "The evidence suggests that the present pattern of drawing district lines to force blacks into overwhelmingly black districts wastes their votes and influence (and)...place(s) them in districts where their policy preferences can become separated from the majority in their states" [1993, 235].

ocratic side. The newly created black-majority district had one potential problem for progressively ambitious black candidates: a white Democratic incumbent. The new 1st was carved out of parts of four old congressional districts that had produced well-entrenched incumbents who almost never faced major challengers. In 1991, it seemed likely that these incumbents would run for reelection in the following year, with the possible exception of Walter Jones, Sr., the 1st district incumbent. A challenge to Jones was out of the question, so prospective candidates were forced to engage in a high-stakes guessing game. Although Jones, the most senior member of the North Carolina congressional delegation, claimed that he was not retiring, most legislators and political elites in the state believed that he would. At 78 years of age, the incumbent suffered from poor health and had to be wheeled through the halls of Congress by an aide. Furthermore, if Jones retired by 1993, current law allowed him to convert his $300,000 campaign war chest to personal use. Those predicting that Jones *would* retire also reasoned that the redistricting committees would never have included so much of his old district in the new 1st if he *were not* retiring. A fellow U.S. Democratic House member told us that Jones initially accepted the redistricting plan, but he thought that the state redistricting committees should have had more contact with him. This U.S. House member seemed to imply that the state legislature simply assumed that Jones was retiring without consulting him, thus creating a "humiliating" situation for Jones [personal interview, August 8, 1991]. Jones officially announced his retirement on October 5, 1991, citing the new black-majority district as the primary reason for his decision [*News and Observer*, October 5, 1991].

The clearest signal to state lawmakers that Jones would retire, however, was the fact that he took no interest in the redistricting process. Danny Lineberry, a political correspondent covering the redistricting story for the *Durham Herald-Sun*, attended many of the redistricting meetings and saw quite a few congressional staffers, but never saw a staff member from Walter Jones' office. Although Jones publicly indicated his displeasure with his new district and never suggested that he planned to retire, one state lawmaker told the *News and Observer*: "Other congressman were heavily involved in trying to protect their districts, but Mr. Jones made no telephone calls and sent no letters objecting to redistricting proposals" [*News and Observer*, September 25, 1991].

We asked all potential black candidates who were mentioned by newspaper reporters or political leaders in eastern North Carolina whether Jones was a factor in their decision to run in 1992 [See Canon, Schousen, Sellers, 1994]. All of these politicians told us that Jones would have a strong impact on the election if he ran, but none of them believed he would run. For example, Warren County Commissioner Eva Clayton said she thought from the beginning that Jones was going to retire. State Sen. Frank Ballance claimed that Jones' wavering about retirement was merely an attempt to help his son, Walter Jones, Jr., by discouraging others from entering the race [personal interviews, spring and summer 1991].

Although it was too early to file, a number of strong black candidates began organizing their campaigns in the new 1st district. Included in this list of black candidates were Ballance, Clayton, State Rep. Toby Fitch, State Rep. Thomas Hardaway, State Rep. Howard Hunter, Reverend Staccato Powell, and Willie Riddick, a long time aide to Walter Jones Sr.

ACT II--BACK TO THE DRAWING BOARD: PLAN #10

In compliance with the "preclearance" provision of Section 5 of the Voting Right Act of 1965, the General Assembly sent plan #6 to the Justice Department. Democratic lawmakers and party leaders were confident that the plan would be approved. Republicans and members of the black community, however, filed complaints urging rejection of the plan on the grounds that it violated the rights of minorities.

On December 19, 1991, just 17 days before the beginning of the filing period for congressional elections, the Justice Department rejected the North Carolina redistricting plan. The ruling cited the "unusually convoluted" shape of the black-majority district and the fact that the plan created only one such district. Some critics argue that the Justice Department went beyond the intention of the 1982 Amendment [*News and Observer*, 1\19\92, 10A]. Speaker Blue said, "I think that what the Republicans are trying to do is corrupt the Voting Rights Act to the extent they can go beyond what its goal and mission is and use it for their political advantage" [*News and Observer*, 1\5\92, 5A]. Particularly, the Justice Department ignored the "geographic compactness" condition of *Gingles*, thus going beyond the prevention of minority vote dilution to an actual proportional representation test for minority representation in the U.S. House. The possible partisan motivation is clear when one considers that the creation of black-majority districts usually helps the Republican Party by concentrating Democratic voters in a few districts [Brace, Grofman, and Handley, 1987].

Back in North Carolina, the legislature called a special December 30 session to address the Justice Department's decision. Democratic lawmakers knew that a second black-majority district in the southern part of the state could deeply hurt their party, so they scrambled to find a less painful alternative. Some wanted to fight for the current plan in court. John Merrit, an aide to U.S. Rep. Charles Rose (D), proposed plan #10 that created a second minority district by connecting black voters in Charlotte and Durham by a thin line that traveled northeast along Interstate 85 (Figure 4), rather than from Charlotte to Wilmington as the Republicans proposed in the Balmer plan (Figure 3).

Democrats found the Merrit plan appealing because it created a second minority district without diluting Democratic power across the state. In fact, they believed that the new plan might actually increase the number of Democratic seats in the House. In addition to creating another minority district, the plan kept the seven currently Democratic seats in Democrats' hands. Three Republican

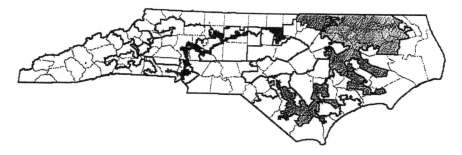

FIGURE 4. Redistricting Plan #10
Proposed by Democrats, January 1992. Approved by General Assembly, January 1992. Approved by Justice Department, February 1992.

incumbents would be placed in even safer Republican strongholds, while the fourth Republican, U.S. Rep. Charles Taylor, would end up in a marginally Democratic district. Thus, under the Merrit plan, Democrats hoped to win nine of the twelve congressional seats in North Carolina. As it turned out, in 1992 the Democrats won only eight seats because Taylor won his reelection bid.

Republicans had been assuming that the second new black district would be in the southern part of the state, and plan #10 left them stunned. They complained bitterly about the new district's odd shape. They had a point; the new "I-85" black-majority district was literally the width of the interstate in some places. In Guilford County, for example, drivers in the southbound lines would be in the Republican-controlled sixth district, while drivers in the northbound lines would be in the new black-majority 12th district. As they traveled down the interstate to Randolph County, the congressional districts actually "changed lanes." Southbound drivers were now in the 12th district, and northbound drivers were in the sixth district [*News and Observer*, January 12, 1992]. The strange "u-turn" on the interstate was necessary to keep the sixth district contiguous (without the lane-change, the 6th would have been cleanly bisected by the 12th district).

Farther south on I-85, drivers traveling either north or south were in the 12th, but the moment they turned onto any exit ramp (on either side of the road) they were in the 9th [*Charlotte Observer*, January 27, 1992]. This strange configuration led Democratic candidate Mickey Michaux to say that in some counties a driver could travel down I-85 with his doors open, and kill everyone in the congressional district. He also joked that it should be an easy district to campaign in because he could meet all the voters by simply stopping at all the rest stops along the interstate.

Plan #10 retained the black-majority district (district 1) in eastern North Carolina. However, the basic outline of the district moved east and south with tentacles extending into Wilmington and Fayetteville. The most significant change for the eastern black-majority district was the exclusion of urban Durham, which accounted for 15.5 percent of the northeastern district under plan #6. The district lines were considerably more contorted than in the earlier plan: the perimeter of the new 1st district is 2,039 miles long, and it contains nine whole counties and parts of 19 others!

The primary filing period was due to open on January 5, but lawmakers postponed it until February 10. Top-ranking Democratic state lawmakers held private meetings with the North Carolina Democratic congressional delegation, state black leaders, and representatives from the NAACP and ACLU. The groups agreed that the Merrit plan was acceptable, and after working out the details, the General Assembly approved plan #10 on January 24, 1992.

ACT III—THE FINAL CHALLENGE BEFORE THE PRIMARIES

Democratic leaders were apologetic while Republicans were apoplectic about the plan. House Speaker Blue said, "It is an ugly plan. I will not stand here and tell you these are the most symmetrical, prettiest districts I have ever seen....There are some funny looking districts." But Blue argued that Democrats were forced to make the new plan because of the Justice Department's ruling [*News and Observer*, January 19, 1992]. Republicans called the plan "idiotic" [*News and Observer*, January 29, 1992]. They offered an amendment to add a third black-majority district, but it was rejected in a party-line vote. State Republican Party chairman Jack Hawke said his party would urge the Justice Department to reject plan #10. If they did not, the Republicans would file suit in court. But in spite of this Republican threat, the Justice Department approved the plan on February 7, just three days before the delayed beginning of the filing period. State legislators immediately said that the 1992 primaries would go on as scheduled, with the filing period running from February 10 to March 2.

Hawke made good on his promise to file suit on behalf of the State Republican Party. He argued that a third black majority congressional district should be added and that the General Assembly of North Carolina has created a "government of the Democratic incumbent, by the Democratic incumbent, for the Democratic incumbent." The suit specifically charged that the new plan violated the voters' rights to "freedom of association and to fair and effective representation" [*News and Observer*, February 29, 1992]. When the suit was filed, the court left open the filing deadline for congressional candidates until the case could be heard. At a hearing in Charlotte, North Carolina on March 9, a three-member U.S. District Court dismissed the case and ruled that the filing period would close immediately. Although the Republicans appealed to the Supreme Court to overturn the lower court decision, Chief Justice William Rehnquist rejected the request on March 11. For the moment, the court challenge was over. When the dust settled, the filing period had ended, and the primary campaign was on.

THE NEW 1ST AND 12TH CONGRESSIONAL DISTRICTS

In plan #10, the final redistricting plan, the North Carolina General Assembly pieced together the new 1st congressional district from parts of four old congressional districts. Each of the old districts contained diverse constituencies. The original 1st, 3rd, and 7th districts included relatively poor farming counties, several sizable military bases, and prosperous coastal counties which relied heavily on tourism for economic growth. The old 2nd district contained both rural counties and the city of Durham, whose urban constituents made up 22.6 percent of the district's population.

The new 1st district is more homogenous than the original four. The plan removed Durham, the coastal areas that rely on tourism, and the military bases from the 1st district. The remaining counties are covered largely by tobacco fields and drying sheds, and their populations rely largely on farming for income. While some businesses have built plants in the new district, many of the available jobs provide low wages. Political leaders from the area frequently devote attention and resources to increasing economic development. In addition, the district clearly meets the Justice Department's requirements for minority representation. In the new 1st district, blacks form a majority of the total population (57.3%) and voting age population (53.4%). Not surprisingly, almost 90 percent of voters in the 1st district are registered Democrats.

The new 12th district is, in several ways, similar to the new 1st. The Democrats have a four to one advantage over Republicans in the 12th, and over 50 percent of its population (56.6%) and voting age citizens (53.3%) are black. Also like the 1st, the 12th was pieced together using bits of several counties and other congressional districts. No single North Carolina country is wholly contained within the snake-line district that winds it way through parts of ten counties and seven of the eleven old congressional districts (the 12th contains parts of districts 2, 4, 5, 6, 8, 9, and 10).

While they do have some similarities, the two black-majority districts also have some fundamental differences. The 1st is primarily a rural district (58% of the people are in rural areas), while the 12th is an urban district made up of voters from Charlotte, Greensboro, Winston-Salem, and Durham (93.2% urban, according to the 1990 U.S. Census). The two districts also differ on a socioeconomic level. The 1st is the poorest district in the state, while 12th tends to be in the middle. For example, in the 1st district only 57.8 percent of those 25 years of age or older hold high school diplomas. In the 12th, the figure is 65.6 percent, which is closer to the 70 percent state average. In median house value and median household income the same holds true. The 1st is last in the state, with a median house value of $46,100 and a household income median of $18,226. The 12th has a median house value of $58,400 (state median $65,800) and household income median of $23,068 (state median $26,647).

The two districts also differ in terms of black political organization. In the 12th, the two largest segments of voters hail from Charlotte and Durham. Both cities have strong black political organizations and each city produced a strong quality black candidate in 1992 (Mel Watt from Charlotte and Mickey Michaux from Durham). In the 1st, as Eva Clayton told us, there are no black political organizations to rally voters or help to get a candidate's message out. Clayton added that she was sorry to hear that Durham was no longer going to be in the 1st district because at least in Durham voters show up at political events. Clayton said that she was tired of going from small town to small town speaking to only a handful of people at a time. When we asked her whether she would like Durham in the 1st if it meant Mickey Michaux would be in the race, she replied "You're darn right." Part of her strategy had been to use Durham as a place to get name recognition, money, and media exposure.

ASSESSING THE STRATEGIC CONTEXT OF REDISTRICTING

Black state lawmakers played an important role in the redistricting process. As noted above, three of the five black state senators served on the Senate Redistricting Committee, and six of the ten black state House members served on the House Redistricting Committee. Of these nine black lawmakers, five of them either ran for a congressional seat or strongly considered running. All five were considered strong candidates. What is most interesting, however, is that until the Justice Department required a second black-majority district, none of these five potential candidates publicly supported plans that called for the creation of two or three black-controlled congressional districts [personal interviews and *Durham Herald-Sun*, January 8, 1992]. Black lawmakers generally believed that a second minority district would limit the effectiveness of black politicians and increase the power of Republicans across the state.

Nevertheless, the redistricting process was subject to manipulation by both blacks and whites. As with many legislative committees, the redistricting committees performed much of their work in informal, "behind-the-scenes" settings, with limited publicity. Consequently, it is difficult to uncover the potential candidates' efforts to draw the district lines in ways that furthered their electoral interests (especially because candidates do not readily admit to self-serving strategic behavior).

In one case, however, we were told by two sources that a black lawmaker did try to influence the redistricting process. According to a newspaper reporter and a politically active Democrat, Thomas Hardaway created the Merrit plan. As the story goes, Hardaway, presented his idea for the "I-85" district to Merrit. The congressional staffer then refined it and presented it as his own plan. Hardaway denies that he was the source of the plan, but if the story is true, it is an interesting twist to the tale.[5]

Under plan #6, Hardaway would have run against Mickey Michaux in North Carolina's new 1st congressional district. Our interviews in eastern North Caro-

---

[5]Another version of the source of the Merrit plan came from Glenn Newkirk, a staffer from the redistricting committee, who claims that a Republican intern concocted the plan at a public access terminal. This story was not confirmed by an independent source; furthermore, it does not make sense that a Republican invented the plan because it was the perfect solution to the Democrats' dilemma of having to create a second black district while protecting their incumbents (or if a Republican did think of it, he or she certainly should have not discussed it with anyone!).

lina revealed that Michaux did not enjoy extensive support in the rural areas of the 1st district; however, he was considered by many political commentators to be the front-runner.

Michaux ran unsuccessfully for an open seat in the old second district in 1982, narrowly losing a runoff election to Tim Valentine after defeating Valentine and one other white candidate in the primary (Michaux had 44 percent, Valentine had 33 percent, and James Ramsey won 23 percent of the vote). Therefore, some of the state's black leaders believed that Michaux deserved the seat that he almost won. During the summer of 1991 Michaux expressed active interest in running for the 1st district congressional seat.[6] Under the Merrit plan, Michaux's home town, Durham, was placed in the new 12th district. As a result, Michaux did not run in the 1st, and the path was cleared for Hardaway and other ambitious state representatives in the 1st district. However, even without Michaux to contend with, Hardaway still could not win the Democratic primary in eastern North Carolina.

Walter Jones, Jr., was at the center of several other redistricting machinations. Jones, Jr. believed that he had been punished in the drawing of state House lines because of his "independent" record in the state House.[7] His old district was split in half, making it much more difficult for him to win reelection to his state house seat. Jones Jr.'s plan to run for his father's seat was complicated when his hometown (Farmville) was removed from the 1st congressional district, after being included in the initial versions of the redistricting plans that were debated in January. Immediately before the final committee vote on the plan, Jones introduced an amendment to return Farmville to the 1st district. The amendment passed with the approval of all nine committee Republicans and several blacks on the committee, who, according to Jones, were later criticized by others in the black community. When the redistricting plan reached the House floor, Jones said that a black representative introduced an amendment to take Farmville back out of the 1st district. The amendment was defeated, but the vote had definite racial overtones, according to Jones. Although he had voted against all the redistricting plans up to this point, he felt compelled to vote for this final one. Jones said that the people of Farmville had suffered enough (with their state House district split), and that the General Assembly had treated his people and his father unfairly.

Potential candidates on the redistricting committee were not the only ones trying to influence the district lines for personal electoral gain. The staff of the current congressional incumbents closely monitored the redistricting process and in some cases played an important role. A local reporter saw incumbents' staffers at many redistricting committee hearings, and one member of the North Carolina

---

[6]We did not find any evidence that Michaux actively resisted the move of his home from the 1st to the 12th district. Michaux may have been aware of his limited rural support and believed that his chances election would be better in a more urban district such as the 12th.

[7]In 1988 Jones, Jr. joined a group of Republicans and independent-leaning Democrats in an overthrow of the established House leadership. Since that time, he has sponsored numerous bills to reform state government and has voted against the House leadership on important legislation.

congressional delegation acknowledged that "we all had people at the redistricting meetings, and we all made suggestions concerning our districts." Private memos that were later made public indicate the extent to which North Carolina Democratic members of Congress were kept informed of the redistricting committee's activities. In one memo, Congressman Price writes that his new district is "satisfactory" so long as East and West Pittsboro are added and parts of Alamance County are removed. In another memo, a staff member from State Senate Redistricting Committee Chairman Dennis Winner's office asks U.S. Rep. Martin Lancaster (D) whether moving several precincts in Duplin and Onslow Counties from the second to the third district would be acceptable. The memo states that the idea is just part of a "draft plan for discussion" and suggests that Lancaster not share the information with others [*News and Observer*, August 25, 1991]. Most significantly, as we pointed out earlier, the staff of U.S. Rep. Rose played an important role in the formulation of the final redistricting plan that the Justice Department approved.

WHITE BACKLASH—*SHAW V. RENO*

After the 1992 election, five white North Carolinians filed a suit [*Shaw v. Reno*, 1993] arguing that the creation of a black majority district violated their 14th Amendment rights to equal protection of the laws. The plaintiffs argued that the North Carolina plan was a racial gerrymander that "violated their constitutional right to participate in a 'color-blind' electoral process" [*New York Times*, June 29, 1993]. The Supreme Court, in a 5-4 ruling, lambasted congressional districts that are based solely on racial composition. Justice Sandra Day O'Connor, writing for the majority, argued that "A reapportionment plan that includes in one district individuals...who may have little in common with one another but the color of their skin bears an uncomfortable resemblance to political apartheid." Unfortunately, the decision created tremendous confusion because it neither ruled in favor of the plaintiffs, nor in favor of the current redistricting plan. O'Connor indicated that the Court was not pleased with the Justice Department's interpretation of the Voting Rights Act (that states must create minority districts whenever physically possible) and remanded the case back to the federal district court. The Court, however, refrained from ruling on the constitutionality of the Voting Rights Act itself.

Shaw v. Reno left open the possibility that the district court could accept the current racially gerrymandered districts, if it can be shown that the districts "further a compelling governmental interest." The district court took up that challenge and upheld the North Carolina districts on August 1, 1994, in *Shaw v. Hunt*. In a rambling decision that is more than one hundred pages long, the district court held that the districts withstand strict scrutiny because they were narrowly tailored to address previous discrimination, and because the Voting Right Act makes the districts necessary. The Court added that the creation of a second district did not constitute a "quota," but rather is a "goal." Part of the reasoning used in *Shaw v. Hunt* was rejected in the more recent *Miller v. Johnson* decision from Georgia [June 29, 1995]. After the Miller decision, the *Shaw v. Hunt* case was appealed to the Supreme Court, and on December 5, 1995 the Court heard the case for a second time.

In a decision handed down on June 13, 1996 the Supreme Court reversed the lower court's decision by declaring North Carolina's 12th district to be unconstitutional. Although the appellants claimed that both minority-majority districts (the 1st and 12th) were unconstitutional, the Court ruled that none of the appellants lived in the 1st district and thus lacked standing to argue the constitutional merits of that district.

The state of North Carolina argued that although race was a prominent factor in its creation of the 12th congressional district, three "compelling state interests" were the primary driving forces for the creation of the new minority-majority district. The state claimed that they were helping to eradicate the effects of past discrimination and complying with sections 2 and 5 of the Voting Rights Act. In a relatively short majority opinion (19 pages), the Court made it clear that North Carolina needed to show that the creation of the 12th district served a "compelling state interest" and "was narrowly tailored to achieve that interest." In a 5 to 4 decision the Court rejected the state's claims. The ruling, however, did not address the question of whether compliance with the Voting Rights Act, under proper conditions, can be a "compelling state interest." In other words, just as in the *Miller* decision, the Court did not decide whether states can use the Voting Rights Act to justify the creation of minority-majority districts.

The exquisite irony of this case is that the North Carolina state legislature initially got into the mess because the Justice Department (under Republican President George Bush) argued that they had not given race *enough* weight in drawing district lines. The conservative wing of the Court then criticized the legislature for giving race *too much* consideration. The current state of law and its interpretation by the Supreme Court leave state legislatures in the uncomfortable position of being sued by black voters if they do not take race into account when redrawing district lines, and being sued by white voters if they are too aggressive in creating minority-majority districts. The question that North Carolina's state legislation must address once again is, "How aggressive is 'too aggressive'?"

THE IMPACT OF REDISTRICTING

The profound changes in North Carolina's congressional districts created a new strategic context for the black community. David Perlmutt of the *Charlotte Observer* claims that "Never in North Carolina has a state or federal election drawn so many black candidates—and shaped a debate so central to black voters in a number of the state's major cities" [*Charlotte Observer*, April 12, 1992]. For this reason many in the black community considered the redistricting process a great success [*Charlotte Observer*, April 12, 1992].

Samuel Moseley, a political scientist at North Carolina A&T State University, argued that qualified black politicians such as Mickey Michaux of Durham simply could not win before the new black-majority districts were created. "It was clear here, that we had a man (Michaux) who was black and qualified and who could not win. After all these years of frustration to see the tide turn to a level playing field is gratifying" [*Charlotte Observer*, April 12, 1992]. (Moseley is referring to Michaux's unsuccessful bid for a U.S. House seat in 1982).

Black politicians also understood the fundamental change that the redistricting process produced. Thomas Hardaway, a black state Rep. who ran in the 1st district, put it this way:

> What we have here is a situation in which blacks have been excluded because whites have written the laws to exclude black participation. They have dammed up the flow to both candidates and voters. Well, the floodgates are open. There are many people who have been waiting for this opportunity [personal interview, March 8, 1992].

Although the redistricting process provided new opportunities for ambitious black politicians and black voters, it also had some serious short-term costs for other candidates. The two quality white Republicans who decided to run in the Republican leaning 12th district under plan #6 where forced out of the race when plan #6 was rejected by the Justice Department and the 12th became a second black-majority district. Coy Privette ended up in the 8th district running against the strongly entrenched nine-term Democratic incumbent, Bill Hefner. Alan Pugh, who had quit his job to run, decided to bow out completely and vowed to refund prorated shares of all contributions given to him [*Charlotte Observer*, May 14, 1992].

Within the black community the late formation of the districts and the uncertainty surrounding their exact location created several problems. In the 12th, all four Democratic candidates got off to a late start. It became difficult for the candidates to get their message out because they lacked sufficient time to organize fund-raising for purchasing TV and radio spots. This gave the advantage to Mickey Michaux and Mel Watt. Michaux was advantaged because he had already decided to run under plan #6 when Durham was in the black-majority district in the eastern part of the state. Watt was in a relatively strong position because he had managed Harvey Gantt's successful campaign for mayor of Charlotte and unsuccessful campaign for Jesse Helms's Senate seat. Consequently, Watt already had a strong political organization in Charlotte.

The late start also influenced the level of voter interest in and awareness of the campaign. The Democratic candidates in the 12th held a series of debates to get their messages out, but the largest meeting in Charlotte drew only 35 people. In another debate, in Salisbury, only five people who were not directly connected to one of the campaigns showed up. Although the two strongest candidates, Michaux and Watt, were able to air radio ads right before the primary, all four of the candidates claimed that it was an "uphill" battle to get their message out to the voters [*Charlotte Observer*, April 12, 1992]. Similar problems were created by the shortened campaign season in the 1st district.

The 12th district is over 80 percent Democratic, and all four of the Democratic candidates were black. These two facts meant that no matter who won the Democratic primary, a black politician would almost certainly be representing the 12th district. The same could not be said of the 1st, where Walter Jones, Jr., could have taken advantage of a divided black vote and a united white vote to win the new black-majority district. This was especially true because the percentage of vote necessary to win a primary outright had recently been reduced from 50 percent to 40 percent. Ironically, this change was intended to help elect more black candidates, but it nearly ended up putting Walter Jones Jr. in office.

Black leaders in the 1st district recognized the potential collective action problem and acted quickly to try to unify behind a single black candidate (see Chapter 4, this volume). The Black Leadership Caucus (BLC), which is organized by congressional district across North Carolina, met on three occasions. Representatives from each county were to cast weighted votes (one voter per 1,000 black voters) for their preferred candidates. However, the process broke down when one candidate, Willie Riddick, was seen by the other candidates as having unfairly manipulated the meetings to his advantage. Two of the leading candidates did not even attend one of the meetings, and others did not have their supporters there. Thus, the process lacked legitimacy and several of the candidates refused to bow out when they did not receive the BLC endorsement.

Four black candidates, Frank Ballance, Howard Hunter, Paul Jones, and Toby Fitch, dropped out to enhance the probability of electing an African-American. However, while Ballance dropped out before the endorsement vote, Hunter, Jones, and Fitch, were pursuing a mix of altruistic and self-interested strategies. Fitch was most explicit about his motives. As co-chair of the redistricting committee, Fitch led the effort to create a majority black district. He believed that the entrance of several black candidates into the race would split the black vote and threaten the election of a black member of Congress. Thus, he did not want to have a part in undermining the collective goal that he worked for a year to achieve; in an interview he emphasized that this was his only reason for deciding to quit the race. At the same time, though, he recognized that by dropping out, his political standing in the 1st district black community improved dramatically. If Jones, Jr. defeated the current group of black candidates, Fitch believed that the black community would unite behind him in 1994 and turn out the first-term white incumbent. The fact that Eva Clayton, a black, won the election did not temper his desire to run for Congress. A local reporter told us that Fitch was seriously considering challenging Clayton in the 1994 Democratic primary [personal interview, October 14, 1993].

The fears of Fitch and other black leaders were almost realized in the 1992 Democratic primary. The white candidate, Walter Jones, Jr., received the greatest number of votes and was only 2.6 percentage points short of winning the primary outright. In the runoff election, however, with a united black community behind her, Eva Clayton defeated Jones by a 55-45 percent margin.

The 1992 congressional elections sent two African-Americans to the U.S. Congress from a state that had not sent a black representative to Capitol Hill since 1899. The results of the 1994 election suggest that the trend will continue. In 1994 the only substantial reelection challenge to Mel Watt and Eva Clayton occurred in the courts. On March 9, 1994 a federal court ruled, in a 2-to-1 decision, that the congressional elections in the two minority-majority districts could go forward even though those districts were being challenged in federal court. Thus, the May primary went forward with Watt and Clayton running unopposed. The next challenge to the two African-American House members came on August 1, 1994, when a three-member federal court ruled [in *Shaw v. Hunt*] that the new black-majority districts passed constitutional muster. Although Watt and Clayton both faced Republican challengers in November, both incumbents won easily. Watt won 66 percent of the district vote against weak Republican challenger Joseph Martin. Clayton faced Republican challenger Ted Tyler again and won 61 percent of the vote.

Walter Jones, Jr. was also back on the campaign trail in 1994. After his defeat in 1992, Jones changed his strategy. He switched parties and congressional districts to run as a Republican in North Carolina's 3rd district. A large portion of the 3rd was made up of the pre-redistricted 1st, which his father held from 1966 to 1992. Although Jones did not live in the district, he had strong name recognition and ran a shrewd campaign, linking the four-term Democratic incumbent, Martin Lancaster, to President Clinton. Jones flooded the district with television spots showing Clinton and Lancaster jogging together and citing Lancaster's support of Clinton's 1993 budget and tax packages. Jones won the general election with 53 percent of the vote.

Jones' win was one of many Republican victories in 1994. While the party won throughout the country, they fared particularly well in the South. The North Carolina congressional delegation shifted from a nine-three advantage for the Democrats to an eight-four advantage for the Republicans. Not surprisingly, redistricting turned a number of safe Democratic districts into marginal or Republican-leaning districts. The two black-majority districts, however, remained safely in Democratic hands.

For the black community in the 1st and 12th districts in North Carolina, redistricting was a success in many ways. The creation of the two black-majority districts sparked political interest within the black community, created avenues for progressively ambitious black politicians, and elected and reelected two black lawmakers to the U.S. House of Representatives. But for some African-Americans, the victory has been bittersweet. While black representation has increased, the creation of minority-majority districts has helped the Republicans increase their power throughout the South and may have helped them gain control of the

House of Representatives [Lublin, 1995a]. Thus, the question of whether an increase in black representation in a Republican controlled House is preferable to fewer black representatives in a Democratically controlled chamber continues to fester in the African-American community.

LEGISLATIVE AND CONGRESSIONAL DISTRICTING IN SOUTH CAROLINA

Orville Vernon Burton

IN ONE OF THE MANY IRONIES OF HISTORY, in the late nineteenth century the South Carolina Democratic Party constructed black districts to minimize the influence of African-Americans and the Republican vote, just the opposite of what has occurred in late twentieth century South Carolina where the creation of black majority districts has been an initiative of African-Americans and the Republican Party.[1] Redistricting was needed after the 1990 census, but as late as May 1994, while all other states had settled their redistricting plans, South Carolina still had not passed a plan. While North Carolina, Georgia, Florida, Texas, and Louisiana all were being challenged for congressional districts "unfair" to white voters, South Carolina was still attempting to prove its proposed plans were not unfair to African-Americans.[2]

In a bizarre tale, the redistricting that was accomplished in May 1992 in the hands of a federal court was then vacated by the Supreme Court on 12 June 1993. The Supreme Court remanded the case to the lower court for further proceedings,[3] and the case went back to the three-judge panel which had submitted the plan. These three judges, U.S. 4th Circuit Court of Appeals Judge Clyde Hamilton and U.S. District Court Judges G. Ross Anderson and Falcon Hawkins, reconvened on a humid afternoon 13 July 1993 in the Strom Thurmond Federal Court House in the state capital of Columbia. The judges, scarcely concealing their annoyance at having been summarily reversed by the Supreme Court, stated that federal judges such as they should not be making reapportionment decisions, that redistricting was a state issue, and the legislature should do it. They gave South Carolina law makers a deadline: if by 1 April 1994 the state had not enacted, and the Justice Department approved, a new redistricting plan, they would take up the matter again at that time. When asked what would happen with a vacancy if a representative were to die in office, the court replied that there were plenty of lawyers in the legislature and they could

---

[1]For a discussion of Districting in late nineteenth century South Carolina, see George Brown Tindall, *South Carolina Negroes, 1877-1900* (Columbia: University of South Carolina Press, 1952).

[2]Columbia *State* 23 May 1994, B1.

[3]*Statewide Reapportionment Advisory Committee v. Theodore,* 113 S. Ct. 2954 (1993), and *Campbell v. Theodore,* 113 S. Ct. 2954 (1993).

figure it out. Thus, South Carolina had no legal redistricting plan in effect.

How did South Carolina's redistricting come to such an impasse? Although both the South Carolina Senate (offering 10 black-majority districts) and the House (offering 28 black-majority districts) devised reapportionment plans after the 1990 census, neither approved the plan of the other. A resolution to extend the session to finalize redistricting failed, and the General Assembly adjourned in June 1991 without a plan. Neither did the governor call a special session of the legislature to handle redistricting, although urged by some to do so. A coalition of African-American leaders, known as the Statewide Advisory Reapportionment Committee (SARC), held a news conference with the Legislative Black Caucus and argued that the cost of a special session would be much less than a lawsuit.

Between the 1991 and 1992 sessions, Republican Governor Carroll Campbell, at the request of the state Senate, offered a plan that provided for 14 black-majority Senate districts. According to the *State*, South Carolina's most influential newspaper, the Senate never responded to the Governor's plan. Veteran white Democrat Marshall Williams, President Pro Temp of the Senate, commented that "the Campbell plan was unacceptable." Marshall explained, "We passed out the best bill that could be passed out for the Senate....But the governor kept saying that ours was a protectionist bill and all that kind of junk." Williams concluded, "Let them sue."[4]

They did. Governor Campbell believed that the Republican Party would benefit from a lawsuit. A national Republican strategy of using the federal courts for redistricting recognized that, except for the four years of President Jimmy Carter, the last quarter century of federal judicial appointments had been by Republican administrations, and the last twelve years under Reagan and Bush had seen particularly partisan appointments.[5] The *State* reported: "Republicans, backed up by the U.S. Justice Department, have embraced a strategy nationally of increasing minority districts. That also has the effect of increasing the number of districts the GOP can win." The paper contended that the Republican strategy "could be particularly effective in South Carolina" where "the electorate is increasingly polarized, with white voters more likely to favor Republicans."[6]

House Speaker Robert Sheheen, a Democrat, criticized Campbell's participation in "reapportionment for purely political purposes." Sheheen accused the Governor of trying "to strengthen the Republican Party....That's his only agenda."[7] Republicans and Campbell countered that "white Democrats in the Legislature have effectively abandoned black citizens to protect their seats."[8]

---

[4]The Columbia *State*, 27 September 1991, 1B and 6B.

[5]"Update on the Republican Strategy of Using the Federal Courts for Redistricting," *Voting Rights Review* (Summer-Fall, 1992) 6.   See also Briefing Paper, prepared by Ellen Spears "The Republicans Go to Court: A Review of Republican Legal Strategies on Minority Rights in the Area of the Voting Rights Act" (Atlanta: Southern Regional Council, 1992). See also The Columbia *State*, 24 January 1992, 1B.

[6]The Columbia *State*, 12 January 1992, 12A; see also ibid., 6 February 1992, 1B.

[7]The Columbia *State*, 11 October 1991, 7B.

In light of this stalemate, on 4 October 1991 Michael Burton, executive director of the South Carolina Republican Party, along with other South Carolina voters
(the *Burton* plaintiffs), filed to have a three-judge district court order interim redistricting.[9] The *Burton* plaintiffs alleged that the existing districts violated the
United States Constitution's provision for one-person one-vote, as well as the Voting Rights Act's Section 2 prohibition against vote dilution of minorities. In addition, the *Burton* plaintiffs argued that the state would not have time before the
1992 elections to redistrict and submit the new district plans to the Justice Department for preclearance as required by Section 5 of the Voting Rights Act.

On 23 October 1991 U.S. Democratic Congressman Robin A. Tallon joined
the Republican *Burton* suit, moving to intervene as a plaintiff. Tallon, whose
sixth Congressional District was commonly recognized as the district to be made
into a majority African-American congressional district, criticized the Congressional plan passed by the State Senate which split 26 of the state's 46 counties, as
"so bad, hell wouldn't have it." The state House Speaker, Democrat Robert Sheheen, retorted that the "main constituency he's protecting is Robin Tallon"; he
characterized Tallon's intervention as "a move toward self-preservation."[10] Confusing partisan lines even further, on 28 October Neil A. Vander Linden et al.,
mostly Republican voters from Dorchester and Berkeley Counties allied with
Republican state senator Mike Rose, moved to intervene as defendants, as did the
Democratic South Carolina Senate.[11]

African-Americans in South Carolina brought suit on 31 October 1991. The
Statewide Advisory Reapportionment Committee (SARC), co-chaired by A.M.E.
Bishop Frederick C. James and State Senator Herbert U. Fielding, the chairman
of the South Carolina Legislative Black Caucus, included most notably the South
Carolina State Conference of the NAACP Branches, the legislative Black Cau-
cus, the Organization of Black County Officials, the Organization of Black
Municipal Officials, other African-American elected officials, the Black Baptist
Organization, various unincorporated associations of private individuals (some
pastors representing their churches), "and other statewide church and civic
groups."[12] This coalition represented, in the words of Greenville dentist William
Gibson, then national director of the National Association for the Advancement
of Colored People (NAACP), "the most united front that we've seen in redistrict-
ing since blacks became involved in the 1970s." The lawsuit was filed on behalf
of SARC by National NAACP General Counsel Dennis Hayes, Staff Attorney
Willie Abrams, and Columbia African-American attorney John Roy Harper II.
They were joined by another veteran voting rights attorney, South Carolina native
Laughlin McDonald, Director of the American Civil Liberties Union Foundation

---

[8]The Columbia *State*, 12 January 1992, 12A.

[9]*Burton v. Sheheen*; 793 F.Supp. 1329 (D.S.C. 1992).

[10]Columbia *State*, 27 October 1991, 3B.

[11]3 November 1991 the additional parties were ordered joined.

[12]The Greenville *News*, 3 November 1992, 10A, col. 2; see also "Stand Up and Let Out Voices Be
Heard," SARC flyer.

(ACLU) Southern Regional Office, so that the litigation for SARC was a joint venture between the NAACP and ACLU. Throughout all phases of reapportionment, SARC and its attorneys also worked closely with the South Carolina legislative black caucus. Throughout the redistricting process the NAACP was working at state and local government levels. The *State* newspaper commented that "Ten years ago, the state NAACP was not so actively involved in reapportionment." Nelson

Rivers, executive director of the state NAACP, explained that "Last time, they (blacks) got ripped off, because there was nobody on a statewide basis, looking out for them in reapportionment."[13]

The *SARC* complaint was similar to the *Burton* complaint and alleged that South Carolina violated black rights under Section 2 of the Voting Rights Act and the First, Thirteenth, and Fifteenth Amendments and Article I, Section 2 of the United States Constitution, as well as Article III, Section 3 of the South Carolina Constitution.[14] The defendants in the *SARC* case were Republican Governor Carroll A. Campbell, Jr., Lieutenant Governor and president of the State Senate Democrat Nick Theodore, Speaker of the South Carolina House of Representatives Democrat Robert Sheheen, and James Ellisor, the Executive Director of the State Election Commission. On 13 November 1991 the *SARC* case was consolidated with the *Burton* Republican case, and will be referred to here as *SARC/Burton*.[15]

In January of 1992, the week the General Assembly was to reconvene, the *State* newspaper, in an article entitled "Clock is running on remap," conducted a survey of the General Assembly concerning redistricting. One hundred ten of the 165 state legislators responded to the question of whether the legislature should create the maximum number of House and Senate districts in which black candidates are likely to be elected; 68 percent agreed, 19 percent disagreed, and 13 percent did not respond. In the same poll, 73 percent disagreed and 26 percent agreed that the legislature was "hopelessly deadlocked over reapportionment" and that the "federal court needs to step in and finish the job."[16]

The panel of three federal judges originally gave a deadline of 30 January 1992 for the General Assembly to complete reapportionment, then gave an extra two weeks, then postponed to 10 February a hearing to decide if the lawmakers

---

[13]The Columbia *State*, 25 June 1992, 2B.

[14]*Statewide Reapportionment Advisory Committee et al.*, Appellants, v. *Nick Theodore et al.*, Appellees, in The Supreme Court of the United States, October Term, 1992, Jurisdictional Statement, pp. 2-3.

[15]The Democratic Party of South Carolina and first-year Democratic legislator Kimberly Burch from Chesterfield, the one House member whose district had been eliminated in the House plan, also intervened in the *Burton/SARC* case, but Burch was later dismissed by consent. In addition, on 12 December 1991, Bufort Blanton, et al. alleged that the South Carolina county legislative delegation system was unconstitutional and sued the *Burton/SARC* defendants and certain members of the state General Assembly. This case was consolidated with the redistricting cases on 14 January 1992. However, before trial, the case concerning the constitutionality of the county delegation system was separated from the redistricting cases. *Blanton v. Campbell*, C.A. No. 2:91-3635-1 (D.S.C.).

[16]The Columbia *State*, 12 January 1992, 1A.

were gridlocked. When the General Assembly reconvened on 14 January, state legislators accomplished what they had failed to do in 1991: they adopted a redistricting plan based on the 1990 census for both the South Carolina House and Senate.

Two plans introduced by the House members of the Black Caucus were defeated. Nevertheless, SARC/NAACP lawyers were willing to accept the General Assembly's compromise plans because SARC believed that their best strategy would be to get a plan before the Justice Department for approval where SARC/NAACP could make their case.[17] Black Caucus chairman State Senator Herbert U. Fielding stated: "We feel we have a much better chance legislatively and going through the Justice Department than going through the courts." SARC believed that the Governor's and the Republican's plans packed African-Americans into districts, diluting their influence in nearby majority-white districts which would tend to then vote Republican.[18]

Traditionally in redistricting, the South Carolina General Assembly sent three separate redistricting bills, for the House, Senate, and U.S. Congress, to the Governor for approval. After the 1990 census, however, the Democrats, who controlled the powerful state Senate, insisted on packaging the three into one bill. Since Republican Governor Carroll Campbell was willing to pass the House plan devised under his hometown ally, House Judiciary Chairman Republican David Wilkins, the Democrats hoped this tactic would preclude Campbell from vetoing the Senate plan.[19] It did not.

On 29 January 1992, Governor Campbell vetoed the General Assembly plan. He argued that neither plan created a sufficient number of majority African-American districts as required by Section 2 of the Voting Rights Act.

Nelson Rivers, state executive director for the NAACP, specifically asked Republican House members to help override Campbell's veto. He explained SARC's strategy to take the plans passed by the General Assembly "and let the Justice Department uphold the rights of black people."[20] Campbell, however, made supporting him in a veto fight a supreme test of party loyalty, and the General Assembly sustained the Governor's veto.[21] With Republican Governor Campbell and a Democratic majority in the General Assembly at such complete odds, all parties agreed at the hearing on 10 February 1992 that the situation was deadlocked. The judges set court hearings on reapportionment plans for 19 February 1992. A three week trial began.

All parties to the 1992 redistricting case stipulated that the current South Carolina legislative and congressional districts were malapportioned according to the 1990 census; the population had grown and was continuing its shift from rural

[17]The Columbia *State*, 24 January 1992, 5B.

[18.]The Columbia *State*, 11 October 1991, 7B, see also 1B.

[19]The Columbia *State*, 12 January 1992, 12A.

[20]The Columbia *State*, 3 May 1992, 1B.

[21]The Columbia *State*, 16 January 1992, 3B. The Senate had only 11 Republicans of 46 members; the House had 42 Republicans of 124 members.

to urban and suburban areas. South Carolina's black population had increased from 948,623 to 1,039,884. However, South Carolina was one of only four states where the proportion of minority population had not increased. Because of white migration to South Carolina, the actual percentage of the black population had decreased from 30.4 to 29.8 percent, and the black voting age population had decreased from 27.3 to 26.9 percent.

The political problems following the 1990 census resembled those following the 1980 census. After the 1980 census, the General Assembly never enacted a plan for congressional districts, so congressional districts drawn by a three-judge court plan in March 1982 were still in effect.[22] In 1981 the General Assembly had redistricted the South Carolina House. However, the General Assembly had only redistricted the Senate following a court-ordered plan in 1984. Not until a special election to fulfill an unexpired term of a state senator on 25 October 1983 was the first African-American elected to the South Carolina Senate in the twentieth century: I. DeQuincey Newman, a grand old man of the South Carolina Civil Rights Movement. At that time the NAACP and the U.S. Department of Justice sued to move the South Carolina Senate to single-member district elections. In 1984 when the General Assembly did implement a court-ordered plan, South Carolina became the last southern state senate to acquire single-member districts or elect African-Americans in regular elections.[23]

By 1992, however, the districts for all three bodies, drawn under the 1980 census, had unacceptable overall deviations using the 1990 Census. The senate districts displayed a deviation of 63.2 percent, and the house districts a ridiculous total deviation of 113.9 percent; the congressional districts had an 8.3 percent total deviation.

As part of the *SARC/Burton* case, the various parties involved in the redistricting cases proposed plans to the three-judge district court for the congressional, senate, and house districts.[24] Attorneys for *SARC* and *Burton* alleged that plans for redistricting must comply with the Voting Rights Act, both Sections 2 and 5. Section 2 applies nationwide and prohibits the use of voting procedures that "result" in discrimination, i.e., are racially unfair. Section 5 applies only in certain jurisdictions, such as South Carolina, with long histories of discrimination in voting and has been held by the Supreme Court to prohibit use of voting procedures which are retrogressive, i.e., which make minorities worse off than they were before enactment of a new practice. A new voting procedure, such as a

---

[22] *S.C. State Conference of Branches of the N.A.A.C.P. v. Riley*, 533 F.Supp. 1178, 1183 (D.S.C. 1982).

[23] *Graham v. South Carolina*, Civil Action No: 3:84-1430-15 (D.S.C. July 31, 1984).

[24] The people who drew plans and testified were Dr. John C. Ruoff for SARC/NAACP, Mark Elann, counsel to the Governor, for the Governor and the Republicans, Robert J. Sheheen, Speaker of the House who consulted with legislative delegations from the House and did a lot of the actual drawing himself, for the House, Marva Smalls, Congressman Robin Tallon's chief of staff, for Tallon, George Fowler, who worked for the state demographer, Bobby Bowers, for Lt. Governor Nick Theodore and amended the plans drawn by the Senate. The Senate had no expert testify, but had plans drawn by a professional staff.

redistricting plan, may be non-retrogressive but still result in discrimination. Accordingly, *SARC* presented evidence proving substantial black vote dilution, including expert testimony as to racially polarized voting, to show that all the factors outlined in *Thornburg v. Gingles*[25] and the 1982 Senate Report that came out of the amendment to the Voting Rights Act were present in South Carolina. An expert for the Republicans presented similar and even more recent analysis of South Carolina elections that demonstrated high racial bloc voting and dilution of the African-American vote. The parties in the case stipulated that "since 1984 there is evidence of racially polarized voting in South Carolina."[26]

Issues argued in federal court were the extent to which African-American voters had the equal opportunity under Sections 2 and 5 to elect candidates of their choice and whether redistricting plans complied with the one-person one-vote standard. *SARC* attorneys claimed that retrogression should be determined by comparing the proposed plans to demonstrate if the plans "provided an undiluted level of minority voting strength."[27] The three-judge court rejected SARC's basis for determining retrogression and ruled that SARC's basis "enshrines the notion that the Voting Rights Act insures proportional representation by race."[28] Instead, the judges used a retrogression standard based upon the plans adopted after the 1980 census. The atmosphere of these hearings was hostile; Dr. Theodore S. Arrington, an experienced expert witness for the Republicans, characterized the attorneys for the defendants as "waspish, intemperate, rude, arrogant, and abusive to virtually every witness." This expert noted, "I have never seen such intense partisan and racial bickering."[29]

The three-judge district court argued that since it, rather than the State of South Carolina, devised the plans, they were not subject to Section 5 preclearance. Still, the court claimed to be aware of the Section 5 requirement that redistricting should not abridge "the right to vote on the basis of race."[30] Moreover, the judges decided (erroneously, as the Supreme Court later held) that the hearings proceeded under Section 5 of the Voting Rights Act and therefore ruled that Section 2 did not fully apply to the redistricting plans. The judges also ruled from the bench they would allow no party a Section 2 hearing on any plan the court adopted. The judges neither understood nor considered that a remedy that fully complied with the racial fairness standard of Section 2 of the Voting Rights Act

[25]478 U.S. 30, 37, 45 (1986).

[26]*Burton v. Sheheen,* 793 F.S. 1329, 1334 (D.S.C. 1992), p. 1334; Solicitor General, Brief for the Untied States as Amicus Curiae, *SARC v. Nick Theodore,* Supreme Court, October 1992, Nos. 92-155 and 92-219, pp. 4, 2. Dr. Theodore S. Arrington was the expert for the Republicans. Dr. John C. Ruoff, James W. Loewen, and Orville Vernon Burton were experts for SARC-NAACP. Nelson B. Rivers III testified for SARC-NAACP about politics in South Carolina.

[27]ibid, p. 10.

[28]SARC Jurisdictional Statement, ibid, p. 10, cites App. 30-31.

[29]Theodore S. Arrington to Dr. Vernon Burton, 5 October 1993, in possession of Burton.

[30]Quoted on p. 9 of the *Statewide Reapportionment Advisory Committee v. Nick Theodore,* In The Supreme Court of the United States, October Term, 1992, Jurisdictional Statement, and cited as in App. 25.

was essential because the *Gingles* conditions prevail in South Carolina.

The plaintiffs never articulated a precise standard for the proportion of a district that needed to be black for an African-American candidate to win. They did make the point, however, that no matter where the level for "reasonable opportunity," the plaintiffs' proposed plans were better than the various legislative plans in moving African-Americans toward equal opportunity to participate and elect candidates of their choice. The plaintiffs emphasized "toward" since none of the plans could pretend to provide full equality of participation.[31]

SARC/NAACP expert Dr. John C. Ruoff analyzed a large number of elections to determine the total percentage of African-American population needed for a candidate of the African-American community to have an 85 percent chance of victory (Ruoff did not have available voting age population data for his analysis). Ruoff determined that, in districts at least 57 or 58 percent black in total population, African-American candidates had won election 85 percent of the time (see table 1). Districts that ranged from 50 to 57 percent black in total population did not provide African-Americans with an equal opportunity to elect candidates of their choice. Statewide, black candidates won only about one-third of the time in these districts. Nevertheless, the court decided that a black voting age population of greater than 50 percent constituted an "opportunity" district for black candidates.

TABLE 1. Elections Won by African-American Candidates, 1980-1992 in 1980 Black Majority Districts with Black Percentage Above and Below 57 Percent

Using 1980 Population

	Total Elections	*African-American Wins*	*African-American % of Wins*
>57%	90	77	86%
50-57%	56	18	32%
Total	146	95	65%

Using 1990 Population

	Total Elections	*African-American Wins*	*African-American % of Wins*
>57%	85	72	85%
50-57%	61	23	38%
Total	146	95	65%

Ultimately, however, the three-judge district court rejected all the proposed plans and constructed its own, using the resources of the state. One of these resources was Bobby Bowers, the longtime state demographer, who receives his

---

[31]Theodore S. Arrington to Dr. Vernon Burton, 5 October 1993, in possession of Burton.

state job by appointment of the South Carolina legislature. An advisor to the court, Bowers was present throughout the hearings. Districts drawn by Bowers, which the court adopted, paid little attention to the plaintiffs' arguments and closely resembled the plans advocated by the state legislature.

All parties, including the court, used computers and mapping software (with the exception of Congressman Tallon, who presented a plan for Congressional districts only). Although some groups had access to larger and faster computers, basically similar computer technology was accessible to all parties because of geographic information systems software available for personal computers.

Until the late 1980s, those who drew redistricting plans had to rely on relatively large census geography (enumeration districts and census tracts) for most of the state. Only in metropolitan areas were data regarding demographic characteristics, such as race or the number of persons of voting age, available at the block level. The only computers available to plan drawers in the 1980s in South Carolina were large and expensive mainframe computers that were owned by government agencies or colleges and universities. Moreover, no geographical information software was readily available for redistricting purposes. As a general matter, redistricting plans had to be drawn by hand on previously published maps.

In the 1990s, however, the redistricting process took place in a new technological environment. Personal computers were widely available and reasonably priced, as were user-friendly redistricting software packages. Moreover, the U.S. Bureau of the Census made census variables available at the block level (and for the existing election precincts) for the entire state in machine readable form. This meant that in the redistricting process, all interested parties could easily draft a variety of alternative districting plans to serve their own interests. As a result, the boundaries of political subdivisions or counties, which had so often served as building blocks for redistricting in the past, were no longer needed, and electoral districts could more accurately conform to the requirements of the one-person one-vote standard and the Voting Rights Act.

The national NAACP provided training to local State Conference members, in particular to State Executive Director Nelson Rivers, so that the South Carolina State Conference could draw maps for its branches within the state. NAACP redistricting expert Sam Walters traveled to South Carolina to aid in designing a computer system.[32] South Carolina Fair Share Executive Director John C. Ruoff worked closely with Rivers and the NAACP, SARC, and the South Carolina legislative black caucus to draw maps and propose various plans.[33]

Although the South Carolina state house and senate, Lt. Governor Theodore, the House, and House Speaker Robert Sheheen objected to creating additional majority African-American seats for their respective legislative bodies, all state policymakers and parties involved in the redistricting suit agreed that a majority African-American congressional district could and should be constructed. Table

---

[32]Dennis Courtland Hayes, General Counsel NAACP to Vernon Burton, 7 June 1993.

[33]Dr. Ruoff has provided us with many of his computations and tables to use in this paper.

2 shows the black proportion of each congressional district proposed by various parties. Republicans actually drew two majority African-American congressional districts, but offered only a plan containing one. The three-judge panel did not rule on whether under the Voting Rights Act it was "required" to create a majority African-American congressional district, but it did construct Congressional District 6 with a 61.8 percent African-American population and a 57.9 voting age black population.[34] Table 3 gives the congressional districts created by the court. Several plans presented at court provided a higher proportion of black voting age population than that implemented by the court. The court's African-American-majority congressional district included all or part of sixteen of the state's forty-six counties. The court drawn congressional plan provided one opportunity and two influence districts for African-Americans.

TABLE 2: Comparison of U.S. Congressional Plans Percent Black in Population

District	1992 Court	SARC/ NAACP	Senate	Lt. Gover- nor	Gover- nor	Repub. Party	House	Sheheen* 1	Sheheen* 2	Tallon
1	20	18	20	20	22	17	25	31	18	24
2	25	21	22	60	24	17	24	36	32	22
3	21	25	24	21	22	50	22	22	21	61
4	20	67	67	20	18	9	20	20	20	19
5	31	19	28	27	26	21	27	32	33	19
6	62	30	18	32	67	65	61	37	55	34
Number of Counties Split to Form a Majority Black District	13	30	25	14	15	NA	11	NA	NA	7

Black majority districts bolded.
*NOT proposed at trial

The bottom row of table 2 shows the number of counties split by the various plans to create a black-majority district. Because the Court argued against splitting counties to increase the number of majority African-American house and senate seats, it is interesting that the court split more counties and precincts in devising a majority African-American congressional district than two of the proposed plans. The majority of these splits increased the African-American population in the majority-black districts. James Clyburn, who handily defeated several

---

[34] According to the Geography Report in the case, the African-American population was 62.15 percent, and the voting age population was actually 58.29 percent. John C. Ruoff to SARC, 12 May 1992, "A preliminary Analysis of Court Ordered Plans," p. 1.

other black candidates in the Democratic primary, was elected over a white Republican in the sixth District in November 1992, the first African-American elected to Congress from South Carolina in the twentieth century.

TABLE 3: U. S. Congressional Districts Created by Federal Court

		Total Population			Voting Age Population		
Dist.	*Total*	*Deviation*	*Black*	*% Black*	*Total*	*Black*	*% Black*
1	581,125	+8	117,022	20.14	427,603	75,536	17.66
2	581,111	-6	147,626	25.40	431,032	98,040	22.75
3	581,104	-13	120,579	20.75	435,406	81,796	18.79
4	581,113	-3	114,332	19.67	437,837	77,739	17.76
5	581,117	0	181,430	31.22	422,294	119,204	28.23
6	*581,133*	*+16*	*358,895*	*61.76*	*412,324*	*238,725*	*57.90*
	3,486,703		1,039,884		2,566,496	691,040	

Table 4 compares the plans for the Senate that were proposed by the various litigators, the plan drawn by the court in 1992 (and the Senate plan finally adopted by the General Assembly in 1995). Both the SARC/NAACP and the Republican Party plans created 13 opportunity districts for African-Americans in the South Carolina Senate. Table 4 presents the number of majority African-American senate districts in total population and voting age population in each proposed plan, the pre-1990 plan, the 1992 court-ordered plan, and the 1995 Senate adopted plan. The court plan provided for 10 majority black voting age population senate districts. Since the existing 1984 district plan with 1980 census data had only seven, and with the 1990 census data only nine, the court found that its plan for 10 districts was not retrogressive. However, plans drawn by others, except that of the Senate and the Senate president, Lt. Governor Theodore, created more black districts than did the court.

Table 5 compares the plans proposed for the House. The court's imposed plan had nine fewer districts with African-American voting age majorities than SARC's and ten fewer than the Governor's and the Republican Party's plans.

In creating the court-ordered districts, the three judges argued that their first precedent was not to violate state policy, which they interpreted as using existing county lines for districts. A careful historical investigation of redistricting in the 1970s and 1980s reveals no such state policy except to comply with the law on one-person one-vote and the Voting Rights Act. Counties had not been used as the basis for redistricting in the House since court ordered redistricting in the 1970s. Furthermore, in 1982 the House plan divided 42 of 46 counties.[35] Astute political and contemporary commentators in the newspapers in the 1970s, 1980s, and 1990s always remarked on the high priority placed on incumbency protection during reapportionment.[36]

---

[35] Orville Vernon Burton, "Report on Reapportionment of the South Carolina House of Representatives," 15 April 1996, for *Able* v. *Wilkins*, No. CV: 3:96-0003 (D.S.C.) in Justice Department Files.

[36] Orville Vernon Burton, "Report on Reapportionment of the South Carolina House of Representatives," 15 April 1996, for *Able* v. *Wilkins*, No. CV: 3:96-0003 (D.S.C.) in Justice Department Files.

TABLE 4. South Carolina Senate Plans

Category	% Black	1984 Plan Based on 1980 Census	1984 Plan Based on 1990 Census	NAACP/ SARC	Senate	Lt. Gov.	Gov.	Repub. Party	1992 Court	1995 Final Senate Plan
*Opport.	57≥	na	na	13	9	7	12	13	8	12
Phantom	50-56	na	na	1	2	5	1	1	3	0
Influence	25-49	na	na	6	13	11	5	2	22	20
Other	<25	na	na	26	22	23	28	30	13	14
≥50% Black Popul.		10	10	14	11	12	13	14	11	12
≥50% Black VAP		7	9	12	9	9	12	13	10	11
Deviation (%)		9.96	63.15	2.74	3.92	3.85	0.01	0.01	1.95	1.9

*Opportunity is 57 percent or elected and African-American from the District to the Senate.

TABLE 5. South Carolina House Plans

Category	% Black	1981 based on 1980 Census	1981 based on 1990 Census	NAACP/ SARC	House	Sheheen	Gov.	Repub. Party	1992 Court	DOJ Objected to 1994 House Plan	Black Caucus Repub. compromise	1994 Final House Plan
*Opport.	58≥	na	na	32	20	18	32	30	19	20	29	29
Phantom	50-57	na	na	0	8	11	3	6	9	7	3	3
Influence	25-49	na	na	23	36	37	15	13	39	38	25	24
Other	<25	na	na	69	60	58	74	75	57	59	67	68
≥50% Black Pop.		26	24	32	28	29	35	36	28	27	32	32
≥50% Black VAP		20	21	32	20	21	33	33	23	21	31	31
Deviation (%)		9.87	113.9	1.95	9.99	2.0	0.98	0.18	1.98	1.99	5.20	5.20

*Opportunity is 58 percent or elected an African-American from the District to the House.

Although they claimed to be cognizant of race, the three-judge panel rejected that they had to judge maps "solely on the effect they have on minority voting rights." The court argued that, although other plans provided for more African-American majority districts, "they do so without regard to any interest but race and without the clear necessity which justifies" a Voting Rights Act remedy.[37] The judges condemned the Republicans and Governor Campbell for partisan motives. "The Republican plan draws lines without regard to any factor except skin color and possibly political affiliation." The judges characterized one Republican Senate district as "overtly racist." The judges also accused SARC of wanting "to defeat white incumbents."[38] The panel announced that it attempted to preserve traditional county and precinct lines as well as "broadly defined community interests."[39] The court wrote "The color of one's skin, in and of itself, does not create a community of interest," anticipating Justice Sandra Day O'Connor's language in *Shaw v. Reno*.[40] Although the judges faulted proposed plans for incumbency protection, the court's imposed plan was criticized as basically an incumbency protection plan.

After all the effort and resources that had gone into redistricting, South Carolina's African-American citizens were greatly disappointed. Nelson B. Rivers III lamented, "The result is a status quo plan, grand incumbency protection."[41] State Senator Kay Patterson, a former chair of the Legislative Black Caucus, commented, "The black community didn't get the seats we were entitled to. I don't think we got a fair shake from the three-judge panel." AME Bishop Frederick C. James and Dr. William F. Gibson, then president of the South Carolina NAACP, released a joint statement as co-chairs of SARC, "The court could have drawn many more predominantly black House and Senate Districts than it did, and the black congressional district could have been much stronger."

With the redistricting plan of the three-judge panel, African-Americans increased their representation by one in Congress, one in the state senate, and three in the house. Nevertheless, they remained underrepresented. The Congressional delegation was 16.7 percent, the senate 15.2 percent, and the house 12.7 percent, while the population was 29.8 percent and the voting age population was 26.9 percent. Continued racial bloc voting, noted among political commentators in newspaper stories, caused African-American candidates to be unable to win except in districts that were majority black, especially more than 57 percent black.

Republicans won more. After the 1992 elections with the new court-ordered districts, the Senate lost five Democrats and gained five Republicans; the House lost eight Democrats and gained eight Republicans. This increase in Republican

[37]The Columbia *State*, 3 May 1992, 12 B. 793 Federal Supplement.

[38]The Columbia *State*, 2 May 1992, 5 A.

[39]The Columbia *State*, 3 May 1992, 12 B; see also 2 May 1992, 5A.

[40]Greenville *News*, 3 Nov. 1992, 1A.

[41]"Update on the Republican Strategy of Using the Federal Courts for Redistricting," *Voting Rights Review* (Summer-Fall, 1992) 6.

seats occurred in the context of a continuing movement of whites toward the Republican party in the state of South Carolina irrespective of the creation of majority black districts. Many in the state of South Carolina believe, however, that the Republican gain could have been much larger if more majority African-American districts had been created. (See Table 6)

TABLE 6: Partisan and Racial Comparison of General Assembly, 1991-1996.

	Democrat*	Republican	Independent	
	HOUSE			
1991	81*	42	1	15*
1993	73*	50	1	18*
current 9-1996	53*	66 (was 68)**	3	25*
*Black **Two districts as of September 1996 are vacant. Republicans held both districts when they became vacant.				
	SENATE			
1991	35*	11	0	6*
1993	30*	16	0	7*
current 9-1996	24*	21	1	6*
*African-Americans are also included among Democrats.				

Knowledgeable South Carolina commentators recognized that neither the GOP nor African-Americans won much. The *State* newspaper announced the three-judge panel decision under the headline, "Blacks, GOP dealt blow by remap." The paper wrote that "by vetoing the General Assembly's redistricting plans, Gov. Campbell rolled the dice in a gamble that the federal courts would make the Republican Party a big winner. But the roll came up snake eyes."[42] The Greenville *News* also noted, "The court-imposed boundaries...essentially mirror what the Democratic-controlled Legislature favored."[43] More than a year later the *State* reiterated that "The plans approved by the three-judge panel were closer to those adopted by the Democrat-led General Assembly than plans with more blacks districts proposed by the GOP and blacks."[44]

Following the 1 May 1992 announcement of the redistricting, Republicans and the Governor stated that, although disappointed, they probably would not appeal to the Supreme Court. Attorneys for SARC, however, did, and Governor Campbell joined as cross-appellant. SARC argued that the three-judge panel had not properly considered Section 2 arguments. Attorney John Roy Harper II explained, "Our position is that the black voters of the state of South

---

[42]The Columbia *State*, 3 May 1992, 1B.
[43]Greenville *News*, 3 Nov. 1992, 1A.
[44]The Columbia *State*, 16 June 1993, 10A.

Carolina were shortchanged by the plan that was drawn by the court."[45]

The Supreme Court asked the Justice Department whether the state's court-drawn election plans complied with voting rights law. In the 7 May 1993 Amicus brief, filed by the Solicitor General, the Justice Department basically agreed with SARC's appeal. According to the *State*, "in a strongly worded brief asking the Supreme Court to make the judges do it over," the Justice Department said that the three-judge panel was in error because they failed properly to consider that the Voting Rights Act "prohibits political processes that dilute black votes."[46] The Justice Department brief stated that the court compounded its error by the "misconception that it was not required to grapple fully with the requirements of Section 2." The three-judge panel "misunderstood the nature of the action before it." The brief specifically questioned the use of 50 percent black voting age population as determining an African-American opportunity district. Moreover, the Justice Department argued the judges "have accorded undue deference to 'state policy' in formulating its plans, placing primary emphasis on preserving county and precinct lines."[47]

The Supreme Court relied on the Justice Department's brief and on 14 June 1993 sent the plan back to the three-judge district court for further hearing on the Section 2 claim.[48] The newspapers all saw this as a victory for African-Americans and possibly for the Republican party. Governor Campbell judiciously commented, "I don't think there would have been a case if the court had felt there were enough minority districts."[49] Local papers throughout the state also questioned whether the three-judge panel had complied with the Voting Rights Act. Both the Columbia and Spartanburg papers reported that the redistricting plans were returned to the three-judge panel to "better determine whether minority voting rights were violated" and reported that the Supreme Court believed the "federal judges who drafted the plan had neglected to ensure minority voters' rights are protected."[50] The *State* reported that the judges were being told by the Supreme Court "to try again, taking care this time to assure minority voters' rights are protected." The Justice Department brief maintained that a Supreme Court decision on the merits of the plans was premature and, according to the newspaper, suggested that "the panel of judges should be forced instead to do the job right, concentrating less on county lines and more on the imperatives of the racial equality in the 1965 Voting Rights Act."[51]

[45]The Columbia *State*, 3 November 1992, B1 and The Greenville *News*, 3 November 1992, 1 and 10A.

[46]The Columbia *State*, 18 May 1993, 1B; see also 16 June 1993, 10A.

[47]William C. Bryson, Acting Solicitor General, Brief for the United States as Amicus Curiae, In the Supreme Court of the United States, October Term, 1992, *Statewide Reapportionment v. ....*, on Appeal, Nos. 92-155 and 92-219, see esp. pp. 6-7, 9, 14, 15, 16, 17, 19.

[48]113 S, Ct. at 2954, 1 and 2.

[49]The Greenville *News*, 15 June 1993, 9A.

[50.]The Columbia *State*, 29 June 1993, 1 and 6 A; see also Spartanburg *Herald-Journal*, June 29, 1993, A9.

[51]The Columbia *State*, 15 June 1993, 1A.

Two weeks after the Supreme Court remanded the redistricting case back to the three-judge district court, South Carolina had to grapple with the Supreme Court decision in *Shaw v. Reno* (28 June 1993) and how that might influence the three-judge panel decision. *Shaw v. Reno* held that a district that was as "bizarre" in shape as to be explainable solely in terms of race could be challenged in federal court.

On 6 July 1993, a week before the three-judge panel was to meet again to reconsider their reapportionment plans, the Columbia newspaper wrote an editorial that asked, "Does drawing voting districts to guarantee the election of black officials actually hurt black voters, by resegregating society and diminishing the number of white Democrats who have tended to support their ideas more than Republicans?" To this, white Democrats responded yes and South Carolina African-American leaders no.[52]

The three-judge panel had hoped the Justice Department would be at the hearing in July 1993, but the department, still at that time without an assistant attorney general for civil rights since President William J. Clinton took office, sent no representatives. After asking questions of the assembled parties, the judges left their decision as it was; they decided not to decide.

The judges gave the redistricting decision back to the state legislators. They had until 1 April 1994 to enact plans for the House of Representatives and Congress. The judges did not set a deadline for the Senate, whose members would not stand for reelection until 1996.[53]

In early January 1994 House Speaker Sheheen announced that he intended to pass legislation similar to the 1992 court plan for redistricting the House.[54] (That plan, of course, had been vacated by the Supreme Court.) The Senate decided not to tie its reapportionment plan to the House or Congressional plan and to take advantage of the extra time allowed them to draw districts that reflected the latest judicial directions on reapportionment. Following a newspaper report that the federal courts had decided it was unconstitutional to create districts with the sole purpose of ensuring victory for black candidates, the Senate wanted to reflect that thinking in their plan.[55]

---

[52]Democrat House Speaker Sheheen was quoted on the North Carolina Congressional decision, "This opinion creates a greater justification for our court's reasoning." The paper stated that the federal judges deciding the South Carolina reapportionment case had "to apply the arguments in the most recent case" and contrasted *Shaw v. Reno* with the Supreme Court decision two weeks earlier which ordered the judges "to justify why there weren't more black-majority districts, or else draw more." The Columbia *State*, 6 July 1993, 14A. A Charleston paper reported that First District U.S. Congressman Republican Arthur Ravenal, Jr. said he was pleased because he had never liked creating a district to ensure the election of a minority; "I'm one of these color-blind people. That Sixth District is an abomination." The Charleston *Post and Courier*, 29 June 1993, 1D and see also 7A.

[53]*State* 17 May 1994, B4.

[54]The day before, according to the newspaper, legislators made clear that they were not going to change the congressional district which had elected James Clyburn as the first African-American from the state since Reconstruction to the U.S. Congress. Columbia *State*, 5 January 1994, 3B. More than half, 76 of the 142 (out of a total of 170) lawmakers who responded to the newspaper's 1994 Legislative Survey would create as many black majority legislative districts as possible. Columbia *State*, 5 January 1994, 3B; ibid, 9 January 1994, 6D.

[55]Columbia *State*, 11 January 1994, 3B.

The General Assembly did agree on the majority black Congressional district, and the 6th Congressional district was left unchanged. Since *Shaw v. Reno* used shape as a factor, legislators felt some uneasiness about the shape of the sixth congressional district. The shape was awkward because three white congressional incumbents insisted on having military bases in their districts instead of in the newly created black majority district. The state submitted the Congressional plan to the Justice Department for preclearance on 8 April 1994, and it was cleared without any problems on 28 April 1994. The first challenge was filed on December 6, 1996 (*Leonard et al.v. Beasley et al.*, USDC, DSC, Columbia Division, Civil No.: 3:96-CV-3640).[56] It was settled on August 6, 1997 with an agreement that the General Assembly would redraw the districts by the end of the session in 1000. If the action is reinstated, everyone stipulates that you can draw a narrowly tailored constitutional majority BVAP district and that the state has a compelling interest in doing that. The parties would also stipulate that traditional districting principles were subordinated to race in drawing the 6th Congressional District, but that the state has a compelling state interest in drawing a 50 percent BVAP district.

The House redistricting, however, was another matter; like Macbeth's lament, it is a "tale told by an idiot, full of sound and fury, signifying nothing." In a letter to all members of the state House of Representatives, Speaker Sheheen briefly outlined what had happened thus far for his colleagues. According to Sheheen, the Court on 13 July 1993 had "stated that no districts now exist" since their "order was vacated by the Supreme Court." Moreover, the judges "made it clear that it deems redistricting as a state legislative matter and one for the federal courts to intervene only as a last resort to ensure timely elections." Sheheen outlined alternatives: start anew, readopt the plan the House had passed in 1992, start from that plan and make changes, adopt the 1992 court plan under which elections had been held, make changes to the court plan, do nothing or "Punt." In a telling penultimate paragraph to the two-page letter Sheheen wrote, "If luck prevails, maybe everyone will write in and say they are well pleased with the district under which they got elected last year and see no need for a change in the court plan."[57]

The white Democrat controlled House basically followed Sheheen's "luck" scheme. The House Judiciary Committee in December, 1993 sent out a notice for a meeting of the Election Laws Subcommittee on 4 January 1995 and on 5 January the Staff of the House Judiciary Committee presented another history of redistricting and attached a copy of *Shaw v. Reno* with the following summary:

---

[56] An interesting footnote. The local lawyer on the case was John Chase, the Democratic candidate who was unable to defeat Clyburn in 1992. Chase ran a racist television advertisement. The campaign ad resembled the American Express commercials but with African-American candidate James Clyburn's picture in the center of the card (the picture purportedly looked like "buckwheat") with a slogan about Clyburn and a "welfare express card."

[57] Robert J. Sheheen to Members of the South Carolina House, 16 July 1993, in Judiciary Committee, Redistricting Papers, South Carolina State Archives and Department of Justice files.

"...a redistricting plan alleged to be so bizarre on its face as to be unexplainable on grounds other than race demands close scrutiny on equal protection grounds, no matter what that motivation underlying its adoption." The memo also announced that Speaker Sheheen had filed bills "which reflect the court ordered plan."[58]

The House Judiciary Committee's plan was nearly identical to the one the Court had drawn in 1992; 20 districts had changes approved by the incumbents. The House approved the plan with only minor changes to districts from which all representatives were elected in 1992. The Judiciary Committee rejected requests for six new majority black districts that black caucus members requested and gave as their reason that they needed to move quickly to beat the April 1 deadline set by the Court. In addition, they relied on the "court decisions that have called into question the practice of creating districts to ensure black representation for government." The House reduced the number of black majority districts from 28 to 27 and majority voting age population districts from 25 to 22. Even so, African-Americans and Republicans calculated that their best opportunity was to get a plan passed and then to make their objections known to the Justice Department. If the House did not pass a plan, the judges who drew the 1992 plans would be in charge and would probably "keep the same districts in place." Thus, Republicans and African-Americans believed "it makes more sense to let white Democrats pass the plan they want so it'll go to the federal Justice Department." Speaker Sheheen, on the other hand, argued that the districts were fair since "three impartial judges" basically had drawn them.[59]

The Senate exercised legislative courtesy and approved the House plan. The Act became law on 15 February 1994, without the signature of Governor Campbell. Speaker Sheheen submitted the plan for preclearance on 23 March 1994.[60] On 2 May 1994 the Justice Department objected to the plan. (See Table 5, page 301, for comparison of the DOJ-objected-to 1994 House Plan.)

In a detailed ten-page letter, Assistant Attorney General Deval L. Patrick noted that under the 1992 court plan, of the 18 elected African-American representatives, all were elected from majority voting age districts and 14 of 18 were from districts that were over 55 percent voting age population. All but one had a black registration majority and 13 were elected from where African-Americans represented 55 percent or more of registered voters. In 10 black majority districts, African-Americans had not been elected, 7 had black voting age populations, but only one had 55 percent black voting age population and none had a 55 percent black registration. These districts were also in rural areas "where it appears that

---

[58]James H. Hodges to Joseph H. Wilder, et al., 23 December 1993 and Staff of the House Judiciary Committee to Members of Election Laws Subcommittee, 5 January 1994, South Carolina House Judiciary Committee, Election Laws Subcommittee, SCDAH and Justice Department Files.

[59]Columbia *State*, 19 and 26 January 1994, B1; Deval L. Patrick to Robert J. Sheheen, 2 May 1994, Objection Letter, p. 4, Justice Department files.

[60]Robert J. Sheheen to Chief, Voting Section, Civil Rights Division, 23 March 1994, Submission Letter, Department of Justice Files.

the present day effects of the state's history of discrimination are more substantial, and thus where a higher black voting age population majority may be necessary to allow black voters an opportunity to elect a candidate of their choice." The legislature could have easily drawn nine additional black majority districts. Instead it actually reduced the number of voting age population black majority districts.

Reviewing South Carolina's recent election history, the Justice Department put special emphasis on the 1992 legislative and congressional elections and concluded that South Carolina elections are characterized "by a pattern of racially polarized voting." Furthermore, it found that "black candidates generally are the candidates of choice of black voters in legislative elections."

The Justice Department also questioned the supposed policy on districts that do not cross county lines. The Justice Department review failed to identify "any state redistricting policies" that guided redistricting for the House. Instead, the Justice Department concluded that incumbency protection drove the process, as the existing court-ordered plan was altered only if all the affected representatives agreed. Thus, it was preordained that no change would be made that would increase the number of districts in which black voters would have the opportunity to elect their preferred candidates. The Justice Department wrote that the lawmakers used a "least-change approach" and advanced only one state policy consideration, "incumbency protection and the ease of administering a plan essentially the same as the 1992 plan." The Justice Department concluded "In sum, our analysis reveals that the redistricting process was designed to ensure incumbency protections, not compliance with the Voting Rights Act."[61]

House Speaker Sheheen responded to the Justice Department objection letter. "Your age-old accusation that the plan...was drawn for incumbency protection is easily advanced when incumbents participate in the drawing of the plan." However, in this case, Sheheen argued that the submitted plan "was primarily penned by the three judge panel" and the plan objected to "was their plan with minor adjustments." Moreover, the Speaker argued that the general assembly had followed state policy and those considerations "have remained constant for my years in the General Assembly: keeping identifiable communities of interest intact; splitting as few county lines as possible to minimize voter confusion; compliance with the Voting Rights Act by allowing identifiable black populations with communities of interest to elect a candidate of their choice; completing the process as expeditiously as possible to allow elections to be held on time while giving candidates and voters the opportunity to know their choices."[62]

An editorial in the Columbia *State* chastised state legislators, "Won't S.C. House ever get remapping right?" Quoting the Justice Department's objection let-

---

[61]Deval L. Patrick to Robert J. Sheheen, 2 May 1994, Objection Letter, p. 4, Justice Department files. Orville Vernon Burton, "Report on Reapportionment of the South Carolina House of Representatives," 15 April 1996, for *Able v. Wilkins*, No. CV: 3:96-0003 (D.S.C.) in Justice Department Files.

[62]Robert J. Sheheen to Honorable Deval L. Patrick, Asst. Atty Genl., 23 May 1994, Submission of Second Plan. See also statements attributed to Sheheen in Columbia *State*, 26 January 1994.

ter that incumbency protection had driven reapportionment of the House, the editors were surprised that "once again" legislators had "failed to follow court mandates concerning the voting rights of blacks." The article emphasized that African-Americans were nearly 30 percent of South Carolina's population and yet were less than 15 percent of members of the House.[63]

Other newspaper accounts commented on white Democratic lawmakers' defiance of "the federal government reminiscent of the Civil Rights era." The Democratic legislators objected to the Department of Justice's objections and argued "other factors...are just as significant as race." House Majority Leader Tim Rogers stated, "I'm not willing to turn over the prerogative the Legislature has carte blanch, to a bunch of bureaucrats." He refused to accept the Justice Department's logic. "Just because they have decided one way does not mean what we did was any less valid or appropriate." One legislator was quoted, "I don't think we can buckle under to a complete Justice Department makeover of the entire state."[64]

According to one newspaper, it was "in the face of that defiance" that African-American legislators refused a compromise to work for three or four additional black districts, and instead demanded all nine that the Justice Department had suggested.[65] Black Representative Don Beatty who spearheaded the reapportionment negotiations for the African-American legislative caucus reported that black Democrats would have accepted a plan that spared more white Democrats had the House's Democratic leadership worked with the black caucus.[66]

Obstinately Speaker Sheheen and white Democrats stalled to keep a reapportionment plan from creating new black majority districts. As white Democrats "filibustered into the night to avoid debate over creating new black-majority districts," frustrated African-American legislators voted unanimously on 10 May, ironically Confederate Memorial Day in South Carolina, to cooperate with Republicans. African-American Representative Joe Neal explained: "Increasing our share of black representation in the South Carolina House is a goal that has been important to our people here in South Carolina since the Civil War."[67] When white Democrats urged African-Americans not to align with Republicans, "black Democrats issued some of the harshest accusations uttered on the House floor in recent memory." Charleston Representative Lucille Whipper reported African-American Democrats were tired of being used. "It reminds me of the days in slavery when we wanted to be free, and our benevolent masters said, 'Why do you want freedom?'"[68]

Finally, in the wee hours of 11 May 1994, a coalition of African-American Democrats and white Republicans successfully ended a 13-hour leadership stall

[63]Columbia *State*, 4 May 1994, A12.

[64]Columbia *State*, 4 May B5 and 3 May A1, 1994

[65]Columbia *State*, 4 May 1994, B5.

[66]Columbia *State*, 13 May 1994, A1 and A7.

[67]Columbia *State*, 11 May 1994, A1 and A6.

[68]Columbia *State*, 12 May 1994, A1 and A7.

on reapportionment. They forced House Speaker Robert Sheheen to recall a reapportionment bill from the Judiciary Committee that would allow them to adopt a coalition amendment creating nine additional African-American majority House districts. House Speaker Sheheen had ruled that the House could not, even with a majority vote, go to a section of the calendar, specifically to the motion period, customarily closed to the floor. In an unusual maneuver, African-American representative Don Beatty moved to appeal the ruling of the chair, declaring that it was out of order to invoke such a rule. Rather than have his procedural rule overturned and his authority diminished, Sheheen relented.

On 11 May 1994 the reapportionment plan passed the House 88-22 over quiet objections of white Democrats. The faithful Sons of the Confederacy who on the previous day and evening were outfitted in the traditional Confederate gray and stood sentinel before the monument to their ancestors on the State House grounds were gone when the legislature adjourned. On May 14, the South Carolina Senate passed and the Lieutenant Governor ratified the South Carolina House Reapportionment plan as it came from the House. Quite likely, historians will remember May 11 as a significant political watershed, the end of white Democratic party ascendancy that had held power in the state house of Representatives and Senate since 1876. Democratic Representative Joe Wilder of Barnwell underscored the significance of the moment, "I'm very disturbed by what happened in here, because it dramatically changes the balance of political power we've had in this House up until now in this century." Although some white and black Democrats predicted a permanent alliance of Republicans and African-American legislators, Roger Young, Republican of Charleston, placed the moment in perspective. When African-American legislators come to the Republican Party and suggest "'Let's talk about the Confederate flag', I think you're going to have a problem."[69]

The federal judges had extended the April 1 deadline to give the House the opportunity to pass the new plan. The coalition of Republicans and African-American legislators hurried to get their plan passed knowing that the judges would order elections held in the districts that they had drawn in 1992, and that those districts protected white Democratic incumbents. A special session was called at the cost of $10,300.[70] That week, as districts were redrawn, one member of the House characterized the last minute efforts to negotiate compromises "a zoo."[71] The finalized plan was adopted on May 19. The House plan was fedexed for preclearance on 23 May 1994 and cleared by the Justice Department on 31 May 1994. In his letter of submission, Speaker Sheheen warned, "I do fear that the additional balkanization of certain communities may lead to legitimate challenges on other grounds which probably will not affect preclearance by your department."[72] The next day the *State* newspaper reported that for the second

---

[69]Columbia *State*, 12 May 1994, A1 and A7.

[70]Columbia *State*, 17 May 1994, B4.

[71]Columbia *State*, 19 May 1994, A10.

time since passage of the 1965 Voting Rights Act, state legislators would be elected from districts drawn by state legislators instead of federal judges.[73]

Republicans gained control of the House after the 1994 election. African-American legislators Sen. John Matthews, Reps. Don Beatty and Gilda Cobb-Hunter believed that "most, if not all, the districts where white Democrats lost to white Republicans were unaffected by redistricting."[74] Between the 1992 and 1994 general elections, two elected Democrats switched parties. Another Democratic district was won by a Republican in a special election. Redistricting in 1994 actually effected a difference of only one in the Democratic-Republican balance. Otherwise, the new or enhanced African-American districts resulted only in Democrats replacing Democrats (although in one district a Republican replaced a Democrat and in another a Democrat replaced a Republican). The other seven districts were simply Republican wins in a Republican year in districts essentially untouched by the 1994 redistricting and in which Democrats won in 1992. After the general election in 1994, eight elected Democrats switched parties, and one black Democrat replaced a white Democrat in a special election. After the 1992 redistricting African-Americans increased in the House from 15 to 18; with the 1994 redistricting they now have 24 of the 124 House seats to make up 19 percent of the members of the House (See Table 6, page 303).

The reapportionment of the Senate is not so dramatic as the House. On 30 March 1994 the South Carolina Senate Judiciary Committee's subcommittee on Reapportionment and Redistricting adopted guidelines for Legislative and Congressional Redistricting. These rules for reapportionment were carefully arranged in a descending order of importance: equality of population, compliance with the Voting Rights Act, contiguity, communities of interest where one-person, one-vote and the Voting Rights Act are not violated, adherence to voting precinct boundary lines, use of only the 1990 census for data, and compactness.[75] According to the *State* newspaper, black and white Democrats in the Senate worked together to create the minimum change to satisfy the Justice Department's demand for more black districts. One of two African-American members of the eight person map-drawing Senate subcommittee, Darrell Jackson, blamed "Democrats' loss of control of the House to a redistricting plan passed last year by a coalition of black Democrats and white Republicans."[76] According to the Charlotte *Observer*, Senate Democrats tried "to create districts where white Democrats depend on both white voters and a solid minority of blacks."[77] Thus, black

[72]Robert J. Sheheen to Honorable Deval L. Patrick, 23 May 1994, letter of submission, Department of Justice files.

[73]Columbia *State*, 1 June 1994, A1.

[74]Charlotte *Observer*, 10 April 1995, 1 and 4 C.

[75]The South Carolina Senate Judiciary Committee's Subcommittee on Reapportionment and Redistricting's Guidelines for Legislative and Congressional Redistricting, 30 March 1994, Files of

[76]Columbia *State*, 29 and 31 March 1995. The paper reported that one white Democratic Senator would be sacrificed to make room for a black Democrat.

and white Democrats rejected a Republican plan that created twice as many black majority districts.[78]

The Senate Judiciary Committee reported out a plan on 30 March 1995 that created two new majority-minority districts and enhanced the existing majority-minority districts.[79] The plan in place for the 1990 elections had 10 black districts; the 1992 plan had 11 black majority districts. The 1995 Senate plan provided one additional black majority district. The only black majority district that was not also a black voting age majority was Greenville District 7, which had been represented by an African-American since 1985, but was vacant at the time the Senate prepared the plan. The Senate had expelled African-American Theo Mitchell after he served time in prison for failing to report cash transactions. The 51.9 percent black population translated into a 47.7 percent voting age black population in District 7, but since an African-American had won the district in the past, it is counted as an opportunity district (although it is unlikely an African-American again will win the district anytime in the near future.).[80] Thus, the 1995 Senate plan provides 12 (as opposed to 8 in the 1992 Court plan) black opportunity districts where either an African-American had won election or the population was 57 percent black.

African-American Senator Kay Patterson explained why he and other black Democrats supported the Senate bill in 1995. Patterson noted that, under the House Republican-Black Caucus compromise plan, the 1994 elections resulted in Republican gains, and, when a number of white Democrats switched parties, Republicans captured the lower chamber. Patterson then converted to "a born-again Democrat" who saw "a hell of a lot of difference between white Democrats and Republicans." Patterson hopes that "Bubba and them may just wake up," as he did, "when they see how the Republicans are looking out for capital gains folks, them big boys, and taking money out of USC and money out of the schools."[81] Senator Darrell Jackson bluntly stated, "We did not want to make the same mistake the House made."[82] Executive Director of the NAACP, James Felder, was quoted "I think we all learned something" from the House redistricting. "You have to avoid the fire next time."[83]

Democrats held a 27 (6 of whom were African-American) to 18 advantage in the Senate when the bill was drawn up and passed. On 4 April 1995 the Senate approved the plan, it was ratified by the House on 11 May 1995 and went into effect without Republican Governor Governor David M. Beasley's signature on

---

[77]Charlotte *Observer,* 10 April 1995, 1 and 4 (quote) C.

[78]Columbia *State*, 29 September 1995, A9.

[79]Minutes, Reapportionment Subcommittee Meeting, 29 March 1995, part of Submission of Senate Plan to Justice Department, Justice Department Files.

[80]Charlotte *Observer*, 8 March 1995, 1C; Columbia *State*, 31 March 1995, newspaper clipping in Justice Department Submission file.

[81]Columbia *State*, 4 April 1995, B1 and B5, quotes from B5.

[82]Greenville *News*, 31 March 1995; Charlotte *Observer*, 31 March 1995, 5C.

[83]Charlotte *Observer*, 10 April 1995, 1 (quote) and 4 C.

17 May. On 16 May, President Pro Temp of the Senate, Marshall B. Williams, sent the plan to the Justice Department, which precleared the plan on 30 May 1995.

The Senate now has 24 (6 of whom are African-Americans) Democrats, 21 Republicans, and one Independent. A Republican won Greenville District 7 in a special election. One white Democrat became an independent.[84] Another four were party switches after the Republican state and national landslide in 1994. A correspondent who has covered reapportionment reported that Republicans "believe it is only a matter of time before the racial politics that made Democrats the dominant force in South Carolina put the GOP firmly in control." Several newspapers noted that most black South Carolinians vote for Democrats and most whites vote for Republicans. South Carolina House Speaker, Republican David Wilkins, has said, "Republican gains have come and will continue to come regardless of the redistricting plan. It might make a net difference of one or two seats, but on a grand scale it makes little difference. The Republican majority is here to stay." Yet, Democrats, black and white, believe that under the 1995 reapportionment plan they can survive the 1996 elections and control the Senate at least until 2000.[85]

A month after the Senate plan was approved, the Supreme Court announced that congressional redistricting by race was illegal in Georgia. Discussing the issues in that case, South Carolina's most influential newspaper on 30 June 1995 quoted former South Carolina House speaker Sheheen, "I think it would be fairly easy for any plaintiff in South Carolina to attack any of the three plans which have been adopted and prevail."[86] Thus, the powerful and respected Democratic House Representative from Kershaw County, Sheheen practically invited lawsuits challenging the hard-won compromises to get reapportionment completed following the 1990 census. Sure enough, white plaintiffs have challenged both the Senate and the House districting plans—although not the black majority Congressional district. They retained as attorney Lee Parks, who prevailed in the Georgia redistricting trial *Miller v. Johnson*.[87] The fate of the those plans for the South Carolina House of Representatives and the Senate was to be decided by three federal judges after an extremely heated trial in the J. Strom Thurmond federal court house in Columbia that began on 12 August and ended on 27 August 1996. The three-judge panel found six of the nine challenged House districts unconstitutional.

In the Senate case, three districts—two black majority (the one majority white abutted one of the majority black districts; the lead plaintiff was the white

---

[84]Greg Smith, the lead plaintiff in *Smith v. Beasley.*

[85]Columbia *State*, 4 April B1 and 5 (quotes from both 1 and 5), 30 June 1995, A1, A7, quote on A7.

[86]Columbia *The State*, 30 June 1995, quotation p. A2, story continued on page A7 with brief summary of redistricting in South Carolina in 1990s.

[87]*Smith v. Beasley* 946 F. Supp. 1174 (O.S.C. 1996) challenged the Senate; *Able v. Wilkins* C/A # 3:96-3-0 challenged the House, both cited *Miller v. Johnson*, 1995 WL 382020 (U.S.)

senator from that majority white district which had been redrawn unfavorably)—
were challenged. In the 1996 election in the challenged districts, as African-
American candidate, DeWitt Williams, won District 37. All three districts were
found unconstitutional. In the redraw, District 29 (Darlington, Florence, and Marlboro) was simply conceded and redrawn to a white Democratic district. District
37 was the focus of lots of back and forth. The final district was the result of Senator Williams letting white Senator Yancey McGill talk him into a district confor-
mation that left McGill pretty much alone in his county of Williamsburg.
Williams lost the district to a white Republican in the 1997 special election.[88]

---

[88]One of the most interesting aspects of the 1994 redistricting is tht it appears to have reduced
polarizations. Countywide African-American candidates were elected in both Marboro and George-
town.

THE POLITICS OF RACE:
The Virginia Redistricting Experience, 1991-1997

Winnett W. Hagens

RACIAL EMPOWERMENT AND PARTISAN POLITICS IN VIRGINIA HISTORY

IT IS OFTEN MORE REVEALING TO VIEW POLITICAL BEHAVIOR as driven by defensive rather than offensive purposes. Looking at politics as defensive, the dominant and essential wellspring of political action is the conservation and protection of the political actor's existing social and economic realities. Since the power to bestow and revoke protections, privileges, immunities, and penalties reposes in government, the essence of politics is the struggle for control of government. From the perspective of politics as defensive behavior, the question of who rules assumes paramount importance because the answer determines who is best able to protect, preserve and maintain their existing status. People enter politics because politics decides who rules, and those who rule decide who gets what. Looking at politics as defensive, one begins to see that people get involved in politics not so much to pursue their dreams as to hang on to what they have.

In Virginia a single issue, the issue of racial empowerment, has not only shaped but quite nearly defined the partisan struggle for power within the Commonwealth since its inception. As V.O. Key has observed, "in its grand outlines the politics of the South revolves around the position of the Negro....Whatever phase of the southern political process one seeks to understand, sooner or later the trail of inquiry leads to the Negro" (1949, 5). Although the position of Negroes may be the pivotal issue in southern and Virginia politics, Negroes have rarely had much say on what their position would be. Following Reconstruction in the 1870s, as V. O. Key, Jr. noted decades ago, the southern disfranchisement movement "gave the southern states the most impressive systems of obstacles between the voter and the ballot box known to the democratic world" (1949, 555). By the mid 1890s, the vast majority of Virginia's blacks had been disfranchised. "In [the] 1900 [presidential election], 147 votes were cast per thousand of the state's population; in 1904, only 57 votes per thousand were cast. By 1940, aided by the primary election, among other factors, fewer than 10 Virginians per

315

thousand were voting" (Wynes, 1971, 66). By the 1940s very substantial numbers of unskilled, propertyless, and illiterate whites had also been disfranchised by the same medley of mechanisms employed to disfranchise blacks in Virginia.

Disfranchisement defused a perilous political situation that had developed for Virginia's ruling elements at the conclusion of the Civil War. The frightening prospect presented to Virginia's privileged ruling elites with the enfranchisement of blacks under reconstruction was the potential development of a viable opposing political party supported by and championing the needs of large numbers of propertyless, exploited, and oppressed voters emerging from slavery. If such an explosive constituency were ever able to join forces with small farmers and a growing urban working class in the formation of a dynamic political organization as they had in the Readjuster movement of the 1870s, the long domination of Virginia politics by an aristocratic elite would be broken forever.

By virtually abolishing the political rights of a propertyless underclass, disfranchisement also dissolved the potential for two-party government in the Commonwealth. It was no accident that one-party government in Virginia also offered the only effective strategy to thwart federal intervention in Commonwealth politics. A one-party state would assure that Virginia's Congressional delegations would be solidly Democratic, segregationist, and economically conservative. Allied with similar delegations from sister states of the former Confederacy in a unified state's rights front, a Congressional minority sufficient to perpetually stifle federal interference in southern politics could be maintained in Washington. Alarmed and, in some cases, terrified by the specter of democracy in the form of Negro suffrage producing some species of Negro rule, Virginians, prodded by an aristocratic leadership with everything to lose, simply abolished democracy in the Commonwealth.[1] As Key would later say, "the simple fact is that a government founded on democratic doctrines becomes some other sort of regime when large proportions of its citizens refrain from voting" (1949, 508). Given Virginia's tradition of aristocratic government, after disfranchisement the ruling regime that remained was what it had always been in Virginia—"a well-disciplined and ably managed oligarchy, of not many more that a thousand professional politicians, which enjoys the enthusiastic and almost undivided support of the business community and of the well-to-do generally...." (Key, 1949, 26).

The disfranchisement of blacks occurred not because of any real threat of "bayonet-negro rule" as the white nightmare of black political domination was sometimes called (Morto,n 1918, 131). No such threat ever existed in Virginia

---

[1]Charles Wynes provided a telling commentary on this point when he observed that "following the class movement of Readjusterism, the Democratic party and the Democratic press succeeded in convincing white Virginians that the white race, regardless of economic class, must stand together against the Negroes. Economic and social issues had to take second-place to the Negro question. The cry was raised that white men could not divide politically so long as the Negro voted, and a small group of independent Democrats set out to disfranchise the Negro. In the end, Democratic conservatives headed off division of the white vote by rigid machine control of the state and by disfranchisement of the lower class of whites as well as Negroes" (Wynes, 1971, 146).

because the Virginia Negro, trapped in abject poverty and widely scorned by white society, emerged from the Civil War virtually powerless. Even during short intervals during Reconstruction and Readjusterism in localities where they were the majority and they voted the "Negroes and Republicans were placing white men, not black, in county offices—and often white Conservatives" (Wynes, 1971, 27). Three hundred years of slavery had done its work.

Yet, powerless is not useless. The real power of the blacks in Virginia has never been in their political strength. The real power of the blacks derives from the simple reality of their presence in Virginia society because it is a presence that, properly manipulated, can evoke fear in the minds of many southern whites. The haunting white fear of black empowerment has been the primary political resource, the indispensable political asset, employed by Virginia's ruling elite to perpetuate and entrench—defend—their rule. Indeed, for 100 years, from the end of the Civil War to the mid 1960s, the principal importance of blacks to the politics of Virginia has been their usefulness as a powerful illusion artfully crafted to strike fear in the hearts of Virginia's white citizens and justifying a one-party, elitist rule by a coalition of landed gentry and corporate commercial interests. As Charles Wynes pointed out in 1971:

> As a political issue, the Negro was too tempting to leave alone. When the issue of the Negro promised to suit their ends, they used it. When a reduced electorate appeared to be advantageous, they disfranchised him. The Virginia legislators who disfranchised the Negro and segregated him by statute *were not* [sic] led by representatives of that class of white people who competed directly with the Negro economically and who were more likely to be thrown with him socially. Instead, men of good family and social prestige led the fight (1971, 149).

In the end, the race issue in Virginia is and always has been a proxy issue propagated by a narrow ruling elite that knows well how to effectively defend its interests. Were it not for the race question, by all the rules of political behavior post-bellum Virginia would offer receptive ground for a more progressive if not radical political agenda. "A poor, agrarian area, pressed down by the colonial policies of the financial and industrial North and Northeast, it offers fertile ground for political agitation" (Key, 1949, 44). Carefully nurtured racial fear cast Virginia politics into the mold of one-party, elitist politics. Were it not for the race issue, the Democratic Party of Virginia might well have evolved into the progressive liberal force it became in other parts of the nation. Instead, the Democratic Party of Virginia, detached by disfranchisement from its historic national footing among the working class, evolved into an instrument of narrow elitist interests that was Republican in every politically relevant sense but name. In my view, there is no reality more crucial to understanding Virginia politics than the fact that its dominant political party, although Democratic in name, is Republican in the sentiments, ideology, and purposes of its membership. In Virginia it has been Democrats who have restrained labor organization with right-to-work statutes that depress wages while the costs of living rise. In Virginia, pay-as-you-go state financing that starves expenditures for public services like education, public health, environmental protection, and public welfare have been standard planks in the Democratic platform since the 1890s. Virginia ranks twelfth in population among the states of the Union; but in 1996 it led the nation in criminal executions. Clearly, the raw materials for a more liberal politics exist in contemporary Virginia. Yet no such movement is in sight today any more than it was 100 years ago. A single issue—the issue of race—an issue historically promoted and inflamed by ruling elements within Virginia culture, largely explains Virginia's intransigent political conservatism.

Ironically, it has been the success of black struggle for civil rights and ballot access in the 1960s that marked the end of a century of political obscurity for the Republican Party of Virginia. Feeling betrayed by President Johnson's realignment of the Democratic Party behind an agenda of civil rights, voting rights and liberal, "Great Society' economics, Virginia Democrats began abandoning intergenerational loyalties to the Democratic Party and migrated by the thousands into the ranks of Republicanism. To be sure, the civil rights agenda of the Democratic Party has earned it the loyalty of black voters, but the flood of black voters into Democratic ranks has not removed control of the party's institutional machinery or its public agenda from the coalition of commercial and property interests that has always ruled party affairs. By the 1980s Virginia would have a two-party system; but, with the exception of the civil rights issue, the center of effort of both parties is conservative economics, limited social programs, and right-to-work labor policy. In truth, the development of two-party competition in the state has been a boon principally for commercial interests in the Commonwealth who find themselves not only without serious challenge to their prerogatives, but also often find themselves in the enviable position of having both major parties in the state aggressively competing for their support.

Minority Ballot Access

Whatever gains African-Americans have achieved in political representation over the last 30 years in Virginia have come only through contentious federal intervention that has invariably been stridently resisted (Davidson and Grofman, 1994). Although Virginia may cling to an "image of moderation in race relations" as Thomas Morris suggests (Davidson and Grofman, 1994), and despite some cosmetic gains in black empowerment, deep divisions between the races persist. Virginia has come a long way since 1960 and the days of "massive resistance" to school desegregation. L. Douglas Wilder, an African-American, was elected Governor in 1989. Nevertheless, in 1991, Virginia, a state with a substantial African-American population, had the smallest proportion of African-American representatives in its legislature of any Southern state (Morris, 1994). By the eve of the 1991 Virginia General Assembly redistricting sessions, the Commonwealth had not elected a single black person to Congress since 1890.

Currently, in some areas Virginia clearly lags behind other states in democratizing its institutions of government. A thorough evaluation of the basic fairness of the Commonwealth's representational system requires at least a look at African-American representation in local government. In Virginia today, the most common mode of minority vote dilution occurs through the operation of at-large election systems in local governments that often submerge substantial black populations in a majority of white voters. Thirty-two of the state's 41 cities and 181 of the state's 188 towns employ the at-large method of electing their governing bodies. In 1991, the Virginia affiliate of the American Civil Liberties Union (ACLU) identified some 64 Virginia towns with black populations of 15 percent or better holding allegedly discriminatory elections under at-large election systems (American Civil Liberties Union, 1991). As Thomas Morris has ably demonstrated, "the continuing under representation of blacks in the many at-large county and city governments…[and] the virtual absence of blacks from the state's town councils indicates a continuing racial polarization at the grass-roots level.…" (Morris, 1990).

Because all Commonwealth judges are appointed rather than elected, Virginia citizens of all races are denied direct electoral influence in the selection of the judiciary. Fewer than 5 percent of Virginia's judges were black in 1990 in a state with a black population of nearly 19 percent (Morris, 1990). Virginia was the last state in the nation to adopt enabling legislation permitting localities to establish elective school boards. Even access to the ballot in Virginia is a good deal less than what it could be by today's national standards. In August 1992, the Voter Registrars Association of Virginia noted in a news release that the League of Women Voters cited Virginia as one of 13 states with "the worst systems for voter registration."[2] In 1991 only 64.4 percent of eligible voters in Virginia were registered and Virginia ranked 42nd in voting age population registered to vote.

Taken as a whole, facts like these are not convenient for those arguing that representational entitlements under the *Voting Rights Act* are remedies for "past injuries." Clearly, in 1991 on the eve of redistricting sessions in the General Assembly, Virginia still had a long way to go to achieve political equality for all of its citizens.

1991 REDISTRICTING SESSIONS—NEW REALITIES

New Voting Rights Law

As they approached the April 1991 redistricting session, more than a few legislators were astonished by dramatic changes in the redistricting playing field which had occurred over the 1980s. First and foremost among striking changes was a sea change in voting law. By 1990 well defined case law had made it clear that minority voters prevented from electing candidates of choice by racial gerrymanders could find almost certain redress in federal courts under Section 2 and, in covered jurisdictions like Virginia, under Section 5 of the *Voting Rights Act*.

---

[2]Voter Registrars Association of Virginia, "News Release—Update," 10 February, 1993, 3.

Henceforth, if majority-minority districts could be created and organized communities of injured voters demanded it, federal courts seemed likely to enjoin state and local jurisdictions to do so.

African-Americans: New Players at the Redistricting Table

A second fundamental change in the Virginia redistricting landscape in 1991 was the presence of African-Americans throughout the highest recesses of Virginia government. The Black Caucus of the Virginia General Assembly had grown to ten in number (seven in the House and three in the Senate) all of whom were Democrats. If compliance with preclearance is likely an offensive but unavoidable duty for many white, conservative Virginia legislators, it is quite another matter to face black legislative colleagues across computers throughout the redistricting process. Perhaps more importantly, an African-American Governor, L. Douglas Wilder, carrying both veto power and an impressive personal record of minority empowerment achievements, would preside over the entire redistricting process (Parker, 1982).

Accessible Redistricting Technology and Interest Group Participation in Redistricting Politics

Over the decade of the 1980s the Bureau of the Census had completed a coast-to-coast digital map data base called TIGER/Line in CD rom format.[3] The Census PL 94-171 data base containing population and population attribute data (race data) aggregated at the block level of geography as required for redistricting was linked (georeferenced) to this digital base map. By 1991 various software development firms were offering competitive software that utilized Geographic Information Systems (GIS) technology to permit users to automate districting plan creation and publish maps and reports defining a districting proposal. For the first time in Virginia's redistricting history, interest groups like the NAACP and the ACLU were not frozen out of direct influence on the redistricting process for lack of simple technical ability to quickly construct and evaluate plans. With grants from the Ford and Rockefeller Foundations in 1991, Dr. Rudolph Wilson and I were able to establish a Redistricting Research Project, later called the Voting Rights Project, at Norfolk State University (NSU, Norfolk, Virginia). The NSU Voting Rights Project subsequently provided an independent plan creation and evaluation capability to the Virginia Conference of the NAACP and other community groups in Virginia and across the south. By 1991, the ACLU had also established a comparable facility in Richmond, Virginia. At long last the legislature's monopoly on the technical capability to create districting plans ended. No longer could the legislature claim, as it had in past decades, that alternatives to its redistricting plans were technically impractical. Both NSU and the ACLU were

---

[3]"TIGER" is an acronym standing for "Topologically Integrated Geographically Encoded Referencing" system.

able to publish plans for the minority that demonstrated the feasibility of alternative redistricting proposals that increased minority representation above levels proposed by the General Assembly. When legislative plans diluted minority representation as they initially did for both the Virginia House of Delegates and the Senate in 1991, alternative third-party proposals entered into the public record by voting rights advocates would establish a trail of evidence highly relevant to the DOJ preclearance process.

Another rarely mentioned technical development emerging from the 1991 redistricting session in Virginia was the development of a partisan preference data base describing the Virginia electorate. This data set of voter preferences was linked (georeferenced) to the digitized TIGER/Line base map of Virginia and was available exclusively to General Assembly members through the Assembly's Legislative Services facility. Using precinct election histories, algorithms were developed that assigned partisan preference values to census blocks. Since any representational district is basically a collection of census blocks, it became possible to roughly estimate the partisan preference of any district drawn at the Legislative Services facility by aggregating the partisan preference values of its constituent blocks. Among other things, the 1990s redistricting cycle and its attendant technical GIS wizardry may well have ushered in something of a revolution in election campaign management technology (Hagens and Fairfax, 1996).

Unprecedented Partisanship

Unquestionably, one of the most consequential changes in the redistricting battlefield in 1991 was the presence of century high levels of partisan competition within the Virginia General Assembly, especially within the House of Delegates. By 1991 the partisan playing field in the General Assembly had profoundly changed. For the first time in the twentieth century, Democratic legislators embarked on redistricting facing the cumulative results of a quarter century of steady growth in Republican voters driven in part by liberal Democratic racial policies. In 1989, 39 percent of the House and 25 percent of the Senate was Republican. The November 1989 House election had produced "the GOP's best showing of the century, and the Democrats' worst" (Sabato, 1989). Republicans scored a net gain of four seats increasing its House contingent to a century high total of 39 in a 100-member body. More importantly, "the Republicans captured a stunningly large share of the legislative votes: 44.8 percent in all districts and 49.3 percent in party-contested districts" (Sabato, 1989). In the 1991 redistricting session, a popular Republican chant in the House of Delegates—"51 in 1991"—provocatively asserted that control of the House was within Republican reach.

Rising local competition, especially in the House, was the central reality facing Democrats entering a redistricting session offering irresistible opportunities for handicapping opponents. As subsequent developments would reveal, the clearly dominant theme of 1991 Commonwealth redistricting would be historically unparalleled levels of partisan conflict. And, unlike redistricting rounds in the 1970s and 1980s, Republicans would be without the protection of a Republican Governor's veto in the 1990s.

Partisan Redistricting Strategies

Although politics may often masquerade as a conflict of principles, the rhetoric is invariably driven by an underlying conflict of interests. Beneath the surface rhetoric of racial politics that characterized redistricting debates in 1991, a bitter struggle for partisan control of the legislature, especially the House of Delegates, raged. In truth, the conflict over minority seats in the legislature was essentially a substitute or proxy theme masking a more fundamental battle for partisan control of Commonwealth government across the decade of the 1990s. The press seized upon this new race-based redistricting theme and dramatized it throughout the Commonwealth as the dominant reality of the redistricting sessions. The real story, however, was that both parties were exploiting their own versions of new voting law in pursuit of their strategies to wrest control of the General Assembly. Once again in Virginia the issue of race would be manipulated for partisan advantage.

Republican Strategy

To this day the Central Committee of the Republican Party of Virginia remains philosophically opposed in principle to any policies that seek to resolve social ills by racially based reapportionments of economic or political advantages. On the eve of the 1991 redistricting session, decrying the legitimacy of the Voting Rights Act itself, the Central Committee of the Republican Party of Virginia adopted a resolution prohibiting use of its name or application of its "resources to any effort designed to create legislative districts based on race".[4]

In 1991, many Virginia Republican voters and their Republican representatives in the General Assembly were on a collision course when it came to the question of minority entitlements to representation. The Republican Party of Virginia offers growing numbers of Virginians a home in large part because of its adamant hostility to racial preferences of any sort. Indeed, a dramatic turnaround in the appeal of the Republican candidates to Virginia voters coincides almost exactly with the passage of the Civil Rights Act of 1964 and the Voting Rights Act of 1965. For General Assembly Republicans, as distinct from Republican voters, new voting law offered tantalizing opportunities to increase their numbers and, thereby, their power in both the General Assembly and Congress. In open contravention to party principles, Republican legislators, especially Republican Delegates, sought to capitalize on new voting law and demand the creation of the maximum number of black districts achievable. Given lower black registration, turnout, roll-on rates and age cohort disparities between black and white voters, the construction of black districts in Virginia typically requires increasing the

---

[4]*The Virginian-Pilot*, 11 July, 1991, p. D-6.

proportion of total minority voters beyond 55 percent of the voting age population (VAP) (Byrd-Harden, testimony, 1991). Redistricting under new voting law would require Virginia Democrats to do something they would never willingly do to themselves—pack Democratic voters into Democratic districts in numbers exceeding those required to produce Democratic victories but essential to produce victories for African-American candidates. The Democratic districts that remained would be stripped of core black voters and be vulnerable to Republican assault as resident Democratic incumbents eventually retired.

One of the best ways to understand Republican strategy on this score is with the concept of the "influence district." Although during the redistricting sessions there was no consensus on precisely what an "influence district" was or its political significance, the voting rights advocates in the NAACP clung to their impressions that legislators in districts with below 30 percent black VAP could not be relied upon to be responsive to minority concerns (Byrd-Harden, informal interview, 11 May, 1991). This subjective NAACP definition of an 'influence district' as one with less than 50 percent black VAP but more than 30 percent black VAP is adopted here only for the purposes of analysis. Maximizing black population districts would minimize black influence districts. Minimizing black influence districts would maximize Republican electoral opportunities. Insofar as Democratic districts serve black voters even marginally better than Republican districts, minimizing black "influence districts" is simply a special case of squandering the black vote by "packing" black voters into overcrowded black districts. In subsequent pages, I will refer to this strategy as "smart Republican redistricting strategy." Long after the redistricting sessions were over, at least one Virginia Republican would gloat that "for every member of a racial minority elected to state legislatures or Congress as a result of redistricting [in 1991]— two or more Republicans were voted into office" (Goolrick, 1996).

Democratic Redistricting Strategy

In Virginia, the black vote is the bedrock upon which the statewide Democratic plurality is anchored. No one has put this point more forcefully than Governor L. Douglas Wilder when he commented that if they [the Republicans] ever sought the minority vote with open arms, Democrats would be lost forever". Democrats controlled the General Assembly in 1991 and as long as they retained party discipline they had the power to defend their interests. Democratic leaders typically insisted that voting law provided some flexibility to legislatures in meeting Section 5 requirements which they argued did not require maximization of black representation to achieve preclearance. It was true that in the spring of 1991 when the Commonwealth's redistricting sessions got under way the ardor of DOJ voting rights enforcement had yet to be tested. With General Assembly elections scheduled for November of 1991, Virginia competed with Louisiana for first place among the states seeking preclearance for their legislative redistricting plans under new voting law. In outward appearances the Democratic leadership was clearly discomfited by the clamor for optimum black representation voiced by community groups like the NAACP and the ACLU. The source of the Democratic leadership's anxiety was the gathering momentum of a Republican redistricting strategy that, if successful, promised to ultimately dislodge Democratic control of the General Assembly.

The Democratic leadership responded with a two-pronged strategy. First, willing to test DOJ enforcement mettle if need be, the leadership introduced redistricting plans in both chambers that fell far short of maximizing black representation but offered some modest improvements in existing black representation. The second prong of Democratic strategy surfaced in the House of Delegates, where the Democratic leadership pursued a blatant partisan gerrymander designed to handicap Republican resurgence across the decade of the 1990s.

In both these strategies the Democratic leadership enjoyed the sometimes public and sometimes private support of some members of the Black Caucus. African-American voters in Virginia, in contrast to their black representatives in the legislature, are, as a whole, considerably less than enthusiastic about the advantages of Democratic ascendancy in the General Assembly. Black voters and community groups probably understand the true character of the Democratic Party of Virginia better than any other segment of the Virginia electorate. In Virginia black voters are allowed to pick between two parties bearing different names but pursuing essentially the same public policies. Among the politically alert element within black Virginia culture, one often finds the opinion that the Democrats and Republicans are simply two factions of one party—the party of wealth and privilege. For many black voters, voting for white Democratic candidates in Virginia seems to be not so much a matter of supporting the candidate of choice as it is a matter of choosing the lesser of two evils. The Republicans, with their arch-conservative economics, anti-labor politics, reactionary views on government, and strident resistance to affirmative action of any sort, constitute the first evil. The Virginia Democrats, no less conservative in economic policy than their Republican cohorts, the architects of right-to-work statues in the state, and lackluster exponents of racial justice constitute the other evil. Although black voters in the Commonwealth have consistently and overwhelmingly supported Democratic candidates across the state since they gained access to the ballot in the 1960s, they have few tangible benefits to show for over three decades of loyalty.

Like their Republican counterparts during the 1991 redistricting sessions, black legislators would find themselves frequently at cross purposes with their constituents and community organizations like the NAACP and the ACLU who sought to maximize black representation. Black legislators and Governor Wilder, on the other hand, observed first hand the crippling handicaps burdening a minority party within a legislature. What, after all, was the point of increasing black representation only to tip control of the legislature to an opposing party openly hostile to almost any remedy to past or present discrimination? Among black elected officials already seated in the General Assembly, considerations such as

these moved them into a course of moderation that balanced partisan considerations with racial empowerment when it came to the question of which redistricting plan satisfied new voting law.

1991— REDISTRICTING THE HOUSE OF DELEGATES

Since I have already presented a narrative of the 1991 redistricting session for the
General Assembly elsewhere (Persons, 1997), a broad summary outline should
suffice here. In April 1990, concentrated distributions of African-Americans constituted 18.8 percent (University of Virginia 1991, 2) of the Virginia population.
At the same time the Virginia House of Delegates in 1990 also had the lowest
black representation (7 percent) of any southern state—seven Delegates in nine
majority-minority population districts (Shaw, Pittman, et. al. 1991, 5). Debate in
the House centered on the question of which plan, Democratic or Republican,
provided black voters with the best remedy to a patent racial gerrymander in the
Virginia House of Delegates. The Democratic plan, which one reporter called the
"brainchild of the Black Caucus in the House," also delivered 11 black "influence" districts in which black population exceeded 25 percent.[5] According to a
Republican spokesman the plan also delivered "the most vicious statewide gerrymander in the history of America."[6] Thirty-nine percent of all Republican House
incumbents were paired with each other, or, in the case of one, with the Independent representative in the House who generally supports Republican initiatives
(Republican Party of Virginia, 1991). Steve Haner, Executive Director of the
Joint Republican Caucus, had a light-hearted but prescient comment about the
redistricting outcome for Republicans in the House saying: "We will have all
these unemployed delegates wanting to move to the Senate. The real effect of the
plan is to recruit the best crop of Republican Senate candidates ever."[7]

The Virginia Conference of the National Association for the Advancement
of Colored People (NAACP), the ACLU and Republicans all challenged the
Democratic proposal on grounds of minority vote dilution. All these dissenting
groups presented the House Privileges & Elections Committee with alternative
proposals or plans demonstrating or alleging that 13 districts with majority black
populations, two more than the Democratic plan, could be built. The ACLU and
Republicans both introduced plans showing that another viable majority-minority
district (57.73 percent black VAP in the Republican plan) could be drawn in the
Richmond-Henrico-Charles City area. A weaker district (56 percent VAP in the
NAACP plan and 55 percent VA in the ACLU plan) could also be built in the
Danville-South Boston-Halifax-Pittsylvania area.

Passage of the Democratic plan was, in the end, little more than an exercise
in majority rule. With members of both parties, including the Black Caucus, voting along strictly partisan lines the Democratic redistricting bill sailed through

---

[5]*The Richmond Times Dispatch,* 5, April, 1991.
[6]*The Richmond News Leader,* 5, April, 1991, p 5.
[7]*The Winchester Star,* 6, April, 1991, p A6.

the General Assembly. Despite rigorous pleas from the NAACP and the ACLU, Governor Wilder, who well appreciated the ominous trend of growing Republican strength in the House, signed off on the Democratic bill.

In the view of the NAACP, by failing to establish two additional majority-minority districts and two additional minority influence districts the Democratic plan diluted minority voting strength for the purpose of incumbent protection .[8] Attached to the NAACP's Comment Letter to the DOJ was the NAACP plan for the Danville area containing an additional 56 percent black VAP district. The ACLU and Republicans also submitted cogent Comment Letters corroborating NAACP claims.

Department of Justice Objections to the House Plan

At the statewide redistricting conference held at Norfolk State University on December 7, 1990, J. Gerald Hebert, Acting Chief of the Voting Section, doffed his coat, rolled up his sleeves, and told all in attendance that "redistricting plans which contain districts which dilute minority voting strength can never be justified and will not be tolerated" (Hebert, remarks, 1990). Among African-Americans attending the conference, such rhetoric fired expectations of bold DOJ voting law enforcement. "Optimization" and "maximization" became buzz words in the vernacular of voting rights advocates in Virginia as they began to draw new black legislative districts.

It was not to be. From the perspective of voting rights advocates including the NAACP, the limited scope of DOJ objections to the House plan were plainly disappointing. The single objection to the House plan was a very narrowly drawn complaint that focused entirely on the submergence of 4,000 black voters in Charles City County in a majority white district while rejecting available alternatives (Dunne, 1991, letter, July 16, p 2). Not a word was written regarding the other potential black majority district in the Danville area or the two additional putative influence districts drawn by voting rights advocates.

With lawmakers on both sides of the aisle voting along clearly partisan lines, House amendments answering DOJ objections with the construction of a single additional black House district sailed through both chambers of the General Assembly, were endorsed by the Governor, and survived DOJ scrutiny.

Allegedly injured by a partisan gerrymander, Republicans had no choice but to turn to the courts for redress. In August 1991, Republicans entered a motion in federal court seeking injunctive relief to forestall legislative elections under an alleged gerrymander plan which promised grievous injury to Republican rights protected under the First and Fourteenth Amendments. True to the ideological doctrine of Virginia Republicans, race-based Voting Rights Act issues were conspicuously absent from the complaint. Ultimately, adroit career moves into Senate contests by several paired Republican delegates consider-

---

[8]Byrd-Harden, Comment Letter, 8, July, 1991, pp 1-11.

ably mitigated injuries. The 4th Circuit Court of Appeals finally denied the Republican motion.

1991—REDISTRICTING THE VIRGINIA SENATE

Throughout the 1991 redistricting sessions the Virginia Senate was eminently less partisan than the House. With a three-to-one majority, Senate Democrats savored an almost unassailable advantage over Republicans. Unlike their counterparts in the House, Republican Senators followed their historic redistricting strategy of accommodation and compromise, which could protect their numbers without provoking partisan reprisals. Where partisan incumbent protection was the clearly dominant theme of House redistricting, the controlling theme of Senate redistricting was unambiguously bipartisan incumbent protection.

African-Americans entered the Senate redistricting session with two solid majority-minority districts, one in Richmond and another in Norfolk. A third minority Senator, Bobby Scott (D-Newport News), represented a district that was 65 percent white. The voting rights question confronting the chamber was how many additional black districts would Virginia Senators, left to their own devices, create?

Consistent with their strategy, the Democratic leadership's redistricting bill offered a single additional (53.6 percent) black Senate district. Both the NAACP and the ACLU had published plans demonstrating that five winnable black Senate districts could be built. Voting rights advocates were clearly indignant with the arrogance of a legislative chamber openly contravening established law. Nevertheless the leadership's bill, with some minor amendments, cleared both chambers of the General Assembly only to be vetoed by Governor Wilder. The governor returned the bill to the Senate with message that "the Senate should have the opportunity to demonstrate that it can and will adhere to the law and will not turn back the clock on the commendable progress that has been made in the Commonwealth."[9] On the same day, Lt. Gov. Donald S. Beyer Jr. commented to the press that "it's going to be a very painful process for a lot of people who spent a long time building safe seats for themselves...."[10] The Senate P & E Committee amended their original plan and delivered a new version bearing five black districts which kept "most incumbents in separate districts" but drew a Wilder ally into a black district.[11]

A coalition of disgruntled Democratic senators in collaboration with most Republican Senators submitted an alternative bill which spared the governor's ally but drew "two of the administration's sternest critics—both holdovers from the segregationist Byrd machine" into predominantly black districts.[12] By offer-

[9]*The Virginian-Pilot*, 20, April, 1991, p A1.
[10]*The Virginian-Pilot,* 20, April, 1991, p A1.
[11]*The Virginian-Pilot,* 24, April, 1991, p A1.
[12]*The Richmond Times Dispatch,* 1, May, 1991.

ing concessions in the form of a few stronger Republican districts, the insurgents' plan clearly induced Republican support by explicitly weakening Democratic districts.[13] In a historic departure from tradition, the insurgents' bill, with the support of 9 of 10 Republicans and all black Senators, passed on a 21-18 vote. The plan subsequently cleared the House and was signed by Governor Wilder. Since the plan created the maximum number of achievable black Senate districts, DOJ preclearance quickly followed. For the first time in the post-reconstruction redistricting history of Virginia, insurgent Democratic senators had defeated the leadership's redistricting plan and prevailed with an alternative enthusiastically endorsed by Republicans. Much to the alarm of the Senate Democratic leadership, the 1991 Virginia Senate redistricting bill would in a very real sense be a Republican plan.

A Compactness Challenge

A prophetic court challenge to the Senate plan surfaced in Halifax County Circuit Court shortly after the plan's adoption. A group of elected officials from eight Southside counties challenged the predominantly black 18th Senatorial District on the grounds that it violated Virginia Constitutional requirements for a "compact and contiguous district."[14] As proposed, the 18th Senatorial District, which is 57.39 percent black (1990 VAP), stretches 178 miles across 12 localities in Southside Virginia. Although prescient in 1991, the lawsuit apparently failed to gather sufficient support for appeals after its initial rejection.

CONGRESSIONAL REDISTRICTING

Population growth in the Commonwealth over the 1980s increased Virginia's Congressional apportionment from 10 to 11 seats. By the time Congressional redistricting got under way in November 1991, it was a foregone conclusion that the additional seat would sustain Virginia's first black Congressional district since 1890. The issue was where would the district be built and which incumbent(s), if any, would be injured by Democrats in control of the process. The Assembly's initial plan created a 61.5 percent black population majority district (the 3rd Congressional District) in a sprawling geography connecting Norfolk, Richmond and the Northern Neck. Owing to some very vigorous "arm-twisting" by the state's largest single employer—Newport News Shipbuilding—Republican Herbert Bateman's 1st District was carefully contoured to avoid excessive black population, thus preserving a Republican incumbency and the interests, including a sizable number of black jobs, it allegedly protected.[15]

Both the NAACP and the ACLU appealed to Governor Wilder to oppose

---

[13] *The Richmond Times Dispatch*, 1, May, 1991.

[14] *The Richmond News Leader*, 18, July, 1991, p 1.

the plan on the grounds that the minority population was insufficient to insure the election of a minority candidate.[16] Wilder subsequently offered amendments increasing the black population in the 3rd District to 63.9 percent and the Assembly concurred. DOJ approval quickly followed almost guaranteeing the election of Virginia's first black congressman in 102 years.

SUMMARY—1991 GENERAL ASSEMBLY GAINS IN BLACK POPULATION MAJORITY DISTRICTS FOR AFRICAN-AMERICANS

Tables 1 and 2 summarizing majority-black and black influence districts in 1990 (Table 1) and 1991 (Table 2) provide a basis for summarizing overall gains in majority-minority population districts for African-Americans during the 1991 redistricting session. In the House, majority-black population districts increased from 9 (nine percent of House seats) to 12 (twelve percent of House seats), a gain of three seats. In the Senate, majority-black population districts increased from 2 (five percent of Senate seats) to 5 (over twelve percent of Senate seats), a gain of three seats. Overall, then, majority-black population districts in the General Assembly (House and Senate combined) increased from 11 (slightly over seven percent) to 17 (twelve percent).

As the tables show, the cost of African-American increases in majority black population General Assembly districts was a substantial decrease in black influence districts. By Ms. Byrd-Harden's "influence district" definition (greater than 30 percent black VAP, but less than 50 percent VAP) overall thirteen black influence districts (seven in the House and six in the Senate) were sacrificed to gain six additional majority-black population General Assembly districts. The dissolution of thirteen black influence districts no doubt gave Republicans some cause for celebration because it was in these weakened Democratic districts that Republicans placed their hopes of eventually capturing the General Assembly.

In Congressional redistricting I have adopted a slightly less demanding threshold—20 percent black VAP—as a definition for a black influence district. As Table 3 illustrates, using a 20 percent minimum minority population standard reveals that the creation of the single black Congressional district also had its price in the loss of three black influence districts. This will become important later when we examine the question of whether or not Republican "smart redistricting strategy" succeeded.

---

[15]Bateman serves on two Congressional committees which oversee the defense procurement upon which Newport News Shipbuilding is almost entirely dependent. As a lobbyist for the shipyard put it: "replacing Bateman could (threaten) our position in Congress and ultimately (contribute) to putting many minority workers on the street without a job." *The Virginian-Pilot,* 20, November, 1991, p A1.

[16]*The Virginian-Pilot,* 22, November, 1991, p. D5.

TABLE 1. Majority Black and Black Influence Districts, VA, 1990

HOUSE OF DELEGATES		SENATE	
Majority Black Population Districts (equal to or greater than 50% Black VAP)			
District Number	*% Black (VAP)*	*District Number*	*% Black (VAP)*
62nd	54	5th	50
63rd	61	9th	77
70th	85	Sum = 2	Average % = 64%
71st	70		
80th	64		
89th	67		
90th	66		
92nd	62		
95th	60		
Sum = 9	Average % = 65%		
Black Influence Districts (greater than 30%, less than 50% Black VAP)			
20th	35	1st	36
23rd	31	2nd	35
59th	33	10th	31
60th	39	13th	49
61st	39	15th	42
64th	31	16th	42
69th	44	18th	33
74th	47	Sum = 7	Average % = 38%
75th	41		
76th	42		
77th	36		
79th	33		
100th	36		
Sum = 13	Average % = 37%		

Shading reveals districts with non-black incumbents. All percentages are rounded.

Source: Commonwealth of Virginia, Division of Legislative Services, *Drawing the Line, 1991 Redistricting in Virginia,* No. 3 (January), 1991.

TABLE 2. Majority Black and Black Influence Districts, VA, 1991

HOUSE OF DELEGATES		SENATE	
Majority Black Population Districts (equal to or greater than 50% Black VAP)			
District Number	*% Black (VAP)*	*District Number*	*% Black (VAP)*
63rd	60	2nd	56
69th	61	5th	62
70th	60	9th	64
71st	59	16th	60
74th	60	18th	60
75th	57	Sum = 5	Average % = 60%
77th	58		
80th	62		
89th	64		
90th	57		
92nd	62		
95th	59		
Sum = 12	Average % = 60%		
Black Influence Districts (greater than 30%, less than 50% Black VAP)			
20th	34	15th	35
59th	31	Sum = 1	Average % = 35%
60th	36		
61st	39		
62nd	31		
100th	36		
Sum = 6	Average % = 35%		

Shading reveals districts with non-black incumbents. All percentages are rounded.
Sources: Commonwealth of Virginia, Division of Legislative Services, *Drawing the Line, 1991 Redistricting in Virginia,* Nos. 5 & 6 (May and July), 1991.

TABLE 3. Congressional Black Influence Districts, 1981 and 1991*

1981		1991	
District Number	*% Back (VAP)*	*District Number*	*% Black (VAP)*
1st	30	4th	32
2nd	24	5th	25
3rd	29		
4th	39		
5th	24		
Sum = 5	Average % = 29	Sum = 2	Average % =28

* The influence district definition used here is any district with over 20% black VAP but less than 50% VAP.
Sources: Commonwealth of Virginia, Division of Legislative Services, News Release, Public Hearing - Congressional Redistricting, October 1991, 2; and Drawing the Line, December 2, 1991, 1-2.

1991, 1993, AND 1995 ELECTION OUTCOMES FOR AFRICAN-AMERICANS

Building majority-black population districts and electing African-American candidates to those districts are two vastly different things. In Virginia elections are often won or lost at the nomination stage. Indeed, for African-American candidates without the advantages of incumbency, the 1991 Democratic primaries and conventions repeatedly proved to be insurmountable obstacles. Although the African-American community fielded minority candidates at the nomination stage in every predominantly black district, despite a preponderance of black voting age population in these districts no minority candidate was able to defeat a white incumbent in a primary contest. Since white incumbents occupied 5 of 12 majority-minority House seats, blacks were unable to advance to the general election as Democratic candidates in any of the three newly created black House districts. In the end, the only black candidates able to win House seats were the seven African-Americans who already had them. A central reality of the 1991 House elections for African-Americans was that blacks gained no additional seats in the House of Delegates.

Assuming all majority-minority House districts created in the 1990s round of redistricting elude or survive newly accessible court challenges occasioned by yet another upheaval in voting law, representational gains for blacks in the Virginia House of Delegates over the 1990s will be a protracted, incremental struggle. The first success in this process was scored by Lionel Spruill Sr. (D, Chesapeake) who advanced to occupy the 77th House District (58 percent black VAP) in 1993 elections after the white incumbent accepted a local District Court appointment. A second conversion occurred in 1995 when Donald McEachin, an African-American attorney from Henrico, was finally able to dislodge the powerful Robert B. Ball, Sr. from the 74th House District (56 percent black VAP) in an uphill primary battle (Sabato, 1995).

African-American gains in the Virginia Senate were a different matter. Unlike the House, the Senate, created a plan maximizing black Senate representation with three new majority-minority districts. White incumbents retired in two of the new black Senate districts permitting black candidates to run and win in contests for open seats. Senator Bobby Scott retained the third new district which was reshaped from a majority-white to a majority-black district.

Congress

As widely predicted, African-American Senator Bobby Scott (D-Newport News), who represented a Virginia Senate constituency which was 65 percent white in 1990, walked away from competitors in both the 1992 primary and general elections. Scott, a graduate of Harvard College and Boston College Law School, is now Virginia's first black congressman since reconstruction.

1991, 1993, 1995 ELECTIONS—THE PARTISAN OUTCOME

House of Delegates

As House elections in 1991, 1993 and 1995 have shown, the Democratic gerrymander was prescient. In 1991, despite the pairings of 15 Republicans in redistricting, Republicans picked up two additional House seats capturing 41 of 100 seats with 51.0 percent of total vote for all contested House races. The Republican statewide vote share for all House seats (contested and uncontested) was less impressive at 43 percent in 1991.

In the 1993 House elections, for the first time in this century, the GOP received a majority of all votes cast (contested and uncontested) in House elections. Republicans picked up an additional six seats bringing their total to 47. The Republican proportion of the statewide House vote share had increased a full 8.2 percent from 43 percent in 1991 to 51.2 percent in 1993. In the 1995 legislative elections, the Republican vote share rose to an all-time high of 53 percent. Despite the GOP's majority status in the House electorate, the Democratic gerrymander and vigorous Democratic campaigning continued to deny Republicans control of the chamber. In fact, the Republican seats-votes ratio (calculated as the GOP percent of House seats divided by the percent of voters statewide endorsing GOP House candidates) diminished slightly from .95 in 1991 to .91 in 1993. Republicans would very likely control the Virginia House of Delegates today (1997) were it not for the Democratic redistricting gerrymander. House Democrats in high places well pleased with the result may, however, live to regret their handiwork. Given Republican gains in the electorate, the 2001 redistricting round could well provide the GOP with both a precedent and an opportunity to even the score.

Senate

Elections in 1991 delivered startling consequences for Senate Democrats. Reaching their high-water mark for the century, the GOP gained eight Senate seats overall increasing their numbers from 10 to 18 in a 40 member chamber. A fascinating aspect of this landslide is revealed by the seats-votes ratios for the GOP's Senate contingent. With only 41.3 percent of the statewide Senate vote total Republicans captured 45 percent of Senate seats yielding a seats-votes ration of 1.08. By contrast, the Democratic share of the statewide Senate vote total was 54.4 percent and their share of Senate seats was 55 percent (22 of 40) yielding a seats-votes ratio of 1.01. Actually, both Democrats and Republicans enjoyed some over-representation at the expense of Independents who are substantially underrepresented in their seat-votes ration. The 1991 elections confirmed the worst fears of the Democratic Senate leadership—the Senate redistricting plan had apparently tilted the playing field to Republican advantage. In the 1995 Senate elections, with Democrats failing to contest 12 Republican incumbents, Republicans garnered two additional Senate seats and scored their best Republican performance of the century while quite nearly capturing control of the Virginia Senate.

BLACK EMPOWERMENT IN PERSPECTIVE

How does one evaluate the overall gains African-Americans in Virginia scored in the 1991 redistricting sessions and subsequent elections through 1995? Following elections in 1995, three predominantly black population districts were retained by white incumbents so that African-Americans occupied only 14 of 17 black majority General Assembly Seats. Between 1990 and 1995 the African-American share of General Assembly seats had increased from 7.1 percent to 10 percent.[17] African-Americans also gained their first predominantly black population Congressional District in 1991. There is no question that these are notable accomplishments for a state that historically had the lowest levels of black representation in the South (Morris, 1994).

Yet, this gain in political empowerment for black Virginians bears a number of critical qualifications. To begin with, a 102 year wait for a single Congressional seat can hardly be viewed as swift justice. As the Virginia Conference of the NAACP insists, it is also by no means certain that every potential black district was in fact legislated. Even if African-Americans eventually capture every legislated majority black population district they will remain underrepresented because they will hold 12 percent of the seats of the governing body in a state where they are 18.8 percent of the population. Furthermore, as observers universally agree, none of these gains were graciously volunteered by Virginia lawmakers in search of more equitable representation for minorities. On the contrary, the new black districts in Virginia were wrenched as concessions from a body legislating under the duress of well defined federal voting law that protected minorities from vote diluting districting schemes.

---

[17]African-American Senator Bobby Scott (D, Newport News) achieved office in a 65 percent white district bringing the African-American seat total to 10 seats, or 7.1 percent of the General Assembly in 1990.

All in all, the struggle in the 1991 General Assembly redistricting sessions for minority voting rights in the Commonwealth has produced a very mixed bag of results. Those who seek to maintain an image of moderation in race relations in Virginia can point to important African-American gains in the General Assembly and Congress. Others will doubtless argue that beneath the veneer of these cosmetic gains little has changed for blacks in the Commonwealth. In any event, a troubling reality of minority voting rights advances over the last three decades in Virginia is that virtually every increase in black representation depended on federal intervention for its success. A reversal in federal policy could have a potentially devastating impact on the cause of minority empowerment in Virginia. As recent events suggest, such a turnaround in federal policy is now clearly under way.

Did "Smart" Republican Redistricting Strategy Work?

Did the GOP strategy to use voting law to pack Democrats into black districts produce legislative gains for Republicans? In Virginia there is no simple answer to this question and in one sense it's still too soon to venture a complete assessment. Republicans in this context are employing a long-term redistricting strategy that contemplates assaulting currently Democratic districts as their occupants retire. Since Virginia legislators do not, as a rule, retire quickly, it will take several more years before the strategy can be completely evaluated. African-Americans sacrificed 13 General Assembly 'influence districts' in the 1991 round of redistricting. Clearly many black voters were indeed stripped from previously racially mixed districts leaving behind 13 General Assembly seats (seven in the House and six in the Senate) with swollen margins of white voters presumably less committed to the Democratic agenda than black voters. Accompanying this redistricting outcome which weakened Democratic districts has been a pronounced increase in Republican voter appeal to whites across the South. Merle Black, a political scientist at Emery University, has documented a rather striking recent upsurge in Southern white Republican voters noting that "whites voting Republican shot up from the low 50s in 1992 to 65 percent in 1994" (Edsall and Yang, 1996). In 1991, 1993, and 1995, Republican General Assembly strength reached century high levels. Redistricting, however, could only create the potential for Republican gains not, the reality.

The reality was that 1991 and 1993 were not good years for the "in party"—Democrats—in Virginia. A national recession was underway and the Virginia economy was anemic. Elections in 1991 and 1993 offered Virginia voters opportunities to vent their dissatisfaction with the status quo in general and the administration of Democratic Governor L. Douglas Wilder in particular. In 1991, Governor Wilder had the least favorable approval rating of any governor since opinion surveys were started in the state (Sabato, 1991, 1993). The other titular head of the Virginia Democratic Party—Senator Charles Robb—was plagued by womanizing and alleged drug abuse scandals. All of which is to say that Republican gains in the General Assembly are probably strongly linked to both changes in the mood of the electorate and changes in election geographies effected by redistricting. The 1995 elections tend to confirm this conclusion. With Governor Wilder and Senator Robb offstage and the Virginia economy beginning to revive, Democrats were able to capture a slight majority (51.4 percent) of votes in contested General Assembly elections (Sabato, 1995).

Congressional elections since redistricting also contradict the proposition that 'smart redistricting strategy' actually worked to Republican benefit. Despite the loss of three black congressional influence districts in redistricting (see Table 3, page 332), Democrats were able to actually increase their share of the congressional delegation to its highest proportion since 1964—7 of the 11 House seats. And, unlike other southern states, in the 1994 congressional elections there was no Republican Revolution in Virginia. Democrats did, however, lose a seat as Republicans won in the Eleventh District in an extraordinarily rare election in which the challenger out spent the incumbent (Sabato, 1995).

If the GOP redistricting strategy worked anywhere in Virginia, one might be able to say it worked in the Virginia Senate. In the Senate, GOP strategy succeeded only because of the unprecedented failure of a complacent and fractured Democratic majority to pursue partisan election advantages available in redistricting. Yet, given the tidal shift of the Virginia electorate in a Republican direction, it would be inaccurate to say that Republican Senate gains were the sole product of smart redistricting strategy.

AN UPHEAVAL IN VOTING LAW: IMPLICATIONS FOR VIRGINIA

It has been argued that it is easier to unring a bell than withdraw liberties once granted. Yet, in voting rights, recent Supreme Court decisions (*Shaw* v. *Reno, Miller* v. *Johnson, Shaw* v. *Hunt,* and *Bush* v. *Vera*) have accomplished the political equivalent of unringing a bell. What the Court majority seems to be saying is that districting plans shown to be based predominantly on race at the Congressional level will not survive Court scrutiny unless they satisfy "strict scrutiny, our most rigorous and exacting standard of constitutional review" (Kennedy, 1995). Compactness, although undefined, can be one of several indices used to detect the presence of districting that is predominantly race-based. With one exception the Supreme Court has now sustained every challenge to a race-based congressional district it has heard since 1993. The exception was a challenge to North Carolina's 1st Congressional District (*Shaw* v. *Hunt*) which the Court dismissed because none of the white plaintiffs actually lived in the district (Greenhouse, L., 1996).

Although I have presented my interpretation of these decisions elsewhere (Persons, 1997), a summary is pertinent here. In every case since 1993 where the Court has sustained a challenge to race-based redistricting, the evidence established that the predominant motive for and justification of race-based redistricting plans was compliance with DOJ enforcement of Section 5 of the Voting

Rights Act. As I reread the opinions of Kennedy, O'Connor, and Rehnquist in these cases, I am struck by their rebuke of voting rights enforcement policy within the DOJ. Conservatives see a fundamental difference between a case specific remedy for well proven instances of vote dilution and the "optimization" or "maximization" enforcement strategies pursued at DOJ under Section 5 of the Voting Rights Act. A case specific approach implies the relentless regimen of jurisdiction-by-jurisdiction litigation in an adversarial context to deliver narrowly tailored relief to discrete victims of proven vote dilution injuries. "Optimization" and "maximization" standards for minority representation, on the other hand, offer blanket protection to a class of putatively injured minorities without the rigors of case-by-case litigation. In my view, the cement holding a tenuous conservative majority together in this reversal of voting law is a common distrust of the motives or justifications driving race-based redistricting and not race-based redistricting per se. Yet, in these new rulings the Court has certainly not invalidated race-based districting remedies resulting from Sec. 2 proceedings.

In the often acrimonious debates trailing in the wake of *Shaw, Miller* and *Bush* the critical distinction between Section 5 preclearance protections and Section 2 judicial relief has, in my view, sometimes been overlooked even by seasoned scholars. It is worth remembering, as the DOJ argued in *Miller*, that "Congress enacted Section 5 of the Voting Rights Act in 1965, and extended its coverage—because it found that 'case by case litigation was inadequate to combat widespread and consistent discrimination in voting' and that it was necessary to 'shift the advantages of time and inertia from the perpetrators of evil to its victims' " (Carter, 1996). The essence of the difference between Section 5 and Section 2 of the Voting Right Act is, in the end, a matter of expediency. It's the difference between wholesale minority empowerment under DOJ enforcement of Section 5—and case specific or retail vote dilution remedies under Section 2. In light of this critical distinction it is simply inaccurate and dangerously misleading to argue that recent Supreme Court decisions abolish all remedies available to voters victimized by vote diluting practices. I say "dangerously misleading" because such arguments conceal the availability of Section 2 remedies as a still powerful tool in the arsenal of voting rights advocates. Although it is true that there may be members of the conservative Court majority propelling this new racial jurisprudence who might be willing to invalidate Section 2 of the Voting Rights Act, until Section 2 is overturned it is simply self-defeating for voting rights advocates to argue that minority voters are without remedy to vote dilution practices. Yet and still, the invalidation of districting plans enacted under the influence of DOJ Section 5 enforcement may well undermine African-American representational gains in Virginia.

In 1995, at about the same time as the *Miller* decision was announced, Bobby Scott's 3rd Congressional District was challenged in Federal District Court in a suit remarkably similar to the plaintiffs' arguments in *Shaw, Miller*, and *Bush*. The plaintiffs in this case, *Moon v. Meadows*, argued that by assigning citizens on the basis of classification by race to certain congressional districts the districting plan adopted by General Assembly constitutes an unconstitutional racial gerrymander in violation of the Equal Protection clause of the Fourteenth Amendment. The plaintiffs, assisted in their suit by the Campaign for a Color-blind America, did not assert or allege that a tangible or demonstrable injury resulted from adoption of the districting plan apart from the alleged violation of their 14th Amendment protections.

The defense in the case was ably provided by the Commonwealth's Office of the Attorney General. "Smart Republican redistricting strategy" had apparently not lost its appeal to George Allen, a Republican, who replaced L. Douglas Wilder as Governor. Arguments in the case followed what has come to be a familiar course in this new jurisprudence of racial redistricting. Plaintiffs proffered an assortment of evidence and experts (the record of legislative intent, shape, and racial characteristics) supporting their contention that race dominated considerations in the configuration of the 3rd Congressional District. They also argued that traditional districting principles including locality integrity, respect for regional identities, and compactness were all subordinated to racial considerations.

The defense tendered evidence and expert testimony that incumbency protection and the economic vitality of the Commonwealth that incumbents served, not race, was the preeminent consideration shaping the contours of the 3rd Congressional District. Further, the defense argued that the district was not bizarre; and, was, in fact, more compact than the least compact districts from the 1980s plan. Indeed, as the defense noted, a plan advanced by Senator Hunter Andrews for a majority black district that was extremely regular in shape by the "eyeball" test was rejected in behalf of competing political and economic interests. The defense went on to insist that as single-member General Assembly districts and equal population standards were established in past years, the tradition of respect for political subdivisions or communities of interests had diminished in Virginia redistricting practice. Nevertheless, in the eyes of the defense, Virginia did not neglect traditional districting practices.

Post-trial briefs filed by the litigants revealed that both sides perceived that the center of the controversy rested in large measure on the question of whether or not Virginia had a compelling state interest in avoiding liability under Section 2 of the Voting Rights Act sufficient to satisfy a strict scrutiny inquiry. The Commonwealth argued almost stridently that **"Even if strict scrutiny is applied to the third congressional district, the state had a strong basis in evidence for creating a majority black district to avoid potential liability under section 2 of the voting rights act** [sic]."[18] In subsequent argument the Attorney General laid out compelling evidence establishing a vote dilution case against his own state had it failed to create a majority-minority district in the 1991 redistricting

---

[18]Joint Post-Trial Brief Of Defendant Bruce Meadows and Defendant-Intervenors Curtis Harris, et al, C.A. No. 3:95cv942, 11.

session. Point by point, attorneys for the Commonwealth sought to demonstrate that it satisfied all three criteria of Section 2 liability established in *Thornburg v. Gingles,* 478 U.S. 30, 50-51 (1986). To make this case the Commonwealth went on to provide convincing evidence on the three preconditions of a Section 2 liability—(1) that the minority is sufficiently large and geographically compact to constitute a majority single-member district; (2) that the majority was politically cohesive; and (3) that racially polarized voting was such that white voters usually prevented black voters from electing their candidates of choice. The plaintiffs, although conceding the second precondition (political cohesion within the minority community), vigorously contended the Commonwealth's arguments on the first and third preconditions.

On February 7, 1997 a three-judge federal panel delivered its decision. Writing for the unanimous panel, Judge Robert R. Merhige Jr., a jurist historically sympathetic to minority rights, opined that "the evidence, in our view, is overwhelming that the creation of a safe black district predominated in the drawing of the boundaries of the Third Congressional District."[19] "In other words," Merhige wrote, quoting from an earlier Supreme Court ruling, "race was the criterion that, in the State's view, could not be compromised."[20] Virginia became the sixth state to have a congressional district overturned since the 1995 upheaval in voting law.

The outcome in *Moon v. Meadows* raises, in my mind, a fascinating question. Accepting for the purposes of argument the Attorney General's compelling case that Virginia was indeed liable to a Section 2 lawsuit, would the outcome have been different had the Commonwealth failed to draw a majority-minority district in 1991 and the minority sought redress in a Section 2 claim? In other words, would a majority black 3rd Congressional District created in a successful Section 2 proceeding succeed even though an equivalent geography erected under Section 5 compulsion failed? We will, of course, never have the answer to this question. Yet, in my view, for reasons elaborated above, I suspect that such a Section 2 district might well have succeeded.

Under this new racial jurisprudence, every General Assembly majority-minority district fashioned in the 1991 redistricting session, six seats in all, could face constitutional challenge. I say "could" because whether or not black representational gains in Virginia are vulnerable to court challenge hinges in part on the question of what representational benchmark is used to define an unlawful representational retrogression prohibited by Court precedent in *Beer v. United States* (1976). In *Miller,* The Georgia District Court ruled that "the proper benchmark, in our view, is the 1982 plan, which is the last legislative plan in effect before the unconstitutional 1992 plan was enacted" (Carter 1996). If such reasoning is followed in potential Virginia litigation, none of the majority-minority population districts (3 in the House of Delegates, 3 in the Senate and the 3rd Congressional District) created in 1991 will be immune from legal challenge.

---

[19]*The Virginian-Pilot,* 12, February, 1997, p. A18.
[20]*Ibid.*

Yet, even if Rep. Bobby Scott ultimately loses the advantage of a black population majority in the 3rd, it seems highly unlikely to me that he will also lose his career in Congress. Scott is a very capable politician with proven appeal to white voters that will serve him well even if the 3rd is redrawn. The same observation can be made regarding the new African-American seats in the Virginia General Assembly. It is by no means a foregone conclusion that incumbent African-Americans in the General Assembly will necessarily lose them should their districts succumb to constitutional challenge.

The turnaround in voting law may well have profound consequences for the partisan balance in Virginia government as it will simply outlaw what I have referred to as "smart Republican redistricting strategy." Another redistricting session precipitated by a successful court challenge to the current districting plan must be a frightening prospect for Republican legislators. Reducing black population in the six new black General Assembly districts and the single black Congressional district will very likely achieve its judicial purpose of reducing the proportion of black voters in black districts to levels below those essential to insure the election of black candidates. The resulting districts, especially if they are drawn by a legislature controlled by a thin majority of embattled Democrats, would be drawn to retain proportions of black voters too high to elect Republicans but ideal for maximizing Democratic representation. At least one alarmed Virginia Republican activist has appealed publicly to the "purists" within his party to abandon their challenges to minority-majority districts (Goolrick, 1996). It turns out that author of this public appeal to Republicans to forsake their hostility to race-based districting is an aide to Virginia Republican Congressman Herbert Bateman. A flood of minority voters into Bateman's 1st Congressional District would almost certainly foreshorten his political career.

New voting law is also already impacting local governments in Virginia. On June 29, 1995 the Supreme Court released its ruling in *Miller v. Johnson.* On August 28, 1995 the Office of the Attorney General in a highly unusual move withdrew its outstanding objection to the adoption of an at-large School Board election method in Chesapeake, Virginia. Chesapeake, Virginia's fastest growing city, had requested reconsideration of the DOJ Section 5 objection interposed on June 20, 1994. Correspondence from the City's retained attorneys, Hunton & Williams (Richmond, Virginia), clearly identified decisive changes in court rulings as the pivotal factor in the withdrawal of the objection (Greever, A. G., 1995, August 31). On September 14, 1995, the City Council of a contiguous sister city—Portsmouth, Virginia—followed suit and announced its intention to adopt an at-large method of election for its School Board. I had direct knowledge of Portsmouth's intention to consider single-member districting alternatives prior to the Chesapeake reversal because my consulting services had been sought in the matter.

Local redistricting in Virginia is, however, a much different animal than General Assembly or congressional redistricting. Local redistricting has most often been precipitated by lawsuits mounted by an organized group of aggrieved minority voters challenging an at-large method of election. In the course of such litigation the painful local history of vote diluting practices and patterns of racial block voting are thoroughly documented. When minority plaintiffs succeed in such challenges, the judicially supervised, race-based remedial districting plans which emerge are justified by a record of discrimination that has withstood adversarial scrutiny. This, of course, stands in marked contrast to redistricting bills legislated under the threat or existence of DOJ objections during the 1991 General Assembly redistricting sessions. Consequently, in my opinion, minority voters in Virginia communities injured by vote diluting practices should not abandon the courts in their struggle against discrimination in the voting place unless and until the Court invalidates race-based districting altogether. Indeed, it is not inconceivable that Virginia cities, counties and towns with significant black populations employing at-large methods of elections could prove to be fertile grounds for Section 2 lawsuits in the years immediately ahead.

CONCLUSIONS

Overall, then, it seems fair to say that as districting cases move through the courts in the years ahead, the recent turnaround in voting law is more likely to incrementally erode gains in African-American empowerment than to reverse them. Yet, an erosion in African-American empowerment will have at least one potentially volatile consequence. For decades African-Americans in Virginia and elsewhere have been told that if they were patient, if they played by the rules, eventually they would realize a coequal status in American society. In 1993, at the very moment when empowerment seemed finally within reach, an upheaval in voting law has shattered the dream. For many African-Americans recent reversals in civil rights law will constitute an embittering betrayal of a social compact. I fear that in the end these current decisions of the Court will only heap another grievance onto the tinderbox of racial tension now building in our republic.

I began this analysis with a discussion of the disfranchisement of the blacks in Virginia in the 1890s following reconstruction. In the 1890s the policy of disfranchisement was invented by an alliance of landed gentry and commercial interests to preserve their privileged advantages in Commonwealth rule. Today, African-Americans have access to the ballot in Virginia; but, given this new jurisprudence of race, candidates preferred by black voters—black candidates—are no longer assured of political geographies that will support their election. No matter how one turns these new precedents in voting law, the political result is the same—majority black population districts created under the compulsion of Section 5 enforcement to remedy current or past discrimination will not survive strict scrutiny in federal courts. Predominantly white districts, on the other hand, suffer no such legal prejudice. From the perspective of black voters, when all is said and done and the smokescreen of litigation lifts, the net result is that whites have the vote and their candidates but blacks have only the vote. The disfranchisement this new law sustains doesn't deny blacks the ballot, it denies them choice. It is virtual disfranchisement. Like the disfranchisement of the 1890s, the disfranchisement of the 1990s also preserves and defends the advantages, prerogatives and conservative policies of the aristocratic tradition that has always ruled in Virginia.

PART IV

Districting Commissions and Minority Empowerment

IS THERE A BETTER WAY TO REDISTRICT?[1]

Donald E. Stokes

THIS CHAPTER IS A REPORT ON NEW JERSEY'S EXPERIMENT IN REDISTRICTING. The experiment is, in effect, designed to see whether a way can be found that allows the practical political wisdom of the parties to flow into the redistricting process while contraining the process to meet clear tests of the public interest. Such a method of redistricting would lie somewhere between the British and Commonwealth practice of assigning the task to neutral commissioners who are notably short on practical wisdom and the American practice of leaving the drawing of boundaries to the ordinary political process, with results that are notably short on public interest. The two most important tests of public interest have to do with fairness between the parties and the fair representation of minorities, *desiderata* of current redistricting that are conceptually linked. I will sketch here the background of New Jersey's experiment, summarize the results thus far, and draw conclusions of general importance for the redistricting process.

THE ORIGIN OF NEW JERSEY'S EXPERIMENT

When the U. S. Supreme Court was remaking American representation in the wake of *Baker v. Carr,* it came upon an upper house in New Jersey's legislature composed of one senator from each county. The Court was unimpressed by claims that such an arrangement might be appropriate for the state that had once sold the rest of the country on the idea of the equal representation of states in the United States Senate. It declared this "little New Jersey Plan" to be a violation of

---

[1]This a revision of a paper prepared for delivery at the Western Political Science Association, San Francisco, March 21, 1992. It is a pleasure to acknowledge the research assistance of Frank Hoke and the skilled help I received as a public member of several redistricting commissions from Joseph A. Irenas, Mark M. Murphy, Ernest C. Reock, and David M. Satz, Jr.

the U.S. Constitution and mandated the state legislature to call a limited constitutional convention to fix it. Since the legislature was then divided, with the General Assembly in the hands of the Democrats and the Senate strongly tilted toward the Republicans, it summoned a finely balanced convention, and the two sides worked out a redistricting procedure that was itself finely balanced between the parties.

Under this procedure, redistricting begins in a census year with the appointment of a highly partisan but balanced Apportionment Commission of ten members, five chosen by each of the two state party chairmen. These party delegations have a month to agree on the boundaries of the state's forty legislative districts.[2] If they do reach agreement, these boundaries hold for the next decade unless they are overturned by the courts. But if the ten party commissioners are unable to reach agreement, the Chief Justice of the State Supreme Court chooses an eleventh, public member, and the expanded Commission has another month to finish the job. The constitution does not say what will happen if it fails to do so, but no public member worth her or his salt will let the second month run out.

This procedure differs from the ordinary political process first of all by taking redistricting out of the hands of the legislature. Yet it is easy to exaggerate this difference. There is no bar to the appointment of Senators or Assembly members, and the Commission has included members of the legislature on each of the four occasions—after the 1966 constitutional convention and after the 1970, 1980, and 1990 censuses—when the procedure has been used. There is also a dense flow of (accurate and inaccurate) information to and from the legislature as the Commission does its work. In practical terms, the Commission may not be more removed from the legislature than would be a special committee selected from the Senate and Assembly to draw the new boundaries, although the legislature does not vote on the Commission's plan after the boundaries are fixed.

What *does* set the Commission's work fundamentally apart from the ordinary political process is the equal weighting of the parties and the procedure for moving a deadlocked Commission to an agreement without tilting it toward one party or the other. The appointment of ten members by the party chairmen guarantees that the Commission will be exquisitely political, in keeping with the character of New Jersey as a strongly partisan state. It has been more than twenty years since a party delegation split on a Commission vote, and the Commission is awash with the practical wisdom of its partisan members. But neither delegation can dominate the other on a straight party vote, unlike the situation in the legislature when both houses (and the governor's office) are controlled by the same party. And if this balanced, ten-member Commission is deadlocked at the end of a month of working on its own, the neutral public member supplied by the Chief Justice will not simply deliver control into the hands of one party or the other.

---

[2]The ten party members of the Apportionment Commission are appointed by the party chairmen by November 15 of the census year. The Commission has until February I or until one month after the census data are delivered to the state, whichever is later, to reach an agreement on the new boundaries.

I should underscore this last point, since it is so easy to suppose that a public member inserted into a deadlocked Commission will break the tie simply by choosing one or the other of two partisan plans. The "tiebreaker" phrase is a staple of newspaper comment, and it easily slipped into the assignment I was given by the organizer of our panel, who has observed New Jersey from a distance. But a public member who broke a tie by choosing one or the other of two biased plans would reduce fairness between the parties to the very limited terms either of a lottery between the parties or of choosing the marginally less biased of two partisan plans. Either way, the tiebreaker would give one party an advantage for the next ten years, unless the courts intervened. The positive promotion of the public interest requires a more activist role by a public member who has a clear idea of what fairness between the parties *means.*

Moreover, limiting tiebreakers to choosing one or the other of two biased plans could easily undercut the neutrality of the Chief Justice, who appoints the eleventh member, since confining the tiebreaker to such a role would create powerful incentives for governors and senators to nominate and confirm a Chief Justice likely to pick a tiebreaker who would vote right. We had a glimpse of such a future when the current Chief Justice was renominated in 1986.[3] Conservative senators who opposed him on other grounds charged that he had appointed a registered Democrat to produce a 6 to 5 Democratic vote in 1981 and urged the Republican governor to nominate a Chief Justice who could be relied on to produce a 6 to 5 Republican vote in the Apportionment Commission to be appointed in 1991. This argument might have been more influential if the tiebreaker had not played a far more activist role in moving both party delegations toward a fair agreement, in a manner I will now describe.

BREAKING THE TIE IN 1981

The Census Bureau delivered New Jersey's 1980 census data to the governor's office on the last day of February in 1981, only six weeks before the statutory date on which the secretary of state must notify the county clerks of the boundaries of the legislative districts so that prospective candidates will know where they can run.[4] The ten party commissioners appointed by the two party chairmen hammered out the framework of an agreement during March, the month allotted

---

[3]Justices of New Jersey's Supreme Court are initially appointed by the Governor and confirmed by the State Senate for a term of years. If renominated and reconfirmed at the end of this term, they serve until retirement.

[4]New Jersey is divided into forty legislative districts, each of which sends to the legislature a Senator and two members of the General Assembly elected at large. All 80 members of the Assembly are elected to two-year terms in each of the odd-numbered years of the decade. All 40 Senators are elected to two-year terms in the odd-numbered year at the beginning of the decade and to four-year terms in the second and fourth odd-numbered years of the decade. Hence, the year after the census is always a major election year, and New Jersey has a brisker timetable for redistricting than states where a major election does not occur until the second year after the census.

them. By agreement, the Democrats were given a free hand in drawing boundaries in Hudson County and Newark; the most urban part of the state, the Republicans a free hand in drawing boundaries in the suburban and rural northwestern part of the state. The Republicans also accepted their rivals' objective of creating a new Democratic district in New Jersey's rapidly expanding waist, although they expected something in return. On this and a series of other issues the party delegations were genuinely deadlocked when the month ran out.

Toward the end of March the Chief Justice contacted me about becoming the public member if the Commission deadlocked, and I joined the Commission at the beginning of April, with the starting date of the state's electoral timetable only two weeks away. After becoming acquainted with my new colleagues and the issues dividing them, I proposed that we move to an agreement by three stages:

- that we first of all go through the outstanding issues and see whether some could be resolved on their merits, knowing that others would be resolved only in the context of an overall agreement;
- that I then set out a plan I believed to be fair between the parties (and that also met the equal-population, compactness, and contiguity requirements) and see if it had six votes;
- that if it did not, I would then ask each party to submit an alternative plan and would support whichever was closer to mine.

These steps moved the expanded commission to an agreement within the two weeks before the secretary of state's notice to the county clerks was due. Several particular issues were disposed of on their merits. Although the plan I then proposed enjoyed support in both party delegations, neither voted for it, and I then asked each party to offer me an alternative plan, on the understanding that I would give my vote to the alternative closer to mine if it met the required tests. The result was a pair of alternatives that were virtual photocopies of my own. Although both of the other plans met my test of fairness between the parties, the Democrats' was marginally closer than the Republicans' to mine. I therefore supported the slight modification of my own plan offered by the Democrats.

This agreement enjoyed substantial support in both of the party delegations, and this consensus is reflected by the fact that the counsel for the two parties filed a common brief and successfully defended the plan when it was later confronted by a minor challenge in the courts. But at the late-evening hour when the agreement was reached I knew that its Republican support would melt away before the Commission formally voted the new boundaries the following day.

With the public member and Democratic commissioners guaranteeing the state the plan everyone knew was needed if we were not to make a mess of the electoral timetable of the state, the Republicans were free to vote against the plan and ward off the brickbats of those who objected to particular provisions. Despite the appearance of conflict created by the 6 to 5 vote on the final plan, the fact is that it would have made not a particle of difference to any of the major issues on which the parties were previously deadlocked *which* of the three virtually identical final plans was chosen. Yet it was essential to the goal of fairness between the parties that we chose one of *these* plans, rather than one of the two conspicuously biased plans on which the parties were deadlocked when I joined the Commission, for reasons I will explain after I describe the operation of this constitutional procedure following the 1990 census.

BREAKING THE TIE IN 1991

The Census Bureau delivered New Jersey's data to the state on the first day of February in 1991, four weeks ahead of its 1981 delivery, indeed early enough for the expanded commission also to have a month for its work without missing the start of the state's election timetable, if a deadlock forced the procedure to this further stage. But the context of the commission's work was drastically changed by the collapse of the Democrats' prospects after their newly elected governor, Jim Florio, put through the largest tax increase in the history of the state in his early weeks in office. Both of the party delegations named to the Apportionment Commission in November of 1990 saw a Republican avalanche coming. As a result, the Democrats had no stomach for negotiating from what they thought was a position of extreme weakness. They went not into the committee room but into the courts, where they challenged the census figures as seriously undercounting blacks and Hispanics. The U.S. government had responded to this same challenge from the City of New York by promising a federal district court in Brooklyn that the Secretary of Commerce would announce July 1 whether the Department would release revised data. In view of this promise, the Democratic members of the Apportionment Commission asked New Jersey's courts to sanction the view that the data released by the Census Bureau were merely "preliminary" and that redistricting should be deferred until the "official" data were released during the summer. This position appealed to a number of Democrats in the legislature because it would put over from the spring until the fall the primary election in which Democratic incumbents would need to explain to challengers within their own party why they had voted for the Florio tax increases.

With the weeks in which the Republican and Democratic Commissioners would ordinarily have fashioned the framework of an agreement running out, this legal challenge reached New Jersey's Supreme Court. On the last day of February the Court unanimously ruled, with the Chief Justice absenting himself, that the data released by the Census Bureau were sufficient for New Jersey's redistricting process. Since the month allowed the unexpanded Commission had elapsed, the Chief Justice appointed the public member, and the expanded Commission had the month of March to get the job done.

If I thought anything was clear when the process triggered by the census ten years earlier came to an end, it was that no one would ever ask me to do the job again. But I was wrong, and on the first of March a year ago I accepted the Chief Justice's call and entered a totally changed situation. Far from hammering out the framework of an agreement, the parties had not even met. Each of the delegations and their staffs, with coaching from Washington, had done a good deal of preliminary work. But the *tabula* of principles agreed to between the two parties was simply *rasa,* and I started talking with the parties separately to find out how they saw the world and where the goals they wanted to achieve might overlap. I was again helped by the legal counsel and chief analyst I had used ten years before, and from the day I came on board we began to draw maps of our own.

Since I believed in the logic of direct negotiation between the parties, I told the two delegations that I would keep out of their way for the first of the four weeks that remained to see if they could make headway on their own, in a mini first phase of the process envisaged by New Jersey's constitution. But the looming Republican avalanche and cleavages within the Democratic ranks so impaired the bargaining between the parties that this week produced as little as the prior month had. If there was to be an agreement, it would need to emerge from the parallel bargaining of the public member with the two party delegations.

This created a different channel by which the parties' practical wisdom flowed into the bargaining process, but I believed in this wisdom's again playing a role. I needed in particular to have the parties' view of the value of the members of the Senate and Assembly whose fortunes could be affected by changes in the legislative districts. Given the population shifts in New Jersey during the 1980s, no one could have drawn the boundaries of a new set of compact, contiguous, and equally populous districts without pitting some incumbents against others or separating some incumbents from most of their constituents. The redistricting procedure written into New Jersey's constitution clearly intended these decisions to reflect the views of the parties and not to be left only to the wisdom of the public member.

Although this required an intensive effort, the work could have been completed well before the end of the month allotted us. Little change was needed in a band of districts across New Jersey's waist. But, the population north of this mid-section was down by the equivalent of one legislative district, and the population south of this mid-section was up by an equal amount. Hence, a district would need to disappear above this waist and reappear below it, with the additional changes this would entail in the surrounding districts. As the constitutional deadline approached, I set out a plan I thought was fair between the parties and met the other legal requirements, including those on the representation of minorities, but also reflected the practical wisdom of the parties on a swarm of particular points. In this case, the plan had six votes—the public member's and the five Republicans'—although I was unclear until the last moment which party would supply the additional votes to carry a plan.

Hence, the role played by the public member in the extraordinary circumstances of 1991 was very far removed from the idea of breaking a tie by choosing one of the other of two partisan plans. The 1991 experience demonstrated the resiliency of New Jersey's constitutional procedure under a complete breakdown of negotiations between the parties. Since the public member played a role akin to that of a court-appointed master working with the counsel of leaders from each party, it is all the more important to know whether such a master can be guided by principles that genuinely serve the public interest—or whether this constitutional procedure is simply an occasion for politics in a different form. We should ask whether the idea of fairness between the parties can be given objective meaning rather than being in the end a subjective judgment call. I will answer strongly in the affirmative and outline the objective criteria I have twice put into practice, before turning to minority representation and the other tests a plan should meet.

FAIRNESS BETWEEN THE PARTIES

When I joined the 1981 Apportionment Commission I was struck by how difficult it was for my fellow commissioners to say in general terms what the idea of fairness between the parties meant. Although an agreement they reached on their own would probably have been fair by a process akin to the "unseen hand" of competitive markets, they were unable to give conceptual meaning to this idea. We can make a start toward clarifying the idea of fairness between the parties if we see that it involves a *relationship*, between popular votes received and legislative seats won. A set of district boundaries will be fair between the parties if the party that wins a majority of votes ends up with a majority of seats. This idea implies two essential tests of fairness:

- *lack of bias:* if there is a dead heat in popular votes, there should not be a built-in reason for expecting one of the parties, rather than the other, to control a majority of seats
- *responsiveness*: if a political tide moves the electorate away from a dead heat, the party toward which the tide is moving should build up a majority of seats

Each of these tests has to do with the functional form of the relationship between popular votes and legislative seats sketched in Figure 1. If one of the major parties had virtually no support in a particular election, we would expect it to win virtually no seats in the legislature; and if it had overwhelming support, we would expect it to win virtually all of the seats. In between, the party's proportion of seats should increase with its share of votes cast, according to the sort of relationship sketched by the figure.

No single curve of this sort describes the relationship of votes to seats. On the contrary, the shape and location of the curve depend on how the boundaries of the legislative districts are drawn and on how those who are predisposed to vote for one party or the other are distributed across the districts. Since accidental factors will affect the number of seats produced by a particular share of statewide votes in a particular election, it makes more sense to regard the vertical axis of Figure I as the share of seats a party would, in the statistician's sense, *expect* to have on the basis of a given share of the statewide vote in a given election.

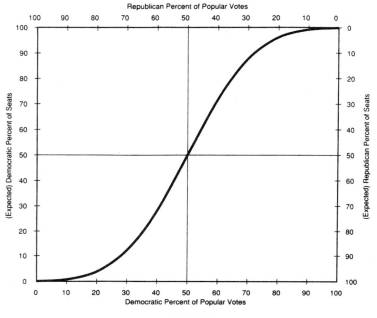

FIGURE 1

It is important to see that a party's expected share of seats would not increase in direct proportion to its share of votes, as a straight line from the lower left to the upper right corner of Figure 1. If the party had virtually no popular support and held no seats, its first increases in votes would win it very few seats. Similarly, if the party had overwhelming support and already held almost all of the seats, its last increases in votes would win it very few additional seats. In between, in the more competitive range, a given percentage increase in the party's share of votes will typically bring a greater percentage increase in its expected share of seats. These facts together give the curve describing this relationship in Figure 1 its "S" shape and a slope greater than one in the competitive, central range—properties noted by those who first saw that a "cube law" governs this relationship under widely different sets of boundaries. This slope in the central range describes how responsive the division of seats in the legislature is to the electoral tides that may move toward one or the other of two fairly evenly matched parties.

The aspect of this relationship of votes to seats that bears on the first of the tests articulated above *(lack of bias)* is the question of whether a party's expected

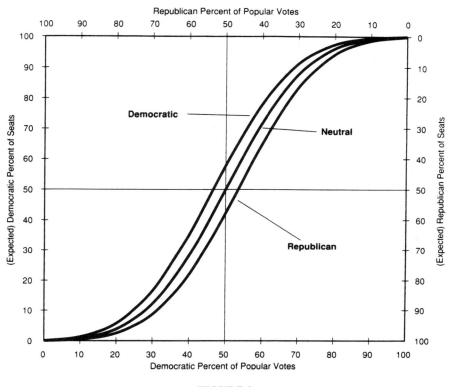

FIGURE 2

share of seats is at 5O percent—or is above or below 50 percent—when its share of the statewide vote is at 50 percent; that is, whether neither party can *expect* to have more than half the seats when there is a dead heat in the popular vote. Figure 2 shows three alternative relationships between votes and seats. The first of these, the curve to the left, is biased toward the Democrats, since the expected Democratic share of seats passes 50 percent before the party polls 50 percent of the statewide vote. The second, the middle curve, is fair between the parties, since neither party expects to have a majority of seats when the statewide vote is a dead heat. The third, the curve to the right, is biased toward the Republicans, since the expected Republican share of seats passes 50 percent without the party having polled 50 percent of the statewide vote. In an intensely partisan redistricting, the goal of the Democrats will be to draw the boundaries of the legislative districts so that a left-biased curve, such as the one labeled "Democratic" in Figure 2, describes the relationship between votes and seats. The goal of the Republicans will be to draw the boundaries so that a right-biased curve, such as the one labeled "Republican" in Figure 2, describes this relationship. The goal of the public member will be to draw the boundaries so that the curve is unbiased and passes through the joint 50 percent point of Figure 2, as the one labeled "Neutral" does.

Each of the curves in Figure 2 gives an idealized account of the relationship between votes and seats. Since there are few legislative elections from which we might chart this relationship empirically, we need some added assumptions to apply these tests to a set of proposed boundaries. The steps by which I have proceeded are these:

- First, we have aggregated the vote in the most recent legislative election (or other past elections) within a set of proposed boundaries to reconstruct how these proposed districts would have voted if these new boundaries had been in force at the time of the election in question.
- Second, we reduced the share of votes the party that won statewide would have polled in each of these proposed districts by the proportion by which its statewide share of the vote exceeded 50 percent in order to simulate, within the proposed districts, an election in which there was a dead heat in the state-wide vote.
- Third, we calculated the share of the proposed seats each of the parties would have captured in this simulated dead heat.

The proposed boundaries are fair between the parties if, under this simulation of a dead heat in the popular vote, each of the parties would expect to win half of the seats.

The relationship of votes to seats is, however, complicated by the fact that a higher fraction of the total population goes to the polls in legislative districts won by the Republicans than in legislative districts won by the Democrats. For example, in the 1985 legislative elections in New Jersey, the average turnout was 25.6 percent as a proportion of the total population in Assembly districts won by the Republicans and only 20.3 percent in Assembly districts won by the Democrats, a difference of more than 5 percent. Several reasons explain this difference. One has to do with the proportion of the population that is of voting age; since those living in Democratic districts have more children than do those living in Republican districts, a greater proportion of the population in Democratic districts is below voting age. But the reasons for this difference also have to do with rates of participation; those of voting age who live in Democratic districts are less likely to register and to go to the polls than are those of voting age who live in Republican districts. These factors together account for the considerable spread between the fraction of the total population that votes in Republican and Democratic seats.

This difference needs to be taken into account as we describe the relationship of popular support to legislative seats under a fair plan of representation. If the preferences of those who go to the polls reflect the interests and preferences of everyone who lives in their districts, the lower turnout in the Democratic seats produces a leftward shift of the curve that describes the relationship between popular support and seats. This shift is illustrated by Figure 3. As the figure suggests, the different rates of turnout between Democratic and Republican seats could produce a Democratic advantage in the relationship of seats to actual support even if there were a potential Republican advantage in the relationship of seats to potential support.

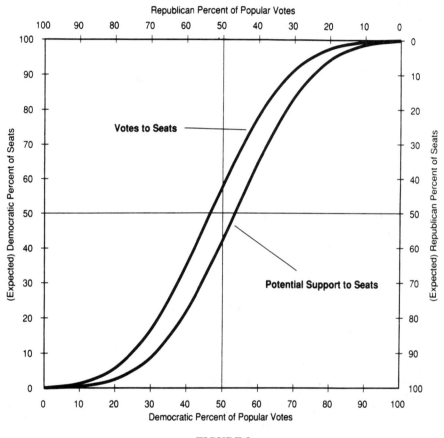

FIGURE 3

It is far from clear what allowance should be made for this difference in turnout in redrawing the legislative boundaries of the state. On the one hand, it could be argued that a system of representation should take account only of those who are willing to register and vote. On the other hand, the courts have long since made clear that representation is about whole populations, and not only about those who vote or those who are registered or those who are qualified to register. It is about everyone, including children and illegal aliens. From this perspective, a set of boundaries will be fair between the parties if the Democrats and Republicans have a 50-50 chance of winning control of the legislature when they are evenly divided among *potential* supporters across the state. Hence, a set of boundaries could still be judged fair if the Democrats have a majority of seats before they have half of the actual votes cast for the legislature. Under the assumption that those who do vote represent the interests and preferences of those who don't, this complication can be removed from the relationship of votes to seats by redefining the horizontal axis of Figure 3 as the average of the parties' share of the popular vote calculated district by district across the state, rather than the parties' share of the vote pooled across all districts of the state. If my assumption holds, such a redefinition removes the effects of the differences in demography and participation between Democratic and Republican districts, and the graph of the relationship between votes and seats will pass through the 50-50 point under a fair plan.

Hence, there is a clear answer to the question of what fairness between the parties means, and a clear algorithm a public member can use to test the fairness of particular plans. I applied this test to alternative plans in the 1981 redistricting. The plan I proposed met this test, as did both of the virtual photocopies submitted as alternatives by the parties. As the 1991 redistricting neared, I published this test and the associated algorithm in a report to the Fund for New Jersey that circulated widely in the parties. Hence, the party commissioners and their staffs understood in this latter year that there is an objective criterion of fairness and a means of saying whether a particular plan was fair. This was a genuine resource in bargaining with the party delegations, and the plan that in the end won six votes met this test of fairness between the parties.

HOW FAIR HAVE THE RESULTS BEEN?

However clear this standard of fairness may be, a public member who rallies his fellow commissioners to such a standard is all too aware that subsequent elections will be an unsparing test of how correctly this standard and its associated algorithm were applied. There have now been ten legislative elections since this standard was first applied in 1981—six for the Assembly and four for the State Senate. How well have the results in these elections upheld the belief that the boundaries of the legislative districts have been fair?

Lack of bias. From the plot of the parties' share of popular votes and seats for these elections in Figure 4 we can see that the party winning a statewide majority of popular votes also won a majority of seats in the Assembly and State Senate in each of the legislative elections from 1981 to 1991, except for the 1981 election for the General Assembly. And this exception vanishes when the horizontal dimension of the chart is redefined as the average of the parties' share of the vote calculated district by district across the state. The fairness of boundaries drawn by this test was most severely pressed by the results of the legislative elections of 1987, when one party, the Republicans, received a statewide majority of votes for the Assembly and the opposite party, the Democrats, received a statewide majority of votes for the Senate. When these votes were translated into seats, each of the parties controlled the house for which it polled a statewide majority, as it should have under a fair plan.

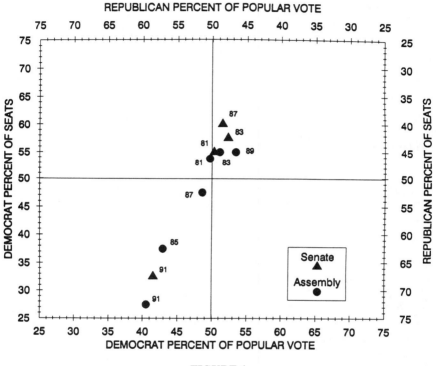

FIGURE 4

Responsiveness. The tides of popular support that moved back and forth between the parties in these legislative elections were translated into substantial changes in their shares of seats in the Senate and Assembly. This was notably clear as the electoral tide moved toward the Republicans in 1985 and 1991. In the first of these years, a 14 percent spread in the parties' share of votes cast for the Assembly was translated into a 25 percent spread in the Republican and Democratic shares of Assembly seats. In the latter year, a 17 percent spread in the parties' share of votes for the Senate and 19 percent spread in the parties' share of votes for the Assembly were translated into a spread in shares of seats of 35 percent in the Senate and of 45 percent in the Assembly. Over this central competitive range, the redistricting plans adopted in 1981 and 1991 were found to translate a one percent swing in the division of votes received into more than a

two percent swing in the division of seats won when this relationship was estimated by appropriate regression methods for the ten legislative elections from
1981 to 1991. And when the abscissa is redefined as the average of the parties'
share of the vote calculated district by district the regression line lies still closer
to the 50-50 point of the figure. These results confirm the conclusion that a public
member, working in the context of a mixed redistricting commission, can use
objective standards to draw boundaries that are responsive to electoral tides and
unbiased between the parties.

These are not, however, the sole tests of the acceptability of a set of district
boundaries. Four others have become a standard part of the redistricting repertory
—equality of population, compactness, the contiguousness of a district's territory,
and the representation of minorities. I will say a word about the first three before
turning to minority representation, which seems to me the most important and
difficult of the requirements now imposed by constitutional law and by statute.

OTHER REQUIREMENTS

The U.S. Supreme Court has pursued the equality of population to a precision far
beyond the capacity of the Census Bureau to say what the true population of districts is.[5] Mercifully, the Court has been more relaxed about equality of population in redistricting state legislatures, out of respect for the desire of the states to
keep their civil divisions whole as they sort these into legislative districts. A 10
percent variation between the largest and smallest legislative district is still coun-
tenanced for the states -- and for their counties and municipalities. The legislative
districts drawn by New Jersey's 1981 and 1991 Apportionment Commissions varied by less than half this difference. The Court has so emphasized the standard of
one person/one vote in its congressional decisions that the boundaries emerging
from the current redistricting of state legislatures are likely to partition civil divisions more often and to keep more closely to population equality than the courts
would in fact require.

The requirement of contiguous territory is nowadays under pressure less
from partisan gerrymanderers than it is from those who are trying to sort out
racial and ethnic communities. Contiguous territory presented no difficulty to
New Jersey's Apportionment Commissions in 1981 and 1991, although their
experience highlights anomalies in the definition of contiguity. Historically the
courts have said that a district can be contiguous across water as well as land, an
interpretation that accepts such anomalies as a river boundary's wandering inland
to remove a bit of territory from the district on one side of the river to the district
on the other. However odd it may have seemed on other grounds, the agreement
among the partisan members of the 1981 Apportionment Commission to remove

---

[5]In *Karcher* v. *Daggett,* 1983, a case New Jersey had the doubtful honor of presenting, the Court set
aside a Democratic map for New Jersey's congressional districts as failing to be a good faith effort to
meet the requirement of reasonable population equality between districts even though the most populous exceeded the least populous of the new districts by less than 0.7 percent of the statewide average.

a potential candidate from a district on one side of the Toms River to a district on the other side of the river was consistent with the legal doctrine that water as well as land can keep a district whole.

The criterion of compactness will increasingly be subjected to automated tests in a computerized world. One formula, for example, calculates the ratio of the actual area of a district to the area of the smallest circle that could be circumscribed around the district. In fact, however, the naked eye needs no assistance to see whether districts are reasonably compact, as it needed none to spot Elbridge Gerry's "Gerrymander" for what it was. The Senate and Assembly districts laid out by New Jersey's Apportionment Commissions in 1981 and 1991 were conspicuously compact—and vastly closer to this ideal than were the congressional districts drawn by the ordinary legislative process in 1982.

REPRESENTING MINORITIES

Although minority representation became a central concern of redistricting with the enactment of the 1982 amendments of the Civil Rights Act of 1965 and court decisions involving the 14th and 15th amendments to the U.S. Constitution, the tests in this area remain elusive and difficult to apply. The efforts to enfranchise minorities launched by the 1965 act had as their initial target racial gerrymandering in the southern states, especially efforts to disfranchise blacks by excessively concentrating their voting strength in a few districts (*packing*) or excessively diluting their voting strength among several districts (*cracking*), as well as submerging black voters in larger electorates that chose all of their representatives at large. The goal of this intervention was therefore the *initializing* one of completing the admission of newly enfranchised black voters to the political process. The courts and the Justice Department intervened in the redistricting process to prevent racial gerrymanders from keeping newly enfranchised black voters from electing representatives of their choice—in many cases black representatives—in accord with the experience of other groups that have gained access to the political process. The principal means of achieving this goal was believed to be the creation of heavily minority (*majority* minority) districts, and this belief gave rise to the working rule that districts needed to be 65% minority to achieve this result in view of past discrimination against blacks, the polarization of voting by race, and the limited influence of blacks on the nominating process.[6]

In time, the attention of the law and of the Department of Justice shifted from *negative* racial gerrymandering in the South to *positive* racial gerrymandering elsewhere in the country. With this shift the initializing goal of empowering

---

[6]Commentaries on this controversial rule are almost a growth industry within the literature of redistricting. The Justice Department never intended it to be an absolute guide, and the fraction of the population that needs to be minority to permit such a local majority to elect a representatives of their own choosing turns on such factors as the fraction of the minority and non-minority populations that are of voting age, their relative rates of participation, and the degree to which the vote is polarized along racial lines.

concentrations of minority voters was transformed into the goal of *maximizing* the number of minority representatives. It is here that the problem of minority representation is linked to the problem of fairness between the parties. A geographic system of representation places racial and ethnic minorities under the same disadvantage in translating votes into seats that is faced by a small political party, even if its supporters are fairly concentrated. The shape of the curves in Figures 1 to 3 suggest how difficult it is for a minority element of the population to claim a share of seats proportional to its share of votes, since the functional relationship between votes and seats is by no means the proportional one represented by a straight line running from 0-0 to 100-100. This home truth is reflected by the fact that, whereas African-Americans constituted 13.4% of New Jersey's population and Hispanics 9.6% in 1990, [7] the last elections prior to the census gave blacks 7.5% of the seats in the Assembly and 5% of the seats in the Senate and gave Latinos 1.5% of the seats in the Assembly and no seats at all in the Senate. Therefore, both minorities fell short in these terms, with the somewhat greater success of blacks reflecting their greater numbers, residential concentration, and influence within local party organizations.

Under our system of geographical representation, no minor party is assured a share of seats equal to its share of votes. If anything, this lack of proportionality is thought to be a virtue, since it limits the legislative presence of splinter parties until they have a substantial hold on the electorate. But the tendency of a geographic system to limit the legislative presence of minorities evokes a quite different response. Constitutional and statute law and the American ethos of inclusion create a sense of obligation to bring the proportion of seats held by these minorities as close as possible to the proportion they are of the population.[8] Hence, an appropriate goal of redistricting in New Jersey is sending more black and Latino representatives to Trenton.

The 1982 amendments to the Voting Rights Act of 1965 made the issue of minority representation far more central in legislative redistricting after the 1990 census than it was ten years before. In view of New Jersey's need to be quick off the mark to be ready for a major election in the first year after a census, the national parties treated the state as an early testing ground for their emerging strategies on redistricting, especially for the Republican effort to create majority minority districts as a means of packing Democratic votes. Staff representatives of

---

[7]Although the Department of Commerce did not release figures corrected for the undercount, informal conversations with the Census Bureau suggest that the undercount could be corrected by multiplying the black and Hispanic population by 1.06 and everyone else by 1.02. Such a correction would raise the estimate of the African-American proportion of New Jersey's population to 13.9%, of the Hispanic proportion to 10%.

[8]Neither Congress nor the Supreme Court has equated this commitment with the representation of African-Americans by blacks or of Hispanics by Latinos. They instead have required district boundaries to be drawn to give these minorities a chance to elect representatives (of any race or ethnicity) of their own choosing. But the classic pattern of American politics is for a rising minority to establish its claims on the political system by electing its own to public office.

the Republican National Committee recruited part of the state's NAACP leadership to the idea that a district should be at least 65 percent black to guarantee the conversion of African-American votes into actual representation in the legislature.

This issue was most directly joined in Essex County (Newark and its northern and western suburbs), where the Republicans wanted two heavily black and Hispanic districts, and the Democrats wanted three less tightly packed minority districts. Both the Republicans and Democrats argued that their plans would send more black legislators to Trenton. The Republicans gave great weight to the Justice Department's guidelines, which were said to require at least 65 percent minority districts. The Democrats countered that these guidelines were developed to cope with discriminatory districting in the South, that the Republicans wanted to pack largely Democratic minority voters into two districts, which would be overwhelmingly majority-minority when Hispanics were also counted, and that a greater number of African-American legislators would be elected if the blacks in Newark and its suburbs were spread over three less heavily majority-minority districts.

As this clash of views suggests, the translation of minority voting strength into seats is conditioned by the realities of local politics, especially those of the nominating process. In this respect the politics of Newark and Essex County are dramatically unlike those of the areas of the South for which the Justice Department's guidelines were orginally drawn. Although the blacks of Essex County are economically less prosperous than the whites, their political empowerment in Newark and its near-suburbs is well advanced. This power ensures the nomination of black candidates for the Assembly and Senate from the legislative districts where they are in the majority, except for cases where a white incumbent is for a period able to retain office in a district in which blacks have become the majority. Such survivors are sometimes replaced by minority representatives when district boundaries are changed.

In view of these realities, I believed that three black-dominated Essex districts were likely to produce a greater number of minority representatives than the two overwhelmingly minority districts proposed by the Republicans, which could produce a maximum of six black legislators. It seemed likely that three moderately majority-minority districts would send seven minority representatives to Trenton after the 1991 election and might send as many as nine by the end of the decade. Accordingly, I worked out with the Democrats the boundaries of three such districts that would also replace a surviving white incumbent by a black representative in 1991 and made clear to the Republicans that I could not vote for a plan that packed an excessive number of black and Hispanic voters into two districts. The Republicans accepted this decision readily enough, since their main interest lay in clearing the way for the statewide election they expected to win handsomely. But this outcome led to the irony that the final 1991 plan, which was carried by an alignment of the five Republicans commissioners with the public member, was one on which the Republicans had lost on the most difficult issue we faced, while the Democrats voted against a plan on which they had won on our most difficult issue. This irony underscores the fact that much more than a simple tiebreaker's role was required to reach a fair agreement.

DIFFUSION TO OTHER LEVELS OF GOVERNMENT

The success of New Jersey's experiment has progressively persuaded the state's political activists, journalists, and citizen groups that the mixed model of redistricting written into the state's constitution is a better way of redrawing constituency boundaries and should be extended to other levels of government. But as is so often true, this "better idea" spread to other levels when it suited the interests of those who effected the transfer. The lame duck Democratic legislative leadership that was swept from power by the 1991 elections canceled the control of congressional redistricting by the incoming, veto-proof Republican legislature and assigned this task to a balanced partisan commission instead. The statute passed by the outgoing Democratic legislature provided that in each party each of three leaders—the state chairman and the leader in the Assembly and the Senate—would name two members of this 12-person commission, which would be presided over by a neutral chairman playing the tiebreaker's role.

Although this extension of the Commission idea reflected the success of the constitutional procedure for redistricting the legislature, the holdover Democratic legislature prescribed a somewhat different role for the neutral chairman of the commission redistricting the congressional seats. It is not difficult to read into these provisions the mixed feelings of the Democratic leadership about their experience with a strongly activist public member in the commission redistricting the legislature. As a result, their statute provided for the neutral chairman to be chosen not by the Chief Justice but by the party commissioners themselves, who would be turned out of office if they failed to reach a choice within a specified time of their own appointment. Moreover, the neutral chairman would have no vote unless the Commission was deadlocked as it neared the end of the month allotted it. In this case, the chairman could vote only on the two plans with the widest support, playing a "tiebreaker's" role in the strictest sense. Indeed, the statute creating the congressional redistricting commission took the remarkable additional step of also seeking to constrain the State Supreme Court to the most limited tiebreaker's role by requiring the Court, if it became involved, to pick only one or the other of the two plans with the largest number of votes in the Commission. It is by no means clear that the Court could be bound by such a constraint.

Meanwhile, it served the political interests of the incoming, veto-proof Republican legislature to extend the better idea of a balanced commission to yet another level of government. In early March of this year the governor signed into law a statute creating such commissions to redraw the boundaries of the districts from which county freeholders are chosen in the three counties of the state that elect at least some of their freeholders from districts, rather than at large. The existing law had placed the drawing of freeholder districts in the hands of county election boards, to which each of the county party chairmen appointed two members, with the deciding vote cast by the county clerk. Since the county clerk was a Democrat in each of the counties—Atlantic, Essex, and Hudson—with freeholder districts, the new law in effect canceled Democratic control of the process in these counties. Indeed, in Essex County it canceled a new set of boundaries sponsored by the Democrats that almost certainly would have reduced the Republicans on a nine-member board of freeholders from two seats to one, and very possibly to none at all.

Reflecting the success of New Jersey's experiment with a "mixed" model of redistricting, the new statute declared that "fairness can be strengthened by adopting a method of selecting district commissioners based on the provisions in the New Jersey Constitution for the selection of members of the Apportionment Commission, which establishes legislative districts after each decennial Federal census." The act thereupon reproduced the main features of the experimental model, including the designation of a public commissioner by the Chief Justice of the Supreme Court of New Jersey if the party commissioners are deadlocked at the end of a first stage. In accord with the prior norms for the size of the county election boards, each of the county chairmen would appoint two, rather than five, commissioners. Hence, each of these commissions would have five members when they were joined by their public commissioners.

Because Atlantic County was preparing to elect district freeholders this year, candidates entering the April primary in that county needed to know the district boundaries by early April. In view of this, the legislature prescribed a crash timetable for this year's redistricting in all three counties if the governor signed the act by March 9. Under this timetable, the county chairmen were to name the party commissioners, the Chief Justice and the public commissioner within three days of the date the act took effect, and the commissions were to complete their work within ten days of their appointment—not only in Atlantic County, where there would be a freeholder election this year, but also in Hudson and Essex Counties, where the earliest freeholder elections were a year off. Assisted by the staff who helped the public member of the 1991 legislative redistricting, the public commissioners got the job done within deadline in all three counties.

This time my assignment from the Chief Justice was to return to Essex County, where the issue of minority representation had sharply divided the commission redistricting the state legislature and where a Democratic-controlled election board had recently marched through the northern and western suburbs of the county laying waste to previously Republican districts. The public commissioner was therefore called upon to promote the public interest in terms both of fairness between the parties and of the fair representation of minorities. Detailing what then happened will again make clear how I view the "tiebreaker's" role in New Jersey's mixed model of redistricting.

I felt that my responsibility to assure fairness between the parties extended only to the five district freeholders and not to the four elected at large; the distinction between these two kinds of seats was a charter issue for the county rather than an issue for the redistricting commission and its public member. My analysis of party registrations and the returns from prior elections for the board of freeholders and for the Assembly and State Senate suggested that the Democrats enjoyed something like a three-to-two edge over the Republicans in potential electoral support countywide. It was also clear that a three-to-two split in district freeholders better matched this latent strength than did a four-to-one or five-to-zero split, even allowing for the greater shifts of seats than of votes in the mid-range of party competitiveness. I therefore made it plain that I could not support the boundaries recently drawn by the Democrats, and the commission readily enough agreed that the Republicans should have two winnable seats.

We then turned to the question of minority representation. Although the blacks in Newark and its near suburbs were economically much worse off than the suburban whites in the north and west of Essex County, they were equally empowered in a political sense. But this was not yet true of the county's growing Hispanic element, the Puerto Ricans in Newark's north and central wards and the Portuguese in Newark's east ward; the politics of inclusion had yet to reach these groups, where the county's legislative body was concerned. It was clear that a district could be created from Newark's north and east wards and parts of its central ward in which Hispanics would be the largest population group, although they would not constitute a majority. Seeing that I had the Republican votes to create this district if the Democrats failed to support it, the key Democratic commissioner, the leader of Newark's east ward, moved with astonishing speed to lead the parade.

In twenty-four hours he won the blessing of the county Democratic leadership for moving the incumbent freeholder, an Italian-American in the east ward, from this district to an at-large seat and asked the leadership of the Hispanic community in the north ward to find a candidate to run as a Democrat for the district seat. As a result, the plan adopted within the statute's very tight deadline made headway on the issues both of fairness between the parties and the fair representation of minorities.

EVALUATING NEW JERSEY'S EXPERIMENT

The results of the state's redistricting experiment thus far show that New Jersey has had substantial success in finding a way between the practice in Britain and the older Commonwealth countries of leaving the redrawing of constituency boundaries to neutral commissioners, who have little of the practical wisdom of those who operate the representative institutions in these countries, and the typical American practice of leaving the redrawing of boundaries to the ordinary legislative process, with results that have blackened the reputations of legislatures since the days of Elbridge Gerry. It is hard to give legitimacy to a party's exploiting its control of the legislative process in the redistricting season to

strengthen its hold on the state legislature or the state's congressional delegation for the next decade—and perhaps beyond—since its skill in doing so will
increase its chances of controlling the next redistricting, a decade hence. An
inherent conflict of interest is involved when a majority party draws boundaries
that increase its likelihood of retaining control. And this conflict of interest is
even more troubling when individual legislators use their influence on the
redistricting process to advance their particular interests—for example, by having the boundaries of their constituency redrawn to exclude the home of a
potential opponent. We have a multiple form of this conflict when a legislature
redraws the boundaries of its constituencies to protect incumbents from both
parties.

Apart from the reluctance of those who are for the moment in control to give
up their influence on the political process, the main barrier to reform is the difficulty of devising an alternative. Unlike Britain and the older Commonwealth
countries, the U.S. has almost no tradition of neutral commissioners performing
such politically sensitive tasks, although the courts have increasingly played this
role, ignoring Justice Frankfurter's admonition to stay out of this "political
thicket." But the courts also lack the practical wisdom of those who make our
representative institutions work and are a cumbersome source of neutral judgment on redistricting plans. Boundary issues reach the courts only when an original plan is challenged on constitutional or statutory grounds, and the courts are
often limited to the unhappy choice between two or more plans that serve the
interests of the parties proposing them.

The success of New Jersey's experiment with a mixed procedure for redistricting its legislature is underscored by the biased results of leaving the redistricting of its congressional seats to the ordinary political process. This contrast
ten years ago was telling. After the state Apportionment Commission redrew the
boundaries of the legislative districts in 1981, the Democratic legislature and
governor drew a set of boundaries for New Jersey's congressional districts that
Congressional Quarterly called "a four-star gerrymander [that] twisted crazily
through counties and townships all over the state to create a Democratic advantage." Their handiwork was soon overturned by the courts, which supplanted the
Democratic boundaries with an alternative plan drawn by the Republicans, to further their own party's advantage. After comparing these parallel reapportionments triggered by the 1980 census, any fair observer would say that the framers
of New Jersey's constitutional amendments had found a better way of redrawing
constituency boundaries.

This observation is given greater force by the fact that a version of the
"mixed" commission model has been extended by statute to the redrawing of congressional districts after the 1990 census—and has also been extended by statute
to the redrawing of freeholder districts. We can learn more about the essential
requirements of the mixed commission model by studying the variations introduced by these statutory extensions, especially the restrictions on the role of the

neutral chairman written into the statute creating the commission redistricting New Jersey's congressional seats after the 1990 census. We can also learn more by studying the repeated use of the mixed commission model, under the very different conditions of 1981 and 1991, for redrawing the boundaries of the state's legislative districts.

NEW YORK CITY REDISTRICTING:
A View from Inside

Alan Gartner

REDISTRICTING IS ABOUT POWER, ITS ALLOCATION AND REALLOCATION. Laswell's definition of politics—"Who gets what, when, and how"—provides a useful framework within which to reflect upon recent experience in New York.[1]

BACKGROUND

WHILE THE DECENNIAL CENSUS RESULTS REQUIRED a realignment of the City Council districts to reflect population shifts, a new City Charter required more substantial changes. In *New York City Board of Estimate v. Morris* (1989), the Supreme Court of the United States held that the voting structure of the city's Board of Estimate violated the "one person, one vote" standard. (The five Borough Presidents each had one vote, although Brooklyn had nearly seven times the population of Staten Island. Furthermore, according to the 1990 census, Brooklyn's population was 60 percent non-white, while that of Staten Island was 20 percent non-white.) In response to this decision, a Charter[2] Revision Commission was appointed by Mayor Edward I. Koch. The revised Charter, adopted by the voters in November 1989 (the same election at which David N. Dinkins was elected Mayor), abolished the Board of Estimate and transferred the bulk of its legislative authority to the City Council. Key was the authority to adopt the budget, as well as power concerning land use and contracts.

An additional change implemented under the revised Charter was expanding the City Council from 35 to 51 members. The purpose of this expansion was two-

---

[1]The basis of this discussion is the author's work first as Executive Director, New York City Districting Commission, 1990-91, and then as a court-appointed expert in the development of the lines for New York's congressional delegation, 1992. For a fuller treatment of these topics, see Gartner, 1993.

[2]The Charter of the City of New York is the city's primary guiding document, or essentially its constitution.

fold: First, to enhance the representativeness of the council members by reducing the number of their constituents; and second, to increase the opportunity for members of racial and language minorities to elect representatives of their choice. While the size of the Council had varied over time, from 25 to 78 members, the 45 percent increase from 35 to 51 members is unique in the city's history. Combined with the enhancement of the Council's authority, the change represented an unprecedented shift in the city's political geography.

In order to implement the expansion of the City Council, the Charter established a Districting[3] Commission, set the procedure for appointing its members, established the criteria the Commission was to use in conducting its work, set a schedule to assure that the new City Council would take office in January, 1992, set the basis for adoption of its plan, and adjusted the term of office for the new Council members to two years (1992-1994) for those elected in 1991 and then returning to the four-year term for those elected in 1993.

Three of the Commission's 15 members were appointed by the minority party of the City Council (that is the then one Republican Council member appointed three Commission members), five by its majority party, and the remaining seven by the Mayor. The Commission was to have at least one member from each borough, not have a majority from any one political party, and overall reflect the population of the city, including members of those groups protected by the Voting Rights Act.[4] The Commission included four African-Americans, three Hispanic members, one Asian-American member, and seven non-Hispanic white members.

In crafting the districts, the Districting Commission heard testimony in 27 hearings it conducted, gained information presented at more than 400 community meetings its staff organized or attended, and from scores of meetings with advocacy organizations and groups.

In addition to this extensive program of community outreach activities, the Commission recognized that real access for the community required access to the computer technology. Toward that end, the Commission staff conducted "map drawing" training programs for community members, as well as developed a dis-

---

[3]Members of the Commission took the name "Districting Commission," as opposed to the more common "redistricting", as meaning that the work of the Commission was to start with a blank slate, that is to craft 51 *new* seats not to build upon the existing 35. Thus, for example, among the myriad of "levels" of maps that the Commission developed in its data base, it did not include the lines of the 35 districts. The City Council did hire a consultant who developed a data base for them that included these lines. And, of course, incumbents frequently talked about how "their" district was to be reshaped!

[4]This requirement was challenged as a "quota". The suit, *Ravitch et al. v. City of New York*, was decided on August 3, 1992. District Court (S.D.N.Y.) Judge Mary Johnson Lowe, while finding the race-conscious measure justified by a compelling governmental interest to remedy past discrimination, deemed it unconstitutional because it was not narrowly tailored to achieve its goals; i.e., was too rigid, contained no expiration date, and had the potential to harm innocent people who might be precluded by race from serving on the Districting Commission. The plaintiffs asserted they were engaged in an act of principle and that they did not wish to thwart the work of the Commission; to this end, they stipulated that a decision in this case would not take effect until after the election (1991) pursuant to the work of the Districting Commission.

tricting "game" for high school students. Most importantly, and uniquely, the Commission established a "public access" terminal, loaded with all the data the Commission used, that was available to members of the public to draw their own maps. Commission staff members were available to assist (but not to interfere) in this process. More than 200 members of the public used the "public access" terminal, and many alternative plans so developed were presented to the Commission. The "public access" terminal was housed in mid-Manhattan at The Graduate School and University Center, The City University of New York.[5,6]

Of the 51 districts in the plan adopted by the Commission,[7] twelve had an African-American population in excess of 50 percent, nine an Hispanic population in excess of 50 percent, and six had a combined "minority" population in excess of 50 percent. Following rejection by the Department of Justice of the Commission's initial submission, minor revisions were made in three areas, and a week later the plan was approved. In the November 1991 election, twelve African-Americans were elected, along with nine Hispanics. As a percentage of the City Council, "minority" members grew from 25 percent in the 35-member Council to 41 percent of the new 51-member body.

"When"

Nationally, as in New York, the broad population trends are that while the numbers of Hispanics and Asian-Americans are sharply increasing, those of African-Americans (and non-Hispanic whites) are growing at a lesser rate. A consequence of this played itself out in the districting process in New York, with Hispanics generally arguing for districts with smaller population concentrations, in the expectation that they would "grow into" the districts. Additional factors were involved as well. They included belief in the greater likelihood of white crossover votes for Hispanic (and Asian-American candidates), as well as the far greater racial segregation of the African-American population.

While the city's African-American and Hispanic populations are nearly the same (1.847 million and 1.783 million, respectively), their population concentrations across the city sharply differ. For example, 41 percent of the city's African-American population live in Voter Tabulation Districts (VTDs) that are 80 percent or greater black; only 10 percent of the city's Hispanic population live in such VTDs. This is true at the 50 percent population concentration level as well: 68 percent of the African-American population live in such areas, while only 47 percent of the Hispanic population do so.[8] As districting is a matter of both geography *and*

---

[5]When picket lines closed The Graduate School as a result of a strike, an exception was made to allow use of the "public access" terminal.

[6]After the Commission finished its work, the terminal was turned over to the CUNY Data Bank, where it continues to be used by community organizations.

[7]The plan was supported by all four of the Commission's African-American members, one of the three Hispanic members, the one Asian-American member, and five of the seven non-Hispanic white members.

[8]The non-Hispanic white population is the most segregated with 53 percent living in 80 percent white VTDs and 84 percent living in 50 percent white VTDs.

demography, even with essentially equivalent populations, it is not possible to create districts with Hispanic population concentrations at the same level as it is for
African-Americans. As districting is about voting, two further factors affect these
efforts. First, the Hispanic population is younger than the African-American population, and second, the Hispanic population includes a higher percentage of non-citizens than does the African-American population.[9] These factors further conduce
toward differences in approach between the African-American and Hispanic communities encouraging the latter's "growing into" strategy.[10]

"What"

At its simplest level, what is being allocated are legislative seats. And per *Baker v.
Carr,* these are to be based upon people, not land area or political sub-units. However, land areas are involved. While never explicitly stated as a matter of policy, in
practice the City Districting Commission chose to place important unpopulated
areas in "minority" districts. This included such assets as the city's major parks and
waterfront areas. Underlying the design of this process was the understanding that
"control" over such assets was an important aspect of gaining political power.

---

[9]While historically the city's Hispanic population was predominantly Puerto Rican (i.e., citizens),
increasingly growth has been among non-Puerto Rican groups, especially Dominicans.

[10]Contemporary Geographic Information Systems (GIS) permit achievement of zero population
deviation. To do so, as now is the practice for congressional districting is, I believe, a mindless quest.

First it is time and resource consuming. With current computer capacity, population equality
within reasonable deviations of several percentage points is fairly easy to achieve. Driving to zero
population deviation requires a qualitative increase in time (and resources) expended. A further consequence of this is to make it harder for citizen organizations effectively to participate.

Second, there is something anomalous in the requirement of zero population deviation among the
congressional districts within a state at the same time as there are huge interstate differences in the number of individuals in a congressional district. For example, the single district in Wyoming has an official
count of 455,975 persons, but the average congressional district is several hundred times larger.

Third, even in equal population districts there is a substantial disparity in the number of persons
who are citizens, as well as in the ratio between the district with the largest number of voters and the
smallest.

Fourth, it is at the least peculiar to insist upon honoring the "one person, one vote" standard at
zero population deviation in light of the acknowledged inaccuracy of the census, both overall and specifically among poor people and people of color.

Fifth, with congressional districts in the range of a half million persons, there can be no credible
argument that deviations among districts within a state of as many as several thousand persons would
have substantial statistical or political consequence for the equal weight given to each individual's vote.

Sixth, driving to zero population deviation not only results in peculiarly shaped districts, it
requires a near absolute disregard for any semblance of community.

None of this is to quarrel with the requirement of equally weighted votes nor is it an argument to
return to the pre-*Baker* era. However, the standards applied to legislative and local districting, as per
the Charter is true for the City Council, would suffice, such as accepting deviations of plus or minus a
small statistically insignificant percent from the mean when (1) uniformly applied, (2) done without
implicating the protection guaranteed by the Voting Rights Act, and (3) done for the purpose of maintaining communities. The governing case, *Karcher v. Dagget* (1982), would seem to permit application of these principles. However, rather than be subjected to challenge for a deviation of a percentage
point (or less), those who do redistricting find it prudent to go to zero population deviation, regardless
of its consequences, costs, and foolishness. The courts would do well to send a more sensible message.

"Who"

Incumbents versus the Protected Classes They Represent
The voting Rights Act protects the rights of communities of persons from the "protected classes." Too often, however, this has come to mean protecting the rights of incumbents from these communities. While there is an argument to be made as to the importance of selecting candidates from among the members of these communities,[11] it is not the intent of the Act. Indeed, in too many cases the interest of incumbents has been a factor impeding communities gaining enhanced opportunities. For example, the political leaders of the Hispanic community in the Bronx supported creating three safer (for them) Hispanic seats, while the City Districting Commission plan adopted four. While unsuccessful with the Commission, they were able to convince their legislative colleagues to craft five (rather than the possible six) Assembly seats in the Bronx. And in Manhattan, an incumbent Council member sought to maximize the percentage of African-Americans in "her" district, at the consequence of reducing the possibility of crafting a second African-American majority district in the borough. Of course, incumbent protection is not limited to "minority" communities; and, in fact, after honoring the strictures of the Voting Rights Act, attention to issues of incumbency is not precluded.

Conflict Among Protected Classes
New York is unique it its inclusion of sizable populations of three "protected classes": per the 1990 census, non-Hispanic Blacks represent 25.2 percent of the population, Hispanics 24.4 percent, and non-Hispanic Asians 6.7 percent (The Voting Age Population (VAP) figures are 23.4 percent, 22.0 percent, and 6.7 percent, respectively.) While non-Hispanic whites have become a minority of the population by 1990, they remained a majority of the city's electorate, representing an estimated 56 percent of those who voted in the 1989 elections.[12]

Given these demographic facts and the facts of geography noted earlier, the work of the Commission involved less issues of "minority" vs. "majority" than divisions between and among "minority" groups.[13] As noted earlier, while African-Americans and Hispanics constitute about the same number of people, the greater dispersal of the latter made it impossible to craft as many Hispanic majority districts as African-American. So long as redistricting is understood as a zero sum game the tension between the two groups will continue. In a paper prepared for a Harvard University conference on African-American-Hispanic relations, Charles Kamaski, vice-president for research at La Raza, wrote:

[W]e assumed for a long time that because African-Americans have gone through the

---

[11]See, for example, Reed (1992).

[12]Mollenkopf (1992), Table 4.1.

[13]The Bronx Democratic machine and its appointee to the Commission argued for dividing the six districts in the county evenly, with "whites" keeping three districts despite the fact that they constituted less than a third of the population. This claim was dismissed, if not without some political turmoil and the loss of that member's vote for the Commission's plan.

can't rely
zero-sum game

kind of searing discrimination—some would argue worse, some would argue not as bad as what Latinos have gone through—that they naturally would be more sympathetic and receptive to the kinds of concerns and grievances Latinos have. That was an assumption we've found was not true.

In his paper for the same conference, Milton Morris, director of research for the Joint Center for Political and Economic Studies, wrote:

> The Hispanic community is, compared to blacks, a relative newcomer to this whole effort. So it is logical that there should be greater representation in our case than in theirs. It's just the reality of our history.

And, perhaps appropriately, the last word (here) on this should be left to a New Yorker. Ruben Franco, then president, Puerto Rican Legal Defense and Education Fund (PRLDEF) and later an unsuccessful candidate in the new tri-county congressional district, wrote, "When we were going for the crumbs, we were bickering. Now we're for the big stuff and we're fighting".[14]

OTHER GROUPS

Considering issues that go beyond the Voting Rights Act raises whether other population groups should be given attention when crafting legislative lines. In New York, members of the gay and lesbian community argued that they were a community, similar to those protected by the Voting Rights Act, who suffered discrimination and deserved representation. This was an argument that the Commission accepted and after addressing the areas of "minority" population concentrations, the Commission crafted a district which elected an openly gay candidate.[15] Other groups sought representation as well: some argued for class-based districts, and others for attention to gender.

CONCLUSION

If this "big stuff" is power for individuals, whether people of color or not, then not only is it a zero sum game, it is politics as usual. The community benefits which the Voting Rights Act seeks to guarantee are matters of more substance. Those, such as Thernstrom[16], who challenge the post-1982 implementation of the Voting Rights as race-based, ignore that the Act is remedy to the consequences of housing segregation and racial bloc voting not their cause. On the other hand, Guinier is correct in noting that, "[V]oting rights case law...[has] accepted as its premise the fact that people of different races often lived and

---

[14]These excerpts are from Morris (1991).

[15]As census data do not identify gays and lesbians, the community marshaled an impressive array of ancillary data to make their case. These included maps showing the electoral success of previous gay and lesbian candidates, the location of community "institutions" (e.g., book stores, social service agencies, bars and bath houses), and the residences (by zip code) of contributors to gay and lesbian causes

[16]Thernstrom (1987).

voted differently from each other. Rather than insisting that such separateness and difference be eradicated…the Voting Rights Act model of racial justice recognized racial difference."[17]

A concern expressed by many critics, both nationally and in the city, of the current stage of implementation of the Voting Rights Act is that the race-conscious basis of crafting districts would lead to "Balkanization" of the polity. While the current City Council has been in office for only a few years, to date this seems not to be the case. Perhaps in only a single instance was race the fracture line in a divided vote. More important, it seems, has been geography. For example, in a decision as to the siting of a major recycling facility, all but one of the votes against were cast by those members (African-American, Hispanic, and white) whose districts were closest to the proposed plant, while all the votes for it were cast by those members (African-American, Hispanic, and white) whose districts were farthest away. This is not to say that the expanded "minority" presence on the City Council has had no effect. It seems clear, for example, that the majority support for a Civilian Review Board (of police misconduct) had much to do with the increase in "minority" members of the Council.[18]

John Lewis, now a congressman from Georgia, whose heroism at Selma and elsewhere in the civil rights movement gives him unique standing, once again offers a vision for the future:

> The goal of the struggle for the right to vote was to create an interracial democracy in America. It was not to create separate enclaves or townships. The Voting Rights Act should lead to a climate in which people of color will have an opportunity to represent not only African-Americans, but also Hispanic Americans and all Americans.[19]

---

[17]Guinier (1991a).

[18]Beyond the scope of what we can discuss here are those "third stage" issues that Guinier has so cogently addressed. In a sense, it is an achievement of note that we must now address issues beyond access to the polling booth (stage 1) and equality *of votes (stage 2)*. (Guinier, 1991a, b, 1992)

[19]Cited in R. Pear (1992)

References/Author Index

NUMBERS IN BRACKETS FOLLOWING EACH REFERENCE indicate the page or pages on which the work is cited. Below is an alphabetical listing of coauthors cited in references, followed by the name of the senior author under whose name a complete entry will be found. Many of these coauthors are also listed as senior authors for other works.

At the end of the References section there is a separate listing of court cases, each followed by page number(s) in brackets indicating where the case was cited. Principal discussions are in **boldface**.

Aldrich, J.H., *See* Abramson, P.R.
Alston, D.A., *See* Pettigrew, T.F.
Brace, K.W., *See* Niemi, R.G.
Cain, B., *See* Butler, D.
Caridas-Butterworth, V.M., *See* Engstrom, R.L.
Carlucci, C., *See* Niemi, R.G.
Comer, J., *See* Basehart, H.
Dannehl, C., *See* Costantini, E.
Davidson, C., *See* Grofman, B.
Denton, N.A., *See* Massey, D.S.
Desposato, S., *See* Petrocik, J.
DeWitt, T.A., *See* Smith, A.H.
Edsall, M.D., *See* Edsall, T.B.
Engstrom, R.L., *See* Halpin, S.A.
Epstein, C., *See* Cameron, C.
Esolin, G., *See* Rose, D.D.
Glazer, A., *See* Grofman, B.
Greenberg, M., *See* Plano, J.C.
Griffin, R., *See* Grofman, B.
Grofman, B., *See* Brace, K.
Guinier, L., *See* Days, D.S.
Halpin, S.A., *See* Engstrom, R.L.
Handley, L., *See* Brace, K.
————. *See* Grofman, B.
Hendricks, G., *See* Cook, R.
Hill, D.B., *See* Cassel, C.A.
Hill, Jean A., *See* Engstrom, R.L.

Hill, Jeffrrey, *See* Niemi, R.G.
Hofeller, R., *See* Niemi, R.G.
Issacharoff, S., *See* Aleinikoff, T.A.
Jackman, S., *See* Niemi, R.G.
Kernell, S., *See* Jacobson, G.
King, G., *See* Gelman, A.
Lawson, K., *See* Fay, J.
Lowenstein, D.H., *See* Brown, R.H.
Luskin, R.C., *See* Cassel, C.A.
Niemi, R., *See* Brace, K.
————, *See* Pildes, R.H.
O'Halloran, S, *See* Cameron, C.
Parsons, S.K., *See* Llorens, J.L.
Perry, H., *See* Llorens, J.L.
Robbins, M., *See* Glazer, A.
Rogers, C.B., *See* Renstrom, P.G.
Rosenthal, H., *See* Poole, K.T.
Schousen, M.M., *See* Canon, D.T.
Sellers, P.J., *See* Canon, D.T.
Smith, A.B., *See* Bullock, C.S.
Sousa, D.J., *See* Canon, D.T.
Stewart, J., *See* McClain, P.
Stimson, J., *See* Carmines, E.G.
Thomas, B., *See* Samish, A.H.
Welch, S., *See* Sigelman, L.
Whicker, M.L., *See* Strickland, R.A.
Wright, J.R., *See* Krehbiel, K.
Yang, J.E., *See* Edsall, T.B

References

Abramson, Paul. R. and John H. Aldrich. 1982. "The decline of electoral participation in America." *American Political Science Review* 76: 502-521. [54]

Adams, Bruce. 1977. "A Model State Reapportionment Process: The Continuing Quest for 'Fair and Effective Representation.'?" *Harvard Journal on Legislation* 14: 825-904. [155]

Aleinikoff, T. Alec and Sam Issacharoff. 1993. "Race and redistricting—drawing constitutional lines after Shaw v. Reno." *Michigan Law Review*, 92 No. 3 (December): 588-651. [70]

Alt, James. 1994. "The impact of the Voting Rights Act on Black and White voter registration in the South." In Chandler Davidson and Bernard Grofman (Eds.). 1994. *Quiet Revolution in the South: The Impact of the Voting Rights Act, 1965-1990*. Princeton NJ: Princeton University Press, 351-377. [69, 71]

American Civil Liberties Union (Virginia Affiliate), 1991. "Press release," February 19. [318]

Atwater, Lee. 1990. "Altered States: Redistricting Law and Politics in the 1990s." *Journal of Law and Politics* 6: 661-72. [159, 189]

Baker, Gordon E. 1962. "The California Senate: Sectional Conflict and *Vox Populi*." In Malcolm E. Jewell, ed., *The Politics of Reapportionment*. New York: Atherton Press: 51-63.[134, 135, 136]

Baker, Gordon E. 1989. "Judicial Determination of Political Gerrymandering: A `Totality of Circumstances' Approach." *Journal of Law and Politics* 3:1-19. [164, 170]

Ballard, Gregory G. 1991. "Application of Section-2 of the Voting-Rights Act to Runoff Primary Election Laws." *Columbia Law Review* 91: 1127-1157. [39, 45]

Barclay, Thomas S. 1951. "The Reapportionment Struggle in California in 1948." *Western Political Quarterly* 4:313-24. [136]

Basehart, Harry and John Comer. 1991. "Partisan and Incumbent Effects in State Legislative Redistricting." *Legislative Studies Quarterly*. 16: 65-79.

Black Elected Officials: A National Roster. Washington, D.C.: Joint Center for Political Studies, 1987, 1991. [15]

Born, Richard. 1985. "Partisan Intentions and Election Day Realities in the Congressional Redistricting Process." *American Political Science Review* 79:309. [159]

Boyd, R. W. 1981. "Decline of U.S. voter turnout: Structural explanations." *American Politics Quarterly.* 9: 133-160. [55]

Brace, Kimball, Bernard Grofman and Lisa Handley. 1987. "Does Redistricting Aimed to Help Blacks Necessarily Help Republicans?" *Journal of Politics* 49: 169-85. [39]

Brace, Kimball, Bernard Grofman, Lisa Handley, and Richard Niemi. "Minority Voting Equality: The 65 Percent Rule in Theory and Practice." *Law and Policy*, Vol. 10, No. 1 (January 1988), 43-62.

Brady, David and Bernard Grofman. 1991. "Sectional differences in partisan bias and electoral responsiveness in U.S. House elections, 1850-1980." *British Journal of Political Science*, 21: 247-256. [52]

Brazil, Eric. 1982. "A mixed bag of messages from those ballot propositions." *California Journal* 13:

Brown, Ronald H. And Daniel Hays Lowenstein. 1990. "A Democratic Perspective on Legislative Districting." *Journal of Law and Politics*. 6: 673-81.

Brunell, Thomas and Bernard Grofman, 1996. "Explaining divided U.S. Senate delegations, 1788-1994." Prepared for delivery at the Annual Meeting of the Public Choice Society, Houston, Texas, March (A revised version presented at the Conference on Strategy and Politics, Center for the Study of Collective Choice, University of Maryland, College Park, MD, April 12, 1996.). [63]

Bullock, Charles S. III, and Smith, A. Brock. 1990. "Black Success in Local Runoff Elections." *Jour-*

nal of Politics 52: 1205-20. [39]

Butler, David, and Bruce Cain. 1992. *Congressional Redistricting: Comparative and Theoretical Perspectives*. New York: Macmillan.[1, 149, 153, 189, 232, 272, 273]

Byrd-Harden, L. 1991. "Remarks before House Committee on Privileges and Elections: Rules and criteria for redistricting in Virginia—committee meeting with participation," Richmond, Virginia, March 20. [332]

Cain, Bruce E. 1984. *The Reapportionment Puzzle*. Berkeley: University of California Press. [134, 170]

Caldeira, Gregory. 1992 "Litigation, lobbying and voting rights law." In Chandler Davidson and Bernard Grofman (eds.). 1994. *Quiet Revolution in the South: The Impact of the Voting Rights Act, 1965-1990*. Princeton NJ: Princeton University Press, 230-260.

California Journal. 1972a. "Scholar Says Legislature Shouldn't Reapportion." 2:59-63. [143]

California Journal. 1972b. Legislature v. Reinecke, Brown v. Reagan, and Members of the House of Representatives v. Reagan. 3:7-11. [141]

California Journal. 1973. "The Courts and Legislature Follow Separate Courses Toward Reapportionment." 4:153-54. [142]

Cameron, Charles, David Epstein, and Sharyn O'Halloran. 1995. "Do majority-minority districts maximize black representation in congress?" Paper presented at the annual meeting of the Midwest Political Science Association. Chicago, April 6-8. [59]

Campagna, Janet C. 1991. "Bias and Responsiveness in the Seat-Vote Relationship." *Legislative Studies Quarterly* 16:81-89 [181].

Canon, David T. 1990. *Actors, Athletes, and Astronauts: Political Amateurs in the United States Congress*. Chicago: University of Chicago Press.

Canon, David T. and David J. Sousa. 1992. "Party System Change and Political Career Structures in the United States Congress." *Legislative Studies Quarterly* 17: 347-63. [39]

Canon, David T., Matthew M Schousen, and Patrick J Sellers,. 1994. "A Formula for Candidate Uncertainty: Creating a Black-Majority District." In *Who Runs for Congress? Ambition, Context, and Candidate Emergence*. Edited by Thomas A. Kazee. Washington, D.C.: CQ Press, 23-44. [49, 273, 277

Canon, David T., Schousen, Matthew M, and Sellers, Patrick J. 1996. "The Supply-Side of Congressional Redistricting: Race and Strategic Politicians, 1972-1992." *Journal of Politics*, 58: 837-53. [263]

Carmines, Edward G. and James Stimson. 1989. *Issue evolution: Race and the transformation of American politics*. Princeton, NJ: Princeton University Press. [63, 77]

Carter, Selwyn (1996). "Justice, Section 5 Targeted - Limits on Race Cost Minority State Seats," Voting Rights Review, Southern Regional Council, Summer, p. 1, 15-20. [336]

Cassel, Carol A. and D.B. Hill. 1981. "Explanations of turnout decline: A Multivariate test." *American Politics Quarterly*. 9: 181-196. [54

Cassel, Carol A. and R.C. Luskin. 1988. "Simple explanations of turnout decline." *American Political Science Review*. 82: 1321-1330. [54, 55]

Cavanagh, Thomas E. 1981. "Changes in American voter turnout, 1964-1976." *Political Science Quarterly*. 96: 53-65.

Cavanagh, Thomas E. "Voting rights in a new key: Using seats/votes models to evaluate African-American representation." Paper presented at the annual meeting of the American Political Science Association, September. [55]

Clay, William L. 1993. *Just Permanent Interests: Black American in Congress, 1870-1992*. New York: Amistad. [40]

Congressional Quarterly. 1973. *Congressional Districts in the 1970s*. Washington, D.C.: Congressional Quarterly, Inc. [146]

Congressional Quarterly. 1974. *Congressional Districts in the 1970s*, 2nd ed. Washington, D.C.: Congressional Quarterly, Inc. [145]

Congressional Quarterly. 1983. *Congressional Districts in the 1980s*. Washington, D.C.: Congressional Quarterly, Inc. [160]

Costantini, Edmond and Charles Dannehl. 1993. "Party Registration and Party Vote: Democratic Fall-Off in Legislative Elections." *Legislative Studies Quarterly* 18:33. [146]

Crouch, Winston W., et al. 1967. *California Government and Politics*, 4th ed. Englewood Cliffs: Prentice-Hall. [150]

D'Agostino, Carl, 1972. "Declaration of Carl D'Agostino Regarding the Republican-CSI Plan," in Legislature v. Reinecke, 6 Cal.3d 595 (1972). (Copy in Institute of Governmental Affairs Library, University of California, Berkeley.) [138, 146]

Davidson, Chandler. 1984. *Minority Vote Dilution*. Washington, DC: Howard University Press. [39]

Davidson, Chandler and Bernard Grofman (eds.) 1994. *Quiet revolution in the South, the impact of the Voting Rights Act of 1965-1990*. Princeton: Princeton University Press. [3, 70, 317]

Dawson, Michael C. *Behind the Mule: Race and Class in African-American Politics*. Princeton, N.J.: Princeton University Press, 1994. [78]

Days, Drew S. III and Lani Guinier 1984. "Enforcement of Section 5 of the Voting Rights Act," in Chandler Davidson (ed.) *Minority Vote Dilution*. Howard University Press. [105]

Duncan, Phil. 1992. Blacks Hope to Win House Seat After a Century of Waiting." Congressional Quarterly Weekly Reports, August 22, 1992, 2536-37. [45, 46, 47]

Dunne, John R. 1993. "Remarks of [Assistant Attorney General] John R. Dunne," *Cardozo Law Review*, 14: 1127-. [95]

Dymally, Mervyn M. 1971. *The Black Politician: His Struggle for Power*. Belmont, Cal.: Duxbury Press. [46]

Edsall, T. B. & Yang, J. E., (1996). "Effect of ruling on districts uncertain," *Washington Post*, June 14, A33. [334]

Edsall, Thomas Byrne, and Mary D Edsall. 1991. *Chain Reaction: The Impact of Race, Rights, and Taxes on American Politics*. New York: W.W. Norton. [42, 63]

Ehrenhalt, Alan. 1991. *The United States of Ambition: Politicians, Power, and the Pursuit of Office*. New York: Random House. [39]

Ehrenhalt, Alan. 1993. "Redistricting and the Erosion of Community." *Legislative Studies Section Newsletter* (APSA), (June) 18, 20.

Engstrom, Richard L. 1980. "The Hale Boggs Gerrymander: Congressional Redistricting, 1969." *Louisiana History* 21:59-66. [243, 256]

Engstrom, Richard L. 1986. "Repairing the Crack in New Orleans' Black Vote: VRA's Results Test Nullifies 'Gerryduck'." *Publius* 16:109-121. [232]

Engstrom, Richard L. 1989. "When Blacks Run for Judge: Racial Divisions in the Candidate Preferences of Louisiana Voters." *Judicature* 73:87-89. [241]

Engstrom, Richard L. 1992. "Modified Multi-Seat Election Systems as Remedies for Minority Vote Dilution." *Stetson Law Review* 21:743-770. [267]

Engstrom, Richard L. 1995. "Shaw, Miller and the Districting Thicket." *National Civic Review* 84:323-336. [266]

Engstrom, Richard L., Stanley A. Halpin, Jr., Jean A. Hill, and Victoria M. Caridas-Butterworth. 1994. "Louisiana." In Chandler Davidson and Bernard Grofman (eds.) *Quiet Revolution in the South*. Princeton, N.J.: Princeton University Press. [232, 233. 241]

Fay, James and Kay Lawson. 1992. "Is California Going Republican?" In *Party Realignment and State Politics*, ed. Maureen Moakley. Columbus: Ohio State University Press. [188]

Gartner, A. 1992. Drawing the lines: Redistricting and the politics of racial succession in New York, unpublished manuscript. [9, 10]

Gelman, Andrew and Gary King. 1990. "Estimating the Electoral Consequences of Legislative Redistricting." *Journal of the American Statistical Association 85:277-78.* [181]

Gelman, Andrew and Gary King. 1994. "A unified method of evaluating electoral systems and districting plans." *American Journal of Political Science*, 38: 514-554.

Glazer, Amihai, Bernard Grofman and Marc Robbins. 1987. "Partisan and Incumbency Effects of 1970s Congressional Redistricting." *American Journal of Political Science* 30:680-707. [139, 189]

Goolrick, John, (1996) Virginia's minority-majority district aids Republicans. *The Virginian Pilot*, August 22, p. A14. [332, 339]

Gottlieb, Stephen E. 1988. "Fashioning a Test for Gerrymandering." *Journal of Legislation* 15:1-14. [181]

Greenhouse, L. (1996). High court voids race-based plan for redistricting. *The New York Times*, June

14, p. A24. [335]

Greever, A. G. (1995). School board preclearance. [Letter from Hunton & Williams, Richmond, Virginia, to City Attorney, City of Chesapeake], August 31. [339]

Griffith, Elmer C. 1907. *The Rise and Development of the Gerrymander*. Chicago: Scott, Foresman and Co. [230}

Grofman, Bernard.1982a. "For Single Member Districts Random Is Not Equal." In Bernard Grofman, Arend Lijphart, Robert McKay, and Howard Scarrow (eds.). *Representation and Redistricting Issues*. Lexington, Mass.: D.C.Heath and Company, 55-59.

Grofman, Bernard. 1982b. "Should Representatives Be Typical of Their Constituents?" In Bernard Grofman, Arend Lijphart, Robert McKay, and Howard Scarrow (eds.) *Representation and Redistricting Issues*. Lexington, Mass.: D.C.Heath and Company, 97-99.

Grofman, Bernard. 1983. "Measures of bias and proportionality in seats-votes relationships." *Political Methodology* 9: 295-278.

Grofman, Bernard. 1985. "Criteria for Districting: A Social Science Perspective." *UCLA Law Review*, 33, No. 1 (October): 77-184 [77]

Grofman, Bernard (ed.) 1990. *Political gerrymandering and the courts*. New York: Agathon Press. [73]

Grofman, Bernard. 1991a. "Multivariate methods and the analysis of racially polarized voting: Pitfalls in the use of social science by the courts." *Social Science Quarterly*, 72 No. 4 (December): 826-833. [77]

Grofman, Bernard. 1991b. Statistics without substance: A critique of Freedman et al. and Clark and Morrison. *Evaluation Review*, 15 No. 6 (December): 746-769. [77]

Grofman, Bernard. 1991c. Radcially polarized voting in Alaska. Study done for the Reapportionment Board.

Grofman, Bernard. 1992a. "Expert Witness Declaration in Pope v. Blue." Civ. No. 3: 92CV71-P (W.D., Charlotte Division), March 15. [3]

Grofman, Bernard. 1992b. "Voting Rights, Voting Wrongs: The Legacy of Baker v. Carr. A Report of the Twentieth Century Fund." New York: Priority Press (distributed through the Brookings Institution). [1, 69]

Grofman, Bernard. 1992c. "An Expert Witness Perspective on Continuing and Emerging Voting Rights Controversies: From One Person, One Vote to Partisan Gerrymandering." *Stetson Law Review* 21 No. 3 (Summer): 783-818. [1, 69, 74]

Grofman, Bernard 1993a."Would Vince Lombardi Have Been Right If He Had Said: 'When it comes to redistricting, race isn't everything, it's the only thing'? "*Cardozo Law Review* 14 (April): 1237 -1276. [3 4, 70, 71, 72, 73, 74, 75, 98]

Grofman, Bernard. 1993b. Voting rights in a multi-ethnic world. *Chicano-Latino Law Review*. 13: 15-37. [77]

Grofman, Bernard. 1993c. "The use of ecological regression to estimate racial bloc voting." *University of San Francisco Law Review*, 27 No. 3 (Spring): 593-625 . [77]

Grofman, Bernard. 1995. New methods for valid ecological inference. In Munroe Eagles (ed.), *Spatial and Contextual Models in Political Research*. London: Taylor and Francis, 127-149. [77]

Grofman, Bernard 1997. "The Supreme Court, the Voting Rights Act and Minority Representation." In Anthony A. Peacock (ed.) *Affirmative Action and Representation: Shaw v. Reno and the Future of Voting Rights*. Durham, North Carolina: Carolina Academic Press, 173-200. [3, 70, 74]

Grofman, Bernard and Chandler Davidson (eds). 1992a. *Controversies in Minority Voting: The Voting Rights Act in Perspective*. Washington, D.C.: Brookings Institution.

Grofman, Bernard and Chandler Davidson. 1992b. "Postscript: What is the Best Route to a Color-Blind Society?" In Bernard Grofman and Chandler Davidson (Eds.), *Controversies in Minority Voting: The Voting Rights Act in Perspective*. Washington, D.C.: The Brookings Institution, 300-317. [74, 78]

Grofman, Bernard and Chandler Davidson. 1994."The effect of municipal election structure on black representation in eight southern states." In Chandler Davidson and Bernard Grofman (eds.) *Quiet revolution in the South, the impact of the Voting Rights Act of 1965-1990*. Princeton: Princeton University Press, 301-334. [3]

Grofman, Bernard, Robert Griffin and Amihai Glazer. "The effects of black population on electing Democrats and liberals to The House of Representatives." *Legislative Studies Quarterly*, 1992, 17 (3): 365-379. [2, 59, 60, 61, 64]

Grofman, Bernard and Lisa Handley. 1989a. "Black Representation: Making Sense of Electoral Geography at Different Levels of Government." *Legislative Studies Quarterly,* 14: 265-79. [39]

Grofman, Bernard, and Lisa Handley. 1989b. "Minority Population Proportion and Black and Hispanic Congressional Success in the 1970s and 1980s." American Politics Quarterly 17:436-45; reprinted in revised and updated form under the title "Preconditions for Black and Hispanic Congressional Success," in Wilma Rule and Joseph Zimmerman (Eds.) *The Election of Women and Minorities*. New York. Greenwood Press, 1992a. [19, 39]

Grofman, Bernard and Lisa Handley. 1991. "The Impact of the Voting Rights Act on Black Representation in Southern State Legislatures." *Legislative Studies Quarterly*, Vol. 16, No. 1 (February), 111-127. [14, 56]

Grofman, Bernard and Lisa Handley. 1992b. "Identifying and Remedying Racial Gerrymandering." *Journal of Law and Politics*, Vol. 8, No. 2 (Winter), 345-404. [70]

Grofman, Bernard and Lisa Handley. 1995a. "1990s issues in voting rights.Ó *University of Mississippi Law Journal*, 65 (No. 2, Winter): 205- 270. [59, 69, 73, 77]

Grofman, Bernard and Lisa Handley. 1995b. "Racial context, the 1968 Wallace vote, and southern presidential dealignment: Evidence from North Carolina and elsewhere." In Munroe Eagles (ed.), *Spatial and Contextual Models in Political Research*. London: Taylor and Francis.[77]

Grofman, Bernard, Lisa Handley and Richard G. Niemi. 1992. *Minority Representation and the Quest for Voting Equality*. New York: Cambridge University Press. [1, 3, 69, 70]

Grofman, Bernard, Arend Lijphart, Robert McKay, and Howard Scarrow (eds.). 1982. *Representation and Redistricting Issues*. Lexington, MA: D. C. Heath and Company.

Grofman, Bernard, Michael McDonald, William Koetzle, and Thomas Brunell. 1996. Split Ticket Voting: A Comparative Midpoints Approach. Presented at the Conference on Strategy and Politics, Center for the Study of Collective Choice, University of Maryland, College Park, MD, April 12. [64]

Guinier, Lani. 1991a. "The triumph of tokenism: The Voting Rights Act and the theory of black electoral success." *Michigan Law Review*, 89 (March), 1077-1154. [39, 40, 373]

Guinier, Lani. 1991b. No two seats: the elusive quest for political equality. *Virginia Law Review*, 77, (November), 1413-1514.

Guinier, Lani. 1992. Voting rights and democratic theory: Where do we go from here? In Bernard Grofman and Chandler Davidson (eds.), *Controversies in minority voting: The Voting Rights Act in Perspective*. Washington, D.C.: The Brookings Institute, 283-292.

Hadley, Charles D. 1986. "The Impact of the Louisiana Open Elections System Reform." *State Government* 58:152-157. [235]

Hagens, W.W., and A.E. Fairfax. 1996. Precision voter targeting: GIS maps out a strategy. *Geo Info Systems* 6(11).

Halpin, Stanley A., Jr., and Richard L. Engstrom. 1973. "Racial Gerrymandering and Southern State Legislative Redistricting: Attorney General Determinations Under the Voting Rights Act." *Journal of Public Law* 22:37-66.

Hancock, Paul F. and Lora L. Tredway. 1985."The Bailout Standard of the Voting Rights Act: An Incentive to End Discrimination," *Urban Law.* 17: 379-. [85]

Handley, Lisa and Bernard Grofman. 1994."The impact of the Voting Rights Act on minority representation: Black officeholding in southern state legislatures." In Chandler Davidson and Bernard Grofman (eds.) *Quiet revolution in the South, the impact of the Voting Rights Act of 1965-1990*. Princeton: Princeton University Press, 335-350. [3]

Hardin, Garrett. 1968. "The Tragedy of the Commons." *Science* 162: 1243-48. [41]

Hebert, J. G. (1990), Remarks of J. Gerald Hebert, Acting Chief, Voting Section, Civil Rights Division, Department of Justice, at "A statewide conference on advancing minority representation: redistricting federal, state and local government in Virginia, 1991-1992," Norfolk State University, Norfolk, Virginia, December 7. [325]

Hill, Kevin A. 1995. "Did the creation of majority black districts aid Republicans? An analysis of the 1992 congressional elections in eight southern states." *Journal of Politics*, 57 No. 2 (May): 384-

401. [58, 60]

Hinderaker, Ivan, and Laughlin E. Waters. 1952. "A Case Study in Reapportionment—California 1951." *Law and Contemporary Problems* 17:440-69. [134, 136]

Holden, Matthew, Jr. 1973. *The Politics of the Black "Nation"*. New York: Chandler Publishing. [46]

Holmes, Robert, "Reapportionment Politics in Georgia," *Phylon*, XLV, No. 3, (1984). [192]

Huckabee, David C. 1994. *Congressional Districts: Objectively Evaluating Shapes*. Washington D.C.: Congressional Research Service. [229]

Huckfeldt, Robert and Caole W. Kohfeld. 1989. *Race and the decline of class in American politics*. Urbana, Illinois: University of Illinois Press. [63, 77]

Hurley, Patricia. 1991. "Partisan Representation, Realignment, and the Senate in the 1980s." *Journal of Politics*, 53: 3-33.

Issacharoff Sam. 1992."Polarized voting and the political process - the transformation of voting rights jurisprudence." *Michigan Law Review*, 90 No. 7 (June): 1833-1891.

Issacharoff, Sam. 1996. "The constitutional contours of race and politics." In Dennis J. Hutchinson, David A. Strauss, and Geoffrey R. Stone (eds.). *Supreme Court Review 1995*. Chicago: University of Chicago Press, 45-70. [76]

Jacobson, Gary C. 1990. *The Electoral Origins of Divided Government: Competition for U.S. House Elections, 1946-1988*. Boulder, Co.: Westview Press [39].

Jacobson, Gary C. 1992. *The Politics of Congressional Elections*. 3d. ed. New York: HarperCollins Publishers Inc.

Jacobson, Gary C., and Kernell, Samuel. 1983. *Strategy and Choice in Congressional Elections*. New Haven: Yale University Press. [39]

Jewell, Malcolm E. 1967. *Legislative Representation in the Contemporary South*. Durham, N.C.: Duke University Press.

Karlan, Pamela S. 1989. "Maps and Misreadings: The Role of Geographic Compactness in Racial Vote Dilution Litigation.*" Harvard Civil Rights—Civil Liberties Law Review*. Vol. 24, No. (Winter), 173-248.

Karlan, Pamela S. 1993. "All Over the Map: The Supreme Court's Voting Rights Trilogy." In Denis J. Hutchinson, David A Strauss, and Geoffrey R. Stone (eds.). *The Supreme Court Review*, 1993. Chicago: University of Chicago Press, 245-287. [70, 73]

Karlan, Pamela S. 1995. "Apres Shaw le deluge.*" Political Science & Politics*. 28 (March): 50-54. [70]

Karlan, Pamela S. 1997. "The Application of the Voting Rights Act to Judicial Elections." In Georgia A. Pesons (ed.), *Race and Representation*. Ann Arbor: University of Michigan Press. [73, 76]

Kennedy, A.M. 1995. Excerpts from hight court ruling in racial resdistricing case. *The New York Times,* June 30, p. 22.

Key, V. O. 1949. *Southern politics in state and nation* (3rd printing, 1994). Knoxville: University of Tennessee Press. [314, 315, 316]

Key, V.O. 1956. *American State Politics: An Introduction*. New York: Alfred A. Knopf. [45]

Kousser, J. Morgan. 1991. "How to Determine Intent: Lessons from L.A." *The Journal of Law and Politics* 7: 591-732. [138]

Kousser, J. Morgan. 1993. "Beyond *Gingles*: Influence Districts and the Pragmatic Tradition in Voting Rights Law." *University of San Francisco Law Review*. 27: 551-92. [174]

Kousser, J. Morgan. 1995a. "Estimating the Partisan Consequences of Redistricting—Simply." Caltech Social Science Working Paper 929. [139, 149, 179, 184]

Kousser, J. Morgan. 1995. "Shaw v. Reno and the Real World of Redistricting and Representation. *"Rutgers Law Journal*, 26. [70, 78]

Krehbiel, Keith and John R. Wright. 1993. "An Incumbency Effect in Congressional Elections: A Test of the Explanations." *American Journal of Political Science*. 27: 140-157. [56]

Ladd, Everett Carll, ed. 1995. *America at the Polls: 1994*. Storrs, Conn.: Roper Center [179]

Livermore, Sarah. 1985/86. *The American Bench: Judges of the Nation*. Sacramento: Reginald Bishop Forster and Associates, Inc. 3rd ed.

Loewen, James. W. 1990. "Racial Bloc Voting and Political Mobilization in South Carolina." *Review of Black Political Economy*, 19: 23-37.

Llorens, James L., Sharon K. Parsons, and Huey Perry. 1996. "The Election of Troy Carter to the Louisiana House of Representatives." In Huey L. Perry (ed.) *Race, Politics, and Governance in the United States*. Gainesville, FL: University of Florida Press. [264]

Lowell, Frederick K., and Teresa A. Craigie. 1985. "California's Reapportionment Struggle: A Classic Clash Between Law and Politics." *Journal of Law and Politics* 2:245-61. [134, 156]

Lowenstein, Daniel Hays, 1972. "Brief of Petitioner Edmund G. Brown Jr." in *Legislature v. Reinecke*, 6 Cal. 3d 595 (1972). (Copy in Institute of Governmental Affairs Library, University of California, Berkeley.) [14, 137, 138]

Lublin, David. 1995a. "Racial redistricting and the new republican majority: A critique of the NAACP Legal Defense Fund 'Report on the 1994 Congressional Elections'." Unpublished manuscript. [3, 53, 60, 289]

Lublin, David. 1995b. "The election of African-Americans and Latinos to the U.S. House of Representatives." Unpublished manuscript. [51, 60, 61]

Lublin, David. 1997. *The Paradox of Representation: Racial Gerrymandering and Minority Interests in Congress.*

Maisel, L. Sandy. 1986. *From Obscurity to Oblivion: Running in the Congressional Primary.* Knoxville: University of Tennessee Press.

Massey, Douglas S. and Nancy A. Denton. l993. *American Apartheid: Segregation and the Making of the Underclass*. Cambridge, MA: Harvard University Press. [78]

Mayhew, David R. 1971. "Congressional Representation: Theory and Practice in Drawing the Districts." In Nelson W. Polsby, ed., *Reapportionment in the 1970s*. Berkeley: Univ. Of California Press: 249-85. [138]

McClain, Paula and Joseph Stewart Jr.(eds.) l995. "Minisymposium: The Voting Rights Act After Shaw." *PS* (March): 24-56. [1, 70]

McCrary, P. 1990. "Racially Polarized Voting in the South - Quantitative Evidence from the Courtroom." *Social Science History* 14: 507-531. [39]

McDonald, Laughlin. 1995. "The counterrevolution in minority voting rights." *Mississippi Law Journal*, 65 (Winter, No. 2): 271-314. [70]

McKaskle, Paul L. 1995. "The Voting Rights Act and the 'conscientious redistricter'." *University of San Francisco Law Review*, 30 (Fall): 1-94. [70]

Mollenkopf, J. 1992. *A phoenix in the ashes: The conservative politics of economic boom in New York City*. New York: Russell Sage. [371]

Morrill, Richard L. 1996. "Territory, Community, and Collective Representation." *Social Science Quarterly* 77:3-5. [268]

Morris, M. 1991. Black electoral participation and the distribution of public benefits. In *The Right to vote: A Rockefeller Foundation conference*. New York: The Rockefeller Foundation. 164-188. [372]

Morris, T. R. 1994. Virginia. In C. Davidson & B. Grofman (eds.), *Quiet revolution in the South: The impact of the Voting Rights Act 1965-1990*. Princeton, New Jersey: Princeton University Press, 271-298. [317, 333]

Morris, T. R. 1990. "Virginia and the Voting Rights Act." *The University of Virginia News Letter*, 66 (10) (June). [318]

Morton, Richard L. 1918. *The Negro in Virginia Politics, 1865-1902*. A dissertation presented to the faculty of the University of Virginia. Charlottesville: University of Virginia Press.

NAACP Legal Defense and Educational Fund. l994. "The Effect of Section 2 of the Voting Rights Act on the 1994 Congressional Elections." New York: NAACP Legal Defense and Educational Fund, November 30. [51]

Nakanishi, Don T. 1991. "The Next Swing Vote? Asian Pacific Americans and California Politics." In *Racial and Ethnic Politics in California*, ed. Bryan Jackson and Michael Preston. Berkeley: IGS Press. [188]

"The New Congress: Younger, More Diverse House and Senate Take Aim at Political Gridlock." *Congressional Quarterly*. 1993: 51, Supplement to No. 3, January 16.

Niemi, Richard G. and Kimball W. Brace. 1993. "Bright Lines, Guidelines, and Tradeoffs: The Conflict Between Compactness and Minority Representation in the Congressional Districts of the 1990s." Paper Presented at the Annual Meeting of the Midwestern Political Science Association. Chicago, Illinois, April 17. [39]

Niemi, Richard G., Bernard Grofman, Carl Carlucci, and Thomas Hofeller. 1990. "Measuring Compactness and the Role of a Compactness Standard in a Test for Partisan and Racial Gerrymandering." *Journal of Politics* 52: 1182-1204. [39, 74, 272]

Niemi, Richard G., Jeffrey Hill and Bernard Grofman. 1985. The impact of multimember districts on party representation in U.S. state legislatures. *Legislative Studies Quarterly*, 10, No. 4: 441-455. [69]

Niemi, Richard G. And Simon Jackman. 1991. "Bias and Responsiveness in State Legislative Redistricting." *Legislative Studies Quarterly*. 16: 183-202. [165]

Olson, Mancur. 1965. The Logic of Collective Action: Public goods and the theory of groups. Cambridge: *Harvard University Press*, 1965. [41]

Owen, Guillermo and Bernard Grofman. 1997. Estimating the likelihood of fallacious ecological inference: Linear ecological regression in the presence of context effects. *Political Geography*, 16(8): 657-690.

Parent, Wayne. 1988. "The Rise and Stall of Republican Ascendancy in Louisiana Politics." In *The South's New Politics: Realignment and Dealignment*, eds. Robert H. Swansbrough and David M. Brodsky. Columbia, SC: University of South Carolina Press. [244]

Parker, Frank R. 1982. The Virginia legislative reapportionment case, *GMU Law Review*, 5 no.73. [319]

Parker, Frank R. 1990. *Black votes count: Political empowerment in Mississippi after 1965*. Chapel Hill: The University of North Carolina Press. [70]

Parker, Frank R. 1993. "Voting Rights Enforcement in the Bush Administration: The Four-Year Record," in *New Opportunities: Civil Rights At a Crossroads*. Citizens' Commission of Civil Rights. [98]

Peacock, Anthony A. (ed.) 1997. *Affirmative Action and Representation: Shaw v. Reno and the Future of Voting Rights*. Durham, North Carolina: Carolina Academic Press, 1997. [1, 70]

Pear, R. (1992). "Redistricting expected to bring surge in minority law makers." *New York Times*, August 3, A17. [373]

Perry, Huey L. 1990. "Black Electoral Success in 1989: Symposium". *PS: Political Science and Politics*, 23: 141-62. [47]

Persons, Georgia A. (ed.). 1997. *Race and Representation*. Ann Arbor: University of Michigan Press.

Petrocik, John and Scott Desposato. 1995. "The partisan consequences of majority-minority districting in the South." Paper presented at the Annual Meeting of the American Political Science Association, September. [58]

Pettigrew, Thomas F. And Denise A. Alston. 1988. *Tom Bradley's Campaigns for Governor: The Dilemma of Race and Political Strategies*. Washington: Joint Center for Political Studies. [155]

Pildes, Richard H and Richard G. Niemi. 1993. "Expressive harms, bizarre districts" and voting rights: Evaluating election district appearances after Shaw v. Reno." *Michigan Law Review*, 92:483-587. [70, 74, 229]

Pitkin, Hanna Fenichel. 1967. *The Concept of Representation*. Berkeley, CA: University of California Press. [231]

Plano, Jack C., and Milton Greenberg. 1993. *The American Political Dictionary*. 9th. ed. New York: Harcourt Brace College Publishers. [[229]

Poole, Keith T. and Howard Rosenthal. 1987. "Analysis of congressional voting patterns: a unidimensional spatial model." *Legislative Studies Quarterly*. 12 (February). [61]

Quinn, T. Anthony. 1981. "California." In Leroy Hardy, Alan Heslop, and Stuart Anderson, eds., *Reapportionment Politics: The History of Redistricting in the 50 States*. Beverly Hills: Sage Publications: 53-57. [134, 136]

Quinn, T. Anthony. 1984. "Carving Up California: A History of Redistricting, 1951-1984." Mimeo. Claremont, CA: Rose Institute of State and Local Government.

Reed, J. 1992. "Of boroughs, boundaries and bullwinkles: The limitation of single-member districts in a multiracial context." *Fordham Urban Law Journal*, 19, 3 (Spring), 759-780. [371]

Renstrom Peter G., and Chester B. Rogers. 1989. *The Electoral Politics Dictionary*. Santa Barbara, CA: ABC-CLIO, Inc. [229]

Republican Party of Virginia, et al. 1991. "Plaintiffs' memorandum of points and authorities in support of motion for preliminary injunction." [324]

Research Division, North Carolina General Assembly. 1991. "Redistricting 1991: Legislator's Guide to North Carolina Legislative and Congressional Redistricting." Mimeo.

Rose, Douglas D. 1992. "Six Explanations in Search of Support: David Duke's U.S. Senate Campaign." *In The Emergence of David Duke and the Politics of Race*. Douglas D. Rose (ed.). Chapel Hill, NC: University of North Carolina Press.

Rose, Douglas D., with Gary Esolin. 1992. "DuKKKe for Governor: 'Vote for the Crook, It's Important'." In Douglas D. Rose (ed.) *The Emergence of David Duke and the Politics of Race*. Chapel Hill, NC: University of North Carolina Press. [267]

Rosengarten, Dick. 1991. *Calpeek: California Political Week* 13(45):3. [146]

Sabato, L. 1989. "Highlights of Sabato Analysis—1989 General Election for Governor," University of Virginia,.Woodrow Wilson Department of Government. [320]

Sabato, L. 1991. "Highlights of Sabato analysis—1991 General Assembly elections," University of Virginia, Woodrow Wilson Department of Government. [334]

Sabato, L. 1993. "Highlights of the Sabato Analysis—1993 general election for governor," University of Virginia, Woodrow Wilson Department of Government. [334]

Sabato, L. 1995. "Highlights of the Sabato analysis—1995 elections for the Virginia General Assembly," University of Virginia, Woodrow Wilson Department of Government. [331, 335]

Salzman, Ed. 1973. "Masters' redistricting outlook." *California Journal* 4:333-38. [144]

Salzman, Ed. 1974. "Double trouble for Republicans—redistricting and Watergate." *California Journal* 4:195-96. [146, 149]

Salzman, Ed. March 1982a. "Will the redistricting ruling boomerang against Democrats?" *California Journal* 13:97-98. [154]

Salzman, Ed. 1982b. "Will the GOP complete its reapportionment parlay?" *California Journal* 13:281-82. [154]

Samish, Arthur H. and Bob Thomas. 1971. *The Secret Boss of California: The Life and High Times of Art Samish*. New York: Crown Publishers. [135]

Savage, David G., "The Redistricting Tangle," Vol. 21, No. 8. *State Legislatures* (September 1995), 20-24. [206, 210]

Schockley, Evelyn Elaine. 1991. "Voting-Rights Act Section-2 - Racially Polarized Voting and the Minority Community Representative of Choice." *Michigan Law Review* 89: 1038-1067. [199]

Schuck, Peter H. 1987. "What Went Wrong with the Voting Rights Act." *Washington Monthly* (November): 51-55. [74]

Shaw, Pittman, Potts & Trowbridge, 1991. Section 5 comment letter, June 25. [324]

Sigelman, Lee and Susan Welch. 1991. *Black Americans' Views of Racial Inequality: The Dream Deferred*. Cambridge, England: Cambridge University Press.

Smith, Arlo Hale, and Timothy A. DeWitt. 1995. "Jurisdictional Statement" in U.S. Supreme Court, in *DeWitt v. Wilson*. (mimeo.) [185]

Spears, Ellen. 1992. Briefing paper, "The Republicans Go to Court: A Review of Republican Legal Strategies on Minority Rights in the Area of the Voting Rights Act," (Atlanta: Southern Regional Council). [291]

Stern, Mark. 1992. *Calculating Visions: Kennedy, Johnson and Civil Rights*. New Brunswick, New Jersey. Rutgers University Press.

Stokes, Donald E. 1993. *Legislative Redistricting by the New Jersey Plan*. New Brunswick, New Jersey: Fund for New Jersey, March. [10, 74]

Strickland, Ruth Ann, and Whicker, Marcia Lynn. 1992. "Comparing the Wilder and Gantt Campaigns: A Model for Black Candidate Success in Statewide Elections." *PS: Political Science and Politics* 25: 204-212.

Swain, Carol. 1993. *Black Faces, Black Interests: The Representation of African Americans In Congress*. Cambridge: Harvard University Press. [47]

Tate, Katherine. 1993. From Protest to Politics: *The New Black Voters in American Elections*. Cambridge, Mass.: Harvard University Press. [78]

Thernstrom, Abigail M. 1979. "The Odd Evolution of the Voting Rights Act." *Public Interest* 55 (Spring): 49-76.

Thernstrom, Abigail. 1987. *Whose Votes Count? Affirmative Action and Minority Voting Rights*. Cambridge, MA: Harvard University Press. [39, 74, 372]

Tindall, George Brown. 1952. *South Carolina Negroes, 1877-1900*. Columbia: University of South Carolina Press.

Turner, James P. 1992. "Case-Specific Implementation of the Voting Rights Act," in Bernard Grofman and Chandler Davidson (eds.) *Controversies in Minority Voting*. Washington, D.C.: The Brookings Institution. [97]

University of Virginia, Center for Public Service. 1991. "Census highlights." (1) p. 2. [324]

"Update on the Republican Strategy of Using the Federal Courts for Redistricting," *Voting Rights Review* (Summer-Fall, 1992) 6. [291, 302]

Vanderleeuw, James M. 1991. "The Influence of Racial Transition on Incumbency Advantage in Local Elections." *Urban Affairs Quarterly* 27: 36-50. [39]

Watson, S.M. 1984. "The Second Time Around: A Profile of Black Mayoral Election Campaigns." *Phylon* 45: 165-75. [39]

Wattenberg, Martin. 1991, *The Rise of Candidate-Centered Politics: Presidential Elections of the 1980s*. Cambridge, Mass.: Harvard University Press. [63]

Waxman, Henry A. 1972. "Declaration of Henry A. Waxman" in *Legislature v. Reinecke*, 6 Cal. 3d 595 (1972). (Copy in Institute of Governmental Affairs Library, University of California, Berkeley.) [138]

Way, H. Frank. 1962. "'Brutal Butchery of the Two-Party System?" In Malcolm E. Jewell, ed., *The Politics of Reapportionment*. New York: Atherton Press: 249-64. [135, 146]

Weber, Ronald E. 1993. "Louisiana." In *Redistricting in the 1980s: A Fifty State Survey*, eds. Leroy Hardy, Alan Heslop, and George S. Blair. Claremont, CA: The Rose Institute of State and Local Government.[233]

Wilkening, David L. 1977. "Political History of California: State Legislative Reapportionment 1849-1977." Unpub. M.A. Thesis: California State Univ., Sacramento.[134, 140, 142]

Will, George F. 1995. "The Voting Rights Act at 30: Racial gerrymandering is one reason Newt Gingrich is Speaker." *Newsweek* (July 10). [51, 74]

Wynes, Charles. 1971. *Race Relations in Virginia, 1870-1902*. Totowa, NJ: Rowman and Littlefield.

Young, H.P. 1988. "Measuring Compactness of Legislative Districts." *Legislative Studies Quarterly*. 13 No. 1 (February): 105-115.

Court Cases

PAGE NUMBERS IN BRACKETS INDICATE PAGES ON WHICH citations to each case appear. Page numbers in **boldface** refer to principal discussions.

Able v. Wilkins, No. CV 3:96-0003 (D.S. C.) [107, 300, 308]

Abrams v. Johnson, 117 S. Ct. 1925, 1939 (1997). [99]

Accord, Texas v. United States, 866 F. Supp. 20 (D.D.C. 1994) [100]

Almager v. Gaines County, Texas, No. 5-92-CV-66-W (N.D. Tex. June 1, 1993) [113]

Arizona Hispanic Community Forum v. Symington, 506 U.S. 969 (1992) [91]

Arizonans for Fair Representation v. Symington, No. CIV 92-256-PHX-SMM (D. Ariz. May 5, 1992), aff'd mem. sub nom., Hispanic Chamber of Commerce v. Arizonans for Fair Representation, 507 U.S. 981 (1993) [91, 92]

Avery v. Midland County, 390 U.S. 474 (1968) [81]

Badham v. Eu, 694 F.Supp. 664 (N. D. Cal 1988). [159, 273

Baker v. Carr 369 U.S. 186 (1962) [69, 137, 370

Baker v. McKeithen, CV 92-0973 (W.D. La. 1992) [245]

Beer v. United States, 374 F. Supp. 363 (D.D.C. 1974), vacated and remanded, 425 U.S. 130 (1976), on remand, No. 1495-73 (July 29, 1976) [77, 98, 112, 338

Bolivar County, Mississippi v. United States, No. 91-2186 (D.D.C. Dec. 20, 1994) [111]

Bossier Parish School Board v. Reno, No. 94-1495 (D.D.C. May 1, 1998) [100, 112]

Brewer v. Ham, 876 F.2d 448 (5th Cir. 1989) [109]

Briscoe v. Bell, 432 U.S. 404 (1977) [85]

Brown v. Board of Education, 347 U.S. 483 (1954) [185]

Burton v. Sheheen, 793 F. Supp. 1329 (D.S.C. 1992), vacated and remanded sub nom., *Statewide Reapportionment Advisory Committee v. Theodore*, 508 U.S. 968 (1993) [92, 107, 292, 296]

Busbee v. Smith, 549 F. Supp. 494 (D.D.C. 1982), aff'd mem., 459 U.S. 1116 (1983) [100, 112]

Bush v. Vera, 517 U.S. 952 (1996) [186, 189, 335]

Calhoun County, Texas v. United States, No. 92-1890 (D.D.C.) [111]

Camp v. Wesch, 504 U.S. 902 (1992) [91]

Campbell v. Theodore, 113 S. Ct. 2954, 508 U.S. 968 (1993) [???]

Campos v. City of Baytown, 840 F.2d 1240 (5th Cir. 1988) [81, 102, 104

Campos v. City of Houston, 776 F. Supp. 304 (S.D. Tex. 1991), stay pending appeal denied, 502 U.S. 1301 (1991) (Scalia, Circuit Justice), vacated and remanded, 968 F.2d 446 (5th Cir. 1992), cert. denied, 508 U.S. 941 (1993) [114]

Carpenter v. Hammond, 667 P. 2d (Alaska, 1983) [121, 130]

Casares v. Cochran County, Texas, No. 5-92-CV-184-C (N.D. Tex. Oct. 9, 1992) [112]

Castro County, Texas v. United States, No. 93-1792 (D.D.C. Dec. 17, 1993) [111, 113]

Chisom v. Roemer, 501 U.S. 380 (1991) [105]

Citizens for a Better Gretna v. City of Gretna, 636 F. supp 1113 (E. D. Ls 1986);834 F.2d 496 (5th Cir. 1987), cert. denied, 492 U.S. 905 (1989) [81, 102, 249]

City of Pleasant Grove v. United States, 479 U.S. 462 (1987) [100]

City of Port Arthur v. United States, 517 F. Supp. 987 (D.D.C. 1981), aff'd, 459 U.S. 159 (1982) [101, 112]

City of Richmond v. United States, 422 U.S. 358 (1975) [100, 101]

King v. *State Board of Elections*, 979 F. Supp. 619 (N.D. Ill. 1997), *aff'd mem. sub. nom. King* v. *Illinois Board of Elections*, 118 S. Ct. 877 (1998). [95]

Lawyer v. *Department of Justice* 117 S. Ct. 2186 (1997). [95]

Lee County, Mississippi v. United States, No. 93-0708 (D.D.C.) [111]

Legislature v. Deukmejian, 34 Cal. 3d 658 (1993) [157]

Legislature v. Reinecke, 10 Cal. 3d 396 (1973) [139]

Lewis v. Alamance County, 99 F. 3rd. 600 (4th Cir. November 4, 1996) [76]

Lopez v. Hale County, Texas, 797 F. Supp. 547 (N.D. Tex. 1992), aff'd mem. 506 U.S. 1042 (1993) [114]

Louisiana v. Hays, 114 S. Ct 2731, 512 U.S. 1230 (1994); 115 S Ct. 2431, 515 U.S. 737 (1995) [256, 264]

LULAC v. Clements, 999 F. 2d 831(5th Cir. 1993), cert. denied 114 S. Ct. 878 (1994) [4, **76-77**]

LULAC v. Monahan-Wickett-Pyote Independent School District, No. P-92-CA-007 (W.D. Tex. Apr. 16, 1992) [113]

Major v. Treen, 574 F. Supp. 325 (E.D. La. 1983) [232, 243, 249, 254]

McCain v. Lybrand, 465 U.S. 236 (1984) [83]

McDaniel v. Sanchez, 452 U.S. 130 (1981) [86]

McMillan v. Escambia County, 748 F.2d 1037 (5th Cir. 1984) [81]

McNeil v. Springfield Park District, 851 F.2d 937 (7th Cir. 1988), cert. denied, 490 U.S. 1031 (1989) [109]

Members of the California Democratic Congressional Delegation v. Eu, Case No. C91-3383 FMS, Civil U.S. District Court, Northern District of California [174, 188]

Mexican American Political Action Committee v. Calhoun County, Texas, No. V-92-013 (S.D. Tex. Nov. 5, 1992) [113]

Miller v. Johnson, 115 S. Ct. 2475, 515 U.S. 900 (1995) [3, 4, 6, 42, 74, 80, 82, 95, 105, 135, 186, **209-212,** 260, 272, 313, 335, 339]

Mississippi v. United States, 490 F. Supp. 569 (D.D.C. 1979), aff'd mem., 444 U.S. 1050 (1980) [99, 103, 112]

Mobile v. Bolden, 446 U.S. 55 (1980) [81]

Moon v. Meadows and Harris, 1997 WL 57432 (E. D. Va. February 7, 1997) [9, 75, 336, 338]

Morris v. Gressette, 432 U.S. 491 (1977) [83]

New York City Board of Estimate v. Morris, 489 U.S. 688 (1989) [105, 367]

Nixon v. Kent County, 76 F.3d 1381 (6th Cir. 1996) (en banc) [104]

Pope v. Blue, 809 F. Supp. 392 (W.D. N.C. 1992) aff'd mem 506 U.S. 801 (1992) [7, 239]

Puerto Rican Legal Defense & Education Fund v. City of New York, 769 F. Supp. 74 (E.D.N.Y. 1991), vacated and injunction denied, No. CV 91 2026 (E.D.N.Y. June 18, 1991) (three-judge court), further relief granted, (E.D.N.Y. July 30, 1991) (three-judge court) [113]

Ravitch et al. v. City of New York (S.D.N.Y.) August 3, 1992) [368]

Reno v. Bossier Parish School Board, 520 U.S. 471 (1997) [84, 100]

Republican Party of North Carolina v. Hunt, 841 F. Supp (E.D.N.C. 1994), aff'd mem as modified, Repubican Party of North Carolina v. North Carolina State Board of Elections, No. 94-1507, 1994 WL 263955 (4th Cir. June 17, 1994) [73]

Reyna v. Castro County, Texas, C.A. No. 2-92-CV-168-J (N.D. Tex. Oct. 14, 1992) [113]

Reynolds v. Sims, 377 U.S. 533 (1964) [81, 136, 186, 266]

Romero v. City of Pomona, 883 F.2d 1418 (9th Cir. 1989) [109]

Sanchez v. Anaya, No. 82-0067M (D.N.M. Dec. 17, 1984) [85]

Senate of California v. United States, No. 81-2767 (D.D.C. Apr. 26, 1982) [112]

Shaw v. Barr, 808 F. Supp. 461 (E.D.N.C.) 1992) [239]

Shaw v. Hunt, 517 U.S. 899 (1996) [8, 42, 72, 82, 95, 100, 285]

Shaw v. Reno, 509 U.S. 630, 113 S.Ct. 2816 (1993) [3, 4, 7, 42, 65, 70, **71-79**, 95, 96, 105, 185, 186, 189, 209, 239, 253, 258, 261, 266, 269, 272, 284, 302, 306, 335]

Silver v. Brown, 63 Cal. 2D 270 (1965) [139]

Slagle v. Terrazas, 506 U.S. 801 (1992) [86, 92]

Smith v. Beasley, 946 F. Supp. 1174 (D.S.C. 1996) [312]

South Carolina v. Katzenbach, 383 U.S. 301 (1966)

South Carolina State Conference of Branches of the NAACP v. Riley, 533 F. Supp. 1178 (D.S.C. 1982) [295]

Southeast Conference v. Hickel, CN IJU-91-1608 Civil; SCN S-5156, December 29, 1995. [121, 125, 126, 127, 128, 129, 130]

Statewide Reapportionment Advisory Committee v. Campbell, No. 3:91-3310-1 (D.S.C. Aug. 22, 1994) [86]

Statewide Reapportionment Advisory Committee v. Theodore, 508 U.S. 968 (1993) [92, 290, **293-303**]

Terrazas v. Ramirez, 829 S.W.2d 712 (1991) [92]

Terrazas v. Slagle, 789 F. Supp. 828 (W.D. Tex. 1991), aff'd mem. sub nom., Richards v. Terrazas, 504 U.S. 939 (1992) and Slagle v. Terrazas, 506 U.S. 801 (1992) [91, 92]

Terrazas v. Slagle, 821 F. Supp. 1162 (W.D. Tex. 1993) [104]

Texas v. United States, 785 F. Supp. 201 (D.D.C. 1992) [86, 98, 99]

Texas v. United States, 802 F. Supp. 481 (D.D.C. 1992) [92]

Thornburg v. Gingles, 478 U.S. 30 (1986). [42, 65, 70, 71, 73, 74, 75, 81, 94, 96, 102, 209, 271, 296, 338]

United Jewish Organizations of Williamsburgh, Inc. v. Carey, 430 U.S. 144 (1977) [103]

United States v. Board of Supervisors of Warren County, 429 U.S. 642 (1977) [83]

United States v. Cibola County, No. 93-1134 LH/LFG (D.N.M. Apr. 21, 1994) [85]

United States v. City of Houston, 800 F. Supp. 504 (S.D. Tex. 1992) [114]

United States v. Dallas County Commission, 850 F.2d 1430 (11th Cir. 1988), cert. denied, 490 U.S. 1030 (1989) (county commission) [81]

United States v. Dallas County Commission, 850 F.2d 1433 (11th Cir. 1988), cert. denied, 490 U.S. 1030 (1989) (county school board) [81]

United States v. Graham County, No. CIV-93-598 (D. Ariz. Apr. 18, 1994) [113]

United States v. Hayes, 115 S. Ct. 2431, __U.S. __ (1995) [260]

United States v. McKinley County, No. 86-0029-C (D.N.M. Jan. 13, 1986) [85]

United States v. Sandoval County, No. 88-1457-SC (D.N.M. Sept. 9, 1994) [85]

United States v. Socorro County, No. 93-1244 JP (D.N.M. Apr. 11, 1994) [85]

United States v. Yuma County, No. 92-2024 (D. Ariz. Oct. 30, 1992 & Mar. 12, 1993) [113]

Village of Arlington Heights v. Metropolitan Housing Development Corp., 429 U.S. 252, 265-66 (1977). [100]

Wade v. Nolan, 414 P. 2d (Alaska 1966) [121]

Watkins v. Fordice, 771 F. Supp. 789 (S.D. Miss.), aff'd mem. in part and vacated as moot in part, 502 U.S. 954 (1991) [91]

Watkins v. Mabus, 771 F. Supp. 789 (S.D. Miss.), aff'd mem. in part and vacated as moot in part, 502 U.S. 954 (1991) [91]

Wells v. Edwards, 347 F. Supp. 453 (M.D. La. 1972), aff'd mem., 409 U.S. 1095 (1973) [105]

Wesberry v. Sanders, 376 U.S. 1 (1964) [81]

Wesch v. Hunt, 785 F. Supp. 1491 (S.D. Ala.), aff'd mem. sub nom., Camp v. Wesch, 504 U.S. 902 (1992) [91, 241]

White v. Regester, 412 U.S. 755 (1973) [81]

Wilson v. Eu (California, 1992). [171, 172, 174, 184, 185, 190]

Zimmer v. McKeithen, 485 F.2d 1297 (5th Cir. 1973) (en banc), aff'd on other grounds sub nom., East Carroll Parish School Board v. Marshall, 424 U.S. 636 (1976) [81]

Index

Organization of Black County Officials, 292
Organization of Black Municipal Officials, 292

P

packed district
  and election of minority-preferred candidates, 249, 359
Parks, A. Lee, 212, 216, 217, 223, 225, 313
partisan fairness
  and partisanship of outcomes, 184
partisan gerrymander[ing], 239, 272-273
partisan politics
  and ethnic concerns, 187
partisan reference database, 321
partisan representation. *See* representation
partisan self-interest, 269
partisanship
  and district racial composition, 247
  and minority influence/power, 172-173, 186
Patrick, Deval L., 97, 256, 265, 307, 311
Patterson, Kay, 312
Peace, Steve, 171
Peeler, Mary L., 276
Perdue, Sonny, 220
Perlmutt, David, 285
personal ambition
  African-American, 269, 270
  and collective action problem, 41
policy
  and collective action problem, 41
policy liberalism, and descriptive minority representation, 61
political behavior
  defensive, 315
political geography
  and minority redistricting, 39
political subdivisions
  and socio-economic integration, 128-129
Pollard, Jake, 215
Population concentrations. *See also* African-American population concentrations; Hispanic-American popoulation concentrations

minority, 104-105, 122
  equality of, 153-154, 186, 358
minority percentages
  recognition of increase, 108
non-resident military
  and redistricting, 127-128
Powell, Adam Clayton, 46
Powell, Staccato, 278
preclearance
  administrative request for, 86
  and court-ordered plan, 86
  denial, 87
    in Alabama, 240-241
    in Georgia, 239-240, 260
    in North Carolina, 239
    in Louisiana, 233-241
  obtaining, 83-84
  and post-1990 plans, 88-96
  and redistricting plan adoption, 85, 86n
  U.S. Justice Department powers under Section 5 of VRA, 4, 69, 80-117
Price, David, 271, 284
Privette, Coy, 276, 286
proportional representation
  and minority representation, 278
  and racial representation, 296
Proposition 6 (contiguity/boundaries), 151
Proposition 13 (property tax reduction), 150
Proposition 14 (redistricting commission), 154-156, 159
Proposition 39 (redistricting commission), 157-159
Proposition 118 (redistricting commission), 165-166
Proposition 119 (redistricting commission), 166
public interest, 345
Pugh, Alan, 276, 286

R

race
  -based disfranchisement
    and Section 5 of VRA, 233
  -based districting
    and Fourteenth Amendment strict scrutiny, 253, 336, 338
  of candidates, 49-50

ABOUT THE EDITOR

Bernard Grofman is Professor of Political Science and Social Psychology at the University of California, Irvine. He is a specialist in the theory of representation. His major fields of interest are in American politics, comparative election systems, and social choice theory. He is co-author, with Lisa Handley and Richard N. Niemi, of *Minority Representation and the Quest for Voting Equality*, Cambridge, 1992; and he has also edited a number of books including *Choosing An Electoral System* (co-edited with Arend Lijphart), Praeger, 1984; *Electoral Laws and Their Political Consequences* (co-edited with Arend Lijphart), Agathon Press, 1986; *Information Pooling and Group Decision Making* (co-edited with Guillermo Owen), JAI Press, 1986; *The Federalist Papers and the New Institutionalism* (co-edited with Donald Wittman, Agathon Press, 1989; *Political Gerrymandering and the Courts*, Agathon Press, 1990; *Controversies in Minority Voting: The Voting Rights Act in Perspective* (co-edited with Chandler Davidson), The Brookings Institution, 1992; *Information, Participation & Choice: An Economic Theory of Democracy in Perspective*, Michigan, 1993; *Quiet Revolution in the South: The Impact of the Voting Rights Act, 1965-1990* (co-edited with Chandler Davidson), Princeton, 1994.

ABOUT THE AUTHORS

Wayne Arden has served as counsel to many elected officials and organizations, including the Democratic Legislative Leaders Association, IMPAC 2000 (the redistricting committee for the Democratic Members of Congress) and the Democratic National Committee.

Tuckerman Babcock is a government affairs consultant in Alaska. He served as director of the Governor's Reapportionment Board during the 1990 redistricting, was director of Boards and Commissions for the Governor, and served as a legislative assistant in both the Alaska House of Representatives and State Senate in many sessions during 1984-1997.

Orville Vernon Burton is Professor of History and Sociology and a Senior Research Scientist at the National Center for Supercomputing Applications, where he heads the initiative for Humanities and Social Science projects at the University of Illinois at Urbana-Champaign. He was named a University Scholar in 1988. He is the author of numerous articles, mostly on race relations, rural society, and the American South. He is the author or editor of six books, including *In My Father's House Are Many Mansions: Family and Community in Edge-field, South Carolina* (1985, fourth printing, 1995, University of North Carolina Press). He received his Ph.D. from Princeton University in 1976. His current research focuses on race and the law.

David T. Canon is Associate Professor of Political Science at the University of Wisconsin in Madison. He received his Ph.D. from the University of Minnesota in 1987. His teaching and research interests are in American political institutions, especially Congress. He is author of *Actors, Athletes, and Astronauts: Political Amateurs in the U.S. Congress,* various articles and book chapters, and several edited collections of readings in American politics (with Ken Mayer and Anne Khademian). He is currently working on two forthcoming books: *Race, Redistricting, and Representation* and *The Dilemma of Congressional Reform* (with Ken Mayer). He is also involved in the Relational Database on Historical Congressional Statistics Project, which is related to his interests in realignments and political careers.

Richard L. Engstrom is a Research Professor of Political Science at the University of New Orleans. His extensive research on electoral systems has been published in *the American Political Science Review, Journal of Politics, Electoral Studies, Social Science Quarterly, Journal of Law and Politics,* and many other journals and books. He serves as Chair of the Representation and Electoral Systems Section of the American Political Science Association.

Alan Gartner is Dean for Research, The Graduate School and University Center, The City University of New York. He served as Executive Director, New York City Districting Commission (1990-92) and as a court-appointed expert in the drawing of lines for New York's congressional districts. He is the author of more than a score of books concerning issues of equity, educational reform, disability, and social policy. On the topic of redistricting, he is the author of two articles in the *Cardozo Law Review* (1993), and a monograph, *Drawing the Lines: Redistricting and the Politics of Racial Succession in New York* (1993).

Winnett W. Hagens was co-founder in 1990 and later Co-Director and Co-Principal Investigator of the Norfolk University (NSU) Voting Rights Project in Norfolk, Virginia, the first sustained redistricting research facility within a Historically Black College or University (HBCU). In the years since its founding, the NSU Voting Rights Project has completed more than 200 redistricting plans delivered to clients in 60 localities. Until late 1997 Hagens was also Assistant Professor of Political Science in the Political Science and Economics Department at NSU, where his research interests included innovation in the application of Geographic Information Science (GIS) to the methodology of political inquiry, minority politics, campaign finance reform, and normative political theory. He has an ABD from the University of Iowa. In December 1997 he was appointed Director of the Fair Representation Program for the Southern Regional Council in Atlanta, Georgia.

Lisa Handley is Senior Research Analyst at Election Data Services, Inc., a Washington, D. C. political consulting firm, and an adjunct professor of political science at George Washington University. She received her Ph.D. from George Washington University in 1991. She is co-author of *Minority Representation and the Quest for Voting Equality* (Cambridge University Press, 1992), and has published a number of articles in political science journals on the subject of minority voting rights. In addition, she has consulted with clients in over thirty voting rights lawsuits, testifying as an expert witness in a number of these cases.

Bob Holmes is Director of the Southern Center for Studies in Public Policy at Clark Atlanta University and in 1996 was re-elected to his twelfth term in the Georgia House of Representatives. He received his Ph.D. from Columbia University in 1969. He serves as co-editor of the annual publication *Georgia Legislative Review* and is past president of the Georgia Legislative Black Caucus and the National Conference of Black Political Scientists. He has authored or co-authored more than 60 publications in the areas of legislative politics, public policies and the Black community and Atlanta city politics.

Jason F. Kirksey is the Hannah D. Atkins Endowed Chair for Political Science at Oklahoma State University. His research has been published in *Women and Politics,* the *National Political Science Review,* the *Voting Rights Review,* and *Oklahoma Politics.* During the writing of this chapter in this volume he was in the graduate program at the University of New Orleans.

J. Morgan Kousser is Professor of History and Social Science at Caltech. A graduate of Princeton and Yale, he has taught at Caltech since 1969 and has held visiting professorships at Michigan, Harvard, Oxford, and Claremont Graduate School. The author of *The Shaping of Southern Politics: Suffrage Restriction and the Establishment of the One-Party South, 1880-1910* and numerous articles on southern history, race relations, education, redistricting, voting rights, and quantitative methods, he has served as an expert witness in 19 minority vote dilution cases. His book*, "Colorblind" Justice: Race, Election Law, and the Undoing of the Second Reconstruction,* will be published soon.

Mark A. Posner is an attorney in the Civil Rights Division of the United States Department of Justice. From 1980 through 1995, he was a member of the Division's Voting Section, where he played an integral role in enforcing the administrative preclearance requirement of Section 5 of the Voting Rights Act of 1965. From 1992 to 1995, he served as Special Section 5 Counsel. His current work focuses on obtaining civil remedies for police misconduct. Prior to joining the Justice Department, he clerked for United States District Court Judge Harry Pregerson (now a member of the Ninth Circuit Court of Appeals), and graduated as Order of the Coif in 1978 from Boalt Hall School of Law at the University of California at Berkeley. The views expressed in Mr. Posner's essay do not necessarily represent the views of the Department of Justice of the United States.

Matthew M. Schousen is an Assistant Professor of Government at Franklin & Marshall College. He received his Ph.D. from Duke University in 1993 and has published in the areas of voting behavior, congressional redistricting and candidate recruitment. His current research interests include congressional rules and institutions.

Patrick Sellers is Assistant Professor of Political Science at Indiana University. He has published articles on race and redistricting and on campaigns and elections. He was an APSA Congressional Fellow in Senate Minority Leader Tom Daschle's office in 1996-1997. His current research focuses on congressional leadership and the framing of the policy agenda inside and outside Congress.

Donald Stokes (1927-1997) was a distinguished and pioneering scholar of American voting behavior using survey research methods. He served as Dean of the Woodrow Wilson School at Princeton from 1974 to 1992. His approach to bipartisan districting, as outlined in his posthumously published essay in this volume, provide one important model to achieve fair and reasonable districting outcomes.